Human Resource Management

Tenth
Edition

Human Resource Management

R. Wayne Mondy, SPHR

McNeese State University

In collaboration with

Judy Bandy Mondy

McNeese State University

PEARSON

Prentice Hall

Upper Saddle River, New Jersey 07458

Library of Congress Cataloging-in-Publication Data

Mondy, R. Wayne
   Human resource management / R. Wayne Mondy. — 10th ed.
     p. cm.
   Includes bibliographical references and index.
   ISBN 0-13-222595-6
    1. Personnel management—United States.   2. Personnel management.   I. Title.
   HF5549.2.U5M66 2007
   658.3—dc22   2007003107

Senior Acquisitions Editor: Michael Ablassmeir
Editorial Assistant: Susan Osterlitz
Editor-in-Chief: David Parker
Assistant Editor: Keri Molinari
Product Development Manager: Ashley Santora
Marketing Manager: Anne Howard
Marketing Assistant: Ian Gold
Managing Editor, Production: Renata Butera
Production Editor: Marcela Boos
Permissions Coordinator: Charles Morris
Manufacturing Buyer: Diane Peirano
Design/Composition Manager: Christy Mahon
Art Director: Pat Smythe
Interior Design: John Romer
Cover Design: Liz Harasymczuk
Cover Illustration: Kenneth Batelman
Composition: GGS Book Services
Full-Service Project Management: GGS Book Services
Printer/Binder: Courier Kendallville
Typeface: 10/12.5 Janson text

Credits and acknowledgments borrowed from other sources and reproduced, with permission, in this textbook appear on appropriate page on page.

Pearson Education LTD.
Pearson Education Singapore, Pte. Ltd
Pearson Education, Canada, Ltd
Pearson Education—Japan

Pearson Education Australia PTY, Limited
Pearson Education North Asia Ltd
Pearson Educación de Mexico, S.A. de C.V.
Pearson Education Malaysia, Pte. Ltd.

10 9 8 7 6 5 4 3 2 1
ISBN-13: 978-0-13-222595-3
ISBN-10:   0-13-222595-6

To Bob Noe, my good friend and co-author through nine editions of **Human Resource Management**; *my friend for life. Take a hip-pocket with you.*

RWM

Brief Contents

Contents

Preface

Human resource management is arguably the most exciting area within the field of business. Much has changed in the world since the writing of the ninth edition of this book. Your author personally witnessed and experienced the devastating effect that Mother Nature can have on human resource management when Hurricane Rita struck his hometown in 2005. Some of the current examples put in your text are truly real world. Major technological changes appear to be increasing geometrically with no end in sight. The interrelationship of human resource management functions and the increasing utilization of technology is reflected throughout this book.

As will be noted throughout the tenth edition, much has occurred with regard to who performs the human resource tasks. HR outsourcing, HR shared service centers, professional employer organizations, and line managers now assist in the accomplishment of human resource activities. As a shift is made in the allocation of those who perform the human resource function, many HR departments continue to get smaller. This shift should permit HR to shed its administrative image and focus on strategic and mission-oriented activities.

The tenth edition of *Human Resource Management* reveals this strategic function in a practical, realistic manner yet maintains its balance of pragmatism and theoretical concepts. And, the strategic role of HR in planning and operating organizations is apparent as each major human resource function is discussed. This book is intended primarily for students who are being exposed to human resource management for the first time. It is designed to put them in touch with the field through the use of numerous examples and company material, and will reinforce the notion that, by definition, all managers are necessarily involved with human resources. The book provides helpful insights for those students who aspire to management positions.

FEATURES OF THE BOOK

NEW

The following features have been included to promote the readability and understanding of important human resource management concepts.

- A model (see Figure 1-2) is developed which provides a vehicle for relating all human resource management topics. It is hoped that this overview will serve as an excellent teaching device.
- HRM in Action, which discusses current topics in human resource management, is provided at the beginning of each chapter to set the tone for a discussion of the major topics included within the chapter. Most of the HRM in Action features are new to the tenth edition.

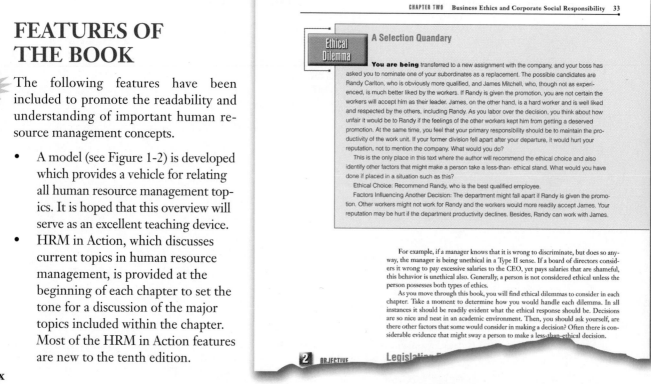

CHAPTER TWO Business Ethics and Corporate Social Responsibility 33

Ethical Dilemma

A Selection Quandary

You are being transferred to a new assignment with the company, and your boss has asked you to nominate one of your subordinates as a replacement. The possible candidates are Randy Carlton, who is obviously more qualified, and James Mitchell, who, though not as experienced, is much better liked by the workers. If Randy is given the promotion, you are not certain the workers will accept him as their leader. James, on the other hand, is a hard worker and is well liked and respected by the others, including Randy. As you labor over the decision, you think about how unfair it would be to Randy if the feelings of the other workers kept him from getting a deserved promotion. At the same time, you feel that your primary responsibility should be to maintain the productivity of the work unit. If your former division fell apart after your departure, it would hurt your reputation, not to mention the company. What would you do?

This is the only place in this text where the author will recommend the ethical choice and also identify other factors that might make a person take a less-than- ethical stand. What would you have done if placed in a situation such as this?

Ethical Choice: Recommend Randy, who is the best qualified employee.

Factors Influencing Another Decision: The department might fall apart if Randy is given the promotion. Other workers might not work for Randy and the workers would more readily accept James. Your reputation may be hurt if the department productivity declines. Besides, Randy can work with James.

For example, if a manager knows that it is wrong to discriminate, but does so anyway, the manager is being unethical in a Type II sense. If a board of directors considers it wrong to pay excessive salaries to the CEO, yet pays salaries that are shameful, this behavior is unethical also. Generally, a person is not considered ethical unless the person possesses both types of ethics.

As you move through this book, you will find ethical dilemmas to consider in each chapter. Take a moment to determine how you would handle each dilemma. In all instances it should be readily evident what the ethical response should be. Decisions are so nice and neat in an academic environment. Then, you should ask yourself, are there other factors that some would consider in making a decision? Often there is considerable evidence that might sway a person to make a less-than-ethical decision.

2 OBJECTIVE

Legislation

- A brief exercise called Ethical Dilemma is included in the body of each chapter. These exercises are designed to permit students to make ethical decisions regarding real-world situations. A debriefing guide is provided for the instructor in the Instructor's Manual.

- A Trends & Innovations section is included in each chapter to highlight current developments in the field of human resource management. Most of the Trends & Innovations features are new to this edition.

- A Global Perspective is included at the end of each chapter that highlights HRM in the global environment. Most of the Global Perspectives features are new to this edition.

- Exploring With HR Web Wisdom provides a Website for selected topics in each chapter. A minimum of three Websites are furnished in each chapter.

- Two HRM Incidents are provided at the end of each chapter. These short cases highlight material covered in the chapter. Many of these are new to this edition.

- Actual company examples and materials are used throughout the book to illustrate how a concept is implemented in organizations.

IMPROVEMENTS TO THE TENTH EDITION

The previous editions of this book have enjoyed considerable success. Many adopters offered suggestions for improving the ninth edition. All topics have been updated to provide the most recent coverage available. Topics that have been added are described below.

- New to Chapter 1: Strategic Human Resource Management: An Overview Sections: Unanticipated Events; Human Capital Metrics: Measuring HR's Effectiveness; The Evolution of Human Resource Management; The Evolving HR Organization; HRM in Action: HR Branding; HR Trends & Innovations: Cyberwork; Global Perspective: British versus American Culture: It's Different.

- New to Chapter 2: Business Ethics and Corporate Social Responsibility Sections: HRM in Action: Developing an Ethical Culture at Tyco International; HR Trends & Innovations: One Person's Ethical Stand.

- New to Chapter 3: Workforce Diversity, Equal Employment Opportunity, and Affirmative Action Sections: Services Employment and Reemployment Rights Act; Veterans' Benefits Improvement Act; HRM in Action: Sequencing Moms, Bringing Them Back; HR Trends & Innovations: Superdads; Global Perspective: Not the Glass Ceiling, the Bamboo Ceiling.

- New to Chapter 4: Job Analysis, Strategic Planning, and Human Resource Planning Sections: Strategic Planning Process; Employee Self-Service; HRM in Action: Planning for Disasters—Up Close and Personal with Hurricane Rita; HR Trends & Innovations: Manager Self-Service.

- New to Chapter 5: Recruitment Sections: 2006 criteria to determine whether an individual is an Internet applicant; Corporate Career Website, Weblogs (blogs for short); High-Tech Competition; Going Paperless at Continental Airlines; HRM in Action: Hiring Temporary Executives; HR Trends & Innovations: Social Network Recruiting; Global Perspective: China: Running Out of People?

- New to Chapter 6: Selection Sections: Sending Résumés via the Internet; Metrics for Evaluating Recruitment/Selection Effectiveness; HRM in Action: Substance Abuse Testing; HR Trends & Innovations: Liars Index; Global Perspective: Selecting a Buddy.

- New to Chapter 7: Training and Development Sections: Training & Development Delivery Systems; Online Higher Education; Orientation at Monster.com; Onboarding (Executive Orientation); HR Trends & Innovations: Virtual Instructor-Led; Global Perspective: Learning the Culture of China.

- New to Chapter 8: Performance Management and Appraisal Sections: Performance Management; HRM in Action: Identifying those in the Middle is Also Important; HR Trends & Innovations: 720-Degree Review.

- New to Chapter 9: Direct Financial Compensation: Equity Theory; Point Method Example; HRM in Action: Are Top Executives Paid Too, Much?; HR Trends & Innovations: Outrageous Severance Pay Examples?; Global Perspective: Costs of Expatriates.

- New to Chapter 10: Benefits, Nonfinancial Compensation, and Other Compensation Issues Sections: Health Savings Accounts; Flexible Spending Account; On-Site Health Care; Scholarships for Dependents; Work-Life Balance; Customized Benefit Plans; Pension Protection Act; More Work, Fewer Hours; HRM in Action: Nontraditional Benefits; HR Trends & Innovations: Two in a Box; Global Perspective: China's Work Week.

- New to Chapter 11: A Safe and Healthy Work Environment Sections: A Substance-Abuse-Free Workplace; Smoke-Free Workplaces; HRM in Action: A New Security Threat: Identity Theft; HR Trends & Innovations: Paying You to Be Healthy; Global Perspective: Global Safety Programs.

- New to Chapter 12: Labor Unions and Collective Bargaining Sections: Organizing Several Big Companies at Once; Organizing through the Card Check; HRM in Action: Change to Win Coalition; HR Trends & Innovations: Virtual Strikes.

- New to Chapter 13: Internal Employee Relations Section: HRM in Action: Continuous Background Checking.

- New to Chapter 14: Global Human Resource Management Sections: Background Investigation; Global Bribery; HRM in Action: Cultural Differences Affecting Global Human Resource Management; HR Trends & Innovations: Global E-learning.

TEACHING AND LEARNING RESOURCES

- ### HUMAN RESOURCE MANAGEMENT CD-ROM
  Developed by Mary Gowan of George Washington University, this student CD-ROM focuses on essential HR skills such as Strategic Planning and Recruitment, Job Analysis, and Total Rewards. Each module contains an introduction, a skills section that allows the student to apply his or her knowledge though interactive exercises, and finally a quiz that tests students on the material covered in the module. This item may be value-packed with the text at a nominal cost. For more information, please contact your local sales representative.

- ### STUDY GUIDE
  This study guide assists students in learning human resource management. The guide includes chapter descriptions, key terms, chapter study outlines, exercises, "You and HR" memos, and study quizzes consisting of discussion questions, fill-in questions, true/false questions, multiple choice questions, matching exercise, and answers.

- **COMPANION WEBSITE AT WWW.PRENHALL.COM/MONDY**

- **INSTRUCTOR'S MANUAL**

  This helpful Instructor's Manual includes, chapter descriptions, key terms, lecture outlines, possible answers to Ethical Dilemma exercises, answers to all end-of-chapter review questions, possible answers to all HRM Incidents, daily quizzes and a sample syllabi.

- **TEST ITEM FILE**

- **INSTRUCTOR'S RESOURCE CD-ROM**

  A brand new interface plus searchable database means accessing and finding resources has never been easier. Resources included on this CD: Instructor's Manual, Test Item File, TestGen electronic test manager software and class-tested PowerPoint slides that provide a comprehensive training delivery system for teaching human resource management.

- **HUMAN RESOURCE MANAGEMENT SKILLS VIDEO**

  In these compelling part-ending video segments, students will watch a panel of real-life HR executives from companies like BMG and HotJobs.com discuss current human resource issues like sexual harassment and discrimination, recruiting, the complexities of restructuring, incentives and benefits, labor relations, and the successes and failures of expatriate employees.

- **COURSE MANAGEMENT CONTENT IN WEBCT, BLACKBOARD, AND COURSECOMPASS**

ACKNOWLEDGMENTS

I would like to personally thank Dr. Bob Noe, my co-author on the first nine editions and friend for life, for his continued support and encouragement on the tenth edition. His words continue to ring through out the book. As with the previous editions, the support and encouragement of many practicing HRM professionals has made this book possible.

I especially appreciate the efforts of the professionals who reviewed this edition. These individuals are:

Linda Hefferin, Elgin Community College

Daniel Lybrook, Purdue University

Anne Murray, Pfeiffer University

Patrick Schutz, Mesa State College

Carolyn Waits, Cincinnati State Technical Community College

R. Wayne Mondy, SPHR
McNeese State University

PART ONE

Introduction

CHAPTER OBJECTIVES

After completing this chapter, students should be able to:

1 Define human resource management.

2 Identify the human resource management functions.

3 Identify the external environmental factors that affect human resource management.

4 Explain who performs human resource management tasks.

5 Explain the need for the human resource manager to be a strategic partner.

6 Describe human capital metrics.

7 Describe the various human resource classifications, including executives, generalists, and specialists.

8 Describe the evolution of human resource management.

9 Explain the evolving HR organization.

Strategic Human Resource Management: An Overview

HRM IN *Action:*

HR Branding

Branding:
Firm's corporate image or culture.

Discussing the topic of **branding** in an HR book may at first appear strange, since it is a topic more likely to be used in marketing or personal selling. But, in today's competitive world where firms are constantly competing for the best talent, developing the correct HR brand is quite important. In HR terms, branding refers to the firm's corporate image or culture.[1]

A brand embodies the values and standards that guide people's behavior. Through branding, people get to know what the company stands for, the people it hires, the fit between jobs and people, and the results it recognizes and rewards. "Every company has a brand," says Joel Head, president of Headwinds Ltd., a human resources consulting company in Independence, Ohio. "The brand could be from the company of choice to the company of last resort."[2]

Jane Paradiso, national practice director for workforce planning at Watson Wyatt Worldwide defines branding as "spending money up front to attract the right people in the beginning. If [a company can convey] that 'We're a great place to work' concept, [it] can attract the right people."[3]

Brands imply what employees will get from working there, and why working for the company is a career and not just a job.[4]

An employer's culture is known for such things as, "it's fun to work at this company," "we have a passionate and intelligent culture," or "there is a strong team feeling here." These brands are quite important in getting the highest-quality applicants to join the firm.[5]

It is especially important as the competition for talent intensifies.[6] Being recognized as a great place to work is a strategy that makes a difference. Employment branding is an extension of product or business branding," says Jeffrey St. Amour, national practice leader for PricewaterhouseCoopers' HR Services strategic communication group. "They're both trying to create the same thing, which is product loyalty or a feeling that this is a high-quality company." The brand a company establishes will have a major impact on the type of employee who will want to work for that company. Individuals within the organization are indeed a part of the culture of the company.[7]

Achieving acknowledgment by an external source is a good way that a brand can be recognized. Being listed on *Fortune* magazine's 100 Best Companies to Work For is so desirable that some organizations try to change their culture and philosophies to get on the list.[8]

Think about how being on the following lists might assist in a company's recruitment and retention programs:

- *Working Mother* list of 100 best companies
- *Fortune* magazine list of 100 fastest-growing companies in the United States
- *Money* magazine list of 100 best places to live
- *Business Ethics* magazine list of 100 Best Corporate Citizens
- *BusinessWeek* list of 100 best small companies
- *Computerworld* list of Best Places to Work
- *Black Enterprise* list of Best Companies for Diversity

In the first part of this chapter, HR branding is discussed. Next, human resource management and the human resource management functions are described. Then the dynamic human resource management environment is presented. Next, the changing role of HR and the development of the human resource manager into a strategic partner with upper management are addressed. Measuring HR effectiveness through the use of HR capital metrics is then described and human resource designations are discussed. The evolution of HRM and the evolving HR organization are described, and a description of the scope of this book is provided. The chapter concludes with a global perspective entitled "British versus American Culture: It's Different."

1 OBJECTIVE

Define human resource management.

Human resource management (HRM):
Utilization of individuals to achieve organizational objectives.

Human Resource Management

Human resource management (HRM) is the utilization of individuals to achieve organizational objectives. Consequently, managers at every level must concern themselves with HRM. Basically, all managers get things done through the efforts of others; this requires effective HRM. Individuals dealing with human resource matters face a multitude of challenges, ranging from a constantly changing workforce to ever-present government regulations, a technological revolution, and the effects of 9/11 and natural disasters such as hurricanes and tornadoes. Furthermore, global competition has forced both large and small organizations to be more conscious of costs and productivity. Because of the critical nature of human resource issues, these matters must receive major attention from upper management.

2 OBJECTIVE

Identify the human resource management functions.

Human Resource Management Functions

People who are engaged in the management of human resources develop and work through an integrated HRM system. As Figure 1-1 shows, five functional areas are associated with effective HRM: staffing, human resource development, compensation, safety and health, and employee and labor relations. These functions are discussed next.

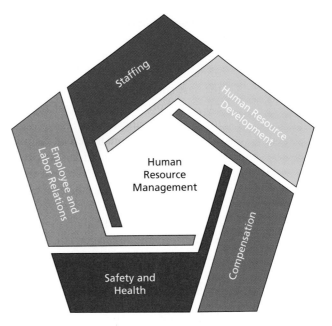

Figure 1-1 Human Resource
Management Functions

Staffing

Staffing is the process through which an organization ensures that it always has the proper number of employees with the appropriate skills in the right jobs, at the right time, to achieve organizational objectives. Staffing involves job analysis, human resource planning, recruitment, and selection, all of which are discussed in this text.[9]

Job analysis is the systematic process of determining the skills, duties, and knowledge required for performing jobs in an organization. It impacts virtually every aspect of HRM including planning, recruitment, and selection. Human resource planning (HRP) is the systematic process of matching the internal and external supply of people with job openings anticipated in the organization over a specified period of time. The data provided set the stage for recruitment or other HR actions. Recruitment is the process of attracting individuals on a timely basis, in sufficient numbers, and with appropriate qualifications, to apply for jobs with an organization. Selection is the process of choosing from a group of applicants the individual best suited for a particular position and the organization. Successful accomplishment of these three tasks is vital if the organization is to effectively accomplish its mission. Chapters 4, 5, and 6 are devoted to these topics, which are collectively referred to as staffing.

Human Resource Development

Human resource development (HRD) is a major HRM function consisting not only of training and development but also of individual career planning and development activities, organization development, and performance management and appraisal. Training is designed to provide learners with the knowledge and skills needed for their present jobs. Development involves learning that goes beyond today's job and has a more long-term focus. Training and development is covered in Chapter 7.

Career planning is an ongoing process whereby an individual sets career goals and identifies the means to achieve them. This is a continuing and difficult process because the average person graduating from college today may face five to seven career changes (career, not employer) in his or her working years.[10]

Career development is a formal approach used by the organization to ensure that people with the proper qualifications and experiences are available when needed. Individual careers and organizational needs are not separate and distinct. Organizations should assist employees in career planning so the needs of both can be satisfied. Career planning and development is discussed in the appendix to Chapter 7. Students may find that the information provided is useful in evaluating their careers.

Organization development (OD) is the planned process of improving an organization by developing its structures, systems, and processes to improve effectiveness and achieving desired goals. OD applies to an entire system, such as a company or a plant. A number of interventions are discussed that serve to improve a firm's performance.

Performance management is a goal-oriented process that is directed toward ensuring that organizational processes are in place to maximize productivity of employees, teams, and ultimately, the organization. Performance appraisal is a formal system of review and evaluation of individual or team task performance. It affords employees the opportunity to capitalize on their strengths and overcome identified deficiencies, thereby helping them to become more satisfied and productive employees. Performance management and appraisal is discussed in Chapter 8.

Compensation

The question of what constitutes a fair day's pay has plagued management, unions, and workers for a long time. A well-thought-out compensation system provides employees with adequate and equitable rewards for their contributions to meeting organizational goals. As used in this book, the term *compensation* includes the total of all rewards provided employees in return for their services. The rewards may be one or a combination of the following:

- **Direct Financial Compensation:** Pay that a person receives in the form of wages, salaries, commissions, and bonuses.
- **Indirect Financial Compensation (Benefits):** All financial rewards that are not included in direct compensation such as paid vacations, sick leave, holidays, and medical insurance.
- **Nonfinancial Compensation:** Satisfaction that a person receives from the job itself or from the psychological and/or physical environment in which the person works.

Direct financial compensation is discussed in Chapter 9 and benefits, nonfinancial rewards, and other compensation issues are discussed in Chapter 10.

Safety and Health

Safety involves protecting employees from injuries caused by work-related accidents. Health refers to the employees' freedom from physical or emotional illness. These aspects of the job are important because employees who work in a safe environment and enjoy good health are more likely to be productive and yield long-term benefits to the organization. Today, because of federal and state legislation that reflects societal concerns, most organizations have become attentive to their employees' safety and health. Chapter 11 is devoted to topics related to safety and health.

Employee and Labor Relations

Private-sector union membership has fallen from 39 percent in 1958 to about 7.8 percent in 2005.[11] This was the lowest percentage since 1901. Even so, a business is required by law to recognize a union and bargain with it in good faith if the firm's employees want the union to represent them. In the past, this relationship was an accepted way of life for many employers, but most firms today would rather have a union-free environment. When a labor union represents a firm's employees, the human resource activity is often referred to as industrial relations, which handles the job of collective bargaining. Chapter 12 relates strictly to labor unions and collective bargaining; Chapter 13 relates to both union and nonunion internal employee relations.

Human Resource Research

Although human resource research is not a distinct HRM function, it pervades all functional areas, and the researcher's laboratory is the entire work environment. For instance, a study related to recruitment may suggest the type of worker most likely to succeed in a particular firm. Research on job safety may identify the causes of certain work-related accidents. The reasons for problems such as excessive absenteeism or excessive grievances may not be readily apparent. However, when such problems occur, human resource research can often shed light on their causes and possible solutions. Human resource research is clearly an important key to developing the most productive and satisfied workforce possible.

Interrelationships of HRM Functions

All HRM functional areas are highly interrelated. Management must recognize that decisions in one area will affect other areas. For instance, a firm that emphasizes recruiting top-quality candidates but neglects to provide satisfactory compensation is wasting time, effort, and money. In addition, a firm's compensation system will be inadequate unless employees are provided a safe and healthy work environment. If a firm's compensation system pays below-market wages, the firm will always be hiring and training new employees only to see the best leave for a competitor's higher wages. The interrelationships among the HRM functional areas will become more obvious as these topics are addressed throughout the book.

OBJECTIVE

Identify the external environmental factors that affect human resource management.

External environment:
Factors outside an organization's boundaries that affect a firm's human resources makeup.

Dynamic Human Resource Management Environment

Many interrelated factors affect the five previously identified HRM functions. Factors outside an organization's boundaries that affect a firm's human resources make up the **external environment**.

The firm often has little, if any, control over how the external environment affects management of its human resources. As illustrated in Figure 1-2, external factors include the labor market, legal considerations, society, unions, shareholders, competition, customers, technology, the economy, and unanticipated events. Each factor, either separately or in combination with others, can place constraints on how HRM tasks are accomplished.

Labor Market

Potential employees located within the geographic area from which employees are recruited comprise the labor market. The capabilities of a firm's employees determine to a large extent how well the organization can perform its mission. Since new employees are hired from outside the firm, the labor market is considered an external environmental factor. The labor market is always changing, and these shifts inevitably cause changes in the workforce of an organization. In turn, changes in individuals within an organization affect the way management must deal with its workforce. This topic will be discussed later in Chapter 3 under the heading "Diversity and Diversity Management."

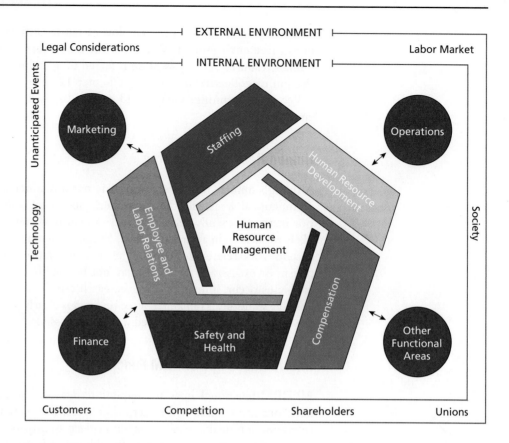

Figure 1-2 Environment of Human Resource Management

Legal Considerations

Another significant external force affecting HRM relates to federal, state, and local legislation and the many court decisions interpreting this legislation. In addition, presidential executive orders have had a major impact on HRM. These legal considerations affect virtually the entire spectrum of human resource policies. Chapter 3 highlights the most significant ones, which affect equal employment opportunity. Laws, court decisions, and executive orders affecting other HRM activities will be described in the appropriate chapters.

Society

Society may also exert pressure on HRM. The public is no longer content to accept, without question, the actions of business. This was forcefully brought to the forefront by the wrongful actions of such large companies such as Enron, WorldCom, Arthur Andersen, Tyco International, Adelphia Communications, and others. To remain acceptable to the general public, a firm must accomplish its purpose while complying with societal norms.

The title of Chapter 2 is "Business Ethics and Corporate Social Responsibility." When a firm responds effectively to social interests, it is said to be socially responsible. Social responsibility is the implied, enforced, or felt obligation of managers, acting in their official capacity, to serve or protect the interests of groups other than themselves.[12]

Social responsibility is closely related to ethics; the discipline dealing with what is good and bad, or right and wrong, or with moral duty and obligation.

Unions

Union:

Employees who have joined together for the purpose of dealing with their employer.

Wage levels, benefits, and working conditions for millions of employees reflect decisions made jointly by unions and management. A **union** is comprised of employees who have joined together for the purpose of dealing with their employer. Unions are treated as an environmental factor because, essentially, they become a third party when dealing with the company. In a unionized organization, the union rather than the individual employee negotiates an agreement with management.

Shareholders

Shareholders:
Owners of a corporation.

The owners of a corporation are called **shareholders**.

Because shareholders, or stockholders, have invested money in the firm, they may at times challenge programs considered by management to be beneficial to the organization. Stockholders are wielding increasing influence and management may be forced to justify the merits of a particular program in terms of how it will affect future projects, costs, revenues, profits, and even benefits to society as a whole.

Competition

Firms may face intense competition in both their product or service and labor markets. Unless an organization is in the unusual position of monopolizing the market it serves, other firms will be producing similar products or services. A firm also must maintain a supply of competent employees if it is to succeed, grow, and prosper. But other organizations are also striving for that same objective. A firm's major task is to ensure that it obtains and retains a sufficient number of employees in various career fields to allow it to compete effectively. A bidding war often results when competitors attempt to fill certain critical positions in their firms. As will be discussed in Chapter 5, firms are sometimes forced to resort to unusual means to recruit and retain such employees.

Customers

The people who actually use a firm's goods and services also are part of its external environment. Because sales are crucial to the firm's survival, management has the task of ensuring that its employment practices do not antagonize the customers it serves. Customers constantly demand high-quality products and after-purchase service. Therefore, a firm's workforce should be capable of providing top-quality goods and services. These conditions relate directly to the skills, qualifications, and motivations of the organization's employees.

Technology

The world has never before seen technological changes occur as rapidly as they are today. The development of HR technology has created new roles for HR professionals but also places additional pressures on them to keep abreast of the technology.[13]

According to a survey by the Society for Human Resource Management (SHRM), a leading trend identified by the panel of experts was the expanded use of the Web for delivery and utilization of HR applications on a service basis.[14]

Companies are automating many or all of the human resource administrative functions.[15] Both employee and manager self-service will be discussed in Chapter 4. Most of this technology did not exist only a short time ago. "We have seen more technological changes in the last 36 months than we have seen over the last 18 years," says Suzanne Zuniga, chief operating officer at CorVirtus, a recruitment and hiring consulting firm based in Colorado Springs, Colorado.[16]

Further, according to HR technology researcher IDC, spending by U.S. companies on workforce optimization and other hiring-process automation services is expected to reach $720 million by 2008, up from $260 million in 2004.[17]

According to a recent survey, the use of HR technology has had a measurable impact on the growth of operating income.[18] The impact of technology on these practices is noted throughout this book.

Economy

The economy of the nation, on the whole and in its various segments, is a major environmental factor affecting HRM. As a generalization, when the economy is booming, it is more difficult to recruit qualified workers. On the other hand, when a downturn is experienced, more applicants are typically available. To complicate this situation even further, one segment of the country may be experiencing a downturn, another a slow recovery, and another a boom.

Unanticipated Events

Unanticipated events are occurrences in the external environment that cannot be foreseen. Perhaps the author has been influenced to identify unanticipated events as an external environment factor after personally seeing the impact of Hurricane Rita on human resource management in his hometown (see HR Incident 1 at the end of this chapter for a real-life case). Many of the human resource functions required modification. The author would venture a guess that every disaster, whether manmade or by nature, requires a tremendous amount of adjustment with regard to human resource management. Certainly, 9/11 impacted HR in ways yet to be fully determined. On a global perspective think of the many different ways that HR was affected when the tsunami struck Indonesia.

Cyberwork:
Possibility of a never-ending workday.

Trends & Innovations

Cyberwork

Technology has created an assortment of possibilities that will be rewarding for some individuals, but not for others. Development of the Internet has had significant implications for the job. Cyberspace engineers are intent on giving users anywhere, anytime access to the Internet. The wireless industry, whose market has already surpassed that of personal computers, has created the potential for **cyberwork**, a possibility of a never-ending workday. BlackBerrys, cell phones, text messaging, and e-mail create endless possibilities for communication.[19] Workers have around-the-clock access to software.[20]

Everything has become blurred with technology. Some workers believe that their employer wants them to be available 24/7. What will employees scattered across the globe do when their managers need information from them at an inconvenient hour? Managers will not likely be content to wait until 8:00 a.m. (your time). Obviously, workers could turn off their smart phones, notebooks, or pocket devices to prevent such inconvenient intrusions, but that might be detrimental to career security. In one survey, a respondent said, "I am required to carry a cell phone 24/7. I am called any time there is a problem, and expected to answer. We have had people terminated for not answering phones." Others said they are expected to respond to cell phone calls and the "constant e-mail traffic, even on vacation." Another respondent said, "We are a worldwide company with customers and engineering staff all over the world. To accommodate and manage the time zones, I am expected to make myself available at any time. [For example,] answering e-mail and phone calls on Sunday to accommodate the 12-hour time difference in other countries is expected."[21]

Even the cruise lines appear to be accommodating the 24/7 workday. In 2006, cruise lines began implementing the technology that permits passengers to use their cell phones while cruising. Perhaps the days of getting away from it all have ended.

Many career-minded people who want to advance will choose to be available when needed. They may believe the 24/7 workday may be less a corporate mandate and more a natural consequence of ambitious people working hard together. Some employees will jump at the chance to be maximally involved, while others will place greater value on their privacy and more work-life balance (discussed in Chapter 10).

How Human Resource Management Is Practiced in the Real World

At the beginning of each chapter, there is an HRM in Action that focuses on an important topic related to the chapter. Features entitled Ethical Dilemmas are included in all but the first chapter to see how you would react in an ethical situation. A Trends & Innovations feature is included in each section to highlight current developments in the field of human resource management. A Global Perspective is included at the end of each chapter that highlights HRM in the global environment. Two HRM Incidents are provided at the end of each chapter to highlight material covered in the chapter.

 OBJECTIVE

Explain who performs human resource management tasks.

HR's Changing Role: Who Performs the Human Resource Management Tasks?

The person or units who perform the HRM tasks have changed dramatically in recent years and today there is no typical HR department.[22] This restructuring has often resulted in a shift in who carries out each function, not the elimination of the previously identified five HR functions. Some organizations continue to perform the majority of HR functions within the firm. However, as internal operations are reexamined, questions are raised, such as: Can some HR tasks be performed more efficiently by line managers or outside vendors? Can some HR tasks be centralized or eliminated altogether? Can technology perform tasks that were previously done by HR personnel? One apparent fact is that all functions within today's organizations are being scrutinized for cost cutting, including HR. All units must operate under a lean budget in this competitive global environment and HR is no exception.[23] The Hackett Group, the Atlanta-based business process advisory firm, reports that world-class HR organizations spend less per employee on HR than their peers and they operate with 35 percent fewer HR staff.[24]

As a shift is made in determining who will perform the human resource function, many HR departments continue to get smaller because others are now accomplishing certain functions. Outsourcing, shared service centers, professional employer organizations, and line managers now assist in the accomplishment of many traditional human resource activities. This shift should ultimately permit HR to shed its administrative image and focus on more strategic and mission-oriented activities[25] (to be discussed later). Let us first look at the role of the traditional human resource manager.

Human Resource Manager

Human resource manager:
Individual who normally acts in an advisory or staff capacity, working with other managers to help them deal with human resource matters.

Historically, the **human resource manager** was responsible for each of the five HR functions. Although this all-encompassing position has disappeared in most companies, the actual HRM tasks remain. A human resource manager is an individual who normally acts in an advisory or staff capacity, working with other managers to help them deal with human resource matters. Often, large HR departments were created with the central figure being the HR manager or executive. The human resource manager was primarily responsible for coordinating the management of human resources to help the organization achieve its goals. There was a shared responsibility between line managers and human resource professionals. Frequently the line manager went to HR for guidance in topics such as promotion, hiring, discipline, or discharge. The distinction between human resource management and the human resource manager is illustrated by the following account:

Bill Brown, the production supervisor for Ajax Manufacturing, has just learned that one of his machine operators has resigned. He immediately calls Sandra Williams, the human resource manager, and says, "Sandra, I just had a Class A machine operator quit down here. Can you find some qualified people for me to interview?" "Sure Bill," Sandra replies. "I'll send two or three down to you within the week, and you can select the one that best fits your needs."

In this instance, both Bill and Sandra are concerned with accomplishing organizational goals, but from different perspectives. As a human resource manager, Sandra identifies applicants who meet the criteria specified by Bill. Yet, Bill will make the final decision as to the person who is hired because he is responsible for the machine operators' performance. His primary responsibility is production; hers is human resources. As a human resource manager, Sandra must constantly deal with the many problems related to human resources that Bill and the other managers face. Her job is to help them meet the human resource needs of the entire organization. As previously mentioned, today many HR departments continue to get smaller because others are now accomplishing certain functions.

HR Outsourcing

Outsourcing:

Process of hiring an external provider to do the work that was previously done internally.

Outsourcing is the process of hiring an external provider to do the work that was previously done internally. The market for human resource outsourcing is growing dramatically.[26] The total value of all human resource outsourcing contracts was $3.6 billion worldwide in 2005 but is expected to reach $7.4 billion by 2009.[27] William Martorelli, a principal analyst with Forrester Research Inc., said, "The HRO market is changing and evolving very rapidly."[28] The key to outsourcing success is to determine which functions to outsource, the extent to which they should be outsourced, and which ones to keep in-house.[29] In a recent survey, 65 percent of respondents said that the leading motivation for outsourcing an HR function was to "employ use of experts." In the same survey, only 31 percent of respondents said that the reason for outsourcing was to reduce costs.[30] HR outsourcing is done in three ways: discrete services, multiprocess services, and total HR outsourcing.[31]

With discrete services, one element of a business process or a single set of high-volume repetitive functions is outsourced to a third party. A large majority of companies outsource transactional HR activities, such as 401(k) administration. Multiprocess services involve the complete outsourcing of one or more human resource processes. Examples might be the outsourcing of benefits administration and payroll. Procter & Gamble has outsourced its entire training operations.[32]

Total HR outsourcing represents the transfer of the majority of HR services to a third party. Whirlpool Corporation signed a 10-year deal to outsource HR business processes for 68,000 employees to Convergys Corporation.[33] However, as Michael Cornetto, senior HR delivery consultant at Watson Wyatt, said, "Despite much speculation otherwise, there is no headlong rush toward the total outsourcing of all HR services."[34]

Although most organizations expect to outsource more in the future, the strategic components of HR will likely remain within the organization.[35] HR executives would remain within the organization and be involved with strategic matters related to people management and other key HR functions.[36] In one survey, more than 90 percent of respondents say their compensation management and performance management functions are in-house.[37] "If you outsource HR correctly, it can improve service quality, save money and time, and free HR time for core functions," noted Geoffrey Dubiski, director of operations at Yoh HR Solutions of Philadelphia, an HR outsource vendor.[38]

Major outsourcing firms have evolved to accomplish many of the HR tasks that were formally done in-house. For example, Accenture HR is a global management consulting, technology services, and outsourcing company, with net revenues of $15.55 billion.[39] Accenture is capable of handling the outsourcing needs of a single HR activity or the HR activities of an entire company. For example, in 2006 Unilever announced a 7-year human resources outsourcing contract with Accenture with an estimated value of $1.1 billion.[40]

HR Shared Service Centers

Shared service center (SSC):
Centers that take routine, transaction-based activities dispersed throughout the organization and consolidate them in one place.

A **shared service center (SSC)**, also known as a center of expertise, takes routine, transaction-based activities dispersed throughout the organization and consolidates them in one place. For example, a company with 20 strategic business units could consolidate routine HR tasks and perform them in one location. Shared service centers provide an alternative to HR outsourcing and can often provide the same cost savings and customer service. Approximately 50 percent of the *Fortune* 500 companies use shared service centers for some of their HR tasks.[41] Financial services company Capital One began consolidating its HR activities in 1999 and, in the opinion of HR Vice President Doug Krey, "There is really nothing that HR does that can't be done through a shared services approach."[42]

The most common HR functions that use SSCs are benefits and pension administration, payroll, relocation assistance and recruitment support, global training and development, succession planning, and talent retention.

Professional Employer Organization (Employee Leasing)

Professional employer organization (PEO):
A company that leases employees to other businesses.

A **professional employer organization (PEO)** is a company that leases employees to other businesses. When a decision is made to use a PEO, the company releases its employees who are then hired by the PEO. The PEO then manages the administrative needs associated with employees. It is the PEO that pays the employees; it also pays workers' compensation premiums, payroll-related taxes, and employee benefits. The company reimburses the PEO and typically charges a fee of from 1 to 4 percent of the customer's gross wages, with percentages based on the number of leased employees. The PEO is the employees' legal employer and has the rights to hire, fire, discipline, and reassign an employee, whereas the client company maintains enough control so it can run the day-to-day operations of its business. The company that hires the PEO is sometimes termed a *co-employer*. Typically small and medium-sized firms are the primary users of PEOs.[43] It is estimated that the PEO industry generates approximately $51 billion in gross revenues annually.[44] PEOs permit business owners to focus on their core business while the PEO handles HR activities.[45]

Leasing has advantages for employees. Because leasing companies provide workers for many companies, they often enjoy economies of scale that permit them to offer a wider selection of benefits at considerably lower cost, due to the large numbers of employees in their pools. In addition, workers frequently have greater opportunities for job mobility. Some leasing firms operate throughout the nation. The relocation of one employed spouse in a dual-career family may be more satisfactory if the leasing company offers the other spouse a job in the new location too. For instance, Administaff, a Houston-based PEO, has more than 5,000 clients across the country.[46] In addition, if a client organization suffers a downturn, the leasing company offers job security. The PEO can transfer employees to another client, avoiding both layoffs and loss of seniority. Finally, according to the Small Business Administration, business owners spend up to 25 percent of their time on employee-related paperwork. Since smaller companies are less likely to have a dedicated human resources specialist, the PEO can handle the compliance requirements of programs such as 401(k) programs.

A potential disadvantage to the client is erosion of employee loyalty because workers receive pay and benefits from the leasing company. Regardless of any shortcomings, use of employee leasing is growing.

Line Managers

Line managers:
Individuals directly involved in accomplishing the primary purpose of the organization.

Individuals directly involved in accomplishing the primary purpose of the organization are **line managers**. As the traditional work of HR managers diminishes, line managers are stepping up and performing some duties typically done by human resource professionals. Managers are being assisted by manager self-service, the use of software and the corporate network to automate paper-based human resource processes that require a manager's approval, record-keeping or input, and processes that support the manager's job. This topic will be discussed in further detail in Chapter 4.

The success or failure of managers is largely based on the quality of their subordinates. Therefore, line managers are increasingly involved in the selection process. In addition, all managers understand that their workers must be continuously trained and developed. And, if the organization is unionized, the line manager must know how to deal effectively with the union.

HR as a Strategic Partner

5 OBJECTIVE

Explain the need for the human resource manager to be a strategic partner.

Strategic Management of Human Capital, Office of Personnel Management, the Federal Government's Human Resource Agency

http://apps.opm.gov/ humancapital/

This site is dedicated to providing information and resources that can be used to assess, formulate, and implement human capital strategies.

In Chapter 4, strategic planning will be defined as the process by which top management determines overall organizational purposes and objectives and how they are achieved. If HR is a strategic partner, HR executives must work with top management in achieving concrete plans and results. They must understand the operational side of the business and comprehend the complex organizational design, and they must be able to determine the capabilities of the company's workforce, both today and in the future. HR executives must ensure that human resources support the firm's mission. That means participating in and being responsive to the rapid changes that are occurring in business today. Harold W. Burlingame, longtime AT&T HR executive, has been hailed as a model HR executive for his continued emphasis on HR involvement in the business end of an organization.[47] Michael Maccoby, an executive consultant, said this about Mr. Burlingame: "He was before his time. A generation ago many HR people were more like policemen than managers of human capital, but Burlingame was always very strategic. He had a deep understanding of how to connect HR to business strategy."[48]

HR professionals must assume a strategic role when it comes to the management of human resources.[49] In companies such as Procter & Gamble, Yahoo!, Southwest Airlines, American Express, JetBlue, and Home Depot, HR operates at the highest strategic level.[50] Myrna Hellerman, a senior vice president with Sibson Consulting, said, "HR executives must have a seat at the board of directors' table to help the CEO and board make appropriate decisions about employee pay and compensation."[51]

There are currently three critical issues that boards must address and HR can contribute expertise to all three. These are: Do we have the right CEO? How well is the CEO's compensation linked to actual performance? Do we have the right strategy?[52]

HR professionals must change the way they work. Working as a business partner, rather than in a transactional HR role, requires a much deeper and broader understanding of the business issues. What exactly should HR be doing? Richard Pinola, chair and CEO of Right Management Consultants, Inc. (Philadelphia), during a session at a SHRM conference, listed the following tasks that CEOs want from HR:

- Make workforce strategies integral to company strategies and goals.
- Leverage HR's role in major change initiatives, such as strategic planning; mergers; and acquisitions: more HR professionals are being asked to join the team that previews mergers and explores potential merger partners,[53] systems implementation, and reorganizing/downsizing.
- Earn the right to a seat at the corporate table.
- Develop awareness and/or an understanding of the business.
- Understand finance and profits.
- Help line managers achieve their goals.[54]

The above list is a sharp deviation from what has traditionally been an administrative-type role for HR. It is now necessary for HR professionals to integrate the goals of HR with the goals of the organization and focus on expanding its strategic and high-level corporate participation with an emphasis on adding value. In doing so, HR must demonstrate that it can produce a return on investment for its programs. The CEO needs help in matters that human resource professionals are qualified to handle. As HR expert and author David Bratton said, "They (HR) are the enablers, they are the ones who should know about change and develop strategies to make it work."[55]

Human resource professionals can give the CEO and CFO a powerful understanding of the role human capital plays in the organization and the way it combines with business processes to expand or shrink shareholder value. To answer the question of whether the HR executive is involved strategically, William Schiemann, chair and CEO of Metrus Group, suggests that the following questions be answered:

1. Is HR present at mergers and acquisitions planning meetings, strategy reviews, and restructuring discussions?

2. Does HR provide an annual report on its ROI?

3. Does HR lead the people strategy? Has it developed performance indicators for the success of that strategy?

4. Is HR rated by its customers?

5. Does the organization conduct strategic versus entitlement employee surveys?

6. Are employee and other survey initiatives linked to customer and financial metrics?

7. Is there an ROI process to evaluate HR initiatives connected to the business strategy?[56]

P. O. Mak, head of HR for GE Capital Asia-Pacific, said, "You have to think in terms of a business leader and understand the big picture. Either you confine yourself in a room and work on policy, or you can get out in front of what's going on globally in business."[57] If today's HR managers are to become strategic partners in their organizations, they must run their departments according to the same rigid criteria that apply to other units, and be able to use data available in their unit to forecast outcomes and become real partners with upper management. HR units must be able to show how they add value to the company. Tied closely to strategic human resources is human capital metrics, the focus of the next discussion.

6   OBJECTIVE

Describe human capital metrics.

Human capital metrics:
Measures of HR performance.

Human Capital Metrics: Measuring HR's Effectiveness

Human capital metrics are measures of HR performance.[58] Even though employees account for as much as 80 percent of the worth of a corporation, the task of measuring and understanding how they contribute to the bottom line is often difficult. Jac Fitzenz, founder and chairman of the Saratoga Institute, a human capital management consulting firm in Santa Clara, California, says, "I can put a value on everything in my office: my clock, my desk. But I can't put a value on people."[59] Part of HR's becoming a strategic business partner includes being able to measure the effectiveness of the various HR tasks. Management has for years been able to measure the success or failure of a production process. They focused on return on investment, the bottom line, and profit. Today, HR is under the same scrutiny and management wants to know how HR activities contribute to the organization's bottom line.[60]

Bob Proctor, managing director of CLC Metrics, a measurement firm, said, "Measurement is critical when resources are finite, because HR cannot be all things to all people." This often includes, at a minimum, a serious focus on return-on-investment (ROI).[61]

Human capital metrics have been developed to determine how HR activities contribute to a company's profits.[62] Metrics associated with HR will continue to become more important and HR professionals must become adept at using metrics to show progress with their initiatives. For example, some employers gather data on where hires come from—such as through advertising, referrals, college recruitment programs, or lateral moves. The return on investment from those various sources can then be determined.[63]

Employee productivity metrics are also increasingly being used by HR professionals,[64] who are now analyzing hiring data in greater depth to better determine the value of their hiring practices and to better align them with business priorities. The metrics that can be collected in order to assess HR efficiency include productivity and cost metrics for the HR function such as time to fill open positions, HR head-count ratios, and administrative cost per employee. Other metrics might include turnover cost and training return on investment.[65]

A comprehensive set of metrics can be produced to evaluate HR's administrative activities. Upper management wants to know if the expenditure on HR activities is contributing sufficiently to the bottom line.[66] It has been estimated that the cost per employee for HR administration ranges from $1,200 to $1,600. Some have even placed the median per-employee investment close to $2,955.[67] Certainly upper management should want to know if this expenditure is contributing sufficiently to the bottom line.

It has been suggested that top performers in an organization contribute anywhere from 5 to 22 times more value to their companies than mid-level or low performers.[68] If that statement is anywhere correct, think of the metrics that HR professionals could use as they track progress in such areas as quality of hires, improved recruitment, and the selection processes.[69]

There is, however, no one-size-fits-all approach that employers can adopt to achieve greater hiring efficiency. The metrics that will best suit each company depends on a variety of factors, including its business goals.[70]

Wachovia Corporation, a consumer banking and financial services company based in Charlotte, North Carolina, has shifted its hiring metrics to emphasize success in the recruiting process. A scorecard is a report card of the effectiveness of a specific person. The monthly scorecard given for individual recruiters at Wachovia includes the following metrics: number of hires, time to fill, percentage of diverse candidates, percentage of diverse hires, interview-to-offer ratio, and offer-to-acceptance rate. The scorecard also includes metrics that are not yet connected to incentive compensation such as hiring manager satisfaction; new hire satisfaction; and a series of efficiency measures, including number of internal hires and number of external hires by source (such as employee referral, Internet, advertising, agency, college recruiting, career fair, etc.).[71]

Human Resource Designations

Various designations are used within the human resource profession; among these are HR executives, generalists, and specialists. An **executive** is a top-level manager who reports directly to the corporation's chief executive officer (CEO) or to the head of a major division. A **generalist**, who may be an executive, performs tasks in a variety of HR-related areas. The generalist is involved in several, or all, of the five HRM functions. A **specialist** may be an HR executive, manager, or nonmanager who is typically concerned with only one of the five functional areas of HRM. Figure 1-3 helps clarify these distinctions.

The vice president of industrial relations, shown in Figure 1-3, specializes primarily in union-related matters. This person is both an executive and a specialist. An HR

Web **Wisdom**

Saratoga

http:www.pwc.com/http://www.pwc.com/extweb/service.nsf/docid/de40ffb0d40981d385256f17005397cd

Saratoga is highly recognized as a world leader in the field of HR metrics and analysis, dedicated to the premise that intelligent measurement is fundamental to performance improvement.

 OBJECTIVE

Describe the various human resource classifications, including executives, generalists, and specialists.

Executive:

A top-level manager who reports directly to a corporation's chief executive officer or to the head of a major division.

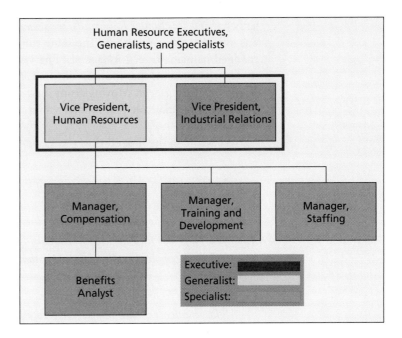

Figure 1-3 Human Resource Executives, Generalists, and Specialists

 OBJECTIVE

Describe the evolution of human resource management.

vice president is both an executive and a generalist, having responsibility for a wide variety of functions. The compensation manager is a specialist, as is the benefits analyst. Whereas a position level in the organization identifies an executive, the breadth of such positions distinguishes generalists and specialists.

Evolution of Human Resource Management

It seems appropriate, as the tenth edition of *Human Resource Management* is published, to see how HR management has evolved over the past 30 years. Traditionally, separate functions such as staffing, training and development, compensation, safety and health, and labor relations (if the firm was unionized) were created and placed under the direction of a human resource manager or executive (see Figure 1-4). Large firms might have had a manager and staff for each HR function that reported to the HR executive. The HR vice president worked closely with top management in formulating corporate policy.

The title of the book says much about the HR evolution. In the first edition, the book was titled *Personnel: The Management of Human Resources*, and the focus was more on personnel as a staff or advisory function. By the fourth edition, the title of the book

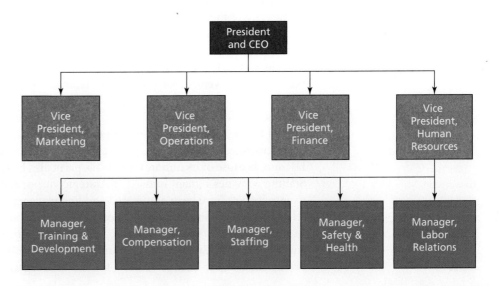

Figure 1-4 Traditional Human Resource Functions in a Large Firm

had changed to *Human Resource Management* and a more general management focus was evolving. This was about the same time that the journal *Personnel Administrator* changed its name to *HR Magazine*. The journal entitled *Personnel* changed its name to *HR Focus*, and the journal entitled *Personnel Journal* changed its name to *Workforce Management*. Moving from the more narrow focus of personnel suggested the more important role that human resource management would play out in the business world.

We wrote in the first edition:

> *Not many decades ago, people engaged in human resource work had titles such as welfare secretary and employment clerk. Their duties were rather restrictive and often dealt only with such items as workers' wages, minor medical problems, recreation, and housing.*[72] *Personnel, as human resources was most commonly called, as a profession was generally held in low esteem, and its organizational position was typically near the bottom of the hierarchy. As one personnel director said, "the personnel executive was the 'glad hander' or 'back slapper' who kept morale up in a company by running the company picnic and making sure the recreation program went off well"*
>
> *These days are over in many organizations. The personnel director's position is no longer a retirement position given to managers who cannot perform adequately anywhere else in the organization.*

Today, the person or persons who perform HR tasks are certainly different than they were even a decade ago. As more and more companies use alternative means to accomplish HR tasks, the role of the traditional HR manager is diminishing. As mentioned earlier, HR must now enter into the business of strategic HR, focus more on the bottom line of the organization, and leave the more administrative tasks to technology or others.

OBJECTIVE

Explain the evolving HR organization.

Evolving HR Organizations

In previous editions, the manner in which the human resource tasks changed as the firm grew was presented. HR functions in small businesses, medium-sized businesses, and in a large firm were described. These days the HR organization is much more difficult to describe. As previously discussed, line managers, HR outsourcing, HR shared service centers, and professional employer organizations are now handling many more of the traditional HR tasks. In discussion with numerous human resource managers in various sized organizations, the conclusion was that there is no pattern for how human resource tasks are now achieved. The only certainty is that the five previously identified HR functions must still be accomplished. Each company must choose the appropriate vehicle for doing these tasks based upon its specific needs and goals. A possible example of an evolving HR organization is presented in Figure 1-5. Here, the company has outsourced training and development, a function previously performed by the Training & Development Department. The compensation function is now performed at a shared service center. Safety and health has been removed from HR and, because of its importance in this particular firm, reports directly to the CEO. Staffing activities remain under the strategic vice president for human resources but many activities have been automated and line managers are now more involved in the selection process. Since the firm is nonunion, there is no Industrial Relations Manager. In this example, as the title suggests, the HR vice president is now more concerned with the strategic human resource matters. Because of the many changes that have occurred in HR in recent years, a typical HR organization realistically cannot be

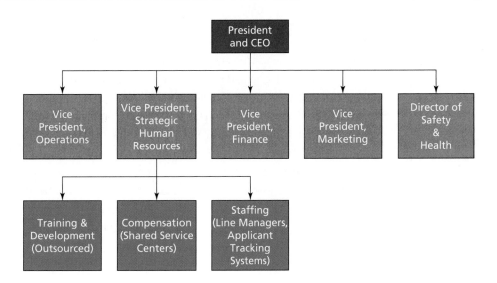

Figure 1-5 A Possible Evolving HR Organization Example

shown. Some firms have chosen to totally outsource their HR function: others choose different options. The organization of HR in today's environment is truly a work in progress.

A Global Perspective

British and American Culture Are Different

When Christina Seckar left her HR job in New Jersey for a manager's position in England, her British boss offered her a warning: "Watch yourself. British people are different from Americans." Seckar had also heard that the highest number of failed international assignments involve Americans in the United Kingdom and Britons in the United States. She says, "I thought, 'OK, if you ever thought it was going to be simple, keep that in mind.'" A year after her move abroad, Seckar is still learning the ropes of British business culture at the oil field technology services company where she works in Southampton, England. "It hasn't been easy," she says. "I didn't realize in the beginning how much each and every thing you do is going to be a challenge."[73]

Seckar's case is by no means unique. The United Kingdom might seem to require less adjustment for Americans than countries such as China or Japan, where English is not the official language and where cultural differences are obvious. But that assumption can set up Americans for difficulty, disappointment, and underachievement. "The United Kingdom really is a foreign country—and HR departments that ignore that fact are at their peril," says Dean Foster, a New York–based consultant on intercultural business issues. "It's that expectation of similarity that throws everyone off."[74]

U.S. expatriates on assignment in the United Kingdom must deal with a language that they know, but it is full of different turns of phrase and unexpected meanings. British attitudes about work, personal ambition, individualism, efficiency, business meetings, and communications may run counter to a person's experiences and expectations.[75]

Americans tend to rely on sports metaphors in business talk, which may confuse Britons. Experts suggest that employees avoid using phrases such as "step up to the plate," "cover all the bases," "I'll touch base with you," "ballpark figure," "off the wall," and "out in left field." Britons tend to say more with fewer words and lots of nuance.[76]

Craig Storti, author of *Old World, New World—Bridging Cultural Differences: Britain, France, Germany and the U.S.*, said, "Americans come across loud and clear. But because the English are relatively understated and indirect, a lot of what they say is in what they do not say. Americans hear the words, and they understand the words, but they do not interpret the meaning correctly." "Differences in communication style are the biggest surprise" for American expatriates with assignments in the United Kingdom, he adds.[77] "A Brit might say, 'We have a bit of a problem,'" says Matthew J. Kapszukiewicz, a London-based HR manager for Europe, the Middle East, and Asia at PricewaterhouseCoopers. "That could mean it's a big problem; it might mean it's a small problem, but you're not quite sure, and you have to explore that," he says. Misunderstandings go both ways. Britons harbor a degree of distrust toward Americans in the workplace because of fine distinctions in language and expression, says Cary Cooper, professor of organizational psychology and health at Lancaster Management School, Lancaster University, in England. "Americans use words that disguise what they're doing: 'process re-engineering,' 'restructuring,' 'fight-sizing,' 'involuntary career events,'" says Cooper, a longtime U.K. resident with dual U.S.-U.K. citizenship. "They have to learn not to use jargon."[78]

Scope of This Book

Effective HRM is crucial to the success of every organization. To be effective, managers must understand and competently practice HRM. This book was designed to give you the following:

- An insight into the role of strategic HRM in today's organizations, the strategic role of HR functions, and the impact of technology and global competition.
- An awareness of the importance of business ethics and corporate social responsibility in HRM.
- An understanding of job analysis, human resource planning, recruitment, and selection.
- An awareness of the importance of human resource development, including training and developing, for employees at all levels.
- An understanding of performance appraisal and its role in performance management.
- An appreciation of how compensation programs are formulated and administered.
- An understanding of safety and health factors as they affect the firm's profitability.
- An opportunity to understand employee and labor relations.
- An appreciation of the global dimension of HRM.

Students often question whether the content of a book corresponds to the realities of the business world. In writing and revising this book, the comments, observations, and experiences of HR practitioners are integrated throughout, along with extensive research efforts. HR practices of leading business organizations are provided to illustrate how theory can be applied in the real world. The intent is to enable you to experience human resource management in action.

This book is organized in eight parts, as shown in Figure 1-6; combined, they provide a comprehensive view of human resource management. As you read it, hopefully you will be stimulated to increase your knowledge in this rapidly changing and challenging field.

HUMAN RESOURCE MANAGEMENT, 10TH EDITION

PART I. INTRODUCTION
Chapter 1: Strategic Human Resource Management: An Overview

PART II. ETHICAL, SOCIAL, AND LEGAL CONSIDERATIONS
Chapter 2: Business Ethics and Corporate Social Responsibility
Chapter 3: Workforce Diversity, Equal Employment Opportunity, and Affirmative Action

PART III. STAFFING
Chapter 4: Job Analysis, Strategic Planning, and Human Resource Planning
Chapter 5: Recruitment
Chapter 6: Selection

PART IV. HUMAN RESOURCE DEVELOPMENT
Chapter 7: Training and Development
Appendix Chapter 7: Career Planning and Development
Chapter 8: Performance Management and Appraisal

PART V. COMPENSATION
Chapter 9: Direct Financial Compensation
Chapter 10: Benefits, Nonfinancial Rewards, and Other Compensation Issues

PART VI. SAFETY AND HEALTH
Chapter 11: A Safe and Healthy Work Environment

PART VII. EMPLOYEE AND LABOR RELATIONS
Chapter 12: Labor Union and Collective Bargaining
Appendix Chapter 12: History of Unions in the United States
Chapter 13: Internal Employee Relations

PART VIII. OPERATING IN A GLOBAL ENVIRONMENT
Chapter 14: Global Human Resource Management

Figure 1-6 Organization of This Book

Summary

1. Define human resource management.

Human resource management is the utilization of individuals to achieve organizational objectives. Consequently, all managers at every level must concern themselves with HRM.

2. Identify the human resource management functions.

The HRM functions include staffing, human resource development, compensation, safety and health, and employee and labor relations.

3. Identify the external environmental factors that affect human resource management.

External factors include the labor force, legal considerations, society, unions, shareholders, competition, customers, technology, economy, and unanticipated events. Each factor, either separately or in combination with others, can place constraints on how HRM tasks are accomplished.

4. Explain who performs human resource management tasks.

HR outsourcing is the process of hiring an external provider to do the work that was previously done internally. HR shared service centers take routine, transaction-based activities that are dispersed throughout the organization and consolidate them in one place. A professional employer organization is a company that leases employees to other businesses. Line managers in certain firms are being used more frequently than before to deliver HR services.

5. Explain the need for the human resource manager to be a strategic partner.

If HR is to be a strategic partner, HR executives must work with top management in achieving concrete plans and results. It is necessary for them to understand the operational side of the business and comprehend the complex organizational design. They must also be able to determine the capabilities of the company's workforce, both today and in the future, and ensure that human resources support the firm's mission.

6. Describe human capital metrics.

Human capital metrics are measures of HR performance.

7. Describe the various HR classifications, including executives, generalists, and specialists.

Executives are top-level managers who report directly to the corporation's CEO or the head of a major division. Generalists (who are often executives) are persons who perform tasks in a wide variety of HR-related areas. A specialist may be a human resource executive, manager, or nonmanager who typically is concerned with only one of the functional areas of HRM.

8. Describe the evolution of human resource management.

It seems appropriate as the tenth edition of this text is published to view HR as it has evolved over the past 30 years. The title of the book says much about the HR evolution. In the first edition, the book was titled *Personnel: The Management of Human Resources* and the focus was more on personnel as a staff or advisory function. By the fourth edition, the title of the book had been changed to *Human Resource Management* and a more general management focus was evolving.

9. Explain the evolving HR organization.

The HR organizational structure of firms changes as they outsource, use professional employer organizations and shared service centers, and involve line managers more in traditional HR tasks. Regardless of an organization's design, the five previously identified HR functions must still be accomplished.

Key Terms

- Branding, 3
- Human resource management (HRM), 4
- Staffing, 5
- Human resource development (HRD), 5
- External environment, 7
- Union, 8
- Shareholders, 9

- Cyberwork, 10
- Human resource manager, 11
- Outsourcing, 12
- Shared service center (SSC), 13
- Professional employer organization (PEO), 13
- Line managers, 13

- Human capital metrics, 15
- Executive, 16
- Generalist, 17
- Specialist, 17

Questions for Review

1. Define human resource management. What human resource management functions must be performed regardless of the organization's size?

2. What are the external environmental factors that affect human resource management? Describe each.

3. This chapter describes HR's changing role in business. Describe each component that is involved in human resource management.

4. How should HR act as a strategic partner?

5. What are human capital metrics?

6. What are the various designations associated with human resource management?

HRM Incident 1

HR after a Disaster

After Hurricane Rita struck Lake Charles, in southwest Louisiana, on September 24, 2005, many businesses wondered if they would ever return to their former selves. Massive destruction was everywhere. Lake Charles, known for its large and beautiful oak and pine trees, now had the job of removing those downed trees from homes, businesses, and lots. You could see for miles through what used to be thick forests. Huge trucks designed for removing massive tree trunks were everywhere. While driving down a street, downed trees could be seen stacked two stories high, waiting to be picked up. The town grew rapidly in size as debris and repair crews set about recovery operations. The noise created by chain saws could be heard from daylight until dark. The sounds of hammers were everywhere as homeowners scrambled to get their roofs repaired. Often repair crews would just find an empty lot and set up tents for the night because all motels were full. Traffic was unbelievably slow and it appeared as if everyone was attempting to get on the road at the same time. Just driving from Point A to Point B could often be quite an adventure. As might be expected in conditions such as these, accidents were numerous. Often police did not have the resources to ticket every fender bender, so unless there were injuries, insurance cards were exchanged and the police went on to the next accident.

Months after Hurricane Rita struck, large and small businesses were still frantically trying to find workers so they could start up again. It appeared that every business in the town had a "Help Wanted" sign out front. Individuals who wanted a job could get one and could command a premium salary. Wal-Mart, known for remaining open 24 hours a day, could only stay open on an abbreviated schedule. It even bussed in employees from Lafayette, Louisiana, 70 miles away, each morning and returned them at night because there were not enough workers available in the local area. Restaurants that normally remained open late into the evening closed at 6:00 p.m., if they opened at all. Compensation scales that were in use prior to the hurricanes had to be thrown out and new plans implemented. Minimum-wage jobs were nonexistent. Employees who earned minimum wage before the storm could now command $10 per hour just for being a flagger (a person who directs traffic). Fast-food restaurants that normally paid $6 per hour now paid $9 or $10. Burger King was even offering a $1,500 bonus for entry-level workers. Upscale restaurants that normally paid minimum wage plus tips now paid premium rate plus tips. Restaurants that remained open often had a much younger staff and it was evident that the managers and assistant managers were working overtime to train these new workers.

Restaurant patrons had to learn patience because there would be mistakes by these eager, but largely untrained workers.

Questions

1. How were the human resource functions affected by Hurricane Rita?
2. Do you believe that the HR situation described regarding Hurricane Rita would be typical in a disaster? Explain.

HRM Incident 2

Downsizing

As the largest employer in Ouachita County, Arkansas, International Forest Products Company (IFP) is an important part of the local economy. Ouachita County is a mostly rural area in south central Arkansas. It employs almost 10 percent of the local workforce, and few alternative job opportunities are available in the area.

Scott Wheeler, the human resource director at IFP, tells of a difficult decision he once had to make. According to Scott, everything was going along pretty well despite the economic recession, but he knew that sooner or later the company would be affected. "I got the word at a private meeting with the president, Janet Deason, that we would have to cut the workforce by 30 percent on a crash basis. I was to get back to her within a week with a suggested plan. I knew that my plan would not be the final one, since the move was so major, but I knew that Ms. Deason was depending on me to provide at least a workable approach.

"First, I thought about how the union would react. Certainly, workers would have to be let go in order of seniority. The union would try to protect as many jobs as possible. I also knew that all of management's actions during this period would be intensely scrutinized. We had to make sure that we had our act together.

"Then there was the impact on the surrounding community to consider. The economy of Ouachita County had not been in good shape recently. Aside from the influence on the individual workers who were laid off, I knew that our cutbacks would further depress the area's economy. I knew that there would be a number of government officials and civic leaders who would want to know how we were trying to minimize the harm done to the public in the area.

"We really had no choice but to make the cuts, I believed. First of all, I had no choice because Ms. Deason said we were going to do it. Also, I had recently read a news account that one of our competitors, Johns Manville Corporation in West Monroe, Louisiana, had laid off several hundred workers in a cost-cutting move. To keep our sales from being further depressed, we had to ensure that our costs were just as low as those of our competitors. The wood products market is very competitive and a cost advantage of even 2 or 3 percent would allow competitors to take many of our customers.

"Finally, a major reason for the cutbacks was to protect the interests of our shareholders. A few years ago a shareholder group disrupted our annual meeting to insist that IFP make certain antipollution changes. In general, though, the shareholders seem to be more concerned with the return on their investments than with social responsibility. At our meeting, the president reminded me that, just like every other manager in the company, I should place the shareholders' interests above all else. I really was quite overwhelmed as I began to work up a human resource plan that would balance all of these conflicting interests."

Questions

1. List the elements in the company's environment that will affect Scott's suggested plan. How legitimate is the interest of each of these?
2. Is it true that Scott should be concerned first and foremost with protecting the interests of shareholders? Discuss.

Notes

1. Melissa Johnson and Phil Roberts, "Rules of Attraction," *Marketing Health Service* 26 (Spring 2006): 38–40.
2. Julie Barker, "How to Pick the Best People (And Keep Them)," *Potentials* 38 (November 2005): 33–36.
3. "HR Brand-Building in Today's Market," *HR Focus* 82 (February 2005): 1–15.
4. Jason Averbook, "Connecting CLOs with the Recruiting Process," *Chief Learning Officer* 4 (June 2005): 24–27.
5. Fabian Hieronimus, Katharina Schaefer, and Jürgen Schröder, "Using Branding to Attract Talent," *McKinsey Quarterly* (2005): 12–14.
6. "Employer Brands Catch on, but Few Measure Effectiveness Yet," *HR Focus* 83 (August 2006): 8.
7. "Building on Brand to Attract Top Employees," *Workforce Management* 85 (February 27, 2006): 31–32.
8. Jack J. Phillips, "The Value of Human Capital: What Logic and Intuition Tell Us," *Chief Learning Officer* 4 (August 2005): 50–52.
9. R. Wayne Mondy, Robert M. Noe, and Robert E. Edwards, "What the Staffing Function Entails," *Personnel* 63 (April 1986): 55–58.
10. Russ Westcott, "Has Your Work Life Plateaued?" *Quality Progress* 34 (October 2001): 60.
11. "Union Members in 2005," U.S Department of Labor, Bureau of Labor Statistics, January 20, 2006.
12. Kenneth E. Goodpaster and John B. Matthews, Jr., "Can a Corporation Have a Conscience?" *Harvard Business Review* 60 (January-February 1982): 132–141.
13. Jennifer Schramm, "HR Technology Competencies: New Roles for HR Professionals," *HR Magazine* 51 (April 2006): 1–10.
14. Jennifer Schramm, "HR's Tech Challenges," *HR Magazine* 50 (March 2005): 152–152.
15. "Train Managers and Executives to Avoid Legal 'Danger Zones,'" *HR Focus* 83 (August 2006): 4–7.
16. Alice Andors, "Tech Smarter," *HR Magazine* 50 (October 2005): 66–72.
17. Michelle V. Rafter, "Unicru Breaks Through in the Science of 'Smart Hiring'," *Workforce Management* 84 (May 2005): 76–78.
18. "HR Technology Is Fueling Profits, Cost Savings, & Strategy," *HR Focus* 83 (January 2006): 7–10.
19. Mike Hogan, "Life without Limits," *Entrepreneur* 34 (April 2006): 6–7.
20. John A. Ryder, "Future of HR Technology," *HR Magazine* 50 (2005 Anniversary Issue): 67–69.
21. Rick Merritt, "Working Harder in Tough Times," *Electronic Engineering Times* (August 22, 2005): 37–52.
22. "SHRM Predicts the Human Capital Metrics of the Future," *HR Focus* 82 (August 2005): 7–10.
23. Richard P. Rison and Jennifer Tower, "How to Reduce the Cost of HR and Continue to Provide Value," *Human Resource Planning* 28 (2005): 14–17.
24. "Advice to HR: Simplify and Save," *HR Magazine* 50 (September 2005): 18.
25. "HR Departments Struggle to Move up from 'Administrative' to 'Strategic' Status," *HR Focus* 83 (March 2006): 8.
26. Paul Harris, "Outsourcing Spreads Its Wings," *Employee Benefit News* 20 (April 2006): 22–30.
27. "A Watershed Year Predicted for HR Outsourcing," *HR Magazine* 51 (February 2006): 16–20.
28. Pamela Babcock, "A Crowded Space," *HR Magazine* 51 (March 2006): 68–74.
29. Roseanne White Geisel, "Get Star-Quality Service," *HR Magazine* 51 (March 2006): 78–86.
30. "HR Outsourcing," *Controller's Report* (July 2006): 8–9.
31. Leslie A. Weatherly, "HR Outsourcing: Reaping Strategic Value for Your Organization," *HR Magazine* 50 (September 2005): 1–11.
32. Alan Bellinger, "Outsourcing Needs a Training Element," *ITTraining* (April 2005): 12.
33. Patrick Thibodeau and Marc L. Songini, "HR Outsourcing Picking up Steam," *Computerworld* 39 (August 8, 2005): 7.
34. Ann Pomeroy, "Outsourcing, One Step at a Time," *HR Magazine* 50 (June 2005): 12.
35. "HR Technology Is Fueling Profits, Cost Savings, & Strategy," *HR Focus* 84 (January 2006): 7–10.
36. Steve Davolt, "The Half-truth of Total HRO," *Employee Benefit News* 20 (June 2006): 27–28.
37. Pomeroy, "Outsourcing, One Step at a Time."
38. "Why Outsourcing Succeeds—or Not," *HR Focus* 82 (July 2005): 1–14.
39. http://www.accenture.com/Global/About_Accenture/Company_Overview/CompanyDescription.htm (June 12, 2006).
40. Jessica Marquez, "Accenture May Make Move into Global Benefits," *Workforce Management* 85 (June 26, 2006): 16.
41. Martha Frase-Blunt, "Keeping HR on the Inside," *HR Magazine* 49 (October 2004): 57–61.
42. Ibid.
43. Max Chafkin, "Fed up with HR?" *Inc.* 28 (May 2006): 50–52.
44. Fiona Haley, "PEOs to the Rescue," *Black Enterprise* 36 (July 2006): 62.
45. Chafkin, "Fed up with HR?"
46. Haley, "PEOs to the Rescue."
47. Steve Bates, "His True Calling," *HR Magazine* 47 (August 2002): 38–43.
48. "Tips for Expanding Your Corporate Role," *HR Focus* 80 (September 2003): 1–15.
49. "HR's Growing Role in M&A Due Diligence," *HR Focus* 82 (August 2005): 1–15.
50. Susan Meisinger, "Fast Company: Do They Really 'Hate' HR?" *HR Magazine* 50 (September 2005): 12.
51. "What Lies Ahead for HR?" *HR Focus* 81 (October 2004): 1–15.
52. Roger Kenney, "The Boardroom Role of Human Resources," *Corporate Board* 26 (January/February 2005): 12–16.
53. "HR's Growing Role in M&A Due Diligence," *HR Focus* 82 (August 2005): 1–15.
54. Richard Pinola, "What CEOs Want from HR," *HR Focus* 79 (September 2002): 1.
55. David Brown, "The Future Is Nigh for Strategies HR," *Canadian HR Reporter* 15 (June 17, 2002): 7.

56. "Trends to Watch in HR's Future," *HR Focus* 79 (December 2002): 7.

57. Kevin Voigt, "The New Face of HR," *Far Eastern Economic Review* 165 (September 5, 2002): 61.

58. Gary T. Smith, "A Primer on Metrics," *Intelligent Enterprise* 7 (March 6, 2004): 26–30.

59. Steve Bates, "Accounting for People: HR Executives and Academics Are Searching for the Holy Grail of HR–Measurements of the Value of Human Capital," *HR Magazine* 47 (October 2002): 30.

60. "Getting Real and Specific with Measurements," *HR Focus* 82 (January 2005): 11–13.

61. "Hey, Workplace Learning Pro! You're Next!" *T+D* 59 (September 2005): 10.

62. "SHRM Predicts the Human Capital Metrics of the Future," *HR Focus* 82 (August 2005): 7–10.

63. Charlotte Garvey, "Next Generation Hiring Metrics," *HR Magazine* 50 (April 2005): 70–76.

64. Karen M. Krol, "Repurposing Metrics for HR," *HR Magazine* 51 (July 2006): 64–69.

65. Craig Schneider, "The New Human-Capital Metrics," *CFO* 22 (February 2006 Special Issue): 22–27.

66. Edward E. Lawler III, Alec Levenson, and John W. Boudreau, "HR Metrics and Analytics: Use and Impact," *Human Resource Planning* 27 (2004): 27–35.

67. Richard P. Rison and Jennifer Tower, "How to Reduce the Cost of HR and Continue to Provide Value," *Human Resource Planning* 28 (2005): 14–17.

68. Megan Santosus, "Loyalty, Shmoyalty," *CIO* 15 (April 15, 2002): 40.

69. "SHRM Predicts the Human Capital Metrics of the Future," *HR Focus* 82 (August 2005): 7–10.

70. Charlotte Garvey, "Next Generation Hiring Metrics," *HR Magazine* 50 (April 2005): 70–76.

71. Ibid.

72. Henry Eibirt, "The Development of Personnel Management in the United States," *Business History Review* 33 (August 1969): 348–349.

73. DeeDee Doke, "Perfect Strangers," *HR Magazine* 49 (December 2004): 62–68.

74. Ibid.

75. Ibid.

76. Ibid.

77. Ibid.

78. Ibid.

PART TWO

Ethical, Social, and Legal Considerations

CHAPTER OBJECTIVES

After completing this chapter, students should be able to:

1 Define ethics and understand the model of ethics.

2 Explain the attempts at legislating ethics.

3 Understand the importance of a code of ethics and describe human resource ethics.

4 Describe the professionalization of human resource management.

5 Describe the concept of corporate social responsibility.

6 Explain what is meant by stakeholder analysis and the social contract.

7 Describe how a corporate social responsibility program is implemented.

Business Ethics and Corporate Social Responsibility

2

CEOs who take over companies that have been torn apart by scandal have many battles to fight to repair the company's reputation.[1] Some have said that changing Tyco's corporate image must rank as one of the toughest jobs in recent history.[2]

Dennis Kozlowski, CEO at Tyco International, resigned in 2002 after being charged with fraud. In the aftermath, Tyco was viewed as an example of a company whose ethics had gone astray. Under Kozlowski's leadership, there were reports of extraordinary excesses: a $6,000 shower curtain, a birthday party on the island of Sardinia, and even a private performance by singer-songwriter Jimmy Buffet, who sang "Wasting away again in Margaritaville."[3]

Tyco's new CEO, Edward Breen, appointed Eric Pillmore to change this image in the wake of the Kozlowski scandal. He was chosen to head the company's corporate governance efforts two weeks after Breen took office. Pillmore faced an uphill battle of winning over the largely new executive team and the very concerned employees. "I was hired with the charter to develop an ethics and compliance program," he said, "and was given the latitude by the board of directors to architect the job as I saw fit—and so that everyone could sleep at night." Pillmore had to determine where to start in an organization that has facilities in more than 60 countries and employs more than 200,000.[4]

One of the first steps Breen and Pillmore took was to establish "four critical corporate values: integrity, excellence, teamwork, and accountability." A framework for accountability also had to be established.[5] Pillmore reports to the board of directors, not the CEO. Also, the directors do not just hear from the CEO. At Tyco the board now meets about six times a year, and managers of different units join the board for dinner. In addition, directors regularly visit business units, typically without CEO Breen or other senior staff.[6] Tyco also established the position of ombudsperson with the responsibility of preventing a recurrence.[7]

Once the ethical guidelines were developed, the policy and accompanying materials were drafted in the 26 languages spoken within Tyco. The four critical values provided the basis for Tyco's 32-page guide for ethical conduct, which tries to make it perfectly clear what is, and what is not, appropriate business behavior. The guide includes stories on every page that show employees examples of how things can go wrong in everyday business activities. Purchasing employees, for example, are shown what constitutes a conflict of interest. The guide encourages employees to examine where there might be problems.[8]

Dov Seidman, CEO of corporate ethics consultancy LRN, said, "It takes a while to weave ethics into the fabric of a corporate culture. Right now, ethics is where quality was 20 to 30 years ago—it's a separate discipline within the company. Employees used to figure that quality control was a back-end responsibility and that somebody else would catch any given defect." Now, he says, anyone can stop a production line if they see a problem. "Quality has been designed into people's job descriptions. Ethics will happen the same way."[9]

In 2005, a jury convicted Kozlowski of stealing millions of dollars from Tyco. He was found guilty of grand larceny, conspiracy, securities fraud, and eight of nine counts of falsifying business records. By 2006, the scandal left by Tyco's now-jailed former CEO had been cleaned up.[10] The company had also recovered its financial health and reputation.[11]

This chapter begins by examining how an ethical culture was developed at Tyco International. This is followed by a discussion of ethics and the presentation of a model of ethics. Next, attempts that have been made to legislate ethics are presented. Then, the importance of a code of ethics and human resource ethics are discussed. The professionalization of human resource management is described, followed by a discussion of the concept of corporate social responsibility and what is meant by stakeholder analysis and the social contact. Next, we examine how a corporate social responsibility program is implemented, and the chapter concludes with a global perspective feature entitled "'When in Rome, Do as the Romans' Does Not Work Today."

Ethics

Ethics is the discipline dealing with what is good and bad, or right and wrong, or with moral duty and obligation.

It was not long ago that many organizations paid only lip service to ethics. Headlines have exposed the far-from-ethical exploits of Enron, Arthur Andersen, WorldCom, Global Crossing, Adelphia Communications, Tyco International, and others. The ruthless self-interest that motivated the leaders of some large corporations has been revealed. Often corporate executives made decisions that did not parallel the expectations of society. The same seems to be true of boards of directors, who often used a rubber-stamp approach. The image of Enron is now a vital presence in every boardroom. To have served on the Enron board literally has become a badge of shame. At Enron, the firm's stated values, respect, integrity, communication, and excellence were once proudly etched on paperweights. But, because of unethical leaders, the company was destroyed.[12] "CEOs have to be clear and say, 'That's never what I want,' and make sure people understand norms," says Bob Shoemaker, director of programs for the Center for Ethical Business Cultures.[13] General Norman Schwarzkopf, hero of Desert Storm, has a piece of advice that all CEOs should follow. He calls it Rule 14: "When in doubt, do what's right."[14] The image of the business world would be in much better shape if this simple advice had been followed.

Trends & Innovations

One Person's Ethical Stand

Everyone is not as ethical as Leonard Roberts, the former CEO of Arby's, the fast-food restaurant chain. He took over the chain when it was losing money and made Arby's profitable, but then resigned from the board of directors when Arby's owner threatened to withhold bonuses for Roberts's staff and not to give promised help to Arby's franchisees, in order to further increase profits. In retaliation for his ethical stand, Roberts was fired. He was then hired as CEO of the Shoney's restaurant chain. Soon after arriving he discovered that the company was the subject of the largest racial discrimination suit in history. After investigating and discovering that the company was, in fact, in the wrong, Roberts promised the suit would be settled fairly. Shoney's owner agreed to pay and settle, but only if Roberts would resign afterward. "My stand on integrity was getting a little hard on my wife and kids," Roberts said. "However, I knew it had to be done. There was no other way. You cannot fake it. You must stand up for what is right regardless. You cannot maintain your integrity 90 percent and be a leader. It's got to be 100 percent." Later Roberts became CEO of RadioShack Corporation. Because of his work at RadioShack, *Brandweek* magazine named him Retailer of the Year.[15] He retired in 2006.

Web Wisdom

International Business Ethics Institute

http://www.business-ethics.org

The Institute was founded in 1994 in response to the growing need for transnational in the field of business ethics.

Most of the 500 largest corporations in the United States now have a code of ethics, which encompasses written conduct standards, internal education, and formal agreements on industry standards, ethics offices, social accounting, and social projects. Even so, business ethics scandals continue to be headline news today. Lying on resumes, obstruction of justice, destruction of records, stock price manipulation, cutting corners to meet Wall Street's expectations, fraud, waste, and abuse, unfortunately, are occurring all too often when those in business go wrong ethically.[16]

However, business is not alone. There is virtually no occupation that has not had its own painful ethical crises in recent years. There was the coach who altered his star pitcher's birth certificate in the Little League World Series and the teachers who provided answers on standardized tests to improve their schools' performance.[17]

But certainly a devastating blow to society was dealt by business, and ethical breaches in business continue today. Recently, enforcers at the Securities & Exchange Commission (SEC) have opened inquiries and investigations of executives who have switched the dates of their stock option grants to favor their own bank accounts.[18]

In a study conducted by TheLadders.com, an executive job search service, 83 percent of the survey's 1,020 respondents rated a company's record of business ethics very important when deciding whether to accept a job.[19]

A Model of Ethics

According to Kenneth D. Lewis, Chairman and Chief Executive Officer at Bank of America, "There is a difference between what's legal and what's ethical. But we don't often talk about it, and I've wondered why. Maybe people think it's too soft . . . too hard to define . . . or, in corporate language, not 'actionable.' Maybe it's easier for us to defer to new laws and regulations as the solution. But new laws are only part of the solution. And, in my view, they don't get to the heart of the problem."[20] There must be leaders who are able and willing to instill ethics throughout the culture of the organization.[21]

Ethics is about deciding whether an action is good or bad and what to do about it if it is bad. Ethics is a philosophical discipline that describes and directs moral conduct. Those in management make ethical (or unethical) decisions every day. Do you hire the best-qualified person, who is a minority? Do you forget to tell a prospect about the dangerous aspect of a certain job? Some ethical decisions are major and some are minor. But decisions in small matters often set a pattern for the more important decisions a manager makes.

A model of ethics is presented in Figure 2-1. As can be seen, ethics consists mainly of two relationships, indicated by the bold horizontal arrows. A person or organization is ethical if these relationships are strong and positive. Notice that the first element in the model is sources of ethical guidance. One might use a number of sources to determine what is right or wrong, good or bad, moral or immoral. These sources include the Bible and other holy books. They also include the still, small voice that many refer to as conscience. Millions believe that conscience is a gift of God or the voice of God. Others see it as a developed response based on the internalization of societal mores. Another source of ethical guidance is the behavior and advice of the people psychologists call significant others—our parents, friends, and role models, and members of our churches, clubs, and associations. For most professionals, there are codes of ethics that prescribe certain behavior. Without this conscience that has developed it might be easy to say, "Everyone does it," "Just this once won't hurt," or "No one will ever know."[22]

Laws also offer guidance to ethical behavior, prohibiting acts that can be especially harmful to others. If a certain behavior was illegal, most would consider it to be unethical as well. There are exceptions, of course. For example, through the 1950s, laws in most southern states relegated black persons to the backs of buses and otherwise assigned them inferior status. Martin Luther King Jr. resisted such laws and, in fact, engaged in civil disobedience and other nonviolent forms of resistance to their enforcement. King won the Nobel Peace Prize for his efforts.

Notice in Figure 2-1 that the sources of ethical guidance should lead to our beliefs or convictions about what is right or wrong. Most would agree that people have a responsibility to avail themselves of these sources of ethical guidance. In short, individuals should care about what is right and wrong and not just be concerned with what is expedient. The strength of the relationship between what an individual or an organization believes to be moral and correct and what available sources of guidance suggest is morally correct is **Type I ethics**.

For example, suppose a manager believes it is acceptable to not hire minorities, despite the fact that almost everyone condemns this practice. This person is unethical, but perhaps only in a Type I sense.

Having strong beliefs about what is right and wrong and basing them on the proper sources may have little relationship to what one does. Figure 2-1 illustrates that **Type II ethics** is the strength of the relationship between what one believes and how one behaves.

Type I ethics:
Strength of the relationship between what an individual or an organization believes to be moral and correct and what available sources of guidance suggest is morally correct.

Type II ethics:
Strength of the relationship between what one believes and how one behaves.

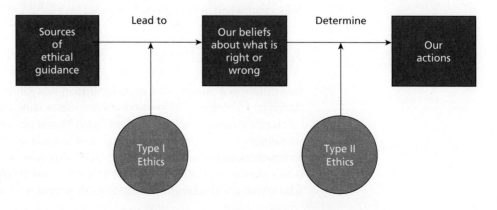

Figure 2-1 A Model of Ethics
Source: R. Wayne Mondy and Shane R. Premeaux, *Management: Concepts, Practices, and Skills,* 7th ed. (Upper Saddle River, NJ: Prentice Hall, 1995), p. 91.

A Selection Quandary

You are being transferred to a new assignment with in the company, and your boss has asked you to nominate one of your subordinates as a replacement. The possible candidates are Randy Carlton, who is obviously more qualified, and James Mitchell, who, though not as experienced, is much better liked by the workers. If Randy is given the promotion, you are not certain the workers will accept him as their leader. James, on the other hand, is a hard worker and is well liked and respected by the others, including Randy. As you labor over the decision, you think about how unfair it would be to Randy if the feelings of the other workers kept him from getting a deserved promotion. At the same time, you feel that your primary responsibility should be to maintain the productivity of the work unit. If your former division fell apart after your departure, it would hurt your reputation, not to mention the company. What would you do?

This is the only place in this text where the author will recommend the ethical choice and also identify other factors that might make a person take a less-than-ethical stand. What would you have done if placed in a situation such as this?

Ethical Choice: Recommend Randy, who is the best qualified employee.

Factors Influencing Another Decision: The department might fall apart if Randy is given the promotion. Other workers might not work for Randy and the workers would more readily accept James. Your reputation may be hurt if the department productivity declines. Besides, Randy can work with James.

For example, if a manager knows that it is wrong to discriminate, but does so anyway, the manager is being unethical in a Type II sense. If a board of directors considers it wrong to pay excessive salaries to the CEO, yet pays salaries that are shameful, this behavior is unethical also. Generally, a person is not considered ethical unless the person possesses both types of ethics.

As you move through this book, you will find ethical dilemmas to consider in each chapter. Take a moment to determine how you would handle each dilemma. In all instances it should be readily evident what the ethical response should be. Decisions are so nice and neat in an academic environment. Then, you should ask yourself, are there other factors that some would consider in making a decision? Often there is considerable evidence that might sway a person to make a less-than-ethical decision.

2 OBJECTIVE

Explain the attempts at legislating ethics.

Legislating Ethics

In 1907, Teddy Roosevelt said, "Men can never escape being governed. If from lawlessness or fickleness, from folly or self-indulgence, they refuse to govern themselves, then in the end they will be governed [by others]."[23] Many contend that ethics cannot be legislated. Although laws cannot mandate ethics, they may be able to identify what is good ethics.[24] Much of the current legislation was passed because of business ethics breakdowns. There have been three attempts to legislate business ethics since the late 1980s. The first, the Procurement Integrity Act of 1988, prohibits the release of source selection and contractor bid or proposal information. Also, a former employee who served in certain positions on a procurement action or contract in excess of $10 million is barred from receiving compensation as an employee or consultant from that contractor for one year.[25] The Act was passed after there were reports of military contracts for $500 toilet seats. There was also a $5,000 hammer.[26]

The second attempt occurred with the passage of the 1992 Federal Sentencing Guidelines for Organizations Act that outlined an effective ethics training program.[27]

It promised softer punishments for wayward corporations that already had ethics programs in place. In the law were recommendations regarding standards, ethics training, and a system to report misconduct anonymously. Executives were supposed to be responsible for the misconduct of those lower in the organization. If executives were proactive in their efforts to prevent white-collar crime it would lessen a judgment against them and reduce the liability. Organizations responded by creating ethics officer positions, installing ethics hotlines, and developing codes of conduct. But, it is one thing to have a code of ethics and quite another to have this code instilled in all employees from top to bottom. For example, the Enron debacle was not supposed to happen. The Enron Code of Ethics was 62 pages long and had a foreword by Kenneth L. Lay, who was then the company's chairman, saying "Enron's reputation finally depends on its people, on you and me. Let's keep that reputation high."[28] Even with the ethical code, it is apparent that top management pursued business as usual. That ethics program obviously served as a smoke screen to deflect attention or culpability resulting from illegal actions.

The third attempt at legislating business ethics was due not only to Enron and others but also to the way the public viewed the world after September 11. The Corporate and Auditing Accountability, Responsibility and Transparency Act criminalized many corporate acts that were previously relegated to various regulatory structures. Known as the Sarbanes-Oxley Act, its primary focus is to redress accounting and financial reporting abuses in light of corporate scandals.[29] The Act contains broad employee whistle-blower protections that subject corporations and their managerial personnel to significant civil and criminal penalties for retaliating, harassing, or discriminating against employees who report suspected corporate wrongdoing. The whistle-blower protections of the Act apply to corporations listed on U.S. stock exchanges; companies otherwise obligated to file reports under the Securities & Exchange Act; and officers, employees, contractors, subcontractors, and agents of those companies.[30]

The Act states that management may not discharge, demote, suspend, threaten, harass, or in any other manner discriminate against an employee protected by the Act. It protects any employee who lawfully provides information to governmental authorities concerning conduct he or she reasonably believes constitutes mail, wire, or securities fraud; violations of any rule or regulation issued by the Securities & Exchange Commission (SEC); or violations of any other federal law relating to fraud against shareholders. The Act evidently has teeth, because in the 2003 *Bechtel v. Competitive Technologies Inc.* Supreme Court case involving wrongful termination under Sarbanes-Oxley's whistle-blower-protection rule, the Court ruled that the company violated the Act by firing two employees and ordered them reinstated. They were fired because during a meeting they had raised concerns about the company's decision not to report, on its SEC filing, an act they thought should have been disclosed.[31]

The law prohibits loans to executives and directors. It requires publicly traded companies to disclose whether or not they have adopted a code of ethics for senior officers.[32] The Act does not require SEC reporting banks and bank-holding companies to have a code of ethics, but if an SEC reporting company does not have one, it must explain why. However, as former Securities and Exchange Commission Chairman Arthur Levitt said, "While the Sarbanes-Oxley Act has brought about significant change, the greatest change is being brought about not by regulation or legislation, but by humiliation and embarrassment and private rights of action."[33]

Although many of the Sarbanes-Oxley tasks fall outside of the responsibilities of human resources, HR professionals need to take action with regard to the Act's non-retaliation provisions. In addition, if HR is to be a strategic partner in corporate affairs, HR professionals must understand where the Act's corporate mandates intersect with existing HR policies and practices so they can fit them together with corporate compliance efforts.

Even with the passage of the Corporate Reform Bill, the Blue Ribbon Conference Board Commission on Public Trust and Private Enterprise has recommended additional executive compensation reforms designed to restore trust in America's publicly traded corporations. Among the suggestions are:

- Any outside compensation consultants should be retained by the board's compensation committee and should report solely to the committee.
- Stock options should be expensed on a uniform and broadly accepted basis.
- Senior managers and executives should be required to own a meaningful amount of company stock on a long-term basis.
- Executive officers should be required to give public notice before selling company stock.[34]

In retrospect, Congress itself may have caused many of the problems leading to the passage of CAART. In 1997, it blocked an attempt by the SEC and the AICPA (American Institute of Certified Public Accountants) to pass a rule banning auditors from doing most kinds of lucrative consulting work for the same companies they audited. Some 46 members of Congress from both parties sent letters opposing the measure.[35]

Code of Ethics

3 OBJECTIVE

Understand the importance of a code of ethics and describe human resource ethics.

For organizations to grow and prosper, good people must be employed. Today college job seekers believe that corporate leadership ethics is important in their search for the right firm to work for. In one survey, 82 percent said that finding an ethical firm was important in their job search.[36]

Some companies are searching for new employees who have a sound ethical base because they have discovered that a person who is ethical tends to be more successful. Many organizations are approaching these challenges by examining ways to strengthen their cultural underpinnings. By fostering a strong ethical culture, firms are better able to gain the confidence and loyalty of their employees and other stakeholders, which can result in reduced financial, legal, and reputation risks, as well as improvements in organizational performance. As part of this examination, organizations are redesigning their ethics programs to facilitate a broader and more consistent process that incorporates the analysis of outcomes and continual improvement. To build and sustain an ethical culture, organizations need a comprehensive framework that encompasses communication of behavior expectations, training on ethics and compliance issues, stakeholder input, resolution of reported matters, and analysis of the entire ethics program.[37]

What exactly is a code of ethics? The code is a statement of the values adopted by the company, its employees, and its directors, and sets the official tone of top management regarding expected behavior.[38] Many industry associations adopt such codes, which are then recommended to members. Some consultants specialize in helping companies embed ethical principles in their corporate cultures. And most business schools now include business ethics in their courses. There are many kinds of ethical codes. An excellent example of a code of ethics was developed by the Society for Human Resource Management (SHRM). Major provisions in the SHRM code of ethics include: professional responsibility, professional development, ethical leadership, fairness and justice, conflicts of interest, and use of information. With regard to conflicts of interest, the code states, "As HR professionals, we must maintain a high level of trust with our stakeholders. We must protect the interests of our stakeholders as well as our professional integrity and should not engage in activities that create actual, apparent, or potential conflicts of interest."[39]

It is vitally important that those who work in human resource management understand those practices that are unacceptable and ensure that organizational members behave ethically in dealing with others. A code of ethics establishes the rules by which the organization lives and becomes part of the organization's corporate culture.[40] However, as Samuel A. DiPiazza Jr., Global CEO of Pricewaterhouse-Coopers, said, "It is easy to talk about ethics but it is a lot harder to create an ethical, effective, diverse organization that stands for truth and integrity."[41]

Once these rules are published, everyone within and outside the firm knows the rules that company employees should live by. A broad-based participation of those subject to the code is important. Michael Coates, CEO of Hill and Knowlton Canada, said, "For a company to behave ethically, it must live and breathe its code of conduct, train its personnel and communicate its code through its visioning statements. It cannot just print a manual that sits on a corporate shelf."[42]

Just what should be included in a code of ethics? Topics typically covered might be business conduct, fair competition, and workplace and HR issues. For example, employees in purchasing or other disciplines would be shown what constitutes a conflict of interest. Most U.S. workers say their employers provide clear standards for ethical behavior.[43] At Wal-Mart, it is considered unethical to accept gifts from suppliers. Gifts are either destroyed or given to charity.

To keep the code on the front burner for employees, larger firms appoint an ethics officer (remember, this was done in the case of Tyco International). This individual should be a person who understands the work environment. To obtain the involvement of others within the organization, an ethics committee is often established. Typically, representatives from legal, human resources, corporate compliance, corporate communications, external affairs, and training departments are included.

There are reasons to encourage industry associations to develop and promote codes of ethics. It is difficult for a single firm to pioneer ethical practices if its competitors take advantage of unethical shortcuts. For example, U.S. companies must comply with the Foreign Corrupt Practices Act, which prohibits bribes of foreign government officials or business executives. Obviously, the law does not prevent foreign competitors from bribing government or business officials to get business and such practices are common in many countries. This sometimes puts U.S. companies at a disadvantage (a topic discussed in greater detail in Chapter 14).

Even the criteria for winning the Baldrige National Quality Award have changed and an increased emphasis on ethics in leadership is now stressed. The criteria say senior leaders should serve as role models to the rest of their organizations. Baldrige applicants are asked questions as to how senior leaders create an environment that fosters and requires legal and ethical behavior, and how the leaders address such governance matters as fiscal accountability and independence in audits.[44]

The Adolph Coors Company of Golden, Colorado, has developed one of the nation's most comprehensive ethics programs. The company offers its 8,500 employees considerable resources including interactive online courses, ethics leadership training, a decision map, a highly detailed set of policies, and a help line.[45] Warren Malmquist, who developed the program and serves as director of Coors Audit Services, says, "The goal of the program is to step beyond rules and guidelines and teach employees how to think, clarify, and analyze situations." When the program was started in 1990, the company's ethics policy was little more than a basic code of conduct and set of guidelines. Since then, the firm has continually added features that are deliberately focused on a strategy of prevention rather than investigation."[46]

"We realized that it was essential to develop a code of ethics that is meaningful rather than a legal-based document that's difficult to understand," said Caroline McMichen, group manager of ethics and audit services.[47]

Coors was the winner of the 2005 Optimas Award for Ethical Practice for implementing a customized program that has directly affected the way employees perceive their work and do their jobs.[48]

Human Resource Ethics

Human resource ethics:
Application of ethical principles to human resource relationships and activities.

Human resource ethics is the application of ethical principles to human resource relationships and activities.

Some believe that those in human resources have a great deal to do with establishing an organization's conscience. Certainly, some of the ethical lapses of recent years occurred in the field referred to as human resource management. During the corporate scandals of recent years, some say that HR played a seemingly invisible role, and that attention to corporate governance and executive compensation was sadly neglected.[49] Perhaps the HR executives were themselves too weak politically to be champions of organization transformation.[50] The inference being made was that if HR professionals in these firms had been more strategically focused, perhaps the scandals could have been avoided or the impact lessened. Some believe that HR should have questioned the salaries, stock options, and related perks received by some corporate executives even as the company was reduced to penny stock. That being said, many believe that it is now the duty of the HR professional to help restore trust in organizations. In fact, one of the core principles of the SHRM Code of Ethical and Professional Standards in HR Management states that "As HR professionals, we are responsible for adding value to the organizations we serve and contributing to the ethical success of those organizations."[51]

The HR manager can help foster an ethical culture, but that means more than just hanging the codes-of-conduct posters on walls. Instead, since the HR professionals' primary job is dealing with people, they must help to instill ethical practices into the corporate culture. In fact, promoting corporate ethics was a Top-10 trend among HR professionals in the SHRM 2004–2005 Workplace Forecast.[52] They need to help establish an environment where employees throughout the organization work to reduce ethical lapses.[53] The ethical bearing of those in HR goes a long way in establishing the credibility of the entire organization.

There are two areas where HR professionals can have a major impact on ethics and, therefore, corporate culture. These areas are corporate governance and executive compensation. HR should review and enforce organizational governance policies and implementation methods to ensure a high level of executive integrity and effectiveness. All employees should know what is ethical and unethical in their specific area of operations. It is insufficient to say that everyone should be ethical. Dialogue should be developed so that workers in different areas know what is ethical. For example, ethical questions confronting a salesperson will be different from those in research or production.

The second area HR should focus on is executive compensation. It is perhaps in the area of compensation that HR executives could have the greatest impact on corporate behavior. The HRM in Action in Chapter 9 is entitled "Are Top Executives Paid Too Much?" If top-level HR professionals know the strategic nature of the organization and know the company thoroughly, they can play a major supporting role in establishing and adjusting compensation for the CEO and other top managers. Obviously, the present method of determining executive compensation is under close public scrutiny, including stock options, success-to-reward equations, and equity of separation packages. "HR can make sure that the compensation committee has relevant, fair and accurate information for decision making, in collaboration with consultants and management," says Edward Graskamp, national practice leader for executive compensation at consulting firm Watson Wyatt. HR executives must become recognized in their organizations as being able to contribute to strategic deliberations. The HR executive can provide the needed guidance and information so that informed compensation decisions can be made. It is the duty of HR professionals to promote ethical compensation practices.[54]

4 **OBJECTIVE**

Describe the professionalization of human resource management.

Profession:
Vocation characterized by the existence of a common body of knowledge and a procedure for certifying members.

Professionalization of Human Resource Management

A **profession** is a vocation characterized by the existence of a common body of knowledge and a procedure for certifying members.

Performance standards are established by members of the profession rather than by outsiders; that is, the profession is self-regulated. Most professions also have effective representative organizations that permit members to exchange ideas of mutual concern. These characteristics apply to the field of human resources, and several well-known organizations serve the profession. Among the more prominent are the Society for Human Resource Management (SHRM); Human Resource Certification Institute (HRCI); American Society for Training and Development (ASTD); and the WorldatWork.

Society for Human Resource Management

The largest national professional organization for individuals involved in all areas of human resource management is the Society for Human Resource Management (SHRM). The basic goals of the society include defining, maintaining, and improving standards of excellence in the practice of human resource management. Membership consists of 200,000 professionals with more than 550 affiliated chapters within the United States and members in more than 100 countries. There are also numerous student chapters on university campuses across the country.[55]

SHRM publishes a monthly journal, *HR Magazine*, and a monthly newspaper, *HR News*. A major subsidiary of SHRM, the Recruiting & Staffing Focus Area (formerly EMA), offers in-depth information on issues addressing employment and retention issues, whereas SHRM offers a broader coverage of HR issues.[56]

Human Resource Certification Institute

One of the more significant developments in the field of HRM has been the establishment of the Human Resource Certification Institute (HRCI), an affiliate of SHRM. Founded in 1976, HRCI's goal is to recognize human resource professionals through a certification program. Today, more than 80,000 professionals are certified.[57] HRCI offers three certifications for HR professionals which are PHR (Professional in Human Resources), SPHR (Senior Professional in Human Resources), and GPHR (Global Professional in Human Resources).[58]

Certification encourages human resource professionals to update their knowledge and skills continuously. It provides recognition to professionals who have met a stated level of training and work experience. A number of years ago, Wiley Beavers, a former national president of SHRM, stated that human resource certification would:

- Allow students to focus on career directions earlier in their education.
- Provide sound guidelines for young practitioners in important HR areas.
- Encourage senior practitioners to update their knowledge.

American Society for Training and Development

Founded in 1944, the American Society for Training and Development (ASTD) is the world's largest association dedicated to workplace learning and performance professionals. ASTD's 70,000 members and associates come from more than 100 countries and thousands of organizations. The membership consists of individuals who are concerned specifically with training and development. The society publishes a monthly

Human Resource Certification Institute (HRCI)

http://www.hrci.org/

The Professional Certification Program in HR Management is for individuals seeking to expand their formal HR training.

journal, *T+D Magazine*. Numerous other publications are also available to help its members remain current in the field.[59]

WorldatWork

WorldatWork was founded in 1955 as the American Compensation Association (ACA) and currently has a worldwide membership that exceeds 23,000.[60] This organization consists of managerial and human resource professionals who are responsible for the establishment, execution, administration, or application of compensation practices and policies in their organizations. The WorldatWork's quarterly journal contains information related to compensation issues. WorldatWork focuses on human resource disciplines associated with attracting, retaining, and motivating employees. In addition to serving as the membership association of the profession, WorldatWork provides education programs, the monthly *workspan*® magazine, online information resources, surveys, publications, conferences, research, and networking opportunities. An affiliate organization, WorldatWork Society of Certified Professionals® administers and issues the certification designations: Certified Compensation Professional (CCP®), Certified Benefits Professional® (CBP), and Global Remuneration Professional (GRP®).[61]

OBJECTIVE

Describe the concept of corporate social responsibility.

Corporate social responsibility (CSR):

Implied, enforced, or felt obligation of managers, acting in their official capacity, to serve or protect the interests of groups other than themselves.

Corporate Social Responsibility

What do the following United States companies have in common: Agilent Technologies, Inc.; Alcoa Inc.; Bank of America Corporation; Baxter International Inc.; Coca-Cola Company; Eastman Kodak Company; FPL Group, Inc.; General Electric Company; Hewlett-Packard Company; Intel Corporation; Johnson and Johnson; Masco Corporation; Nike Inc., Pinnacle West Capital Corporation; Schlumberger Limited; United Parcel Service, Inc.; and United Technologies Corporation? They have been identified as having a commitment to excellence in the area of corporate social responsibility Global 100. These companies have demonstrated the ability to manage the "triple bottom line" of social responsibility (society, environment, and economy). There were included in the 100 firms across the globe as representing the top five percent of socially responsible companies.[62]

Corporate social responsibility (CSR) is the implied, enforced, or felt obligation of managers, acting in their official capacity, to serve or protect the interests of groups other than themselves.

When a corporation behaves as if it has a conscience, it is said to be socially responsible. It is how a company as a whole behaves toward society. It is certainly more than words being said. Social responsibility has moved from nice-to-do to must-do. More and more companies are issuing corporate social responsibility reports that detail their environmental, labor, and corporate-giving practices. A study by the Social Investment Research Analyst Network found that 40 percent of the S&P 100 issue CSR reports.[63]

Apparently, socially responsible behavior pays off on the bottom line;[64] in one study, 82 percent of companies noted that good corporate citizenship helps the bottom line. General Electric joined a growing crowd of big companies, such as Hewlett-Packard, GAP, and IBM, that issue comprehensive statements about their efforts in governance, the environment, and corporate responsibility.[65]

When GE CEO Jeffrey Immelt announced that the company would double its spending on green technology research, it was no grand attempt to save the planet. It was an example of astute business strategy. Immelt said, "We plan to make money doing it."[66] That is also the conclusion of research based on business ethics' 100 best corporate citizens list, which shows that the financial performance of these companies was significantly better than others in the Standard & Poor's 500. The rankings were based on corporate service to the following stakeholder groups: stockholders, employees, customers, the community, the environment, overseas stakeholders, and women and minorities.[67]

Procter & Gamble has long believed it has a responsibility for the long-term benefit of society as well as the company. Over the years, P&G has pursued programs to strengthen U.S. education, to encourage employment opportunities for minorities and women, to develop and implement environment-protection technology, and to encourage employee involvement in civic activities and the political process.[68]

Intel has established a set of core values that drive its actions, both internally and externally. It has created an impression of being a great place to work and of the company as an asset to the communities where it operates. Following these principles, its employees volunteer time and contribute a great deal of money in global education support. As another example, about 50,000 of Home Depot's 325,000 employees donated 2 million hours to community service.[69]

An organization's top executives usually determine a corporation's approach to social responsibility. For example, when McDonald's began, it was Ray Kroc's philosophy to be a community-based business. His philosophy from the very beginning was to give back to the communities that McDonald's served.[70]

One of the best benchmarks for defining social responsibility in manufacturing is the one-page set of operating principles developed 60 years ago by Robert Wood Johnson, then Johnson & Johnson's chairman of the board. The document is still in use today and addresses supporting good works and charities.[71]

Business for Social Responsibility

http://www.bsr.org/

This is a global organization that helps member companies achieve success in ways that respect ethical values, people, communities, and the environment.

 OBJECTIVE

Explain what is meant by stakeholder analysis and the social contract.

Organizational stakeholder:
Individual or group whose interests are affected by organizational activities.

Social contract:
Set of written and unwritten rules and assumptions about acceptable interrelationships among the various elements of society.

Stakeholder Analysis and the Social Contract

Most organizations, whether profit or nonprofit, have a large number of stakeholders. An **organizational stakeholder** is an individual or group whose interests are affected by organizational activities.

Society is increasingly holding corporate boards of directors and management accountable for putting the interest of stakeholders first.[72] However, managers may not acknowledge responsibility for all of them. Some of the stakeholders for Crown Metal Products, a fictitious manufacturer, are shown in Figure 2-2. But only a few, identified by bold arrows, are viewed as constituencies by Crown management. Each firm will have different stakeholders based on the organization's mission and the focus of social responsibility efforts.

The actions of many corporate executives are designed to serve interests other than those of the common shareholder. For example, a number of managements have placed large amounts of company stock in employee stock ownership trusts for the purpose of avoiding takeover attempts that were clearly in the interests of common shareholders. This benefited the employees, of course, but it also helped the managers keep their jobs. Other companies make gifts of company resources, often cash, to universities, churches, clubs, and so forth, knowing that any possible benefit to shareholders is remote. Some authorities favor this trend and suggest that members of the public should be placed on major corporate boards to protect the interests of nonowner stakeholders.

One approach to stakeholder analysis involves consideration of the social contract. The **social contract** is the set of written and unwritten rules and assumptions about acceptable interrelationships among the various elements of society.[73]

Much of the social contract is embedded in the customs of society. For example, in integrating minorities into the workforce, society has come to expect companies to do more than the law requires. "Shareholder activism has focused on HR issues since the mid-1970s," says Timothy Smith, a senior vice president at Walden Asset Management in Boston and president of the Social Investment Forum, a trade association. He says HR should actually feel supported, rather than irritated by shareholders, "especially if they find executive management isn't paying enough attention to certain workplace issues. This is a chance for shareholders to actually help."[74]

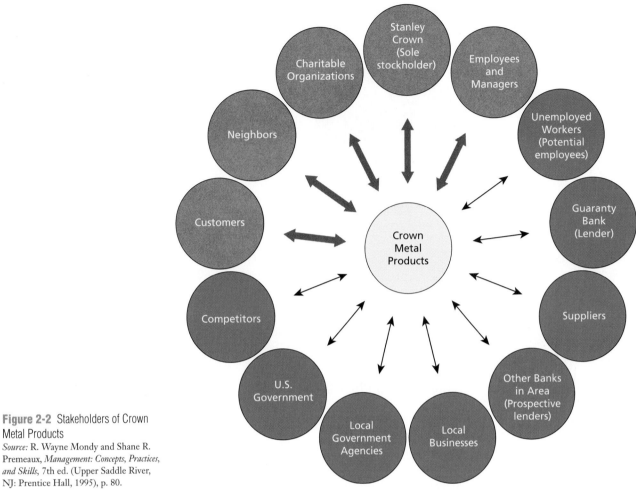

Figure 2-2 Stakeholders of Crown Metal Products
Source: R. Wayne Mondy and Shane R. Premeaux, *Management: Concepts, Practices, and Skills*, 7th ed. (Upper Saddle River, NJ: Prentice Hall, 1995), p. 80.

Some of the contract provisions result from practices of the parties to the contract. Like a legal contract, the social contract often involves a quid pro quo (something exchanged for something). One party to the contract behaves in a certain way and expects a certain pattern of behavior from the other. For example, a relationship of trust may have developed between a manufacturer and the community in which it operates. Because of this, each will inform the other well in advance of any planned action that might cause harm, such as the phasing down of a plant's operations by the company. The widespread belief that such a relationship was rare prompted Congress to pass the Worker Adjustment and Retraining Notification Act of 1988. That law requires firms employing 100 or more workers to give 60 days' notice to employees and local government officials when a plant closing or layoff affecting 50 or more employees for a 90-day period is planned.

The social contract concerns relationships with individuals, government, other organizations, and society in general, as Figure 2-3 illustrates. Each of these relationships will be considered individually in the following sections.

Obligations to Individuals

Organizations have certain obligations to their employees. Individuals often find healthy outlets for their energies through joining organizations. From their employers, they expect a fair day's pay for a fair day's work, and perhaps much more. Many expect to be paid for time off to vote, perform jury service, and so forth. To the extent that individuals' expectations are acknowledged as responsibilities by the organization, they become part of the social contract. Many individuals are now voicing their

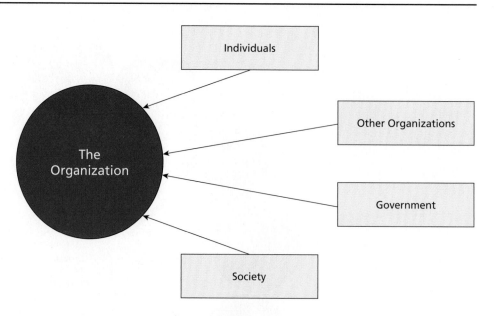

Figure 2-3 The Social Contract
Source: R. Wayne Mondy and Shane R. Premeaux, *Management: Concepts, Practices, and Skills,* 7th ed. (Upper Saddle River, NJ: Prentice Hall, 1995), p. 82.

opinions by purchasing stock from firms that have a reputation for being socially responsible.

Obligations to Other Organizations

Managers must be concerned with relationships involving other organizations, both organizations that are like their own, such as competitors, and very different ones. Commercial businesses are expected to compete with one another on an honorable basis, without subterfuge or reckless unconcern for their mutual rights. However, some organizations appear to have a certain amount of disdain for competitors, especially when it comes to recruiting. Charities, such as the United Way, expect support from businesses, often including the loan of executives to help with annual fund drives. At the same time, such institutions are expected to come, hat in hand, to business managers, requesting rather than demanding assistance.

In the traditional view of social responsibility, businesses best meet obligations through pursuit of their own interests. Some companies view the social contract mainly in terms of the company's interests. For example, FMC Corporation, a major diversified manufacturer, has firm policies about how it will direct its contributions. The basic criteria FMC applies are that contributions must help areas around company facilities or where its employees live and that their gifts must improve the corporation's business environment. FMC might contribute to a university in an area where it has a plant, but it would not give gifts to distant universities.

Obligations to Government

Government is an important party to the social contract for every kind of organization. Under the auspices of government, companies have a license to do business, along with patent rights, trademarks, and so forth. Churches are often incorporated under state laws and given nonprofit status. Many quasi-governmental agencies, such as the Federal Deposit Insurance Corporation, regional planning commissions, and local school boards, have been given special missions by government.

In addition, organizations are expected to recognize the need for order rather than anarchy and to accept some government intervention in organizational affairs. They are expected to work with the guidelines of governmental organizations such as the Equal Employment Opportunity Commission and the Office of Federal Compliance Programs (discussed in Chapter 3).

Obligations to Society in General

The traditional view of business responsibility has been that businesses should produce and distribute goods and services in return for a profit. Businesses have performed this function effectively, giving the United States one of the highest overall standards of living in the world. A high percentage of the population has its basic needs for food, clothing, shelter, health, and education reasonably well satisfied. And most citizens are afforded some leisure time. Profitable firms are able to pay taxes to the government and make donations to charities. All this should be a matter of some pride for business owners and managers.

Businesses operate by public consent with the basic purpose of satisfying the needs of society. As those needs are more fully met, society demands more of all of its institutions, particularly large business firms. Possible social issues that private companies might be involved with include environmental protection, support of education, and economic development in poor communities.[75]

At the same time, remember that in order to survive, businesses must make a profit over the long run. If they fail, they will not be able to contribute. As responsible corporate citizens, businesses should follow the spirit of the law as well as the letter. There is a major difference in adhering to equal employment laws and being an equal opportunity employer.

In the sixteenth century, Sir Thomas More said, "If virtue were profitable, common sense would make us good and greed would make us saintly."[76]

More knew that virtue is not profitable, so people must make hard choices from time to time. Common sense hardly makes one good. In the United States today, the consensus is clear. Corporate strategists are being held to a higher standard than just pursuing their own interests, or even those of stockholders; they must consider the interests of other groups too.

 OBJECTIVE

Describe how a corporate social responsibility program is implemented.

Social audit:
Systematic assessment of a company's activities in terms of its social impact.

Implementing a Corporate Social Responsibility Program

To overcome the negative publicity of corporate misdeeds and to restore trust, businesses are now conducting audits of their social responsibility activities, not just financial audits. A **social audit** is a systematic assessment of a company's activities in terms of its social impact.

Some of the topics included in the audit focus on such core values as social responsibility, open communication, treatment of employees, confidentiality, and leadership. Firms are now acknowledging responsibilities to various stakeholder groups other than corporate owners.[77]

Some even set specific objectives in social areas. They are attempting to formally measure their contributions to various elements of society and to society as a whole. An increasing number of companies, as well as public and voluntary sector organizations, are trying to assess their social performance systematically. Three possible types of social audits are currently being utilized: (1) simple inventory of activities, (2) compilation of socially relevant expenditures, and (3) determination of social impact. The inventory is generally a good starting place. It consists of a listing of socially oriented activities undertaken by the firm. Here are some examples: (1) minority employment and training, (2) support of minority enterprises, (3) pollution control, (4) corporate giving, (5) involvement in selected community projects by executives, and (6) a hardcore unemployment program. The ideal social audit would go well beyond a simple listing and involve determining the true benefits to society of any socially oriented business activity.

The following steps are recommended for establishing and implementing a corporate social responsibility (CSR) program. First, a person should be assigned the responsibility for the program and a structure should be developed. This individual should, at a very minimum, report to senior management or a board member. Second, a review of what the company is presently doing with regard to CSR should be determined. The difference between where the company is at present and where it wants to be should be determined (a gap analysis). Third, shareholders' expectations and perspectives are determined. Fourth, a policy statement is written covering CSR areas such as environmental, social, and community issues. Fifth, a set of corporate objectives and an action plan to implement the policies should be developed. Sixth, company-wide quantitative and qualitative targets and key performance indicators over a two- to five-year period, together with the necessary measurement, monitoring, and auditing mechanisms, should be created. These actions and strategies should focus on the core business of the organization. Seventh, communicate to stakeholders and fund managers the direction of CSR for the company. Eighth, the progress of the CSR program should be determined. Finally, the progress of the CSR program should be reported.[78]

The CSR program should not be a one-time-only activity but rather a continuing effort to monitor and report the firm's achievements in the area of social responsibility.

A Global Perspective

"When in Rome, Do as the Romans Do" Does Not Work Today

The old adage, "When in Rome do as the Romans do," made ethical decisions easy. The new one, yet to be written, will make ethical decisions harder. Dennis Bakke, CEO of AES Corporation, the world's largest independent power producer, based in Arlington, Virginia, is a proclaimed "cultural imperialist." He will not lower the ethical standards for his $9.3 billion corporation in any of the 31 nations in which it owns or invests in 184 power plants. That includes countries like corruption-plagued Uganda. Recently, AES gained final approval to build a 250-megawatt hydroelectric dam on Uganda's upper Nile River. Bakke says that in a decade of project development, so far he has forbidden the paying of bribes. Outsiders hearing about the $550 million project say that resisting corruption must have been impossible. But Bakke maintains otherwise. He says he would not even approve of paying Ugandan reporters fees for writing positive stories, a routine Ugandan practice, despite heavy criticism leveled at AES for destroying the Bujagali rapids, for displacing poor farmers, and for backroom political dealing. Bakke deals regularly with an issue facing all firms that do business globally. He must decide what is ethically acceptable when home and host country practices conflict. But the dilemmas he and other CEOs handle have become much more complex, and more quickly attract the media spotlight.[79]

"If we believe that the nation-state has some moral responsibility," says Rushwood Kidder, president of the Institute for Global Ethics in Camden, Maine, "then we have to extend [the same to the multinational corporation], the entity that is taking the nation-state's place in more and more parts of society." John Browne, CEO of BP, feels the same. "If globalization marks the end of sovereignty for national governments," he said in a speech at Cambridge University last year, "it should equally end any sense of splendid isolation that exists in the corporate world." The old adage that was once accepted in many quarters, "When in Rome, do as the Romans do," has become unacceptable. The new CEO challenge is to act like an ethical leader for society as a whole, to act before crises demand it, to engage outsiders in decision making, and to adhere to standards of behavior that locals embrace.[80]

Summary

1. Define ethics and understand the model of ethics.

Ethics is the discipline dealing with what is good and bad, or right and wrong, or with moral duty and obligation. Ethics consists mainly of two relationships. The first element in the model is sources of ethical guidance. The strength of the relationship between what an individual or an organization believes to be moral and correct and what available sources of guidance suggest is morally correct is Type I ethics. Type II ethics is the strength of the relationship between what one believes and how one behaves. Generally, a person is not considered ethical unless the person possesses both types of ethics.

2. Explain the attempts at legislating ethics.

There have been three attempts to legislate business ethics since the late 1980s. The Procurement Integrity Act of 1988 prohibits the release of source selection and contractor bid or proposal information. Also, a former employee who served in certain positions on a procurement action or contract in excess of $10 million is barred from receiving compensation as an employee or consultant from that contractor for one year. The second attempt occurred with the passage of the 1992 Federal Sentencing Guidelines for Organizations that outlined an effective ethics program. The third attempt at legislating business ethics was the Corporate and Auditing Accountability, Responsibility and Transparency Act, which focused on the accounting and financial reporting abuses in light of recent corporate scandals.

3. Understand the importance of a code of ethics and describe human resource ethics.

A code of ethics establishes the rules that the organization lives by. The HR manager can help foster an ethical culture.

4. Describe the professionalization of human resource management.

Several well-known organizations serve the profession. Among the more prominent are the Society for Human Resource Management (SHRM); Human Resource Certification Institute (HRCI); American Society for Training and Development (ASTD); and the WorldatWork (formerly the American Compensation Association).

5. Describe the concept of corporate social responsibility.

Corporate social responsibility is the implied, enforced, or felt obligation of managers, acting in their official capacity, to serve or protect the interests of groups other than themselves. It is how a company as a whole behaves toward society.

6. Explain what is meant by stakeholder analysis and the social contact.

Protecting the diversity of stakeholder interests requires answering questions regarding how you will treat the various stakeholders. Answering such questions is termed stakeholder analysis. The social contract is the set of written and unwritten rules and assumptions about acceptable interrelationships among the various elements of society.

7. Describe how a corporate social responsibility program is implemented.

First, a person should be assigned the responsibility for the program and a structure should be developed. Second, a review of what the company is presently doing with regard to CSR should be determined. Third, shareholders' expectations and perspectives are determined. Fourth, a policy statement is written covering CSR areas such as environmental, social, and community issues. Fifth, a set of corporate objectives and an action plan to implement the policies should be developed. Sixth, company-wide quantitative and qualitative targets and key performance indicators should be created. Seventh, communicate to stakeholders and fund managers the direction of CSR for the company. Eighth, the progress of the CSR program should be determined. Finally, the progress of the CSR program should be reported.

Key Terms

- Ethics, 30
- Type I ethics, 32
- Type II ethics, 32
- Human resource ethics, 37
- Profession, 38
- Corporate social responsibility (CSR), 39
- Organizational stakeholder, 40
- Social contract, 40
- Social audit, 43

Questions for Review

1. Describe the model of ethics presented in your text. Distinguish between Type I and Type II ethics.
2. What laws have been passed in an attempt to legislate ethics?
3. What are human resource ethics?
4. Why is it important to have a code of ethics?
5. What are the areas where HR professionals can have a major impact on ethics?
6. Define profession. Do you believe that the field of human resource management is a profession? Explain your answer.
7. What is corporate social responsibility?
8. What is meant by the terms stakeholder analysis and social contract?
9. What are the steps that are involved in implementing a corporate social responsibility program?

HRM Incident 1

An Ethical Flaw

Amber Davis had recently graduated from college with a degree in general business. Amber was quite bright, although her grades did not reflect this. She had thoroughly enjoyed school, dating, playing tennis, swimming, but found few academic endeavors. When she graduated, she had not found a job. Her dad was extremely upset when he discovered this, and he took it upon himself to see that Amber became employed.

Amber's father, Allen Davis, was executive vice president of a medium-sized manufacturing firm. One of the people he contacted in seeking employment for Amber was Bill Garbo, the president of another firm in the area. Mr. Davis purchased many of his firm's supplies from Garbo's company. After telling Bill his problem, Allen was told to send Amber to Bill's office for an interview. Amber went, as instructed by her father, and before she left Bill's firm, she was surprised to learn that she had a job in the accounting department. Amber may have been lazy, but she certainly was not stupid. She realized that Bill had hired her because he hoped that his action would lead to future business from her father's company. Although Amber's work was not challenging, it paid better than the other jobs in the accounting department.

It did not take long for the employees in the department to discover the reason she had been hired; Amber told them. When a difficult job was assigned to Amber, she normally got one of the other employees to do it, implying that Mr. Garbo would be pleased with that person if he or she helped her out. She developed a pattern of coming in late, taking long lunch breaks, and leaving early. When the department manager attempted to reprimand her for these unorthodox activities, Amber would bring up the close relationship that her father had with the president of the firm. The department manager was at the end of his rope.

Questions

1. From an ethical standpoint, how would you evaluate the merits of Mr. Garbo's employing Amber? Discuss.
2. Now that she is employed, what course would you follow to address her on-the-job behavior?
3. Do you feel that a firm should have policies regarding practices such as hiring people like Amber? Discuss.

| HRM Incident 2 | "You Can't Fire Me" |

Norman Blankenship came in the side door of the office at Consolidation Coal Company's Rowland mine, near Clear Creek, West Virginia. He told the mine dispatcher not to tell anyone he was there. Norman was general superintendent of the Rowland operation. He had been with Consolidation for 23 years, having started out as a mining machine operator.

Norman had heard that one of his section bosses, Tom Serinsky, had been sleeping on the job. Tom had been hired two months earlier and assigned to the Rowland mine by the regional personnel office. He had gone to work as section boss, working the midnight to 8:00 a.m. shift. Because of his age and experience, Serinsky was the senior person in the mine on his shift.

Norman took one of the battery-operated jeeps used to transport personnel and supplies in and out of the mine and proceeded to the area where Tom was assigned. Upon arriving, he saw Tom lying on an emergency stretcher. Norman stopped his jeep a few yards away from where Tom was sleeping and approached him. "Hey, you asleep?" Norman asked. Tom awakened with a start and said, "No, I wasn't sleeping."

Norman waited for Tom to collect his senses and then said, "I could tell that you were sleeping. But that's beside the point. You weren't at your workstation. You know that I have no choice but to fire you." After Tom had left, Norman called his mine foreman and asked him to come in and complete the remainder of Tom's shift.

The next morning, Norman had the mine HR manager officially terminate Tom. As part of the standard procedure, the mine HR manager notified the regional HR manager that Tom had been fired and gave the reasons for firing him. The regional HR manager asked the mine HR manager to get Norman on the line. The regional HR manager said, "Norm, you know Tom is Eustus Frederick's brother-in-law, don't you?" Frederick was a regional vice president. "No, I didn't know that," replied Norman, "but it doesn't matter. The rules are clear. I wouldn't care if he was Frederick's son."

The next day, the regional human resource manager showed up at the mine just as Norman was getting ready to make a routine tour of the mine. "I guess you know what I'm here for," said the HR manager. "Yeah, you're here to take away my authority," replied Norman. "No, I'm just here to investigate," said the regional HR manager.

By the time Norman returned to the mine office after his tour, the regional HR manager had finished his interviews. He told Norman, "I think we're going to have to put Tom back to work. If we decide to do that, can you let him work for you?" "No, absolutely not," said Norman. "In fact, if he works here, I go." A week later, Norman learned that Tom had gone to work as section boss at another Consolidation coal mine in the region.

Questions

1. What would you do now if you were Norman?
2. Do you believe the regional HR manager handled the matter in an ethical manner? Explain.

Notes

1. Debby Young, "Repairing a Damaged Reputation," *Electronic Business* 31 (June 2005): 11–20.
2. Beth Snyder Bulik, "Best & Brightest Media Strategists: Seb Maitra," *B to B* 90 (November 14, 2005): 37.
3. Alan S. Rutkin, "A Litigious State of Mind," *Best's Review* 106 (October 2005): 110.
4. Barbara Jorgensen, "Do the Right Thing—the Right Way," *Electronic Business* 31 (June 2005): 16–18.
5. Ibid.
6. Joseph Weber, Roger O. Crockett, Michael Arndt, Brian Grow, and Nanette Byrnes, "How the Best Boards Stay Clued In," *Business Week* (June 27, 2005): 40.
7. Jorgensen, "Do the Right Thing—the Right Way."
8. Ibid.
9. Ibid.
10. Harry Maurer, "Breakup of the Week," *Business Week* (November 28, 2005): 35.
11. Nicholas Varchaver and Joan L. Levinstein, "What Is Ed Breen Thinking?" *Fortune* (March 20, 2006): 134–140.
12. Ann Pomeroy, "Ethical Leaders Needed," *HR Magazine* 50 (July 2005): 16.
13. Jonathan Pont, "Doing the Right Thing to Instill Business Ethics," *Workforce Management* 84 (April 2005): 26–27.
14. Robert C. Hazard, Jr., "Corporate Ethics, Corporate Pay and the Lodging Industry," *Lodging Hospitality* 58 (November 2002): 65.

15. Victor M. Parachin, "Integrity—The Most Important Trait to Cultivate," *Supervision* 63 (February 2002): 3.

16. Joan E. Dubinsky, "Business Ethics: A Set of Practical Tools," *Internal Auditing* 17 (July/August 2002): 39–45.

17. Owen C. Gadeken, "Ethics in Program Management," *Defense & AT-L* 34 (July/August 2005): 32–35.

18. Elizabeth MacDonald and Erika Brown, "Thumbs on the Scale," *Forbes* 176 (October 28, 2005): 56.

19. Ann Pomeroy, "Tarnished Employment Brands Affect Recruiting," *HR Magazine* 49 (November 2004): 16.

20. Kenneth D. Lewis, "The Responsibility of the CEO: Providing Ethical and Moral Leadership," *Vital Speeches of the Day* 69 (October 15, 2002): 6–9.

21. David Gebler, "Creating an Ethical Culture," *Strategic Finance* 87 (May 2006): 29–34.

22. Patricia Wallington, "Honestly! Ethical Behavior Isn't Easy, Just Essential. Here's How to Run an Honest Organization and Be an Ethical Leader," *CIO* 16 (March 15, 2003): 41–41.

23. Kenneth D. Lewis, "The Responsibility of the CEO: Providing Ethical and Moral Leadership," *Vital Speeches of the Day* 69 (October 15, 2002): 6–9.

24. Paul Fiorelli, "How to 'Pump Up' Your Organization's 'Ethical Muscle Memory'," *Journal of Health Care Compliance* 8 (May/June 2006): 23–79.

25. http://www.usdoj.gov/jmd/ethics/procurea.htm, March 9, 2006.

26. Alynda Wheat, "Keeping an Eye on Corporate America," *Fortune* 146 (November 25, 2002): 44–46.

27. Kathryn Tyler, "Do the Right Thing," *HR Magazine* 50 (February 2005): 99–102.

28. Alec Wilkinson, "The Enron Example," *New Yorker* 81 (July 4, 2005): 30–31.

29. Connie N. Bertram, "A Whistle Stop for Whistle-blowers," *Community Banker* 14 (April 2005): 48–49.

30. "How HR Can Facilitate Ethics," *HR Focus* 82 (April 2005): 1–14.

31. Cathleen Flahardy, "SOX Gives DOL Power to Reinstate Whistleblowers," *Corporate Legal Times* 15 (August 2005): 24–26.

32. Kathryn Tyler, "Do the Right Thing," *HR Magazine* 50 (February 2005): 99–102.

33. Howard Stock, "Ethics Trump Rules, Levitt Says," *Investor Relations Business* (April 7, 2003): 1.

34. Steve Bates, "Tough Reforms Suggested for Executive Compensation," *HR Magazine* 47 (November 2002): 12–14.

35. "Con gress' Own Corporate Scandals," *Business Week* 3801 (September 30, 2002): 126.

36. Steve Bates, "Corporate Ethics Important to Today's Job Seekers," *HR Magazine* 47 (November 2002): 12.

37. David Childers and Norman Marks, "Ethics as a Strategy," *Internal Auditor* 62 (October 2005): 34–38.

38. Greg Boudreaux and Tracy Sterner, "Developing a Code of Ethics," *Management Quarterly* 46 (Spring 2005): 2–19.

39. http://www.shrm.org/ethics/code-of-ethics.asp, September 8, 2003.

40. Childers and Marks, "Ethics as a Strategy."

41. Samuel A. DiPiazza, "Ethics in Action," *Executive Excellence* 19 (January 2002): 15–16.

42. Peter R. Kensicki, "Create Your Own Ethical Statement," *National Underwriter* 106 (October 21, 2002): 33–34.

43. "Unethical Workplace Conduct Continues, Despite Standards, Surveys Say," *HR Focus* 84 (January 2006): 8–9.

44. Debbie Phillips-Donaldson, "Corporate Ethics Rule," *Quality Progress* 36 (April 2003): 6.

45. Samuel Greengard, "Golden Values," *Workforce Management* 84 (March 2005): 52–53.

46. Ibid.

47. Ibid.

48. Ibid.

49. Susan Meisinger "Trust in the Top" *HR Magazine* 47 (October 2002): 8.

50. "7 Steps Before Strategy," *Workforce* 81 (November 2002): 40–44.

51. Meisinger, "Trust in the Top."

52. "How HR Can Facilitate Ethics," *HR Focus* 82 (April 2005): 1–14.

53. Ann Pomeroy, "The Ethics Squeeze," *HR Magazine* 51 (March 2006): 48–55.

54. Meisinger, "Trust in the Top."

55. http://www.shrm.org/about/, September 8, 2006.

56. http://www.shrm.org/ema/, September 8, 2006.

57. http:www.hrci.org, September 8, 2006.

58. http://www.hrci.org/Certification/OV/, September 8, 2006.

59. http://www.astd.org/ASTD/About_ASTD, September 8, 2006.

60. http://www.worldatwork.org/worldatwork.html, September 8, 2006.

61. http://www.WorldatWork.org, September 8, 2006.

62. http://www.global100.org/2006/index.asp

63. Laura Demars, "Beyond the Bottom Line," *CFO* 21 (September 2005): 17.

64. Nancy R. Lockwood, "Corporate Social Responsibility: HR's Leadership Role," *HR Magazine* 49 (December 2004): 1–10.

65. Elizabeth Woyke and Dan Beucke, "GE is Rewriting the Book," *Business Week* (June 27, 2005): 13.

66. Simon Zadek, "Responsibility Isn't a Blame Game," *Fortune (Europe)* 152 (October 3, 2005): 70–73.

67. http://www.business-ethics.com/chart_100_best_corporate_citizens_for_2004.htm, October 31, 2005.

68. John S. McClenahen, "Devising Strategies," *Industry Week* 254 (May 2005): 58–59.

69. Brian Grow, Steve Hamm, and Louise Lee, "The Debate Over Doing Good," *Business Week* (August 15, 2005): 76–78.

70. "Social Responsibility: An Ongoing Mission for a Good Corporate Citizen," *Nation's Restaurant News* (April 11, 2005): 60–66.

71. John S. McClenahen, "Defining Social Responsibility," *Industry Week* 254 (March 2005): 64–65.

72. Telis Demos, "Managing Beyond the Bottom Line," *Fortune (Europe)* 152 (October 3, 2005): 68–70.

73. "The Social Contract," *Canada & the World Backgrounder* 70 (May 2005): 6.

74. Eilene Zimmerman, "Shareholders Are Watching HR," *Workforce* 81 (October 2002): 18.

75. Curtis C. Verschoor, "Good Corporate Citizenship Is a Fundamental Business Practice," *Strategic Finance* 87 (March 2006): 21–22.

76. Quoted in Robert Bolt, *A Man for All Seasons* (New York: Random House, 1962).

77. John Peloza, "Using Corporate Social Responsibility as Insurance for Financial Performance," *California Management Review* 48 (Winter 2006): 52–72.

78. Andreas King, "How to Get Started in Corporate Social Responsibility," *Financial Management* (October 2002): 5.

79. Bill Birchard, "Global Profits, Ethical Perils," *Chief Executive* 179 (June 2002): 48–54.

80. Ibid.

CHAPTER OBJECTIVES

After completing this chapter, students should be able to:

1 Describe the projected future diverse workforce.

2 Describe diversity and diversity management.

3 Explain the various components of the present diverse workforce.

4 Identify the major laws affecting equal employment opportunity.

5 Identify some of the major Supreme Court decisions that have had an impact on equal employment opportunity.

6 Describe the Equal Employment Opportunity Commission.

7 Explain the purpose of the *Uniform Guidelines on Employee Selection Procedures*.

8 Describe disparate treatment and adverse impact.

9 Describe the *Uniform Guidelines* related to sexual harassment, national origin, and religion.

10 Explain affirmative action as required by presidential Executive Orders 11246 and 11375.

11 Describe affirmative action programs.

Workforce Diversity, Equal Employment Opportunity, and Affirmative Action

HRM IN *Action:*

Sequencing Moms, Bringing Them Back

Today, more new mothers are leaving the labor force only to return later; they are often referred to as sequencing moms.

To get them to return, many companies are going beyond federal law and giving mothers a year or more for maternity leave. Other businesses are specifically trying to recruit them.[1]

Several factors are behind this change in corporate attitude. Mothers who leave the labor force today tend to be older and have more career experience and proven skills than they did in the past, making them desirable job candidates. And, employer attitudes have changed. Flexible work schedules, telecommuting and other family-friendly programs can now be found at many major companies.[2] Major employers are reaching out to sequencing moms to be sure they do not make a permanent exit. It is important to let them know that they are a valuable resource and that the company wants them back.[3]

Deloitte & Touche has a program that allows qualifying employees to leave the company for up to five years to focus on personal goals such as family. During that time, the participants, who are called alumni, stay connected to the firm and use company resources to keep their skills current. Participants are paired with a mentor and they receive subsidized training and semiannual check-ins to evaluate the program and their plans to return to work. Participants can also request temporary, paid assignments with the company. The program is designed to help employees move in and out of the workforce for personal reasons; it is also open to male employees and those who have personal goals other than raising children.[4]

There appears to be a tangible shift toward companies accepting returning women professionals. "A lot of these women have MBAs. They've been senior vice presidents," says Kathryn Sollman, co-founder of WomenAtWork Network in Wilton, Connecticut, which helps professional women who have taken time off return to the workplace. "Employers get their profiles and salivate. There is a whole 'woe is me' attitude out there (among some mothers), but it's simply not true. Employers are extremely receptive."[5]

While some companies are recruiting these women, other employers have programs that help their own employees leave and later return. IBM offers a program that allows employees to take up to three years off. Typically, working mothers who use the program take a year or more off, and then they use the remainder of their leave to re-enter work on a part-time basis. After the three years are up, they have the option of returning either full- or part-time. IBM surveyed employees who had taken the leave and found 59 percent would have left the company if the program had not been available. "We didn't want a situation where women had to opt out," says Maria Ferris, manager of work-life and women's initiatives at IBM. "We've invested in them, trained them. We want to retain them."[6]

Sequencing moms:
New mothers who leave the labor force only to return later.

In this chapter, we first describe **sequencing moms**, new mothers who leave the labor force only to return later. Then the projected future diverse workforce is explained, followed by a discussion of diversity and diversity management and the various components of the present diverse workforce. The development of this diverse workforce did not just happen; laws, executive orders, and Supreme Court decisions have had a major impact in formulating this new work environment. Therefore, the second part of this chapter provides an overview of the major EEO legislation that impacted human resource management and helped to create this diverse workforce. Toward this end, significant equal employment opportunity laws affecting human resource management are discussed; significant Supreme Court decisions are presented, and the Equal Employment Opportunity Commission is described. The *Uniform Guidelines on Employee Selection Procedures* are then explained and the issues of disparate treatment and adverse impact are addressed. Additional guidelines on employee selection procedures are also explained, and we discuss the importance of presidential Executive Orders 11246 and 11375 and affirmative action programs. This chapter concludes with a Global Perspective feature entitled "Not the Glass Ceiling, the Bamboo Ceiling."

1 OBJECTIVE

Describe the projected future diverse workforce.

Projected Future Diverse Workforce

The U.S. labor force in 2005 was 147 million.[7] By 2010, the civilian labor force is projected to increase to 158 million, and in the future the overall U.S. workforce will become more diverse.[8]

The Department of Labor's Bureau of Labor Statistics projects that the numbers of Asian and other employees (including Pacific Islanders, American Indians, and Alaskan Natives) in the U.S. workforce will increase 44.1 percent by 2010; Hispanic workers will increase 36.3 percent; and African-American workers 20.7 percent. The numbers of men and women in the labor force will grow, but the number of men will grow at a slower rate than the number of women. As a result, men's share of the labor force is expected to decrease while women's share is expected to increase. The youth labor force, aged 16 to 24, is projected to increase its share, growing more rapidly than the overall labor force. The large group, 25 to 54 years old, is projected to decline by 2010. The number of workers 55 or older is predicted to grow 50 percent by 2012, due to the aging of the baby-boomer generation.[9]

The Bureau of Labor Statistics estimates that by the year 2010, the median age of the labor force will be over 40, women will make up nearly half of the workforce (48 percent), and they will be the majority (59 percent) of the new additions to the labor force.[10]

Employees with disabilities are being included in increasing numbers. According to the 2000 Census, 19.3 percent of Americans have a disability of some kind, and 41.9 percent of Americans aged 65 or older are disabled.[11] Many immigrants from developing areas, especially Southeast Asia and Latin America, have joined the labor force. As evidenced from the above discussion, the labor force in the United States is expanding. However, evidently it is not doing so at a fast enough pace. It is estimated that more than 70 million baby boomers will reach age 65 over the next 15 years. However, only 40 million new workers will enter the workforce.[12] The U.S. Department of Labor projects that by 2013, available jobs will outnumber workers by 6.7 million and by 2030, available jobs will outnumber workers by 30 million.[13]

Diversity and Diversity Management

OBJECTIVE

Describe diversity and diversity management.

Diversity:
Any perceived difference among people: age, race, religion, functional specialty, profession, sexual orientation, geographic origin, lifestyle, tenure with the organization or position, and any other perceived difference.

Diversity refers to any perceived difference among people: age, race, religion, functional specialty, profession, sexual orientation, geographic origin, lifestyle, tenure with the organization or position, and any other perceived difference.

The challenge for managers in the future will be to recognize that people with common, but different characteristics from the mainstream, often think, act, learn, and communicate differently. Because every person, culture, and business situation is unique, there are no simple rules for managing diversity, but diversity experts say that employers need to develop patience, open-mindedness, acceptance, and cultural awareness. Diversity is more than equal employment and affirmative action,[14] topics to be discussed later in this chapter. Diversity aims to create workforces that mirror the populations and customers that organizations serve. R. Roosevelt Thomas Jr., former president of the American Institute for Managing Diversity, clarified some misconceptions about diversity in corporate America when he said, "People vary along an infinite number of possibilities." Thomas also believes, "They vary according to race and gender, but they also vary according to age, sexual orientation, and when they joined the company. Some workers are union members; some are not. Some are exempt; some are nonexempt. The variety is endless. Your definition has to be sufficiently broad to encompass everyone."[15] Many believe that workers in a diverse workforce are more satisfied in their work environment.[16] Diversity has been achieved in some areas, but perhaps other areas have a way to go.[17]

Diversity management:
Ensuring that factors are in place to provide for and encourage the continued development of a diverse workforce by melding these actual and perceived differences among workers to achieve maximum productivity.

Diversity management is ensuring that factors are in place to provide for and encourage the continued development of a diverse workforce by melding these actual and perceived differences among workers to achieve maximum productivity.

"If organizations want to remain competitive in the marketplace, diversity has to be a part of the strategic goal," said Susan Meisinger, president and CEO of SHRM.[18]

According to the SHRM 2005 Workplace Diversity Practices Survey, 78 percent of the respondents said diversity practices have helped reduce costs and 74 percent said the practices improved the financial bottom line.[19] In a Gallup survey, 61 percent of respondents who placed their company's diversity efforts in the upper third of companies surveyed said they are extremely satisfied with their company. But among employees who rate their company's diversity efforts in the lower third, only 21 percent said they were extremely satisfied with their company.[20]

Diversity management is about pursuing an inclusive culture where newcomers feel welcome, and everyone sees the value of his or her job. It involves creating a supportive culture where all employees can be effective. In creating this culture it is important that top management strongly support workplace diversity as a company goal and include diversity initiatives in their companies' business strategies. It has grown out of the need for organizations to recognize the changing workforce and

OBJECTIVE

Explain the various components of the present diverse workforce.

Web **Wisdom**

Workforce diversity

http://www.doi.gov/diversity/

Current diversity news is provided.

other social pressures that often result. Achieving diversity is more than being politically correct; it is about fostering a culture that values individuals and their wide array of needs and contributions. Promoting diversity can be a sound business strategy that leads to increased market share and a reputation as being a place people want to work.[21]

In a recent study conducted by the National Urban League it was shown that at the companies where diversity is a fact of life, productivity growth in the past four years exceeded that of the economy as a whole by 18 percent.[22] Components that combine to make up the diverse workforce will be discussed next.

Single Parents and Working Mothers

The number of single-parent households in the United States is growing.[23] Although the divorce rate peaked in the early 1980s, the number of divorces remains around 50 percent.[24] Often, one or more children are involved. Of course, there are always widows and widowers who have children, and there are some men and women who choose to raise children outside of wedlock. Approximately 72 percent of mothers with children under 18 are in the workforce, a figure up sharply from 47 percent in 1975.[25]

Breakdowns in primary child-care arrangements cost U.S. companies billions in lost productivity each year. Traditionally, child-care needs were viewed as being outside the realm of the business world, a responsibility workers had to bear and manage alone. This situation was particularly difficult for single parents; but even when both parents worked, they often could not afford a full-time, live-in housekeeper. For many workers, child care has been managed with the help of family or friends.

Many women who formerly remained at home to care for children and the household now need and want to work outside the home. If this valuable segment of the workforce is to be effectively utilized, organizations must fully recognize the importance of addressing work/family issues. Businesses have begun to see that providing child-care services and workplace flexibility may influence workers' choice of employers. More and more companies provide paid maternity leave, and some offer paternity leave. For instance, Google's maternity- and paternity-leave program allows for 75 percent of pay for up to six weeks, a $500 stipend for new parents to spend on takeout meals, adoption assistance, nearby child-care centers and a backup child-care center.[26]

Managers need to be sensitive to the needs of working parents. At times, management also needs to be creative in accommodating this most valuable segment of the workforce. The topic of workplace flexibility will be discussed in greater detail in Chapter 10.

Women in Business

Numerous factors have contributed to the growth and development of the U.S. labor force. However, nothing has been more prominent than the rise in the number of women in the labor force. Therefore, the base of building a diverse workforce rests on an employer's ability to attract and retain females. The number of women in the labor force rose from 18 million in 1950 to 66 million in 2000, an annual growth rate of 2.6 percent.[27]

Today, women account for 45 percent of the workforce.[28] Research by the Department of Labor revealed that women now hold half of all management, professional, and related occupations.[29] According to the Center for Women's Business Research, women-owned businesses grew by 28 percent between 1997 and 2004, which is three times the growth rate for U.S. businesses overall.[30]

Because of the number of women who are entering the workforce, there is an increasing number of nontraditional households in the United States. These households include those headed by single parents and those in which both partners work full-time.

Dual-Career Family

Dual-career family:
A situation in which both husband and wife have jobs and family responsibilities.

The increasing number of **dual-career families**, where both the husband and wife have jobs and family responsibilities, presents both challenges and opportunities for organizations. The majority of children growing up today have both parents working outside the home.[31]

Today, employees have turned down relocations because of spouses' jobs and concerns about their children. As a result, some firms have revised their policies against nepotism to allow both partners to work for the same company. Other firms have developed polices to assist the spouse of an employee who is transferred. Some companies are offering assistance in finding a position for the spouse of a transferred employee.

As the number of dual-career families increases, organizations must become even more flexible. For example, customized benefit plans (discussed in Chapter 10) may need to be available for today's workers. With dual-career families, only one of the spouses might pick up a health care plan, and the second spouse might select additional vacation. Some companies are actually designing their buildings to help dual-career families. At Procter & Gamble, the company specifically incorporated into the plant a dry cleaner, a shoe repair shop, and a cafeteria that prepares food employees can take home at night, relieving them of the need to prepare an evening meal. More than anything, dual-career families want more workplace flexibility (a topic of Chapter 10). Included in these work-life balance choices are flextime, compressed work weeks, job sharing, customized benefit plans, telecommuting, and part-time work.

Some dual-career families have established long-distance jobs to ensure that both couples are able to advance in their careers. The shift is coming as job relocations create a mobile workforce, leaving many professional couples grappling with career tracks that diverge. More are choosing to live in separate cities so both partners can get ahead.

Workers of Color

Workers of color (including Hispanics, African Americans, and Asians) are at times stereotyped. They may encounter misunderstandings and expectations based on ethnic or cultural differences. Members of ethnic or racial groups are socialized within their particular culture. Many are socialized as members of two cultural groups, the dominant culture and their racial or ethnic culture. Ella Bell, professor of organizational behavior at MIT, refers to this dual membership as biculturalism. In her study of African-American women, Bell identifies the stress of coping with membership in two cultures simultaneously as bicultural stress. She indicates that role conflict; competing roles from two cultures; and role overload, too many expectations to comfortably fulfill, are common characteristics of bicultural stress. Although these issues can be applied to other minority groups, they are particularly intense for women of color. This is because this group experiences dynamics affecting both minorities and women.[32]

Socialization in one's culture of origin can lead to misunderstandings in the workplace. This is particularly true when the manager relies solely on the cultural norms of the majority group. According to these norms, within the American culture it is acceptable, even considered positive, to publicly praise an individual for a job well done. However, in cultures that place primary value on group harmony and collective achievement, this method of rewarding an employee may cause emotional discomfort. Some employees feel that, if praised publicly, they will lose face within their group.

Older Workers

The population of the United States is growing older and will have a tremendous impact on workplace issues, because of increasing longevity and delaying of retirement.[33] The nation's workforce is hitting middle age, and the threat of a long-term labor shortage is developing.[34] The growing segment of Americans 65 or older is widely considered a critical part of the current and future workforce.[35] Many organizations today are actively courting older employees to entice them to remain on the job longer, especially in fields such as health care. They are doing everything from restructuring jobs to offering phased-retirement plans.[36]

Older workers not only provide a large hiring pool, but there are now more of them who want, or need, to work longer. One AARP study showed that 68 percent of workers between the ages of 50 and 70 plan to work in some capacity during retirement or never retire at all.[37]

As the workforce grows older, its needs and interests may change. Many will become bored with their present careers and desire different challenges. The graying of the workforce has required some adjustments. Some older workers favor less demanding full-time jobs, others choose semiretirement, and still others prefer part-time work. Many of these individuals require retraining because their technical skills may not be current.

People with Disabilities

Common disabilities include limited hearing or sight, limited mobility, mental or emotional deficiencies, and various nerve disorders. Such disabilities limit the amount or kind of work a person can do or make its achievement unusually difficult. In jobs for which they are qualified, however, disabled workers do as well as the unimpaired in terms of productivity, attendance, and average tenure. In fact, in certain high-turnover occupations, disabled workers have lower turnover rates.

A serious barrier to effective employment of disabled persons is the preconceived notions that have developed with time.[38] Managers should examine their own biases and attitudes toward such individuals. Many individuals experience anxiety just being around workers with disabilities, especially if the disabilities are severe. Fellow workers may show pity or feel that a disabled worker is fragile. Some even show disgust. The manager can set the tone for the proper treatment of workers with disabilities. If someone is unsure about how to act or how much help to offer, the disabled person should be asked for guidance. Managers must always strive to treat employees with disabilities as they treat other employees, and must hold them accountable for achievement.

Immigrants

Large numbers of immigrants from Asia and Latin America have settled in many parts of the United States. Some are highly skilled and well educated and others are only minimally qualified and have little education. They have one thing in common: an eagerness to work. They have brought with them attitudes, values, and mores particular to their home country cultures.

After the end of hostilities in Vietnam, Vietnamese immigrants settled along the Mississippi and Texas Gulf Coast. At about the same time, thousands of Thais fleeing the upheaval in Thailand came to the Boston area to work and live. New York's Puerto Rican community has long been an economic and political force there. Cubans who fled Castro's regime congregated in southern Florida, especially Miami. A flood of Mexicans and other Hispanics continues across the southern border of the United States. The Irish, the Poles, the Italians, and others who came here in past decades have long since assimilated into, and indeed become, the culture. Newer immigrants require time to adapt. Meanwhile, they generally take low-paying and menial jobs, live in substandard housing, and form enclaves where they cling to some semblance of the cultures they left.

Wherever they settle, members of these ethnic groups soon begin to become part of the regular workforce in certain occupations and break out of their isolation. They begin to adopt the English language and American customs. They learn new skills and adapt old skills to their new country. Managers can place these individuals in jobs appropriate to their skills, with excellent results for the organization. As corporations employ more foreign nationals in this country, managers must work to understand the different cultures of their employees.

Young Persons with Limited Education or Skills

Each year, thousands of young, unskilled workers are hired, especially during peak periods, such as holiday buying seasons. These workers generally have limited education, sometimes even less than a high school diploma. Those who have completed high school often find that their education hardly fits the work they are expected to do. Many of these young adults and teenagers have poor work habits; they tend to be tardy or absent more often than experienced or better-educated workers.

Although the negative attributes of these workers at times seem to outweigh the positive ones, they are a permanent part of the workforce. Certainly, when teenagers are hired, an organization is not hiring maturity or experience; but young people possess many qualities such as energy, enthusiasm, excitement, and eagerness to prove themselves. There are many jobs they can do well. More jobs can be de-skilled, making it possible for lower-skilled workers to do them. A well-known example of de-skilling is McDonald's substitution of pictures for numbers on its cash register keys. Managers should also look for ways to train unskilled workers and to further their formal education.

Educational Level of Employees

Another form of diversity now found in the workplace concerns the educational level of employees. The United States is becoming a bipolar country with regard to education, with a growing number of very educated people on one side and an alarming

---

Trends & Innovations

Superdads

The majority of men today are vastly more involved in the rearing of their children and maintenance of their households than their fathers were.[39] The job of stay-at-home dad is becoming more attractive to today's working dads. The number of working fathers who say they would be willing to give up the breadwinner role if their spouse or partner earned enough to support their families rose from 43 percent in 2004 to 49 percent in 2005, according to a CareerBuilder.com survey.[40]

Men appear to be adjusting to this new role, but not without some stress. "There's a push-pull," says Kevin Lee, 40, a photographer in Salt Lake City, Utah, with two small children and a wife who works part-time. "I feel like when I'm with the kids, it's great, and I enjoy that time. But in the back of my mind, I'm always thinking that I've got all these other things to do, like work around the house or job-related work." These fathers also have the disadvantage of having few role models to show them the way.[41] Traditionally, a man went out into the world and worked with other men, and when he came home, the rest of the family busied themselves to make him comfortable. Now, as with women of a generation ago, men are experiencing the notion of a second shift. Dr. Scott Haltzman, a psychiatrist in Barrington, Rhode Island, said, "Historically, men felt that if they applied themselves and worked hard, they would continue to rise within an organization. Now they must contend with a shaky economy, buyouts, layoffs and mergers, not to mention rapidly evolving technological advances."[42]

increase in the illiteracy rate on the other. In September 2005, the overall unemployment rate was 5.1 percent. But the percentage does not tell the whole story with regard to educational level of employees. The unemployment rate for those with a bachelor's degree was 2.4 percent; for those with a two-year degree, it was 3.6 percent; for those with a high school diploma, it was 5 percent; and for those without a high school diploma, it was 8.2 percent.[43]

Complicating this situation even more is the estimate that more than half of the new jobs will require some education beyond high school. Adding even more complexity is the trend in the workplace to empower workers. Empowerment is possible because of the advanced educational level required of the new workforce; however, those with limited education will be left out of this empowerment effort.

Equal Employment Opportunity: An Overview

As can be seen from the above discussion, the workforce of today has become truly diverse. But, this was not the case in the early 1960s; in fact, little of the workforce of those days remotely resembles that of today. Then, few mainstream opportunities were available to women, minorities, and those with disabilities. If this were so today, our economy would certainly grind to a halt. But diversity did not just happen. Legislation (federal, state, and local), Supreme Court decisions, and executive orders have encouraged both public and private organizations to tap the abilities of a workforce that was largely underutilized before the mid-1960s. The concept of equal employment opportunity has undergone much modification and fine-tuning since the passage of the Equal Pay Act of 1963, the Civil Rights Act of 1964, and the Age Discrimination in Employment Act of 1967.[44]

Numerous amendments to these acts have been passed, as well as other acts in response to oversights in the initial legislation. Major Supreme Court decisions interpreting the provisions of the act have also been handed down. Presidential executive orders were signed into law that provided for affirmative action. Over four decades have passed since the introduction of the first legislation, and equal employment opportunity has become an integral part of the workplace.

Although equal employment opportunity has come a long way since the early 1960s, continuing efforts are required because some problems still exist.[45]

In a recent Gallup Organization poll, 9 percent of respondents said they experienced some form of workplace discrimination in the last year that is barred under federal law.[46] While perfection is elusive, the majority of businesses today do attempt to make employment decisions based on who is the best qualified, as opposed to whether an individual is of a certain gender, race, religion, color, national origin, age, or is disabled. Throughout the remainder of this chapter, hiring standards to avoid will be identified based on some of the laws, executive orders, and Supreme Court decisions that have had a major impact in creating this diverse workforce.

OBJECTIVE

Identify the major laws affecting equal employment opportunity.

Laws Affecting Equal Employment Opportunity

Numerous national laws have been passed that have had an impact on equal employment opportunity. The passage of these laws reflects society's attitude toward the changes that should be made to give everyone an equal opportunity for employment. The most significant of these laws will be described in the following sections.

Civil Rights Act of 1866

The oldest federal legislation affecting staffing is the Civil Rights Act of 1866, which is based on the Thirteenth Amendment to the U.S. Constitution. Specifically, this Act provides that all citizens have the same right "as enjoyed by white citizens . . . to inherit, purchase . . . hold, and convey . . . property, [and that] all persons . . . shall have the same right to make and enforce contracts . . . as enjoyed by white citizens." As interpreted by the courts, employment, as well as membership in a union, is a contractual arrangement. Blacks and Hispanics are covered by this Act if they are discriminated against on the basis of race. Until 1968, it was assumed that the Act was applicable only when action by a state or state agency, and not by private parties, was involved. That year the Supreme Court overruled this assumption and broadened the interpretation of the Act to cover all contractual arrangements. There is no statute of limitations to the Act as evidenced by the fact that it continues to be used today in race discrimination in housing cases.

Equal Pay Act of 1963

The Equal Pay Act of 1963 prohibits an employer from paying an employee of one gender less money than an employee of the opposite gender, if both employees do work that is substantially the same. Jobs are considered substantially the same when they require equal skill, effort, and responsibility and they are performed under similar working conditions.

The Act covers work within the same physical place of business.[47] For example, an employer could pay a female more in San Francisco than a male working in the same position in Slippery Rock, Pennsylvania, even if the jobs were substantially the same, because of the cost-of-living difference. The EPA permits pay distinctions based on the following factors:

- Unequal responsibility
- Dissimilar working conditions
- Differences due to seniority
- Differences resulting from a merit pay system
- Differences based on quantity or quality of production

In 2003, median weekly earnings for women who were full-time workers were 80 percent of their male counterparts, which is up from 63 percent in 1979.[48] While pay inequities obviously exist and no doubt reflect gender discrimination to some degree, there may be legitimate reasons for part of the problem. Supply-and-demand factors help explain the persistence of pay inequity. Traditionally, many women held occupations that men did not consider, such as schoolteacher, secretary, social worker, nurse, and waitress. However, times have changed. For example, after only three decades as members of the mainstream workforce, one in three wives now earn more than their spouses, up from one in five in 1980. Women with MBAs are doing even better, as nearly 60 percent have direct deposits larger than their spouses. The picture will even get brighter for women since 20 percent more women than men are graduating from college, and more women are joining the managerial ranks every year.[49]

One thing is certain, the Equal Pay Act has teeth and they will get sharper because the U.S. Department of Labor is aggressively enforcing the Act and seeking harsher penalties against companies that violate it. Recently, the EEOC resolved more than 10,000 sex discrimination complaints in favor of the charging party and recovered $100.8 million in monetary benefits for charging parties and other aggrieved individuals. Morgan Stanley settled a sex discrimination suit filed by the EEOC for $54 million. The lead plaintiff, Allison Schieffelin, claimed that, for reasons relating to her gender, the investment firm discriminated against her, withholding opportunities for promotions and higher pay.[50]

Title VII of the Civil Rights Act of 1964, Amended 1972

The statute that has had the greatest impact on equal employment opportunity is Title VII of the Civil Rights Act of 1964, as amended by the Equal Employment Act of 1972. Under Title VII, it is illegal for an employer to discriminate in hiring, firing, promoting, compensating, or in terms, conditions, or privileges of employment on the basis of race, color, sex, religion, or national origin. The Act also forbids retaliation against an employee who has participated in an investigation, proceeding, or hearing.[51]

Title VII covers employers engaged in or affecting interstate commerce who have 15 or more employees for each working day in each of 20 calendar weeks in the current or preceding calendar year. Also included in the definition of employers are state and local governments, schools, colleges, unions, and private employment agencies

---

Joint Reporting Committee

- Equal Employment Opportunity Commission
- Office of Federal Contract Compliance Programs (Labor)

EQUAL EMPLOYMENT OPPORTUNITY

EMPLOYER INFORMATION REPORT EEO—1

1997

Standard Form 100
(Rev. 4–92)

O.M.B. No. 3048–0007
EXPIRES 12/31/93
100-213

Section A—TYPE OF REPORT
Refer to instructions for number and types of reports to be filed.

1. Indicate by marking in the appropriate box the type of reporting unit for which this copy of the form is submitted (MARK ONLY ONE BOX).

　　(1) ☐ Single-establishment Employer Report

Multi-establishment Employer:
　(2) ☐ Consolidated Report (Required)
　(3) ☐ Headquarters Unit Report (Required)
　(4) ☐ Individual Establishment Report (submit one for each establishment with 50 or more employees)
　(5) ☐ Special Report

2. Total number of reports being filed by this Company (Answer on Consolidated Report only) _____

Section B—COMPANY IDENTIFICATION (To be answered by all employers)				OFFICE USE ONLY
1. Parent Company				
a. Name of parent company (owns or controls establishment in item 2) omit if same as label				a.
Address (Number and street)				b.
City or town	State		ZIP code	c.

2. Establishment for which this report is filed. (Omit if same as label)
　　a. Name of establishment

Address (Number and street)	City or town	County	State	ZIP code	d.
					e.
b. Employer identification No. (IRS 9-DIGIT TAX NUMBER)				☐☐☐☐☐☐	f.

Was an EEO–1 report filed for this establishment last year? ☐ Yes ☐ No

Section C—EMPLOYERS WHO ARE REQUIRED TO FILE (To be answered by all employers)

☐ Yes ☐ No　1. Does the entire company have at least 100 employees in the payroll period for which you are reporting?

☐ Yes ☐ No　2. Is your company affiliated through common ownership and/or centralized management with other entitles in an enterprise with a total employment of 100 or more?

☐ Yes ☐ No　3. Does the company or any of its establishments (1) have 50 or more employees AND (b) is not exempt as provided by 41 CFR 60–1.5, AND either (1) is a prime government contractor or first-tier subcontractor, and has a contract, subcontract, or purchase order amounting to $50,000 or more, or (2) serves as a depository for Government funds in any amount or is a financial institution which is an issuing and paying agent for U.S. Savings Bonds and Savings Notes?

　　If the response to question C–3 is yes, please enter your Dun and Bradstreet Identification number (if you have one): ☐☐☐☐☐☐☐☐☐

NOTE: If the answer is yes to questions 1, 2, or 3, complete the entire form, otherwise skip to Section G.

NSN 7540–00–180–6384

Figure 3-1(a) Equal Employment Opportunity Employer Information Report

Section D ñ EMPLOYMENT DATA

SF 100 ñ Page 2

Employment at this establishment ñ Report all permanent full- and part-time employees including apprentices and on-the-job trainees unless specifically excluded as set forth in the instructions. Enter the appropriate figures on all lines and in all columns. Blank spaces will be considered as zeros.

Job Categories	Number of Employees (Report employees in only one category)														
	Race/Ethnicity														
	Hispanic or Latino		Not-Hispanic or Latino												Total Col A - N
			Male						Female						
	Male	Female	White	Black or African American	Native Hawaiian or Other Pacific Islander	Asian	American Indian or Alaska Native	Two or more races	White	Black or African American	Native Hawaiian or Other Pacific Islander	Asian	American Indian or Alaska Native	Two or more races	
	A	B	C	D	E	F	G	H	I	J	K	L	M	N	O
Executive/Senior Level Officials and Managers 1.1															
First/Mid-Level Officials and Managers 1.2															
Professionals 2															
Technicians 3															
Sales Workers 4															
Administrative Support Workers 5															
Craft Workers 6															
Operatives 7															
Laborers and Helpers 8															
Service Workers 9															
TOTAL 10															
PREVIOUS YEAR TOTAL 11															

1. Date(s) of payroll period used: _____   (Omit on the Consolidated Report.)

Approval

O.M.B. No. 3046-0007
Revised 01/2006
Expires 1/2009

Figure 3-1(b) *(continued)*

that procure employees for an employer with 15 or more employees. All private employers who are subject to the Civil Rights Act of 1964 as amended with 100 employees or more must annually submit an EEO-1 (see Figure 3-1). Changes to the EEO-1 have been approved to take place in 2007 with the new form having more categories than the present form and with additional questions for soliciting employee self-identification about race and ethnic data.[52]

Three notable exceptions to discrimination as covered by Title VII are bona fide occupational qualifications (BFOQs), seniority and merit systems, and testing and educational requirements. According to the act it is not: an unlawful employment practice for an employer to hire and employ employees . . . on the basis of his religion, sex, or national origin in those certain instances where religion, sex, or national origin is a bona fide occupational qualification reasonably necessary to the normal operation of the particular business or enterprise.

Thus, for example, religious institutions, such as churches or synagogues, may legally refuse to hire teachers whose religious persuasion is different from that of the hiring institution. Likewise, a maximum-security correctional institution housing only male inmates may decline to hire females as security guards. The concept of bona fide occupational qualification was designed to be narrowly, not broadly, interpreted and has been so construed by the courts in a number of cases. The burden of proving the necessity for a BFOQ rests entirely on the employer.

The second exception to discrimination under Title VII is a bona fide seniority system such as the type normally contained in a union contract. Differences in employment conditions among workers are permitted provided that such differences are not the result of an intention to discriminate because of race, color, religion, sex, or national origin. Even if a bona fide seniority system has an adverse impact on those individuals protected by Title VII (i.e., it affects a class or group), the system can be invalidated only by evidence that the actual motives of the parties to the agreement were to discriminate.

In the matter of testing and educational requirements, Title VII states that it is not "an unlawful employment practice for an employer to give, and to act upon, the results of any professionally developed ability test provided that such test, its administration, or action upon the results is not designed, intended or used to discriminate because of race, color, religion, sex, or national origin." Employment testing and educational requirements must be job related, and the burden of proof is on the employer when adverse impact is shown to establish that a demonstrable relationship exists between actual job performance and the test or educational requirement.

Persons not covered by Title VII include aliens not authorized to work in the United States and members of the communist party. Homosexuals are also not protected under Title VII. The courts have consistently ruled that where the term "sex" is used in any federal statute that term refers to biological gender and not to sexual preference.

The Civil Rights Act of 1964 also created the Equal Employment Opportunity Commission (EEOC) and assigned enforcement of Title VII to this agency. Consisting of five members appointed by the president, the EEOC is empowered to investigate, conciliate, and litigate charges of discrimination arising under provisions of Title VII. Additionally, the commission has the responsibility of issuing procedural regulations and interpretations of Title VII and the other statutes it enforces. The most significant regulation issued by EEOC is the *Uniform Guidelines on Employee Selection Procedures*.

The Act continues to have teeth. A $15 million settlement was been reached between printing company R. R. Donnelley & Sons and some 600 class members consisting of former employees who took their race bias claims to the Supreme Court during an eight-year case. In recent years there have been more gender discrimination cases involving hiring and firing, pay and promotion, leave related to pregnancy and motherhood, sexual harassment, and retaliation for complaining about sexual harassment.[53]

In 2006, the Supreme Court ruled in favor of Sheila White, a forklift operator at Burlington Northern & Santa Fe Railway Co., who alleged that the company unfairly retaliated against her charge of sexual discrimination when it reassigned her to more physically demanding work in the rail yard.[54] The Abercrombie & Fitch Stores, Inc. settled for $50 million in three lawsuits alleging race and sex discrimination.[55] A multimillion dollar agreement was reached between Ford Motor Co. and the Equal Employment Opportunity Commission to settle allegations that Ford discriminated against black employees in its apprenticeship program. Ford agreed to eliminate a long-standing apprenticeship admissions test, offer positions to nearly 300 current and former black employees, and provide monetary awards to a class of up to 3,400 individuals.[56]

Age Discrimination in Employment Act of 1967, Amended in 1978 and 1986

As originally enacted, the Age Discrimination in Employment Act (ADEA) prohibited employers from discriminating against individuals who were 40 to 65 years old. The 1978 amendment provided protection for individuals who were at least 40, but less than 70 years old. In a 1986 amendment, employer discrimination against anyone age 40 or older is illegal. Questions asked about an applicant's age or date of birth may be ill-advised. However, a firm may ask for age information to comply with the child labor law. For example, the question could be asked, "Are you under the age of 18?" Also, questions about the ages of children, if any, could be potentially discriminatory because a close approximation of the applicant's age often is obtained through knowledge of the ages of the children. The EEOC is responsible for administering this Act. The Act pertains to employers who have 20 or more employees for 20 or more calendar weeks (either in the current or preceding calendar year); unions with 25 or more members; employment agencies; and federal, state, and local government subunits.

Age discrimination suits are now the fastest-growing category of discrimination complaints filed with the U.S. Equal Employment Opportunity Commission. Recently, 16,585 age discrimination claims were filed with the agency. They are also the most expensive; in 2005 awards amounting to $77 million was collected.[57]

The Supreme Court continues to refine the law. In 2005, the Supreme Court made it easier for workers to file age discrimination claims.[58] Before the ruling, in order to bring a claim to court, plaintiffs had to show that a company's policies were deliberately biased. In *Smith v City of Jackson*, it was determined that if a company has a policy or practice that adversely affects a disproportionate number of workers age 40 or older, even if it is not intentional, the organization becomes vulnerable to accusations of age discrimination.[59]

Enforcement begins when a charge is filed, but the EEOC can review compliance even if no charge is filed. The Age Discrimination in Employment Act differs from Title VII of the Civil Rights Act in providing for a trial by jury and carrying a possible criminal penalty for violation of the Act. The trial-by-jury provision is important because juries are thought to have great sympathy for older people who may have been discriminated against. The criminal penalty provision means that a person may receive more than lost wages if discrimination is proved. The 1978 amendment also makes class action suits possible.

Age Can Actually Be a Bona Fide Occupational Qualification

Age can actually be a bona fide occupational qualification where it is reasonably necessary to the essence of the business, and the employer has a rational or factual basis for believing that all, or substantially all, people within the age class would not be able to perform satisfactorily. Courts have continued to rule that the Federal Aviation Administration adequately explained its long-standing rule that it can force commercial pilots to retire at age 60. The age 60 rule was first imposed in 1959 and had long been controversial.

This ruling supported the 1974 Seventh Circuit Court decision that Greyhound did not violate the ADEA when it refused to hire persons 35 years of age or older as intercity bus drivers. Again, the likelihood of risk or harm to its passengers was involved. Greyhound presented evidence concerning degenerative physical and sensory changes that humans undergo at about age 35 that have a detrimental effect upon driving skills, and that the changes are not detectable by physical tests.[60]

Rehabilitation Act of 1973

The Rehabilitation Act prohibits discrimination against disabled workers who are employed by certain government contractors and subcontractors and organizations that receive federal grants in excess of $2,500. Individuals are considered disabled if they have a physical or mental impairment that substantially limits one or more major life activities or if they have a record of such impairment. Protected under the Act are diseases and conditions such as epilepsy, cancer, cardiovascular disorders, AIDS, blindness, deafness, mental retardation, emotional disorders, and dyslexia.

There are two primary levels of the Act. All federal contractors or subcontractors exceeding the $2,500 base are required to post notices that they agree to take affirmative action to recruit, employ, and promote qualified disabled individuals. If the contract or subcontract exceeds $50,000, or if the contractor has 50 or more employees, the employer must prepare a written affirmative action plan for review by the Office of Federal Contract Compliance Programs (OFCCP), which administers the Act. In it, the contractor must specify that reasonable steps are being taken to hire and promote disabled persons.

In a recent interpretation of Section 8 of the Rehabilitation Act, federal technology buyers are forced to think about people who are blind, deaf, paralyzed, or have other disabilities before they buy software, computers, printers, copiers, fax machines, kiosks, telecommunications devices, or video and multimedia products. Federal Website designers also have to make their sites accessible to disabled users, and anyone in government who develops or maintains technology products has to make sure those technologies are accessible. Thus far, federal law exempts corporate America from complying with the guidelines. However, companies wanting to obtain government business must fully comply.

Pregnancy Discrimination Act of 1978

Passed as an amendment to Title VII of the Civil Rights Act, the Pregnancy Discrimination Act prohibits discrimination in employment based on pregnancy, childbirth, or related medical conditions. Questions regarding a woman's family and childbearing plans should not be asked. Similarly, questions relating to family plans, birth control techniques, and the like may be viewed as discriminatory because they are not also asked of men. The basic principle of the Act is that women affected by pregnancy and related conditions must be treated the same as other applicants and employees on the basis of their ability or inability to work. A woman is therefore protected against such practices as being fired or refused a job or promotion merely because she is pregnant or has had an abortion. She usually cannot be forced to take a leave of absence as long as she can work. If other employees on disability leave are entitled to return to their jobs when they are able to work again, so too are women who have been unable to work because of pregnancy. Also, limiting job advancement opportunities while a woman is pregnant may be a violation of the Act.[61]

The same principle applies in the benefits area, including disability benefits, sick leave, and health insurance. A woman unable to work for pregnancy-related reasons is entitled to disability benefits or sick leave on the same basis as employees unable to work for medical reasons. Also, any health insurance provided must cover expenses for pregnancy-related conditions on the same basis as expenses for other medical conditions. However, health insurance for expenses arising from an abortion is not required except where the life of the mother would be endangered if the fetus were carried to term or where medical complications have arisen from an abortion.

In a class action suit originally filed in 1978, but not settled until July 1991, American Telephone & Telegraph Company (AT&T) agreed to settle a pregnancy discrimination suit with the EEOC for $66 million. This suit was the largest cash recovery in the agency's history and involved more than 13,000 then-present and former female AT&T workers. The 1978 suit charged that Western Electric required pregnant workers to leave their jobs at the end of their sixth month of pregnancy, denied them seniority credit, and refused to guarantee them a job when they returned. Pregnancy discrimination cases continue and pregnancy-discrimination settlements are at an all-time high. Recently the Equal Employment Opportunity Commission received 4,512 complaints.[62] "We recover about $12 million or $13 million a year through litigation," says David Grinberg, a spokesman with the EEOC in Washington, D.C., "and that is in addition to what we recover in the pre-litigation process where most of the charges are settled."[63]

Immigration Reform and Control Act of 1986

The desire to stem illegal immigration prompted Congress to enact the Immigration Reform and Control Act (IRCA) of 1986. The IRCA granted amnesty to approximately 1.7 million long-term unauthorized workers in an effort to bring them out of the shadows and improve their labor market opportunities. It also established criminal and civil sanctions against employers who knowingly hire unauthorized aliens. The act also makes unlawful the hiring of anyone unless the person's employment authorization and identity are verified. When dealing with the national origin provision of the Civil Rights Act, IRCA reduces the threshold coverage from 15 to 4 employees. The IRCA toughened criminal sanctions for employers who hire illegal aliens; denied illegal aliens federally funded welfare benefits, and legitimized some aliens through an amnesty program. To comply with the IRCA, candidates for employment are not required to be U. S. citizens but they must prove they are eligible to work in the United States. Employers must require all new employees to complete and sign a verification form (Form I-9) to certify their eligibility for employment. These individuals can establish their eligibility for employment by presenting a U.S. passport, alien registration card with photograph, or a work permit that establishes the person's identity and employment eligibility. Employers should recognize that faked documents are not uncommon and should protect themselves by conducting a background investigation.

Illegal Immigration Reform and Immigrant Responsibility Act of 1996

The Illegal Immigration Reform and Immigrant Responsibility Act of 1996 was passed partly in response to the fact that at least one of the terrorists who blew up the World Trade Center in 1993, killing six people and wounding 1,000, had legally entered on a student visa. The law places severe limitations on persons who come to the United States and remain in the country longer than permitted by their visas and/or persons who violate their nonimmigrant status. Anyone unlawfully present in the United States for 180 days, but less than one year, is subject to a three-year ban for admission to the United States. Anyone unlawfully present in the United States for one year or more is subject to a 10-year ban from admission to the United States. There are certain exceptions, however, such as extreme hardship. However, since 9/11, the law has been enforced more rigorously.[64]

Americans with Disabilities Act of 1990

The Americans with Disabilities Act (ADA), passed in 1990, prohibits discrimination against qualified individuals with disabilities. The ADA prohibits discrimination in all employment practices, including job application procedures, hiring, firing, advancement, compensation, training, and other terms, conditions, and privileges of employment. It applies to recruitment, advertising, tenure, layoffs, leaves, benefits, and all other employment-related activities. The employment provisions apply to private employers, state and local governments, employment agencies, and labor unions. Persons discriminated against because they have a known association or relationship with a disabled individual is also protected. Employers with 15 or more employees are covered.

The ADA defines an individual with a disability as a person who has, or is regarded as having, a physical or mental impairment that substantially limits one or more major life activities, and has a record of such an impairment, or is regarded as having such an impairment.[65] However, the Supreme Court has ruled that people with correctable physical limitations, like poor eyesight or high blood pressure, may not seek the protection of the Americans with Disabilities Act.

The EEOC guidelines on pre-employment inquiries and tests regarding disabilities prohibit inquiries and medical examinations intended to gain information about applicants' disabilities before a conditional job offer. In the Supreme Court case of *Leonel v American Airlines*, the Court ruled that the airline violated the ADA'S required sequence for pre-hire medical inquiries/examinations by making medical inquiries and requiring individuals to take medical examinations before completing and making its hiring decisions.[66]

The guiding principle is to ask only about potential employees' ability to do the job, and not about their disabilities. Lawful inquiries include those regarding performance of specific functions or possession of training, while illegal inquiries include those that ask about previous medical conditions or extent of prior drug use. The ADA does not protect people currently using illegal drugs. It does protect those in rehabilitation programs who are not currently using illegal drugs, those who have been rehabilitated, and those erroneously labeled as drug users.

Coverage under the ADA continues to evolve. Recently the Equal Employment Opportunity Commission issued guidelines on the employment of individuals with intellectual disabilities. As defined by the EEOC, people are considered to have an intellectual disability if they meet all three of the following criteria: their intellectual functioning level (IQ) is below 70–75; they have significant limitations in adaptive skills—the basic conceptual, social, and practical skills needed for everyday life; and their disability began before age 18.[67]

Civil Rights Act of 1991

During 1988–1989, the Supreme Court rendered six employment discrimination decisions of such magnitude that a congressional response was required to overturn these decisions.[68] The result was passage of the Civil Rights Act of 1991. The Act amended five statutes: (1) the Civil Rights Act of 1866; (2) Title VII of the Civil Rights Act of 1964, as Amended; (3) the Age Discrimination in Employment Act of 1967, as Amended; (4) the Rehabilitation Act of 1973; and (5) the Americans with Disabilities Act of 1990.

The Civil Rights Act of 1991 had the following purposes:

- To provide appropriate remedies for intentional discrimination and unlawful harassment in the workplace.
- To codify the concepts of *business necessity* and *job related* pronounced by the Supreme Court in *Griggs v Duke Power Co.*
- To confirm statutory authority and provide statutory guidelines for the adjudication of disparate impacts under Title VII of the Civil Rights Act of 1964. Disparate impact occurs when certain actions in the employment process work to the disadvantage of members of protected groups. The concept of disparate impact will be discussed later under the topic of adverse impact.
- To respond to recent decisions of the Supreme Court by expanding the scope of relevant civil rights statutes in order to provide adequate protection to victims of discrimination.

Under this Act, a complaining party may recover punitive damages if the complaining party demonstrates that the company engaged in a discriminatory practice with malice or with reckless indifference to the law. However, the following limits, based on the number of people employed by the company, were placed on the amount of the award:

- Between 15 and 100 employees—$50,000
- Between 101 and 200 employees—$100,000

- Between 201 and 500 employees—$200,000
- More than 500 employees—$300,000

In each case, aggrieved employees must be with the firm for 20 or more calendar weeks in the current or preceding calendar year.

With regard to burden of proof, a complaining party must show that a particular employment practice causes a disparate impact on the basis of race, color, religion, sex, or national origin. It must also be shown that the company is unable to demonstrate that the challenged practice is job related for the position in question and consistent with business necessity. The Act also extends the coverage of the Civil Rights Act of 1964 to extraterritorial employment. However, the Act does not apply to U.S. companies operating in other countries if it would violate the law or the customs of the foreign country. The Act also extends the nondiscrimination principles to Congress and other government agencies, such as the General Accounting Office and the Government Printing Office.

Also included in the Civil Rights Act of 1991 is the Glass Ceiling Act. The **glass ceiling** is the invisible barrier in organizations that impedes women and minorities from career advancement.

This act established a Glass Ceiling Commission to study the manner in which businesses fill management and decision-making positions, the developmental and skill-enhancing practices used to foster the necessary qualifications for advancement to such positions, and the compensation programs and reward structures currently utilized in the workplace. It was also to study the limited progress made by minorities and women. It established an annual award for excellence in promoting a more diverse skilled workforce at the management and decision-making levels in business. Some industries, such as hospitality, appear to have broken the glass ceiling. It appears the glass ceiling in corporate America may be showing a few cracks, but more work needs to be done. Andrea Jung, Chief Executive of Avon Products Inc., said, "I'm actually optimistic. In the next five years, I think you're going to see dimensionally different opportunities for women."[69]

Glass ceiling:
Invisible barrier in organizations that impedes women and minorities from career advancement.

Uniformed Services Employment and Reemployment Rights Act (USERRA) of 1994

The Uniformed Services Employment and Reemployment Rights Act provides protection to Reservists and National Guard members. Under this Act those workers are entitled to return to their civilian employment after completing their military service. The Act is intended to eliminate or minimize employment disadvantages to civilian careers that can result from service in the uniformed services. USERRA was enacted to protect the reemployment benefits and nondiscrimination rights of individuals who voluntarily or involuntarily take a leave of absence from employment to serve in the military. As a general rule, a returning employee is entitled to reemployment in the same job position that he or she would have attained with reasonable certainty if not for the absence to serve in the military. Known as the escalator principle, this requirement is designed to ensure that a returning employee is not penalized (by losing a pay raise, promotion, etc.) for the time spent on active duty. There are no special rights for temporary workers or the new hires taking over reservists' jobs under USERRA.[70]

Sue King, management attorney with Littler Mendelson's Washington, D.C., office said, "If a replacement employee complains that he lost his job when a reservist reclaims it, employers should follow whatever general state or federal labor laws would apply, and company policies and procedures."[71]

USERRA requires the individual to apply for reemployment within a specified time period upon completion of military service. For service over 180 days, the person must reapply with the employer within 90 days after completion of service. These limits are extended for up to two years by hospitalization or convalescence from an injury caused during or aggravated by active military duty, and may be extended further by the minimum time required to make reporting for work reasonable for the injured person.

Veterans' Benefits Improvement Act (VBIA) of 2004

The VBIA amends portions of the USERRA. The VBIA enhances housing, education, and other benefits for veterans. Two provisions are of particular importance to employers: (1) a provision requiring employers to post a notice informing employees of their rights under USERRA; and (2) a provision increasing the health care continuation period for employees on military leave from 18 months to 24 months.[72]

State and Local Laws

Numerous state and local laws also affect equal employment opportunity.[73] A number of states and some cities have passed fair employment practice laws prohibiting discrimination on the basis of race, color, religion, gender, or national origin. Even prior to federal legislation, several states had anti-discrimination legislation relating to age and gender. For instance, New York protected individuals between the ages of 18 and 65 prior to the 1978 and 1986 ADEA amendments, and California had no upper limit on protected age. Recently, San Francisco voted to ban weight discrimination. The Board of Supervisors added body size to city laws that already bar discrimination based on race, color, religion, age, ancestry, sex, sexual orientation, disability, place of birth, or gender identity. The State of California even has a law that requires sexual harassment prevention training.[74] In 2006, Washington became the eighth state to explicitly prohibit bias against transgender people.[75]

When EEOC regulations conflict with state or local civil rights regulations, the legislation more favorable to women and minorities applies. For instance, whereas the threshold coverage for the Civil Right Act of 1964 is 15, in Chicago companies with just a single employee can be sued for discrimination.[76]

OBJECTIVE

Identify some of the major Supreme Court decisions that have had an impact on equal employment opportunity.

Significant U.S. Supreme Court Decisions

Knowledge of the law is obviously important for those involved with human resource management; however, the manner in which the courts interpret the law is vitally important. Also, court interpretations continuously change, even though the law may

---

Ethical Dilemma

What Was the Real Message?

You were recently hired as information technology manager and one of your first tasks was to pre-screen candidates for an IT position with a subsidiary. After interviewing 20 candidates, you recommend an individual you consider the most qualified for upper management for the second interview. A day later, you are taken aside by a friend and told in vague phrases, accompanied by less ambiguous body language, that you should not waste management's time by sending certain types (nudge-nudge-wink-wink) for an interview.[77]

The intent of the message was clear: if you want to be accepted as a team player with this company, you had better get with the program.

What would you do?

not have been amended. Discussions of some of the more significant U.S. Supreme Court decisions affecting equal employment opportunity follow.

Griggs v Duke Power Company

A major decision affecting the field of human resource management was rendered in 1971. A group of black employees at Duke Power Company had charged job discrimination under Title VII of the Civil Rights Act of 1964. Prior to Title VII, the Duke Power Company had two workforces, separated by race. After passage of the Act, the company required applicants to have a high school diploma and pass a paper-and-pencil test to qualify for certain jobs. The plaintiff was able to demonstrate that, in the relevant labor market, 34 percent of the white males but only 12 percent of the black males had a high school education. The plaintiff was also able to show that people already in those jobs were performing successfully even though they did not have high school diplomas. No business necessity could be shown for this educational requirement. The *Griggs v Duke Power Company* case continues to be a benchmark case in employment law.[78]

In an 8-0 vote, the Supreme Court ruled against Duke Power Company and stated, "If an employment practice which operates to exclude Negroes cannot be shown to be related to job performance, the practice is prohibited." A major implication of the decision is that when human resource management practices eliminate substantial numbers of minority or women applicants (prima facie evidence), the burden of proof is on the employer to show that the practice is job related. This Court decision significantly affected the human resource practices of many firms. Questions in employment procedures that should be avoided if not job related include credit record, conviction record, garnishment record, and education. It should be noted that actually asking non-job-related questions is not illegal; it is how a hiring person uses the gained information that makes it illegal.[79] For instance, asking a person his or her age is not in and of itself illegal. Using this information to systematically eliminate older workers from consideration older is illegal.[80] Stating that a job requires a college degree when it could be accomplished effectively by a high school graduate can potentially be discriminatory. Even work experience requirements that are not job related should be avoided.

Albermarle Paper Company v Moody

In 1966, a class action suit was brought against Albermarle Paper Company and the plant employees' labor union. A permanent injunction was requested against any policy, practice, custom, or usage at the plant that violated Title VII. In 1975, the Supreme Court, in *Albermarle Paper Company v Moody*, reaffirmed the idea that any test used in the selection process or in promotion decisions must be validated if it has an adverse impact on women and minorities. The employer has the burden of proof for showing that the test is valid. Subsequently, the employer must show that any selection or promotion device actually measures what it is supposed to measure.

Phillips v Martin Marietta Corporation

In 1971, the Court ruled that Martin Marietta had discriminated against a woman because she had young children. The company had a rule prohibiting the hiring of women with school-age children. The company argued that it did not preclude all women from job consideration, only those women with school-age children. Martin Marietta contended that this was a business requirement. The argument was obviously based on stereotypes and was rejected. A major implication of this decision is that a firm cannot impose standards for employment only on women. For example, a firm cannot reject divorced women if it does not also reject divorced men. Neither application forms nor interviews should contain questions for women that do not also apply to men. Examples of questions that should not be asked are: "Do you wish to be addressed as Ms., Miss, or Mrs.?" "Are you married?" "Do you have children?" "Do you plan on having any more children?" "Where does your husband work?"

Espinoza v Farah Manufacturing Company

In 1973, the Court ruled that Title VII does not prohibit discrimination on the basis of lack of citizenship. The EEOC had previously said that refusing to hire anyone who was a noncitizen was discriminatory as this selection standard was likely to have an adverse impact on individuals of foreign national origin. Because 92 percent of the employees at the Farah facility in question were Hispanics who had become American citizens, the Court held that the company had not discriminated on the basis of national origin when it refused to hire a Hispanic who was not a U.S. citizen.

Dothard v Rawlingson

At the time Rawlingson applied for a position as correctional counselor trainee, she was a 22-year-old college graduate whose major course of study had been correctional psychology. She was refused employment because she failed to meet the minimum height and weight requirements. In this 1977 case, the Supreme Court upheld the U.S. District Court's decision that Alabama's statutory minimum height requirement of five feet, two inches and minimum weight requirement of 120 pounds for the position of correctional counselor had a discriminatory impact on women applicants. The contention was that minimum height and weight requirements for the position of correctional counselor were job related. However, the Court stated that this argument does not rebut prima facie evidence showing these requirements have a discriminatory impact on women, whereas no evidence was produced correlating these requirements with a requisite amount of strength thought essential to good performance.

University of California Regents v Bakke

This Supreme Court decision dealt with the first major test involving reverse discrimination. The University of California had reserved 16 places in each beginning medical school class for minorities. Allen Bakke, a white man, was denied admission even though he scored higher on the admission criteria than some minority applicants who were admitted. The Supreme Court ruled 5–4 in Bakke's favor. As a result, Bakke was admitted to the university and later received his degree. But, at the same time, the Court reaffirmed that race may be taken into account in admission decisions.

American Tobacco Company v Patterson

This 1982 Supreme Court decision allows seniority and promotion systems established since Title VII to stand, although they unintentionally hurt minority workers. Under *Griggs v Duke Power Co.*, a prima facie violation of Title VII may be established by policies or practices that are neutral on their face and in intent, but that nonetheless discriminate against a particular group. A seniority system would fall under the *Griggs* rationale if it were not for Section 703(h) of the Civil Rights Act, which provides:

> *Notwithstanding any other provision of this subchapter, it shall not be an*
> *unlawful employment practice for an employer to apply standards of*
> *compensation, or different terms, conditions, or privileges of employment*
> *pursuant to a bona fide seniority or merit system . . . provided that such*
> *differences are not the result of an intention to discriminate because of race,*

color, religion, sex, or national origin, nor shall it be an unlawful employment practice for an employer to give and to act upon the results of any professionally developed ability test provided that such test, its administration or action upon the results is not designed, intended or used to discriminate because of race, color, religion, sex, or national origin.

Thus, the court ruled that a seniority system adopted after Title VII may stand even though it has an unintended discriminatory impact.

O'Connor v Consolidated Coin Caterers Corp.

The U.S. Supreme Court unanimously ruled that an employee does not have to show that he or she was replaced by someone younger than 40 to bring suit under the ADEA. The Court declared that discrimination is illegal even when all the employees are members of the protected age group. The case began in 1990 when James O'Connor's job as a regional sales manager was eliminated. The company did not select O'Connor, age 56, to manage either of its two remaining sales territories. He later was fired. His replacement was 40 years old. O'Connor was evidently doing so well that he earned a bonus of $37,000 the previous year. Apparently, O'Connor's new boss told him he was too damn old for the kind of work he was doing and that what the company needed was new blood.

Writing for the Court, Justice Scalia stated, "The ADEA does not ban discrimination against employees because they are aged 40; it bans discrimination against employees because of their age, but limits the protected class to those who are 40 or older." Thus, it is not relevant that one member in the protected class has lost out to another member in that class, so long as the person lost out because of his or her age. The Court also found that being replaced by someone substantially younger was a more reliable indicator of age discrimination than being replaced by someone outside the protected class.

Adarand Constructors v Pena

In a 5–4 decision, the U.S. Supreme Court in 1995 criticized the moral justification for affirmative action, saying that race-conscious programs can amount to unconstitutional reverse discrimination and even harm those they seek to advance. The *Adarand* case concerned a Department of Transportation policy that gave contractors a bonus if they hired minority subcontractors. A white contractor challenged the policy in court after losing a contract to build guardrails, despite offering the lowest bid. A federal appeals court upheld the program as within the proper bounds of affirmative action. The Supreme Court decision did not uphold or reject that ruling, but instead sent the case back for further review under new, tougher rules. As a result, the ruling seems to invite legal challenges to other federal affirmative action programs. However, since the 2003 rulings in the case of *Grutter v Bollinger* and *Gratz v Bollinger* (discussed next), organizations are unsure how the Supreme Court will address affirmative action in the private sector in the future.

Grutter v Bollinger

The Supreme Court appeared to support the *Bakke* decision. In the case of *Grutter v Bollinger*, the Court ruled in a 5–4 decision that colleges and universities have a compelling interest in achieving diverse campuses. Schools may favor black, Hispanic, and other minority students in admissions as long as administrators take the time to assess each applicant's background and potential. Justice Sandra Day O'Connor, in writing for the majority opinion, said, "Effective participation by members of all racial and ethnic groups in the civic life of our nation is essential if the dream of one nation, indivisible, is to be realized."[81]

Gratz v Bollinger

In the case involving *Gratz v Bollinger*, the Court, in a 6–3 decision, said that in trying to achieve diversity, colleges and universities could not use point systems that blindly give extra credit to minority applicants. The university used a point system to determine admissions criteria in its College of Literature, Science and the Arts, with minority applicants receiving bonus points. The court determined that Michigan's 150-point index for screening applicants, which gave an automatic 20 points to minority applicants, was not the proper way to achieve racial diversity.

OBJECTIVE

Describe the Equal Employment Opportunity Commission.

Equal Employment Opportunity Commission

Title VII of the Civil Rights Act, as amended, created the Equal Employment Opportunity Commission that is charged with administering the act. Under Title VII, filing a discrimination charge initiates EEOC action. The EEOC continually receives complaints. Recently, approximately 80,000 employees filed complaints with the Equal Employment Opportunity Commission. Employers paid more than $420 million in damages to employees who won claims.[82]

Charges may be filed by one of the presidentially appointed EEOC commissioners, by any aggrieved person, or by anyone acting on behalf of an aggrieved person. Charges must be filed within 180 days of the alleged act; however, the time is extended to 300 days if a state or local agency is involved in the case. Because of this time restriction, the Civil Rights Act of 1866 may be called into play because it has no statute of limitation.

Notice in Figure 3-2 that when a charge is filed, the EEOC first attempts a no-fault settlement. Essentially, the organization charged with the violation is invited to settle the case with no admission of guilt. Most charges are settled at this stage.

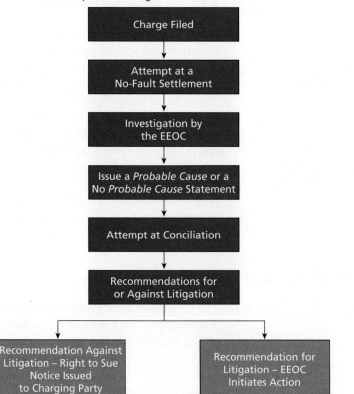

Figure 3-2 EEOC Procedure Once a Charge Is Filed
Source: © 2008 by Prentice Hall

EEOC

http://www.eeoc.gov

The home page for the Equal Employment Opportunity Commission is presented.

Failing settlement, the EEOC investigates the charges. Once the employer is notified that an investigation will take place, no records relating to the charge may be destroyed. During the investigative process, the employer is permitted to present a position statement. After the investigation has been completed, the district director of the EEOC will issue a probable cause or a no probable cause statement.

In the event of a probable cause statement, the next step involves attempted conciliation. In the event this effort fails, the case will be reviewed for litigation potential. Some of the factors that determine whether the EEOC will pursue litigation are (1) the number of people affected by the alleged practice; (2) the amount of money involved in the charge; (3) other charges against the employer; and (4) the type of charge. Recommendations for litigation are then passed on to the general counsel of the EEOC. If the recommendation is against litigation, a right-to-sue notice will be issued to the charging party. The EEOC files suit in only about 1 percent of all charges.[83] Note that the Civil Rights Act of 1964 prohibits retaliation against employees who have opposed an illegal employment practice. The Act also protects those who have testified, assisted, or participated in the investigation of discrimination.

Burdened with thousands of backlogged employment-discrimination cases, the EEOC is trying a new approach. The enforcement agency has launched a voluntary mediation program in cities around the country. The goal is to resolve a significant number of disputes before the EEOC even begins its investigation by bringing the contesting parties together in a neutral forum. Chair Cari Dominguez said that the Equal Employment Opportunity Commission (EEOC) will focus primarily on prevention, strategic enforcement, and litigation.[84]

 OBJECTIVE

Explain the purpose of the *Uniform Guidelines on Employee Selection Procedures.*

Uniform Guidelines on Employee Selection Procedures

Prior to 1978, employers were faced with complying with several different selection guidelines. In 1978, the Equal Employment Opportunity Commission, the Civil Service Commission, the Department of Justice, and the Department of Labor adopted the *Uniform Guidelines on Employee Selection Procedures.* These guidelines cover several federal equal employment opportunity statutes and executive orders, including Title VII of the Civil Rights Act, EO 11246, and the Equal Pay Act. They do not apply to the Age Discrimination in Employment Act or the Rehabilitation Act.

The *Uniform Guidelines* provide a single set of principles that were designed to assist employers, labor organizations, employment agencies, and licensing and certification boards in complying with federal prohibitions against employment practices that discriminate on the basis of race, color, religion, gender, and national origin. The *Uniform Guidelines* provide a framework for making legal employment decisions about hiring, promotion, demotion, referral, retention, licensing and certification, the proper use of tests, and other selection procedures. Under the *Uniform Guidelines*, recruiting procedures are not considered selection procedures and therefore are not covered.

Regarding selection procedures, the *Uniform Guidelines* state that a test is

> *any measure, combination of measures, or procedures used as a basis for any employment decision. Selection procedures include the full range of assessment techniques from traditional paper-and-pencil tests, performance tests, testing programs or probationary periods, and physical, education, and work experience requirement through informal or casual interviews and unscored application forms.*

Using this definition, virtually any instrument or procedure used in the selection decision is considered a test.

8   **OBJECTIVE**

Describe disparate treatment and adverse impact.

Disparate treatment:
Employer treats some people less favorably than others because of race, religion, color, sex, national origin, or age.

Concept of Disparate Treatment

Unlawful employment discrimination, as established through various Supreme Court decisions, can be divided into two broad categories: adverse impact and disparate treatment. **Disparate treatment** means that an employer treats some people less favorably than others because of race, religion, color, sex, national origin, or age. It is the most easily understood form of discrimination.

For example, males are treated differently than females; whites are treated differently than blacks. The crux of disparate treatment is different treatment on the basis of some non-allowable criterion. It may be thought of as direct discrimination. Common forms of disparate treatment include selection rules with a racial, sexual, or other premise; prejudicial action; unequal treatment on an individual basis; and different hiring standards for different groups.

McDonald v Santa Fe Trail Transportation Company offers an example of disparate treatment. Three of the company's employees, two whites and one black, had allegedly misappropriated 60 gallons of antifreeze. Santa Fe took disciplinary action against the workers by terminating the two whites, but not the black employee. The discharged white workers filed suit against the company, charging that their termination violated both Title VII and the Civil Rights Act of 1866. The Supreme Court, in a 1977 decision, agreed with the plaintiffs that they had been the recipients of unequal treatment on the basis of their race. Central to disparate treatment is the matter of proof. The plaintiff must first be able to establish a prima facie case, and, second, be able to establish that the employer was acting on the basis of a discriminatory motive.

Concept of Adverse Impact

Prior to the issuance of the *Uniform Guidelines*, the only way to prove job relatedness was to validate each test. The *Uniform Guidelines* do not require validation in all cases. Essentially, it is required only in instances where the test or other selection device produces an adverse impact on a minority group. **Adverse impact**, a concept established by the *Uniform Guidelines*, occurs if women and minorities are not hired at the rate of at least 80 percent of the best-achieving group.

Under the *Uniform Guidelines*, adverse impact has been described in terms of selection rates, the selection rate being the number of qualified applicants hired or promoted, divided by the total number of qualified applicants. This has also been called the four-fifths rule, which is actually a guideline subject to interpretation by the EEOC. The groups identified for analysis under the guidelines are (1) blacks, (2) Native Americans (including Alaskan natives), (3) Asians, (4) Hispanics, (5) women, and (6) men.

The following formula is used to compute adverse impact for hiring:

Adverse impact:
Concept established by the *Uniform Guidelines*, occurs if women and minorities are not hired at the rate of at least 80 percent of the best-achieving group.

$$\frac{\text{Success rate for women and minority applicants}}{\text{Success rate for best-achieving group applicants}} = \text{Determination of adverse impact}$$

The success rate for women and minority applicants is determined by dividing the number of members of a specific group employed in a period by the number of qualified women and minority applicants in a period. The success rate of best-achieving group applicants is determined by dividing the number of people in the best-achieving group employed by the number of the best-achieving group applicants in a period.

Using the formula, let us determine whether there has been adverse impact in the following case. During 2007, 400 people were hired for a particular job. Of the total, 300 were white and 100 were black. There were 1,500 qualified applicants for these jobs, of whom 1,000 were white and 500 were black. Using the adverse formula, you have:

$$\frac{100/500}{300/1,000} = \frac{0.2}{0.3} = 66.67\%$$

Thus, adverse impact exists.

Evidence of adverse impact involves more than the total number of minority workers employed. Also considered is the total number of qualified applicants. For instance, assume that 300 blacks and 300 whites were hired. But there were 1,500 qualified black applicants and 1,000 qualified white applicants. Putting these figures into the adverse impact formula, it can be concluded that adverse impact still exists.

$$\frac{300/1,500}{300/1,000} = \frac{0.2}{0.3} = 66.67\%$$

Thus, it is clear that firms must monitor their recruitment efforts very carefully. Obviously, firms should attempt to recruit qualified individuals because once in the applicant pool, they will be used in computing adverse impact.

Assuming that adverse impact is shown, employers have two avenues available to them if they still desire to use a particular selection standard. First, the employer may validate a selection device by showing that it is indeed a predictor of success. For instance, the employer may be able to show a strong relationship between the selection device and job performance, and that if it did not use this procedure, the firm's training costs would become prohibitive. If the device has proved to be a predictor of job performance, business necessity has been established.

The second avenue available to employers should adverse impact be shown is the bona fide occupational qualification (BFOQ) defense. The BFOQ defense means that only one group is capable of performing the job successfully. Courts have narrowly interpreted this defense because it almost always relates to sex discrimination. For instance, courts have rejected the concept that because most women cannot lift 100 pounds, all women should be eliminated from consideration for a job requiring heavy lifting.

Creators of the *Uniform Guidelines* adopted the bottom-line approach in assessing whether a firm's employment practices are discriminatory. For example, if a number of separate procedures are used in making a selection decision, the enforcement agencies will focus on the end result of these procedures to determine whether adverse impact has occurred. Essentially, the EEOC is more concerned with what is occurring than how it occurs. It admits that discriminatory employment practices that cannot be validated may exist; however, the net effect, or the bottom line, of the selection procedures is the focus of the EEOC attention.

9   OBJECTIVE

Describe the *Uniform Guidelines* related to sexual harassment, national origin, and religion.

Additional Guidelines on Employment Selection Procedures

Since the *Uniform Guidelines* were published in 1978, they have been modified several times. Some of these changes reflect Supreme Court decisions; others clarify implementation procedures. The three major changes discussed are the Guidelines on Sexual Harassment, Guidelines on Discrimination because of National Origin, and Guidelines on Discrimination because of Religion.

Guidelines on Sexual Harassment

The United States Equal Employment Opportunity Commission recently fielded more than 13,000 charges of sexual harassment. Awards to charging parties amounted to more than $37 million, not counting monetary benefits obtained through litigation.[85]

As previously mentioned, Title VII of the Civil Rights Act generally prohibits discrimination in employment on the basis of gender. The EEOC has also issued guidelines that state that employers have a duty to maintain a workplace free from sexual harassment. The OFCCP has also issued similar guidelines. Managers in both

Table 3-1   **EEOC Definition of Sexual Harassment**

Unwelcome sexual advances, requests for sexual favors, and verbal or physical conduct of a sexual nature that occur under any of the following situations:

1. When submission to such conduct is made either explicitly or implicitly a term or condition of an individual's employment
2. When submission to or rejection of such contact by an individual is used as the basis for employment decisions affecting such individual
3. When such conduct has the purpose or effect of unreasonably interfering with an individual's work performance or creating an intimidating, hostile, or offensive working environment

for-profit and not-for-profit organizations must be particularly alert to the issue of sexual harassment. The EEOC issued the guidelines because of the belief that sexual harassment was a widespread problem. Table 3-1 contains the EEOC's definition of sexual harassment. As you see, there are two distinct types of sexual harassment: (1) where a hostile work environment is created, and (2) when there is a quid pro quo, for example, an offer of promotion or pay raise in exchange for sex.

According to these guidelines, employers are totally liable for the acts of their supervisors, regardless of whether the employer is aware of the sexual harassment act. In *Faragher v City of Boca Raton* and *Burlington Industries, Inc. v Ellerth*, the Supreme Court held that an employer is strictly liable, meaning that it has absolutely no defense, when sexual harassment by a supervisor involves a tangible employment action.[86]

Where co-workers are concerned, the employer is responsible for such acts if the employer knew, or should have known, about them. The employer is not responsible when it can show that it took immediate and appropriate corrective action on learning of the problem.[87]

Another important aspect of these guidelines is that employers may be liable for acts committed by nonemployees in the workplace if the employer knew, or should have known, of the conduct and failed to take appropriate action. Firms are responsible for developing programs to prevent sexual harassment in the workplace. They must also investigate all formal and informal complaints alleging sexual harassment. After investigating, a firm must take immediate and appropriate action to correct the situation. Failure to do so constitutes a violation of Title VII, as interpreted by the EEOC. To prevail in court, companies must have clear procedures for handling sexual harassment complaints. Typically, employers choose an impartial ombudsperson to hear and investigate charges before lawyers get involved. If the sexual harassment complaint appears legitimate, the company must take immediate and appropriate action. There have been numerous sexual harassment court cases and the Supreme Court continues to refine the concept.[88]

In *Miller v Bank of America*, a U.S. Circuit Court of Appeals held an employer liable for the sexually harassing acts of its supervisors, even though the company had a policy prohibiting such conduct, and even though the victim did not formally notify the employer of the problem. Another U.S. Circuit Court of Appeals ruled that sexual harassment, in and of itself, is a violation of Title VII. The court ruled that the law does not require the victim to prove that she or he resisted harassment and was penalized for that resistance. The first sexual harassment case to reach the U.S. Supreme Court was the case of *Meritor Savings Bank v Vinson* in 1986. In the *Vinson* decision, the Supreme Court recognized for the first time that Title VII could be used for offensive environment claims. According to the EEOC, specific actions that could create a hostile workplace include a pattern of threatening, intimidating, or hostile acts and remarks, negative sexual stereotyping, or the display of written or graphic materials considered degrading. The Supreme Court decision in *Harris v Forklift Systems, Inc.* in 1993 expanded the hostile workplace concept and made it easier to win sexual harassment claims. In a unanimous decision, the Supreme Court held that "to be accountable as abusive work environment harassment, conduct need not seriously affect . . . the psychological well-being or lead the plaintiff to suffer injury." No longer does severe psychological injury have to be proved. Under this ruling, the plaintiff only needs to show that his or her employer allowed a hostile-to-abusive work environment to exist. In a Seventh U.S. Circuit Court of Appeals ruling, a company president's one-time sexual proposition to a subordinate was sufficient to constitute a hostile work environment. The decision was made in light of the president's position of significant authority and the closeness in which the individual worked.[89]

Complaints still occur all too regularly. Dial Corporation agreed to pay $10 million to settle a class action sexual harassment lawsuit brought by the EEOC. The case, which involved lurid allegations about male employees' behavior at the Aurora factory, was filed on behalf of 90 female employees who worked at the plant.[90]

For a long time an unresolved question in employment law has been whether same-sex harassment (for example, males harassing males) is unlawful under Title VII of the Civil Rights Act of 1964. The Supreme Court, in the case of *Oncale v Sundowner Offshore Services*, held that same-sex sexual harassment may be unlawful under Title VII. The Supreme Court decided that a plaintiff could make out a claim for sexual harassment as long as the harassing conduct was because of sex. The Court emphasized that Title VII does not prohibit all verbal or physical harassment in the workplace, only that which constitutes discrimination because of sex.

Guidelines on Discrimination Because of National Origin

Both EEOC and the courts have interpreted national origin protection under Title VII as extending far beyond discrimination against individuals who came from, or whose forebears came from, a particular country. National origin protection also covers (1) marriage or association with a person of a specific national origin; (2) membership in, or association with, an organization identified with, or seeking to promote the interests of national groups; (3) attendance at, or participation in, schools, churches, temples, or mosques generally used by persons of a national origin group; and (4) use of an individual's or spouse's name that is associated with a national origin group. As Table 3-2 shows, the EEOC has identified certain selection procedures that may be discriminatory.

National origin discrimination cases have been increasing and have doubled in a decade.[91] Harassment on the basis of national origin is a violation of Title VII. Employers have a duty to maintain a working environment free from such harassment. Ethnic slurs and other verbal or physical conduct relating to an individual's national origin constitute harassment when this conduct (1) has the purpose or effect of creating an intimidating, hostile, or offensive working environment; (2) has the purpose or effect of unreasonably interfering with an individual's work performance; or (3) otherwise adversely affects an individual's employment opportunity.

Of interest with regard to national origin is the English-only rule. Courts have generally ruled in the employer's favor if the rule would promote safety and product quality and stop harassment. For example, suppose a company has a rule that only English must be spoken except during breaks. That rule must be justified by a compelling business necessity. In *Garcia v Spun Steak*, the Ninth Circuit Court of Appeals (the Supreme Court refused to review) concluded that the rule did not necessarily violate Title VII.

Table 3-2   Selection Procedures That May Be Discriminatory with Regard to National Origin

1. Fluency in English requirements: One questionable practice involves denying employment opportunities because of an individual's foreign accent or inability to communicate well in English. When this practice is continually followed, the Commission will presume that such a rule violates Title VII and will study it closely. However, a firm may require that employees speak only in English at certain times if business necessity can be shown.
2. Training or education requirements: Denying employment opportunities to an individual because of his or her foreign training or education, or practices that require an individual to be foreign trained or educated may be discriminatory.

Spun Steak's management implemented the policy after some workers complained they were being harassed and insulted in a language they could not understand. The rule allowed workers to speak Spanish during breaks and lunch periods. However, English-only policies that are not job related have been challenged and eliminated.[92]

Guidelines on Discrimination because of Religion

The number of religion-related discrimination complaints filed with the Equal Employment Opportunity Commission (EEOC) continues to increase.[93] Employers have an obligation to accommodate religious practices unless they can demonstrate a resulting hardship. The most common claims filed under the religious accommodation provisions involve employees objecting to either Sabbath employment or membership in or financial support of labor unions. Consideration is given to identifiable costs in relation to the size and operating costs of the employer and the number of individuals who actually need the accommodation. These guidelines recognize that regular payment of premium wages constitutes undue hardship, whereas these payments on an infrequent or temporary basis do not. Undue hardship would also exist if an accommodation required a firm to vary from its bona fide seniority system.

These guidelines identify several means of accommodating religious practices that prohibit working on certain days. Some of the methods suggested included voluntary substitutes, flexible scheduling, lateral transfer, and change of job assignments. Some collective bargaining agreements include a provision that each employee must join the union or pay the union a sum equivalent to dues. When an employee's religious beliefs prevent compliance, the union should accommodate the employee by permitting that person to make an equivalent donation to a charitable organization.

Affirmative Action: Executive Order 11246, as Amended by Executive Order 11375

10 OBJECTIVE

Explain affirmative action as required by presidential Executive Orders 11246 and 11375.

An **executive order** (EO) is a directive issued by the president and has the force and effect of a law enacted by Congress as it applies to federal agencies and federal contractors. Many believe that the concept of affirmative action got its beginning in 1948 when President Harry S. Truman officially ended racial segregation in all branches of the military by issuing Executive Order 9981.[94]

However, officially it began in 1965 when President Lyndon B. Johnson signed EO 11246, which establishes the policy of the U.S. government as providing equal opportunity in federal employment for all qualified people. It prohibits discrimination in employment because of race, creed, color, or national origin. The order also requires promoting the full realization of equal employment opportunity through a positive, continuing program in each executive department and agency. The policy of equal opportunity applies to every aspect of federal employment policy and practice.

A major provision of EO 11246 requires adherence to a policy of nondiscrimination in employment as a condition for the approval of a grant, contract, loan, insurance, or guarantee. Every executive department and agency that administers a program involving federal financial assistance must include such language in its contracts. Contractors must agree not to discriminate in employment because of race, creed, color, or national origin during performance of a contract.

Affirmative action, stipulated by EO 11246, requires covered employers to take positive steps to ensure employment of applicants and treatment of employees during employment without regard to race, creed, color, or national origin.

Covered human resource practices relate to employment, upgrading, demotion, transfer, recruitment or recruitment advertising, layoffs or termination, rates of pay or other forms of compensation, and selection for training, including apprenticeships. Employers are required to post notices explaining these requirements in conspicuous places in the workplace. In the event of contractor noncompliance, contracts can be

Executive order (EO):
Directive issued by the president that has the force and effect of law enacted by Congress as it applies to federal agencies and federal contractors.

Affirmative action:
Stipulated by Executive Order 11246, it requires employers to take positive steps to ensure employment of applicants and treatment of employees during employment without regard to race, creed, color, or national origin.

canceled, terminated, or suspended in whole or in part, and the contractor may be declared ineligible for future government contracts. In 1968, EO 11375, which changed the word "creed" to "religion" and added sex discrimination to the other prohibited items, amended EO 11246. These EOs are enforced by the Department of Labor through the Office of Federal Contract Compliance Programs (OFCCP).

Affirmative Action Programs

An **affirmative action program (AAP)** is an approach developed by organizations with government contracts to demonstrate that workers are employed in proportion to their representation in the firm's relevant labor market.

An affirmative action program may be voluntarily implemented by an organization. In such an event, goals are established and action is taken to hire and move minorities and women up in the organization. In other situations, an AAP may be mandated by the OFCCP.

The degree of control the OFCCP will impose depends on the size of the contract, with contracts of $10,000 or less not covered. The first level of control involves contracts that exceed $10,000 but are less than $50,000. These contractors are governed by the equal opportunity clause, as shown in Table 3-3. The second

Table 3-3 Equal Opportunity Clause—Government Contracts

1. The contractor will not discriminate against any employee or applicant for employment because of race, color, religion, sex, or national origin. The contractor will take affirmative action to ensure that applicants are employed, and that employees are treated during employment, without regard to their race, color, religion, sex, or national origin. Such action shall include, but not be limited to the following: employment, upgrading, demotions, or transfer; recruitment or recruitment advertising, layoff or termination; rates of pay or other forms of compensation; and selection for training, including apprenticeship. The contractor agrees to post in conspicuous places, available to employees and applicants for employment, notices to be provided by the contracting officer setting forth the provisions for this nondiscrimination clause.
2. The contractor will in all solicitations or advertisements for employees placed by or on behalf of the contractor, state that all qualified applicants will receive consideration for employment without regard to race, color, religion, sex, or national origin.
3. The contractor will send to each labor union or representative of workers with which he or she has a collective bargaining agreement or other contract or understanding, a notice to be provided by the agency contracting officer, advising the labor union or workers' representative of the contractor's commitments under section 202 of Executive Order 11246 of September 24, 1965, and shall post copies of the notice in conspicuous places available to employees and applicants for employment.
4. The contractor will comply with all provisions of Executive Order 11246 of September 24, 1965, and the rules, regulations, and relevant orders of the Secretary of Labor.
5. The contractor will furnish all information and reports required by Executive Order 11246 of September 24, 1965, and by the rules, regulations, and orders of the Secretary of Labor, or pursuant thereto, and will permit access to his or her books, records, and accounts by the contracting agency and the Secretary of Labor for purposes of investigation to ascertain compliance with such rules, regulations, and orders.
6. In the event of the contractor's noncompliance with the nondiscrimination clauses of this contract or with any of such rules, regulations, or orders, this contract may be canceled, terminated, or suspended in whole or in part and the contractor may be declared ineligible for further Government contracts in accordance with procedures authorized in Executive Order 11246 of September 24, 1965, or by rule, regulation, or order of the Secretary of State, or as otherwise provided by law.
7. The contractor will include the provisions of paragraphs (1) through (7) in every subcontract or purchase order unless exempted by rules, regulations, or orders of the Secretary of Labor issued pursuant to section 204 of Executive Order 11246 of September 24, 1965, so that such provisions will be binding upon each subcontractor or vendor. The contractor will take such action with respect to any subcontract or purchase order as may be directed by the Secretary of Labor as a means of enforcing such provisions including sanctions for noncompliance: Provided, however, that in the event the contractor becomes involved in, or is threatened with litigation with a subcontractor or vendor as a result of such direction, the contractor may request the United States to enter into such litigation to protect the interests of the United States.

Source: Federal Register, 45, no. 251 (Tuesday, December 30, 1980): 86230.

level of control occurs if the contractor (1) has 50 or more employees; (2) has a contract of $50,000 or more; (3) has contracts which, in any 12-month period, total $50,000 or more or reasonably may be expected to total $50,000 or more; or (4) is a financial institution that serves as a depository for government funds in any amount, acts as an issuing or redeeming agent for U.S. savings bonds and savings notes in any amount, or subscribes to federal deposit or share insurance. Contractors meeting these criteria must develop a written affirmative action program for each of their establishments and file an annual EEO-1 report. Note that the threshold is 50 employees here, but it was 100 with regard to those covered by the Civil Rights Act of 1964.

The third level of control on contractors is in effect when contracts exceed $1 million. All previously stated requirements must be met, and in addition, the OFCCP is authorized to conduct pre-award compliance reviews. In determining whether to conduct a pre-award review, the OFCCP may consider, for example, the items presented in Table 3-4.

If an investigation indicates a violation, the OFCCP first tries to secure compliance through persuasion. If persuasion fails to resolve the issue, the OFCCP serves a notice to show cause or a notice of violation. A show cause notice contains a list of the violations, a statement of how the OFCCP proposes that corrections be made, a request for a written response to the findings, and a suggested date for a conciliation conference. The firm usually has 30 days to respond. Successful conciliation results in a written contract between the OFCCP and the contractor. In a conciliation agreement, the contractor agrees to take specific steps to remedy noncompliance with an EO. Firms that do not correct violations can be passed over in the awarding of future contracts. The procedures for developing affirmative action plans were published in the *Federal Register* of December 4, 1974. These regulations are referred to as Revised Order No. 4. The OFCCP guide for compliance officers, outlining what to cover in a compliance review, is known as Order No. 14.

The OFCCP is very specific about what should be included in an affirmative action program. A policy statement has to be developed that reflects the CEO's attitude regarding equal employment opportunity, assigns overall responsibility for preparing and implementing the affirmative action program, and provides for reporting and monitoring procedures. The policy should state that the firm intends to recruit, hire, train, and promote persons in all job titles without regard to race, color, religion, gender, or national origin, except where gender is a bona fide occupational qualification (BFOQ). The policy should guarantee that all human resource actions involving such areas as compensation, benefits, transfers, layoffs, return from layoffs, company-sponsored training, education, tuition assistance, and social and recreational programs will be administered without regard to race, color, religion, gender, or national origin. Revised Order No. 4 is quite specific with regard to dissemination of a firm's EEO policy, both internally and externally. An executive should be appointed to manage the firm's equal employment opportunity program. This person should be given the necessary support by top management to accomplish the assignment. Revised Order No. 4 specifies the minimum level of responsibility associated with the task of EEO manager.

Table 3-4 **Factors That the OFCCP May Consider in Conducting a Preaward Review**

1. The past EEO performance of the contractor, including its current EEO profile and indications of underutilization.
2. The volume and nature of complaints filed by employees or applicants against the contractor.
3. Whether the contractor is in a growth industry.
4. The level of employment or promotional opportunities resulting from the expansion of, or turnover in, the contractor's workforce.
5. The employment opportunities likely to result from the contract in issue.
6. Whether resources are available to conduct the review.

An acceptable AAP must include an analysis of deficiencies in the utilization of minority groups and women. The first step in conducting a utilization analysis is to make a workforce analysis. The second step involves an analysis of all major job groups. An explanation of the situation is required if minorities or women are currently being underutilized. A job group is defined as one or more jobs having similar content, wage rates, and opportunities. Underutilization is defined as having fewer minorities or women in a particular job group than would reasonably be expected by their availability. The utilization analysis is important because the calculations determine whether underutilization exists. For example, if the utilization analysis shows that the availability of blacks for a certain job group is 30 percent, the organization should have at least 30 percent black employment in that group. If actual employment is less than 30 percent, underutilization exists, and the firm should set a goal of 30 percent black employment for that job group.

The primary focus of any affirmative action program is on goals and timetables, with the issue being how many and by when. Goals and timetables developed by the firm should cover its entire affirmative action program, including correction of deficiencies. These goals and timetables should be attainable; that is, they should be based on results that the firm, making good-faith efforts, could reasonably expect to achieve. Goals should be significant and measurable, as well as attainable. Two types of goals must be established regarding underutilization: annual and ultimate. The annual goal is to move toward elimination of underutilization, whereas the ultimate goal is to correct all underutilization. Goals should be specific in terms of planned results, with timetables for completion. However, goals should not establish inflexible quotas that must be met. Rather, they should be targets that are reasonably attainable. Some techniques that can be used to improve recruitment and increase the flow of minority and women applicants are shown in Table 3-5.

Table 3-5   Techniques to Improve Recruitment of Minorities and Women

- Identify referral organizations for minorities and women.
- Hold formal briefing sessions with representatives of referral organizations.
- Encourage minority and women employees to refer applicants to the firm.
- Include minorities and women on the Personnel Relations staff.
- Permit minorities and women to participate in Career Days, Youth Motivation Programs, and related activities in their community.
- Actively participate in job fairs and give company representatives the authority to make on-thespot-commitments.
- Actively recruit at schools having predominant minority or female enrollments.
- Use special efforts to reach minorities and women during school recruitment drives.
- Undertake special employment programs whenever possible for women and minorities. These might include technical and nontechnical co-op programs, after-school and/or work-study jobs, summer jobs for underprivileged individuals, summer work-study programs, and motivation, training, and employment programs for the hardcore unemployed.
- Pictorially present minorities and women in recruiting brochures.
- Include the minority news media and women's interest media when expending help wanted advertising.

Source: Federal Register, 45, no. 251 (Tuesday, December 30, 1980): 86243.

A Global Perspective

Not the Glass Ceiling, the Bamboo Ceiling

Asian Americans are the fastest-growing minority in the United States, having increased by 72 percent since 1990, versus just 13 percent for the U.S. population as a whole. Then why are there are so few Asian Americans at the very highest levels of U.S. companies? Lack of education is certainly not the reason since the Census Bureau reports that 44 percent of Americans of Asian heritage are college graduates, which is well above the national average of 27 percent. Although they make up 4.4 percent of the workforce, only a few, such as Avon CEO Andrea Jung, are CEOs. Only 1 percent of corporate directors are Asian. Even in the Silicon Valley, where about 30 percent of tech professionals are from the Pacific Rim countries, Asian Americans account for only 12.5 percent of managers with 80 percent of tech managers being Caucasian.[95]

Jane Hyun, a former human resources executive at J.P. Morgan, who now has her own consulting company, has written a book entitled *Breaking the Bamboo Ceiling: Career Strategies for Asians*. She tries to explain why Asian Americans are not getting ahead in big companies, and what they can do about it. Hyun was born in Korea and grew up in New York City. Her family came to the United States when she was eight. Hyun says, "What many Americans don't understand is that people like me have one foot in two worlds. Of course I've assimilated, but I still feel Asian." She points out that most Asians share certain cultural values that are the opposite of what it takes to succeed in the corporate world.[96]

Hyun says "Most Asians are taught from an early age to be self-effacing and to put the community ahead of one's own interests. Pacific Rim cultures are full of sayings like, 'The tallest nail gets hammered down.' So the idea of putting your ideas forward or marketing yourself or even taking credit for your own achievements—these are alien concepts." Asian Americans also have been taught to respect authority and defer to elders. "Often, in meetings, Asians will not speak up," Hyun observes. "Unfortunately, this reticence gets mistaken for aloofness or arrogance or inattention, when it is usually just the Asian habit of respecting authority. We wait for our turn to speak—and often our turn just never comes."[97]

"The first step is self-awareness," she says. "Asian Americans may not know how we're perceived by our Caucasian peers and bosses, so we need to get honest feedback. This is why mentoring relationships can be so valuable, if you're paired up with a non-Asian mentor. You'll never be able to deal with issues and problems that remain unspoken." Hyun advises Asians "to learn the skills you need to succeed, seek out companies that are interested in developing all their people, not just a chosen few, and that offer lots of opportunities for training, coaching, and mentoring." Hyun urges people of Asian extraction to "practice taking the credit for your own work as well as acknowledging the contributions of others. You don't need to blow your own horn all the time, but train yourself to seize the right moments when they arise."[98]

Summary

1. Describe the projected future diverse workforce.

The U.S. workforce will become more diverse by 2010.

2. Describe diversity and diversity management.

Diversity refers to any perceived difference among people: age, race, religion, functional specialty, profession, sexual orientation, geographic origin, lifestyle, tenure with the organization, or position, and any other perceived difference. Diversity management is ensuring factors are in place to provide for and encourage the continued development of a diverse workforce by melding these actual and perceived differences among workers to achieve maximum productivity.

3. Explain the various components of the present diverse workforce.

The workforce is made up of the following: single parents and working mothers, women in business, dual-career families, workers of color, older workers, people with disabilities, immigrants, young persons with limited education or skills, and educational level of employees.

4. Identify the major laws affecting equal employment opportunity.

Major laws include the Civil Rights Act of 1866; Equal Pay Act of 1963; Title VII of the Civil Rights Act of 1964, as Amended in 1972; Age Discrimination in Employment Act of 1967, as Amended in 1978 and 1986; Rehabilitation Act of 1973; Pregnancy Discrimination Act of 1978; Immigration Reform and Control Act (IRCA) of 1986; Immigration Act of 1990; Illegal Immigration Reform and Immigrant Responsibility Act of 1996; Civil Rights Act of 1991; Uniformed Services Employment and Reemployment Rights Act of 1994; and Veterans' Benefits Improvement Act of 2004.

5. Identify some of the major Supreme Court decisions that have had an impact on equal employment opportunity.

Major decisions include *Griggs v Duke Power Company*, *Albermarle Paper Company v Moody*, *Phillips v Martin Marietta Corporation*, *Espinoza v Farah Manufacturing Company*, *Dothard v Rawlingson*, *University of California Regents v Bakke*, *American Tobacco Company v Patterson*, *O'Connor v Consolidated Coin Caterers Corp.*, *Adarand Constructors v Pena*, *Grutter v Bollinger*, and *Gratz v Bollinger*.

6. Describe the Equal Employment Opportunity Commission.

Title VII of the Civil Rights Act, as amended, created the Equal Employment Opportunity Commission. It was initially charged with administering the Act.

7. Explain the purpose of the *Uniform Guidelines on Employee Selection Procedures*.

The *Guidelines* adopted a single set of principles that were designed to assist employers, labor organizations, employment agencies, and licensing and certification boards to comply with requirements of federal law prohibiting employment practices that discriminated on the basis of race, color, religion, sex, and national origin. They were designed to provide a framework for determining the proper use of tests and other selection procedures.

8. Describe disparate treatment and adverse impact.

With disparate treatment, an employer treats some people less favorably than others because of race, religion, sex, national origin, or age. Adverse impact is a concept established by the *Uniform Guidelines* and occurs if women and minorities are not hired at the rate of at least 80 percent of the best-achieving group.

9. Describe the *Uniform Guidelines* related to sexual harassment, national origin, and religion.

The EEOC has also issued interpretive guidelines that state that employers have an affirmative duty to maintain a workplace free from sexual harassment. The EEOC broadly defined discrimination on the basis of national origin as the denial of equal employment opportunity because of an individual's ancestors or place of birth or because an individual has the physical, cultural, or linguistic characteristics of a national origin group. Employers have an obligation to accommodate religious practices unless they can demonstrate a resulting hardship.

10. Explain affirmative action as required by presidential Executive Orders 11246 and 11375.

Affirmative action, stipulated by EO 11246, requires covered employers to take positive steps to ensure employment of applicants and treatment of employees during employment without regard to race, creed, color, or national origin. The order prohibited discrimination in employment because of race, creed, color, or national origin. EO 11375 changed the word "creed" to "religion" and added sex discrimination to the other prohibited items, amended EO 11246.

11. Describe affirmative action programs.

An affirmative action program is an approach that an organization with government contracts develops to demonstrate that women or minorities are employed in proportion to their representation in the firm's relevant labor market.

Key Terms

- Sequencing moms, 52
- Diversity, 53
- Diversity management, 53
- Dual-career family, 55

- Glass ceiling, 67
- Disparate treatment, 74
- Adverse impact, 74
- Executive order (EO), 78

- Affirmative action, 78
- Affirmative action program (AAP), 79

Questions for Review

1. What is meant by the term "sequencing moms?"
2. What is the expected composition of the future diverse workforce?
3. Define diversity and diversity management.
4. What are the components that combine to make up the present diverse workforce? Briefly describe each.
5. Briefly describe the following laws:
   a. Civil Rights Act of 1866
   b. Equal Pay Act of 1963
   c. Title VII of the Civil Rights Act of 1964, as amended in 1972
   d. Age Discrimination in Employment Act of 1967, as amended in 1978 and 1986
   e. Rehabilitation Act of 1973
   f. Pregnancy Discrimination Act of 1978
   g. Immigration Reform and Control Act (IRCA) of 1986
   h. Americans with Disabilities Act of 1990
   i. Civil Rights Act of 1991.
   j. Uniformed Services Employment and Reemployment Rights Act of 1994
6. What is the purpose of the Office of Federal Contract Compliance Programs?
7. What are the significant U.S. Supreme Court decisions that have had an impact on equal employment opportunity?
8. What is the purpose of the *Uniform Guidelines on Employee Selection Procedures*?
9. Distinguish between disparate treatment and adverse impact.
10. How does the Equal Employment Opportunity Commission (EEOC) define sexual harassment?
11. What is a presidential executive order? Describe the major provisions of EO 11246, as amended by EO 11375.
12. What is an affirmative action program?

HRM Incident 1

I Feel Great

Les Partain, manager of the training and development department for Gazelle Corporation, was 64 years old and had been with the firm for over 30 years. For the past 12 years he had served as Gazelle's training and development manager and felt that he had been doing a good job. This belief was supported by the fact that during the last five years he had received excellent performance reports from his boss, LaConya Caesar, HR director.

Six months before Les's birthday, he and LaConya were enjoying a cup of coffee together. "Les," said LaConya, "I know that you're pleased with the progress our T&D section has made under your leadership. We're really going to miss you when you retire this year. You'll certainly live the good life because you'll receive the maximum retirement benefits. If I can be of any assistance to you in developing the paperwork for your retirement, please let me know."

"Gee, LaConya," said Les. "I really appreciate the good words, but I've never felt better in my life, and although our retirement plan is excellent, I figure that I have at least five more good years. There are many other things I would like to do for the department before I retire. I have some excellent employees, and we can get many things done within the next five years."

After finishing their coffee, both returned to their work. As LaConya left, she was thinking, "My gosh, I had no idea that character intended to hang on. The only reason I gave him those good performance appraisals was to make him feel better before he retired. He was actually only an average worker and I was anxious to move a more aggressive person into that key job. We stand to lose several good people in that department if Les doesn't leave. From what they tell me, he's not doing too much of a job."

Questions

1. From a legal viewpoint, what do you believe LaConya can do regarding this situation? Discuss.
2. What actions should LaConya have taken in the past to avoid her current predicament?

HRM Incident 2

So, What's Affirmative Action?

Supreme Construction Company began as a small commercial builder located in Baytown, Texas. Until the late 1990s, Alex Boyd, Supreme's founder, concentrated his efforts on small, free-standing shops and offices. Up to that time, Alex had never employed more than 15 people.

In 2000, Alex's son Michael graduated from college with a degree in construction management and immediately joined the company full-time. Michael had worked on a variety of Supreme jobs while in school, and Alex felt his son was really cut out for the construction business. Michael was given increasing responsibility, and the company continued its success, although with a few more projects and a few more employees than before. In 2002, Michael approached his father with a proposition: "Let's get into some of the bigger projects now. We have the capital to expand and I really believe we can do it." Alex approved, and Supreme began doing small shopping centers and multistory office buildings in addition to work in its traditional area of specialization. Soon, employment had grown to 75 employees.

In 2006, the National Aeronautics and Space Administration (NASA) released construction specifications for two aircraft hangars to be built southeast of Houston. Although Supreme had never done any construction work for the government, Michael and Alex considered the job within the company's capabilities. Michael worked up the $1,982,000 bid and submitted it to the NASA procurement office.

Several weeks later the bids were opened. Supreme had the low bid. However, the acceptance letter was contingent on submission of a satisfactory affirmative action program.

Questions

1. Explain why Supreme must submit an affirmative action program.
2. Generally, what should the program be designed to accomplish?

Notes

1. Stephanie Armour, "Moms Find It Easier to Pop Back into Workforce," *USA Today* (September 23, 2004): Money, 1b.
2. Kathy Gurchiek, "Good News for Moms Reconsidering Work," *HR Magazine* 51 (July 2006): 30.
3. Kelley M. Butler, "Today's Working Women Seek Mentors, Motherhood Transition," *Employee Benefit News* 20 (April 2006): 17–19.
4. Armour, "Moms Find it Easier to Pop Back into Workforce."

5. Ibid.

6. Ibid.

7. Diana Furchtgott-Roth, "Challenges in Staffing," *HR Magazine* 50 (2005 Anniversary): 69–70.

8. Desda Moss, "Diversifying Demographics," *HR Magazine* 50 (2005 Anniversary): 37.

9. Lisa Daniel, "Checking the Exits," *HR Magazine* 50 (August 2005): 101–104.

10. Peter Francese, "The American Work Force," *American Demographics* 24 (February 2002): 40–41.

11. Bob Regan, "Design for Diversity," *American City & County* 120 (July 2005): 34.

12. "The Present & Future Job Market: Top Trends & How to Prepare," *HR Focus* 83 (June 2006): 8.

13. Jason Averbook, "Connecting CLOs With the Recruiting Process," *Chief Learning Officer* 4 (June 2005): 24–27.

14. Nancy R. Lockwood, "Workplace Diversity," *HR Magazine* 50 (June 2005): Special section 1–10.

15. Barbara Ettorre, Donald J. McNerne, and Bob Smith, "HR's Shift to a Center of Influence" (American Management Association's 67th Annual Human Resources Conference and Exposition) *HR Focus* 73 (June 1996): 12.

16. Kelley M. Butler, "Workplace Diversity Can Increase Employee Loyalty," *Employee Benefit News* 20 (March 2006): 16–17.

17. David C. Wilson, "When Equal Opportunity Knocks," *Gallup Management Journal Online* (April 13, 2006).

18. "Diversity Pays Financially As Well As in Other Ways," *HR Focus* 82 (December 2005): 9.

19. Ibid.

20. Bill Leonard, "Gallup: Workplace Bias Still Prevalent," *HR Magazine* 51 (February 2006): 34.

21. Richard Haugh, "Diversity and the Bottom Line," *Hospitals & Health Networks* 79 (June 2005): 67–70.

22. Ann Fisher, "How You Can Do Better on Diversity," *Fortune* 150 (November 15, 2004): 60.

23. Jane Bennett Clark, "Doing It All on Your Own," *Kiplinger's Personal Finance* 60 (April 2006): 84–87.

24. Linda Wasmer Andrews, "Coping with Divorce," *HR Magazine* 50 (May 2005): 58–63.

25. Claudia Wallis, Esther Chapman, Wendy Cole, Lrostom Kloberdanz, Sarah Sturmon Dale, Julie Rawe, Betsy Rubiner, Spmka Steptoe, and Deirdre van Dyk, "The Case for Staying Home," *Time* 163 (March 22, 2004): 50–59.

26. Deborah Rothberg, "Tech's Glass Ceiling Shows Some Cracks," *eWeek* 23 (June 19, 2006): 26.

27. Mitra Toossi, "A Century of Change: The U.S. Labor Force, 1950–2050," *Monthly Labor Review* 125 (May 2002): 15–28.

28. Jonathan A. Segal, "Shatter the Glass Ceiling," *HR Magazine* 50 (April 2005): 121–126.

29. "Women in the Labor Force: A Databook," Bureau of Labor Statistics, U.S. Department of Labor, February 2004.

30. Karen E. Klein, "Make Way for Female Entrepreneurs," *Business Week Online* (March 6, 2006): 4.

31. "Mother Load," *New Republic* 234 (May 1, 2006): 9.

32. Ella Bell, "The Bicultural Life Experience of Career Oriented Black Women," *Journal of Organizational Behavior* 11 (November 1990): 459–478.

33. "Keeping Graying Baby Boomers at Work and Productive," *Employee Benefit Plan Review* 60 (October 2005): 9–10.

34. "Turning Boomers into Boomerangs," *Economist* 378 (February 18, 2006): 65–67.

35. Kenneth Mitchell, "Productivity Does Not End with Age," *Business Insurance* 40 (March 27, 2006): 10.

36. Melissa Hennessy, "The Retirement Age," *CFO* 20 (February 2006): 42–45.

37. Kenneth Terrell, "When Experience Counts," *U.S. News & World Report* 140 (March 20, 2006): 48–50.

38. "Hiring Disabled Workers Won't Handicap Business; the Challenge Is Getting Past Preconceived Notions," *Nation's Restaurant News* 40 (March 20, 2006): 25.

39. Michele Orecklin, Sonja Steptoe, and Sarah Sturmon, "Stress and the Superdad," *Time Canada* 164 (August 23, 2004): 32–33.

40. "Mr. Mom?" *Credit Union Management* 28 (September 2005): 64.

41. Orecklin, Steptoe, and Sturmon, "Stress and the Superdad."

42. Ibid.

43. Furchtgott-Roth, "Challenges in Staffing."

44. Paul Salvatore, Daniel Halem, Allan Weitzman, Gershom Smith, and Lan Schaefer, "How the Law Changed HR," *HR Magazine* 50 (2005 Anniversary): 47–56.

45. "How Widespread Is the Gender Pay Gap?" *HR Focus* 83 (June 2006): 5.

46. "9% of Workers Report Bias & Discrimination at Their Workplaces," *HR Focus* 83 (February 2006): 2.

47. Declan C. Leonard, "Virtually Identical' Job Duties Needed for Equal Pay Claim," *HR Magazine* (February 2005): 116.

48. Mark Dolliver, "And Women Used to Be Such a Good Bargain!" *Adweek* 45 (November 8, 2004): 34.

49. Michelle Conlin, "Look Who's Bringing Home More Bacon," *Business Week* (January 27, 2003): 85.

50. Janet Stites, "Equal Pay for the Sexes," *HR Magazine* 50 (May 2005): 64–69.

51. Judy Greenwald, "Ruling Protects Worker Witness," *Business Insurance* 39 (August 29, 2005): 19.

52. Allan Smith, "Expert: Wait Until 2007 to Use New EEO-1 Categories," *HR Magazine* 51 (January 2006): 25–30.

53. "Gender Wage Gaps Bring More Bias Lawsuits," *HR Focus* 82 (July 2005): 2.

54. Mark Schoeff, Jr., "Ruling Expands Grounds for Retaliation Case," *Workforce Management* 85 (July 17, 2006): 10.

55. "Bias Lawsuits: Two Cases Settle & One Class Action Allowed," *HR Focus* 82 (January 2005): 2.

56. "Settlement in Ford Discrimination Case," *HR Focus* 82 (April 2005): 2.

57. "Train Managers and Executives to Avoid Legal 'Danger Zones,'" *HR Focus* 83 (August 2006): 4–7.

58. Darren Darren, "A New Wrinkle on Age Bias," *Inc.* 27 (July 2005): 36.

59. "ADEA Prevention Not Panic," *HR Magazine* 50 (September 2005) 58–62.

60. Donald L. Caruth, Robert M. Noe III, and R. Wayne Mondy, *Staffing the Contemporary Organization* (New York: Quorum Books, 1988): 49.

61. Patrick Mirza, "New Life for Pregnancy Discrimination Claims," *HR Magazine* 50 (July 2005): 10.

62. Stephanie Clifford, "Pregnancy Claim Settlements Rise," *Inc.* 27 (September 2005): 30.

63. Nancy Hatch Woodward, "Pregnancy Discrimination Grows," *HR Magazine* 50 (July 2005): 78–82.

64. Stephen Davis, "Deported from America," *New Statesman* 133 (November 22, 2004): 14–16.

65. Kelly Collins Woodford and Thomas J. Woodford, "The Duty to Accommodate a Person Who Is Perceived as Disabled: Say It Isn't So," *Labor Law Journal* 57 (Summer 2006): 71–82.

66. Anne G. Scheer, "Rulings Stiffen Rules for Pre-hire Medical Testing," *New Hampshire Business Review* 27 (September 16, 2005): 26.

67. Linda Wasmer Andrews, "Hiring People With Intellectual Disabilities," *HR Magazine* 50 (July 2005): 72–77.

68. The six cases are *Ward Cove Packing Co., Inc., v Antonio, Price Waterhouse v Hopkins, Patterson v McClean Credit Union, Martin v Wilks, West Virginia Hospitals v Casey,* and *Lorence v AT&T.*

69. "Avon, the Net, and Glass Ceilings," *Business Week* (February 6, 2006): 104.

70. Jonathan A. Segal, "They Go and Come . . . and Go," *HR Magazine* 51 (April 2006): 127–129.

71. "Managing Military Service Employees," *HR Focus* (June 2005): 3–4.

72. Michael D. Rosenbaum and Kathleen Shell Scheidt, "Military Leave," *Employee Benefit Plan Review* 59 (June 2005): 32–33.

73. Gerald L. Maatman, Jr., "New Workplace Laws Challenge RMs, HR," *National Underwriter / Property & Casualty Risk & Benefits Management* 110 (June 12, 2006): 30–32.

74. "Lawsuits Could Follow Failure to Train," *HR Focus* 82 (September 2005): 2–2.

75. Matthew Heller, "Diversity," *Workforce Management* 85 (June 26, 2006): 62–63.

76. Jennifer Gill, "Gender Issues," *Inc.* 27 (April 2005): 38–40.

77. Peter de Jager, "Ethics: Good, Evil, and Moral Duty," *Information Management Journal* (September/October 2002): 82–85.

78. "Age Discrimination Decision Mean for Your Company?" *HR Focus* 82 (May 2005): 4–5.

79. Liz Ryan, "Scuttling Some Job-Hunt Myths," *Business Week Online* (March 23, 2006): 4.

80. "Train Managers and Executives to Avoid Legal Danger Zones"

81. Charles Proctor, "Supreme Court Votes to Uphold Affirmative Action in U. Michigan Case," *University Wire* (June 24, 2003): 1.

82. Shawn Zeller, "EEOC," *National Journal* 37 June 18, 2005): 1971.

83. Nancy J. Arencibia, "Is Arbitration Right for Your Company?" *Financial Executive* 18 (December 2002): 46–47.

84. "Faster, Better Service and EEOC Enforcement on the Way," *HR Focus* 79 (June 2002): 8.

85. "Zero Tolerance," *T+D* 59 (August 2005): 50–52.

86. Jonathan A. Segal, "I Quit! Now Pay Me," *HR Magazine* 49 (October 2004): 129–134.

87. Anna West, "Romantic Liaisons," *Cabinet Maker* (March 17, 2006): 16

88. Mark Schoeff Jr., "High Court Sides with Plaintiffs in Pair of Cases," *Workforce Management* (March 13, 2006): 10.

89. Maria Greco Danaher, "Exec's Isolated Come-On Supports Hostile Environment Claim," *HR Magazine* 48 (February 2003): 105.

90. Sarah Ellison and Joann S. Lublin, "Dial to Pay $10 Million to Settle a Sexual-Harassment Lawsuit," *Wall Street Journal* (April 30, 2003): B4.

91. Mary-Kathryn Zachary, "Labor Law," *Supervision* 66 (April 2005): 23–26.

92. D. Diane Hatch, James E. Hall, Mark T. Kobata, and Marty Denis, "English Only Rule Questioned," *Workforce Management* 85 (February 13, 2006): 7.

93. Judy Greenwald, "Employers Facing More Claims of Religious Discrimination," *Business Insurance* 39 (August 15, 2005): 33.

94. *Military Integration's 50th Birthday, http:members.aol.com /WarLib/Lib/9881.htm*

95. Anne Fisher, "Piercing the 'Bamboo Ceiling'," *Fortune* 152 (August 22, 2005): 122.

96. Ibid.

97. Ibid.

98. Ibid.

PART THREE

Staffing

CHAPTER OBJECTIVES

After completing this chapter, students should be able to:

1 Explain why job analysis is a basic human resource tool and explain the reasons for conducting job analysis.

2 Describe the types of information required for job analysis and describe the various job analysis methods.

3 Identify who conducts job analysis and describe the components of a job description.

4 Explain the timeliness of job analysis, job analysis for team members, and describe how job analysis helps satisfy various legal requirements.

5 Explain the strategic planning process and the human resource planning process.

6 Describe forecasting human resource requirements and availability and how databases can assist in matching internal employees to positions.

7 Identify what a firm can do when either a shortage or a surplus of workers exists.

8 Explain downsizing and succession planning in today's environment.

9 Explain the importance of a human resource information system and describe manager and employee self-service.

10 Describe some job design concepts.

Job Analysis, Strategic Planning, and Human Resource Planning

HRM IN *Action:*

Disaster Planning—Up Close and Personal with Hurricane Rita

Disaster plans should focus on catastrophes that range from natural calamities such as hurricanes, earthquakes, and floods to man-made crises such as 9/11.[1] Your author personally witnessed the destruction that resulted when Hurricanes Katrina and Rita struck the Gulf Coast in 2005. The area in Lake Charles, a town in southwest Louisiana, where I lived, truly looked like a war zone.

Businesses were not only damaged by wind but some also faced flood damage and products were destroyed. For a long time there was no electricity, mail service, or newspaper delivery. Employees were scattered across the country. Business owners often had to also contend with the destruction of their own homes. Where a dense forest once stood, one could now see clearly because trees lay broken and twisted on the ground or on top of homes. Houses that had withstood the wind often had a blue tarp, compliments of FEMA. Looking at the massive destruction, one might wonder if businesses in the area could ever recover. It quickly became evident that quite a few organizations had poorly designed disaster plans, or none at all.

Many wished that they had devoted more time to disaster planning. However, some businesses had excellent disaster plans. Although the petroleum refineries were hit hard, they were able to quickly recover because of their detailed disaster recovery plans. In speaking with managers and workers alike, I found that workers knew precisely what their roles were. The plan called for a few critical workers to remain in safe havens within the refineries, to be able to hasten the recovery after the hurricane passed. These individuals were able to tell those returning individuals the extent of the damage and what resources were needed to begin repairs. Many predicted recovery would take years; but because of the detailed disaster planning, they were up and running in record time.

In the aftermath of Hurricanes Katrina and Rita, companies lost track of their employees because the mandatory evacuation order had sent them in all directions. Organizations that had disaster plans in place to communicate with their employees were back in operation rapidly, even though their headquarters might have been inoperative. When Katrina struck New Orleans, financial planners from Wachovia set up shop in Lake Charles and conducted business there until they had to move to Lafayette, Louisiana, due to Hurricane Rita. McNeese State University, located in Lake Charles, Louisiana, was severely damaged by the hurricane. Plans were already in place to move the Internet server that connected students and faculty to another location. Plans had also been made for payroll to be processed at another university in the state and employees could access their money through Western Union anywhere in the country. Even though the buildings at McNeese were inoperative, learning continued. Within a week after the storm, some students and faculty were again at work, and some students who had evacuated to their homes in Mexico were conducting research, writing papers, and communicating with their professors over the Internet. Without a well-developed disaster plan, it is likely that the semester would have had to be cancelled.

When disaster strikes business, there are always significant human resource issues to address.[2] Plans should focus on a wide variety of catastrophes that range from natural calamities to man-made crises. They should also cover day-to-day occurrences such as power failures, server malfunctions, and virus attacks. These plans need to address how the company will respond when employees who play a critical role or possess unique skills and knowledge suddenly become incapacitated or unavailable for some extended period of time.

To fill these voids, it is necessary to identify which positions and personnel within the company are critical to the organization's continued ability to accomplish its primary mission. Critical positions are those that cannot be left vacant even briefly without disastrous results and which would be very difficult to fill. Databases are valuable here also. For critical positions the company should identify the name of the person, key responsibilities, required competencies, classification, pool of candidates for progression, the candidate's existing competencies, and training required for candidates. That information should serve as the basis for the contingency plan, which should document those who could potentially step in to fulfill that role, the person with the authority to invoke that contingency, and other information required to ensure a smooth transition.[3]

This chapter begins by providing an example of the importance of planning for disasters. Next, the reason why job analysis is a basic human resource management tool is shown and the reasons for conducting job analysis are explained. Then, the types of job analysis information required are reviewed and the job analysis methods are discussed. Conducting job analysis is then presented, and the components of a job description are explained. The timeliness of job analysis, job analysis for team members, and the way job analysis helps to satisfy various legal requirements are then discussed, along with the strategic planning process and human resource planning process. Next, the forecasting of human resource requirements and availability is shown, and how HR databases can assist matching internal employees to positions is also explained. Then, actions that can be taken should either a shortage or a surplus of workers exist are presented and downsizing and succession planning are described. Several sections are devoted to human resource information systems (HRIS), manager and employee self-service, and some job design concepts, and the chapter concludes with a Global Perspective entitled "A Database of Repatriate Skills."

OBJECTIVE

Explain why job analysis is a basic human resource tool and explain the reasons for conducting job analysis.

Job analysis:
Systematic process of determining the skills, duties, and knowledge required for performing jobs in an organization.

Job:
Group of tasks that must be performed for an organization to achieve its goals.

Position:
Collection of tasks and responsibilities performed by one person.

Job Analysis: A Basic Human Resource Management Tool

Job analysis is the systematic process of determining the skills, duties, and knowledge required for performing jobs in an organization.[4]

With job analysis, the tasks needed to perform the job are identified. Traditionally, it is an essential and pervasive human resource technique and the starting point for other human resource activities.[5] In today's rapidly changing work environment, the need for a sound job analysis system is critical. New jobs are being created, and old jobs are being redesigned or eliminated. A job analysis that was conducted only a few years ago may now be obsolete. Some have even suggested that changes are occurring too fast to maintain an effective job analysis system.

A **job** consists of a group of tasks that must be performed for an organization to achieve its goals.

A job may require the services of one person, such as that of the president, or the services of 75, as might be the case with data entry operators in a large firm. A **position** is the collection of tasks and responsibilities performed by *one* person; there is a position for every individual in an organization.

In a work group consisting of a supervisor, two senior clerks, and four word-processing operators, there are three jobs and seven positions. A small company might have 25 jobs for its 75 employees, whereas in a large company 2,000 jobs may exist for 50,000 employees. In some firms, as few as 10 jobs may make up 90 percent of the workforce.

The purpose of job analysis is to obtain answers to six important questions:

1. What physical and mental tasks does the worker accomplish?
2. When is the job to be completed?
3. Where is the job to be accomplished?
4. How does the worker do the job?
5. Why is the job done?
6. What qualifications are needed to perform the job?

Job analysis provides a summary of a job's duties and responsibilities, its relationship to other jobs, the knowledge and skills required, and working conditions under which it is performed. Job facts are gathered, analyzed, and recorded, as the job exists, not as the job should exist. Determining how the job should exist is most often assigned to industrial engineers, methods analysts, or others. Job analysis is conducted after the job has been designed, the worker has been trained, and the job is being performed.

Job analysis is performed on three occasions. First, it is done when the organization is founded and a job analysis program is initiated for the first time. Second, it is performed when new jobs are created. Third, it is used when jobs are changed significantly as a result of new technologies, methods, procedures, or systems. Job analysis is most often performed because of changes in the nature of jobs. Job analysis information is used to prepare both job descriptions and job specifications.

Job description:
Document that provides information regarding the essential tasks, duties, and responsibilities of a job.

Job specification:
A document that outlines the minimum acceptable qualifications a person should possess to perform a particular job.

The **job description** is a document that provides information regarding the essential tasks, duties, and responsibilities of the job. The minimum acceptable qualifications a person should possess in order to perform a particular job are contained in the **job specification**.

Both types of documents will be discussed in greater detail later in this chapter.

Reasons for Conducting Job Analysis

As Figure 4-1 shows, data derived from job analysis can have an impact on virtually every aspect of human resource management.

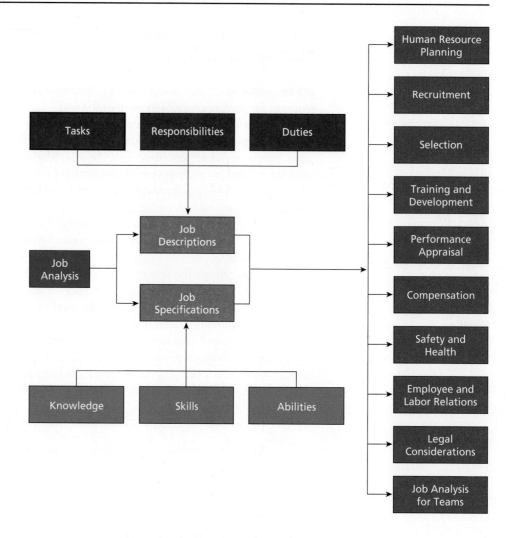

Figure 4-1 Job Analysis: A Basic Human Resource Management Tool

Staffing

All areas of staffing would be haphazard if the recruiter did not know the qualifications needed to perform the various jobs. A major use of job analysis data is found in the area of human resource planning (discussed in this chapter). Merely knowing that the firm will need 1,000 new employees to produce goods or services to satisfy sales demand is insufficient. Each job requires different knowledge, skills, and ability levels (KSAs). Obviously, effective human resource planning must take these job requirements into consideration. Also, lacking up-to-date job descriptions and specifications, a firm would have to recruit and select employees for jobs without having clear guidelines; this practice could have disastrous consequences.[6]

Training and Development

Job description information often proves beneficial in identifying training and development needs. If it suggests that the job requires a particular knowledge, skill, or ability, and the person filling the position does not possess all the qualifications required, training and/or development are probably in order. Training should be directed at assisting workers in performing duties specified in their present job descriptions or developing them for broader responsibilities.

Performance Appraisal

Employees should be evaluated in terms of how well they accomplish the duties specified in their job descriptions and any other specific goals that may have been established.[7] A manager who evaluates an employee on factors not clearly predetermined is left wide open to allegations of discrimination.

Compensation

In the area of compensation, it is helpful to know the relative value of a particular job to the company before a dollar value is placed on it. From an internal perspective, the more significant its duties and responsibilities, the more the job is worth. Jobs that require greater knowledge, skills, and abilities should be worth more to the firm. For example, the relative value of a job calling for a master's degree normally would be higher than that of a job that requires a high school diploma. This might not be the case if the market value of the job requiring only a high school diploma was higher, however. Such a situation occurred in a major West Coast city a number of years ago. It came to light that city *sanitation engineers* (garbage collectors) were paid more than better-educated public schoolteachers.

Safety and Health

Information derived from job analysis is also valuable in identifying safety and health considerations. For example, employers are required to state whether a job is hazardous. The job description/specification should reflect this condition. In addition, in certain hazardous jobs, workers may need specific information about the hazards in order to perform their jobs safely.

Employee and Labor Relations

Job analysis information is also important in employee and labor relations. When employees are considered for promotion, transfer, or demotion, the job description provides a standard for evaluation and comparison of talent. Regardless of whether the firm is unionized, information obtained through job analysis can often lead to more objective human resource decisions.

Legal Considerations

A properly prepared job analysis is particularly important for supporting the legality of employment practices. In fact, the importance of job analysis is well documented in the *Uniform Guidelines on Employee Selection Procedures*.[8] Job analysis data are needed to defend decisions involving termination, promotion, transfers, and demotions. Job analysis provides the basis for tying the HR functions together and the foundation for developing a sound human resource program.

Types of Job Analysis Information

OBJECTIVE **2**

Describe the types of information required for job analysis and describe the various job analysis methods.

Considerable information is needed for the successful accomplishment of job analysis. The job analyst identifies the job's actual duties and responsibilities and gathers the other types of data shown in Table 4-1. Essential functions of the job are determined in this process. Note that work activities; worker-oriented activities; and the types of machines, tools, equipment, and work aids used in the job are important. This information is used later to help determine the job skills needed. In addition, the job analyst looks at job-related tangibles and intangibles, such as the knowledge needed, the materials processed, and the goods made or services performed.

Table 4-1   **Types of Data Collected in Job Analysis**

Summary of Types of Data Collected through Job Analysis[a]

1. **Work activities**
   a. Work activities and processes
   b. Activity records (in film form, for example)
   c. Procedures used
   d. Personal responsibility

2. **Worker-oriented activities**
   a. Human behaviors, such as physical actions and communicating on the job
   b. Elemental motions for methods analysis
   c. Personal job demands, such as energy expenditure

3. **Machines, tools, equipment, and work aids used**

4. **Job-related tangibles and intangibles**
   a. Knowledge dealt with or applied (as in accounting)
   b. Materials processed
   c. Products made or services performed

5. **Work performance**[b]
   a. Error analysis
   b. Work standards
   c. Work measurements, such as time taken for a task

6. **Job context**
   a. Work schedule
   b. Financial and nonfinancial incentives
   c. Physical working conditions
   d. Organizational and social contexts

7. **Personal requirements for the job**
   a. Personal attributes such as personality and interests
   b. Education and training required
   c. Work experience

[a]This information can be in the form of qualitative, verbal, narrative descriptions or quantitative measurements of each item, such as error rates per unit of time or noise level.
[b]All job analysis systems do not develop the work performance aspects.
Source: Reprinted by permission of Marvin D. Dunnette.

Some job analysis systems identify job standards. Work measurement studies may be needed to determine how long it takes to perform a task. With regard to job content, the analyst studies the work schedule, financial and nonfinancial incentives, and physical working conditions. Specific education, training, and work experience pertinent to the job are identified. Because many jobs are often performed in conjunction with others, organizational and social contexts are also noted. Subjective skills required, such as *strong interpersonal skills*, should be identified if the job requires the jobholder to be personable.

Job Analysis Methods

Job analysis has traditionally been conducted in a number of different ways because organizational needs and resources for conducting job analysis differ. Selection of a specific method should be based on the purposes for which the information is to be used (job evaluation, pay increases, development, and so on) and the approach that is most feasible for a particular organization. The most common methods of job analysis are discussed in the following sections.

Questionnaires

Questionnaires are typically quick and economical to use. The job analyst may administer a structured questionnaire to employees, who identify the tasks they perform. In some cases, employees may lack verbal skills, a condition that makes this method less useful. Also, some employees may tend to exaggerate the significance of their tasks, suggesting more responsibility than actually exists.

Observation

When using the observation method, the job analyst watches the worker perform job tasks and records his or her observations. This method is used primarily to gather information on jobs emphasizing manual skills, such as those of a machine operator. It can also help the analyst identify interrelationships between physical and mental tasks. Observation alone is usually an insufficient means of conducting job analysis, however, particularly when mental skills are dominant in a job. Observing a financial analyst at work would not reveal much about the requirements of the job.

Interviews

An understanding of the job may also be gained through interviewing both the employee and the supervisor. Usually, the analyst interviews the employee first, helping him or her describe the duties performed. Then, the analyst normally contacts the supervisor for additional information, to check the accuracy of the information obtained from the employee, and to clarify certain points.

Employee Recording

In some instances, job analysis information is gathered by having employees describe their daily work activities in a diary or log. With this method, the problem of employees exaggerating job importance may have to be overcome. Even so, valuable understanding of highly specialized jobs, such as, for example, recreational therapist, may be obtained in this way.

Combination of Methods

Usually an analyst does not use one job analysis method exclusively. A combination of methods is often more appropriate. In analyzing clerical and administrative jobs, the analyst might use questionnaires supported by interviews and limited observation. In studying production jobs, interviews supplemented by extensive work observations may provide the necessary data. Basically, the analyst should employ the combination of techniques needed for accurate job descriptions/specifications.

Over the years, attempts have been made to provide more systematic methods of conducting job analysis. Several of these approaches are discussed in Table 4-2.

Conducting Job Analysis

3 OBJECTIVE

Identify who conducts job analysis and describe the components of a job description.

The person who conducts job analysis is interested in gathering data on what is involved in performing a particular job. The people who participate in job analysis should include, at a minimum, the employee and the employee's immediate supervisor. Large organizations may have one or more job analysts, but in small organizations line supervisors may be responsible for job analysis. Organizations that lack the technical expertise may use outside consultants to perform job analysis.

Table 4-2 Other Methods Available for Conducting Job Analysis

Department of Labor Job Analysis Schedule

The U.S. Department of Labor established a method of systematically studying jobs and occupations called the job analysis schedule (JAS). When the JAS method is used, a trained analyst gathers information. A major component of the JAS is the Work Performed Ratings section. Here, what workers do in performing a job with regard to data (D), people (P), and things (T) is evaluated. Each is viewed as a hierarchy of functions, with the items higher in the category being more difficult. The codes in the worker functions section represent the highest level of involvement in each of the three categories.

The JAS component "Worker Traits Ratings" relates primarily to job requirement data. The topics general education designation (GED), specific vocational preparation (SVP), aptitudes, temperaments, interests, physical demands, and environmental conditions are included. The Description of Tasks section provides a specific description of the work performed. Both routine tasks and occasionally performed tasks are included.

Functional Job Analysis

Functional job analysis (FJA) is a comprehensive job analysis approach that concentrates on the interactions among the work, the worker, and the organization. This approach is a modification of the job analysis schedule. It assesses specific job outputs and identifies job tasks in terms of task statements.

Position Analysis Questionnaire

The position analysis questionnaire (PAQ) is a structured job analysis questionnaire that uses a checklist approach to identify job elements. It focuses on general worker behaviors instead of tasks. Some 194 job descriptors relate to job-oriented elements. Advocates of the PAQ believe that its ability to identify job elements, behaviors required of job incumbents, and other job characteristics makes this procedure applicable to the analysis of virtually any type of job. Each job descriptor is evaluated on a specified scale such as extent of use, amount of time, importance of job, possibility of occurrence, and applicability.

Each job being studied is scored relative to the 32 job dimensions. The score derived represents a profile of the job; this can be compared with standard profiles to group jobs into known job families, that is, job of a similar nature. In essence, the PAQ identifies significant job behaviors and classifies jobs. Using the PAQ, job descriptions can be based on the relative importance and emphasis placed on various job elements. The PAQ has been called one of the most useful job analysis methods.

Management Position Description Questionnaire

The management position description questionnaire (MPDQ) is a method of job analysis designed for management positions; it uses a checklist to analyze jobs. The MPDQ has been used to determine the training needs of individuals who are slated to move into managerial positions. It has also been used to evaluate and set compensation rates for managerial jobs and to assign the jobs to job families.

Guidelines-Oriented Job Analysis

The guidelines-oriented job analysis (GOJA) responds to the legislation affecting staffing and involves a step-by-step procedure the work of a particular job classification. It is also used for developing selection tools, such as application forms, and for documenting compliance with various legal requirements. The GOJA obtains the following types of information: (1) machines, tools, and equipment; (2) supervision; (3) contacts; (4) duties; (5) knowledge, skills, and abilities; (6) physical and other requirements; and (7) differentiating requirements.

Regardless of the approach taken, before conducting job analysis, the analyst should learn as much as possible about the job by reviewing organizational charts and talking with individuals acquainted with the jobs to be studied. Before beginning, the supervisor should introduce the analyst to the employees and explain the purpose of the job analysis. Although employee attitudes about the job are beyond the job analyst's control, the analyst must attempt to develop mutual trust and confidence with those whose jobs are being analyzed. Failure in this area will detract from an otherwise technically sound job analysis. Upon completion of the job analysis, two basic human resource documents, job descriptions and job specifications, can be prepared. In practice, both the job description and job specification are combined into one document with the job specification presented after the job description.

Job Description

Information obtained through job analysis is crucial to the development of job descriptions. Earlier, *job description* was defined as a document that states the tasks, duties, and responsibilities of the job. It is vitally important that job descriptions are both relevant and accurate.[9] They should provide concise statements of what employees are expected to do on the job, how they do it, and the conditions under which the duties are performed.[10] Concise job descriptions put an end to the possibility of hearing "that's not my job."

Among the items frequently included in a job description are these:

- Major duties performed
- Percentage of time devoted to each duty
- Performance standards to be achieved
- Working conditions and possible hazards
- Number of employees performing the job, and to whom they report
- The machines and equipment used on the job

The contents of the job description vary somewhat with the purpose for which it will be used. The next sections address the parts of a job description.

Job Identification

The job identification section includes the job title, the department, the reporting relationship, and a job number or code. A good title will closely approximate the nature of the work content and will distinguish that job from others. Unfortunately, job titles are often misleading. An executive assistant in one organization may be little more than a highly paid clerk, whereas a person with the same title in another firm may practically run the company. For instance, one former student's first job after graduation was with a major tire and rubber company as an *assistant district service manager*. Because the primary duties of the job were to unload tires from trucks, check tread wear, and stack tires in boxcars, a more appropriate title would probably have been *tire checker and stacker*.

O*NET™ OnLine

http://online.onetcenter .org/

Making occupational information interactive and accessible for all.

O*NET, the Occupational Information Network, is a comprehensive, government-developed database of worker attributes and job characteristics. As the replacement for the *Dictionary of Occupational Titles* (DOT), O*NET is the nation's primary source of occupational information. O*NET is a flexible, easy-to-use database system that provides a common language for defining and describing occupations. Its flexible design also captures rapidly changing job requirements. It provides the essential foundation for facilitating career counseling, education, employment, and training activities by containing information about knowledges, skills, abilities (KSA); interests; general work activities (GWA); and work context.[11]

Date of the Job Analysis

The job analysis date is placed on the job description to aid in identifying job changes that would make the description obsolete. Some firms have found it useful to place an expiration date on the document. This practice ensures periodic review of job content and minimizes the number of obsolete job descriptions.

Job Summary

The job summary provides a concise overview of the job. It is generally a short paragraph that states job content.

Duties Performed

The body of the job description delineates the major duties to be performed.[12] Usually, one sentence beginning with an action verb (such as *receives, performs, establishes,* or *assembles*) adequately explains each duty. As stated earlier, essential functions may be shown in a separate section to aid in complying with the Americans with Disabilities Act. An example of a job description of a records clerk is shown in Figure 4-2.

Job Specification

Recall that *job specification* was defined as a document containing the minimum acceptable qualifications that a person should possess in order to perform a particular job. Job specifications should always reflect the minimum, not the ideal qualifications for a particular job. Several problems may result if specifications are inflated. First, if specifications are set so high that they systematically eliminate minorities or women from considerations for jobs, the organization runs the risk of discrimination charges. Second, compensation costs will increase because ideal candidates will have to be

---

Administrative Information
Job Title: Records Clerk
Department: Loan Operations
Reports To: Loan Operation Manager
Job Number:11

Date of Job Analysis
January 21, 2007

Expiration Date
January 2010

Job Summary
Returns all consumer paid loan documents to customers. Supervises the daily activities of two clerks.

Essential Functions Performed
Receives monthly files for accounts that have been paid in full and require the return of contracts, mortgage documents, auto titles, and other documents.
Answers telephone and e-mail inquiries from customers or loan officers concerning documents.
Maintains file on temporary automobile titles until permanent title is received.
Files permanent automobile titles, contracts, mortgage documents, and other documents in customer files on a daily basis.
Supervises two file clerks who maintain correspondence and other general files.
Performs file clerk duties as needed.
Performs other duties, as required, on a temporary basis, to maintain section or departmental operations and services.

Job Specifications

Education
High school diploma preferred, but not required
Experience
Six months or more in a financial institution and familiarity with various loan documents
Skills Required
Working knowledge of Microsoft Word and Excel
Ability to data enter 35 words per minute

Figure 4-2 Job Description/Specification Example

compensated more than candidates with minimum skills. Third, job vacancies will be harder to fill because ideal candidates are more difficult to find than minimally qualified candidates.

Determining the appropriate qualifications for a job is undoubtedly the most difficult part of job analysis. It requires a great deal of probing on the part of the job analyst as well as a broad understanding of the skills needed to perform varieties of work. Items typically included in the job specification are factors that are job related, such as educational requirements, experience, personality traits, and physical abilities. As previously mentioned, in practice, job specifications are often included as a major section of job descriptions. Figure 4-2 also provides an example of a job specification for the position of records clerk. Another example of an actual job description provided by Conoco for an administrative support position is show in Figure 4-3. Some of the critical skills needed for the job include interpersonal skills/team player, ability to influence others, and knowledge of software applications.

After jobs have been analyzed and the descriptions written, the results should be reviewed with the supervisor and the worker to ensure that they are accurate, clear, and understandable. The courtesy of reviewing results with employees also helps to gain their acceptance.

Position Title: **Administrative Support**	Code:	Salary Grade:
Work Location:	Report To:	Function:

Basic Purpose/Accountabilities:
Responsible for providing and coordinating administrative support to assigned functional groups. Focus is on aligning contributions to department needs and company goals.

Primary Functions/Responsibilities:	Critical Skills/Leadership Criteria:
—Preparation of time sheets —Track employee attendance —Manage fixtures, furniture, and equipment necessary to support the function —Process invoices, monitor expenditures —Coordinate and support meetings —Participate in planning process on projects —Type documentation to individuals external to Conoco —Assist with presentation preparation and planning —Coordinate large-scale documentation reproduction —External mailing/facsimile transmission —Coordinate central office supplies —Resource computer software applications —Coordinate work activities with other functions —Generate alternatives and make recommendations on improving area work process —Record retention/filing	**CRITICAL SKILLS** —Interpersonal skills/team player —Ability to influence others —Knowledge of business software applications —Confidentiality —Planning, organizing, and time management —Written and oral communication —Customer orientation —Knowledge of operations and organization **LEADERSHIP CRITERIA** —Able to lead others —Engenders trust —Understands and uses functional expertise to contribute —Accepts ownership, is accountable, and delivers on commitments —Oriented towards continuous learning

Quantitative Factors/Business Model Activities:	
<u>Quantitative</u>	<u>Business Model</u>

Figure 4-3 A Conoco Job Description
Source: Conoco, Inc.

OBJECTIVE

Explain the timeliness of job analysis, job analysis for team members, and describe how job analysis helps satisfy various legal requirements.

Timeliness of Job Analysis

The rapid pace of technological change makes the need for accurate job analysis even more important now and in the future. Historically, job analysis could be conducted and then set aside for several years. Today, however, job requirements are changing so rapidly that they must be constantly reviewed to keep them relevant. Recall from Chapter 1 that the average person graduating from college today may face five to seven career changes in his or her working years. If this projection is accurate, the need for accurate and timely job analysis is becoming even more important. Further, because of the fast-paced world we live in today, the amount of time that can be devoted to job analysis has diminished. Streamlined methods of job analysis have had to be developed. Darin E. Hartley has developed what he calls *Job Analysis at the Speed of Reality* which is a speeded-up version of the interview method of job analysis. Through this process, a validated job analysis can be completed in between two and three hours as opposed to two or three days.[13]

Job Analysis for Team Members

Historically, companies have established permanent jobs and filled these jobs with people who best fit the job description. The jobs then continued in effect for years to come. In many firms today, people are being hired as team members. Whenever someone asks a team member, "What is your job description?" the reply might well be "Whatever." What this means is that if a project has to be completed, individuals do what has to be done to complete the task.

With team design, there are no narrow jobs. Today, the work that departments do is often bundled into teams. The members of these teams have a far greater depth and breadth of skills than would have been required in traditional jobs. Formerly, there might have been 100 separate job classifications in a facility. With team design, there may be just 10 or fewer broadly defined roles of teams. Another dimension is added to job analysis when teams are considered: Job analysis may determine how important it is for employees to be team players and work well in group situations. Other traits that might be discovered through job analysis include the ability to work in more than one system.

Jobs are changing by getting bigger and more complex. The last duty shown on the proverbial job description, "And any other duty that may be assigned," is increasingly becoming *THE* job description. This enlarged, flexible, complex job changes the way many tasks are performed. Managers cannot simply look for individuals who possess narrow skills required to perform a job. They must go deeper and seek competencies, intelligence, ability to adjust, and ability and willingness to work in teams. Today more than ever, people go from project to project and from team to team. Job definitions become blurred, and titles become almost meaningless as job descriptions have become even more all-encompassing.[14] Basically, what matters is what you know and how well you apply it to the business.

Job descriptions frequently focus heavily, if not exclusively, on minimum objective requirements, such as education and job experience. However, these documents often pay little or no attention to the more subjective behavioral competencies essential to a job, such as flexibility, agility, and strategic insight. When you recruit and hire for one task, it will not be long before the firm asks the employee to do several others as well. With such wide-ranging expectations from the company, the employee will obviously need a broader variety of skills and abilities. Some firms are dealing with this situation by striving to employ individuals who are bright, adaptable, and can work effectively in teams. Hiring for organizational *fit* is discussed in Chapter 6.

Job Analysis and the Law

Effective job analysis is essential to sound human resource management as an organization recruits, selects, and promotes employees. Legislation requiring thorough job analysis includes the following acts.

- *Fair Labor Standards Act:* Employees are categorized as exempt or nonexempt, and job analysis is basic to this determination. Nonexempt workers must be paid time and a half when they work more than 40 hours per week. Overtime pay is not required for exempt employees.

- *Equal Pay Act:* Men are sometimes paid higher salaries than women, even though they perform essentially the same job. If jobs are not substantially different, the employees performing them must receive similar pay. When pay differences exist, job descriptions can be used to show whether jobs are substantially equal in terms of skill, effort, responsibility, or working conditions.

- *Civil Rights Act:* Human resource management has focused on job analysis because selection methods need to be clearly job related. As with the Equal Pay Act, job descriptions may provide the basis for an equitable compensation system and an adequate defense against unfair discrimination charges in initial selection, promotion, and all other areas of human resource administration. When job analysis is not performed, defending certain qualifications established for the job is usually difficult. Remember in the *Griggs v Duke Power Company* case in Chapter 3, the company stated that supervisors must have a high school diploma. However, the company could show no business necessity for this standard. Placing a selection standard in the job specification without having determined its necessity through job analysis makes the firm vulnerable in discrimination suits.

- *Occupational Safety and Health Act:* Job descriptions are required to specify elements of the job that endanger health or are considered unsatisfactory or distasteful by the majority of the population. Showing the job description to the employee in advance is a good defense.

- *Americans with Disabilities Act (ADA):* Employers are required to make reasonable accommodations for workers with disabilities who are able to perform the *essential functions* of a job. It is important that organizations distinguish these essential functions from those that are marginal. The EEOC defines *reasonable accommodation* as any modification or adjustment to a job, an employment practice, or the work environment that makes it possible for an individual with a disability to enjoy an equal employment opportunity. What constitutes reasonable accommodation depends on the disability and the skills of the person in question.

OBJECTIVE

Explain the strategic planning process and the human resource planning process.

Strategic Planning Process

In Chapter 1, it was stressed that HR executives are now focusing their attention on how human resources can help the organization achieve its strategic objectives. Thus, HR executives must now be highly involved in the strategic planning process; in the

Strategic planning:
Process by which top management determines overall organizational purposes and objectives and how they are achieved.

past they often waited until the strategic plan was formulated before beginning human resource planning. **Strategic planning** is the process by which top management determines overall organizational purposes and objectives and how they are achieved.

It is an ongoing process that is dynamic and ever changing.[15] At times an organization may see the need to diversify and increase the variety of the goods that are made or sold. At other times, downsizing may be required in response to the external environment. Or, the strategic plan may see integration, the unified control of a number of successive or similar operations, which was the case when Mercedes-Benz and Chrysler combined. Strategic planning attempts to position the organization in terms of the external environment. Remember the many external environmental factors that were described in Chapter 1.

Strategic planning at all levels of the organization can be divided into four steps: (1) determination of the organizational mission, (2) assessment of the organization and its environment, (3) setting of specific objectives or direction, and (4) determination of strategies to accomplish those objectives (see Figure 4-4). The strategic planning process described here is basically a derivative of the SWOT (Strengths, Weaknesses, Opportunities, and Threats) framework that affects organizational performance, but it is less structured.

Mission Determination

The first step in the strategic planning process is to determine the corporate mission. The **mission** is a unit's continuing purpose, or reason for being.

Mission:
Unit's continuing purpose, or reason for being.

The corporate mission is the sum total of the organization's ongoing purpose. Arriving at a mission statement should involve answering the questions: What are we in management attempting to do for whom? Should we maximize profit so shareholders will receive higher dividends or so share price will increase? Or should we emphasize stability of earnings so employees will remain secure? Certainly, these are questions to which HR can provide valuable assistance.

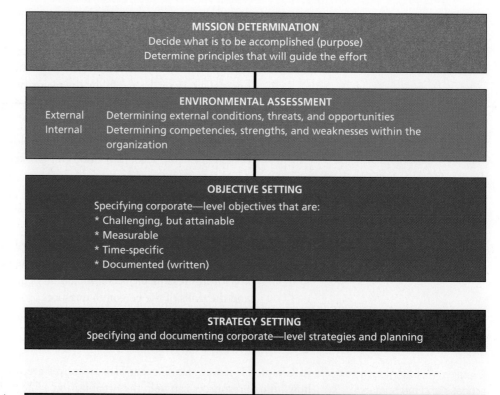

Figure 4-4 Formulating Strategy and Implementation

There are many other mission possibilities. Mission determination also requires deciding on the principles on which management decisions will be based. Will the corporation be honorable or dishonorable, ruthless or considerate, devious or forthright, in dealing with its various constituencies? The answers to these questions tend to become embedded in a corporate culture and help determine the organizational mission. Top management expects HR activities to be closely aligned to this mission and add value toward achieving these goals.

Environmental Assessment

Once the mission has been determined, the organization should assess its *strengths* and *weaknesses* in the internal environment and the *threats* and *opportunities* from the external environment (often referred as a SWOT analysis).[16] Making strategic plans involves information flows from both the internal and the external environments. From inside comes information about organizational competencies, strengths, and weaknesses. Scanning the external environment allows organizational strategists to identify threats and opportunities, as well as constraints. In brief, the job in the planning phase is to develop strategies that take advantage of the company's strengths and minimize its weaknesses in order to grasp opportunities and avoid threats.

HR professionals are in the best position to identify workforce strengths and weaknesses. Through the use of databases, the demographics of the present workforce can be determined. Should the company be considering, for instance, a merger or acquisition, HR would be able to work with top management to determine if the present workforce can be effectively integrated into the workforce of the merged company. For example, does the workforce of the merged company improve the overall value of the company or is there only duplication of talent? If reorganization is being considered, HR professionals should be in a position to know if workers are available in-house to provide the talent needed for a successful reorganization. Any reorganization affects people and HR professionals must be in the forefront of people-related matters.

Objective Setting

Objectives are the desired end results of any activity. Objectives should have four basic characteristics: (1) They should be expressed in writing, (2) they should be measurable, (3) they should be specific as to time, and (4) they should be challenging but attainable. Remember that HR metrics were discussed in Chapter 1. Strategic objectives might be directed at such factors as profitability, customer satisfaction, financial returns, technological leadership, and operating efficiency. Objectives should be developed only after a cost-benefit analysis of each alternative is considered. Since HR professionals are in the people business, it is difficult to imagine any strategic objective that would not involve them in some manner.

Strategy Setting

Strategies can now be developed for accomplishing those objectives. Strategies should be developed to take advantage of the company's strengths and minimize its weaknesses in order to grasp opportunities and avoid threats. It is the task of organizational strategists to clearly communicate how the organization tends to accomplish its goals. HR professionals should be highly involved in these activities since the composition of the workforce will certainly influence the strategies chosen.

Strategy Implementation

Once the strategic planning process is complete, the strategy must be implemented. Some people argue that strategy implementation is the most difficult and important part of strategic management. No matter how creative and well formulated the strategic plan, the organization will not benefit if it is incorrectly implemented. Strategy implementation requires changes in the organization's behavior, which can be brought about by changing one or more organizational dimensions, including management's leadership ability, organizational structure, information and control systems, production technology, and human resources.[17]

Leadership. A leader is able to get others to do what he or she wants them to do. Managers must influence organization members to adopt the behaviors needed for strategy implementation. Top-level managers seeking to implement a new strategy may find it useful to build coalitions and persuade others to go along with the strategic plan and its implementation. HR must take the leadership role in dealing with human resource matters. Basically, leadership is used to encourage employees to adopt supportive behaviors and, when necessary, to accept the required new values and attitudes.

Organizational Structure. A company's organizational structure is typically illustrated by its organizational chart. This structure indicates individual managers' responsibilities and degrees of authority, and incorporates jobs into departments. The structure also pertains to the degree of centralization and the type of department that will be utilized. HR should be in a good position to recommend the most effective structure needed by the organization.

Information and Control Systems. Among the information and control systems are reward systems; incentives; objectives-oriented systems; budgets for allocating resources; information systems; and the organization's rules, policies, and implementations. Certainly, HR should be a valuable asset in developing and working with these systems. A proper mix of information and control systems must be developed to support the implementation of the strategic plan.

Technology. The knowledge, tools, and equipment used to accomplish an organization's assignments are its technology. As with other aspects of strategy implementation, the appropriate level of technology must be found for proper implementation of the strategic plan. It was mentioned in Chapter 1 that the world has never before seen technological changes occur as rapidly as they are today.

Human Resources. Consideration to human resources in the implementation phase of strategic planning is extremely important. The human resource functions must be properly aligned to successfully implement the strategic plan.[18] HR will be central to understanding the future of an asset that is increasingly important to the organization—the intellectual and productive capacity of its workforce.[19] In essence, a proper balance of human resources must be developed to support strategy implementation. Once strategic planning has taken place, human resource plans may be developed to help implement the strategic plan.

Human Resource Planning

Human resource planning (HRP) is the systematic process of matching the internal and external supply of people with job openings anticipated in the organization over a specified period of time.

Effective staffing decisions begin with human resource planning.[20] The human resource planning process is illustrated in Figure 4-5. Note that strategic planning precedes human resource planning. Human resource planning has two components: *requirements* and *availability*. A **requirements forecast** involves determining the number, skill, and location of employees the organization will need at future dates in order to meet its goals.

These projections will reflect various factors, such as production plans and changes in productivity. The determination of whether the firm will be able to secure

Web Wisdom

Bureau of Labor Statistics

http://stats.bls.gov

Vital information related to human resource planning is available on this site.

Human resource planning (HRP):

Systematic process of matching the internal and external supply of people with job openings anticipated in the organization over a specified period of time.

Requirements forecast:

Determining the number, skill, and location of employees the organization will need at future dates in order to meet its goals.

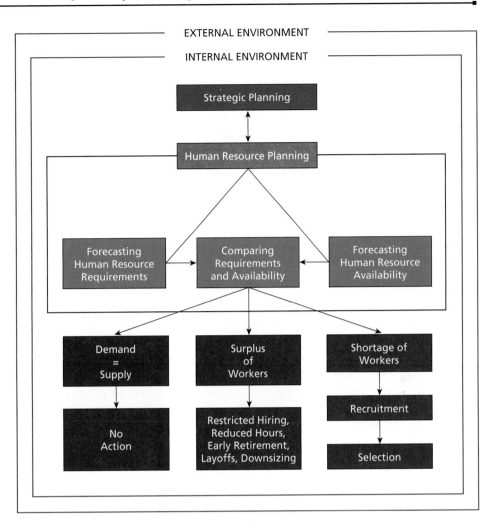

Figure 4-5 The Human Resource Planning Process

Availability forecast:
Determination of whether the firm will be able to secure employees with the necessary skills, and from what sources.

6 **OBJECTIVE**

Describe forecasting human resource requirements and availability and how databases can assist in matching internal employees to positions.

employees with the necessary skills, and from what sources, is called an **availability forecast**.

In order to forecast availability, the human resource manager looks to both internal sources (presently employed employees) and external sources (the labor market). When employee requirements and availability have been analyzed, the firm can determine whether it will have a surplus or shortage of employees. Ways must be found to reduce the number of employees if a surplus is projected. If a worker shortage is forecast, the firm must obtain the proper quantity and quality of workers from outside the organization. In this case, external recruitment and selection are required.

Because conditions in the external and internal environments can change quickly, the human resource planning process must be continuous. Changing conditions could affect the entire organization, thereby requiring extensive modification of forecasts. One of the biggest challenges facing human resource managers is determining how their companies will be affected by the departures of those now eligible, or soon to be eligible, to retire.[21] Planning, in general, enables managers to anticipate and prepare for changing conditions, and HR planning in particular allows flexibility in the area of human resource management.

Forecasting Human Resource Requirements

As previously defined, a *requirements forecast* involves determining the number, skill, and location of employees the organization will need at future dates in order to meet its goals. Before human resource requirements can be projected, demand for the firm's goods or services must be forecasted. This forecast is then converted into people requirements for the activities necessary to meet this demand. For a firm that manufactures personal computers, activities might be stated in terms of the number of units to be produced, number of sales calls to be made, number of vouchers to be processed, or a variety of other activities. For example, manufacturing 1,000 notebook computers each week might require 10,000 hours of work by assemblers during a 40-hour week. Dividing the 10,000 hours by the 40 hours in the work week gives 250 assembly workers needed. Similar calculations are performed for the other jobs needed to produce and market the computers.

Several techniques for forecasting human resource requirements are currently used by HR professionals. Some of the techniques are qualitative in nature, and others are quantitative. Several of the better-known methods are described in this section.

Zero-Base Forecasting

Zero-base forecasting:
Forecasting method which uses the organization's current level of employment as the starting point for determining future staffing needs.

The **zero-base forecasting** method uses the organization's current level of employment as the starting point for determining future staffing needs.

Essentially, the same procedure is used for human resource planning as for zero-base budgeting, whereby each budget must be justified each year. If an employee retires, is fired, or leaves the firm for any other reason, the position is not automatically filled. Instead, an analysis is made to determine whether the firm can justify filling it. Equal concern is shown for creating new positions when they appear to be needed. The key to zero-base forecasting is a thorough analysis of human resource needs. Frequently, the position is not filled and the work is spread out among remaining employees. Plans may also involve outsourcing or other approaches as an alternative to hiring.

Bottom-Up Approach

Bottom-up approach:
Forecasting method in which each successive level in the organization, starting with the lowest, forecasts its requirements, ultimately providing an aggregate forecast of employees needed.

In the **bottom-up approach**, each successive level in the organization, starting with the lowest, forecasts its requirements, ultimately providing an aggregate forecast of employees needed.

It is based on the reasoning that the manager in each unit is most knowledgeable about employment requirements. Beginning with the lowest-level work units in the organization, each unit manager makes an estimate of personnel needs for the period of time encompassed by the planning cycle. As the process moves upward in the company, each successively higher level of management in turn makes its own estimates of needs, incorporating the input from each of the immediately preceding levels. The result, ultimately, is an aggregate forecast of needs for the entire organization. This process is often highly interactive in that estimated requirements from the previous level are discussed, negotiated, and reestimated with the next level of management as the forecast moves upward through the organization. The interactive aspect of managerial estimating is one of the advantages of this procedure because it forces managers to justify their anticipated staffing needs.

Relationship between Volume of Sales and Number of Workers Required

One of the most useful predictors of employment levels is sales volume. The relationship between demand and the number of employees needed is a positive one. As you can see in Figure 4-6, a firm's sales volume is depicted on the horizontal axis, and the number of employees actually required is shown on the vertical axis. In this illustration, as sales decrease, so does the number of employees. Using such a method, managers can approximate the number of employees required at different demand levels.

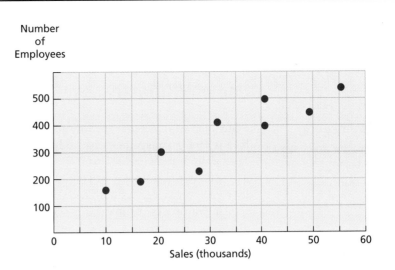

Number
of
Employees

Sales (thousands)

Figure 4-6 The Relationship of Sales Volume to Number of Employees

Simulation Models

Simulation:
Forecasting technique for experimenting with a real-world situation through a mathematical model.

Simulation is a forecasting technique for experimenting with a real-world situation through a mathematical model.

A model is an abstraction of the real world. Thus, a simulation model is an attempt to represent a real-world situation through mathematical logic to predict what will occur. Simulation assists managers by permitting them to ask many *what-if* questions without having to make a decision resulting in real-world consequences. In human resource management, a simulation model might be developed to represent the interrelationships among employment levels and many other variables. The manager could then ask *what-if* questions such as these:

- What would happen if we put 10 percent of the present work-force on overtime?
- What would happen if the plant utilized two shifts? Three shifts?

The purpose of the model is to permit managers to gain considerable insight into a particular problem before making an actual decision.

Forecasting Human Resource Availability

Forecasting requirements involves determining the number, skill, and location of employees the organization will need at future dates in order to meet its goals. The determination of whether the firm will be able to secure employees with the necessary skills, and from what sources, is an *availability forecast*. It helps to show whether the needed employees may be obtained from within the company, from outside the organization, or from a combination of the two sources. Another possibility is that the required skills are not immediately available from any feasible source. Consider the following example.

A large manufacturing firm on the West Coast was preparing to begin operations in a new plant. Analysts had already determined there was a large long-term demand for the new product. Financing was available and equipment was in place. But production did not begin for two years! Management had made a critical mistake: It had studied the demand side of human resources but not the supply side. There were not enough qualified workers in the local labor market to operate the new plant. New workers had to receive extensive training before they could move into the newly created jobs.

HR Planning Organization

http://www.hrps.org

The Website for the Human Resource Planning Society is provided.

The illustration above provides one more instance of the importance of HR involvement in strategic planning.

Use of HR Databases

Many of the workers needed for future positions may already work for the firm. If the firm is small, management probably knows all the workers sufficiently well to match their skills and aspirations with the company's needs. Suppose the firm is creating a new sales position. It may be common knowledge in the company that Mary Garcia, a five-year employee, has both the skills and the desire to take over the new job. This unplanned process of matching people and positions may be sufficient for smaller firms. As organizations grow, however, the matching process becomes increasingly difficult. Databases are being used by organizations that take human resources seriously in matching people with positions. Also, succession planning helps to ensure an internal supply of highly qualified management personnel.

Technology improvements have created ways of managing and analyzing information.[22] Databases now include information on all managerial and nonmanagerial employees. IBM's Workforce Management Initiative involves building a profile of the skills and background of every employee so that, as one example, consultants in its Business Consulting Services unit can be deployed more efficiently. "We wanted smarter utilization of our labor," says Harold Blake, IBM's director of workforce optimization.[23] Information that might appear in such databases includes the following:

- Work history and experience
- Specific skills and knowledge
- Licenses or certifications held
- Organizational training completed
- Educational background
- Previous performance appraisal evaluations
- Assessment of strengths and weaknesses
- Developmental needs
- Promotion potential at present, and with further development
- Current job performance
- Field of specialization
- Job preferences
- Geographic preferences
- Career goals and aspirations
- Anticipated retirement date
- Personal history, including psychological assessments

Before it is necessary to begin an external source, companies can use these databases to search within their own company to see if employees with needed qualifications already exist. A growing trend is for companies to automatically notify qualified employees of new positions. This is discussed further in the next chapter.

OBJECTIVE

Identify what a firm can do when either a shortage or a surplus of workers exists.

Shortage of Workers Forecasted

When firms are faced with a shortage of workers, organizations will have to intensify their efforts to recruit the necessary people to meet the needs of the firm. Some possible actions will be discussed next.

Creative Recruiting

A shortage of personnel often means that new approaches to recruiting must be used. The organization may have to recruit in different geographic areas than in the past, explore new methods, and seek different kinds of candidates. Chapter 5 will describe numerous other creative recruiting approaches.

Compensation Incentives

Firms competing for workers in a high-demand situation may have to rely on compensation incentives. Premium pay is one obvious method; however, this approach may trigger a bidding war that the organization cannot sustain for an extended period. More subtle forms of rewards may be required to attract employees to a firm, such as four-day work weeks, flexible working hours, telecommuting, part-time employment, and child-care centers. These topics are discussed in Chapter 10.

Training Programs

Special training programs may be needed to prepare previously unemployable individuals for positions with a firm. Remedial education and skills training are two types of programs that may help attract individuals to a particular company. For example, a small firm in Los Angeles expanded its market by hiring people with few, if any, qualifications. The firm was willing to spend the necessary time and money needed to provide even basic training.

Different Selection Standards

Another approach for dealing with shortages of workers is the lowering of employment standards. Selection criteria that screen out certain workers may have to be altered to ensure that enough people are available to fill jobs. Instead of desiring extensive work experience, a firm may be willing to hire an inexperienced worker and train the individual to do the job.

Ethical Dilemma

Which "Thinker" Should Go?

Your company is a leading producer of advanced microchips. You are the chief researcher in your firm's *think tank*, which consists of eight people with various specialties. Your group has generated most of the ideas and product innovations that have kept the company an industry leader for 10 years. In fact, the think tank has been so successful that another one has been organized to support the company's newest manufacturing operation on the West Coast. The individuals included in the new think tank have already been selected, but your boss has just assigned you the task of deciding who from your group of thinkers will head the new organization.

The person best qualified for the job is Tim Matherson. Tim is an MIT graduate, the informal team leader, and the individual who personally spearheaded three of the team's five most successful product advancements. However, if Tim is given the promotion, the void created by his leaving will be difficult to fill. On the other hand, the boss forced his nephew, Robert Jones, into the group. He is a sharp graduate of the local state university, but he is not a team player and he is always trying to push you around. You can either recommend Tim, illustrating those who produce the most benefit the most, or you can recommend Robert, making the boss happy, getting rid of a problem, and, most important of all, keeping your best performer.

What would you do?

Surplus of Employees Forecasted

When a comparison of requirements and availability indicates a worker surplus will result, restricted hiring, reduced hours, early retirements, and downsizing may be required to correct the situation. Downsizing will be discussed later as a major section.

Restricted Hiring

When a firm implements a restricted hiring policy, it reduces the workforce by not replacing employees who leave. New workers are hired only when the overall performance of the organization may be affected. For instance, if a quality control department that consisted of four inspectors lost one to a competitor, this individual might not be replaced. If the firm lost all its inspectors, however, it would probably replace at least some of them to ensure continued operation.

Reduced Hours

A company can also react to a reduced workload requirement by reducing the total number of hours worked. Instead of continuing a 40-hour week, management may decide to cut each employee's time to 30 hours. This cutback normally applies only to hourly employees because management and other professionals typically are exempt employees and therefore not paid on an hourly basis.

Early Retirement

Early retirement of some present employees is another way to reduce the number of workers. Some employees will be delighted to retire, but others will be somewhat reluctant. However, the latter may be willing to accept early retirement if the total retirement package is made sufficiently attractive.

OBJECTIVE

Explain downsizing and succession planning in today's environment.

Downsizing:
Reverse of a company growing and suggests a one-time change in the organization and the number of people employed (also known as restructuring, and *rightsizing*).

Downsizing

Downsizing, also known as *restructuring* and *rightsizing*, is essentially the reverse of a company growing and suggests a one-time change in the organization and the number of people employed.

Typically, both the organizational structure and the number of people in the organization shrink. Hewlett-Packard in 2005 announced that it was restructuring along with layoffs of 14,500 workers.[24] In November 2005, GM announced a plan to close 12 plants and parts facilities and cut 30,000 jobs. Early in 2006, Ford Motor Co. announced it would shut down 14 manufacturing plants and lay off 30,000-plus workers.[25] In some cases downsizing has been successful. Such would be a case if a company was selling off unprofitable assets and the reason for reducing payroll was to improve profitability.

Workers should understand when they are hired how the system will work in the event of downsizing. When the firm is unionized, the layoff procedures are usually stated clearly in the labor management agreement. Seniority usually is the basis for layoffs, with the least senior employees laid off first. The agreement may also have a clearly spelled-out *bumping procedure*. When senior-level positions are eliminated, the people occupying them have the right to bump workers from lower-level positions, assuming that they have the proper qualifications for the lower-level job. When bumping occurs, the composition of the workforce is altered. Union-free firms should also establish layoff procedures prior to facing downsizing decisions. In union-free firms, productivity and the needs of the organization are typically key considerations.

When productivity is the primary factor, management must be careful to ensure that productivity, not favoritism, is the actual basis for the layoff decision. Workers may have an accurate perception of their own productivity level and that of their fellow employees. Therefore, it is important to define accurately both seniority and productivity considerations well in advance of any layoffs.

An interesting situation has occurred as corporations downsize, offshore, outsource, merge, make acquisitions, close plants, relocate, and restructure. There is a growing need to temporarily retain employees who are earmarked for separation. *Retention bonuses* are used to entice terminated employees to remain for short periods of time to ensure continued services.[26] Recently, Tommy Hilfiger Corporation set up a retention bonus plan of up to $12 million for key employees to persuade them to stay on with the company after its pending merger with Apax Partners.[27]

Negative Aspects of Downsizing

When downsizing is chosen, companies typically describe the positive aspects that will result, such as improving the bottom line. There may also be a negative side to downsizing. First, there is the cost associated with low morale of those that remain.[28] These workers become very concerned about their own futures and may not want to stick their necks out and take risks, which is exactly what the company needs in order to generate new products, new markets, and new customers. Workers often become preoccupied with their own personal finances and the security of their families.[29] It is difficult to think about the best way to satisfy a client when your last day of employment is unknown.

Second, often layers are pulled out of a firm, making advancement in the organization more difficult. Thus, more and more individuals are finding themselves plateaued in the same job until they retire.[30] Many well-educated people who entered the workforce and rapidly moved up the corporate ladder in the 1990s have found themselves plateaued.

Third, workers begin seeking better opportunities because they believe they may be the next in line to be laid off. Often the best workers find other jobs, leaving the business staffed by those unable to find better or more secure jobs elsewhere. This is exactly the type of employee the company does not need. Workers are needed who can move easily through the uncertainty of being acquired, of layoffs, or the stress of new technology.

Fourth, employee loyalty is often significantly reduced. For workers who remain after downsizing, the loyalty level is often low.[31] These workers believe that it might happen to them the next time. A common thought pattern is that "I must take care of myself, because the company will not take care of me." Employees who would never have considered changing jobs prior to downsizing may soon start thinking about this option, especially if their present company does not provide them with the necessary development to keep up with industry trends.[32]

Fifth, institutional memory (how the organization comes across to customers in all their dealings)[33] or corporate culture is lost. The fewer seasoned people the company has to pass these on, the less it will be able to maintain the soul of the organization.[34]

Sixth, remaining workers are being required to do more. Companies often take the same amount of work and give it to fewer workers, which may produce stress in the long term.[35] Hamilton Beazley, chairman of the Strategic Leadership Group, coined the term *ghost work* to describe the additional workload taken on by surviving employees. "It's as if they're suddenly asked to start speaking Greek," says Beazley. "It can be totally demoralizing and can cripple the individual as well as the organization."[36]

Finally, when demand for the products or services returns, the company often realizes that it has cut too deeply. It then begins looking for ways to get the job done. Frequently, the company brings back former workers as independent contractors, which costs the company significantly more than if they had stayed on the payroll.

At times, with downsizing comes an increase in the number of discrimination lawsuits.[37] If a disproportionate number of employees subject to layoff fall into one racial, age, or other protected category, then the layoff decisions should be reconsidered. To prevent a layoff from triggering a lawsuit, the criteria for who gets eliminated should be nondiscriminatory. If the layoffs are based on performance, it is important to make sure the laid-off workers have lower performance appraisals than do the retained workers. A two-step process should be followed. One group of managers should perform the employee evaluations and another group should select which employees will be terminated. Potential lawsuits can often be avoided through this process.[38]

Another problem is that when companies go through major layoffs, they often try to eliminate people at higher pay levels. The employees who generally hold those positions are age 40 or older. So if these older workers get laid off disproportionately to younger workers, they may make a disparate impact claim.

Outplacement

Outplacement:
A procedure whereby laid-off employees are given assistance in finding employment elsewhere.

As a result of downsizing, some organizations are assisting laid-off employees in locating jobs. The use of outplacement began at the executive level, but it has also been used at other organizational levels. In **outplacement**, laid-off employees are given assistance in finding employment elsewhere.

Through outplacement, the firm tries to soften the impact of displacement.[39] Some of the services provided by group outplacement include the following:

- A financial section that covers pension options, Social Security benefits, expenses for interviews, and wage/salary negotiations.
- Career guidance, perhaps using aptitude/interest and personality profile tests and software.
- Instruction in self-appraisal techniques, which helps in the recognition of the skills, knowledge, experience, and other qualities recruiters may require.
- Tutoring in personal promotional techniques, research, and gaining an entry to potential employers.
- Help with understanding the techniques that lead to successful interviews.
- Development of personal action plans and continuing support.[40]

When organization change takes place, there will be a psychological impact on both the individuals who were dismissed *and* those who remain. Because of downsizing, companies use outplacement to take care of employees by moving them successfully out of the company rather than having to do it on their own.[41] This proactive response will also likely have a positive influence on those who remain with the company after downsizing.

Succession Planning

Succession planning:
Process of ensuring that qualified persons are available to assume key managerial positions once the positions are vacant.

Succession planning is the process of ensuring that qualified persons are available to assume key managerial positions once the positions are vacant.

This definition includes untimely deaths, resignations, terminations, or the orderly retirements of company officials. The goal is to help ensure a smooth transition and operational efficiency, but the transition is often difficult.[42] However, the Corporate Leadership Council (CLC), a human resource research organization, recently surveyed 276 large companies and found that only 20 percent of responding HR executives were satisfied with their top-management succession processes.[43] In a recent survey of board members, nearly half of survey respondents (43 percent) have no clear process for a CEO transition. Almost half of companies with revenue greater than $500 million have no meaningful CEO succession plan, according to the National Association of Corporate Directors.[44] The stripping out of middle-ranking executives has left the question of succession wide open. There was a time when future leaders were carefully groomed, but today the top job often goes to an outsider.

The events of 9/11 reinforced the uncertainty of today's business world and the need for succession planning. Merrill Lynch, Morgan Stanley, Bank of New York, and Deutsche Bank, among others, activated their comprehensive disaster plans and were back up and running almost immediately after the World Trade Center tragedy. As another example, when the chief information officer at Parsons Brinckerhoff, the international engineering and construction management firm, died suddenly, the company immediately replaced him with a designated short-term successor, who filled the job for eight months until a permanent replacement took over.[45]

Because of the tremendous changes that will confront management in this century, succession planning is taking on more importance than ever before. It is not only deaths that have created an increased focus on succession planning. The premature firing of CEOs is no longer a rare event. CEOs are being terminated faster than in the past. Approximately 20 percent of CEOs in the S&P 500 have been CEOs for more than 10 years.[46] Many expect the tenure for CEOs to continue to grow shorter.[47]

Approximately one-third of the CEOs of the *Fortune* 1000 companies were recruited externally. However, hiring CEOs from external sources poses problems because boards of directors cannot know them as well as they know their own people.[48] Also, in the search for a new CEO, boards tend to be harder on internal candidates than on external ones. However, the internal candidates are well known. Boards have had the opportunity to see them perform over a long period of time and have witnessed their successes and failures. In contrast, because external candidates present themselves in the best possible light, they may appear to be a perfect match.[49] But, studies show that outsiders perform no better on average. Although at times there are justifications for going external for top-level executives, an internal succession process may be best.

Of recent, succession planning is going much deeper in the workforce.[50] "The biggest thing that is going on is a movement away from traditional succession planning, which was focused on top executives of the company," says James Holincheck, a research vice president at Gartner Inc. in Chicago. "Today, instead of focusing on the top 25 or 50 employees, companies are pushing it further down in the organization and using it more as a development tool as opposed to a disaster recovery tool." Many organizations are now using succession planning at other levels of the organization. The availability of newer software associated with performance management systems permits organizations to deal with larger numbers of employees at more levels in the firm.[51]

OBJECTIVE

Explain the importance of a human resource information system and describe manager and employee self-service.

Human resource information system (HRIS):
Any organized approach for obtaining relevant and timely information on which to base human resource decisions.

Human Resource Information Systems

Earlier in this chapter the ways that databases could to be used to identify talent currently existing within a company were presented. Human resource planning and succession planning were also discussed. These and virtually all human resource management functions can be enhanced through the use of a **human resource information system (HRIS)**, any organized approach for obtaining relevant and timely information on which to base human resource decisions.

It must also be cost-effective. An HRIS should be designed to provide information that is:

- **Timely.** A manager must have access to up-to-date information.
- **Accurate.** A manager must be able to rely on the accuracy of the information provided.

- **Concise.** A manager can absorb only so much information at any one time.

- **Relevant.** A manager should receive only the information needed in a particular situation.

- **Complete.** A manager should receive complete, not partial information.

The absence of even one of these characteristics reduces the effectiveness of an HRIS and complicates the decision-making process. Conversely, a system possessing all these characteristics enhances the ease and accuracy of the decision-making process.

Firms realize that a properly developed HRIS can provide tremendous benefits to the organization. Although many HR professionals and managers at small organizations shoulder HRIS in addition to their many other responsibilities, larger organizations have specific staff to address technology issues. Figure 4-7 presents an overview of the human resource information system designed for one organization. Utilizing numerous types of input data, the HRIS makes available many types of output data that have far-reaching human resource planning and operational value. Connie Muscarella, vice president of HR and administration at Thomas & Betts Corp., an electrical component manufacturer based in Memphis, Tennessee, said, "I remember the old days of EEOC [Equal Employment Opportunity Commission] reporting, and it took months to pull the numbers and complete the reports."[52] The HRIS ties together all human resource information into a system.

Data from various input sources are integrated to provide the needed outputs. Information needed in the firm's human resource decision-making process is readily available when the system is properly designed.[53] For instance, many firms are now studying historical trends to determine the best means of securing qualified applicants. In addition, complying with statutes and government regulations would be extremely difficult were it not for the modern HRIS.

Manager self-service (MSS):
The use of software and the corporate network to automate paper-based human resource processes that require a manager's approval, record-keeping or input, and processes that support the manager's job.

HUMAN RESOURCE INFORMATION SYSTEM
Goal: Integrate Core Processes into Seamless System

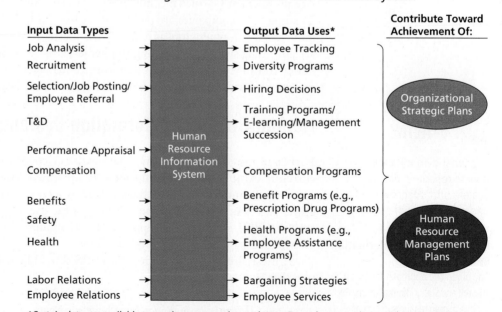

*Certain data are available to employees at work or at home. Examples: supervisors might access just-in-time training for conducting performance appraisal reviews. Operative employees might enter time and labor data. All employees may be able to review 401(k) balances, transfer funds, make benefit elections, set annual performance goals, update personnel data.

Figure 4-7 Human Resource Information System

There are numerous firms that provide human resource information systems. Prominent HR software companies include Sage Abra HRMS, MS Great Plains HRM, Success Factors—Performance Mgmt, Ultipro HR, Kronos Workforce Central Suite, PeopleSoft HCM, and Sage MAS 500 Human Resources.[54]

Trends & Innovations

Manager Self-Service

Technology is increasingly available to permit managers to perform tasks that were previously done by HR.[55] **Manager self-service (MSS)** is the use of software and the corporate network to automate paper-based human resource processes that require a manager's approval, record-keeping or input, and processes that support the manager's job.

There are distinct levels of self-service, from basic administrative tasks to strategic MSS. The basis MSS automates paper, workflow, and processes associated with routine transactions, such as awarding pay increases, arranging transfers, and approving vacation time and travel expenses. More advanced processes include recruiting, compensation planning, and performance management. Even before MSS was implemented, many companies had already automated recruitment processes, using public Websites and commercial software.

MSS can help managers develop and grow staff and assist employees in determining their career paths and developing required competencies, according to a recent survey by Towers Perrin. Self-service for managers is also expanding into planning of annual merit raises/base salary and reviewing and updating employees' performance appraisals online.[56] "We're going to see wider use of MSS over the next three to five years," says Katherine Jones, an analyst at the Aberdeen Group Inc., a Boston IT consulting company. She predicts MSS will be nearly "ubiquitous" among companies with $1 billion or more in revenues. "The decision to adopt MSS is basically a no-brainer," she says.[57]

The decision to go with an MSS system may be easy, but implementation has been difficult.[58] At times, the culture of the organization may need to change and that takes time. There is the difficulty of getting people to accept a new way of doing things. Managers have gotten used to telling the HR department to handle the transactions that MSS now requires managers to perform. MSS could be viewed as extra work placed on managers. Monica Barron, an analyst at IT consulting firm AMR Research Inc. of Boston, said, "Managers may complain, 'Why am I doing HR's work?' When that happens, MSS has not been properly presented as beneficial to the organization."[59]

Examples of success with MSS are numerous. Mapics Inc. had a million-dollar problem. Managers at the Atlanta-based developer of enterprise resource planning software did not know how much vacation time their several hundred workers took each year because their paper-based tracking system was inadequate. Many of their employees did not even use all the vacation they had. "The vacation accrual was worth more than $1 million," says Sandra Hofmann, CIO and chief people officer (a rare combination). After it adopted manager self-service software, Mapics eliminated accrued vacation and implemented a new vacation policy, saving $1 million.[60]

Florida Power & Light Co. has a workforce of 11,500 in 20 states and 1,000 managers using MSS applications, including those for a broad range of transactions such as making organization and payroll changes, tracking employee vacation and sick days, and generating reports for everything from employee emergency phone numbers to compensation histories. Gary McBean, general manager for HR shared services, says, "it hasn't been easy." "Change management is by far the biggest issue and an ongoing challenge," says McBean. The successful implementation of several applications occurred in a short time. And, while the company stressed change management, an additional priority was to make sure managers were comfortable with the applications and how to use them.[61]

Employee Self-Service

Employee self-service (ESS):
Processes that automate transactions that previously were labor-intensive for both employees and HR professionals.

Employee self-service (ESS) consists of processes that automate transactions that previously were labor-intensive for both employees and HR professionals.

ESS applications can free up valuable HR staff time, reducing administrative time and costs.[62] In a recent survey by Towers Perrin, 33 percent of respondents intend to offer employees the ability to plan their careers. A similar percentage will allow workers to update performance goals online, and 52 percent will allow employees to enroll in training courses online.[63] In addition, a growing number of employers provide access to tools and information that can give employees an accurate picture of their financial health.[64] When ESS systems are used, employees become responsible for entering the required changes.[65] Instead of calling or mailing a change of address to payroll, the employee uses the firm's electronic notification system.[66]

Employee self-service systems can certainly help the payroll department, especially in labor savings. But the entire process must be carefully planned and implemented to be cost-effective and user-friendly.[67] Although substantial savings can result from using ESS, there will likely be resistance from some employees.

 OBJECTIVE

Describe some job design concepts.

Job design:
Process of determining the specific tasks to be performed, the methods used in performing these tasks, and how the job relates to other work in an organization.

Job enrichment:
Changes in the content and level of responsibility of a job so as to provide greater challenge to the worker.

Job Design Concepts

We previously said that new jobs were being created at a rapid pace. If this is so, jobs have to be designed. **Job design** is the process of determining the specific tasks to be performed, the methods used in performing these tasks, and how the job relates to other work in the organization.

Several concepts related to job design will be discussed next.

Job Enrichment

Strongly advocated by Frederick Herzberg, **job enrichment** consists of basic changes in the content and level of responsibility of a job so as to provide greater challenge to the worker. Job enrichment provides a vertical expansion of responsibilities.

The worker has the opportunity to derive a feeling of achievement, recognition, responsibility, and personal growth in performing the job. Although job enrichment programs do not always achieve positive results, they have often brought about improvements in job performance, and in the level of worker satisfaction in many organizations.

According to Herzberg, five principles should be followed when implementing job enrichment:

- *Increasing job demands:* The job should be changed in such a way as to increase the level of difficulty and responsibility.
- *Increasing the worker's accountability:* More individual control and authority over the work should be allowed, while the manager retains ultimate accountability.
- *Providing work scheduling freedom:* Within limits, individual workers should be allowed to schedule their own work.
- *Providing feedback:* Timely periodic reports on performance should be made directly to workers rather than to their supervisors.
- *Providing new learning experiences:* Work situations should encourage opportunities for new experiences and personal growth.[68]

Today, job enrichment is moving toward the team level, as more teams become autonomous, or self-managed.

Job Enlargement

Job enlargement:
Increasing the number of tasks a worker performs, with all of the tasks at the same level of responsibility.

There is a clear distinction between job enrichment and job enlargement. **Job enlargement** is defined as increasing the number of tasks a worker performs, with all of the tasks at the same level of responsibility.

Job enlargement involves providing greater variety to the worker. For example, instead of knowing how to operate only one machine, a person is taught to operate two or even three, but no higher level of responsibility is required. Both job enrichment and job enlargement can be used with workers who have progressed as far as they can in their present jobs or are victims of burnout.

Reengineering

Reengineering:
Fundamental rethinking and radical redesign of business processes to achieve dramatic improvements in critical, contemporary measures of performance such as cost, quality, service, and speed.

Reengineering is "the fundamental rethinking and radical redesign of business processes to achieve dramatic improvements in critical contemporary measures of performance, such as cost, quality, service, and speed."[69]

Reengineering essentially involves the firm rethinking and redesigning its business system to become more competitive. When Hewlett-Packard developed its new product line of low-cost printers, engineers were told to ignore the models then being sold and to start from scratch. Through reengineering, the CEO wanted an entire product line to be brought out at one time. He also wanted to take it from concept to store shelves in less than three years, 18 months faster than HP had ever accomplished a product launch. Radical design had to be considered and engineers had to "think outside the box," but the task was accomplished.[70]

Reengineering emphasizes the radical redesign of work in which companies organize around process instead of by functional departments. Incremental change is not what is desired; instead, radical changes are wanted that will alter entire operations at one time. Essentially, the firm must rethink and redesign its business system from the ground up.

Reengineering focuses on the overall aspects of job designs, organizational structures, and management systems. It stresses that work should be organized around outcomes as opposed to tasks or functions. Reengineering should never be confused with downsizing (discussed previously in this chapter), even though a workforce reduction often results from this strategy. Naturally, job design considerations are of paramount concern because as the process changes, so do essential elements of jobs.

A Global Perspective

A Database of Repatriate Skills

Brenda Fender, director of international initiatives for the Employee Relocation Council in Washington, D.C., believes that many organizations still have a long way to go in taking advantage of the experience and knowledge of repatriates. "Many companies just don't track it," she says. J. Stewart Black, president of the Center for Global Assignments, a research and consulting organization in Alpine, Utah, says that "the vast majority" of U.S. companies have failed to realize the importance of creating databases of repatriate skills. If an employee leaves the company, his or her skills and knowledge will be lost for good. The resultant cost of losing a valuable employee, Black says, can be "staggering." Black says that the $2 million cost of a four-year overseas assignment becomes even higher when the usual 25 percent attrition rate is factored in.[71]

Colgate-Palmolive Company recognized the wealth of information it already had on expatriate skills in a system not originally designed for that purpose. Coleen Smith, New York–based vice president for global people development, says the company began putting together a global succession-planning database almost 10 years ago. "It has taken a variety of forms over the years," she says. While Colgate-Palmolive's database is primarily for succession planning, it also contains data on each manager's experience with or awareness of particular cultures. The information is made available throughout the company's worldwide network. "Senior leaders," Smith says, "have come to expect a certain level of information, which we really manage through our global succession-planning database."[72]

Colgate-Palmolive sees a foreign assignment as part of an extended overseas career track rather than as a one-off assignment. A successful foreign assignment tends to lead to another and another. "Our top priority is to identify, develop and retain the next two to three generations of leaders," Smith says. And part of that strategy includes directly using the knowledge of the company's current and former expatriates. Seventy-five percent of Colgate-Palmolive's $9.5 billion in annual sales comes from outside North America. The company has a global expatriate population of about 300, a figure that has remained steady over the past decade. Forty percent of these expatriates have had four or more global assignments. Seventy-five percent have had two or more. The system has gained upper-level support given that the company's senior executives, Smith says, "have all worked in multiple locations around the world." Colgate-Palmolive's wide geographical spread puts enormous emphasis on detailed knowledge of local markets. In Europe, the company must respond to pressure from both consumers and governments for environmentally friendly packaging. In Latin America, managers might have to cope with the complexities growing out of recurrent hyperinflation or periodic currency devaluations. Such swings can affect both product pricing and business planning. All this knowledge about local markets must reach every corner of Colgate-Palmolive's global operations. And this is where a database of expatriate knowledge comes into play.[73]

Summary

1. Explain why job analysis is a basic human resource tool and explain the reasons for conducting job analysis.

Job analysis is the systematic process of determining the skills, duties, and knowledge required for performing jobs in an organization. It is an essential and pervasive human resource technique. In today's rapidly changing work environment, the need for a sound job analysis system is extremely critical. New jobs are being created, and old jobs are being redesigned or eliminated.

Without a properly conducted job analysis, it would be difficult, if not impossible, to satisfactorily perform the other human resource–related functions.

2. Describe the types of information required for job analysis and describe the various job analysis methods.

Work activities, worker-oriented activities, and the types of machines, tools, equipment, and work aids used in the job are important. This information is used to help determine the job skills needed. In addition, the job analyst looks at job-related tangibles and intangibles.

The job analyst may administer a structured questionnaire, witness the work being performed, interview both the employee and the supervisor, or ask them to describe their daily work activities in a diary or log. A combination of methods is often used.

3. Identify who conducts job analysis and describe the components of a job description.

The people who participate in job analysis should include, at a minimum, the employee and the employee's immediate supervisor. Large organizations may have one or more job analysts, but in small organizations line supervisors may be responsible for job analysis. Organizations that lack the technical expertise may use outside consultants to perform job analysis.

Components include the job identification section, which includes the job title, department, reporting relationship, and a job number or code; the job analysis date; the job summary; and the body of the job description that delineates the major duties to be performed.

4. Explain the timeliness of job analysis, job analysis for team members, and describe how job analysis helps satisfy various legal requirements.

The rapid pace of technological change makes the need for accurate job analysis even more important now and in the future.

In many firms today, people are being hired as team members. Whenever someone asks a team member, "What is your job description?" the reply might well be "Whatever." What this means is that if a project has to be completed, individuals do what has to be done to complete the task.

Legislation requiring thorough job analysis includes the following acts: Fair Labor Standards Act, Equal Pay Act, Civil Rights Act, Occupational Safety and Health Act, and the Americans with Disabilities Act.

5. Explain the strategic planning process and the human resource planning process.

Strategic planning is the process by which top management determines overall organizational purposes and objectives and how they will be achieved. It is an ongoing process that is dynamic and ever changing. Strategic planning at all levels of the organization can be divided into four steps: (1) determination of the organizational mission, (2) assessment of the organization and its environment, (3) setting of specific objectives or direction, and (4) determination of strategies to accomplish those objectives.

After strategic plans have been formulated, human resource planning can be undertaken. Human resource planning (HRP) is the systematic process of matching the internal and external supply of people with job openings anticipated in the organization over a specified period of time. Human resource planning has two components: requirements and availability.

6. Describe forecasting human resource *requirements* and *availability* and how HR databases can assist in matching internal employees to positions.

A requirements forecast is an estimate of the numbers and kinds of employees the organization will need at future dates in order to realize its goals. Determining whether the firm will be able to secure employees with the necessary skills and from what sources these individuals may be obtained is called an availability forecast.

Databases are being used by organizations to enable human resources to match people with positions.

7. Identify what a firm can do when either a surplus or a shortage of workers exists.

When a surplus of workers exists a firm may implement one or more of the following: restricted hiring, reduced hours, early retirement, and layoffs.

When a shortage of workers exists, creative recruiting, compensation incentives, training programs, and different selection standards are possible.

8. Explain downsizing and succession planning in today's environment.

Downsizing, also known as restructuring and rightsizing, is essentially the reverse of a company growing and suggests a one-time change in the organization and the number of people employed.

Succession planning is the process of ensuring that qualified persons are available to assume key managerial positions once the positions are vacant. This definition includes untimely deaths, resignations, terminations, or the orderly retirements of company officials.

9. Explain the importance of a human resource information system and describe manager and employee self-service.

A human resource information system is any organized approach for obtaining relevant and timely information on which to base human resource decisions.

Manager self-service is the use of software and the corporate network to automate paper-based human resource–related processes that require a manager's approval, record-keeping or input, and processes that support the manager's job. Employee self-service consists of processes that automate transactions that used to be labor-intensive for both employees and HR professionals.

10. Describe some job design concepts.

Job design is the process of determining the specific tasks to be performed, the methods used in performing the tasks, and how the job relates to other work in the organization. Job enrichment consists of basic changes in the content and level of responsibility of a job so as to provide greater challenge to the worker. Job enrichment provides a vertical expansion of responsibilities. Job enlargement is defined as increasing the number of tasks a worker performs, with all of the tasks at the same level of responsibility. Reengineering is the fundamental rethinking and radical redesign of business processes to achieve dramatic improvements in critical contemporary measures of performance, such as cost, quality, service, and speed.

Key Terms

- Job analysis, 91
- Job, 91
- Position, 91
- Job description, 91
- Job specification, 91
- Strategic planning, 102
- Mission, 102
- Human resource planning (HRP), 104

- Requirements forecast, 104
- Availability forecast, 105
- Zero-base forecasting, 106
- Bottom-up approach, 106
- Simulation, 107
- Downsizing, 110
- Outplacement, 112
- Succession planning, 112

- Human Resource Information System (HRIS), 113
- Manager self-service (MSS), 115
- Employee self-service (ESS), 116
- Job design, 116
- Job enrichment, 116
- Job enlargement, 117
- Reengineering, 117

Questions for Review

1. Why is disaster planning important?
2. What is the distinction between a job and a position? Define job analysis.
3. Why is job analysis considered to be a basic human resource tool?
4. When is job analysis performed?
5. What are the types of information required for job analysis?
6. What are the methods used to conduct job analysis? Describe each type.
7. What are the basic components of a job description? Briefly describe each.
8. Describe how effective job analysis can be used to satisfy each of the following statutes: (a) Fair Labor Standards Act, (b) Equal Pay Act, (c) Civil Rights Act, (d) Occupational Safety and Health Act, and (e) Americans with Disabilities Act.
9. What are the steps involved in the strategic planning process?
10. What are the steps involved in the human resource planning process?
11. What are the human resource forecasting techniques?
12. Distinguish between forecasting human resource requirements and availability.
13. What actions could a firm take if it forecasted a shortage of workers?
14. What actions could a firm take if it had a worker surplus?
15. Define succession planning. Why is it important?
16. Define human resource information system (HRIS). Why is a human resource information system needed?
17. What are manager and employee self-service?
18. Define each of the following: (a) job design, (b) job enrichment, (c) job enlargement, and (d) reengineering.

HRM Incident 1

A Degree for Meter Readers

Judy Anderson was assigned as a recruiter for South Illinois Electric Company (SIE), a small supplier of natural gas and electricity for Cairo, Illinois, and the surrounding area. The company had been expanding rapidly and this growth was expected to continue. In January 2006, SIE purchased the utilities system serving neighboring Mitchell County. This expansion concerned Judy. The company workforce had increased by 30 percent the previous year, and Judy had struggled to recruit enough qualified job applicants. She knew that new expansion would intensify the problem.

Judy is particularly concerned about meter readers. The tasks required in meter reading are relatively simple. A person drives to homes served by the company, finds the gas or electric meter, and records its current reading. If the meter has been tampered with, it is reported. Otherwise, no decision making of any consequence is associated with the job. The reader performs no calculations. The pay was $8.00 per hour, high for unskilled work in the area. Even so, Judy had been having considerable difficulty keeping the 37 meter reader positions filled.

Judy was thinking about how to attract more job applicants when she received a call from the human resource director, Sam McCord. "Judy," Sam said, "I'm unhappy with the job specification calling for only a high school education for meter readers. In planning for the future, we need better-educated people in the company. I've decided to change the education requirement for the meter reader job from a high school diploma to a college degree."

"But, Mr. McCord," protested Judy, "the company is growing rapidly. If we are to have enough people to fill those jobs we just can't insist that college graduates get paid to do such basic tasks. I don't see how we can meet our future needs for this job with such an unrealistic job qualification."

Sam terminated the conversation abruptly by saying, "No, I don't agree. We need to upgrade all the people in our organization. This is just part of a general effort to do that. Anyway, I cleared this with the president before I decided to do it."

Questions

1. Should there be a minimum education requirement for the meter reader job? Discuss.
2. What is your opinion of Sam's effort to upgrade the people in the organization?
3. What legal ramifications, if any, should Sam have considered?

HRM Incident 2

Strategic HR?

Brian Charles, the vice president of marketing for Sharpco Manufacturing, commented at the weekly executive directors' meeting, "I have good news. We can get the large contract with Medord Corporation. All we have to do is complete the project in one year instead of two. I told them we could do it."

Charmagne Powell, vice president of human resources, brought Brian back to reality by reminding him, "Remember the strategic plan we were involved in developing and we all agreed to? Our present workers do not have the expertise required to produce the quality that Medord's particular specifications require. Under the two-year project timetable, we planned to retrain our present workers gradually. With this new time schedule, we will have to go into the job market and recruit workers who are already experienced in this process. We all need to study your proposal further. Human resource costs will rise considerably if we attempt to complete the project in one year instead of two. Sure, Brian, we can do it, but with these constraints, will the project be cost-effective?"

Questions

1. Was Charmagne considering the strategic nature of human resource planning when she challenged Brian's "good news" forecast? Discuss.

2. How did the involvement in developing the corporate strategic plan assist Charmagne in challenging Brian?

Notes

1. "Emergency Preparedness: Are You Taking These Steps?" *HR Focus* 82 (April 2005): 8.

2. Kathy Gurchiek, "Disaster Preparedness Is a Full-Time HR Job," *HR Magazine* 51 (January 2006): 26–34.

3. Selvaraju Balaji, "Could Key Personnel Losses Create Chaos?" *Security Management* 46 (July 2002): 184.

4. R. Wayne Mondy, Robert M. Noe, and Robert E. Edwards, "What the Staffing Function Entails," *Personnel* 63 (April 1986): 55–58.

5. Donald M. Truxillo, Matthew E. Paronto, Michelle Collins, and Jefferson L. Sulzer, "Effects of Subject Matter Expert Viewpoint on Job Analysis Results," *Public Personnel Management* 33 (Spring 2004): 33–46.

6. Inag Pioro and Nina Baum, "How to . . . Design Better Job Application Forms," *People Management* 11 (July 16, 2005): 42–43.

7. "Performance Management: Getting It Right from the Start," *HR Magazine* 49 (March 2004): Special Section 2–10.

8. *Uniform Guidelines on Employee Selection Procedures, Federal Register*, Friday, August 25, 1978, Part IV.

9. Clyde E. Witt, "The Right Stuff: Be a Better Talent Scout," *Material Handling Management* 61 (March 2006): 44–49.

10. Howard Lewinter, "Be Creative Looking for Your Next Job Candidate," *Business Journal Serving Fresno & the Central San Joaquin Valley* (March 11, 2005): 4.

11. http://online.onetcenter.org/help/onet/, June 20, 2006.

12. Clint Parry, "Make Position Description Work for You," *Inside Tucson Business* 15 (August 22, 2005): 17.

13. Darin E. Hartley, "Job Analysis at the Speed of Reality," *T+D* 58 (September 2004): 20–22.

14. Diane Brady, "Rethinking the Rat Race Technology Is Making 'All Work and No Play' a Real Possibility: How Will We Strike the Proper Balance of Work and Life?" *BusinessWeek* 3796 (August 26, 2002): 142–143.

15. "Why Strategic Planning Comes First—and How to Prepare for Succession Plans," *HR Focus* 82 (July 2005): S2–S3.

16. Alan P. Brache, "Choosing the Future," *Leadership Excellence* 22 (May 2005): 14.

17. J. R. Gallbraith and Robert K. Kazannian, *Strategy Implementation: Structure, Systems, and Process*, 2nd ed. (St. Paul, MN: West Publishing, 1986), p. 115.

18. Patricia Buhler, "Managing in the New Millennium," *Supervision* 66 (January 2005): 20.

19. Jennifer Schramm, "Planning Ahead," *HR Magazine* 50 (October 2005): 152.

20. Martin W. Anderson, "The Metrics of Workforce Planning," *Public Personnel Management* 33 (Winter 2004): 363–378.

21. Lisa Daniel, "Checking the Exits," *HR Magazine* 50 (August 2005): 101–104.

22. Jennifer Schramm, "Slicing the Data," *HR Magazine* 51 (March 2006): 60.

23. Scott Leibs, "Building a Better Workforce," *CFO* 21 (Fall 2005): 20–25.

24. Eric Lundquist, "HP Faces Changed World," *eWeek* 22 (July 25, 2005): 25.

25. "Avoiding a Downsizing Disaster," *Aftermarket Business* 116 (March 2006): 12.

26. "Retention Bonuses Grow More Popular in Company Terminations," *HR Focus* 83 (March 2006): 12.

27. Vicki M. Young, "Bonus Plan for Hilfiger Execs," *WWD: Women's Wear Daily* 191 (January 3, 2006): 2.

28. "Avoiding a Downsizing Disaster," *Aftermarket Business*.

29. Audrey Canaff and Wanda Wright, "High Anxiety: Counseling the Job-insecure Client," *Journal of Employment Counseling* 41 (March 2004): 2–10.

30. Donna Rosato, "21 Ways to Jumpstart Your Career," *Money* 34 (April 2005): 162–166.

31. John A. Challenger, "Return on Investment of High-quality Outplacement Programs," *Economic Perspectives* 29 (2005, 2nd Quarter): 86–93.

32. Joel Brockner, "Why It's So Hard to Be Fair," *Harvard Business Review* 84 (March 2006): 122–129.

33. Douglas McCormick, "Outsourcing Atrophy," *Pharmaceutical Technology* 29 (September 2005): 16.

34. Ibid.

35. Melissa Master, "Wayne Cascio Is Down on Downsizing," *Across the Board* 39 (November/December 2002): 13–14.

36. Lisa Takeuchi Cullen, "Where Did Everyone Go?" *Time* 160 (November 18, 2002): 64–66.

37. Brockner, "Why It's So Hard to Be Fair."

38. Michael Price "Anti-discrimination Training Useful to Prevent Bias Claims," *Business Insurance* 37 (January 27, 2003): 12.

39. Michael Carrillo, "Outplacement Assistance Good for Everyone," *Business Credit* 106 (July 2005): 32.

40. Tony Simper, "Outplacement—A Justifiable Expense," *Insurance Brokers' Monthly and Insurance Advisor* 50 (June 2000): 31.

41. Challenger, "Return on Investment of High-quality Outplacement Programs."

42. Stephen Mader, "Succession Planning, the Microsoft Way," *BusinessWeek Online* (June 27, 2006): 18.

43. Ram Charan, "Ending the CEO Succession Crisis," *Harvard Business Review* 83 (February 2005): 72–81.

44. Ann Pomeroy, "Failing at Succession Planning," *HR Magazine* 51 (July 2006): 14–15.

45. Jeffrey Marshall, "Succession Planning Is Key to Smooth Process," *Financial Executive* 21 (October 2005): 26–28.

46. Diane Brady, "Nothing Succeeds Like Succession," *BusinessWeek Online* (March 25, 2005).

47. Ibid.

48. Diane Brady, "Ending the CEO Succession Crisis," *Harvard Business Review* 83 (February 2005): 72–81.

49. Roselinde Torres and William Pasmore, "How to Successfully Manage CEO Succession," *Corporate Board* 26 (May/June 2005): 1–10.

50. Margery Weinstein, "What's Next? Finding Success in Succession Planning," *Training* 43 (July 2006): 40–44.

51. Drew Robb, "Succeeding with Succession," *HR Magazine* 51 (January 2006): 89–92.

52. John McCormack, "Compliance Tools," *HR Magazine* 49 (March 2004): 95–98.

53. "HR Technology Is Fueling Profits, Cost Savings, & Strategy," *HR Focus* 84 (January 2006): 7–10.

54. http://www.2020software.com/default.asp?ic_campID=26&ic_pkw=human%20resource%20software, January 25, 2006.

55. "Do More to Get More from HR Systems," *HR Focus* 83 (June 2006): 1–15.

56. "Self-Service Will Star in Staff & Performance Development," *HR Focus* 82 (April 2005): 8.

57. Bill Roberts, "Empowerment or Imposition?" *HR Magazine* 49 (June 2004): 157–166.

58. "Manager Self-Service Has Obstacles to Overcome," *Payroll Manager's Report* 6 (June 2006): 13.

59. Roberts, "Empowerment or Imposition?"

60. Ibid.

61. Ibid.

62. Drew Rob, "Unifying Your Enterprise with a Global HR Portal," *HR Magazine* 51 (March 2006): 109–115.

63. "Self-Service Will Star in Staff & Performance Development."

64. Desda Moss, "Portal to Retirement," *HR Magazine* 50 (August 2005): 14.

65. "How to Get Employees to Use Self-Service. . . and Like It," *Payroll Practitioner's Monthly* 2005 (February 2005): 1–6.

66. "Employee Self-Service: 7 Keys to Getting Your Staff on Board," *Payroll Manager's Report* 5 (November 2005): 5–6.

67. Ibid.

68. Frederick Herzberg, "One More Time: How Do You Motivate Employees?" *Harvard Business Review* 65 (September/October 1987): 109–120.

69. Michael Hammer and James Champy, *Reengineering the Corporation: A Manifesto for Business Revolution* (New York: Harper Collins Publishers, 1993): 32.

70. Noshua Watson, "What's Wrong with This Printer?" *Fortune* 147 (February 17, 2003): 120.

71. Robert O'Connor, "Plug the Expat Knowledge Drain," *HR Magazine* 47 (October 2002): 101–107.

72. Ibid.

73. Ibid.

CHAPTER OBJECTIVES

After completing this chapter, students should be able to:

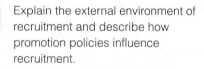 Define recruitment and explain alternatives to recruitment.

Explain the external environment of recruitment and describe how promotion policies influence recruitment.

Describe the recruitment process.

Describe internal recruitment methods.

Explain external recruitment sources.

Describe online recruitment methods.

Identify traditional external recruitment methods.

Describe an applicant tracking system.

Describe how recruitment methods and sources are tailored to each other.

Explain recruitment for diversity.

Recruitment

Hiring executives on a temporary basis has increasingly become a popular practice with some companies.[1] Individuals who have proven their ability as a top-level manager are entering this new arena. Bringing in an interim executive is a tactical approach that is sometimes used to run a department, a division, or even the whole company. Organizations today often view the hiring of a new executive as consisting of two parts. The company begins the search process for the executive in the traditional way, which may take an extended time period. At the same time a temporary executive is hired to cover the position during the time the company is looking for the new CEO.[2] Mike Braun, chief executive of Interim CEO Network in Palo Alto, California, supplies temporary CEOs for companies, mainly in high-technology industries, while the company is conducting an executive search. "The CEO decision is so important that the normal selection process can take six months to a year to play out," he says. "But we can have a seasoned interim CEO in place within four or five weeks." The compensation for temporary executives is usually 15 percent to 20 percent above what the new CEO will earn.[3] Further, research has shown that the average tenure for interim CEOs averages 5.3 months.[4]

Temporary executives appear to thrive on the intellectual challenge and flexibility provided. They are perfect for managing big projects and covering leaves and sudden vacancies. Gord Wilson, managing partner of Mississauga, Ontario–based Pivotal Integrated HR Solutions, said, "In my experience, the pathology of the business executive who manages change effectively is inconsistent with the attributes to manage process. So our recommendation is to bring in an interim for a year and a half to manage the change process, then hand off at that point to someone who is better equipped to manage the ongoing process."[5]

In many instances, temporary executive assignments become a *try-before-you-buy* exercise for both the temporary executive and the company. Mike Braun says, "About 40 percent of his placements become permanent hires."[6] For instance, Carl Camden of Kelly Services did so well as a temporary executive that he ultimately got the job permanently.[7] Another advantage of temporary executives is that they do not have to engage in the political infighting normally found in an organization. "Due to their limited engagement, interim executives can sidestep internal politics and seem more objective in their roles than someone with a long history," says Frances Randle, vice president and managing director of Toronto-based Knightsbridge Interim Management.[8]

This chapter begins by discussing the trend to hire temporary executives. Next, recruitment is defined and alternatives to recruitment are explained. This is followed by a discussion of the external environments of recruitment and promotion policies. A description of the recruitment process precedes a discussion of internal recruitment methods; then external sources of recruitment and online recruitment methods are examined. Traditional external recruiting methods are presented next, and applicant tracking systems are described. Then the importance of tailoring recruitment methods and sources and recruitment for diversity are discussed, and the chapter concludes with a Global Perspective entitled "China: Running Out of People?"

 OBJECTIVE

Define recruitment and explain alternatives to recruitment.

Recruitment:
Process of attracting individuals on a timely basis, in sufficient numbers, and with appropriate qualifications, to apply for jobs with an organization.

Recruitment Defined

Recruitment is the process of attracting individuals on a timely basis, in sufficient numbers, and with appropriate qualifications, to apply for jobs with an organization.

The firm may then select those applicants with qualifications most closely related to job descriptions. Finding the appropriate way of encouraging qualified candidates to apply for employment is extremely important when a firm needs to hire employees. However, recruiting costs can be expensive. Thus, a properly functioning recruiting program can have a major impact on the bottom line of a company.

How many times do we hear CEOs state, "Our employees are our most important asset"? Instead they should be saying, "The right employees are our most important asset."[9] Hiring the best people available has never been more critical than it is today, because of global competition. Therefore, it is crucial to have a finely tuned recruitment process if the selection process is to function properly. However, before beginning the recruitment process, alternatives to recruitment need to be considered.

Alternatives to Recruitment

Even when human resource planning indicates a need for additional or replacement employees, a firm may decide against increasing the size of its workforce. Recruitment and selection costs are significant when you consider all the related expenses: the search process, interviewing, agency fees, relocation, and processing of a new employee. According to the Employment Policy Foundation, it is estimated that replacing a full-time, private-sector employee costs at least 25 percent of that employee's total annual compensation and it could cost up to 150 percent depending on the nature of the position being filled and the supply of talent.[10] The 2005 SHRM Human Capital Benchmarking Study found that the average *cost-per-hire* was $7,123 and the number goes up exponentially when recruiting and hiring knowledge workers.[11] Therefore, a firm should consider alternatives such as outsourcing, use of contingent workers, professional employer organizations (employee leasing), and overtime carefully before engaging in recruitment.

Outsourcing

As defined in Chapter 1, *outsourcing* is the process of hiring an external provider to do the work that was previously done internally. Subcontracting of various functions to other firms has been a common practice in industry for decades. This decision may make sense when the subcontractor can perform a given function, such as maintenance, with perhaps even greater efficiency and effectiveness. Within the past few years, outsourcing has become a widespread and increasingly popular alternative involving virtually every business area, including human resources.[12] Corporations of all sizes have outsourced to providers in India, China, and Eastern Europe to satisfy their business needs.[13] Estimates of the value of offshore information technology and business-process outsourcing totaled $34 billion in 2005 and could double by 2007.[14] But, not all outsourcing efforts are successful. Dell Computers had so many complaints about thick accents and poor service that they relocated the tech-support center they had in India back to the United States.[15]

Contingent Workers

Contingent workers, described as the "disposable American workforce" by a former secretary of labor, work as part-timers, temporaries, or independent contractors.

Contingent workers are the human equivalents of just-in-time inventory. These *disposable workers* permit distinct advantages: maximum flexibility for the employer and lower labor costs. The Bureau of Labor Statistics separates contingents into two groups. First, there are independent contractors and on-call workers, who are called to work only when needed. Second, there are temporary or short-term workers, which the BLS calls *contingent*. As of 2005, the independent contractors and on-call workers consisted of 14.8 million workers, or 10.7 percent of the workforce, which was an increase of 9.3 percent since 2001. Temporary or short-term workers totaled 5.7 million or 4.1 percent of the workforce.[16]

The reasons that organizations choose to use these workers are numerous and include seasonal fluctuations, project-based work, the desire to acquire skill sets that are not available in the employee population, hiring freezes, and rapid growth. The total cost of a permanent employee is about 30 to 40 percent above gross pay.[17] This figure does not include, among other things, the costs of recruitment. Using contingent workers helps to avoid some of these expenses and to maintain flexibility as workloads vary. As HR departments shrink, increasingly temps and contract workers are being used to fill the void during peak periods.[18]

Companies that provide temporary workers assist their clients in handling excess or special workloads. These companies assign their own employees to their customers and fulfill all the obligations normally associated with an employer. Client firms avoid the expenses of recruitment, absenteeism, turnover, and employee benefits. Manpower, a temporary staffing company, provides additional evidence of the growing importance of the temporary workforce. This firm is now one of the largest employers in the United States.

The main unanswered question regarding using contingent workers is whether this staffing approach is healthy for our society in the long run. In the shorter term, the advantages gained by using contingent workers may be essential for success or even survival of many companies.

Professional Employer Organizations (Employee Leasing)

As discussed in Chapter 1, a *professional employer organization (PEO)* is a company that leases employees to other businesses. When a decision is made to use a PEO, the company releases its employees who are then hired by the PEO. The PEO then manages the administrative needs associated with employees. It is the PEO that pays the employees; it also pays workers' compensation premiums, payroll-related taxes, and employee benefits. The PEO is the employees' legal employer. Therefore, the leasing company is responsible for recruiting activities.[19]

Overtime

Perhaps the most commonly used alternative to recruitment, especially in meeting short-term fluctuations in work volume, is overtime. Overtime may help both employer and employee. The employer benefits by avoiding recruitment, selection, and training costs. The employees gain from increased income during the overtime period.

There are potential problems with overtime, however. Some managers believe that when employees work for unusually long periods, the company pays more and receives less in return. Employees may become fatigued and lack the energy to perform at a normal rate. Two additional possible problems relate to the use of prolonged overtime. Consciously or not, employees may pace themselves to ensure overtime. They may also become accustomed to the added income resulting from overtime pay. Employees may even elevate their standard of living to the level permitted by this additional income. Then, when a firm tightens its belt and overtime is limited, employee morale may deteriorate along with the pay.

 OBJECTIVE

Explain the external environment of recruitment and describe how promotion policies influence recruitment.

External Environment of Recruitment

Like other human resource functions, the recruitment process does not occur in a vacuum. Factors external to the organization can significantly affect the firm's recruitment efforts.

Labor Market Conditions

Of particular importance is the demand for and supply of specific skills in the labor market. A firm's recruitment process may be simplified when the unemployment rate in an organization's labor market is high. The number of unsolicited applicants is usually greater, and the increased size of the labor pool provides a better opportunity for attracting qualified applicants. If demand for a particular skill is high relative to supply, an extraordinary recruiting effort may be required. Recruitment efforts must be increased and new sources explored. Although the recruiter's day-to-day activities provide a *feel* for the labor market, accurate employment data, found in professional journals and U.S. Department of Labor reports, can be useful. Local labor market conditions are of primary importance in recruitment for most nonmanagerial, many supervisory, and even some middle-management positions.

Today, the labor market for many professional and technical positions is much broader and truly global. The number of jobs offshored from the United States to India and elsewhere has tripled since 2003, to a total of 1 million in 2006. Approximately a fourth of them are involved high-tech jobs.[20]

Legal Considerations

Legal matters also play a significant role in recruitment practices in the United States. This is not surprising since the candidate and the employer first make contact during the recruitment process. A poorly conceived recruiting process can do much to create problems in the selection process. Therefore, it is essential for organizations to emphasize nondiscriminatory practices at this stage.[21] In 2006, the Labor Department issued guidelines concerning the online recruiting policies of federal contractors and subcontractors. Companies must keep detailed records of each job search they perform online. They must also identify what criteria were used and be able to explain why a person with protected status was not hired.[22] EEOC guidelines suggest that companies with more than 100 employees keep staffing records for a minimum of two years. The threshold coverage is 50 employees if dealing with the OFCCP. This information enables a compilation of demographic data, including age, race, and gender, based on that applicant pool. The EEOC uses these data to determine if a company's hiring practices are discriminatory. Recruitment for diversity is discussed in greater detail later in this chapter.

Dramatic increases in firms using the Internet for recruiting has added to management's challenge. Under the rule that was put into place in 2006, there are four criteria to determine whether an individual is an Internet applicant:

- The job seeker has expressed interest through the Internet. Applicants have gone to the corporate career Website and applied for a particular job that is listed.
- The employer considers the job seeker for employment in a particular open position. If the applicant does not meet specific qualifications spelled out in the job specification section of the job description, the résumé does not have to be considered.
- The job seeker has indicated he or she meets the position's basic qualifications. If the position description calls for three years of experience, and the individual has three years of experience in previous jobs, he or she would believe that meets the basic qualifications.
- The applicant has not indicated he or she is no longer interested in the position, but the name has not been removed from consideration.[23]

Employers must keep records of any and all expressions of interest through the Internet, including online résumés and internal databases. Where possible, the employer is also expected to obtain the gender, race, and ethnicity of each applicant, according to the rule.[24]

Promotion Policies

An organization's promotion policy can have a significant impact on recruitment. A firm can stress a policy of promotion from within its own ranks or one where positions are generally filled from outside the organization. Depending on specific circumstances, either approach may have merit.

Promotion from within (PFW) is the policy of filling vacancies above entry-level positions with current employees.

> **Promotion from within (PFW):**
> Policy of filling vacancies above entry-level positions with current employees.

When an organization emphasizes promotion from within, its workers have an incentive to strive for advancement. When employees see co-workers promoted, they become more aware of their own opportunities. Motivation provided by this practice often improves employee morale.[25] Managers appear to be using internal promotions more and more. A recent study showed that 53 percent of management positions were filled by internal candidates, whereas five years ago it was only 44 percent. Scott Erker, vice president of selection solutions for Development Dimensions International, said, "You know an internal hire understands your culture. It's also positive because of what it communicates in the organization—that you're committed to your workers."[26] David Powell, vice president of marketing for 3M, states, "We have always had a very strong culture of promotion from within. So people who have been successful in jobs have moved up to the next level, and they've taken their knowledge and their skills and their experiences to that level. That's helped to provide a lot of stability also."[27]

Another advantage of internal recruitment is that the organization is usually well aware of its employees' capabilities. An employee's job performance, by itself, may not be a reliable criterion for promotion. Nevertheless, management will know many of the employee's personal and job-related qualities. The employee has a track record, as opposed to being an *unknown entity*. Also, the company's investment in the individual may yield a higher return. Still another positive factor is the employee's knowledge of the firm, its policies, and its people.

It is unlikely, however, that a firm can (or would even desire to) adhere rigidly to a practice of promotion from within. A strictly applied "PFW" policy eventually leads to inbreeding, a lack of cross-fertilization, and a lack of creativity.[28] Although seldom achieved, a good goal would be to fill 80 percent of openings above entry-level positions from within. Frequently, new blood provides new ideas and innovation that must take place for firms to remain competitive. In such cases, even organizations with PFW policies may opt to look outside the organization for new talent. In any event, a promotion policy that first considers insiders is great for employee morale and motivation, which is beneficial to the organization.

Recruitment Process

3 **OBJECTIVE**

Describe the recruitment process.

As previously defined, *recruitment* is the process of attracting individuals on a timely basis, in sufficient numbers, and with appropriate qualifications, to apply for jobs with an organization. Figure 5-1 shows that when human resource planning indicates a need for employees, the firm may evaluate alternatives to hiring. If these alternatives prove to be inappropriate, the recruitment process starts. Frequently, recruitment begins when a manager initiates an **employee requisition**, a document that specifies job title, department, the date the employee is needed for work, and other details.

Employee requisition:
Document that specifies job title, department, the date the employee is needed for work, and other details.

Figure 5-2 shows L3 Communication's employee requisition. With this information, managers can refer to the appropriate job description to determine the qualifications the recruited person needs. However, these qualifications are becoming less clear-cut.

The next step in the recruitment process is to determine whether qualified employees are available within the firm (the internal source) or if it is necessary to

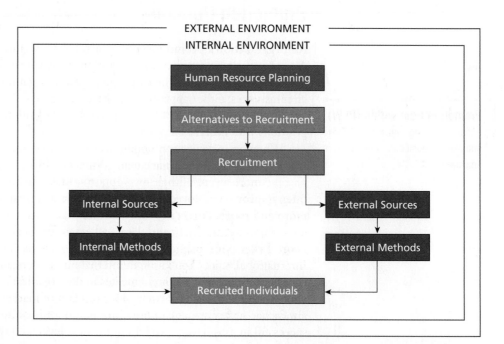

Figure 5-1 The Recruitment Process

L3 communications
Integrated Systems

PERSONNEL REQUISITION FORM		

Figure 5-2 An Employee Requisition for L3 Communications

The form contains the following fields:

- Requisition Number: Date:
- Dept No.   Dept Name:
- Job Type: Full Time ☐   Part Time ☐   Need Date:
- Job Title: Req. Type: Direct ☐   Indirect ☐
- Job Code: Grade: No. Openings:
- Year(s) of Experience: Project Name:
- Additional ☐   Replacement ☐   Replacing:
- Hiring Supervisor: E-Mail:
- Telephone: Fax:
- Dept. Manager: Telephone:
- Job Location: Job Building:
- Security Clearance: None ☐   Confidential ☐   Secret ☐   Top Secret ☐   Existing Clearance: Yes ☐   No ☐
- Minimum Education Level: None ☐   High School ☐   Associate ☐   Bachelor ☐   Master ☐   Ph.D. ☐
- Certification: Yes ☐   No ☐   If yes, specify:
- Degree Fields: May substitute related experience for education?   Yes ☐   No ☐
- Shift: First ☐   Second ☐   Third ☐   Rotating ☐   Overtime Required: Yes ☐   No ☐
- Job Description:
- Required Skills (specialized experience/knowledge/skills for this job):
- Desired Skills (other skills/abilities which will be helpful):
- Describe the physical requirements of the job (e.g. Bending, lifting, overhead work):

	Name/Title	Signature	Date
Manager:			
Director:			
Vice President:			
Finance:			
HR:			

look to external sources, such as colleges, universities, and other organizations. Because of the high cost of recruitment, organizations need to employ the most productive recruitment sources and methods available.

Recruitment sources are where qualified candidates are located, such as colleges or competitors.

Recruitment methods are the specific means used to attract potential employees to the firm, such as online recruiting.

Tapping productive sources of applicants and using suitable recruitment methods are essential to maximizing recruiting efficiency and effectiveness. As Jim Goodnight, CEO of the software giant SAS Institute Inc., stated, "Ninety-five percent of our assets drive out the gate every afternoon at five. I want them to come back in the morning. I need them to come back in the morning."[29]

When a firm identifies the sources of candidates, it employs appropriate methods for either internal or external recruitment to accomplish recruitment objectives. A candidate responds to the firm's recruitment efforts by submitting professional and personal data on either an application for employment form or a résumé, depending upon the company's policy. These two instruments are discussed in the next chapter.

Recruitment sources:
Where qualified candidates are located.

Recruitment methods:
Specific means used to attract potential employees to the firm.

Companies may discover that some recruitment sources and methods are superior to others for locating and attracting potential talent. For instance, one large equipment manufacturer determined that medium-sized, state-supported colleges and universities located in rural areas were good sources of potential managers. Other firms may arrive at different conclusions. To maximize recruiting effectiveness, utilizing recruitment sources and methods tailored to specific needs is vitally important (a topic discussed later in this chapter).

OBJECTIVE

Describe internal recruitment methods.

Internal Recruitment Methods

Management should be able to identify current employees who are capable of filling positions as they become available. Helpful tools used for internal recruitment include employee databases, job postings, and job bidding procedures. As mentioned in Chapter 4, employee databases permit organizations to determine whether current employees possess the qualifications for filling open positions. As a recruitment device, these databases have proven to be extremely valuable to organizations. Databases can be valuable in locating talent internally and supporting the concept of promotion from within.

Job Posting and Job Bidding

Job posting:

Procedure for informing employees that job openings exist.

Job bidding:

Procedure that permits employees who believe that they possess the required qualifications to apply for a posted position.

Job posting is a procedure for informing employees that job openings exist.

Job bidding is a procedure that permits employees who believe that they possess the required qualifications to apply for a posted job.

Hiring managers usually want to give internal candidates priority. Internal candidates already understand the company's culture and know its mission, goals, and priorities. Organizations need to be sure to treat internal candidates properly so they will not be discouraged or prompted to leave if they do not get the job.[30] The job posting and bidding procedures can help minimize the commonly heard complaint that insiders never hear of a job opening until it is filled. Typically, vacant jobs are posted before recruiting externally. A number of forums are available today to advise employees that a vacancy exists. In years past, jobs were literally posted on a bulletin board. Today, companies use the intranet, the Internet, or the company's online newsletter to post jobs. Some companies send out e-mails to selected managers and employees advising them that a vacancy exists. At PricewaterhouseCoopers, the job openings are posted on the company's intranet, and the firm's 123,000 employees are reminded to check the listings by e-mails and voice mails.[31]

Many organizations, including Whirlpool, BMW Manufacturing Co., Kellogg, Hyatt, and Hewlett-Packard, manage internal candidates with Web-based applications. Employees create profiles that detail their skills and interests for their next ideal position and are notified when such a position exists. FedEx's philosophy is that employees should be doing the kind of work they want to do. Its Website helps candidates identify their ideal job. Using drop-down lists, it prompts them to enter data about desires; location, type of work, and so forth; and to describe their skills. When jobs open, managers have instant access to these electronic résumés in which the candidates have specified what they can and want to do.

Now, if a worker does not know about a vacancy, it is because he or she did not check the internal posting system regularly. Yet, even with an online system, a job posting and bidding system has some negative features. For one thing, an effective system requires the expenditure of time, effort, and money. When bidders are unsuccessful, someone must explain to them why they were not selected. Management must choose the most qualified applicant or else the system will lack credibility. Of course, the chosen applicant must also be perceived by peers as the most qualified. Management may have little control over this factor. The key to success in this and many other managerial actions is the degree of trust and confidence that employees have in their supervisors and company. Still, complaints may occur, even in a well-designed and implemented system.

Employee Referrals

Employee referrals continue to be the way that top performers are identified.[32] Todd Davis, senior clinician recruitment consultant with California's largest physician group, said, "Peer referrals are the most powerful recruiting tool. When I get a referral in-house I know the candidate is going to have the skills and the interest, because a colleague has already made the contact."[33] Because of this, many companies are strengthening their employee referral program. These organizations have found that their employees can serve an important role in the recruitment process by actively soliciting applications from their friends and associates. Some firms even pay bonuses for successful referrals[34] (see Figure 5-3 for an example). Often those who are referred by a present employee are more productive.[35] "The most credible indicator of success is someone who worked with that person before," says David Temko, chief technology officer of Laszlo Systems, a software start-up based in San Francisco.[36] A note of caution should be observed in extensive use of employee referral. The new EEOC Compliance Manual, issued in 2006, updates guidance on the prohibition of discrimination under Title VII of the Civil Rights Act of 1964. The manual explicitly warns that recruiting only at select colleges or relying on word-of-mouth recruiting,

Figure 5-3 A Recruitment Poster

Trends & Innovations

Social Network Recruiting

U.S. News & World Report reported that 60.7 percent of job seekers found new jobs through networking.[37] "Social networking" is the business buzzword in recruiting these days. As previously mentioned, it is well known that networking is one of the best recruiting tools and numerous Websites have been developed to utilize social network recruiting.[38] Through social networking technology, databases are searched for contact names, interests, former employers, colleges attended, and other information to identify a network of acquaintances. Social networking technology refers to software and Web-based services that enable users to leverage their personal relationships for networking, hiring, employee referrals, and references.[39]

Social networking technology is also being used as a valuable recruiting tool. Social network recruiting permits employers to put their job postings in front of people who are employed rather than a lot of unemployed people. The system also helps the passive job seeker who is not actively looking for a job but would consider it if the right job came around. These individuals may be hesitant to post their résumé on a job board for fear that their search will be discovered by their company. Another advantage of social networking recruiting is the ability to get *reliable* reference checks. If a job applicant says that he or she worked for XYZ Company from 2000 to 2002, this can be verified by checking with other people who worked for XYZ Company during the same time.[40]

LinkedIn.com is an online network of more than 7 million experienced professionals from around the world, representing 130 industries.[41] As the company co-founder Konstantin Guericke said, "LinkedIn is a relationship jobs networking site that's meant to act a bit like an employee referral program."[42] Jill Pfefferbaum, with Website Priceline.com, has experimented with LinkedIn. "Finding candidates there," she says, "shows that they're innovative in ways of developing their own networks, which is particularly useful for business development."[43]

Social networking technology has attracted a few critics. Privacy advocates are alarmed by the prospect of software that churns through employees' e-mail.

Web Wisdom

Social Network Recruiting

https://www.linkedin.com/

LinkedIn is an online network.

5 OBJECTIVE

Explain external recruitment sources.

which includes employee referral programs, may generate applicant pools that do not reflect diversity in the labor market.[44]

Employee enlistment is a unique form of employee referral where every employee becomes a company recruiter. This is not the same as merely asking employees to refer friends to the company. The firm supplies employees with simple business cards that do not contain names or positions. Instead, these cards have a message similar to: "We are always looking for great _____. For additional information, log on to our Website." Employees then distribute the cards wherever they go, at parties, sports events, family gatherings, picnics, or the park. The purpose is to let people know that the company really does want people to apply.

External Recruitment Sources

At times, a firm must look beyond its own borders to find employees, particularly when expanding its workforce. External recruitment is needed to (1) fill entry-level jobs; (2) acquire skills not possessed by current employees; and (3) obtain employees with different backgrounds to provide a diversity of ideas. As Figure 5-4 shows, even with internal promotions, firms still have to fill entry-level jobs from the outside. Thus, after the president of a firm retires, a series of internal promotions follows. Ultimately, however, the firm has to recruit externally for the entry-level position of

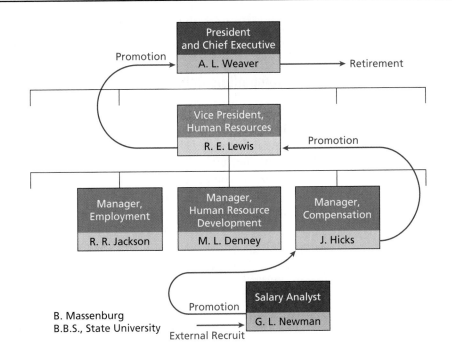

Figure 5-4 Internal Promotion and External Recruitment

salary analyst. If an outside candidate was selected for the president's position, the chain reaction of promotions from within would not have occurred. If no current employee has the desired qualifications, candidates may be attracted from a number of outside sources.

High Schools and Vocational Schools

Organizations concerned with recruiting clerical and other entry-level employees often depend on high schools and vocational schools. Many of these institutions have outstanding training programs for specific occupational skills, such as home appliance repair and small engine mechanics. Some companies work with schools to ensure a constant supply of trained individuals with specific job skills. In some areas, companies even loan employees to schools to assist in the training programs.

Community Colleges

Many community colleges are sensitive to the specific employment needs in their local labor markets and graduate highly sought-after students with marketable skills. Typically, community colleges have two-year programs designed for both a terminal education and preparation for a four-year university degree program. Many community colleges also have excellent mid-management programs combined with training for specific trades. In addition, career centers often provide a place for employers to contact students, thereby facilitating the recruitment process.

Colleges and Universities

Colleges and universities represent a major recruitment source for many organizations. Organizations typically find potential professional, technical, and management employees in these institutions. Placement directors, faculty, and administrators can be helpful to organizations in their search for recruits. Because on-campus recruitment is mutually beneficial, both employers and universities should take steps to develop and maintain close relationships.[45] When a company establishes recruitment programs with educational institutions, it should continue those programs year after year to maintain an effective relationship with each school. It is important that the firm knows the school and the school knows the firm.

Competitors in the Labor Market

A recent study by MetLife found that 22 percent of all employees had changed jobs over an 18-month period.[46] And the trend appears to be continuing since surveys reveal that some 50 percent to 75 percent of employees say they will leave their current companies once the job market starts picking up.[47] When recent experience is required, competitors and other firms in the same industry or geographic area may be the most important source of recruits. In fact, the most highly qualified applicants often come directly from competitors in the same labor market, as people typically do not enter the workforce loaded with experience and job skills. Hardly a day goes by that we do not read about an executive leaving one company for another, often at a huge salary increase. Although the ethics of corporate raiding may be debatable, it is apparent that competitors and other firms do serve as external sources of recruitment for high-quality talent. Even organizations that have policies of promotion from within occasionally look elsewhere to fill positions.

Smaller firms in particular look for employees trained by larger organizations that have greater developmental resources. For instance, an optical firm located in the Midwest believes that its own operation is not large enough to provide extensive training and development programs. Therefore, a person recruited by this firm for a significant management role is likely to have held at least two previous positions with a competitor.

Former Employees

At one time, when employees quit a company, their managers and peers tended to view them as being disloyal, ungrateful, and they were *punished* with no-return policies. A common attitude was that if you left your firm, you did not appreciate what the company had done for you. Today, smart employers try to get their best ex-employees to come back. At Ernst & Young, every former employee who left in good standing is assigned an Ernst & Young staffer who stays in contact. Currently, about 22 percent of hires are employees who had previously left the firm.[48] The advantage of tracking former employees is that the firm knows their strengths and weaknesses and the ex-employees know the company. Tracking, recruiting, and hiring a former employee (called boomeranging)[49] can be a tremendous benefit and can encourage others to stay

Ethical Dilemma

Unfair Advantage?

You are the vice president of human resources for a high-tech company that is competing for a major government project. You believe that one of your key competitors is ahead of you in project development and you would like to recruit some of its engineers who are knowledgeable about the project. You receive an anonymous e-mail that includes the names and phone numbers of key people involved in your competitor's project. If you use the information and are able to hire some of the competitor's key people, your company has a chance to beat the competitor and you will become a hero. If you do not use the information, your company may lose a great deal of money.

What would you do?[50]

with the firm.[51] It sends the message that things are not always greener on the other side of the fence.

Unemployed

The unemployed often provide a valuable source of recruits. Qualified applicants join the unemployment rolls every day for various reasons. Companies may downsize their operations, go out of business, or merge with other firms, leaving qualified workers without jobs. White-collar workers, automotive engineers, and production line workers released by General Motors and Ford Motor Co. could be in demand at companies like Toyota and Hyundai Motor. "It's bad news for them, but it's good news for us," says Kathy Parker, vice president of administrative services at Hyundai Motor America.[52] Employees are also fired sometimes merely because of personality differences with their bosses. Not infrequently, employees become frustrated with their jobs and quit.

Military Personnel

Operation Transition is a program that offers employers two vehicles for tapping into the military labor pool at no cost: the Defense Outplacement Referral System (DORS) and the Transition Bulletin Board (TBB). DORS is an automated résumé and referral system that allows employers to request résumés for open positions. The TBB is a bulletin board where companies can post jobs online. Job seekers at military bases around the world see these listings.

Hiring of former service members may make sense to many employers because many of these individuals typically have a proven work history and are flexible, motivated, and drug free. Another valuable characteristic of veterans is their goal and team orientation.[53] General Electric found an endless supply of talent in junior military officers. Many were graduates of U.S. military academies who had spent four to five years in the service. They were found to be hardworking, smart, and intense; they had leadership experience and were flexible. GE was so impressed with the quality of this recruitment source that it put in place a plan to hire 200 of these former officers each year.[54]

Self-Employed Workers

The self-employed worker may also be a good potential recruit. These individuals may be true entrepreneurs who are ingenious and creative. For many firms, these qualities are essential for continued competitiveness. Such individuals may constitute a source of applicants for any number of jobs requiring technical, professional, administrative, or entrepreneurial expertise within a firm.

6 OBJECTIVE

Describe online recruitment methods.

Online Recruitment Methods

Perhaps the biggest change in the way that organizations recruit has been the rise in the use of online recruiting.[55] Initiating contact with prospective employers by telephone or through the U.S. Postal Service has fast become an outmoded technique for candidates looking for a job. According to SHRM, human resource professionals believe the Internet offers the highest-quality job applicants of all media, and it provides the best recruiting return-on-investment.[56] As previously defined, *recruitment* is the process of attracting individuals on a timely basis, in sufficient numbers, and with appropriate qualifications, to apply for jobs with an organization. When online recruiting is involved, the definition itself does not change. However, words within the definition may take on different meanings. For example, *on a timely basis* may mean within a month or two with traditional recruitment methods. With online recruiting, *timely* may be within a week, a day, or almost immediately. Now consider the term *in sufficient numbers* and see the power of online recruiting. Large numbers of qualified applicants usually can be identified, especially in days of high unemployment. Online recruiting can effectively identify both active and passive applicants. Dissecting the definition still further, we deal with the term *appropriate qualifications*. With online recruiting, there are numerous ways to screen applicants to determine if they have the appropriate qualifications for the job. Finally, *applying for a job with the organization* is easy. Individuals can wake up at midnight, decide to change jobs, and have new résumés out for review before going back to bed. Likewise, companies can place a new job advertisement on their corporate career Website at any time.

Online recruiting has revolutionized the way companies recruit employees and job seekers search and apply for jobs.[57] The speed and expanded talent pool offered by online recruiting makes the recruitment process more efficient and cost-effective for both employer and job candidate. Online recruiting has several advantages over traditional recruiting methods. First, it costs less because online advertising is less expensive. Also, it is easy to post an ad and responses arrive faster and often in greater quantity. Further, the tasks of contacting candidates and processing résumés can be computerized, thereby reducing recruiting time. In addition, advertising online permits the company to search for a wider range of applicants.[58] Another benefit of online recruiting is that the recruiting cycle time, the time from when a vacancy exists until the position is filled, is shortened. Online recruiting permitted Dow Chemical to reduce a hiring cycle from 90 days to 34 and reduce cost per hire by 26 percent.[59]

Although online recruiting can be valuable, it does have certain potential limitations that must be taken into account. Because it is so easy for a person to apply for a job online, processes must be in place to filter out those who do not meet minimum qualifications.[60] Also, there is more competition for qualified employees from small and medium, as well as global, companies. Smaller companies can reach out to applicants from all parts of the country, even globally. Finally, confidentiality could be a problem, since all of the applicant's information is on one or more Websites, which could be violated by hackers.

Unfortunately, online recruiting is changing so fast that it is virtually impossible to keep up to date. New Websites are constantly being created, sites are merging, sites are expanding, and others are being dissolved. Even as this edition was being prepared, numerous Websites changed, and others simply disappeared for no apparent reason. Various recruitment methods involving online recruiting are next discussed.

Internet Recruiter

The **Internet recruiter**, also called *cyber recruiter*, is a person whose primary responsibility is to use the Internet in the recruitment process.

Most companies currently post jobs on their organization's Website. Individuals must be in place to monitor and coordinate these activities. The more companies recruit on the Internet, the greater the need for Internet recruiters. Currently, high-tech firms have the greatest needs, and Internet recruiters can sometimes be quite aggressive. Dan Harris, CEO and senior trainer at Recruiters Dream Network, in Arlington, Texas, says, "Good Internet recruiters can match a potential candidate to a position and present it as a dream job. If the recruiter doesn't come across like a used-car salesman, a reasonable person will listen to a reasonable offer."[61]

At Texas Instruments (TI) once you click the "Submit Your Résumé" button on its corporate career Website, TI has a cyber recruiting team that actually reads the résumés. They read a résumé and do a quick comparison with the positions currently open. Depending upon the number of résumés received, it is possible that someone from TI will contact an applicant the same day. If a strong match to one of the openings exists, they will either call or e-mail the applicant to establish contact. Once

HR
Web Wisdom
HR Internet Guides

www.hr-guide.com

This Website contains links to other Internet-based resources for topics such as recruitment, selection, and EEO.

Internet recruiter:
Person whose primary responsibility is to use the Internet in the recruitment process (also called cyber recruiter).

contact is established, an applicant will likely talk by phone to a recruiter who will ask more questions. Then, the applicant might talk to the program manager or someone else in the department with the job opening. Once a match is determined, the applicant may be invited to visit TI. However, the company can often work with applicants over the phone or use e-mail to make a hiring decision. Everything is done to facilitate the hiring process. TI could hire a person within days or a couple of weeks after receiving a résumé.

Virtual Job Fair

Virtual job fair:
Online recruiting method engaged in by a single employer or group of employers to attract a large number of applicants.

A **virtual job fair** is an online recruiting method engaged in by a single employer or group of employers to attract a large number of applicants.

An online job fair was held for students from 22 colleges and universities throughout Maine. The event allowed students to visit virtual employer booths and submit their résumés online 24 hours a day, seven days a week. It opened up a larger job market to Maine students and graduates. For employers, the virtual job fair reveals a wider range of students than might attend a live fair. "This venue is less expensive for employers and more convenient for students," said Sherry Treworgy, associate director of the Career Center at the University of Maine.[62]

Corporate Career Websites

Corporate career Websites:
Job sites accessible from a company homepage that list available company positions and provide a way for applicants to apply for specific jobs.

Corporate career Websites are job sites accessible from a company homepage that list the company positions available, providing a way for applicants to apply for specific jobs.

They have become a major resource for both job seekers and companies seeking new employees. Today, many firms have established career portals on their corporate Websites. Establishing a career portal starts out by setting up a link on the corporate Website, typically on the homepage, labeled *careers* or *jobs*. Clicking that link transports visitors into the recruiting application, which often has the same look and feel of the corporate Website.[63] Through this link individuals are able to apply for a job with the company.

An excellence award was even established for the top career Websites. In Electronic Recruiting Exchange's First Annual ER Excellence Awards, the top three sites were Enterprise Rent-A-Car, Federated Department Stores, and Whirlpool Corporation.[64] Go to the homepage of Enterprise Rent-A-Car (www.enterprisealive.com) and notice *apply now* is easy to see on the left-hand side of the homepage. Clicking *apply now* takes you to a site that looks very similar to the homepage, but it starts the application process.

A career Website should be upbeat and informative. It should be used as a selling device that promotes the company to prospective job candidates. Writing effective recruitment ads on the Internet is different from the short, one-inch-column ads in the Sunday newspaper. The Internet provides enough space to fully describe the job, location, and company. A good Website should provide a feeling of the kind of corporate culture that exists within the company.[65] Steve Pollock, president of WetFeet Inc., a San Francisco recruitment technology provider, says, "A good website should look different from every other site. It has to capture the unique experience that individual will have at that company. It's like looking at cars; you want them all to have certain standard features, but expect them to be very different in the experience they offer."[66]

Weblogs (blogs for short)

Weblogs, or *blogs*, have changed the ways in which individuals access information.[67] Google or a blog search engine such as Technorati.com can be used. All a person has to do is type in a key phrase like *marketing jobs*.[68] The blogs themselves make it pretty easy to find them, with names like Defensejobs.com, AttorneyJobs.com, and

SalesJobs.com. Google launched blogsearch.google.com, a new indexing tool that points to the latest buzz on any keyword or topic.[69] Some employers and employment agencies have discovered that bloging is a way to do detailed and stealthy background checks.[70] Information of all kinds is available, such as age, martial status, the value of your house, college pranks a person would like to forget, liens, bankruptcies, political affiliations, and the names and ages of your children.[71] Since the individual personally put the information on the Internet, no disclosure is required.

General Employment Websites

Firms utilize employment Websites by typing in key job criteria, skills, and experience, and indicating their geographic location. They next click *Search for Candidates* and in seconds have a ranked list of résumés from candidates who match the firm's requirements. The number of sites seems to expand and contract daily. Therefore, only the most widely recognized general employment Websites, Monster.com, HotJobs.com, and CareerBuilder.com, will be briefly discussed.

Monster.com. The largest employment Website is Monster.com.[72] Information to job seekers such as résumé tips, interview tips, salary information, and networking information is available on the site. One job posting and résumé search for a company for one month with a 100-mile radius costs $1,100.[73]

HotJobs.com. HotJobs.com, a subsidiary of Yahoo!, is a recruiting solutions and software company. Revenue is generated from the fees charged to employers but job seekers are not charged. HotJobs users can search for jobs in several ways: by keyword, job category, location, experience level, or a combination of these choices. Users can create their very own personalized HotJobs to help them organize their job search. Job seekers can block some or all of HotJobs' member companies from viewing a résumé. Site users can also calculate ideal salaries, research plans, and stock options.[74]

CareerBuilder.com. Gannett Co., Inc. has teamed with Knight Ridder and Tribune Company as an equal partner of CareerBuilder.com. With access to 130 newspapers and 400 job sites, CareerBuilder.com has the recruitment industry covered nationwide.[75] Careerbuilder.com offers a confidential personal search agent that will hunt for job opportunities in expressed areas of interest and automatically e-mail them to job seekers. The site provides online career assessment, coaching for interviews, and tips for salary negotiations. CareerBuilder contains 13 million résumés and caters to more than 31,000 employers.[76]

NACElink

NACElink:
National, Web-based system for recruiting college students for all types of employment such as full-time, part-time, internship, co-op, work-study, and alumni.

NACElink is a national, Web-based system for recruiting college students for all types of employment, such as full-time, part-time, internship, co-op, work-study, and alumni.

Organizations desiring to recruit recent college graduates can use NACElink; the result of an alliance between two nonprofit associations—the National Association of Colleges and Employers (NACE) and DirectEmployers Association, Inc.—and an initial collaborating group of career centers. Presently there are 543 schools using the NACElink system. The system includes three components: job posting résumé database, and interview scheduling.[77] It is available to employers to post jobs and search for students and new graduates in several ways.

Niche Sites

Sites that specialize by industry and level of employment are becoming much more common.

Niche sites:

Websites that cater to a specific profession.

Niche sites are Websites that cater to a specific profession; a few of these sites will be identified next.

There seems to be a site for virtually everyone. A few catchy ones include:

- cfo.com (a comprehensive online resource center for senior finance executives).
- accountantsworld.com (an online recruiting service that provides CPA firms with assistance in locating qualified employees).
- careerjournal.com (content comes from the editorial resources of the *Wall Street Journal*. Positions featured include senior and general management, sales, marketing, finance, technology, and a range of related fields).
- dice.com (a leading provider of online recruiting services for technology professionals).
- internships.wetfeet.com (employers who are exclusively looking for interns).
- hospitalsoup.com (global hospital careers).
- joyjobs.com (international employment for teachers).
- techjobbank.com (focuses on the recruiting needs of the technology companies).
- coolworks.com (find seasonal job or career in places such as Yellowstone, Yosemite, or other national parks).
- sixfigurejobs.com (provides executives and experienced professionals with access to some of the most exclusive executive jobs, executive recruiters, and career management tools available).
- TVjobs.com (jobs in broadcasting).
- layover.com (jobs in trucking).
- monstertrak.com (job listings and résumé service that target college students and alumni).
- mfgjobs.com (created exclusively for manufacturing and engineering professionals).
- JobsInLogistics.com (dedicated to logistics jobs and logistics careers).

A niche site is even available for professors who desire to change jobs. Formerly, college and university professors had to go to their library and thumb through the many pages of *The Chronicle of Higher Education* to hunt for a job. Now, sitting in the comfort of their own home they can enter (www.chronicle.com/) *The Chronicle of Higher Education* Website. All the jobs listed with the *Chronicle* are available to view free. Each position announcement has a hot link to a university homepage where additional information can be obtained. The universities pay the fees.

Contract Workers' Sites

Earlier, contract workers were mentioned as part of the contingent workforce as an alternative to recruitment. Sites are available to assist this segment of the workforce. Professionals searching for freelance work turn to Websites that let them market themselves globally. Now, specialized Websites let workers advertise their skills, set their price, and pick an employer. Three such sites are listed below:

- Freelance.com is a company that offers to clients the services of the most talented and carefully selected freelancers.

- AllFreelanceWork.com is a central information base for free-lancers to find everything that they could need all in one place.
- Guru.com is an online marketplace for freelance talent. Through its free service, employers find top freelance and contract talent locally, nationally, or globally.

Hourly Workers' Job Sites

After years of focusing primarily on professionals and their prospective employers, the big general employment job sites are now attracting blue-collar and service workers. The major boards are now listing hourly workers' applications. According to Monster.com CEO Andrew McKelvey, of the 50,000 résumés it receives each day, more than half come from blue-collar workers.[78] Sites such as Monster.com provide an attractive new base of activity because more and more blue-collar workers are using the Internet.

Traditionally, there have been major differences between the ways hourly and salaried workers look for jobs. Most hourly workers pursue jobs by filling out applications rather than creating and sending out résumés. So sites allow job seekers to build an application that can be viewed by employers. Recognizing that some hourly workers do not have computer access, they have set up phone-based services to accept applications. Some job boards have bilingual call center operators who can help job applicants through the process.[79]

Careerbuilder.com enables skilled and hourly workers to apply for hourly jobs by indicating their work preferences, education, and experience. Careerbuilder.com provides Spanish-speaking applicants the ability to gain quick and easy access to employers nationwide. With the bilingual job search center, Hispanics define their job search criteria by company, job type, industry, and city, and receive job postings matching these criteria in Spanish. SnagAJob.com is a large job site for part-time and full-time hourly jobs, recording more than 55 million annual job searches for companies hiring nonexempt employees. Job seekers complete their profile once and then apply to multiple jobs online.[80]

HR Internet Guides

www.hr-guide.com

This Website contains links to other Internet-based resources for topics such as recruitment, selection, and EEO.

 OBJECTIVE

Identify traditional external recruitment methods.

Traditional External Recruitment Methods

Although online recruiting has greatly impacted how recruiting is accomplished, traditional methods continue to be used. Even so, the Internet has made its inroads into the traditional external recruitment methods. Therefore, as the various traditional recruiting methods are discussed, the manner in which the Internet has impacted them will also be discussed.

Media Advertising

Advertising communicates the firm's employment needs to the public through media such as newspapers, trade journals, radio, television, and billboards. The firm's previous experience with various media should suggest the most effective approach for specific types of jobs. Although few individuals base their decision to change jobs on advertising, an ad creates awareness, generates interest, and encourages a prospect to seek more information about the firm and the job opportunities that it provides. A traditional common form of advertising that provides broad coverage at a relatively low cost is the newspaper ad.[81] The firm should attempt to appeal to the self-interest of prospective employees, emphasizing the job's unique qualities. The ad must tell potential employees why they should be interested in that particular job and organization. The message should also indicate how an applicant is to respond: apply in person, by telephone, by mail, or submit a résumé by fax or e-mail.

Recently, the use of newspaper advertising has declined because of online recruiting. Andrew McKelvey, the CEO of Monster.com, suggested the *Fortune* 1000, the companies with at least 2,500 employees, have stopped advertising with the newspapers. He believes that the newspapers were slow in responding and gives the example of the *Sunday Boston Globe*. In 2000 it had around 100 pages of help-wanted classifieds; now it has fewer than 25.[82] Possibly the cause of this decline is the fact that the average cost for an online job advertisement is $377 compared to $3,295 for a newspaper recruitment ad.[83]

Certain media attract audiences that are more homogeneous in terms of employment skills, education, and orientation. Advertisements placed in such publications as the *Wall Street Journal* relate primarily to managerial, professional, and technical positions. The readers of these publications are generally individuals qualified for many of the positions advertised. Focusing on a specific labor market minimizes the likelihood of receiving marginally qualified or even totally unqualified applicants. Like most professional publications, jobs that are advertised in the paper copy of the *Journal* are also available on the publication's Website. Trade journals are also widely utilized.

Qualified prospects who read job ads in newspapers and professional and trade journals may not be so dissatisfied with their present jobs that they will pursue opportunities advertised. Therefore, in high-demand situations, a firm needs to consider all available media resources. Such resources include radio, billboards, and television. These methods are likely to be more expensive than newspapers or journals, but, in specific situations, they may prove successful. For instance, a regional medical center used billboards effectively to attract registered nurses. One large manufacturing firm had considerable success in advertising for production trainees by means of spot advertisements on the radio. A large electronics firm used television to attract experienced engineers when it opened a new facility and needed more engineers immediately. Thus, in situations where hiring needs are urgent, television and radio may provide good results even though these media may not be sufficient by themselves. Broadcast messages can let people know that an organization is seeking recruits. A primary limitation is the amount of information they can transmit.

Employment Agencies

Employment agency:
Organization that helps firms recruit employees and at the same time aids individuals in their attempt to locate jobs.

An **employment agency** is an organization that helps firms recruit employees and at the same time aids individuals in their attempt to locate jobs.

These agencies perform recruitment and selection functions that have proven quite beneficial to many organizations.

Private Employment Agencies. Private employment agencies, often called *head hunters*,[84] are best known for recruiting white-collar employees and offer an important service in bringing qualified applicants and open positions together. However, firms utilize private employment agencies for virtually every type of position. Today, employment agencies often specialize in filling a particular niche in the job market. Engineering is an example of an area where companies call upon niche employment agencies.[85]

Neither the organization nor the job applicant should overlook the use of private employment agencies. The one-time fees that some agencies charge often turn off candidates, although many private employment agencies deal primarily with firms that pay the fees. Employment agencies often have their own Websites to show prospective employees the array of jobs that are available through their agency.

Public Employment Agencies. Public employment agencies, operated by each state, receive overall policy direction from the U.S. Employment Service. Public employment agencies have become increasingly involved in matching people with technical, professional, and managerial positions. Some use computerized job-matching systems to aid in the recruitment process, and they provide their services without charge to either the employer or the prospective employee.

America's Job Bank is a partnership between the U.S. Department of Labor and the state-operated Public Employment Service (http://www.ajb.dni.us/). It is the largest online source for national and international employment. It offers job posting for employers and résumé posting and job searching by occupation, keyword, and zip code for job hunters.

Recruiters

Recruiters most commonly focus on technical and vocational schools, community colleges, colleges, and universities. The key contact for recruiters on college and university campuses is often the student placement director. This administrator is in an excellent position to arrange interviews with students possessing the qualifications desired by the firm. Placement services help organizations utilize their recruiters efficiently. They identify qualified candidates, schedule interviews, and provide suitable rooms for interviews.

The company recruiter plays a vital role in attracting applicants. The interviewee often perceives the recruiter's actions as a reflection of the character of the firm. If the recruiter is dull, the interviewee may think the company is dull; if the recruiter is apathetic, discourteous, or vulgar, the interviewee may well attribute all these negative characteristics to the firm. Recruiters must always be aware of the image they present at the screening interview because it makes a lasting impression. Recruitment success comes down to good personal selling, appealing to the candidate's priorities, and addressing his or her concerns. The recruiter should underscore the job's opportunities and keep the lines of communication open.

Some firms are using videoconferencing with equipment at both corporate headquarters and on college campuses. Recruiters can communicate with college career counselors and interview students through a videoconferencing system without leaving the office.

Job Fairs

Job fair:
Recruiting method engaged in by a single employer or group of employers to attract a large number of applicants to one location for interviews.

A **job fair** is a recruiting method engaged in by a single employer or group of employers to attract a large number of applicants to one location for interviews.

From an employer's viewpoint, a primary advantage of job fairs is the opportunity to meet a large number of candidates in a short time. Conversely, applicants may have convenient access to a number of employers. As a recruitment method, job fairs offer the potential for a much lower cost per hire than traditional approaches.[86] Job fairs are often organized by universities to assist their students in obtaining jobs. Here, employers from many organizations meet at a single point on the campus. Students from disciplines from across the university are represented. Both employers and students can meet to answer questions and drop off a résumé.

At times job fairs are tailored to specific types of individuals. At a Tucson, Arizona, job fair, the event was designed to bring together senior citizens and companies looking to hire them, as well as offer assistance to those seeking to improve their job skills as a first step toward employment. The job fair attracted two dozen companies seeking to fill positions for everything from teachers' aides to bank tellers to tour bus drivers and call-center staff.[87] Job fairs are also held to bring together service members and companies with openings to fill. More than 200,000 people leave the military each year. Dave Suszko, a retired U.S. Air Force recruiter and director of candidate services for MilitaryStars, says, "The military labor market is [the] second largest renewable labor pool in the nation."[88]

Internships

An **internship** is a special form of recruitment that involves placing a student in a temporary job with no obligation either by the company to hire the student permanently or by the student to accept a permanent position with the firm following graduation.

An internship typically involves a temporary job for the summer months or a part-time job during the school year. It may also take the form of working full-time one semester and going to school full-time the next. Many employers today are using the internship as a pipeline to talent. In fact, in a recent study by the National Association of Colleges and Employers, employers rated internships as one of the most effective ways to attract and hire college graduates.[89] Employers are able to *try out* future employees prior to making a job offer.[90] If the trial period proves unsuccessful, there is no obligation on either side.

During the internship, the student gets to view business practices firsthand. At the same time, the intern contributes to the firm by performing needed tasks. In addition to other benefits, internships provide opportunities for students to bridge the gap from business theory to practice. Through this relationship, a student can determine whether a company would be a desirable employer. Similarly, having a relatively lengthy time to observe the student's job performance, the firm can make a better judgment regarding the person's qualifications. Students with internship and co-op experience are often able to find jobs more easily and they progress much further and faster in the business world than those without.

Currently, students find out about many internship programs by using the Internet. Numerous job sites focus on assisting students in obtaining internships.

Executive Search Firms

Executive search firms are organizations used by some firms to locate experienced professionals and executives when other sources prove inadequate. It has been estimated that executive search firms handle more than half of all senior appointments.[91] The typical placement fee for an executive search is 33 percent of the executive's first-year pay. At one time, there was a bias against executive search firms because they were thought to be raiders. However, in time, it became apparent that bringing in outside talent was often healthy and a means to add new capabilities for the firm. The key benefit of executive search firms is the targeting of ideal candidates. In addition, the search firm can find those not actively looking for a job. Searches now often take weeks instead of months.

An executive search firm's representatives often visit the client's offices and interview the company's management. This enables them to gain a clear understanding of the company's goals and the job qualifications required. After obtaining this information, they contact and interview potential candidates, check references, and refer the best-qualified person to the client for the selection decision. Search firms maintain databases of résumés for this process. Other sources used include networking contacts, files from previous searches, specialized directories, personal calls, previous clients, colleagues, and unsolicited résumés. The search firm's task is to present candidates that are eminently qualified to do the job and it is the company's decision whom to hire.

The relationship between a client company and a search firm should be based on mutual trust and understanding. Both parties gain most from their relationship when they interact often and maintain good communication. To ensure success, the search firm must understand in detail the nature of the client's operations, the responsibilities of the open position, and the client's corporate culture. Similarly, the client must understand the search process; work with the consultant; and provide continuous, honest feedback.

There are two types of executive search firms: contingency and retained.

Internship:
Special form of recruitment that involves placing a student in a temporary job with no obligation either by the company to hire the student permanently or by the student to accept a permanent position with the firm following graduation.

Internship Websites

http://www.cofc.edu/~career/internshipwebsites.html

Numerous internship Websites are provided.

Contingency search firms:
Executive search firm that receives fees only upon successful placement of a candidate in a job opening.

Retained search firms:
Executive search firm considered as consultants to their client organizations, serving on an exclusive contractual basis; typically recruit top business executives.

Contingency Search Firms. **Contingency search firms** receive fees only upon successful placement of a candidate in a job opening.

The search firm's fee is generally a percentage of the individual's compensation for the first year. The client pays expenses, as well as the fee. A contingency recruiter goes to work when there is an urgent need to fill a position, an opening exists for a difficult position, or when a hiring executive wants to know about top-notch talent as those people surface, regardless of whether there is an opening.

Retained Search Firms. **Retained search firms** are considered consultants to their client organizations, serving on an exclusive contractual basis, and typically recruit top business executives.

The executive search industry has evolved from a basic recruitment service to a highly sophisticated profession serving a greatly expanded role. These firms assist organizations in determining their human resource needs, establishing compensation packages, and revising organizational structures.

Professional Associations

Virtually every professional group publishes a journal that is widely read by its members. Many professional associations in business areas including finance, marketing, accounting, and human resources provide recruitment and placement services for their members. Jobs advertised are placed in the journal in hard copy and also advertised on the professional group's Website.

The Society for Human Resource Management, for example, operates a job referral service for members seeking new positions and employers with positions to fill. SHRM has a first-rate Website for human resource professionals. At the homepage, click "HR Careers." This will take you to a site where a person is identified as a job seeker or employer. Clicking "HR Jobs' Jobseeker Center" takes you to a board to do a "Quick Search Jobs" and you can do so by title and location. Clicking one will provide you with a position description.[92] Most national professional associations operate their career sites in much the same manner.

Unsolicited Applicants

In Chapter 1 the importance of a company having a positive brand was stressed. If an organization has the reputation of being a good place to work, it may be able to attract qualified prospects even without extensive recruitment efforts. Acting on their own initiative, well-qualified workers may seek out a specific company to apply for a job. Unsolicited applicants who apply because they are favorably impressed with the firm's reputation often prove to be valuable employees. In the Internet age, applicants can go to the firm's corporate career Website and *walk in* by making an application online.

Open Houses

Open houses are a valuable recruiting tool, especially during days of low unemployment. Here, firms pair potential hires and recruiters in a warm, casual environment that encourages on-the-spot job offers. Open houses are cheaper and faster than hiring through recruitment agencies, and they are also more popular than job fairs. There are pros and cons to holding a truly *open* house. If the event is open, it may draw a large turnout, but it also may attract a number of unqualified candidates. Some companies prefer to control the types of candidates they host, and so they conduct invitation-only sessions. In this scenario, someone screens résumés in response to ads, then invites only pre-selected candidates. Advertising of open houses may be through both conventional media and the Internet, where a firm might feature its open house on its homepage.

Event Recruiting

Event recruiting involves having recruiters go to events that individuals the company is seeking attend.

Cisco Systems pioneered event recruiting as a recruitment approach and it has been successful. In the case of programmers in the Silicon Valley, the choice spots have been microbreweries, marathons, and bike races. Companies that participate in these events become involved in some way that promotes their name and cause. For example, they might sponsor or co-sponsor an event, pass out refreshments, and give away prizes. Individuals should know that the company is recruiting and the type of workers it seeks.

Event recruiting gives a company the opportunity to reflect its image. For example, Cisco quickly developed the reputation as the company with *cool* recruiters and, therefore, it must be a *cool* place to work. Everyone was aware of it. Even if a participant was not interested, he or she probably knew someone who was. It became obvious to lots of people that companies such as IBM and Hewlett-Packard were not there, and therefore might not be *cool* places to work. And, *cool* is big for some employees who want an atmosphere of youth, excitement, growth, and perhaps most of all, permission to experiment and make mistakes.[93]

Sign-on Bonuses

Some firms are following the sports industry practice of offering sign-on bonuses to high-demand prospects. For select jobs in select industries, signing bonuses appear to be quite popular. Employers use them to attract top talent, particularly within high-demand fields such as health care, sales, marketing, accounting, and finance.[94] Typical signing bonuses for middle managers and professionals ranges from 5 percent to 10 percent of the base salary.[95] Some highly demanded executives have been able to receive a signing bonus equal to up to 100 percent of salary. Earl Hesterberg, the CEO of Group 1 Automotive Inc., collected a $1 million bonus because he stayed for one year. His annual salary was $1 million.[96]

A Towers Perrin survey indicated that more than 56 percent of employers use sign-on bonuses in all employee categories except clerical staff. Cross-country truck drivers are in high demand so companies such as Paschall Truck Lines ($7,000) and U.S. Xpress ($5,000) have been offering signing bonuses.[97] Cedars Siani Medical Center in Los Angeles offers medical coders/billers a signing bonus of up to $5,000.[98] When hurricanes hit the Gulf Coast in 2005, employers had a difficult time finding workers because a large number of people were displaced. Burger King, an organization that normally employed minimum wage workers, offered a $1,500 bonus.

High-Tech Competitions

Google has a unique way to get individuals interested in applying for technical positions. It sponsors an annual computer programming competition where students from around the world enter and the winners of the competition are sure to be noticed. Recently, Warsaw University student Marek Cygan won the $10,000 grand prize by beating 14,500 competitors from 32 countries in the Code Jam. "We've hired some people through the Google Code Jam, and we're continually exploring opportunities to find brighter, talented engineers to join our team," a Google spokeswoman stated. Cygan got noticed through participating in the Code Jam and will certainly get an interview.[99]

Google is not the only company that uses games as a recruiting tool. TopCoder is a Glastonbury, Connecticut, company that creates software coding competitions. Internet advertising firm DoubleClick hired TopCoder to run a software coding competition contest between students from Columbia University and New York

University. TopCoder identified about 100 programmers to participate in this software competition, and 10 made it to the final round. DoubleClick Chief Information Officer Mok Choe says the company has already hired a few of the winners. "We can filter out the cream of the crop," says Choe.[100]

8   OBJECTIVE

Describe an applicant tracking system.

Applicant tracking system (ATS):
Software application designed to help an enterprise recruit employees more efficiently.

Applicant Tracking System

An **applicant tracking system (ATS)** is a software application designed to help an enterprise recruit employees more efficiently.

Current systems enable human resource and line managers to oversee the entire process, from screening résumés and spotting qualified candidates to conducting personality and skills tests and handling background checks. It allows companies to compile job applications electronically, to more quickly amass candidates, set up interviews, and get new hires on board.[101] An ATS can be used to post job openings on a corporate Website or job board and generate interview requests to potential candidates by e-mail. Other features may include individual applicant tracking, requisition tracking, automated résumé ranking, customized input forms, prescreening questions and response tracking, and multilingual capabilities. In most cases, the goal is not merely to reduce costs but also to speed up the hiring process and find people who fit an organization's success profile. Applicant tracking systems continue to be enhanced to make recruiters more efficient and extend sourcing into the global market.[102] Leading applicant tracking system software providers include Recrutimax, Taleo, and Kenexa.[103]

Going Paperless at Continental Airlines

Recently, Continental Airlines announced that it would move into the international markets and outlined a plan to expand to five continents. The company went from an antiquated, labor-intensive domestic recruiting process to a global, Web-enabled and paperless approach that allows it to staff any location worldwide with half the number of recruiters and at half the cost of the old system in only two months. Under the old system, the airline advertised jobs in U.S. newspapers and then flew recruiters to interview candidates at hotels in major cities. "We had nine full-time employees just scanning in paper résumés or cleaning electronic résumés," recalls Kimberly Paul, manager of global recruiting. iCIMS's iRecruiter was chosen to develop a Web-based operation so that candidates and recruiters could access the system from any of Continental's international flight destinations while still maintaining the company's unique screening and interviewing procedures.[104] Continental no longer uses newspaper advertising in the United States, and uses very little elsewhere. Successful U.S. candidates are flown into Houston, Texas, or Newark, New Jersey, for interviews with a recruiting staff that no longer travels. "I'm not a technical expert, but I was able to train our recruiters to use iRecruiter in a matter of hours," Paul says. Now Continental handles 80,000 applications a year with a very lean staff. Continental began 10 new international destinations in 2005 and used the new technology to recruit 3,200 new hires for locations from Argentina to India.[105]

When Continental enters a new market, it announces the launch in the local media. "This drives people to the Website, where we have posted the open positions," Paul says. "Résumés arrive electronically in Houston, and we e-mail the candidates information for on-site interviews." The Web-based system's automatic screening process culls unqualified candidates before they proceed to the application. Continental's flight attendant candidates, for example, move through 41 questions before completing the formal application.[106]

Significant cost savings have been derived from bringing recruits to a central location, which eliminated the need for local recruiters. Continental's global hiring is located at its Houston headquarters. Colin Day, president and CEO of iCIMS, which produces iRecruiter, said, "The automated global system is far more efficient and allows companies to keep a much leaner staff than they would if they attempted to roll out a global campaign with recruiters. Domestically, companies have been able to cut staff by 50 percent, and the same applies globally."[107]

Applicant tracking systems have made it easier to track EEO data. Web systems also allow companies to track source effectiveness, time to hire, cost per hire, and customized effectiveness measures. "Companies can decide how to advertise for positions and then test different sources and see immediate results for each source," Day says. "The systems track employee performance, so quality of hire can be tracked against expectations. Companies are right on the cusp of adding detailed quality-of-hire metrics."[108]

OBJECTIVE

Describe how recruitment methods and sources are tailored to each other.

Tailoring Recruitment Methods to Sources

Because each organization is unique, so are the needed types and qualifications of workers to fill positions.[109] Thus, to be successful, a firm must tailor its recruitment sources and methods to its specific needs.

Figure 5-5 shows a matrix that depicts sources and methods of recruitment for an information systems manager. Managers must first identify the *source* (where prospective employees are located) before choosing the *methods* (how to attract them). Suppose, for example, that a large firm has an immediate need for an experienced information technology (IT) manager and no one within the firm has these qualifications. It is likely that other firms, possibly competitors, employ such individuals. After considering the recruitment source, the recruiter must then choose the method (or methods) of recruitment that offers the best prospects for attracting qualified candidates. Perhaps it would be appropriate to advertise the job in the classified section of the *Wall Street Journal* and use online recruiting. Alternatively, an executive search firm or a private employment agency may serve as viable options. In addition, the recruiter may attend meetings of professional information technology associations. One or more of these methods will likely yield a pool of qualified applicants.

External Resources	External Methods	Advertising	Private and public employment agencies	Recruiters	Special events	Internships	Executive search firms	Professional associations	Employee referrals	Unsolicited walk-in applicants	Open houses	Event recruiting	Virtual job fairs	Sign-on bonuses
High schools														
Vocational schools														
Community colleges														
Colleges and universities														
Competitors and other firms		X	X				X	X						
Unemployed														
Self-employed														

Figure 5-5 Methods and Sources of Recruitment for an Information Technology Manager

In another scenario, consider a firm's need for 20 entry-level machine operators, whom the firm is willing to train. High schools and vocational schools would probably be good recruitment sources. Methods of recruitment might include newspaper ads, public employment agencies, recruiters, visiting vocational schools, and employee referrals.

OBJECTIVE

Explain recruitment for diversity.

Recruitment for Diversity

According to a recent survey, 82 percent of ethnically diverse online job seekers believe that a company's efforts in diversity recruiting reflect the organization's overall commitment to creating a diverse workforce.[110] Equal opportunity legislation outlaws discrimination in employment based on race, religion, sex, color, national origin, age, disability, and other factors. A few firms abide by these laws solely to avoid the legal consequences of violating them. Most, however, recognize the inherent advantages of heterogeneous groups such as greater creativity and the ability to help a firm expand its customer base. Global competition mandates that firms be innovative. Therefore, organizations actively engage in acquiring a workforce that reflects society and helps the company expand into untapped markets. Organizations that seek to develop a diverse workforce need to use recruitment practices that ensure women, minorities, and those with disabilities are included in their recruitment planning. Firms that are successful in diversity recruitment find that inclusiveness in the workplace quickly becomes self-perpetuating.

Analysis of Recruitment Procedures

To ensure that its recruitment program is diversity oriented, a firm should analyze its recruitment procedures. In identifying sources of possible discrimination, a helpful approach is to develop a *record of applicant flow* or, if feasible, an automated applicant tracking system, as previously described. If the firm has a discriminatory history or operates under an affirmative action program, this record may be mandatory. An applicant flow record includes personal and job-related data concerning each applicant. It indicates whether the firm made a job offer and, if not, an explanation of the decision. Such records enable the organization to analyze its recruitment and selection practices and take corrective action when necessary.

Utilization of Minorities, Women, and Individuals with Disabilities

It is imperative that all recruiters receive training in the use of objective, job-related standards. These individuals occupy a unique position in terms of encouraging or discouraging minorities, women, and the disabled to apply for jobs. Using minorities, women, and individuals with disabilities in key recruitment activities, such as visiting schools and colleges and participating in career days, can pay real dividends. They also are in an excellent position to participate in recruitment planning and can effectively serve as referral sources. Pictures of minorities, women, and disabled employees in help-wanted advertisements and company brochures give credibility to the message, "We are an equal opportunity employer."

Advertising

Business firms emphasize diversity in their advertisements and focus on attracting employees from divergent arenas. This approach augments programs, such as employee referrals, by building internal morale and promoting the company culture.

Some approaches that could encourage diversity:

- Ensuring that the content of advertisements does not indicate preference for any race, gender, or age, or that these factors are a qualification for the job.
- Utilizing media directed toward minorities, such as appropriate radio stations.
- Emphasizing the intent to recruit without regard to race, gender, or disabled status by placing appropriate statements in job ads. A statement such as "We are an Equal Opportunity Employer" might be placed on a newspaper ad.

Employment Agencies

An organization should emphasize its nondiscriminatory recruitment practices when utilizing employment agencies. Even when a business works with private agencies, also covered under Title VII, it is a good idea to list jobs at every level with the state employment service. These agencies can provide valuable assistance to organizations seeking to fulfill diversity goals. In addition, firms should contact agencies and consultant firms that specialize in minority and women applicants.

People with Disabilities

The Social Security Administration (SSA) manages the two largest federal disability benefit programs and made approximately $75 billion in payments to about 8 million beneficiaries (ages 18 through 64) in 2003. Congress passed the Ticket to Work and Work Incentives Improvement Act of 1999 to create a Ticket to Work and Self-Sufficiency Program (the *Ticket* program). The program's goals are to expand the availability of service providers and to help enable beneficiaries to return to work, become self-sufficient, and stop receiving disability benefit payments. Eligible beneficiaries can use their *tickets* as vouchers to request vocational rehabilitation, employment, or other support services.[111] The program also has incentives for key stakeholders. Employers get up to $2,500 per hire in first-year tax credits. SSDI and SSI claimants receive continued medical benefits for up to 8.5 years. They receive a 9-month trial employment period with continuing disability benefits. They also get expedited reinstatement of disability benefits if they are unable to continue to work. Employment networks that assist people with disabilities in obtaining employment receive up to $19,000 per hire in commissions.

Other Suggested Recruitment Approaches

Staffing managers should make contact with counselors and administrators at high schools, vocational schools, and colleges with large minority and/or female enrollments. Joe Watson, head of Strategichire.com, an executive search firm specializing in minorities and women, said, "This is not an instant-access opportunity. You can't ignore certain segments of the population and then access those individuals simply because it's time to do so."[112] Organizations should make counselors and administrators aware that it is actively seeking minorities, women, and disabled individuals for jobs. Also, counselors and administrators should be familiar with the types of jobs available and the training and education needed to perform these jobs. All parties should investigate the possibilities for developing internships and summer employment. Firms should develop contacts with minority, women and other community organizations.[113] These organizations include the National Association for the Advancement of Colored People (NAACP), the League of United Latin American Citizens, the National Urban League, the American Association of University Women, the Federation of Business and Professional Women's Talent Bank, the National Council of Negro Women, and the Veterans Administration. The EEOC's regional offices will assist employers in locating appropriate local agencies.

A Global Perspective

China: Running Out of People?

One would think that China, with a population 1.3 billion, would be an excellent country from which to recruit, but now it appears that China is running short of workers. Although China has a vast pool of unskilled labor, firms in south China now complain that they cannot recruit enough cheap factory and manual workers and the market is even tighter for skilled labor. As the economy grows, China has the challenge of attracting and retaining staff with the skill levels needed. Labor costs continue to rise. "If you think that China is a cheap place for labor, think again," says Vincent Gauthier of Hewitt Associates, a human resources consultancy.[114]

China's history has left it with some peculiar problems. Its Confucian heritage, which emphasizes rote learning and hierarchy, may partly explain why many graduates, despite good paper qualifications and English-language skills, are often cautious about taking the initiative. Some firms also complain that China's one-child policy has made it harder for them to find natural team players. There are also few MBA programs in China. Jeff Barnes, Chief Learning Officer at General Electric in China, says that the "the issue we have is finding mid-level and top-level leadership. The Chinese talent is first-generation. They don't have role models. Their parents worked for state-owned companies."[115]

Chairman Mao's Cultural Revolution in 1966–1976 wiped out a generation of management potential, as millions of Chinese learned that capitalism was evil. After a lifetime under socialism, many lack the mind-set to adopt Western working practices. In China, says Jack Perkowski, manager of Asimco Technologies, a supplier of vehicle parts, "the talent pool consists either of managers from state firms who are too bureaucratic or entrepreneurs who have come up through the private sector and are unconstrained by capital or the law."[116]

Recruitment, retention, and localization of staff is at the top of the agenda for firms in China. Arics Poon, managing director of Oracle for South China and Hong Kong, said, "we need a group of strong, professional managers or we may fail to support our growth in China." Anthony Wu, head of accounting firm Ernst & Young (E&Y) in Hong Kong and China admits that "we have decided not to tender for some major clients because we feel we don't have the staff to service them." Paolo Gasparrini, head of China for L'Oréal, a French cosmetics firm, says that "to find good people in China is not easy. Technically and in administration they are very good. But in marketing—a crucial discipline—there are just a few people with short experience and everyone is competing for them. You find yourself micro-managing more than you'd like."[117]

Fierce competition and a limited supply of talent have resulted in high turnover rates. E&Y's Mr. Wu said, "The biggest issue is retention of people." Pay and benefits are also soaring. A Chinese middle manager at a foreign company in Beijing or Shanghai can now earn total annual cash compensation (salary plus bonus) of $27,000–$32,000. Senior managers receive between $46,000 and $54,000 and top executives can expect $80,000 to $90,000 or more. Bonuses, longer-term incentives, free housing and meals, a mobile phone, and an automobile are becoming standard perks.[118]

Summary

1. Define recruitment and explain alternatives to recruitment.

Recruitment is the process of attracting individuals on a timely basis, in sufficient numbers, and with appropriate qualifications, to apply for jobs with an organization. Alternatives include outsourcing, contingent workers, employee leasing, and overtime.

2. Explain the external environment of recruitment and describe how promotion policies influence recruitment.

Factors external to the organization can significantly affect the firm's recruitment efforts. Of particular importance is the demand for and supply of specific skills in the labor market and legal considerations. An organization's promotion policy can have a significant impact on recruitment. A firm can stress a policy of promotion from within its own ranks or one where positions are generally filled from outside the organization. Depending on specific circumstances, either approach may have merit. Promotion from within is the policy of filling vacancies above entry-level positions with current employees.

3. Describe the recruitment process.

Recruitment frequently begins when a manager initiates an employee requisition. Next, the firm determines whether qualified employees are available from within (the internal source) or must be recruited externally from sources such as colleges, universities, and other firms. Sources and methods are then identified.

4. Describe internal recruitment methods.

Job posting is a method of internal recruitment that is used to communicate the fact that job openings exist. Job bidding is a system that permits individuals in an organization to apply for a specific job within the organization.

5. Identify external recruitment sources.

External sources of recruitment include high schools and vocational schools, community colleges, colleges and universities, competitors and other firms, the unemployed, older individuals, military personnel, and self-employed workers.

6. Describe online recruitment methods.

Perhaps the biggest change in the way that organizations recruit has been the rise in the use of online recruiting. Some online methods include: Internet recruiter, virtual job fairs, corporate career Websites, Weblogs, general employment Websites, NACElink, niche sites, contract workers' sites, and hourly workers' job sites.

7. Identify traditional external recruitment methods.

Traditional external recruitment methods include media advertising, employment agencies, recruiters, job fairs, internships, executive search firms, professional associations, unsolicited applicants, open houses, event recruiting, sign-on bonuses, and high-tech competition.

8. Describe an applicant tracking system.

An applicant tracking system is a software application designed to help an enterprise recruit employees more efficiently. Current systems enable human resource and line managers to oversee the entire process, from screening résumés and spotting qualified candidates, to conducting personality and skills tests and handling background checks.

9. Describe how recruitment methods and sources are tailored to each other.

Recruitment must be tailored to the needs of each firm. In addition, recruitment sources and methods often vary according to the type of position being filled.

10. Explain how to recruit for diversity.

Forward-thinking organizations actively engage in acquiring a workforce that reflects society and helps the company expand into untapped markets. To accomplish this objective, firms may need to use nontraditional recruitment approaches.

Key Terms

- Recruitment, 126
- Contingent workers, 127
- Promotion from within (PFW), 129
- Employee requisition, 130
- Recruitment sources, 131
- Recruitment methods, 131
- Job posting, 132

- Job bidding, 132
- Internet recruiter, 138
- Virtual job fair, 139
- Corporate career Websites, 139
- NACElink, 140
- Niche sites, 141
- Employment agency, 143

- Job fair, 144
- Internship, 145
- Contingency search firms, 146
- Retained search firms, 146
- Event recruiting, 147
- Applicant tracking system (ATS), 148

Questions for Review

1. What are the typical alternatives to recruitment that a firm may use?
2. What are the basic components of the recruitment process?
3. What is meant by the policy of promotion from within?
4. What are the steps involved in the recruitment process?
5. Define job posting and job bidding.
6. Why is employee referral so important in the recruitment process?
7. Define sources and methods of recruitment.
8. What are the external sources of recruitment that are available?
9. What is an Internet recruiter?
10. Define the following:
    a. Virtual job fair
    b. Corporate career Website
    c. NACElink
    d. Niche sites
11. What are the traditional external methods of recruitment that are available?
12. What are the sources and methods of recruitment that might be used for the following jobs:
    a. college professor who just received his or her Ph.D.
    b. senior accountant with a CPA
    c. entry-level accountant
    d. skilled automobile mechanic
    e. entry-level machine operator
13. What is an applicant tracking system?
14. How can a firm improve its recruiting efforts to achieve diversity?

HRM Incident 1

A Problem Ad?

Dorothy Bryant was the new recruiting supervisor for International Manufacturing Company in Salt Lake City, Utah. One of Dorothy's first assignments was to recruit two software design engineers for International. Design engineers are hard to recruit because of the difficulty of their training and the high demand for them. After considering various recruitment alternatives, Dorothy placed the following ad in a local newspaper with a circulation in excess of 1,000,000:

EMPLOYMENT OPPORTUNITY FOR SOFTWARE DESIGN ENGINEERS

2 positions available for software design engineers desiring career in growth industry.

Prefer recent college graduates with good appearance.

Good credit rating

Apply Today! Send your résumé,

in confidence, to: D. A. Bryant

International Manufacturing Co., P.O. Box 1515

Salt Lake City, UT 84115

More than 300 applications arrived in the first week, and Dorothy was elated. When she reviewed the applicants, however, it appeared that few people possessed the desired qualifications for the job.

Questions

1. Dorothy overlooked some of the proper recruiting practices, which resulted in an excessive number of unqualified people applying. What are they?

2. Are there any hiring standards that should be avoided? Identify them and explain why they should be avoided.

HRM Incident 2

I Am Qualified, Why Not Me?

Five years ago when Bobby Bret joined Crystal Productions as a junior accountant, he felt that he was on his way up. He had just graduated with a B+ average from college, where he was well liked by his peers and by the faculty and had been an officer in several student organizations. Bobby had shown a natural ability to get along with people as well as to get things done. He remembered what Roger Friedman, the controller at Crystal, had told him when he was hired: "I think you will do well here, Bobby. You've come highly recommended. You are the kind of guy that can expect to move right on up the ladder."

Bobby felt that he had done a good job at Crystal and everybody seemed to like him. In addition, his performance appraisals had been excellent. However, after five years he was still a junior accountant. He had applied for two senior accountant positions that had come open, but they were both filled by people hired from outside the firm. When the accounting supervisor's job came open two years ago, Bobby had not applied. He was surprised when his new boss turned out to be a hotshot graduate of State University whose only experience was three years with a large accounting firm. Bobby had hoped that Ron Greene, a senior accountant he particularly respected, would get the job.

On the fifth anniversary of his employment at Crystal, Bobby decided it was time to do something. He made an appointment with the controller. At that meeting Bobby explained to Mr. Friedman that he had worked hard to obtain a promotion and shared his frustration about having been in the same job for so long. "Well," said Mr. Friedman, "you don't think that you were all that much better qualified than the people that we have hired, do you?" "No," said Bobby, "but I think I could have handled the senior accountant job. Of course, the people you have hired are doing a great job too." The controller responded, "We just look at the qualifications of all the applicants for each job, and considering everything, try to make a reasonable decision."

Questions

1. Do you believe that Bobby has a legitimate complaint? Explain.

2. Explain the impact of a promotion from within policy on outside recruitment.

Notes

1. Diane Brady, "The Temp in the Corner Office," *BusinessWeek* (July 3, 2006): 13.
2. Terence F. Shea, "Limited Executive Engagements," *HR Magazine* 49 (June 2004): 16–18.
3. Martha Frase-Blunt, "Short-Term Executives," *HR Magazine* 49 (June 2004): 110–114.
4. Del Jones, "Turnover for CEOs Is on Record Pace," *USA Today* (July 12, 2006): 1b.
5. Sue Bowness, "Top Temps," *Profit* 24 (November 2005): 87–88.
6. Frase-Blunt, "Short-Term Executives."
7. Brady, "The Temp in the Corner Office."
8. Bowness, "Top Temps."
9. Bernadette O'Donnell, "In Search of . . . Perfect Employees," *Wenatchee Business Journal* 19 (June 2005): 6.
10. "The Present & Future Job Market: Top Trends & How to Prepare," *HR Focus* 83 (June 2006): 8.
11. Susan Meisinger, "Looming Talent, Skills Gap Challenge HR," *HR Magazine* 50 (October 2005): 12.
12. John W. Rogers Jr., "Farm It Out," *Forbes* 177 (March 13, 2006): 108.
13. Jeff Kaplan, "Downsizing Outsourcing," *Network World* 23 (February 13, 2006): 41.
14. "Learning to Live with Offshoring," *BusinessWeek* (January 30, 2006): 122.
15. Tracy Heffner, "Offshoring: Friend or Foe?" *Printed Circuit Design & Manufacture* 23 (March 2006): 4.
16. "More Contingent Workers Are a Blessing and Sometimes a Challenge for HR," *HR Focus* 83 (January 2006): Special Section S1-S4.

17. Mike Allen, "Staffing Firm's Workload Reveals Telecom Uptick," *San Diego Business Journal* 26 (February 7, 2005): 4.

18. Lisa Daniel "Using Temps in HR," *HR Magazine* 51 (February 2006): 62–66.

19. Max Chafkin, "Fed up with HR?" *Inc.* 28 (May 2006): 50–52.

20. Anne Fisher, "Bringing the Jobs Home," *Fortune* 153 (March 20, 2006): 22.

21. "Internet Recruiting Could Lead to Discrimination," *HR Focus* 84 (February 2006): 2.

22. Ryan McCarthy, "Uncle Sam Wants Your Hiring Data," *Inc.* 28 (April 2006): 28.

23. Judy Greenwald, "Employers Face Bias Rule for Internet Job Applications," *Business Insurance* 40 (January 2, 2006): 4–19.

24. Ibid.

25. Casey J. Dickinson, "Manufacturing Isn't a Dead-end Job," *Business Journal (Central New York)* 19 (April 15, 2005): 11–12.

26. Maggie Rauch, "Study Shows Growing Commitment to Hiring from Within," *Incentive* 179 (March 2005): 7.

27. Jill Jusko, "Secrets to Longevity," *Industry Week* 252 (March 2003): 24.

28. "Inside Versus Outside: Which Is Better?" *Health Care Manager* 24 (April-June 2005): 93–95.

29. Charles Fishman, "Moving Toward a Balanced Work Life," *Workforce* 79 (March 2000): 40.

30. Kathryn Tyler, "Train for Smarter Hiring," *HR Magazine* 50 (May 2005): 89–93.

31. Leslie Gross Klaff, "New Internal Hiring Systems Reduce Cost and Boost Morale," *Workforce Management* 83 (March 2004): 76–79.

32. "Ideas for Improving Your Corporate Web Recruiting Site," *HR Focus* 83 (May 2006): 9.

33. "Be Aggressive, or Be Gone," *Workforce Management* 85 (February 27, 2006): 29–31.

34. "IT Recruiting: Which Way Works Best Today?" *Economics Report* 28 (August 2006): 1–10.

35. "Why Friends Make Great Employees," *Profit* 25 (March 2006): 57.

36. Spence Ante, "Hiring Techies Is as Tricky as Ever," *BusinessWeek Online* (April 4, 2004).

37. Nisha Ramachandran, "How to Find That Perfect Job," *U.S. News & World Report* 138 (March 21, 2005): 45.

38. "Why It Pays to Use High-Tech Candidate Sourcing," *HR Focus* 84 (February 2006): 3–5.

39. Jennifer C. Berkshire, "Social Network Recruiting," *HR Magazine* 50 (April 2005): 95–98.

40. "Career Watch," *Computerworld* 39 (October 12, 2005): 58.

41. https://www.linkedin.com/, September 8, 2006.

42. Douglas Wolk and Jonathan Pont, "At Social Job Sites, It's Who You Know," *Workforce Management* 84 (May 2005): 52–54.

43. Jonathan Pont, "Boom Times for Vendors," *Workforce Management* 84 (May 2005): 51–52.

44. Fay Hansen, "Recruitment & Staffing," *Workforce Management* 85 (June 26, 2006): 59–61.

45. Deborah J. Sessions, "Recruiting Made Easy," *Journal of Accountancy* 201 (May 2006): 31–34.

46. Ed Frauenheim, "Studies: More Workers Look to Switch Jobs," *Workforce Management* 85 (February 13, 2006): 12.

47. Paul Falcone, "Preserving Restless Top Performers," *HR Magazine* 51 (March 2006): 117–122.

48. Jessica Marquez, "Accountants' Book Value Employee Referral Example," *Workforce Management* 84 (June 2005): 74–75.

49. "Return to an Old Job," *Contract Journal* 432 (March 29, 2006): 47.

50. Adapted from case in Winn Schwartau, "Cyber Ethics in the Workplace," *Network World* 19 (January 21, 2002): 47.

51. Judy White House, "Don't Say Goodbye!" *HR Matters* (Winter 2006): 20.

52. Ed Frauenheim, "Ford, GM Cuts May Fuel Hiring at Competitors," *Workforce Management* 85 (February 13, 2006): 6.

53. "Why Soldiers Make Good Employees," *Fair Employment Practices Guidelines* (January 1, 2006): 1–3.

54. John F. Welch, Jr. with John A. Byrne, *Jack Straight from the Gut* (New York: Warner Books, Inc., 2001): 198–199.

55. "Why It Pays to Use High-Tech Candidate Sourcing," *HR Focus* 84 (February 2006): 3–5.

56. "New Internet Domain Will Aid in Job Recruiting and Hiring," *T+D* 59 (June 2005): 15.

57. In Lee, "Evaluation of Fortune 100 Companies' Career Websites," *Human Systems Management* 24 (2005): 175–182.

58. Kanak S. Gautam, "A Summation of Online Recruiting Practices for Health Care Organizations," *Health Care Manager* 24 (July-September 2005): 257–267.

59. Lee, "Evaluation of Fortune 100 Companies' Career Websites."

60. "The Pros and Cons of Online Recruiting," *HR Focus* 81 (April 2004): S2.

61. Sharon Watson, "Hands Off My Staff!" *Computerworld* 35 (January 22, 2001): 50–51.

62. "Virtual Job Fair Offers Opportunities Online," *Bangor Daily News* (February 5, 2003): 5.

63. Drew Robb, "Career Portals Boost Online Recruiting," *HR Magazine* 49 (April 2004): 111–116.

64. "ERE Competition Names the Best Corporate Career Websites," *Human Resources Department Management Report* 5 (April 2005): 8.

65. "Ideas for Improving Your Corporate Web Recruiting Site."

66. Martha Frase-Blunt, "Make a Good First Impression," *HR Magazine* 49 (April 2004): 80–86.

67. Jennifer Schramm, "Revisiting the Internet" *HR Magazine* 50 (August 2005): 168.

68. "Blog Your Way to Work," *Money* 34 (October 2005): 24.

69. Jeremy Caplan, "Blogging 2.0," *Time* 166 (September 26, 2005): 86.

70. Katherine Spencer Lee, "The 21st Century Reference Check" *Certification Magazine* 8 (April 2006): 12.

71. Michelle Conlin, "You Are What You Post," *BusinessWeek* (March 27, 2006): 52–53.

72. Jeremy Caplan, "Résumé Mogul," *Time* 167 (January 9, 2006): A12.

73. http://hiring.monster.com/, September 8, 2006.

74. http://hotjobs.yahoo.com/jobseeker/about/press-center-facts.html, September 8, 2006.

75. Kris Oser, "CareerBuilder Looking to Do a Job on Monster," *Crain's Chicago Business* 28 (January 24, 2005): 21.

76. Olga Kharif, "The Job of Challenging Monster," *BusinessWeek Online* (October 7, 2005).
77. http://www2.nacelink.com/, August 20, 2006.
78. Caplan, "Résumé Mogul."
79. Ibid.
80. http://www.snagajob.com/about_us.aspx, September 8, 2006.
81. Howard Lewinter, "Be Creative Looking for Your Next Job Candidate," *Business Journal Serving Fresno & the Central San Joaquin Valley* (March 11, 2005): 4.
82. Caplan, "Résumé Mogul."
83. "Why It Pays to Use High-Tech Candidate Sourcing."
84. Beverly Nazmi, "How to Get the Best from a Headhunter," *Management Services* 50 (Spring 2006): 42–43.
85. Leslie Stevens-Huffman, "Turning to Niche Staffing Firms to Fill Specialized Hiring Needs," *Workforce Management* (March 3, 2006): 50–52.
86. Fay Hansen, "Far from Obsolete, Career Fairs Are a Low-cost Way for Firms to Hire Quickly and Fill Pipelines," *Workforce Management* 85 (February 27, 2006): 46–47.
87. Philip S. Moore, "Seniors Flood Older Worker Fair," *Inside Tucson Business* 14 (March 3, 2005): 15–17.
88. "U.S. Military Veterans in Demand," *T+D* 59 (July 2005): 14.
89. Alex Kingsbury, "Get a Once and Future Job," *U.S. News & World Report* 138 (April 18, 2005): 70.
90. "Plan for the Most Effective Internship Programs," *HR Focus* 82 (September 2005): 7–11.
91. John Purkiss, "The Smart Way to Stand Out in a Crowd," *Director* 58 (June 2005): 36.
92. http://jobs.shrm.org/jobseekerx/, September 8, 2006.
93. Kevin Wheeler, "Non-Traditional Recruiting Method," *Electronic Recruiting Daily* (March 29, 2000).
94. Fay Hansen, "Refining Signing Bonuses," *Workforce Management* 85 (March 27, 2006): 1–41.
95. "Signing Bonuses Making a Comeback," *Report on Salary Surveys* 5 (June 2005): 8.
96. Gail Kachadourian, "Hesterberg to get $1 million Bonus," *Automotive News* (June 6, 2005): 3.
97. Linda Longton and Andy Duncan, "Big Carriers Offer Better Pay, Benefits," *Overdrive* (January 2005): 11.
98. Mike Scott, "Remote Codes," *Hospitals & Health Networks* 79 (October 2005): 19–20.
99. Thomas Claburn, "One Way to Land a Job at Google," *InformationWeek* (October 10, 2005): 77.
100. Spence Ante, "Hiring Techies Is as Tricky as Ever," *BusinessWeek Online* (April 4, 2004).
101. Michelle V. Rafter, "Unicru Breaks Through in the Science of 'Smart Hiring'," *Workforce Management* 84 (May 2005): 76–78.
102. "Record-keeping Regs, Integration Steer Technology," *Workforce Management* 85 (February 27, 2006): 32.
103. "Applicant Tracking System Software Providers," *Workforce Management* 85 (February 27, 2006): 16.
104. Fay Hansen, "Paperless Route for Recruiting," *Workforce Management* 85 (February 27, 2006): 1–37.
105. Ibid.
106. Ibid.
107. Ibid.
108. Ibid.
109. R. Wayne Mondy, Robert M. Noe, and Robert Edwards, "Successful Recruitment: Matching Sources and Methods," *Personnel* 64 (September 1987): 42–46.
110. "Many U.S. Employers Lack Formal Diversity Recruitment Programs," *HR Focus* 83 (January 2006): 9.
111. Robert E. Robertson, "Social Security Administration: Better Planning Could Make the Ticket Program More Effective," *GAO Reports* (March 2, 2005): 1–47.
112. Evelyn Nussenbaum, "The Lonely Recruiter," *Business 2.0* 4 (October 2003): 132.
113. Ibid.
114. "China's People Problem," *Economist* 375 (April 16, 2005): 53–54.
115. Ibid.
116. Ibid.
117. Ibid.
118. Ibid.

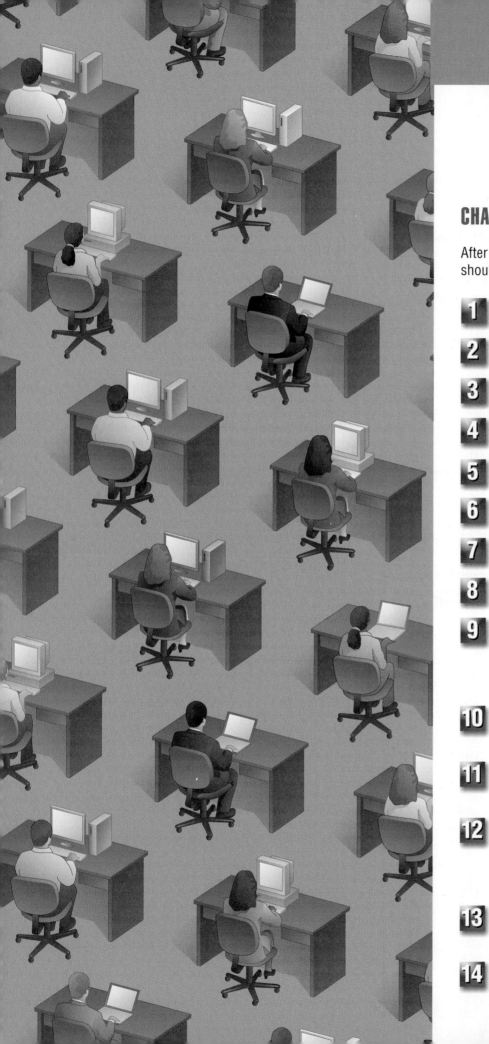

CHAPTER OBJECTIVES

After completing this chapter, students should be able to:

1 Explain the significance of employee selection.

2 Identify environmental factors that affect the selection process.

3 Describe the selection process.

4 Explain the importance of the preliminary interview.

5 Describe reviewing applications and résumés.

6 Describe sending résumés via the Internet.

7 Explain the advantages and potential problems of using selection tests.

8 Describe the characteristics of properly designed selection tests.

9 Explain the types of validation studies; describe types of employment tests, including online testing and the use of assessment center.

10 Explain the importance of the employment interview and describe the general types of interviewing.

11 Describe the various methods of interviewing and potential interviewing problems.

12 Explain the use of pre-employment screening including background investigations, reference checks, negligent hiring, and negligent referral.

13 Describe the selection decision, the medical examination, and notification of candidates.

14 Explain the metrics for evaluating recruitment/selection effectiveness.

Selection

HRM IN *Action:*
Substance Abuse Testing

Failure to test for drugs can sometimes have a disastrous effect on companies large and small. For instance, *Cake for You* is a small specialty bakery. Its service includes making and delivering wedding cakes to receptions. In hiring a delivery driver, *Cake for You* owners were always careful to determine that the potential candidate had a valid driver's license. The owners were quite pleased with their new employee, Mike. He was prompt, neatly attired, and seemed to have a pleasant demeanor. Unfortunately, while making a delivery one morning, Mike was involved in, and in fact caused, a four-vehicle accident that resulted in one fatality. The investigation revealed that Mike was high on marijuana. Had the owners of the firm included drug testing as part of their screening process, they might not be facing a huge lawsuit. In certain industries, such as transportation, for example, drug use on the job is especially hazardous and potentially devastating to the firm. Think of the damage that could be caused by a 40-ton truck careening out of control. Under ideal conditions, a fully loaded truck in daylight on a dry road cannot stop in less than 300 feet, or the length of a football field.

Nearly 80 percent of larger corporations in the United States require some form of workplace drug testing.[1] These proponents of drug testing programs contend that they are necessary to ensure workplace safety, security, and productivity. The National Institute on Drug Abuse reported that drug-abusing employees inflict losses on their companies with both missed time and frequent accidents. They are more than twice as likely to leave work early or miss days, are two-and-a-half times more likely to be absent for eight days or more, and are three times more likely to be late for work. They are also more than three-and-a-half times more likely to be involved in a workplace accident and five times more likely to file a workers' compensation claim.[2]

Urine, blood, oral fluids, or hair samples are possible drug testing methods, with most employers relying on urine testing.[3] However, most experts regard blood tests as the forensic benchmark against which to compare others. The problem with this approach is that it is invasive and requires trained personnel for administration and analysis. The use of hair samples is unique in that drug traces will remain in the hair and will not likely diminish over time. Human hair samples are easy to collect, store, and transport, and they are difficult to change.[4] Although urine and blood testing can detect only current drug use, advocates of hair sample analysis claim it can detect drug use from 3 days to 90 days after drug consumption. This would prohibit an applicant from beating the test by short-term abstinence.

When the oral fluid method is used, the collection pad is saturated and the individual places the swab in a collection vial, snaps off the handle, seals the container, and hands it over for analysis. Oral fluid testing is especially well-suited to cases of reasonable suspicion and post-accident testing. Oral fluid is a great deterrent because it can be done immediately in the workplace and it does not give an individual an opportunity to adulterate or substitute a urine specimen.[5] From a prospective employee's viewpoint, oral fluid and hair testing may be less embarrassing than a urine test. For example, it is humiliating for a candidate to hear, "We're really happy to have you on board. But, will you take this cup and fill it?"

This chapter begins with a discussion of substance abuse testing, followed by a discussion of the significance of employee selection and identification of environmental factors that affect the selection process. Next, the general selection process is described. The next two sections involve the preliminary interview and review of applications and résumés. A section on sending résumés via the Internet follows, and the advantages and potential problems and characteristics of properly designed selection tests are explained. The types of validation studies and types of employment tests are then discussed, and topics related to genetic testing, graphoanalysis, and polygraph tests are described. Aspects of online testing and the use of assessment centers are then presented, and the importance of the employment interview and the general types of interviewing is discussed. Then we examine the various methods of interviewing, realistic job previews, potential interviewing problems, and concluding the interview. Next, the use of pre-employment screening including background investigations and reference checks is presented, followed by a discussion of negligent hiring and negligent referral. Topics related to the selection decision, the medical examination, and notification of candidates are discussed, and metrics for evaluating recruitment/selection effectiveness are explained. The chapter concludes with a Global Perspective entitled "Selecting a Buddy."

1 OBJECTIVE

Explain the significance of employee selection.

Selection:
Process of choosing from a group of applicants the individual best suited for a particular position and the organization.

Significance of Employee Selection

Selection is the process of choosing from a group of applicants the individual best suited for a particular position and the organization.

Properly matching people with jobs and the organization is the goal of the selection process. If individuals are overqualified, underqualified, or for any reason do not *fit* either the job or the organization's culture, they will be ineffective and probably leave the firm, voluntarily or otherwise. As you would expect, a firm's recruitment success has a significant impact on the quality of the selection decision. There are many ways to improve productivity, but none is more powerful than making the right hiring decision. Top performers in an organization contribute anywhere from 5 to 22 times more value to their companies than mid-level or low performers.[6] A firm that selects high-quality employees reaps substantial benefits, which recur every year the employee is on the payroll. On the other hand, poor selection decisions can cause irreparable damage. A bad hire can affect the morale of the entire staff, especially in a position where teamwork is critical. Selecting the wrong person for any job can be costly.[7] This is significant since one in five hires turns out to be a bad choice.[8]

Michael J. Lotito, former chair of the SHRM board of directors, declared, "HR has traditionally been seen as the soft side of business, but I submit that attracting and retaining the right people for your organization is the hard side of business because that is the foundation upon which everything is based."[9] Libby Sartain, vice president of human resources for Southwest Airlines, provides another perspective. She states, "We would rather go short and work overtime than hire one bad apple."[10] If a firm hires many *bad apples*, it cannot be successful for long even if it has perfect plans, a sound organizational structure, and finely tuned control systems. Competent people must be available to ensure the attainment of organizational goals. Today, with many firms having access to the same technology, the *people* make the real difference.

Small businesses, especially, cannot afford to make hiring mistakes. According to Dennis S. O'Reilly, president of O'Reilly Enterprises, a human resource consultant firm, "While an incompetent person's mistake in a large firm may have insignificant consequences, a similar error in a small company may be devastating. In the smaller, less specialized firm, each person typically accounts for a larger part of the business's activity."[11]

Business Owner's Toolkit

http://www.toolkit.cch.com

Offers detailed instructions for the small business owner to hire, manage, and retain employees.

 OBJECTIVE

Identify environmental factors that affect the selection process.

Environmental Factors Affecting the Selection Process

A standardized selection process followed consistently would greatly simplify the selection process. However, circumstances may require making exceptions. The following sections describe environmental factors that affect the selection process.

Other HR Functions

The selection process affects, and is affected by, virtually every other HR function. If the compensation package is inferior to those provided by the firm's competition, hiring the best-qualified applicants will be difficult or impossible. The same situation applies if the firm's safety and health record is substandard. On the other hand, if the selection process provides the firm with only marginally qualified workers, the organization may have to intensify its training efforts.

Legal Considerations

Remember from Chapter 3 that legal matters play a significant role in HR management due to legislation, executive orders, and court decisions. Although the basic purpose of selection is to determine candidates' eligibility for employment, it is also essential for organizations to maintain nondiscriminatory practices. The guiding principle in determining what information I should get from the applicant is: Why am I asking this question? Why do I want to know this information? If the information is job related, usually asking for the information is appropriate.[12]

Speed of Decision Making

The time available to make the selection decision can also have a major effect on the selection process. Research has determined that organizations that fill jobs quickly tend to have a higher total return to shareholders.[13] Conditions also can impact the needed speed of decision making. Suppose, for instance, that the only two quality control inspectors on a production line just had a fight and both resigned, and the firm cannot operate until the positions are filled. In this situation, speed is crucial and a few phone calls, two brief interviews, and a prayer may constitute the entire selection procedure. On the other hand, conducting a national search to select a chief executive officer may take months or even a year. In bureaucracies, it is not uncommon for the selection process to take a considerable amount of time.

Organizational Hierarchy

Organizations usually take different approaches to filling positions at varying levels. For instance, consider the differences in hiring a chief executive officer versus a data entry clerk. Extensive background checks and multiple interviews would most likely apply for the executive position.[14] On the other hand, an applicant for a clerical position would probably take a word-processing test and perhaps have a short employment interview.

Applicant Pool

Applicant pool:
Number of qualified applicants recruited for a particular job.

The number of qualified applicants recruited for a particular job makes up the **applicant pool**.

The process can be truly selective only if there are several qualified applicants. Yet, only a few applicants with the required skills may be available. The selection process then becomes a matter of choosing from whoever is at hand. The expansion and contraction of the labor market also affects the size of the applicant pool. A low unemployment rate often means that the applicant pool is smaller, whereas a high unemployment rate may expand the pool.

Selection ratio:
Number of people hired for a particular job compared to the number of individuals in the applicant pool.

The number of people hired for a particular job compared to the number of individuals in the applicant pool is often expressed as a **selection ratio**, or

$$\text{Selection Ratio} = \frac{\text{Number of people hired}}{\text{Number of qualified applicants (applicant pool)}}$$

A selection ratio of 1.00 indicates that there was only one qualified applicant for an open position. The lower the ratio falls below 1.00, the more alternatives the manager has in making a selection decision. For example, a selection ratio of 0.10 indicates that there were 10 qualified applicants for an open position.

Type of Organization

The type of organization employing individuals such as private, governmental, or not-for-profit can also affect the selection process. A private-sector business is heavily profit oriented. Prospective employees who can help achieve profit goals are the preferred candidates. Consideration of the total individual, including job-related personality factors, is involved in the selection of future employees for this sector.

Government civil service systems typically identify qualified applicants through competitive examinations. Often a manager may select only from among the top three applicants for a position. A manager in this sector may not have the prerogative of interviewing other applicants.

Individuals considered for positions in not-for-profit organizations (such as the Boy Scouts and Girl Scouts, YMCA, or YWCA) confront still a different situation. The salary level in these organizations may not be competitive with those of private and governmental organizations. Therefore, a person who fills one of these positions must be not only qualified but also dedicated to this type of work.

Probationary Period

Many firms use a probationary period that permits them to evaluate an employee's ability based on established performance. This practice may be either a substitute for certain phases of the selection process or a check on the validity of the process. The rationale is that if an individual can successfully perform the job during the probationary period, the process does not require other selection tools. From a legal viewpoint, the use of a probationary period in the selection process is certainly job related. In any event, newly hired employees need monitoring to determine whether the hiring decision was a good one.

Even in unionized firms, the labor/management agreement typically does not protect a new employee until after a certain probationary period. This period is typically from 60 to 90 days. During that time, an employee can be terminated with little or no justification. On the other hand, firing a marginal employee in a union environment may prove to be quite difficult after the probationary period. When a firm is unionized, it becomes especially important for the selection process to identify the most productive workers. Once the probationary period is completed, workers are under the labor/management agreement and the firm must follow its terms in changing the workers' status.

OBJECTIVE

Describe the selection process.

Selection Process

Figure 6-1 illustrates a generalized selection process that may vary by organization. It typically begins with the preliminary interview. Next, applicants complete the firm's application for employment or provide a résumé. Then they progress through a series of selection tests, one or more employment interviews, and pre-employment screening including background and reference checks. The hiring manager then offers the successful applicant a job, subject to successful completion of a medical examination. Notice that an applicant may be rejected at any time during the selection process. To a point, the more screening tools used to assess a good fit, the greater the chance of making a good selection decision. The odds of a successful hire are 14 percent with an interview and a résumé, but 75 percent if tests show that a candidate's skills and personality are compatible with the job and the organization.[15]

OBJECTIVE

Explain the importance of the preliminary interview.

Preliminary Interview

The selection process often begins with a preliminary interview. The basic purpose of this initial screening of applicants is to eliminate those who obviously do not meet the position's requirements. At this stage, the interviewer asks a few straightforward questions. For instance, a position may require specific qualifications such as being a certified public accountant (CPA). If the interview determines that the candidate does not have a CPA, any further discussion regarding this particular position wastes time for both the firm and the applicant.

In addition to eliminating obviously unqualified job applicants quickly, a preliminary interview may produce other positive benefits for the firm. It is possible the position for which the applicant applied is not the only one available. A skilled interviewer will know about other vacancies in the firm and may be able to steer the prospective employee to another position. For instance, an interviewer may decide that although an applicant is not a good fit for the applications-engineering job, she is an excellent candidate for an internal R&D position. This type of interviewing not only builds goodwill for the firm but also can maximize recruitment and selection effectiveness. In addition to face-to-face preliminary interviews, several other options are available. Two of these alternatives are discussed next.

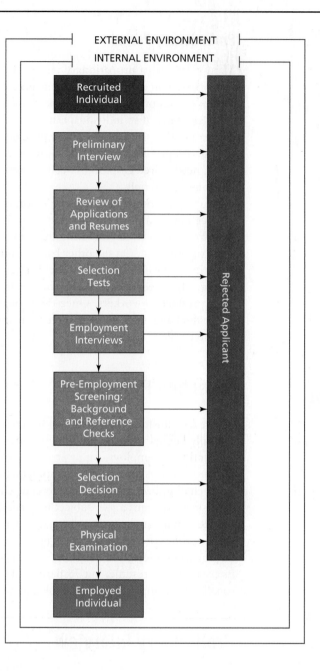

Figure 6-1 Selection Process

Telephone Interview

Telephone interviews are increasingly being used by busy hiring managers who want to narrow the pool of applicants before having a formal face-to-face interview.[16] The goal of the phone interview is to cut down on wasted time and effort in the recruiting process. This method obviously lacks the advantages of face-to-face contact. "The phone eliminates the visual information human beings need to assess a person more completely," says Marjan Bolmeijer, founder of Change-Leaders Inc., a New York–based management consulting group. "There is so much more to a person than what meets the ear."[17] For example, it is not possible to observe nonverbal cues from the candidate that may give hints to aspects of the candidate's interpersonal skills. Also, although the interviewer should not be biased by the candidate's physical appearance, the candidate's voice, particularly any regional accent, may have an even greater effect. Nevertheless, the telephone may be the most economically feasible way to exchange information with applicants in distant locations. In addition, an employer can screen a larger number of candidates using this method.

Videotaped Interview

A videotaped interview is another method that can reduce selection costs in some situations. Organizations may use consulting firms with many interviewers available throughout the nation to assist with this method. Using a structured interview format designed by the hiring firm, the interviewer can videotape the candidate's responses. To assure standardized treatment of other similarly conducted interviews, the interviewer may not interact with the candidate, but only repeat the question, if necessary. The videotaped interview has definite shortcomings and does not replace personal interviews. However, as with the telephone interview, it does allow a firm to conduct a broader search and get more people involved in the selection process.

 OBJECTIVE

Describe reviewing applications and résumés.

Review of Applications

Having the candidate complete an application for employment is another early step in the selection process. This may either precede or follow the preliminary interview. The employer then evaluates it to see whether there is an apparent match between the individual and the position. A well-designed and properly used application form can be helpful since essential information is included and presented in a standardized format. Applications may not be initially required for many management and professional positions. In these cases, a résumé may suffice. A completed application may be obtained at a later time.

The specific information requested on an application for employment may vary from firm to firm, and even by job type within an organization. An application form typically contains sections for name, address, telephone number, military service, education, and work history. Several preprinted statements are usually included on the application form. First, by signing the form, the applicant certifies that information provided on the form is accurate and true. Employers will likely reject candidates who make false claims for major issues. Second, when not prohibited by state law, the form should also state that the position is *employment at will* and that either the employer or the employee can terminate employment at any time for any reason or no reason. Finally, the form should contain a statement whereby the candidate gives permission to have his or her background and references checked.[18]

Conoco provides an example of a well-designed application form. Looking at Figure 6-2, notice the following statement in the employee release and privacy section: "I agree and understand that any employment which may be offered to me will not be for any definite period of time and that such employment is subject to termination by me or by Conoco Inc. at any time, with or without cause." An employment application form must reflect not only the firm's informational needs but also EEO requirements. Potentially discriminatory questions inquiring about such factors as gender, race, age, convictions, national origin, citizenship, birthplace, dependents, disabilities, religion, color, marital status, and sexual orientation do not appear on the form.[19]

Applicants sometimes deliberately leave out information on the application form that may present them in a negative light. To combat this, some employers are requiring all applicants to use online applications that force a person to complete a required field before the application is successfully submitted.[20] Recent research has found that about a third of *Fortune* 500 companies had Web-only application policies.[21] Employment managers compare the information contained in a completed application for employment to the job description to determine whether a potential match exists between the firm's requirements and the applicant's qualifications. As you might expect, this judgment is often difficult.

Application for Employment

Application
No. 125413

Equal Employment Opportunity—It is our policy to provide equal employment opportunity throughout the Company for all qualified persons without regard to race, color, religion, age, sex, national origin, disability, or veteran status.

Instructions
• **Please print in black ink or type information.**

Name (Last, First, Middle)	Are you over 18 years of age? ☐ Yes ☐ No	Social Security Number

Present Address (Street, City, State, ZIP Code)	Phone Number (Area Code First) ( )

Permanent Address (Street, City, State, ZIP Code)	Phone Number (Area Code First) ( )

Date Available for Employment	Employment Desired ☐ Temporary ☐ Regular, Full-Time	Would you accept temporary employment? ☐ Yes ☐ No	Will you perform shift work? ☐ Yes ☐ No

Position Desired—First Preference	Second Preference

Geographical Location Preferred	Geographical Location Where You Will Not Consider Employment

Will you work overtime? ☐ Yes ☐ No	Are you legally authorized to work in the United States on a regular, full-time basis? ☐ Yes ☐ No

Have you been previously employed by Conoco?
☐ No ☐ Yes   If yes, where _____   when _____

Do you have relatives currently employed by Conoco?
☐ No ☐ Yes   If yes, Name _____

Relationship _____ Department _____ Location _____

If you are presently employed, may we contact your employer for a reference?
☐ Yes ☐ No

Indicate Source Which Referred You

☐ Campus Placement Office	☐ Walk-in	☐ Private Employment Agency	☐ Published Advertisement
☐ Employee Referral	☐ Write-In	☐ Governmental Employment Agency	☐ Other (Specify)
	☐ Rehire		

Employment Record (List below your employment in reverse chronological order. Include part-time and summner experience)

From Mo./Yr	To Mo./Yr	/	/	/	/	/	/	/	/
Employer									
Address									
Supervisor's Name and Telephone No. (Area Cose First)		( )		( )		( )		( )	
Position(s) Held									
Reason for Leaving									

Identify and explain any time lapses in your above employment record.

Figure 6-2 An Application for Employment
Source: Courtesy of Conoco, Inc.

Review of Résumés

Résumé
Goal-directed summary of a person's experience, education, and training developed for use in the selection process.

A **résumé** is a goal-directed summary of a person's experience, education, and training developed for use in the selection process.

Professional and managerial applicants often begin the selection process by submitting a résumé. Figure 6-3 illustrates a traditional résumé. Note that the résumé includes the career objective for the specific position the applicant is seeking (a VITA

Education—Circle Highest Grade Completed 1 2 3 4 5 6 7 8 9 10 11 12	Course of Study Major—Minor	Degree Received	Grade Average		Degree Date
			Overall	Major	
High School Attended and Location		Diploma ☐ Yes ☐ No			
Vocational or Technical School Attended		Completed ☐ Yes ☐ No			
College or University					
College or University					
College or University					

Other—1) Include information you believe is important, such as: special training, apprenticeships completed, military experience, other education, or foreign language fluency.

—2) List those machines and/or equipment you are qualified to operate and any other skills you possess.

—3) Titles of these and special research projects.

Completion of this section is optional.

Conoco Inc. is a government contractor subject to Section 503 of the Rehabilitation Act and Section 402 of the Veterans Readjustment Act. As such, we must take affirmative action to employ and advance in employment individuals with disabilities, special disabled veterans, and veterans of the Vietnam era. If you are such an individual and would like to be considered under the affirmative action program, please indicate below.

☐ I am a **special disabled veteran** because **either:** (1) I am entitled to compensation under VA law for disability rated at 30% or more, or for disability rated at 10% or 20% for a serious employment handicap; **or** (2) I was discharged or released from active duty because of a service-connected disability.

☐ I am a **veteran of the Vietnam era** because part or all of my active military service occured between 8/5/64 and 5/7/75 **and either:** (1) I was on active duty for more than 180 days and my discharge or release was not dishonorable; **or** (2) I was discharged or released from active duty because of a service-connected disability.

Submission of this information is voluntary, and disclosure or refusal to provide it will not subject you to adverse treatment. This information shall be used only as allowed by law and shall be kept confidential except that (i) supervisors and managers may be informed about restrictions on work or job duties and necessary accommodations, (ii) first aid or safety personnel may be informed where appropriate in case of an emergency, and (iii) government officials investigating compliance with the law shall be informed.

You may omit references in this section which you feel might reveal age, race, color, sex, national origin, or handicap.

Name and description of scholastic honors received including scholarships.

Name honorary, technical and professional organizations of which you have been a member, or other extracurricular activities in which you have participated, including offices held. (List professional licenses held.)

This form will usually provide the necessary information. It may be supplemented, however, by a letter or personal resume.

PLEASE READ THE FOLLOWING CAREFULLY BEFORE SIGNING.

I authorize any third parties, including former employers, schools, law enforcement authorities, and any persons named above, to give to Conoco Inc. any information they may have regarding me and my background, whether or not such information is contained in written records. I hereby release these third parties from all liability for any damage whatsoever for providing information to Conoco Inc. in connection with this application. I also release Conoco Inc., its agents, employees, and representatives from any liability in connection with their collection and use of information obtained from third parties during the application process. I certify that all information furnished in this application, signed and dated by me this date, is true and complete to the best of my knowledge and belief and that falsification or omission of information requested in this application or in the application process shall be grounds for disqualification from further consideration or for termination.

I understand that if an employment offer is extended, I may be required to undergo a physical examination and/or drug screen test at the expense of Conoco Inc. I further understand that if I do not successfully complete the physical examination or drug screen test, Conoco Inc. may refuse to hire me, and I agree to hold Conoco Inc. harmless for such refusal. I also understand that employment is conditional on my ability to verify my identity and eligibility for employment as required by the Immigration Reform and Control Act of 1986.

I agree and understand that any employment which may be offered to me will not be for any definite period of time and that such employment is subject to termination by me or by Conoco Inc. at any time, with or without cause. I also agree and understand that nothing contained in this application nor any verbal statements made during the application process or during my employment shall be deemed to constitute an employment contract between me and Conoco Inc.

Signature	Date

12-21 (R), 3-92

Figure 6-2 (continued)

does not contain space for the career objective).[22] The remainder of the résumé should be directed toward showing how a person has the necessary skills and competencies necessary to accomplish the position identified in the career objective statement. Only information necessary to show a relationship to the objective should be included. The all-important concept of relevancy is crucial in selling the applicant to the company. In light of the increased threat of identity theft today, individuals should be cautioned to never put their Social Security number, or date of birth on the résumé.[23]

Henry Sanchez

Current Address:
1508 Westwood Dr.
New York, NY 20135
914/555-3869

OBJECTIVE:	To obtain an entry-level position in a public accounting firm.
EDUCATION:	University of New York **Master of Business Administration, December 2003** **Bachelor of Science, Business Administration, May 2000** Concentration: Individual and Corporate Tax with emphasis on Management Information Systems GPA: 3.2 / 4.0
HONORS:	Honors in Accounting and Finance Full academic scholarship President of Summer Conference Program
ACCOMPLISHMENTS:	Conducted TQM seminars Successfully completed ISO-9002 courses Graduate Assistant to the Dean
EXPERIENCE: *November 2003* *Present*	**ASSISTANT ADMINISTRATOR** Touch of Class Foods Corporation Accounting Department • Responsible for building A/P and A/R ledgers • Originated a responsive invoice program • Prepared corporate tax returns and all schedules • Oversaw intern program • Initiated ISO-9002 Certifications in all areas of plant production
May 2001 *November 2003*	**PERSONAL ASSISTANT** Mr. Charles Brandon Park Board of Trustees • Research and Development with City Sewer District • Assisted with general accounting procedures • Assisted with customer-related issues • Assisted with the allocation of public funds
COMPUTER SKILLS:	Microsoft Word, AmiPro, WordPerfect 7.0 Lotus 123, Microsoft Excel, Quattro Pro, Quicken Windows and Windows XP Applications
AFFILIATIONS:	ISO-9002 Certified Consultant TQM National Association

Figure 6-3 Example of a Traditional Résumé

Résumé Tips

http://www.free-resume-tips.com/10tips.html

Résumé tips are offered to improve résumé preparation.

 **OBJECTIVE**

Describe sending résumés via the Internet.

In developing a résumé for mailing, the sender should be careful not to misrepresent the truth. An applicant who is three hours away from graduation has not graduated. Certainly, the résumé should be designed to present the applicant in a positive light but care should be taken to not exaggerate excessively. With regard to job history, pay particular attention to dates of employment being accurate.[24]

Sending Résumés via the Internet

When sending a résumé via the Internet, applicants should realize that most large companies now use automated tracking systems (discussed in Chapter 5). These systems assume a certain résumé style. Résumés that deviate from the assumed style are ignored or deleted. These systems scan résumés into databases, search the databases on command, and rank the résumés according to the number of resulting hits they receive. At times such searches utilize multiple (10–20) criteria. Some systems allow employers to flag résumés that appear to misrepresent the truth, present misleading information, or are in other ways suspicious.[25]

The reliance upon résumé management systems, coupled with the downsizing o human resource departments, has resulted in a situation whereby many résumés are never seen by human eyes once they enter the system. Therefore, a job applicant should make his or her résumé as computer/scanner friendly as possible so that its life in a database will be extended. Kim Isaacs, director of Résumé Power.com, a firm in Doylestown, Pennsylvania, said, "You can be the perfect candidate for the position and never get found if your résumé doesn't have the right language."[26] To make the process work, a keyword résumé style should be used. **Keywords** refer to those words or phrases that are used to search databases for résumés that match.

This match is called a *hit* and occurs when one or more résumés are selected as matching the various criteria (keywords) used in the search. The **keyword résumé** is one that contains an adequate description of the job seeker's characteristics and industry-specific experience presented in keyword terms in order to accommodate the computer search process.

The keywords are often job titles, skills, or areas of expertise related to the position. Keywords tend to be more of the noun or noun phrase type (Word 2006, UNIX, BioChemist) as opposed to power action verbs often found in traditional résumés (developed, coordinated, empowered, organized). Another way to look at keyword phrases is to think in terms of job duties. Detailing an individual's job duties may require a change in mind-set away from traditional résumé writing.

Companies must be careful when searching for keywords. Scott Johnson, a human resources business consultant at Household Finance, a Prospect Heights, Illinois, lender that receives more than 1,000 online résumés each day, said, "Candidates are getting smarter and stuffing résumés with keywords."[27]

An example of a keyword résumé may be seen in Figure 6-4. Job seekers usually need to prepare two versions of their résumé, a keyword résumé and a traditional one

Keywords:
Words or phrases that are used to search databases for résumés that match.

Keyword résumé:
Résumé that contains an adequate description of the job seeker's characteristics and industry-specific experience presented in keyword terms in order to accommodate the computer search process.

HENRY SANCHEZ

1508 Westwood Drive

New York, NY 20135

(914) 555-3869

OBJECTIVE:

To obtain an entry-level position in a public accounting firm.

EMPLOYMENT HISTORY:

11/2003–Present, Assistant Administrator at Touch of Class Foods Corporation

**Built Accounts Payable and Accounts Receivable ledgers.

**Originated a responsive invoice program.

**Prepared corporate tax returns and all schedules.

**Oversaw intern program.

**Initiated ISO-9002 Certifications in all areas of plant production.

05/01–11/2003 *Personal Assistant* at Park Board of Trustees

**Research and Development with City Sewer District.

**Assisted with general accounting procedures.

**Assisted with customer-related issues.

**Assisted with the allocation of public funds.

EDUCATION:

**M.B.A., University of New York, 2003, GPA: 3.8

**B.S. in Business Administration, concentration in Individual and Corporate Taxation with an emphasis in Management Information Systems, 2001, GPA: 3.2

COMPUTER SKILLS:

**Microsoft Word, Excel, Access, PowerPoint

**Quicken

**Windows XP and Windows XP Applications

AFFILIATIONS:

**ISO-9002

**TQM National Association

Figure 6-4 Sample Electronic Résumé of Henry Sanchez

Employee Selection Criteria?

You are the newly appointed sales manager for a large manufacturing organization that has been struggling of late, even though your region is the firm's most successful one. Your office is located in a very close-knit community where people place a high value on local basketball. In fact, it didn't take you long to realize that to most people, local basketball is even more important than the Super Bowl. While you were watching a game the other night with your biggest customer, who purchases almost 40 percent of your yearly volume, told you that the star on the team may soon be leaving the community because his father was laid off. He has heard that your region has an opening for a sales representative, and he asks you to hire the boy's father. You tell him that you will be glad to review the man's résumé, but you think that you have already found an extremely qualified person.

As you are reviewing the résumé of your customer's recommended candidate the next day, the person you are replacing comes by the office to say good-bye. In the conversation he mentions that in this town, people do each other favors, and that is how they build trust. He also tells you that if the boy's father is not hired, the firm may lose most, if not all, of the buyer's business. That is quite a shock because you realize that the customer's candidate lacks some qualifications for the position.

What would you do?

(described previously). The traditional résumé will continue to be designed to be read by real people in 20 *seconds or less* and will follow the various formats presented by untold numbers of résumé writers and résumé-writing programs. The keyword résumé, however, should be added to the job seeker's arsenal, and utilized in any situation where computer scanning or posting online might possibly be involved. The key to success in the future is to prepare both correctly, and then get them to prospective employers.[28]

Here are some additional recommendations to follow if a person believes his or her résumé will be scanned:

- Avoid special characters.
- Do not use tabs; use your space bar.
- Do not use the wordwrap feature when composing your résumé; instead, use hard carriage returns to insert line breaks.
- Use the default font and size.
- Do not use boldface and italics.
- Do not use blocks.
- Do not use columns.
- Do not place names or lines on the sides of résumés.

7 OBJECTIVE

Explain the advantages and potential problems of using selection tests.

Selection Tests: Advantages and Potential Problems

Recognizing the shortcomings of other selection tools, many firms have added pre-employment tests to their hiring process. These tests rate the aptitude, personality, abilities, and motivation of potential employees, allowing managers to choose candidates according to how they will fit into the open positions and corporate culture. Tests alone are not enough to make a sufficient evaluation of a candidate because they are not foolproof. Firms need to use them in conjunction with other selection tools.

Advantages of Selection Tests

Research indicates that customized tests can be a reliable and accurate means to predict on-the-job performance. Also, the cost of employment testing is small in comparison to ultimate hiring costs, and a successful program will bolster a firm's bottom line. The reason organizations use tests is to identify attitudes and job-related skills that interviews cannot recognize. They are a more efficient way to get at that type of information and may result in better-quality people being hired.

Potential Problems Using Selection Tests

Job performance depends on an individual's ability and motivation to do the work. Selection tests may accurately predict an applicant's ability to perform the job, the *can do*, but they are less successful in indicating the extent to which the individual will be motivated to perform it, the *will do*. The most successful employees have two things in common: they identify with their firm's goals and they are highly motivated. For one reason or another, many employees with high potential never seem to reach it. The factors related to success on the job are so numerous and complex that selection may always be more of an art than a science.

Employers should be aware that tests might be unintentionally discriminatory. When it excludes a protected class at a significant rate, the test should be avoided unless the employer can show the test is job related for the position in question and consistent with business necessity. Pre-employment testing carries with it legal liabilities of two types. One is a lawsuit from rejected applicants who claim a test was not job related or that it unfairly discriminated against a protected group, violating federal employment laws. Organizations must ensure that their selection tests do not discriminate against members of protected classes. The second potential legal problem relates to *negligence hiring* lawsuits filed by victims of employee misbehavior or incompetence (a topic discussed later in this chapter).

Test anxiety can also be a problem. Applicants often become quite anxious when confronting yet another hurdle that might eliminate them from consideration. The test administrator's reassuring manner and a well-organized testing operation should serve to reduce this threat. Actually, although a great deal of anxiety is detrimental to test performance, a slight degree is helpful.

The problems of hiring unqualified or less qualified candidates and rejecting qualified candidates, along with other potential legal problems, will continue regardless of the procedures followed. Well-developed tests administered by competent professionals help organizations minimize such consequences.

Characteristics of Properly Designed Selection Tests

8 OBJECTIVE

Describe the characteristics of properly designed selection tests.

Properly designed selection tests are standardized, objective, based on sound norms, reliable, and, of utmost importance, valid. The application of these concepts is discussed next.

Standardization

Standardization:
Uniformity of the procedures and conditions related to administering tests.

Standardization is the uniformity of the procedures and conditions related to administering tests.

In order to compare the performance of several applicants on the same test, it is necessary for all to take the test under conditions that are as identical as possible. For example, the content of instructions provided and the time allowed must be the same, and the physical environment must be similar. If one person takes a test in a room with jackhammers operating just outside and another takes it in a more tranquil environment, differences in test results are likely.

Objectivity

Objectivity in testing occurs when everyone scoring a test obtains the same results.

Multiple-choice and true-false tests are objective. The person taking the test either chooses the correct answer or not.

Norms

Comparison

A **norm** is a frame of reference for comparing an applicant's performance with that of others.

Specifically, a norm reflects the distribution of many scores obtained by people similar to the applicant being tested. A score by itself is insignificant. It becomes meaningful only when compared with other applicants' scores.

When a sufficient number of employees are performing the same or similar work, employers can standardize their own tests. Typically, this is not the case, and a national norm for a particular test is used. A prospective employee takes the test, the score obtained is compared to the norm, and the significance of the test score is then determined.

Reliability

Reliability is the extent to which a selection test provides consistent results.

Reliability data reveal the degree of confidence placed in a test. If a person scores a 130 on a certain intelligence test this week and retakes the test next week and scores an 80, the test reliability would likely be low. If a test has low reliability, its validity as a predictor will also be low. However, the existence of reliability alone does not guarantee the test's validity.

Validity (Job Related)

The basic requirement for a selection test is that it be valid. **Validity** is the extent to which a test measures what it claims to measure.

If a test cannot indicate ability to perform the job, it has no value. And, if used, it will result in poor hiring decisions and a potential legal liability for the employer.

Validity, commonly reported as a correlation coefficient, summarizes the relationship between two variables. For example, these variables may be the score on a selection test and some measure of employee performance. A coefficient of 0 shows no relationship, whereas coefficients of either ± 1.0 indicate a perfect relationship, one positive and the other negative. Naturally, no test will be 100 percent accurate, yet organizations strive for the highest feasible coefficient. If a job performance test has a high positive correlation coefficient, most prospective employees who score high on the test will probably later prove to be high performers.

Title VII requires that employment tests be valid, that is, job related. The test must work without having an adverse impact on minorities, females, and individuals with backgrounds or characteristics protected under the law. If using the test results in an adverse impact on certain members of protected groups, the firm must have a compelling reason why it is used; that is, it must validate the test. Employers are not required to validate their selection tests automatically. Remember from Chapter 3 that validation is required only when the selection process as a whole results in an adverse impact on women or minorities. However, an organization cannot know whether the test is actually measuring desired qualities and abilities without validation.

Types of Validation Studies

The *Uniform Guidelines* established three approaches to validating selection tests: criterion-related validity, content validity, and construct validity.

Criterion-Related Validity

Criterion-related validity is a test validation method that compares the scores on selection tests to some aspect of job performance determined, for example, by performance appraisal.

Performance measures might include quantity and quality of work, turnover, and absenteeism. A close relationship between the score on the test and job performance suggests that the test is valid.

Content Validity

Content validity is a test validation method whereby a person performs certain tasks that are actually required by the job or completes a paper-and-pencil test that measures relevant job knowledge.

Although statistical concepts are not involved, many practitioners believe that content validity provides a sensible approach to validating a selection test. This form of validation requires thorough job analysis and carefully prepared job descriptions. An example of the use of content validity is giving a data-entering test to an applicant whose primary job would be to enter data. Court decisions have supported the concept of content validity.

Construct Validity

Construct validity is a test validation method that determines whether a test measures certain constructs, or traits, that job analysis finds to be important in performing a job.

For instance, a job may require a high degree of creativity or reasoning ability. Or, a sales representative position may require the applicant to be extroverted and aggressive. Construct validity in and of itself is not a primary method for validating selection tests.

Types of Employment Tests

Individuals differ in characteristics related to job performance. These differences, which are measurable, relate to cognitive abilities, psychomotor abilities, job knowledge, work-sample, vocational interests, and personality.

Cognitive Aptitude Tests

Cognitive aptitude tests are tests that determine general reasoning ability, memory, vocabulary, verbal fluency, and numerical ability.

They may be helpful in identifying job candidates who have extensive knowledge bases. As the content of jobs becomes broader and more fluid, employees must be able to adapt quickly to job changes and rapid technological advances. It is likely that testing for more general traits will be necessary to match the broader range of characteristics required for successful performance of these flexible jobs.

OBJECTIVE 9

Explain the types of validation studies; describe types of employment tests, including online testing and the use of assessment center.

Criterion-related validity:
Test validation method that compares the scores on selection tests to some aspect of job performance determined, for example, by performance appraisal.

Content validity:
Test validation method whereby a person performs certain tasks that are actually required by the job or completes a paper-and-pencil test that measures relevant job knowledge.

Construct validity:
Test validation method that determines whether a test measures certain constructs, or traits, that job analysis finds to be important in performing a job.

Cognitive aptitude tests:
Tests that determine general reasoning ability, memory, vocabulary, verbal fluency, and numerical ability.

Psychomotor Abilities Tests

Psychomotor abilities tests are tests that measure strength, coordination, and dexterity.

Miniaturization in assembly operations has accelerated the development of tests to determine these abilities. Much of this work is so delicate that magnifying lenses are necessary, and the psychomotor abilities required to perform the tasks are critical. Standardized tests are not available to cover all these abilities, but those involved in many routine production jobs and some office jobs are measurable.

Job-Knowledge Tests

Job-knowledge tests are tests that measure a candidate's knowledge of the duties of the job for which he or she is applying.

Such tests are commercially available but individual firms may also design them specifically for any job, based on data derived from job analysis.

Work-Sample Tests

Work-sample tests are tests that require an applicant to perform a task or set of tasks representative of the job.

For positions that require heavy use of spreadsheets, having the applicant sit at a computer and construct a sample spreadsheet, with data the firm provides, will be useful in assessing a required ability. Such tests, by their nature, are job related. Not surprisingly, the evidence concerning this type of test is that it is valid, reduces adverse impact, and is more acceptable to applicants. A real test of validity, in the opinion of some experts, should be a performance assessment: take individuals to a job and give them the opportunity to perform it.

Vocational Interest Tests

Vocational interest tests are tests that indicate the occupation a person is most interested in and the one likely to provide satisfaction.

These tests compare the individual's interests with those of successful employees in a specific job. The assumption here is that if a person shows a definite interest in a certain vocation they will be more productive on the job. But, having interest in a job and being able to effectively perform may not be the same. A person may have an interest in being a brain surgeon but not the aptitude for it. Although interest tests have application in employee selection, their primary use has been in counseling and vocational guidance.

Personality Tests

Personality tests are self-reported measures of traits, temperaments, or dispositions.

Personality tests, unlike ability tests, are not time constrained and do not measure specific problem-solving skills. These questionnaires tap into softer areas such as leadership, teamwork, and personal assertiveness. A properly designed personality profile can measure and match the appropriate personality dimensions to the requirements of the job. For example, research indicates that two important predictors for successful salespeople are extroversion and conscientiousness. The ability to test for these traits can mean a significant increase in selection effectiveness. In information technology organization, most large companies now use psychometric testing to identify future managers. These managers are being assessed for their ability to bring about long-term change and their ability to handle day-to-day management tasks, and personality tests can help identify both skills. Generally, fire departments and law enforcement agencies use the Minnesota Multiphasic Personality Inventory (MMPI) test, which consists of 567 statements that help to determine a subject's degree of paranoia, depression, mania, or anxiety.[29] In police departments the MMPI is used to detect the inclination toward substance abuse and psychopathology.[30] These types of tests are typically used in the early stage of the selection process.[31]

Some firms use these tests to classify personality types. With this information, organizations can create diverse teams for creativity or homogeneous teams for compatibility. The use of personality tests as selection tools is controversial, since a great deal of research has concluded that their validity is low relative to other predictors. Nevertheless, use of personality tests is at an all-time high. It has been estimated that 30 to 40 percent of large firms use some form of psychological testing in their employment selection.[32]

Honesty and integrity are important personality traits to consider in the selection process. Since the polygraph test (discussed later) has been effectively banned in the private sector as a hiring tool, other psychological tests, called pen-and-pencil honesty tests, have been used to detect dishonest candidates. However, a more effective way to ensure that employees are honest is to conduct a thorough pre-employment screening including background investigations and reference check prior to hiring and, afterwards, to use appropriate control systems.

Unique Forms of Testing

Three unique forms of testing—genetic testing, graphoanalysis (handwriting analysis), and polygraph testing—will be discussed.

Genetic Testing

Genetic testing is given to identify predisposition to inherited diseases, including cancer, heart disease, neurological disorders, and congenital diseases.

As genetic research progresses, confirmed links between specific gene mutations and diseases are emerging. Scientists have assembled the entire set of genetic instructions for building a human body and world leaders likened this achievement to putting a human being on the moon. This brings both hope and concerns to the forefront in employment testing.

Genetic tests may predict a predisposition to having a disease. However, such tests cannot tell whether a person is certain to get the disease or would become ill at age 30 or 90. In addition, everyone has some disposition to genetic disease and a genetic predisposition is not the same as a pre-existing condition. There are two primary reasons for genetic testing. One is that predictive testing allows employers to reject certain employees and maintain a more productive workforce. Genetic testing offers a way for the firm to foresee likely health care costs and to avoid hiring at-risk candidates. Another purpose is that it enables therapeutic intervention, thereby allowing carriers to get appropriate therapy.

The major concerns with genetic testing relate to the possible misuse of information. Some perceive the process as being highly invasive and believe it communicates to employees that the firm really does not care about them. Also, once the results of a genetic test are in a medical record, they may be made available to employers and insurers without an individual's knowledge or consent. It is one thing knowing that a genetic predisposition might be passed down. It is another thing to record that information in the person's personnel file.

The Equal Employment Opportunity Commission has issued guidelines stating that healthy individuals with a genetic predisposition to a disease, and thus perceived as disabled, are protected by the Americans with Disabilities Act.[33] The United States senate voted 98-0, approving a bill that would provide protection for employees who refuse to have genetic testing because of fears the results might cost them their health insurance, or even their job.[34] An executive order applicable to every aspect of federal employment prohibits discrimination against employees based on genetic information.[35]

Genetic testing:
Tests given to identify predisposition to inherited diseases, including cancer, heart disease, neurological disorders, and congenital diseases.

Web Wisdom
Genetic Testing

http://www. accessexcellence.org/AE/ AEPC/NIH/index.html

Information provided by the U. S. Department of Health and Human Services on genetic testing.

Graphoanalysis (Handwriting Analysis)

The use of handwriting analysis as a selection factor is **graphoanalysis**.

Many in the United States view handwriting analysis in the same context as psychic readings or astrology.[36] In Europe, however, many employers use graphoanalysis to help screen and place job applicants. One study estimated that 85 percent of European companies utilize handwriting analysis.[37] It is not unusual for European companies to have full-time handwriting analysts on staff.

There are two distinct schools of handwriting analysis: the Gestalt theory, developed in Germany, and the trait method, developed mainly in France, England, and the United States. The latter method examines handwriting to determine defined traits, such as how people form certain letters. Although no definitive study exists on the extent of its use in the United States, according to some handwriting experts, graphoanalysis is becoming more common. A basic reason for the reluctance of U.S. employers to use this approach appears to be a concern over the ability to validate such tests. And, there is little research demonstrating the effectiveness of graphology in employee selection. This and the worry about possible legal action seem to make many American employers wary of the process.

Polygraph Tests

For many years, another means used to verify background information has been the polygraph, or lie detector test. One purpose of the polygraph was to confirm or refute the information contained in the application blank. However, the Employee Polygraph Protection Act of 1988 severely limited the use of polygraph tests in the private sector. It made unlawful the use of a polygraph test by any employer engaged in interstate commerce. Even so, the Act does not apply to governmental employers, and there are other limited exceptions. The Act permits use of polygraph tests in the private sector to certain prospective employees of security service firms and pharmaceutical manufacturers, distributors, and dispensers. The Act also permits, with certain restrictions, polygraph testing of certain employees reasonably suspected of involvement in a workplace incident, such as theft or embezzlement. Persons who take polygraph tests have a number of specific rights. For example, they have the right to a written notice before testing, the right to refuse or discontinue a test, and the right not to have test results disclosed to unauthorized persons.

Online Testing

Organizations are increasingly using the Internet to test various skills required by applicants. Firms may design and have their own tests available online or use an external source. For example, tests are available that test job applicants on their alleged technical abilities. Know It All, Inc. offers job-skills testing as a service to firms that lack the resources to evaluate candidates on their own. For a small fee, a company can confirm job candidates' skills online without ever seeing them. The tests are not merely pass-fail, but measure applicants' skill levels as well.[38] Some law enforcement agencies accept applications and conduct initial testing over the Internet.[39]

Assessment Centers

An **assessment center** is a selection approach that requires individuals to perform activities similar to those they might encounter in an actual job.

The assessment center is one of the most powerful tools for assessing managerial talent. Research has established the validity of the assessment center approach to evaluate individuals' current job performance and also to determine how well they are likely to handle new or expanded assignments.[40] Many of America's top companies have set up assessment centers where they can first interview potential employees, then evaluate them in real work situations.[41]

In an assessment center, candidates perform a number of exercises that simulate the tasks they will carry out in the job they seek. Among the typical assessment center tests, the applicants may complete *in-basket exercises* and perform in *management games, leaderless discussion groups, mock interviews,* and other simulations.[42] The traditional in-basket exercise may receive a technological boost by replacing the paper memos with e-mail messages, faxes, or voice mail. Assessment centers measure candidates' skills in prioritizing, delegating, and decision making. The professional assessors who evaluate the candidates' performances usually observe them away from the workplace over a certain period of time, perhaps a single day. The assessors selected are typically experienced managers who may not only evaluate performances, but also participate in the exercises.

An advantage of the assessment center approach is the increased reliability and validity of the information provided. Research has shown that the in-basket exercise, a typical component of assessment centers, is a good predictor of management performance. Its validity provides an alternative to paper-and-pencil tests.

Employment Interview

10 OBJECTIVE

Explain the importance of the employment interview and describe the general types of interviewing.

Employment interview:
Goal-oriented conversation in which an interviewer and an applicant exchange information.

The **employment interview** is a goal-oriented conversation in which the interviewer and applicant exchange information.

Traditionally, interviews have not been valid predictors of success on the job.[43] For 500 years, Leonardo da Vinci's *Mona Lisa* has confounded viewers who try to read her expression. Like the *Mona Lisa*, every job applicant presents a mysterious façade. Nevertheless, interviews continue to be the primary method companies use to evaluate applicants. As discussed later in this chapter, some firms have made significant progress in improving the validity of interviews. The employment interview is especially important because the applicants who reach this stage are the survivors. They have endured the preliminary interview, had their applications reviewed, and scored satisfactorily on selection tests. At this point, the candidates appear to be qualified, at least on paper. Every seasoned manager knows, however, that appearances can be quite misleading. Additional information is needed to indicate whether the individual is willing to work and can adapt to that particular organization.

Interview Planning

Interview planning is essential to effective employment interviews.[44] A primary consideration should be the speed in which the process occurs. Many studies have demonstrated that the top candidates for nearly any job are hired and off the job market within anywhere from 1 to 10 days. It is imperative that interview schedulers keep this in mind.

The physical location of the interview should be both pleasant and private, providing for a minimum of interruptions. The interviewer should possess a pleasant personality, empathy, and the ability to listen and communicate effectively. He or she should become familiar with the applicant's qualifications by reviewing the data collected from other selection tools. As preparation for the interview, the interviewer should develop a job profile based on the job description/specification.[45] After listing job requirements, it is helpful to have an interview checklist that includes these hints:

- Compare an applicant's application and résumé with job requirements.
- Develop questions related to the qualities sought.

- Prepare a step-by-step plan to present the position, company, division, and department.
- Determine how to ask for examples of past job-related applicant behavior.[46]

Content of the Interview

Both the interviewer and the candidate have agendas for the interview. After establishing rapport with the applicant, the interviewer seeks additional job-related information to complement data provided by other selection tools. The interview permits clarification of certain points, the uncovering of additional information, and the elaboration of data needed to make a sound selection decision. The interviewer should provide information about the company, the job, and expectations of the candidate. Other areas typically included in the interview are discussed next.

Occupational Experience. The interviewer will explore the candidate's knowledge, skills, abilities, and willingness to handle responsibility. Although successful performance in one job does not guarantee success in another, it does provide an indication of the person's ability and willingness to work.

Academic Achievement. In the absence of significant work experience, a person's academic record takes on greater importance. Managers should, however, consider grade point average in light of other factors. For example, involvement in work, extracurricular activities, or other responsibilities may have affected an applicant's academic performance.

Interpersonal Skills. An individual may possess important technical skills significant to accomplishing a job. However, if the person cannot work well with others, chances for success are slim. This is especially true in today's world with the increasing use of teams. The biggest mistake an interviewee can make is thinking that firms hire people only for their technical skills.

Personal Qualities. Personal qualities normally observed during the interview include physical appearance, speaking ability, vocabulary, poise, adaptability, and assertiveness. As with all selection criteria, employers should consider these attributes only if they are relevant to job performance.

Organizational fit:
Management's perception of the degree to which the prospective employee will fit in with the firm's culture or value system.

Organizational Fit. A hiring criterion *not* prominently mentioned in the literature is *organizational fit.* **Organizational fit** refers to management's perception of the degree to which the prospective employee will fit in with the firm's culture or value system.

Using *fit* as a criterion raises legal and diversity questions, and perhaps this explains the low profile. Nevertheless, there is evidence that managers use it in making selection decisions and it is not a minor consideration. Complicating the situation further is the fact that the same employee may be a poor fit with one firm and a perfect fit with another.[47] Employees also should consider organizational fit when debating whether or not to accept a job offer. A variety of factors can lead to a bad job fit, ranging from holding opposing views on etiquette or ethics to possessing conflicting views on the direction of the department.[48]

Russell Yaquinto, who coaches managerial job seekers for the outplacement firm Right Management Consultants in Dallas, states that "There's very widespread agreement . . . that you can have the credentials, but if you aren't going to fit [the culture], it doesn't matter. Before long, you'll be out of there." An employee who fits not only the skill requirements but also the culture, values, and belief systems of the organization is typically three times more productive and two times less likely to leave the firm.[49] Maureen Henson, director of recruitment and employment strategies for the

Henry Ford Health System, said, "We are moving away from the get-them-in-the-door-and-get-them-in-the-seat philosophy. A lot more attention is being given to selecting employees for that 'good fit.'"[50]

Candidate's Role and Expectations

While the interviewer will provide information about the company, it is still important that candidates do their homework, including checking the library and the firm's Website. Many sites include information tailored to job seekers. These sites often provide a history of the company and a description of its products and customers. In fact, the candidate should learn as much as possible about the firm. At WetFeet.com, a job seeker can research companies, careers, and industries.[51] A person applying for a management position, especially, should have a thorough understanding of the firm's business priorities, its strengths and weaknesses, and its chief competitors. Applicants should consider how they would address some of the issues facing the company. They need to be able to show how their experiences can help in addressing these issues.

Recruiters need to remember that interviewees also have objectives for the interview. One might be to determine what the firm is willing to pay as a starting salary. Job seekers have other goals that may include the following:

- To be listened to and understood
- To have ample opportunity to present their qualifications
- To be treated fairly and with respect
- To gather information about the job and the company
- To make an informed decision concerning the desirability of the job

Candidates can learn what interviewing skills they need to improve by undergoing a mock interview or two. Having a colleague or friend interview them, then critically reviewing their own responses can be beneficial. This mock interview allows candidates to analyze the strengths and interests that they would bring to a job. The process would also help them prioritize the points they want to make in the real interview.

General Types of Interviews

Types of interviews are often broadly classified as structured, unstructured, and behavioral. A discussion of the differences follows.

Unstructured (Nondirective) Interview

Unstructured interview:
Interview in which the job applicant is asked probing, open-ended questions.

An **unstructured interview** is one in which the interviewer asks probing, open-ended questions.

This type of interview is comprehensive, and the interviewer encourages the applicant to do much of the talking. Questions such as "Tell me about yourself." "What is your greatest strength?" "What is your greatest weakness?" and "How will our company benefit by having you as an employee?" might be asked. The nondirective interview is often more time consuming than the structured interview and results in obtaining different information from different candidates. This adds to the potential legal woes of organizations using this approach. Compounding the problem is the likelihood of discussing ill-advised, potentially discriminatory information. The applicant who is being encouraged to pour his heart out may volunteer facts that the interviewer does not need or want to know. Unsuccessful applicants subjected to this interviewing approach may later claim in court that the reason for their failure to get the job was the employer's use of this information.

Structured (Directive or Patterned) Interview

In the **structured interview**, the interviewer asks each applicant for a particular job the same series of job-related questions.

Although interviews have historically been very poor predictors for making selection decisions, use of structured interviews increases reliability and accuracy by reducing the subjectivity and inconsistency of unstructured interviews.

A structured job interview typically contains four types of questions:

- *Situational questions* are those that pose a typical job situation to determine what the applicant did in a similar situation.

- *Job-knowledge questions* are those that probe the applicant's job-related knowledge; these questions may relate to basic educational skills or complex scientific or managerial skills.

- *Job-sample simulation questions* involve situations in which an applicant may be required to answer questions related to performance of a task.

- *Worker requirements questions* are those that seek to determine the applicant's willingness to conform to the requirements of the job. For example, the interviewer may ask whether the applicant is willing to perform repetitive work or move to another city.

Behavioral Interview

Research shows that traditional interviewing has about a 14 percent chance of predicting job success.[52] Because of this low success rate, the behavioral interview is being increasingly used. The **behavioral interview** is a structured interview where applicants are asked to relate actual incidents from their past relevant to the target job.

Although once used exclusively for senior executive positions, behavioral interviewing is now a popular technique for lower-level positions. The assumption is that past behavior is the best predictor of future behavior.[53] The reason for increased use of behavioral interviews is that older methods have proven to be poor predictors of a candidate's success. The premise that past behavior is the best predictor of future behavior avoids having to make judgments about applicants' personalities and precludes hypothetical and self-evaluative questions.[54]

John Madigan, IT human resource vice president at The Hartford Financial Services Group, Inc., explains that a behavioral job interview reveals a pattern of behavior. "We actually ask what you did in specific situations," Madigan says. "Concrete examples will demonstrate a person's preferred way of dealing with those situations and give you a better idea of that person and how they're likely to act on the job."[55] Behavioral interviewers look for three main things: a description of a challenging situation, what the candidate did about it, and measurable results.[56]

In the behavioral interview, the situational behaviors are selected for their relevance to job success. Questions are formed from the behaviors by asking applicants how they performed in the described situation.[57] For example, when probing for professional or technical knowledge, the candidate might be asked, "Describe a situation where your expertise made a significant difference." Or, if seeking to determine the applicant's enthusiasm, the question might be, "Relate a scenario where you were responsible for motivating others." Benchmark answers derived from behaviors of successful employees are prepared for use in rating applicant responses. A candidate's response to a given situation provides the means to develop an insight into his or her job potential. In behavioral interviews, candidates may unwittingly reveal information about their attitudes, intelligence, and truthfulness. Arrogance, lack of cooperation with team members, and anger can all spill out during such an interview. Although some candidates may think the interview is all about technical skills, it is as much about them as a person as anything. In a recent study of hiring managers, lack of the necessary technical skills was given as the reason for failure only 11 percent of the time. However, 26 percent failed because they could not accept feedback, 23 percent failed because they could not understand and manage emotions, 17 percent failed because they lacked motivation, and 15 percent failed because they had the wrong temperament for the job.[58]

Questions asked in behavior description interviewing are legally safe since they are job related. Equally important, since both questions and answers are related to successful job performance, they are more accurate in predicting whether applicants will be successful in the job they are hired to perform. A positive feature about behavioral interviewing is its ability to serve as a tiebreaker. This technique can help select the one who is most likely to excel in the job when several candidates appear to possess similar skills, experiences, and qualifications. It answers the one question both the hiring manager and the candidate want to know most: Is this a good *fit*?

One difficulty with behavioral interviewing is that some job seekers have gotten wise to the process.[59] A growing number of candidates, especially those coming from business and law schools, deliberately misrepresent themselves during the interview. The stories some concoct about who they are and what they did in real-life situations are pure fiction.

 OBJECTIVE

Describe the various methods of interviewing and potential interviewing problems.

Methods of Interviewing

Organizations conduct interviews in several ways. The level of the open position and the appropriate labor market determine the most fitting approach. A discussion of these methods follows.

One-on-One Interview

In a typical employment interview, the applicant meets one-on-one with an interviewer. As the interview may be a highly emotional occasion for the applicant, meeting alone with the interviewer is often less threatening. The environment this method provides may allow an effective exchange of information to take place.

Group Interview

Group interview:
Meeting in which several job applicants interact in the presence of one or more company representatives.

In a **group interview**, several applicants interact in the presence of one or more company representatives.

This approach, although not mutually exclusive of other interview types, may provide useful insights into the candidates' interpersonal competence as they engage in a group discussion. Another advantage of this technique is that it saves time for busy professionals and executives.

Board (or Panel) Interview

Board interview:
An interview approach in which several of the firm's representatives interview a candidate at the same time.

In a **board interview**, several of the firm's representatives interview a candidate at the same time.

Once the interview is complete, the board members pool their evaluation of the candidate.[60] Most professors who have received a Ph.D. are quite familiar with the board interview, as they were required to defend their dissertation as their professors asked questions. At times some candidates claimed that professors having opposing views were deliberately placed on the board and the candidate had to *tiptoe* through the session, hoping not to offend members.

Multiple Interviews

At times the applicants are interviewed by peers, subordinates, and supervisors. Using multiple interviewers not only leads to better hiring decisions; it also begins the transition process. Amazon.com, IBM, and Motorola use peers to interview and do so successfully. Small firms also find much to praise about this hiring process. The payback is substantial and results in a higher degree of acceptance of a candidate and a higher degree of retention. This approach permits the firm to get a more encompassing view of the candidate. It also gives the candidate a chance to learn more about the company from a variety of perspectives. The result of this type of interview is a stronger, more cohesive team that shares the company's culture and helps assure organizational fit.

Stress Interview

Stress interview:
Form of interview in which the interviewer intentionally creates anxiety.

Most interviewers strive to minimize stress for the candidate. In the **stress interview**, however, the interviewer intentionally creates anxiety.

The interviewer deliberately makes the candidate uncomfortable by asking blunt and often discourteous questions. The purpose is to determine the applicant's tolerance for stress that may accompany the job. Knowledge of this factor may be important if the job requires the ability to deal with a high level of stress.

Stress interviews are not new. The late Admiral Hyman G. Rickover, father of the U.S. Navy's nuclear submarine program, was known to offer interviewees a chair that had one or two legs shorter than the other. The candidates' problems were compounded by the chair's polished seat. The admiral once stated that "they had to maintain their wits about them as they answered questions while sliding off the chair."[61]

Realistic Job Preview

Realistic job preview (RJP):
Method of conveying both positive and negative job information to an applicant in an unbiased manner.

Many applicants have unrealistic expectations about the prospective job and employer. This inaccurate perception may have negative consequences,[62] yet it is often encouraged when interviewers paint false, rosy pictures of the job and company. This practice leads to mismatches of people and positions. What compounds the problem is when candidates exaggerate their own qualifications. To correct this situation from the employer's side, firms should provide a **realistic job preview (RJP)**, conveying both positive and negative job information to the applicant in an unbiased manner.

This should typically be done early in the selection process and, definitely, before a job offer is made.

An RJP conveys information about tasks the person would perform and the behavior required to *fit into* the culture of the organization.[63] This approach helps applicants develop a more accurate perception of the job and the firm. Research shows employers who give detailed RJPs get two results: fewer employees accept the job offer, and applicants who do accept the offer are less likely to leave the firm. Given an RJP, some candidates will take themselves out of the selection process and that will minimize the number of unqualified candidates. Another reason to use RJPs is the benefit a firm receives from being an up-front, ethical employer.

Potential Interviewing Problems

Potential interviewing problems that can threaten the success of employment interviews are discussed next. After studying this information, it becomes clear that being a good interviewer requires careful attention to the task.

Inappropriate Questions

Although no questions are illegal, many are clearly inappropriate. When they are asked, the responses generated create a legal liability for the employer. The most basic interviewing rule is this: "Ask only job-related questions."[64] Recall from Chapter 3 that the definition of a test in the *Uniform Guidelines* includes "physical, education and work experience requirements from *informal or casual interviews*." Because the interview is a test, if adverse impact is shown, it is subject to the same validity requirements as any other step in the selection process. For unstructured interviews, this constraint presents special difficulties. Historically, the interview has been more vulnerable to charges of discrimination than any other tool used in the selection process. One simple rule governs interviewing: *all questions must be job related.* In addition to being a waste of time, irrelevant or personal questions are dangerous and often improper. Since behavioral interviews necessarily consist of job-related questions, their popularity is understandable.

The Americans with Disabilities Act also provides a warning for interviewers. Interviewers should inquire about the need for reasonable accommodations in only a few situations. For example, the topic is appropriate if the applicant is in a wheelchair or has an obvious disability that will require accommodation. Also, the applicant may voluntarily disclose a disability or even ask for some reasonable accommodation. Otherwise, employers should refrain from broaching the subject. Instead, interviewers should frame questions in terms of whether applicants can perform the essential functions of the jobs for which they are applying.

Premature Judgments

Research suggests that interviewers often make judgments about candidates in the first few minutes of the interview. Apparently these interviewers believe their ability to "read" a candidate is superior. When this occurs, a great deal of potentially valuable information is not considered. Even if an interviewer spent a week with an applicant, the sample of behavior might be too small to judge the candidate's qualifications properly. In addition, the candidate's behavior during an interview is seldom typical or natural, thereby making a quick judgment difficult.

Interviewer Domination

In successful interviews, relevant information must flow both ways. Sometimes, interviewers begin the interview by telling candidates what they are looking for, and then are excited to hear candidates parrot back their own words. Other interviewers are delighted to talk through virtually the entire interview, either to take pride in their organization's accomplishments or to express frustrations over their own difficulties. After dominating the meeting for an hour or so, these interviewers feel good about the candidate. Therefore, interviewers must learn to be good listeners as well as suppliers of information.

Permitting Non-Job-Related Information

If a candidate begins volunteering personal information that is not job related, the interviewer should steer the conversation back on course. It might do well to begin the interview by tactfully stating, "This selection decision will be based strictly on qualifications. Let's not discuss topics such as religion, social activities, national origin, gender, or family situations. We are definitely interested in you, personally. However, these factors are not job related and will not be considered in our decision." This enables better decisions to be made while decreasing the likelihood of discrimination charges.

To elicit needed information in any type of interview, the interviewer must create a climate that encourages the applicant to speak freely. However, the conversation should not become too casual. Whereas engaging in friendly chitchat with candidates might be pleasant, in our litigious society, it may be the most dangerous thing an interviewer can do. Asking a woman a question about her children that has nothing to do with the job would not be appropriate.

Contrast Effect

An error in judgment may occur when, for example, a interviewer meets with several poorly qualified applicants and then confronts a mediocre candidate. By comparison, the last applicant may appear to be better qualified than he or she actually is. The opposite can also occur. Suppose that a clearly outstanding candidate is followed by a very good candidate. The second candidate may not be considered even if the first candidate turns down the job offer.

Lack of Training

Anyone who has ever conducted an interview realizes that it is much more than carrying on a conversation with another person. The interviewer is attempting to gain insight into how the applicant answers job-related questions. There should be a reason for asking each question. For instance, suppose the applicant is asked, "Tell me about yourself." A trained interviewer asks this question to determine if the applicant's life experiences qualify the applicant for the job. Interviewers should be trained to have a job-related purpose for asking each question. When the cost of making poor selection decisions is considered, the expense of training employees in interviewing skills can be easily justified.

Nonverbal Communication

Body language is the nonverbal communication method in which physical actions such as motions, gestures, and facial expressions convey thoughts and emotions. The interviewer is attempting to view the nonverbal signals from the applicant. Applicants are also reading the nonverbal signals of the interviewer. Therefore, interviewers should make a conscious effort to view themselves as applicants do to avoid sending inappropriate or unintended nonverbal signals. Research has shown that 90 percent of first impressions are based on nonverbal communication and only 10 percent on verbal communications.[65] It is important for the interviewer to be aware of how he or she is communicating nonverbally.

Concluding the Interview

When the interviewer has obtained the necessary information and answered the applicant's questions, he or she should conclude the interview. Management must then determine whether the candidate is suitable for the open position and organization. If the conclusion is positive, the process continues; if there appears to be no match, the candidate is no longer considered. Also, in concluding the interview, the interviewer should tell the applicant that he or she will be notified of the selection decision shortly. Keeping this promise helps maintain a positive relationship with the applicant.

OBJECTIVE

Explain the use of pre-employment screening including background investigations, reference checks, negligent hiring, and negligent referral.

Pre-Employment Screening: Background Investigations

At this stage of the selection process, an applicant has completed an application form or submitted a résumé, taken the required selection tests, and undergone an employment interview. It is now time to determine the accuracy of the information submitted or to determine if vital information was not submitted. According to a recent study by the Society for Human Resource Management, 96 percent of HR managers conduct some kind of background investigation, which is up from 66 percent 10 years ago.[66] Reasons for leaving jobs or gaps in employment may be cleverly disguised to present a work history that does not provide an accurate or complete picture. Letters of recommendation from companies that are no longer in existence may raise a red flag.[67] Barry Nadell, president of InfoLink Screening Services Inc., said it reviewed thousands of applications it had screened for employers across industries and found 8.4 percent of job applicants had some type of criminal conviction.[68]

Background investigations involve obtaining data from various sources, including previous employers, business associates, credit bureaus, government agencies, and academic institutions, have become increasingly more important. Fingerprinting is becoming a more common part of checks, especially for companies that employ workers in charge of securing a worksite—for example, airports, the financial services industry, hospitals, schools, the gaming industry, and hazardous materials services.[69] An effective and comprehensive background investigation is typically conducted by a third party and includes examination and verification of the following elements:

- previous employment
- education
- personal references
- criminal history
- driving record
- civil litigation
- workers' compensation history
- credit history
- Social Security number

In addition, more and more often, companies are also gathering information regarding an applicant's *mode of living* and his or her *character*.[70] The principal reason for conducting background investigations is to hire better workers. However, there are other critical reasons as well. For example, in a *Security Management Survey* when security directors were asked what the best way to stop insider theft was, background screening was identified as the top preventative measure.[71] The intensity of background investigations depends on the nature of the open position's tasks and its relationship to customers or clients. To be legally safe, employers should ask applicants to sign a liability waiver permitting a background investigation.[72] A comprehensive waiver is typically a statement on the application form that releases former employers, business references, and others from liability. The waiver also authorizes checks of court records and the verification of the applicant's educational history and other credentials.

Rich Zuckennan, a partner at Lamb & Bamosky, who chairs the New York State Bar Association's labor and employment law section, said, "The cost of a background check has come down from what it used to be. Databases are standardized. The background check companies know where to look." Investigations that once cost hundreds of dollars now cost $100–$150. They can range from verifying résumés and college degrees to verifying prior employment periods and, importantly, looking for convictions.[73] Regardless of how they are accomplished, background investigations have become increasingly important in making sound selection decisions and avoiding charges of negligent hiring (to be discussed further shortly). The investigations may provide information critical to selection decisions, since firms can verify virtually every qualification an applicant lists.

Congress created an obstacle for employers when it amended the federal Fair Credit Reporting Act (FCRA). This 1997 amendment places new obligations on employers who use certain information brought to light through background investigations. Employers' obligations are triggered under the Act when they use *consumer* reports that contain information about an individual's personal and credit characteristics, character, general reputation, and lifestyle. The FCRA only covers reports that are prepared by a *consumer reporting agency* such as a credit bureau. In accordance with

Trends & Innovations

Liars Index

It turns out that quite a few executive job seekers have the nerve to claim an advanced degree from an educational institution they never attended. There was so much misrepresentation of degrees on credentials that years ago Jude M. Werra, president of Jude M. Werra & Associates LLC, an executive search firm in Brookfield, Wisconsin, began compiling a "Liars Index." To calculate the percentage of lying executives, Werra divides the number of people who have misrepresented their education on a résumé by the total number of people whose education his company has checked. The Liars Index for the first half of 2005 was 10.73 percent, down slightly from 11.88 percent during the preceding six-month period.[74]

Some of the most common reasons for lying on a résumé, he says, are expecting that employers will not check the facts. "Our semiannual calculation of the percentage of executives who misrepresent their education on their résumés continues to surprise hiring executives, who can easily check the facts," Werra says. In a survey conducted by his firm, nearly 95 percent of these hiring executives said they would not consider hiring candidates who lied about their degree.[75]

Werra has seen plenty of creative résumés in more than 25 years in the industry. A few years ago he reviewed the résumé of a man who claimed to have an executive MBA from the Massachusetts Institute of Technology. A check with MIT revealed no record of the man. Werra went back to the applicant for an explanation, and the man offered to fax a copy of his diploma. Werra showed the document to MIT, which explained that it was given for completing a summer program that lasted a few weeks, not for an executive MBA. The candidate's response: "Picky, picky."[76]

the FCRA, employers using information from such an agency to make employment decisions must take these actions:

- Obtain prior authorization from the applicant.
- Provide a certification of compliance with the Act to the consumer reporting agency.
- Notify the applicant if it takes any adverse employment action based on the report.

Pre-Employment Screening: Reference Checks

Reference checks:
Information from individuals who know the applicant that provide additional insight into the information furnished by the applicant and verification of its accuracy.

Reference checks are validations from those who know the applicant that provide additional insight into the information furnished by the applicant and allow verification of its accuracy.

They are a valuable source of information to supplement the background investigation. Applicants are often required to submit the names of several references that can provide additional information about them. A possible flaw with reference checking is that virtually every living person can name three or four individuals willing to make favorable statements about him or her. Even so, there is anecdotal evidence that personal references do not always provide favorable information. They may not necessarily be committed to shading the truth for the applicant.

A related problem in obtaining information from previous employers is their general reluctance to reveal such data. The Privacy Act of 1974, although limited to the public sector, provides a major reason for this hesitancy. Employers and employees in the private sector have become very sensitive to the privacy issue. There are two schools of thought with regard to supplying information about former employees. One is, "Don't tell them anything." The other is, "Honesty is the best policy." In the more conservative approach, the employer typically provides only basic data, such as starting and termination dates and last job title. The *honesty* approach is based on the reality that facts honestly given or opinions honestly held constitute a solid legal defense. When former employers are unwilling to give any information about a job applicant, both the potential employer and the applicant are at a disadvantage. A red flag is quickly raised when a former employer refuses to talk about a one-time employee. For those firms that freely give out information about previous employees, questions about the applicant's integrity and character are appropriate. It is helpful to know why the person left that job. If the response differs from that given by the applicant, it is definitely a red flag.

The amount of protection given to those who provide references varies greatly. Laws on the books in 37 states and jurisdictions shield employers from liability for harm to an ex-employee based on the contents of a job reference.[77] The intent of this legislation is to make it easier for employers to give and receive meaningful information. A Texas employer can tell a recruiter about the job performance, attendance, attitudes, effort, knowledge, behaviors, and skills of a former employee.[78] Even so, there continues to be some hesitancy on the part of firms to take advantage of it. Although protective laws do exist, apparently there is a wait-and-see attitude among some employers. It will likely take litigation and court rulings before employers fully understand, and have confidence in, the statutes. Negligent hiring and negligent referral, discussed in the next section, provide additional rationale for conducting background investigations.

Negligent Hiring

Negligent hiring:

Liability a company incurs when it fails to conduct a reasonable investigation of an applicant's background, and then assigns a potentially dangerous person to a position where he or she can inflict harm.

Negligent hiring is the liability an employer incurs when it fails to conduct a reasonable investigation of an applicant's background, and then assigns a potentially dangerous person to a position where he or she can inflict harm.[79]

Reasonable investigation varies according to the nature of the job. The risk of harm to third parties, for example, requires a higher standard of care when hiring a taxi driver as opposed to a bank teller. The taxi cab driver is alone and has control of his or her customer for the time the customer is in the car. This would not be the case for the bank teller. Employers who operate home-service businesses, day-care centers, and home health care operations are particularly at risk as are those with employees who drive company vehicles, visit customer locations, handle money, or work with children, the elderly, or the impaired. The primary consideration in negligent hiring is whether the risk of harm from a dangerous employee was reasonably foreseeable.[80] It is imperative that managers exercise due diligence in conducting background investigations of all prospective employees. Hiring organizations cannot avoid the possibility of legal action. However, following sound selection procedures and keeping written records of the investigations will serve them well and may prove to be money well spent.

The average settlement for negligent hiring cases is $1.6 million[81] and, in addition, they are likely to be upheld on appeal. Let us illustrate the problem: a health care employer hired a male applicant as an aide in a home health care program run by a visiting nurses' association. Soon after assignment to the home of a paraplegic, the employee murdered the patient and then robbed him. In an investigation of the situation, it was found that the individual had lied about where he had worked before, had lied about not having a criminal history, had lied about having a nursing degree, and had lied about being licensed. A check on any of these claims would have disqualified the person from employment. In court, the health care organization attempted to defend itself by claiming that it was not standard practice to conduct in-depth background investigations because they were too expensive. The jury was not impressed and the result was a $26.5 million award.[82]

Negligent Referral

Negligent referral is the liability former employers may incur when they fail to offer a warning about a particularly severe problem with a past employee.

Examples of negligent referral are far too numerous. Charles Cullen, a nurse in Pennsylvania and New Jersey, was able to move from hospital to hospital, intentionally killing patients at each hospital. He worked at 10 different hospitals in New Jersey and Pennsylvania, over a period of 16 years, despite the fact that at seven of those hospitals he was under investigation, fired, or forced to resign. Apparently, not one of those institutions gave Cullen a bad reference, or told other hospitals he was trouble.[83]

OBJECTIVE

Describe the selection decision, the medical examination, and notification of candidates.

Selection Decision

At this point, the focus is on the manager, who must take the most critical step of all: the actual hiring decision. If a firm is going to invest thousands of dollars to recruit, select, and train an employee, it is important for the manager to hire the most qualified available candidate according to the firm's criteria. The final choice is made from among those still in the running after reference checks, selection tests, background investigations, and interview information have been evaluated. Usually, the person selected has qualifications that most closely conform to the requirements of the open position and the organization. However, some firms believe that a candidate's development potential is as important as his or her ability to fill the current position. Jim Kutz, IT recruiting director at Capital One Financial Corporation, says, "We often look not only at what the person can do now, but what he can do in the next job."[84]

The person who normally makes the final selection is the manager who will be responsible for the new employee's performance, especially for higher-level positions. In making this decision, the manager will review results of the selection methods used. All will not likely be weighted the same. The question then becomes, "Which data are most predictive of job success?" For each firm or group of jobs, the optimum selection method may be different.

Medical Examination

The Americans with Disabilities Act (ADA) does not prohibit pre-employment medical examinations. However, it does determine the point at which they may be administered during the selection process. ADA explicitly states that all exams must be directly relevant to the job requirements and that a firm cannot order a medical exam until the applicant is offered employment. Typically, a job offer is contingent on the applicant's passing this examination. The basic purpose of the medical examination is to determine whether an applicant is physically capable of performing the work. Managers must be aware of the legal liabilities related to medical examinations. The *Uniform Guidelines* state that these examinations can be used to reject applicants only when the results show that job performance would be adversely affected.

Notification of Candidates

Management should notify both successful and unsuccessful candidates of selection decisions as soon as possible. This action is a matter of courtesy and good public relations. Any delay may also result in the firm losing a prime candidate, as top prospects often have other employment options.

Employers may reject applicants at any time during the selection process. Research has indicated that most people can accept losing if they lose fairly. Problems occur when the selection process appears to be less than objective. It is therefore important for firms to develop and utilize rational selection tools. Time constraints prevent firms from spending much time explaining a decision to an unsuccessful candidate. A rejection letter is a more likely method. However, a letter with a personal touch may reduce the stigma of rejection and avoid the applicant's having a negative feeling about the company. An impersonal letter is likely to have the opposite effect. The best an organization can do is to make selection decisions objectively. Hopefully, most unsuccessful individuals can, with time, accept the fact that they were not chosen.

 OBJECTIVE

Explain the metrics for evaluating recruitment/ selection effectiveness.

Metrics for Evaluating Recruitment/Selection Effectiveness

Metrics available to assess HR efficiency are numerous and a comprehensive set of metrics can be produced to evaluate elements of the recruitment and selection process.[85] This section is devoted to presenting some of these metrics. In the previous chapter, the merit of matching sources and methods of recruitment was discussed. The assumption was made that for each job in an organization, there was an optimum source of recruits and method of recruiting them. An underlying theme regarding matching sources and methods is that of evaluating the cost effectiveness of each recruiting source and method.

Recruiting Costs

In determining the recruiting cost per hire, the total recruiting expense must first be calculated. Then, the cost per hire may be determined by dividing the recruiting expenses by the number of recruits hired. Naturally, the difficulty associated with this measure is in determining the exact costs to include as recruiting expenses. The 2005 SHRM Human Capital Benchmarking Study found that the average cost per hire was $7,123, and the number goes up exponentially in the recruiting and hiring of knowledge workers.[86] It may be beneficial for a firm to use a benchmark cost per hire to compare to the specific cost for the company.

Selection Rate

The number of applicants hired from a group of candidates expressed as a percentage is the *selection rate*. Certainly, the selection rate is affected by the condition of the economy. Also, the validity of the selection process (previously discussed) will impact the selection rate.

Acceptance Rate

Once an offer has been extended, the firm has said that this applicant meets the requirements for the position. The *acceptance rate* is the percent of those who have been offered the job who accept the job offer. If this rate is unusually low, it would be wise to determine the reason that jobs are being turned down. A low acceptance rate increases recruiting cost.

Yield Rate

It has been suggested that the selection process can be viewed somewhat as a funnel with the number of applicants available at each stage of the selection process getting smaller. A *yield rate* is the percentage of applicants from a particular source and method that make it to the next stage of the selection process. For example, if 100 applicants submitted their résumés through the firm's corporate career Website, and 25 were asked in for an interview, the yield rate for the corporate career Website would be 25 percent. Each recruitment method would be analyzed in a similar manner.

Cost/Benefit of Recruitment Sources and Methods

Although not an easy process, companies are beginning to establish metrics to help them assess both quantitative and qualitative aspects of the recruitment and selection process.[87] Gerry Crispin, a principal in the international staffing firm MMC Group, said, "I think one of the key problems that most corporations face is defining what quality really means. Quality is a measure of 'did I get what I wanted?'"[88] Each organization should maintain employment records and conduct its own research in order to determine which recruitment sources and methods are most suitable under various circumstances. For each method, there is a cost attached to it. Likewise, for each method, there should be a benefit attached.

Over time the effectiveness of each recruitment source and method can be determined. The company has information on individuals with such criteria as performance appraisal, turnover, safety record, cost to train, and length of employment, to name a few. Mathematical models can be developed to identify which sources and methods of recruitment produce the best applicants both in terms of quality and quantity. For example, it may be determined that graduates from certain universities produce better-quality employees. The possibilities are unlimited.

Time Required to Hire

The time required to fill an opening is critical for several reasons. First, if the position is unfilled, others must take up the slack or productivity will decline. Also, the longer it takes to fill a position, the more likely it is that the desirable candidates will be off the market. If the process drags on too long, the best candidates will be working for another, more efficient employer. As one Atlanta business owner put it, "If you aren't ready to make a judgment and offer a good prospect a job within 24 hours, they are gone. They've gone to the next guy who can make a decision."[89] This extreme urgency obviously does not exist in all situations. Nevertheless, the point is well made.

Records need to be maintained regarding the average time to fill a position based on the recruitment method used. For example, does Internet recruiting produce faster hires than employment agencies? Or, is your firm's corporate career Website taking too long to move applicants through the selection process?

A Global Perspective

Selecting a Buddy

Many companies are using a formal *buddy* system when sending expatriates on assignments. On one of his first outings in England, South African expatriate Ferdinand Heugh got lost. Fortunately for him, Tony Marsh, his official relocation *buddy*, was there to help him find his way. With Marsh's help, Heugh has navigated a variety of other relocation challenges as well. And along the way, the two have formed a friendship that has eased the transition for Heugh and his family from Cape Town, South Africa, to Sheffield, England. But it all started with a formal buddy program, one that matched Marsh and Heugh in an effort to assist the expatriate's adjustment, inside and outside the office, to a new country.[90]

Buddies at Balfour Beatty often inform expatriates of host-office norms and politics, invite them into their homes, introduce them to friends and networks, and help bolster their credibility in the office. They show expatriates where to receive emergency medical assistance, school their children, buy groceries, and eat out. Balfour Beatty, KPMG International, and some other global companies invest in buddy systems to alleviate the stress new expatriates and their families normally endure, to reduce the time it takes for expatriates to operate at peak productivity, and to help lessen the cost of expatriate programs.[91]

"When you go to a cocktail party for the first time in a new country, you can post yourself in a corner and observe how people behave. You can watch how they greet each other, whether they eat a lot or not at all, and other facets of their behavior," notes Dominique J. Herrmann, executive director of global mobility at KPMG International in Woodcliff Lake, New Jersey. "You don't have that same opportunity when you attend a business meeting for the first time in a new country."[92]

In moving to Colombia, Noel Kreicker, founder of IOR Global Services in Chicago, personally experienced the difficulties expatriates face. When Kreicker, her husband, and their three children arrived in the country, her husband's new colleagues said they were too busy to help the newly relocated family get settled. So the Kreickers had to find, on their own, a school for their son. Fortunately, a parent at the school helped them find housing. That was not the only difficulty to overcome. Their luggage sat on a rain-soaked airport tarmac for three weeks because no one in the host office had informed them that it was customary to give local customs officials a *gift* to have the luggage located and delivered to their hotel. "People can lose it when they're waiting in long lines for their taxpayer ID number or trying to get their car registered" in assignment locations, warns Timothy Dwyer, national director for international HR advisory services at KPMG LLP in New York. "That downtime takes them away from being productive in the office."[93]

When Laura Ponticello, a human resource and leadership adviser at 4C Company, a consulting firm in Skaneateles, New York, took an assignment in London, she encountered difficulty when holding meetings. "I discovered that [organizational] level is very important in the U.K. Had people understood that I occupied a senior level, they would have been more inclined to attend the initial meetings I held." "This is where the expatriate's lack of understanding of the host workplace culture can lead to some messes pretty early on," Dwyer points out.[94]

Summary

1. Explain the significance of employee selection.

Selection is the process of choosing from a group of applicants the individual best suited for a particular position. There are many ways to improve productivity, but none is more powerful than making the right hiring decision.

2. Identify environmental factors that affect the selection process.

The environmental factors that affect the selection process include legal considerations, speed of decision making, organizational hierarchy, applicant pool, type of organization, and probationary period.

3. Describe the selection process.

The selection process typically begins with the preliminary interview where obviously unqualified candidates are rejected. Next, applicants complete the firm's application form, and this is followed by the administration of selection tests and a series of employment interviews with reference and background checks. Once the selection decision has been made, the prospective employee may be given a company medical examination.

4. Explain the importance of the preliminary interview.

The selection process begins with an initial screening of applicants to remove individuals who obviously do not fulfill the position requirements.

5. Describe reviewing applications and résumés.

Having the applicant complete an application for employment is another early step in the selection process. The employer then evaluates it to see whether there is an apparent match between the individual and the position. Historically, managers and HR representatives reviewed résumés manually, a time-consuming process. However, this practice has evolved into a more advanced procedure, with résumés automatically evaluated in terms of typos, spelling errors, and job-hopping.

6. Describe sending résumés via the Internet.

When writing their résumés, applicants should realize that most companies now use automated résumé systems. These systems assume a certain résumé style. Résumés that deviate from the assumed style are ignored or deleted.

7. Explain the advantages and potential problems of using selection tests.

Recognizing the shortcomings of other selection tools, many firms have added pre-employment tests to their hiring process. Research indicates that customized tests can be a reliable and accurate means to predict on-the-job performance. And, the cost of employment testing is small in comparison to ultimate hiring costs; a successful program will bolster a firm's bottom line. The reason organizations use tests is to identify attitudes and job-related skills that interviews cannot recognize.

Job performance depends on an individual's ability and motivation to do the work. Selection tests may accurately predict an applicant's ability to perform the job, the *can do*, but they are less successful in indicating the extent to which the individual will be motivated to perform it, the *will do*. Employers should also be aware that tests might be unintentionally discriminatory. Test anxiety can also be a problem. The problems of hiring unqualified or less qualified candidates and rejecting qualified candidates, along with other potential legal problems, will continue regardless of the procedures followed.

8. Describe the characteristics of properly designed selection tests.

Standardization is the uniformity of procedures and conditions related to administering tests. Objectivity is the condition that is achieved when everyone scoring a given test obtains the same results. Norm is the frame of reference for comparing an applicant's performance with that of others. Reliability is the extent to which a selection test provides consistent results. Validity is the extent to which a test measures what it claims to measure.

9. Explain the types of validation studies; describe types of employment tests, including online testing and the use of assessment center.

Criterion-related validity is determined by comparing the scores on selection tests to some aspect of job performance as determined, for example, by performance appraisal. Content validity is a test validation method whereby a person performs certain tasks that are actually required by the job or completes a paper-and-pencil test that measures relevant job knowledge. Construct validity is a test validation method that determines whether a test measures certain constructs, or traits, that job analysis finds to be important in performing a job.

Types of employment tests include cognitive aptitude, psychomotor abilities, job-knowledge, work-sample, and vocational interest tests. Genetic testing, graphoanalysis, and polygraph testing are three unique forms of testing.

The Internet is increasingly being used to test various skills required by applicants. An assessment center is a selection approach that requires individuals to perform activities similar to those they might encounter in an actual job.

10. Explain the importance of the employment interview and describe the general types of interviewing.

The interview permits clarification of certain points, the uncovering of additional information, and the elaboration of data needed to make a sound selection decision. The interviewer should provide information about the company, the job, and expectations of the candidate.

The general types of interviews are the unstructured interview and the structured interview, including the behavioral interview. The interviewer should provide information about the company, the job, and expectations of the candidate.

11. Describe the various methods of interviewing and potential interviewing problems.

The methods of interviewing include meeting one-on-one with an interviewer, a group interview, the board interview, multiple interviews, the stress interview, and realistic job preview.

Potential interviewing problems include inappropriate questions, premature judgments, interview domination, permitting non-job-related information, contrast effect, lack of training, and nonverbal communication.

12. Explain the use of pre-employment screening including background investigations, reference checks, negligent hiring, and negligent referral.

Background investigations primarily seek data from various sources, including professional references. Reference checks are validations from those who know the applicant that provide additional insight into the information furnished by the applicant and allow verification of its accuracy.

Negligent hiring is the liability an employer incurs when it fails to conduct a reasonable investigation of an applicant's background, and then assigns a potentially dangerous person to a position where he or she can inflict harm. Negligent referral may occur when a former employer fails to offer a warning about a particularly severe problem with a past employee.

13. Describe the selection decision, the medical examination, and notification of candidates.

The selection decision is when the final choice is made from among those still in the running after reference checks, selection tests, background investigations, and interview information are evaluated. The medical examination is used to screen out individuals who have a contagious disease and to determine if an applicant is physically capable of performing the work. The medical examination information may be used to determine if there are certain physical capabilities that differentiate between successful and less successful employees. The selection process results should be made known to both successful and unsuccessful candidates as soon as possible.

14. Explain the metrics for evaluating recruitment/selection effectiveness.

Metrics available to assess HR efficiency are numerous and a comprehensive set of metrics can be produced to evaluate recruitment and selection. Some include recruiting costs, selection rate, acceptance rate, yield rate, cost/benefit of recruitment sources and methods, and time required to hire.

Key Terms

- Selection, 161
- Applicant pool, 162
- Selection ratio, 162
- Résumé, 166
- Keywords, 169
- Keyword résumé, 169
- Standardization, 171
- Objectivity, 172
- Norm, 172
- Reliability, 172
- Validity, 172
- Criterion-related validity, 173

- Content validity, 173
- Construct validity, 173
- Cognitive aptitude tests, 173
- Psychomotor abilities tests, 174
- Job-knowledge tests, 174
- Work-sample tests, 174
- Vocational interest tests, 174
- Personality tests, 174
- Genetic testing, 175
- Graphoanalysis, 176
- Assessment center, 176
- Employment interview, 177

- Organizational fit, 178
- Unstructured interview, 179
- Structured interview, 180
- Behavioral interview, 180
- Group interview, 181
- Board interview, 181
- Stress interview, 182
- Realistic job preview (RJP), 182
- Reference checks, 186
- Negligent hiring, 187
- Negligent referral, 188

Questions for Review

1. What is the significance of employee selection?
2. What environmental factors could affect the selection process? Discuss each.
3. What basic steps normally are followed in the selection process?
4. What is the general purpose of the preliminary interview?
5. What is the purpose of the application form?
6. What types of questions should be asked on an application?
7. What would be the selection ratio if there were 15 applicants to choose from and only 1 position to fill? Interpret the meaning of this selection ratio.
8. What are the advantages and potential problems in the use of selection tests?
9. What are the basic characteristics of a properly designed selection test?
10. What are the types of validation? Define each.
11. Identify and describe the various types of employment tests.
12. What is the purpose of an assessment center?
13. What information should be gained from the interview?
14. What are the general types of interviews?
15. What is a behavioral interview? What types of questions would make up a behavioral interview?
16. What are the various methods of interviewing? Define each.
17. What is a realistic job preview?
18. What are the legal implications of interviewing?
19. Why should a company conduct pre-employment screening?
20. Why should an employer be concerned about negligent hiring and referral?
21. What is the purpose of genetic testing and graphoanalysis?
22. Why should the selection decision be made before conducting a medical examination?
23. What are some metrics for evaluating recruitment and selection?

HRM Incident 1

A Matter of Priorities

As production manager for Thompson Manufacturing, Sheila Stephens has the final authority to approve the hiring of any new supervisors who work for her. The human resource manager performs the initial screening of all prospective supervisors and then sends the most likely candidates to Sheila for interviews.

One day recently, Sheila received a call from Pete Peterson, the human resource manager: "Sheila, I've just spoken to a young man who may be just who you're looking for to fill the final line supervisor position. He has some good work experience and appears to have his head screwed on straight. He's here right now and available if you could possibly see him."

Sheila hesitated a moment before answering. "Gee, Pete" she said, "I'm certainly busy today, but I'll try to squeeze him in. Send him on down."

A moment later Allen Guthrie, the applicant, arrived at Sheila's office and she introduced herself. "Come on in, Allen," said Sheila. "I'll be right with you after I make a few phone calls." Fifteen minutes later Sheila finished the calls and began talking with Allen. Sheila was quite impressed. After a few minutes Sheila's door opened and a supervisor yelled, "We have a small problem on line one and need your help." Sheila stood up and said, "Excuse me a minute, Allen." Ten minutes later Sheila returned, and the conversation continued for ten more minutes before a series of phone calls again interrupted the pair.

The same pattern of interruptions continued for the next hour. Finally, Allen looked at his watch and said, "I'm sorry, Mrs. Stephens, but I have to pick up my wife."

"Sure thing, Allen," Sheila said as the phone rang again. "Call me later today."

Questions

1. What specific policies should a company follow to avoid interviews like this one?
2. Explain why Sheila, not Pete, should make the selection decision.

HRM Incident 2

But I Didn't Mean To!

David Corbello, the office manager of the *Daily Gazette*, a midwestern newspaper, was flabbergasted as he spoke with the HR manager, Amanda Dervis. He had just discovered that he was the target of a lawsuit filed by an applicant who had not been selected. "All I did was make friendly inquiries about her children. She seemed quite receptive about talking about them. She was real proud of her family. She even told me about every aspect of the difficult divorce she had just gone through. She seemed to want to talk so I let her. I thought I was merely breaking the ice and setting the tone for an effective dialogue. I thought nothing of it when she told me that she needed a day-care facility when she went to work. A year later she claims to have been the victim of sexual discrimination because she believes that a man would not have been asked questions about his children. There's nothing to this lawsuit, is there, Amanda?"

Question

1. How should Amanda respond to David's question?

Notes

1. Jennifer Busick, "Workplace Drug Use and Worker Safety: New Strategies, New Solutions," *Safety Compliance Letter* (July 1, 2005): 7–11.
2. William Atkinson, "The Liability of Employee Drug Testing," *Risk Management* 49 (September 2002): 40.
3. Meg Fletcher, "Drug-test Cheats Frustrate Employer Screening Efforts," *Business Insurance* 39 (August 1, 2005): 26.
4. Busick, "Workplace Drug Use and Worker Safety: New Strategies, New Solutions."
5. Robert Cassidy, "Fighting Drub Abuse on the Job Site," *Building Design & Construction* (June 2006): 5.
6. Megan Santosus, "Loyalty, Shmoyalty," *CIO* 15 (April 15, 2002): 40.
7. Michelle Nichols, "Great Employees Make a Great Business," *Business Week Online* (March 31, 2006): 5.
8. "Seeking the 'Perfect Candidate'? Expect Frustration . . . and Costs," *HR Focus* 82 (March 2005): 8.
9. Bill Leonard, "Our Horizons Are Limitless," *HR Magazine* 45 (January 2000): 44–49.
10. Katrina Brooker, "Can Anyone Replace Herb?" *Fortune* 141 (April 17, 2000): 192.
11. Interview with Dennis S. O'Reilly, President, O'Reilly Enterprises, April 3, 2006.
12. "Interviewing Job Applicants: Watching What You Say," *Fair Employment Practices Guidelines* (July 1, 2005): 1–3.
13. "Two Consulting Firm Studies Identify Challenges, Gains for HR," *HR Focus* 82 (October 2005): 8.

14. Justin Menkes, "Multiple Methods Needed to Assess Executive Applicants," *HR Magazine* 51 (February 2006): 20.

15. Michele Bitoun Blecher, "Testing Benefits Entrepreneurs: Screening Helps Avoid Costly Bad Hires," *Crain's Chicago Business* 24 (February 12, 2001): SB16.

16. Diana Domeyer, "Acing the New Job Interview," *Office Pro* 65 (May 2005): 5.

17. Martha Frase-Blunt, "Dialing for Candidates," *HR Magazine* 50 (April 2005): 78–82.

18. Stefan Keller, "Don't Leave the Employment Application Out of the Screening Process," *Security: For Buyers of Products, Systems & Services* 41 (June 2004): 28–30.

19. "Interviewing Job Applicants: Watching What You Say," *Fair Employment Practices Guidelines* (July 1, 2005): 1–3.

20. Ibid.

21. "Why It Pays to Use High-Tech Candidate Sourcing," *HR Focus* 84 (February 2006): 3–5.

22. "Is Your Résumé Recruiter Friendly?" *Machine Design* 77 (December 1, 2005): 81.

23. Anne Fisher, "Job Offer or Identity-theft Scam?" *Fortune* 152 (September 9, 2005): 162.

24. Liz Ryan, "The Elephant in Your Resume," *Business Week Online* (June 6, 2005).

25. Patricia M. Buhler, "Interviewing Basics: A Critical Competency for All Managers," *Supervision* 66 (March 2005): 20–22.

26. Kimberly Lankford and Jessica Anderson, "A New Résumé for a New Year," *Kiplinger's Personal Finance* 59 (January 2005): 87–88.

27. "Myths About Recruiting Technology," *Workforce Management* 83 October 2004): 70.

28. "How to Create a Handy Electronic Résumé," *Library Mosaics* 16 (July/August 2005): 20.

29. Paul J. Antonellis Jr., "Burning Personalities," *Fire Chief* 50 (February 2006): 72–76.

30. "SATS FOR J-O-B-S," *Time* 167 (April 4, 2006): 89.

31. Will Hadfield, "Psychometric Tests Help to Identify IT Bosses' Skills," *Computer Weekly* (August 2, 2005): 31.

32. James Krohe Jr., "Are Workplace Tests Worth Taking?" *Across the Board* 43 (July/August 2006): 16–23.

33. "Genetic Testing: What to Know Before You Test," *HR Focus* 82 (August 2005): 2–2.

34. Meg Green, "Wearing Genes to Work," *Best's Review* 106 (August 2005): 99.

35. "Executive Order to Prohibit Discrimination in Federal Employment Based on Genetic Information," *Regulatory Intelligence Data, Industry Group* 91 (February 8, 2000): 1.

36. Bruce Tennenbaum, "Hire the Write Way," *Pest Control* 73 (August 2005): 112.

37. Michael Alter, "Handwriting Analysis," *Landscape Management* 44 (October 2005): 86.

38. www.proveit.com, September 8, 2006.

39. Taryn Brodwater, "ISP Trooper Exams Now Available Online: Candidates Can File Applications and Get Results 'Almost Immediately'," *Spokesman-Review* (August 9, 2006).

40. Judi Brownell, "Applied Research in Managerial Communication: The Critical Link Between Knowledge and Practice," *Cornell Hotel and Restaurant Administration Quarterly* 44 (April 2003): 39.

41. "How Top U.S. Companies Approach Recruitment," *Des Moines Business Record* 23 (May 5, 2005): Special Section 25.

42. Dino di Mattia, "Testing Methods and Effectiveness of Tests," *Supervision* 66 (August 2005): 4–5.

43. Patricia M. Buhler, "Interviewing Basics: A Critical Competency for All Managers," *Supervision* 66 (March 2005): 20–22.

44. "Interviewing Job Applicants: Watching What You Say," *Fair Employment Practices Guidelines* (July 1, 2005): 1–3.

45. "Train Managers and Executive to Avoid Legal 'Danger Zones'," *HR Focus* 83 (August 2006): 4–7.

46. Paul Falcone, "Career Counselor Interviewing," *HR Magazine* 51 (January 2006): 97–101.

47. Mark Murphy, "Hiring IQ," *Leadership Excellence* 23 (January 2006): 11.

48. Lisa Daniel and Carolyn Brandon, "Finding the Right Job Fit," *HR Magazine* 51 (March 2006): 62–67.

49. Bill Carpitella, "Interviewing 101: Listen for Organizational Fit," *Professional Builder* 66 (December 2001): 30.

50. Carolyn Brandon, "Truth in Recruitment Branding," *HR Magazine* 50 (November 2005): 89–96.

51. http://www.wetfeet.com, September 8, 2006.

52. Jay Zack and Mark Van Beusekom, "Making the Right Hire: Behavioral Interviewing," *The Tax Advisor* 27 (September 1996): 570.

53. John Sullivan, "Be Correctly Prepared," *PM Network* 20 (April 2006): 24.

54. Kathryn Tyler, "Train for Smarter Hiring," *HR Magazine* 50 (May 2005): 89–93.

55. Judith Trotsky, "Oh, Will You Behave?" *Computerworld* 35 (January 8, 2001): 42.

56. Lisa Yoon, "Increasingly, Job Candidates Are Being Asked to Critique Their Own Careers," *CFO.com* (February 27, 2003): 1.

57. John Sullivan, "Be Correctly Prepared," *PM Network* 20 (April 2006): 24.

58. Mark Murphy, "Hiring IQ," *Leadership Excellence* 23 (January 2006): 11.

59. Paul Falcone, "Career Counselor Interviewing," *HR Magazine* 51 (January 2006): 97–101.

60. Sullivan, "Be Correctly Prepared."

61. Martha Frase-Blunt, "Games Interviewers Play," *HR Magazine* 46 (January 2001): 107–108.

62. "Seven Surprises That Can Sink Your Management," *T+D* 59 (September 2005): 17.

63. Carolyn Brandon, "Truth in Recruitment Branding," *HR Magazine* 50 (November 2005): 89–96.

64. "Train Managers and Executive to Avoid Legal 'Danger Zones'."

65. R. Wayne Mondy and Shane R. Premeaux, *Management: Concepts, Practices, and Skills* (Orlando, FL: Harcourt, Inc., 2000): 291.

66. Jessica Marquez, "RadioShack Gaffe Shows Need to Screen Current Employees," *Workforce Management* 85 (March 13, 2006): 3–4.

67. Shelley A. Kirkpatrick, "Plugging Hiring Holes," *Security: For Buyers of Products, Systems & Services* 43 (March 2006): 66–67.

68. Barry Nadell, "Background Checks a Smart Step," *Nation's Restaurant News* 39 (August 15, 2005): 18.

69. Charles Archer, "Electronic Fingerprinting," *HR Magazine* 50 (August 2005): 107–109.

70. Kris Frieswick, "Background Checks," *CFO* 21 (August 2005): 63–65.

71. "Favorite Strategies to Stop Employee Thieves," *Security Director's Report* 6 (March 2006): 8.

72. Steve Albrecht, "Hiring a Good Person as Key as a Skilled Worker," *San Diego Business Journal* 26 (August 15, 2005): 60–61.

73. Claude Solink, "Double Checking," *Long Island Business News* 52 (October 7, 2005): 1B–8B.

74. Jude M. Werra, "Liar, Liar, Pants on Fire," *HR Magazine* 50 (September 2005): 16–18.

75. Ibid.

76. Ibid.

77. Diane Cadrian, "HR Professionals Stymied by Vanishing Job References," *HR Magazine* 49 (November 2004): 31–40.

78. Ibid.

79. Maria Greco Danaher, "Lack of Background Check Leads to Liability," *HR Magazine* 50 (January 2005): 94.

80. Daniel J. Gerber, "Thorough Background Checks Are a Must," *Pest Control* 73 (October 2005): 60.

81. Linda Haugsted, "Slipping Through the Screen," *Multichannel News* (December 12, 2005): 18–20.

82. William Atkinson, "Keeping Violent Employees Out of the Workplace," *Risk Management* 48 (March 2001): 12.

83. Paul Snitzer and Lisa Clark, "'Speak No Evil' Is a Risky Policy," *Modern Healthcare* 35 (December 5, 2005): 23.

84. Trotsky, "Oh, Will You Behave?"

85. Edward E. Lawler III, Alec Levenson, and John W. Boudreau, "HR Metrics and Analytics: Use and Impact," *Human Resource Planning* 27 (2004): 27–35.

86. Meisinger, "Looming Talent, Skills Gap Challenge HR."

87. "SHRM Predicts the Human Capital Metrics of the Future," *HR Focus* 82 (August 2005): 7–10.

88. "Did You Get the Employee You Wanted?" *Workforce Management* 83 (October 2004): 101.

89. Dina Berta, "Chains Tap Psychological Profiling to Trim HR Turnover," *Nation's Restaurant News* 36 (September 30, 2002): 1.

90. Ibid.

91. Ibid.

92. Ibid.

93. Ibid.

94. Ibid.

PART FOUR

Human Resource Development

CHAPTER OBJECTIVES

After completing this chapter, students should be able to:

1 Define training and development.

2 Explain factors influencing T&D.

3 Describe the T&D process.

4 Describe the various T&D methods.

5 Describe training and development delivery systems.

6 Describe management development, mentoring, and coaching.

7 Define orientation and describe the executive orientation concept of onboarding.

8 Identify special training areas.

9 Explain the metrics for evaluating training and development.

10 Describe the Workforce Investment Act.

11 Define organization development (OD) and describe various OD techniques.

Training and Development

HRM IN *Action:*

Job Security versus Career Security

In an article in *Time* magazine entitled "What Will Be the 10 Hottest Jobs? . . . and What Jobs Will Disappear?" the primary jobs identified for extinction included stockbrokers, auto dealers, mail carriers, and insurance and real estate agents. The reason given for the predicted demise of these jobs was that the Internet would eliminate positions in the middle. Other predictions for ultimate career demise included: telephone repair people (wireless technology will take over), computer data entry personnel (voice recognition technology and scanning devices will eliminate the manual effort), and library researchers.[1] The researcher of yesterday pulled journals and books from the shelves, copied pertinent pages, and turned them over to the investigator. Today, the investigator can sit at his or her computer at home and access libraries through the Internet. Automation will also affect the types of jobs needed. Grocery stores will not need as many cashiers, because checkout stands are being automated. FedEx and UPS will not need as many workers, because machines will do more sorting. Not as many loaders will be needed because machines will determine which packages belong on which trucks.

In the above examples, these jobs now identified for extinction were historically very secure careers. In the past, most people remained with one company and career for the majority of their adult years. The term **job security** implies security in one job, often with one company. Historically, this type of security depended upon an employee doing a good job and keeping out of trouble.[2,3] But, for most workers today, this assumption is not valid. As one HR executive stated, "Job security has really become an aberration. No employer can guarantee job security for you. If you depend on things always being the way they are, that's risky business. You don't know what's going to happen."[4] The old social contract between employers and employees no longer exists.[5] The country has become a free-agent nation, in which employees are no more loyal to companies than companies are to employees.[6] Downsizing, reorganization, refocusing business strategies, and of course, executive betrayal in such companies as Enron, WorldCom, and Arthur Andersen changed all the old rules.[7] The decision to leave or stay is

Job security:
Implies security in one job, often with one company.

based not only on an employee's career prospects in the present company, but also on how it might prepare him or her to move on elsewhere.[8] Therefore, the way people approached their careers in the past is history. As John A. Challenger, CEO of global outplacement firm Challenger, Gray & Christmas, said, "The truth is: there are no permanent jobs. Lifetime jobs do not exist. All jobs, in some sense, are temporary and many workers operate as if they could lose their job tomorrow."[9]

Career security:

Requires developing marketable skills and expertise that help ensure employment within a range of careers.

Employability doctrine:

Employees owe the company their commitment while employed and the company owes its workers the opportunity to learn new skills, but that is as far as the commitment goes.

Career security is distinctly different from job security; it requires developing marketable skills and expertise that help ensure employment within a range of careers. Career security results from the ability to perform within a broad range of careers well enough to be marketable in more than one job and to more than one organization. Career security is different from job security in that job security implies security in one job, often with one company. With career security, workers are offered opportunities to improve their skills, and thus their employability in an ever-changing work environment. Under this so-called **employability doctrine**, employees owe the company their commitment while employed and the company owes its workers the opportunity to learn new skills, but that is as far as the commitment goes. Under the employability doctrine, loyalty in either direction is not expected.

The first portion of this chapter is devoted to making a distinction between job and career security. Next, strategic training and development and the factors influencing T&D will be explained. Following this, we examine the T&D process and how training and development needs are determined and objectives established. Then, the numerous T&D methods are discussed and training and development delivery systems are described. Management development, orientation, and the executive orientation concept of onboarding are then discussed. Special training areas are identified, and the means by which T&D programs are implemented are then explained, followed by a discussion of the metrics for evaluating training and development. After that, the Workforce Investment Act is explained, organization development is described and the chapter concludes with a Global Perspective entitled "Learning the Culture of China."

Strategic Training and Development

1 OBJECTIVE

Define training and development.

Training and development (T&D):

Heart of a continuous effort designed to improve employee competency and organizational performance.

Training:

Activities designed to provide learners with the knowledge and skills needed for their present jobs.

Development:

Learning that goes beyond today's job and has a more long-term focus.

Training and development (T&D) is the heart of a continuous effort designed to improve employee competency and organizational performance. **Training** provides learners with the knowledge and skills needed for their present jobs. Showing a worker how to operate a lathe or a supervisor how to schedule daily production are examples of training. On the other hand, **development** involves learning that goes beyond today's job and has a more long-term focus. It prepares employees to keep pace with the organization as it changes and grows. T&D activities have the potential to align a firm's employees with its corporate strategies. Some possible strategic benefits of T&D

include employee satisfaction, improved morale, higher retention, lower turnover, improved hiring, a better bottom line, and the fact that satisfied employees produce satisfied customers.[10]

In virtually every market, customers are demanding higher quality, lower costs, and faster cycle times. To meet these requirements, firms must continually improve their overall performance. Rapid advances in technology and improved processes have been important factors in helping businesses meet this challenge. However, the most important strategic competitive advantage for any firm is its workforce, one that must remain competent through continuous workforce development efforts. Organizations spend over $50 billion every year on formal T&D programs.[11] Recently, the average annual expenditure per employee for training rose to $955 but averaged $1,368 per employee in large organizations.[12] To many, this may seem like a tremendous amount of money. However, successful organizations realize that well-structured and significant employee T&D programs correlate strongly with long-term strategic success.

Improved performance, the bottom-line purpose of T&D, is a strategic goal for organizations.[13] Toward this end, many firms have become or are striving to become learning organizations. A **learning organization** is a firm that recognizes the critical importance of continuous performance-related T&D and takes appropriate action.

A learning management system moves beyond delivering tactical training projects to initiating learning programs aligned to strategic corporate goals.[14] Once undervalued in the corporate world, training programs are now credited with strengthening customer satisfaction, contributing to partnership development, enhancing research and development activities and, finally, reinforcing the bottom line. Being recognized as a company that encourages its employees to continue to grow and learn can be a major plus in recruiting.[15] In a learning organization workers are rewarded for learning and are provided enriched jobs, promotions, and compensation.[16] Organizations with a reputation of being a learning leader tend to attract more and better-qualified employees.[17]

In a recent study of training professionals, approximately 80 percent responded that they plan to expand their training and development efforts to meet expected company growth.[18] What accounts for the increased interest? In its annual coverage of the "100 Best Companies to Work for in America," each of the top 10 on the list was rated highest in the areas of learning and growth opportunities.[19] On nearly every survey, training ranks in the top three benefits that employees want from their employers and they search for firms that will give them the tools to advance in their profession. Remember the discussion at the beginning of this chapter, when it was stated that "With career security, workers are offered opportunities to improve their skills, and thus their employability in an ever-changing work environment." It is clear that T&D is not merely a nice thing to provide. It is a strategic resource; one that firms must tap to energize their organizations in the twenty-first century.

Factors Influencing Training and Development

There are numerous factors that both impact and are impacted by T&D. These issues are discussed next.

Top Management Support

For T&D programs to be successful, leadership support at the top is required. Henry Goldman, managing director of the Goldman-Nelson Group in Huntington Beach, California, can attest to this. His boss, the CEO of Goldman-Nelson, was adamant that the firm's 24 vice presidents understand a new initiative. Goldman asked him to give a short speech at an introductory session so attendees would know that the new

---

Learning organization:
Firm that recognizes the critical importance of continuous performance-related T&D and takes appropriate action.

American Society for Training and Development

http://www.astd.org

The homepage for the American Society for Training and Development is presented. Visit the Press Room to get current information on training and development topics.

 OBJECTIVE

Explain factors influencing T&D.

program was important to the chief executive. On the day of the program launch, however, the CEO did not show up to give the presentation. The message to the vice presidents was clear; the CEO did not think the change was important enough for him to become an active participant. The result: the change never got off the ground.[20] Without top management support, a T&D program will not succeed. The most effective way to achieve success is for executives to take an active part in the training and provide the needed resources.

Commitment from Specialists and Generalists

In addition to top management, all managers, whether they are specialists or generalists, should be committed to and involved in the T&D process. The primary responsibility for training and development lies with line managers, from the president and chairman of the board on down. T&D professionals merely provide the technical expertise.

Technological Advances

Perhaps no factor has influenced T&D more than technology. The computer and the Internet, in particular, are dramatically affecting the conduct of all business functions. As emphasized throughout this chapter, technology has played a huge role in changing the way knowledge is delivered to employees, and this change is constantly being extended.

Organization Complexity

Flatter organization structures resulting from fewer managerial levels give the appearance of a simpler arrangement of people and tasks. This, however, is not the case. The tasks of individuals and teams are now both enlarged and enriched. The result is that American workers are spending more time on the job and performing more complex tasks than ever before. Also, the interactions between individuals and groups have become more complicated. The traditional chain of command, which provided a sense of stability at the expense of efficiency, is outdated in many modern organizations.

Ethical Dilemma

Tough Side of Technology

You are the human resource director for a large manufacturing firm that is undergoing major changes. Your firm is in the process of building two technologically advanced plants. When these are completed, the company will close four of its five old plants. It is your job to determine who will stay with the old plant and who will be retrained for the newer plants.

One old-plant employee is a 56-year-old production worker who has been with your firm for 10 years. He seems to be a close personal friend of your boss, as they are often seen together socially. However, in your opinion, he is not capable of handling the high-tech work required at the new plants, even with additional training. He is not old enough to receive any retirement benefits and there are other qualified workers with more seniority who want to remain at the old plant.

What would you do?

In recent years, the increasingly rapid changes in technology, products, systems, and methods have had a significant impact on job requirements. Thus, successful employees constantly upgrade their skills and develop an attitude that permits them not only to adapt to change, but also to accept and even seek it. Many organizations have changed dramatically as a result of downsizing, technological innovations, and customer demands for new and better products and services. The outcome is often that fewer people must accomplish more work at a more complex level. Supervisors and employees performing in self-directed teams are taking up much of the slack from dwindling middle-management ranks. All these changes translate into a greater need for T&D.

Learning Styles

Although much remains unknown about the learning process, some generalizations stemming from the behavioral sciences have affected the way firms conduct training. Some examples follow:

- Learners progress in an area of learning only as far as they need to in order to achieve their purposes. Research indicates that unless there is relevance, meaning, and emotion attached to the material taught, the learner will not learn.

- The best time to learn is when the learning can be useful. Global competition has dramatically increased the need for efficiency. One way this impacts T&D is the need for training on a timely basis. **Just-in-time training** is training provided anytime, anywhere in the world when it is needed.[21]

- Depending on the type of training, it may be wise to space out the training sessions.

Just-in-time training:
Training provided anytime, anywhere in the world when it is needed.

Computer technology, the Internet, and intranets have made these approaches economically feasible to a degree never before possible. The ability to deliver knowledge to employees on an as-needed basis, anywhere on the globe, and at a pace consistent with their learning styles, greatly enhances the value of T&D.

Research on student learning styles indicates that most college students have a practical orientation to learning, with a preference for concrete learning activities, rather than a theoretical orientation toward learning that is abstract. Active modes of teaching and learning appear to be more effective than the passive modes of learning most familiar to many instructors and students. Active learning is based on the assumption that students learn best by doing. Active learning situations provide students with the opportunity not only to apply and practice what they have learned, but also to see the results of their practice, determine if they really understood what they did, and gain insight for subsequent application.

Steven Covey, author of *The Seven Habits of Highly Effective People*, suggests that organizations create a culture where every learner becomes a teacher and every teacher becomes a learner. The firm supplies not only individual knowledge but also creates institutional knowledge so that when an employee leaves the organization, another individual in the company possesses the same knowledge.[22]

Other Human Resource Functions

Successful accomplishment of other human resource functions can also have a crucial impact on T&D. For instance, if recruitment and selection efforts attract only marginally qualified workers, a firm will need extensive T&D programs. A firm's compensation package may also influence T&D efforts. Organizations with competitive pay systems or progressive health and safety programs will find it easier to attract workers who are capable of hitting the ground running, and to retain employees who require less training.

3   OBJECTIVE

Describe the T&D process.

Training and Development Process

Major adjustments in the external and internal environments necessitate corporate change. You can see the general T&D process that anticipates or responds to change in Figure 7-1. First, an organization must determine its specific training needs. Then specific objectives need to be established. The objectives might be quite narrow if limited to the supervisory ability of a manager, or they might be broad enough to include improving the management skills of all first-line supervisors. In exemplary organizations, there is a close link between the firm's strategic mission and the objectives of the T&D program. Review and periodic updating of these objectives is necessary to ensure that they support the changing strategic needs of the organization. After setting the T&D objectives, management can determine the appropriate methods and the delivery system to be used. Naturally, management must continuously evaluate T&D to ensure its value in achieving organizational objectives.

Determine Specific Training and Development Needs

The first step in the T&D process is to determine specific T&D needs. In today's highly competitive business environment, undertaking a program because other firms are doing it is asking for trouble. A systematic approach to addressing bona fide needs must be undertaken.

Training and development needs may be determined by conducting analyses on several levels.

- *Organizational analysis:* From an *overall organizational* perspective, the firm's strategic mission, goals, and corporate plans are studied, along with the results of human resource planning.

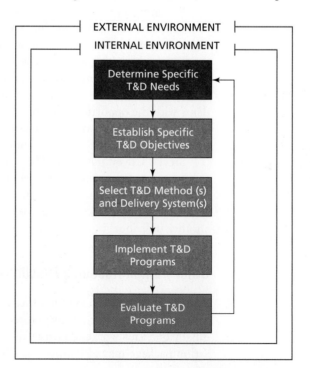

Figure 7-1 Training and Development Process

- *Task analysis:* The next level of analysis focuses on the *tasks* required to achieve the firm's purposes. Job descriptions are important data sources for this analysis level.

- *Person analysis:* Determining *individual training needs* is the final level. The relevant questions are, "Who needs to be trained?" and "What kind of knowledge, skills, and abilities (KSAs) do employees need?" Performance appraisals and interviews or surveys of supervisors and job incumbents are helpful at this level.

Sky Foster, manager for training and associate development for South Carolina–based BMW, states, "We are now training for need, as opposed to rolling out a number of courses. First, it was a check-off list for many of the courses, but now they have more impact and meaning. We specifically ask, 'What knowledge do you want your people to have? What skills do they need? What do they need to do differently from what they're doing today?' We ask more pointed questions and find out exactly what job knowledge and skills the person must have to perform."[23]

Establish Specific Training and Development Objectives

T&D must have clear and concise objectives and be developed to achieve organizational goals.[24] Without them, designing meaningful T&D programs would not be possible. Worthwhile evaluation of a program's effectiveness would also be difficult at best. Consider these purposes and objectives for a training program involving employment compliance:

Training Area: Employment Compliance

Purpose: To provide the supervisor with

1. Knowledge and value of consistent human resource practices
2. The intent of EEO legal requirements
3. The skills to apply them

Objectives: To be able to

1. Cite the supervisory areas affected by employment laws on discrimination
2. Identify acceptable and unacceptable actions
3. State how to get help on equal employment opportunity matters
4. Describe why we have discipline, disciplinary action, and grievance procedures
5. Describe our disciplinary action and grievance procedures, including who is covered

As you see, the *purpose* is established first. The specific *learning objectives* that follow leave little doubt about what the training should accomplish. With these objectives, managers can determine whether training has been effective. For instance, in the example above, a trainee either can or cannot state how to get help on equal employment opportunity matters.

4 **OBJECTIVE**

Describe the various T&D methods.

Training and Development Methods

When a person is working in a garden, some tools are more helpful in performing certain tasks than others. The same logic applies when considering various T&D methods. In some cases, it is not feasible to learn while performing a job at the same time. Although an increasing amount of T&D takes place on the job at the time the employee needs the training, many programs occur away from the work setting. Regardless of whether programs are in-house or outsourced, firms utilize a number of methods for imparting knowledge and skills to the workforce and usually more than one method, called *blended training*, is used to deliver T&D.[25] These T&D methods are discussed next.

Instructor-Led

The instructor-led method continues to be effective for many types of T&D. One advantage of instructor-led T&D is that the instructor may convey a great deal of information in a relatively short time. The effectiveness of instructor-led programs

---

Trends & Innovations

Virtual Instructor-Led

Traditionally, instructors physically lectured in front of a real student body. Now instructors can deliver their lectures virtually. As before, the instructor is still in charge of the class but he or she is not physically standing in front of students. The instructor still lectures but in a different format. Students can do practically anything they could do in a traditional classroom. They can share a whiteboard, communicate as individuals and groups, view video material, and so forth. Students do not have to wait for a professor's office hours since an e-mail may be sent anytime. The largest software provider of virtual instructor-led delivery systems is Blackboard. The Blackboard Learning System is a software application for delivering education online and has powerful capabilities for managing courses and tailoring instruction to enhance student outcomes. It enables instructors to use the full power of the Internet with access to any learning resource at any time from any place. Blackboard has licensed over 1,000 enterprise editions of the Blackboard Learning System.[26]

Your author appreciated firsthand the power of the virtual instructor-led method when his university took a direct hit from Hurricane Rita in 2005. Under the mandatory evacuation order, students and faculty scattered in every direction, going to different states and countries. A few days after the hurricane struck, it was evident that the brick-and-mortar university would be out of service for some time. When your author evacuated to Fort Worth, Texas, he went to Blackboard and e-mailed all his students asking them to reply if they received his e-mail. Luckily, the server had been transferred to another school in the state and Blackboard could still be used by students. Surprisingly, most responded, some from their homes in New York, Mexico, Asia, and the Philippines.

Prior to the hurricane, students had been assigned a term paper which required library research using EBSCOhost, a business research database. They were encouraged to begin their research and to communicate often with their instructor. From Fort Worth, there began a steady flow of communication between instructor and students. Students would attach a rough draft of their research paper for the instructor to review. After review, the papers were returned in the same manner. Lectures were placed on Blackboard for students to read. Apparently other instructors were also using Blackboard to keep in touch with students. The semester was ultimately completed, although weeks later than normal, but only 8 percent of the entire student population failed to complete the semester.

improves when groups are small enough to permit discussion, and when the instructor is able to capture the imagination of the class and utilize multimedia in an appropriate manner. Also, the charisma or personality that the instructor brings to class may excite the students to want to learn.

Case Study

Case study:

T&D method in which trainees are expected to study the information provided in the case and make decisions based on it.

The **case study** is a T&D method in which trainees study the information provided in the case and make decisions based on it.

If an actual company is involved, the student would be expected to research the firm to gain a better appreciation of its financial condition and environment. Research on companies has been significantly enhanced through the availability of library databases such as EBSCOhost. Often, the case study method occurs in the classroom with an instructor who serves as a facilitator.

Behavior Modeling

Behavior modeling:

T&D method that permits a person to learn by copying or replicating behaviors of others to show managers how to handle various situations.

Behavior modeling is a T&D method that permits a person to learn by copying or replicating behaviors of others to show managers how to handle various situations. Behavior modeling has been used to train supervisors in such tasks as conducting performance appraisal reviews, correcting unacceptable performance, delegating work, improving safety habits, handling discrimination complaints, overcoming resistance to change, orienting new employees, and mediating individuals or groups in conflict.

Role-Playing

Role-playing:

T&D method where participants are required to respond to specific problems they may encounter in their jobs by acting out real-world situations.

Role-playing is a T&D method where participants are required to respond to specific problems they may encounter in their jobs by acting out real-world situations. Rather than hearing an instructor talk about how to handle a problem or discussing it, they learn by doing. Role-playing is often used to teach such skills as disciplinary action, interviewing, grievance handling, conducting performance appraisal reviews, team problem solving, effective communication, and leadership style analysis. It has also been used successfully to teach workers how to deal with individuals who are angry, irate, or out of control.[27] Some restaurant chains use role-playing to train servers how to deal with difficult situations such as a couple having an argument at the dining table.[28]

Role-playing may also serve to train managers. Consider this scenario:

> *"Be in the boardroom in 10 minutes," reads the e-mail from Senior Vice President Alan Young. The CEO is out on his boat, and a storm has knocked out all communications. Worse, there has been a massive fire in the call center in South America. "We could lose billions," Young says. The board has given senior staff emergency powers. You're a top manager who has been called in to help. What do you do?*[29]

In the episode above, this is the final setting in a new computer-based role-playing exercise called Virtual Leader.

Business Games

Business games:

T&D method that permits participants to assume roles such as president, controller, or marketing vice president of two or more similar hypothetical organizations and compete against each other by manipulating selected factors in a particular business situation.

Business games is a T&D method that permits participants to assume roles such as president, controller, or marketing vice president of two or more similar hypothetical organizations and compete against each other by manipulating selected factors in a particular business situation. Participants make decisions affecting price levels, production volumes, and inventory levels. Typically, a computer program manipulates their decisions, with the results simulating those of an actual business situation. Participants are able to see how their decisions affect other groups and vice versa. The best thing about this type of learning is that if a poor decision costs the company $1 million, no one gets fired, yet the business lesson is learned.

In-Basket Training

In-basket training:
T&D method in which the participant is asked to establish priorities for and then handle a number of business papers, e-mail messages, memoranda, reports, and telephone messages that would typically cross a manager's desk.

In-basket training is a T&D method in which the participant is asked to establish priorities for and then handle a number of business papers, e-mail messages, memoranda, reports, and telephone messages that would typically cross a manager's desk. The messages, presented in no particular order, call for anything from urgent action to routine handling. The participant is required to act on the information contained in these messages. In this method, the trainee assigns a priority to each particular situation before making any decisions. This form of training has been quite accurate in predicting performance success in management jobs.[30] Assessment centers, discussed in Chapter 6, commonly make use of this training method in the selection process.

On-the-Job Training

On-the-job training (OJT):
An informal T&D method that permits an employee to learn job tasks by actually performing them.

The next four T&D methods involve learning by actually doing work-related tasks. **On-the-job-training (OJT)** is an informal T&D method that permits an employee to learn job tasks by actually performing them. The key to this training is to transfer knowledge from a highly skilled and experienced worker to a new employee, while maintaining the productivity of both workers.[31] Individuals may also be more highly motivated to learn because it is clear to them that they are acquiring the knowledge needed to perform their jobs. At times, however, the trainee may feel so much pressure to produce that learning is negatively affected. Firms should be selective about who provides on-the-job training. The trainers are often supervisors. However, peer-to-peer communication can provide a very powerful means for training. Regardless of who does the training, that person must have a good work ethic and correctly model the desired behavior.

Job Rotation

Job rotation:
T&D method where employees move from one job to another to broaden their experience.

Job rotation (sometimes called cross-training) is a T&D method where employees move from one job to another to broaden their experience. Higher-level tasks often require this breadth of knowledge. Rotational training programs help employees understand a variety of jobs and their interrelationships, thereby improving productivity. Job rotation is often used by organizations to encourage effective teamwork.[32] Organizations are widely applying entry-level rotational training programs. For instance, a college graduate may be given the opportunity to test his or her skills in a number of different roles such as finance, sales, and supply-chain management, before settling on a full-time management role within the company. Streamlined firms have to do more with less so it makes sense to develop employees who can jump in anywhere they are needed.

Internships

As mentioned in Chapter 5, an internship program is a recruitment method typically involving students in higher education who divide their time between attending classes and working for an organization. *Internships* as a T&D method allow participants to integrate theory learned in the classroom with business practices. In a recent

WetFeet survey, 79 percent felt a good internship was essential to meeting their long-term career goals.[33] As evidence of their current popularity, three out of four students now complete internships before graduation; up from one in 36 in 1980.[34] A study by the National Association of Colleges and Employers found that employers offered higher starting salaries to graduates with internship experience.[35]

Apprenticeship Training

Apprenticeship training:
Training method that combines classroom instruction with on-the-job training.

Apprenticeship training is a training method that combines classroom instruction with on-the-job training. Such training is common with craft jobs, such as those of plumber, barber, carpenter, machinist, and printer. While in training, the employee earns less than the master craftsperson who is the instructor. Apprenticeship programs last from two to five years, with four years being the average length.

The days of narrow training just for job skills are past for some crafts. In today's workplace, communication and interpersonal relationships are essential. For example, a Pennsylvania apprenticeship program now requires electrician hopefuls to earn an associate's degree in order to graduate. The program requires academic courses right alongside electrical wiring in a mix of traditional vocational-technical training.[36]

  OBJECTIVE

Describe training and development delivery systems.

Training and Development Delivery Systems

The section above focused on the various T&D methods available to organizations; and, the list is constantly changing. In this section, our attention is devoted to how the training will be delivered to participants.

Corporate Universities

Corporate university:
T&D delivery system provided under the umbrella of the organization.

A T&D delivery system provided under the umbrella of the organization is referred to as a **corporate university**. The corporate T&D institution differs from many traditional education programs in that its focus is on creating organizational change that involves such areas as company training, employee development, and adult learning.[37] It is proactive and strategic rather than reactive and tactical and can be closely aligned to corporate goals.[38] An estimated 2,000 corporate universities exist in the United States today.[39] This number includes many *Fortune* 500 companies. If this growth rate continues, the roughly 3,700 traditional universities will someday be outnumbered. The best-known corporate universities include those at General Motors, McDonald's, Disney, Motorola, GE, and Intel. Intel University in Arizona administers programs developed by 73 training groups located worldwide. Intel offers technology courses ranging from using Microsoft Word to training in lithography, one of the stages of computer-chip manufacturing. The university also teaches nontechnical skills such as dealing with conflict and harassment avoidance.

Growth in the number of corporate universities may be attributed to their flexibility, which permits students to learn on their own time, and the use of various modes including DVDs, audio- and videotapes, and, of course, the Internet. Also, firms are better able to control the quality of training and to ensure that their employees receive the same messages. The remarkable growth rate of corporate universities clearly illustrates that they have something going for them.

Colleges and Universities

For decades, colleges and universities have been the primary delivery system for training professional, technical, and management employees. Many public and private colleges and universities are taking similar approaches to training and education as have the corporate universities. Corporate T&D programs often partner with colleges and universities or other organizations, such as the American Management Association, to deliver both training and development.

Community Colleges

Community colleges are publicly funded higher education establishments that deliver vocational training and associate degree programs. Some employers have discovered that community colleges can provide certain types of training better and more costeffectively than they can.

In a report entitled "The Knowledge Net," the American Association of Community Colleges (AACC) argued that community colleges should increase their collaborations with business, industry, and other educational entities as a primary strategy to develop a higher-quality, better-prepared workforce.[40] Apparently, many organizations agree. Rapid technological changes and corporate restructuring have created a new demand by industry for community college training resources. Here are some examples:

- In Phoenix, PepsiCo Inc., has established its own training program with community college help. Its Gatorade factory in suburban Tolleson and a neighboring container manufacturer host an electricity-theory class taught by Maricopa Community College faculty.[41]

- In Cedar Rapids, Iowa, Kirkwood Community College is part of a development consortium known as the Workplace Learning Connection that helps 700 local firms recruit and train workers.[42]

- Connecticut Community Colleges include as clients some of our nation's most prestigious firms: Cigna, Clairol, Eli Lilly, Frito Lay Inc., General Electric, International Paper, Pitney Bowes, Pratt & Whitney, The Travelers, and United Technologies, to name a few.[43]

The federal government has joined industry in an increased interest in community college involvement in educating the national labor force. The Workforce Investment Act (WIA), discussed later in this chapter, dramatically altered the federal system of job training and workforce development. This huge and comprehensive federal law assures the participation of community colleges, as they are a critical factor in the success of this legislation.

Online Higher Education

Online higher education: Educational opportunities including degree and training programs that are delivered, either entirely or partially, via the Internet.

In recent years, there has been an increase in the use of online higher education as a means of delivering T&D. **Online higher education** is defined as educational opportunities including degree and training programs that are delivered, either entirely or partially, via the Internet.[44] One reason for the growth of online higher education is that it allows employees to attend class at lunchtime, during the day, or in the evening. It also saves employees time since it reduces their need to commute to school. It increases the range of learning opportunities for employees and increases employee satisfaction. According to a recent ASTD survey, approximately 29 percent of corporate tuition reimbursements now go to online or blended programs.[45] Enrollment in online universities continues to grow. The University of Phoenix has over 80,000 degree-seeking undergraduate students.[46] It even has 18,800 online MBA students. General Motors pays for its employees to earn an MBA through an Internet-based school launched two years ago by the New

York Institute of Technology and Cardean University. Schools such as Indiana University and Arizona State University have also entered the online MBA market.[47]

Videoconferencing

For a number of years, many firms in the United States have used videoconferencing and satellite classrooms for delivering T&D and the technology is rapidly improving.[48] The approach is interactive and appears to offer the flexibility and spontaneity of a traditional classroom. A great deal of T&D takes place using this technology, offering the prospect of increasing the number of trainees and at the same time saving companies money. Global firms, in particular, can benefit from this technology. With far-flung operations, videoconferencing cuts the cost of travel.[49] Potential terrorist attacks also make this approach more appealing. Videoconferencing and similar technology can increase access to training, ensure consistency of instruction, and reduce the cost of delivering T&D programs. There is seemingly no limit to its possibility.

Vestibule System

Vestibule system:
T&D delivery system that takes place away from the production area on equipment that closely resembles equipment actually used on the job.

Vestibule system is a T&D delivery system that takes place away from the production area on equipment that closely resembles equipment actually used on the job. For example, a group of lathes may be located in a training center where the trainees receive instruction in their use. A primary advantage of the vestibule system is that it removes the employee from the pressure of having to produce while learning. The emphasis is focused on learning the skills required by the job.

Video Media

The use of video media such as DVDs, videotapes, and film clips continues to be popular T&D delivery systems. The media are especially appealing to small businesses that cannot afford more expensive training methods. In addition, they provide the flexibility desired by any firm. Behavior modeling, previously mentioned, has long been a successful training method that utilizes video media.

E-Learning

E-learning:
T&D delivery system for online instruction.

E-learning is the T&D delivery system for online instruction. It takes advantage of the speed, memory, and data manipulation capabilities of the computer for greater flexibility of instruction. A basic benefit is that it is self-paced and individualized and can be done while at work or off-shift.[50] The concept can be repeated as often as needed. Help screens can also be included in the program to give additional explanation for those who need it. In a computer lab, participants can be working on different parts of a program, at varying speeds and in different languages. E-learning systems may also utilize multimedia to enhance learning with audio, animation, graphics, and interactive video.

By 2008, the e-learning market should more than double, rising to $13.5 billion in the United States and $21 billion globally, according to International Data Group Inc.[51] The versatility of online learning has important implications for T&D since the demand for an educated and empowered workforce is critical in the economy. The advantages of using e-learning are numerous: it is available anytime, anywhere in the world, and in different languages. However, the biggest advantage is cost savings. According to Paul Walliker, Caterpillar Inc.'s collaboration and online training manager, "To create an e-learning module is three times less expensive than it is to create an instructor-led class."[52]

Individuals involved in e-learning are no longer constrained by the need to be in a classroom at a specific location and time. Animation, video, and multimedia make presentations vivid and appealing. E-learning is also considered the most effective way to control training costs.[53] For example, IBM found that using such technology has enabled the company to trim the cost of training by $400 million a year. Companies are treating e-learning strategically, with greater attention to ROI and more awareness of how to use online training.[54] Also, e-learning and classroom learning were found to be equally effective.[55]

For Union Pacific, the largest railroad in North America, both distance and time have been hurdles to learning. About 19,000 of its 48,000 widely disbursed employees work on the railroad's locomotives and freight cars, many on different schedules. So the company uses a blend of traditional learning and e-learning that provides the kind of training far-flung employees require, at a time when they can use it.[56]

Firms that consistently have a high turnover rate are turning to e-learning because classroom learning is not cost-effective. Nike faced a challenge that a number of retailers today are confronting. Nike designed an online training program that the company could offer to employees in its own stores as well as at other retailers that sell Nike products. The program conveys a lot of information quickly, but it is also easy to learn. This is important because the training is directed at 16- to 22-year-olds. The concept of Sports Knowledge Underground (SKU) was developed. The layout for SKU resembles a subway map, with different stations representing different training themes. For example, Apparel Union Station branches off into the apparel technologies line, the running products line, and the Nike Pro products line. The Cleated Footwear Station offers paths to football, whereas the Central Station offers such broad lines as customer skills. Each segment is three to seven minutes long and gives associates the basic knowledge they need about various products. The program is presently reaching approximately 20,000 associates.[57]

Virtual reality is a unique extension of e-learning that permits trainees to view objects from a perspective otherwise impractical or impossible. For example, it is not feasible to turn a drill press on its side so a trainee can inspect it from the bottom. A computer easily permits this type of manipulation.

Simulators

Simulators are T&D delivery system comprised of devices or programs that replicate actual job demands. The devices range from simple paper mock-ups of mechanical devices to computerized simulations of total environments. Training and development specialists may use simulated sales counters, automobiles, and airplanes. Although simulator training may be less valuable than on-the-job training for some purposes, it has certain advantages. A prime example is the training of airline pilots in a simulator; simulated crashes do not cost lives or deplete the firm's fleet of jets.

Automobile mechanics are using the same type of simulation training that was developed to help U.S. Air Force technicians fix jet fighters. An auto technician can take the program wherever the technician has access to a personal computer with an Internet connection. General Motors recognized that a different approach would be needed to train service technicians following the explosion of technology in its vehicles. It felt that if Raytheon could help technicians fix B-2 Stealth bombers and F-15 jet fighters, it was qualified to help mechanics repair cars. "During each simulation, the technician receives a work order to complete. He or she must select the appropriate tools to diagnose the problem and make the repair. A virtual instructor appears at several points to inform, challenge and help technicians discover the concern, much like an instructor would in one of GM's training centers."[58]

Virtual reality:
Unique extension of e-learning that permits trainees to view objects from a perspective otherwise impractical or impossible.

Simulators:
T&D delivery system comprised of devices or programs that replicate actual job demands.

6 OBJECTIVE

Describe management development, mentoring, and coaching.

Management development:
Consists of all learning experiences provided by an organization resulting in upgrading skills and knowledge required in current and future managerial positions.

Management Development

Management development consists of all learning experiences provided by an organization resulting in upgrading skills and knowledge required in current and future managerial positions. Although leadership is often depicted as an exciting and glamorous endeavor, there is another side; failure can quickly result in losing one's position. The risks are especially high due to today's rapid changes. This situation magnifies the importance of providing development opportunities for a firm's management group. Organizations in the United States focus training efforts on managers and professionals.

A firm's future lies largely in the hands of its managers. This group performs certain functions essential to the organization's survival and prosperity. Managers must make the right choices in most of their decisions; otherwise, the firm will not grow and may even fail. Therefore, it is imperative that managers keep up with the latest developments in their respective fields and, at the same time, manage an ever-changing workforce operating in a dynamic environment. Also note that as managers reach higher levels in the organization, it is not so much their technical skills that they need, but their interpersonal skills and their business knowledge.

First-line supervisors, middle managers, and executives may all participate in management development programs. These programs are available in-house, by professional organizations, and at colleges and universities. T&D specialists often plan and present in-house programs, at times utilizing line managers. Organizations such as the Society for Human Resource Management and the American Management Association conduct conferences and seminars in a number of specialties. Numerous colleges and universities also provide management T&D programs. Colleges and universities may possess expertise not available within business organizations. In these cases, academicians and management practitioners can advantageously present T&D programs jointly. Reasons for conducting management training outside and inside the company are presented in Table 7-1.

According to a recent study from global HR consulting firm DDI, nearly a third of global business leaders do not have the skills they need to help their organizations achieve business goals. That's a problem, since researchers found that strong leadership can increase the successful implementation of business strategies by 22 percent. DDI's senior vice president, Rich Wellins, says, "Companies that are worried about their future profitability should be just as worried about the future of their leadership." Paul Bernthal, manager of DDI's Center for Applied Behavioral, says many leaders know they lack necessary skills. "'We're not doing as well as we'd like,' they say, 'but nobody's helping us.'" Only half the leaders surveyed are satisfied with their organization's leadership development opportunities. Although the use of formal workshops is the most common leader development practice, only 42 percent of leaders

Table 7-1 Reasons for Conducting Management Training Outside and Inside the Company

Reasons to conduct management training outside the company include these:
- An outside perspective
- New viewpoints
- Exposure to faculty experts and research
- Broader vision

Reasons for keeping management training inside the company
- Training that is more specific to needs
- Lower costs
- Less time
- Consistent, relevant material
- More control of content and faculty
- Development of organizational culture and teamwork

found training workshops *highly effective*. Working on special projects or assignments and getting help from mentors or coaches were the most effective methods.[59]

Mentoring and Coaching

Mentoring and coaching have become important means of management development. Because the purposes of mentoring and coaching are similar in concept and the terms are often used interchangeably in the literature, they are discussed together. Coaching and mentoring activities, which may occur either formally or informally, are primarily development approaches emphasizing one-to-one learning. **Mentoring** is an approach to advising, coaching, and nurturing, for creating a practical relationship to enhance individual career, personal, and professional growth and development. It focuses on skills to develop protégés to perform to their highest potential, leading to career advancement.[60] Mentors may be anywhere in the organization or even in another firm. For years mentoring has repeatedly been shown to be the most important factor influencing careers of both men and women.[61] **Coaching** is often considered a responsibility of the immediate boss, who provides assistance, much like a mentor. The coach has greater experience or expertise than the protégé and is in the position to offer wise advice. Coaching has become an excellent way to develop managers and executives.[62] Although some companies have become too lean to provide inside coaches, individual managers have independently sought out their own.

> **Mentoring:**
> Approach to advising, coaching, and nurturing, for creating a practical relationship to enhance individual career, personal, and professional growth and development.

> **Coaching:**
> Often considered a responsibility of the immediate boss who provides assistance, much like a mentor.

Mentoring/Coaching for Women and Minorities. How important is it for a manager to have a mentor? Some believe that having a mentor is essential to *make it to the top*, and the lack of one may explain why women and minorities have encountered the glass ceiling.[63] For various reasons, mentors tend to seek out their mirror images. Since women and minorities are not equally represented at the firm's top levels, they are often left without a mentor. Studies show that women who are mentored, particularly by other women, are more likely to enhance and expand career skills, advance in their careers, receive higher salaries, and enjoy their work more. The main point is that women and minorities want and need to have advantages provided by mentors to effectively use their talents and realize their potential, not only for their personal benefit but to assist their firms.[64] Joan Gosier, a business executive, said, "Having a mentor is imperative. Some people think you can just work hard. But without a sponsor, you don't know the unwritten rules that can take you to the next level."[65] According to Katherine Giscombe, Catalyst senior director of research, "African-American women who have a mentor are more likely to get promoted. And those who have more than one mentor are most likely to get promoted."[66]

Specific Roles. Depending on their organizational relationship, mentors may perform various roles: they provide coaching, sponsor advancement, provide challenging assignments, protect employees from adverse forces, and encourage positive visibility. They also offer personal support, friendship, acceptance, counseling, and role modeling. Mentoring has additional advantages for new hires. Days before new hires arrive at Monster.com, they are assigned personal mentors who will guide them through the first few weeks.[67] A study sponsored by Deloitte & Touche found that Generation Xers, discussed in the appendix to this chapter, were entrepreneurial, hardworking, confident, and committed. However, they were less loyal to their employers than their predecessors. What makes a difference for them? The study found that it was mentoring.[68]

Potential Problems. Although mentoring has many obvious advantages, there are reasons why the process is not foolproof. One reason is the mentor; the other is the protégé. Some managers do not have the temperament to become a mentor or coach. The role imposes additional work, and some literally have no time. Others just do not want to be bothered. On the other side, some new hires are argumentative or uninterested. Even if both parties are generally willing, there may be a personality conflict. Ultimately, the proper pairing of individuals in a mentoring/protégé relationship is critical to its success.

Reverse Mentoring

Reverse mentoring:
A process where older employees learn from younger ones.

Reverse mentoring is a process where older employees learn from younger ones.[69] There are people in organizations approaching retirement who do not want to retire, and who have tremendous knowledge that should not go to waste. There are young people who know things others do not know and who are anxious to expand their horizons. The existence of these two diverse, but potentially mutually helpful, populations has led to reverse mentoring. At Procter & Gamble, the reverse mentoring program allows senior management to be mentored in an area such as biotechnology. It pairs scientists and top managers in order to explore the potential impact of biotechnology on P&G's customers, suppliers, and overall business.[70] General Electric's reverse mentoring program was so impressive that the program grew to include the top 3,000 managers in the company. GE even recruited a *mentor* for the board: Scott McNealy, CEO of Sun Microsystems.[71]

According to one study, 41 percent of respondents use reverse mentoring to spread technical expertise and 26 percent rely on younger staff members to help executives gain a more youthful perspective.[72] Benefits can stem from either group. It seems reasonable that *new economy* managers and *old economy* managers can learn from each other. A classic example of this arrangement is Microsoft's CEO Bill Gates, who regularly consults business guru Warren Buffett for advice.[73]

 OBJECTIVE

Define orientation and describe the executive orientation concept of onboarding.

Orientation:
Initial T&D effort for new employees that informs them about the company, the job, and the work group.

Orientation

Orientation is the initial T&D effort for new employees that informs them about the company, the job, and the work group. First impressions are often the most lasting. This lesson may apply to new employees' impressions of their employers, and orientation programs give organizations an opportunity to begin the relationship with a good start. After all, considerable time, money, and effort often have gone into the selection process. Dennis Liberson, executive vice president for human resources at Capital One Financial Corporation, says, "We have programs in place to *immediately* show people what the culture is all about and what it's going to take to succeed."[74]

Purposes of Orientation

In a recent study, 44 percent of employees polled felt they were not given the tools and resources they needed to succeed in the first few weeks on the job.[75] Therefore, effective orientation plays a large part in reducing employee turnover. Orientation formats are unique to each firm. However, some basic purposes are listed below.

- *The Employment Situation.* At an early point in time, it is helpful for the new employee to know how his or her job fits into the firm's organizational structure and goals.
- *Company Policies and Rules.* Every job within an organization must be performed within the guidelines and constraints provided by policies and rules. Employees must understand these to ensure a smooth transition to the workplace.
- *Compensation.* Employees have a special interest in obtaining information about the reward system. Management normally

provides this information during the recruitment and selection process and often reviews it during orientation.

- *Corporate Culture.* The firm's culture reflects, in effect, "How we do things around here."[76] This relates to everything from the way employees dress to the way they talk. Remember our earlier discussion in Chapter 6 of the importance of *organizational fit* to an employee's success.

- *Team Membership.* A new employee's ability and willingness to work in teams were likely determined before he or she was hired. In orientation, the program may again emphasize the importance of becoming a valued member of the company team.

- *Employee Development.* An individual's employment security is increasingly becoming dependent upon his or her ability to acquire needed knowledge and skills that are constantly changing. Thus, firms should keep employees aware not only of company-sponsored developmental programs, but also those available externally.

- *Socialization.* To reduce the anxiety that new employees may experience, the firm should take steps to integrate them into the informal organization. Some organizations have found that employees subjected to socialization programs, including the topics of politics and career management, perform better than those who have not undergone such training.

Responsibility for and Scheduling of Orientation

Although orientation is often the joint responsibility of the training staff and the line supervisor, peers often serve as excellent information agents. There are several reasons for using peers in performing this function. For one thing, they are accessible to newcomers, often more so than the boss. Peers also tend to have a high degree of empathy for new people. In addition, they have the organizational experience and technical expertise to which new employees need access.

Orientation may occupy a new employee's first few days on the job. However, some firms believe that learning is more effective if spread out over time. For example, a company may deliver a program in a system of 20 one-hour sessions over a period of several weeks. Some firms are sensitive to information overload and make information available to employees on an *as-needed* basis. For example, a new supervisor may eventually have the responsibility for evaluating his or her subordinates. But, knowledge of how to do this may not be needed for six months. A training segment on performance evaluation may be placed on the Internet or a firm's intranet and be available when the need arises. This approach is consistent with *just-in-time training*, mentioned earlier.

Orientation at Monster.com

Monster.com dropped its old orientation process and replaced it with one designed primarily to convey the *zing* of the corporate culture. Monster employees attend orientation sessions in which the orientation content is mixed with fun, games, and prizes. Before new hires arrive they are assigned personal mentors who guide them through the first few weeks. The idea behind the new process is to demonstrate to new employees that they are valued, through a well-organized, well-considered, month-long program of activities. On a typical Monday, Monster welcomes 10 to 15 new employees to its group orientation sessions. New hires introduce themselves, discuss how they came to be at Monster, tell positive things about themselves, and discuss other topics intended to help new employees build a rapport. New employees get an overview of Monster's business philosophy, its customer base, its products and services, its facilities, and other information helpful to new employees.[77]

The second part of the orientation program is intended to ensure that a new employee gets off to a smooth start in his or her job. Before the new hire arrives, his or her manager receives a six-page checklist of to-dos. That list itemizes tasks that begin prior to the new employee's arrival such as setting up an employee's work area and creating a departmental organizational chart. In addition, all new employees are assigned mentors from their departments. "The idea is for the new hire to be paired with a veteran employee who is genuinely interested in being a mentor. The activity also can become part of the mentor's performance review," says Kristen Gleason, Monster's professional development manager.[78]

Onboarding (Executive Orientation)

Onboarding:
Process companies use to help new executives quickly learn an organization's structure, culture, and politics so that they can start making contributions to the organization as soon as possible.

Onboarding is the process companies use to help new executives quickly learn an organization's structure, culture, and politics so that they can start making contributions to the organization as soon as possible.[79] However, in one recent survey, only 30 percent of hiring executives were satisfied with their process.[80] For instance, when Bristol-Myers Squibb, the global pharmaceutical manufacturer, studied the retention rates of its recently hired executives it discovered that the company was losing promising new executives because it was not taking steps to ensure their success. It made new executives the object of keen focus during the first 30 to 60 days of their employment, providing guidelines, clarifying roles, setting up meetings with influential colleagues, and fostering each newcomer's understanding of the company's cultural norms. Follow-up meetings are held during the executive's first year to check progress and resolve problems.[81]

As another example, when a new program manager at Intel's Mobile Platforms Group arrived for her first day on the job, Jessica Rocha, her boss, handed her a calendar filled with already-scheduled meetings. These meetings had nothing to do with the usual employee-orientation process, through which new hires learn about Intel's values and HR procedures. Rather, Rocha had scheduled face-to-face interviews with people across Intel who had the technical expertise, cultural lowdown, and political knowledge the newly hired manager would need to accomplish her work.[82]

 OBJECTIVE

Identify special training areas.

Special Training Areas

Many organizations also have extensive programs for supervisors and employees. These programs often emphasize specific tasks required to perform given jobs. Other programs may deal with critical areas that surround the job.

Diversity

Diversity training attempts to develop sensitivity among employees about the unique challenges facing women and minorities and strives to create a more harmonious working environment. Many firms recognize the significance of a diverse workforce and consider diversity training to be essential.[83] A survey by SHRM indicates that about two-thirds of U.S. companies provide some diversity training for employees, mostly mandatory and aimed at executives and managers.[84]

English as a Second Language (ESL)

Training in ESL shows sensitivity to diversity issues and helps firms deal with employees in a way that optimizes personal work relationships. In this spirit, four unrelated Texas restaurants have worked together to create an ESL course that focuses on vocabulary crucial to restaurant settings. It also doubles as a Spanish-language course for English speakers. Restaurant operators have long known that teaching English to Spanish speakers can improve customer service and improve an employee's skill and confidence. La Madeleine, Carlson Restaurants Worldwide, Dave & Buster's (based in Dallas), and San Antonio–based Taco Cabana, each with large numbers of Spanish-speaking employees, wanted a uniform, self-taught program based on the vocabulary needed for restaurants. They also wanted something that would allow English-speaking employees to learn Spanish with the same tools. The group used the brainpower of all four companies to create a system that builds an extensive restaurant vocabulary by using flashcards and pictorials. The tools offer words spelled in English and Spanish and spelled phonetically in both languages.[85]

In regulated environments, such as the pharmaceutical industry, the Food and Drug Administration (FDA) has placed severe regulatory burdens on companies. Companies that employ workers where English is their secondary language may encounter difficulty complying. If the records are in English and the company employees do not read English well, they will not be able to read and follow the directives.[86] Having an ESL training program is especially important in these industries.

Ethics

In the wake of Enron and other corporate scandals, many firms are emphasizing ethics. By stressing fair play and a respect for law, they intend to develop a corporate culture that rewards ethical behavior. This emphasis has a practical side. Under federal guidelines, companies convicted of crimes are eligible for reduced sentences if they have previously established programs to prevent and detect fraud. Recall from Chapter 2 that the Sarbanes-Oxley Act also requires companies to adopt ethics programs.

Telecommuter

Both telecommuters and their supervisors need *telecommuter training*. Telecommuter training should emphasize effective communication strategies that permit managers and employees to define job responsibilities and set goals and job expectations. The primary challenge for the telecommuter is to be able to work without direct supervision; the challenge for the supervisor is to make a shift from *activity-based management* to *results-based management*. This is a difficult transition for the many managers who feel that workers cannot be productive unless they are at their workplace.

Customer Service

Customer service training teaches employees the skills needed to meet and exceed customer expectations. Communication skills, including listening skills and the recognition of diverse customer needs and requirements receive special emphasis.

Conflict Resolution

Conflict resolution training focuses on developing the communication skills needed to resolve gridlock in relationships.[87] Conflict within an organization can be valuable and often aids in growth and change. But, it is critical that the conflict be recognized, managed, and transformed into a positive force for advancing the firm's goals.

Teamwork

Teamwork training strives to teach employees how to work in groups that often have been empowered with considerable authority in making decisions. This type of training is essential because our culture has historically nurtured individual accomplishments, yet organizations are increasingly using teams. Team building as an organizational development intervention is discussed later in this chapter.

Empowerment

Empowerment training teaches employees and teams how to make decisions and accept responsibility for results. It often accompanies teamwork training because some firms have delegated considerable authority to teams. For example, work teams may actually hire employees for their group, determine pay increases, and plan work schedules.

Remedial

Remedial training focuses on foundation skills such as basic literacy and mathematics skills. A large percentage of individuals are entering the workforce without the requisite skills to handle the jobs that technology has produced. It is estimated that as many as one-third of new employees require remedial training after high school to become qualified for work.[88]

Anger Management

Anger management training programs give employers a tool to help prevent domestic abuse and workplace violence. The programs are designed to help participants take control of their angry outbursts. The program helps participants identify and focus on the most crucial aspects of anger management.[89]

Implementing Training and Development Programs

A perfectly conceived training program will fail if management cannot convince the participants of its merits. Participants must believe that the program has value and will help them achieve their personal and professional goals. A long string of successful programs certainly enhances the credibility of T&D.

Implementing T&D programs is often difficult. One reason is that managers are typically action oriented and feel that they are too busy for T&D. According to one management development executive, "Most busy executives are too involved chopping down the proverbial tree to stop for the purpose of sharpening their axes." Another difficulty in program implementation is that qualified trainers must be available. In addition to possessing communication skills, the trainers must know the company's philosophy, its objectives, its formal and informal organization, and the goals of the training program. Training and development requires more creativity than perhaps any other human resource function.

Implementing training programs presents unique problems. Training implies change, which employees may vigorously resist. Participant feedback is vital at this stage because there are often problems in new programs. It may be difficult to schedule the training around present work requirements. Unless the employee is new to the firm, he or she undoubtedly has specific full-time duties to perform. Another difficulty in implementing T&D programs is record keeping. It is important to maintain training records including how well employees perform during training and on the job. This information is important in terms of measuring program effectiveness and charting the employees' progress in the company. The problems mentioned have solutions; however, the more effectively and efficiently they are resolved, the better the chances for success.

9 OBJECTIVE

Explain the metrics for evaluating training and development.

Web Wisdom

Evaluating Training and Development

http://www.astd.org/astd/ Resources/eval_roi_ community/techniques. htm

Excerpts from the original four articles that introduced Kirkpatrick's four-level model of evaluation.

Metrics for Evaluating Training and Development

Managers should strive to develop and use T&D metrics because such information can smooth the way to budget approval and executive buy-in.[90] Most managers agree that training does not cost, it pays, and training is an investment, not an expense. Although corporate America spends billions of dollars a year on employee training, there is no clear consensus within the training community on how to determine its value. What may be missing in programs is a clearly stated business objective for the outcome. It is impossible to evaluate the effectiveness of the activity without clear objectives. And, if you do not collect accurate data and feedback on the effectiveness of your training programs, you just may be wasting money.

Obviously, T&D can enhance its integrity within a firm if it shows tangible benefits to the organization. The three purposes of evaluating include: deciding if a program should be continued, deciding if a program should be modified, and determining the value of training.[91] Thus, the T&D department must document its efforts and demonstrate that it provides a valuable service. Organizations have taken several approaches to evaluate the worth of specific programs. The Kirkpatrick model for training evaluation is widely used in learning environments.[92] The levels in this model are: (1) participants' opinions, (2) extent of learning, (3) behavioral change (transfer of training to the job), and (4) accomplishment of T&D objectives (impact on performance).

Participants' Opinions

Evaluating a T&D program by asking the participants' opinions of it is an approach that provides a response and suggestions for improvements, essentially a level of customer satisfaction. You cannot always rely on such responses, however. The training may have taken place in an exotic location with time for golfing and other fun activities, and the overall experience may bias some reports. Nevertheless, this approach is a good way to obtain feedback and to get it quickly and inexpensively.

Extent of Learning

Some organizations administer tests to determine what the participants in a T&D program have learned. The pretest–posttest control group design is one evaluation procedure that may be used. In this procedure, both groups receive the same test before and after training. The experimental group receives the training but the control group does not. Each group receives randomly assigned trainees. Differences in pretest and posttest results between the groups are attributed to the training provided. A potential problem with this approach is controlling for variables other than training that might affect the outcome.

Behavioral Change

Tests may accurately indicate what trainees learn, but they give little insight into whether the training leads participants to change their behavior. For example, it is one thing for a manager to learn about motivational techniques but quite another matter for this person to apply the new knowledge. A manager may sit in the front row of a training session dealing with empowerment of subordinates, absorb every bit of the message, understand it totally, and then return the next week to the workplace and continue behaving in the same old autocratic way. The best demonstration of value, however, occurs when learning translates into lasting behavioral change.[93] The 360-degree feedback appraisal method (discussed in the following chapter) is often used to measure behavioral changes.[94]

Accomplishment of T&D Objectives

Still another approach to evaluating T&D programs involves determining the extent to which programs have achieved stated objectives and have actually impacted performance. For instance, if the objective of an accident prevention program is to reduce the number and severity of accidents by 15 percent, comparing accident rates before and after training provides a useful metric of success. As another example, a firm might establish a return on investment metric. However, in some circumstances, the actual ROI number may be hard to establish because of the difficulty in isolating the effects of training.[95]

Benchmarking

Benchmarking

http://www.benchnet.com/
The Benchmarking Exchange and Best Practices homepage.

Benchmarking is the process of monitoring and measuring a firm's internal processes, such as operations, and then comparing the data with information from companies that excel in those areas. Because training programs for individual firms are unique, the training measures are necessarily broad. Common benchmarking questions focus on metrics such as training costs, the ratio of training staff to employees, and whether new or more traditional delivery systems are used. Information derived from these questions probably lacks the detail to permit specific improvements of the training curricula. However, a firm may recognize, for example, that another organization is able to deliver a lot of training for relatively little cost. This information could then trigger the firm to follow up with interviews or site visits to determine whether that phenomenon represents a *best practice*. As T&D becomes more crucial to organizational success, determining model training practices and learning from them will become increasingly important.

 OBJECTIVE

Describe the Workforce Investment Act.

Business/Government/Education Training Partnership: Workforce Investment Act

The Workforce Investment Act (WIA) replaced the problem-riddled Job Training Partnership Act (JTPA) and consolidated more than 70 federal job-training programs. It provides states with the flexibility to develop streamlined systems in partnership with local governments. A primary focus of WIA is to meet the needs of business for skilled workers and to satisfy the training, education, and employment needs of individuals.

One-stop service centers are at the heart of the system. These centers provide job seekers with a range of services including career counseling, skill assessments, training, job search assistance, and referrals to programs and services, depending on need.

 **OBJECTIVE**

Define organization development (OD) and describe various OD techniques.

Organization Development

Individuals and groups receive the bulk of T&D effort. However, some firms believe that to achieve needed change, they must move the entire organization in the desired direction. Efforts to achieve this are the focus of *organization development*. **Organization development (OD)** is the planned process of improving an organization by developing its structures, systems, and processes to enhance effectiveness and achieve desired goals. Organization development applies to an entire system, such as a company or a plant. Organization development is a major means of achieving change in the corporate culture. Remember from Chapter 1 that HR branding was discussed as a corporate culture means of affecting the image of a firm. Various factors in the firm's corporate culture affect employees' behavior on the job. To bring about desired changes in these factors and behavior, organizations must be transformed into market-driven, innovative, and adaptive systems if they are to survive and prosper in today's highly competitive global environment. This type of development is increasingly important as both work and the workforce diversify and change.

Numerous OD interventions are available to the practitioner. Interventions covered in the following section include survey feedback, a technique often combined with other interventions; quality circles; team building; and sensitivity training.

Survey Feedback

Survey feedback:
Process of collecting data from an organizational unit through the use of questionnaires, interviews, and objective data from other sources such as records of productivity, turnover, and absenteeism.

Survey feedback is a process of collecting data from an organizational unit using questionnaires, interviews, and objective data from other sources such as records of productivity, turnover, and absenteeism. It enables management teams to help organizations create working environments that lead to better working relationships, greater productivity, and increased profitability. Survey feedback generally involves the following steps:

- Members of the organization, including top management, are involved in planning the survey.
- All members of the organizational unit participate in the survey.
- The OD consultant usually analyzes the data, tabulates results, suggests approaches to diagnosis, and trains participants in the feedback process.
- Data feedback usually begins at the top level of the organization and flows downward to groups reporting at successively lower levels.
- Feedback meetings provide an opportunity to discuss and interpret data, diagnose problem areas, and develop action plans.

Quality Circles

Quality circles:
Groups of employees who voluntarily meet regularly with their supervisors to discuss problems, investigate causes, recommend solutions, and take corrective action when authorized to do so.

America received the concept of quality circles from Japan several decades ago. This version of employee involvement is still in use today, improving quality, increasing motivation, boosting productivity, and adding to the bottom line. **Quality circles** are groups of employees who voluntarily meet regularly with their supervisors to discuss their problems, investigate causes, recommend solutions, and take corrective action when authorized to do so. The team's recommendations are presented to higher-level management for review, and the approved actions are implemented with employee participation.

In order to implement a successful quality circle program, the firm must set clear goals for the program, gain top management's support, and create a climate conducive to participative management. In addition, a qualified manager is essential for the program and the program's goals must be communicated to all concerned. Individuals participating in the program must receive quality circle training. Most organizations that implement continuous improvement cultures, or team systems, teach their employees tools for reaching decisions and solving problems. The tools include four basic steps: problem definition, data collection to confirm the root cause of the problem, solution generation, and action planning. In addition, the firm designs a tracking system to determine results of the action taken.

The key to the success of quality circles is the sincerity of management in dealing with the teams where the participants view their role as an essential part of company decisions. Even those employees who are not part of the circle generally become enthusiastic. Although they have not personally taken part in the planning, they will accept the decisions because their peers, not just the boss, have helped form them. The work becomes more interesting and the employees more motivated when they recognize that successful task completion requires a mutual effort of management and employees.

One thing seems certain: if a firm is to sustain employee interest and enthusiasm for quality circle activities, the employees must share in the economic gain. Nonfinancial rewards are important, as will be discussed in a later chapter. However, if, over the long run, employees are excluded from monetary rewards, they will wonder who really benefits from the programs.

Team Building

Team building:
Conscious effort to develop effective work groups and cooperative skills throughout the organization.

Team building is a conscious effort to develop effective work groups and cooperative skills throughout the organization. It helps members diagnose group processes and devise solutions to problems. Effective team building can be the most efficient way to boost morale, employee retention, and company profitability. Whether it's a lieutenant leading troops into battle or executives working with their managers, the same principles apply. An important by-product of team building is that it is one of the most effective interventions for improving employee satisfaction and work-related attitudes. Individualism has deep roots in American culture. This trait has been a virtue and will continue to be an asset in our society. Now, however, there are work situations that make it imperative to subordinate individual autonomy in favor of cooperation with a group. It seems apparent that teams are clearly superior in performing many of the tasks required by organizations. The building of effective teams, therefore, has become a business necessity.[96]

Organizations must provide much training effort prior to efficient and effective functioning of work teams. Fortunately, most managers know this. Team building utilizes *self-directed teams*, each composed of a small group of employees responsible for an entire work process or segment.[97] Team members work together to improve their operation or product, to plan and control their work, and to handle day-to-day problems. They may even become involved in broader, company-wide issues, such as vendor quality, safety, and business planning.

Team building may begin as soon as an applicant is hired. At Southwest Airlines, the firm divides new employees into teams and gives them a raw egg in the shell, a handful of straws, and some masking tape. Their task is, in a limited amount of time, to protect that delicate cargo from an eight-foot drop. The exercise prepares teams of employees for creative problem solving in a fast-paced environment.[98]

The Lake Forest Graduate School of Management has developed an approach it calls Team Banquets. An internationally recognized executive chef helped develop this program, which brought together people with different knowledge, skills, and experience to accomplish a single goal: create a banquet. The exercise is based on the discovery that some of the most effective, efficient teams in the world are in the kitchens of fine restaurants. These settings serve as models of organization, communication, and results-oriented processes. The Team Banquet brings together 25 to 30 employees and challenges them to prepare a gourmet banquet within two hours. Only the raw ingredients and equipment are provided. The assigned roles may put a mail clerk in charge while a group manager serves as an assistant. Each team is assigned a specific portion of the banquet preparation, from entrée to decorations and food presentation. Participants receive safety instructions but not recipes. Teams must rely on their own knowledge and creativity in devising the dishes they serve. The initial response to this approach was skepticism. However, management and participants soon discovered that the exercise provided an excellent analogy to the workplace and provided an outstanding means for developing teamwork.[99]

Nick Conner, vice president for program development at Tampa-based TeamBuilders, describes the following team-building exercise that he uses with his clients. "The group of managers participated in a 'blind mission,' whereby half the team must guide their peers in carrying a five-gallon bucket with a ball onto a platform of squares that is smaller in diameter than the bucket. The exercise appears simple, but half the team is blindfolded. Participants, especially the individuals who serve as leaders, quickly realize that they are prone to give conflicting orders or to speak in a manner as if it was obvious what needed to be done. The communication gaps that arise in a simple game are a metaphor for the same types of lapses that occur in the workplace. "People start to realize, 'How many times do we speak to others as if we know the same thing,'" Conner says.[100]

Sensitivity Training

Sensitivity training:
Organization development technique that is designed to help individuals learn how others perceive their behavior (also known as T-group training).

Sensitivity training, or T-group training, is a procedure designed to help individuals learn how others perceive their behavior. It is based on the assumption that a number of individuals meeting in an unstructured situation will develop working relations with each other. From this experience, they will learn much about themselves as perceived by the other group members. It differs from many traditional forms of training, which stress the learning of a predetermined set of concepts. When sensitivity training begins, there is no agenda, no leaders, no authority, and no power positions. Essentially, a vacuum exists until participants begin to talk. Through dialogue, people begin to learn about themselves and others. The trainer's purpose is to serve as a facilitator in this unstructured environment. Participants are encouraged to learn about themselves and others in the group. Some objectives of sensitivity training are to increase the participants' self-awareness and sensitivity to the behavior of others. The training also strives to develop an awareness of the processes that facilitate or inhibit group and intergroup functioning, and to increase the participants' ability to achieve effective interpersonal relationships. T-group training was once a prominent OD intervention. A central problem with sensitivity training, according to some, is that its purpose is to change individuals, not necessarily the environment in which they work. When participants attempt to use what they have learned, they often find their co-workers unwilling to accept it, or worse, what they have learned may not be appropriate for their own work situation.

A Global Perspective

Learning the Culture of China

A school that started three years ago to help children of Chinese descent learn about China's history and culture has found another niche for its services. The Chinese Language School of Connecticut Inc., a nonprofit organization, has branched out to help companies wishing to initiate trade with China or learn more about the country's culture and traditions. Susan Serven, the school's president, started the language school initially as a way to incorporate the Chinese culture into the lives of the two children she adopted from China. She and her friends began classes in New Canaan designed for children three years old and up. "We expected 50 children to show up the first day but we had 130 children," Severn said. Since then classes have met in libraries and churches across the county.[101]

Last year, Severn began receiving requests from companies that were interested in having their employees learn the Mandarin language, one of two major languages spoken in China. "It's critical that companies planning to maintain a presence or just do frequent business with China know some Chinese and about the Chinese culture." So the school set out this year to target corporate clients. Classes are held at clients' facilities and are customized. CD-ROM, audio, and video learning technologies are offered so employees can learn practical communication skills.[102] Peter Gioia, an economist with the Connecticut Business Industry Association, the state's largest business group, said China is a huge factor that is likely to loom larger as the years go by. "China is officially an economic superpower. Besides the enormous amount of exports, it imports an awful lot. It seems that the Europeans have been more adept at catching their market than us," Gioia said. Berlitz Languages Inc., Princeton, New Jersey, a language school with classes in Stamford and Westport, also offers classes teaching Mandarin. "Over the last two years we have experienced a noticeable increase in the number of inquiries we receive concerning Mandarin," said John Weckerling, director for the Stamford and Westport schools.[103]

Summary

1. Define training and development.

Training is designed to permit learners to acquire knowledge and skills needed for their present jobs. Development involves learning that goes beyond today's job.

2. Explain factors influencing T&D.

Increasingly rapid changes in technology, products, systems, and methods have had a significant impact on job requirements, making T&D a must. T&D programs must have top management's full support; all managers should be committed to and involved in the T&D process. They must be convinced that there will be a tangible payoff if resources are committed to this effort.

3. Describe the T&D process.

First, an organization must determine their specific training needs. Then specific objectives need to be established. After setting the T&D objectives, management can determine the appropriate methods and the delivery system to be used. Naturally, management must continuously evaluate T&D to ensure its value in achieving organizational objectives.

4. Describe the various training and development methods.

Training and development methods include instructor-led, case study, behavior modeling, role-playing, business games, in-basket training, on-the-job training, job rotation, internships, and apprenticeship training.

5. Describe training and development delivery systems.

Delivery systems include corporate universities, colleges and universities, community colleges, online higher education, videoconferencing, vestibule system, video media, e-learning, and simulators.

6. Describe management development, mentoring, and coaching.

Management development consists of all learning experiences provided by an organization for the purpose of providing and upgrading skills and knowledge required in current and future managerial positions. Mentoring is an approach to advising, coaching, and nurturing, for creating a practical relationship to enhance individual career, personal, and professional growth and development. Coaching, often considered a responsibility of the immediate boss, provides assistance much like a mentor.

7. Define orientation and describe the executive orientation concept of onboarding.

Orientation is the guided adjustment of new employees to the company, the job, and the work group. Onboarding is the process companies use to help new executives quickly learn an organization's structure, culture, and politics, as well as the ways they can start making discernible contributions to the organization as soon as possible.

8. Identify special training areas.

Special training needs include training involving diversity, English as a second language (ESL), ethics, telecommuting, customer service, conflict resolution, teamwork, empowerment, remedial, and anger management.

9. Explain the metrics for evaluating training and development.

The metrics by which T&D programs are evaluated include participants' opinions, extent of learning, behavioral change, accomplishment of T&D objectives, and benchmarking.

10. Describe the Workforce Investment Act.

The Workforce Investment Act (WIA) replaced the problem-riddled Job Training Partnership Act (JTPA) and consolidated more than 70 federal job-training programs. It provides states with the flexibility to develop streamlined systems in partnership with local governments.

11. Define organization development (OD) and describe various OD techniques.

Organization development is the planned process of improving an organization by developing its structures, systems, and processes to improve effectiveness, and achieving desired goals. OD techniques include survey feedback, a technique often combined with other interventions, quality circles, team building, and sensitivity training.

Key Terms

- Job security, 199
- Career security, 200
- Employability doctrine, 200
- Training and development (T&D), 200
- Training, 200
- Development, 200
- Learning organization, 201
- Just-in-time training, 203
- Case study, 207
- Behavior modeling, 207
- Role-playing, 207
- Business games, 207
- In-basket training, 208
- On-the-job training (OJT), 208
- Job rotation, 208
- Apprenticeship training, 209
- Corporate university, 209
- Online higher education, 210
- Vestibule system, 211
- E-learning, 211
- Virtual reality, 212
- Simulators, 212
- Management development, 213
- Mentoring, 214
- Coaching, 214
- Reverse mentoring, 215
- Orientation, 215
- Onboarding, 217
- Benchmarking, 221
- Organization development (OD), 221
- Survey feedback, 222
- Quality circles, 222
- Team building, 223
- Sensitivity training, 224

Questions for Review

1. What is the difference between job security and career security?
2. Define training and development.
3. What is a learning organization?
4. What are some factors that influence T&D?
5. What are the steps in the T&D process?
6. What are the various training and development methods? Briefly describe each.
7. What are the various training and development delivery systems? Briefly describe each.
8. Define management development. Why is it important?
9. Distinguish between mentoring and coaching. What is reverse mentoring?
10. Define orientation and explain the purposes of orientation.
11. Describe the concept of onboarding.
12. What are some metrics for evaluating training and development?
13. What is the Workforce Investment Act?
14. Define each of the following:
    a. organization development
    b. survey feedback
    c. quality circles
    d. sensitivity training
    e. team building

HRM Incident 1

Training at Keller-Globe

Lou McGowen was worried as she approached the training director's office. She supervises six punch press operators at Keller-Globe, a maker of sheet metal parts for the industrial refrigeration industry. She had just learned that her punch presses would soon be replaced with a continuous-feed system that would double the speed of operations. She was thinking about how the workers might feel about the new system when the training director, Bill Taylor, opened the door and said, "Come on in, Lou. I've been looking forward to seeing you."

After a few pleasantries, Lou told Bill of her concerns. "The operators really know their jobs now. But this continuous-feed system is a whole new ball game. I'm concerned, too, about how the workers will feel about it. The new presses are going to run faster. They may think that their job is going to be harder."

Bill replied, "After talking with the plant engineer and the production manager, I made a tentative training schedule that might make you feel a little better. I think we first have to let the workers know why this change is necessary. You know that both of our competitors changed to this new system last year. After that, we will teach your people to operate the new presses."

"Who's going to do the teaching?" Lou asked. "I haven't even seen the new system."

"Well, Lou," said Bill, "the manufacturer has arranged for you to visit a plant with a similar system. They'll also ship one of the punch presses in early so you and your workers can learn to operate it."

"Will the factory give us any other training help?" Lou asked.

"Yes, I have asked them to send a trainer down as soon as the first press is set up. He will conduct some classroom sessions and then work with your people on the new machine."

After further discussion about details, Lou thanked Bill and headed back to the production department. She was confident that the new presses would be a real benefit to her section and that her workers could easily learn the skills required.

Question

1. Evaluate Keller-Globe's approach to training.

HRM Incident 2

Career versus Job Security?

J. D. Wallace, a 30-year-old employee with Bechtel Engineering, headquartered in Houston, Texas, describes his assessment of career development. "My present job is to work with an engineering software design program, Plant Design System (PDS), that is used to create a 3-dimensional model of a petro-chem refinery. PDS is the fastest-growing and most demanded skill in the industry. The system has grown into a major design system that clients prefer. It has become very difficult for designers to find new jobs or keep their current jobs if they do not have the ability to run this system. Unfortunately, a lot of the designers have been caught with their pants down. They didn't see the need to get new skills. They believe, 'I've done it this way for 20 years and I have not needed computer skills. Computers will never replace board drafting. This company needs me and they will not be able to replace me because of my many years of experience.' On the other hand, some designers realize the importance of learning new technology. These designers can, for the most part, write their own ticket. They have become the highest-paid and most sought-after employees. I believe that it is very important to constantly increase your value to the company. For example, my college degree opened the door for me. Once the door opened, it was up to me to keep learning. I had to continue to train, retrain, and learn new systems. Some of the systems that I have invested time in learning have quickly become obsolete. However, I have not lost anything in the process. Improving skills is never a waste of time. It is amazing how fast the industry can change. Skills that you obtain and thought you would never use, can be the only reason you have a job tomorrow.

"Workers today must do whatever it takes to get the training needed to keep their jobs. Some of the things you could do include going back to school, or changing companies to get the necessary training. Very few companies spend the time and money needed to give workers all the training they need. Everybody must realize that they must stay current or they will be left behind.

"In the last year alone the market for designers with PDS training has grown so fast that companies can no longer be assured of having an adequate work pool to draw from. The pay scale has expanded rapidly and is still growing. A good friend of mine has recently quit his present job for a 35 percent pay increase. Another company has lost many of its 10-year-plus employees to huge salary offers. Workers with the needed skills now have a lot of options. They can (for the most part) pick the company they want, by location, benefits, permanent staff, or contract. They currently have a lot of leverage. Workers without those skills have very limited choices because they do not add value to their companies."

Questions

1. Is J. D. concerned more with job security or career security? Discuss.

2. Do you agree with J. D.'s statement that "improving your skills is never a waste of time," considering that he has learned systems which quickly became obsolete? Discuss.

Notes

1. Julie Rawe, "What Will Be the 10 Hottest Jobs? . . . and What Jobs Will Disappear? *Time* 155 (May 22, 2000): 73.

2. "The Myth of Job Security," *InfoWorld* 27 (September 12, 2005): 64.

3. Rick Merritt, "Working Harder in Tough Times," *Electronic Engineering Times* (August 22, 2005): 37–52.

4. Daniel Schoonmaker, "Soper's Focus: Career Security," *Grand Rapids Business Journal* 23 (April 11, 2005): 5–10.

5. Margaret A. White and Suzanne M. Behr, "The New Employees," *Leadership Excellence* (April 2005): 9–10.

6. Scott Leibs, "Building a Better Workforce," *CFO* 21 (Fall 2005): 20–25.

7. Brent M. Longnecker and Nicole Shanklin, "Total Rewards: A Three-Legged Platform Toward Improved Productivity," *Employee Benefit Plan Review* 59 (July 2004): 8–10.

8. Nichole L. Torres, "Perking Up," *Entrepreneur* 34 (April 2006): 30.

9. Merritt, "Working Harder in Tough Times."

10. "How to Develop the Best Training Initiatives," *HR Focus* 82 (August 2005): 11–13.

11. Tammy Galvin, "Industry Report 2002," *Training* 39 (October 2002): 27.

12. "Spending on Learning & Training Is Increasing: ASTD Report," *HR Focus* 83 (March 2006): 9.

13. "What to Do Now That Training Is Becoming a Major HR Force," *HR Focus* 82 (February 2005): 5–6.

14. Josh Bersin, "Learning Management: The Enterprise Approach," *Chief Learning Officer* 4 (November 2005): 48–53.

15. Steve Arneson, "Continuous Learning and Workforce Engagement," *Chief Learning Officer* 5 (January 2006): 24–27.

16. Warren Wilhelm, "Learning Organizations," *Leadership Excellence* 23 (March 2006): 17–18.

17. Jason Averbook, "Connecting CLOs with the Recruiting Process," *Chief Learning Officer* 4 (June 2005): 24–27.

18. "How to Use Training to Accelerate Growth," *HR Focus* 82 (April 2005): 3–4.

19. Averbook, "Connecting CLOs with the Recruiting Process."

20. "Making Change Work—For Real," *HR Focus* 80 (January 2003): S1.

21. David James Clarke IV, "The Nexus of Learning: The Intersection of Formal and Informal Education," *Chief Learning Officer* 5 (February 2006): 22–25.

22. Steven R. Covey, "Teaching Organizations," *Executive Excellence* (March 2000): 20.

23. Holly Ann Suzik, "Built from Scratch," *Quality* 38 (October 1999): 32–34.

24. "Why a Business Approach to Training Is Best," *HR Focus* 82 (July 2005): 5.

25. "Blended Learning Works Best, a New ASTD Survey Reports," *HR Focus* 82 (January 2005): 9.

26. http://www.blackboard.com/company/press/release .aspx?id=791879, September 8, 2006.

27. Andy Edelman, "When Words Fail: 8 Tips for Preparing Your Employees for a Crisis," *Business Credit* 108 (July/August 2006): 70–71.

28. Lisa Jennings, "Learning to Identify What Customers Want," *Nation's Restaurant News* 39 (September 19, 2005):138.

29. Ulrich Boser, "Gaming the System, One Click at a Time," *U.S. News & World Report* 133 (October 28, 2002): 60.

30. Kenneth M. York, David S. Strubler, and Elaine M. Smith, "A Comparison of Two Methods for Scoring an In-Basket Exercise," *Public Personnel Management* 34 (Fall 2005): 271–280.

31. Anthony Urbaniak, "Training Employees," *Supervision* 65 (February 2004): 6–7.

32. Julia Vowler, "Away Days Promote Teamworking," *Computer Weekly* (May 5, 2005): 28.

33. Dawn S. Onley, "Internship Program Dividends," *HR Magazine* (January 2006): 85–87.

34. Malcolm Coco, "Internships: A Try Before You Buy Arrangement," *Advanced Management Journal* 65 (Spring 2000): 41.

35. Alex Kingsbury, "Get a Once and Future Job," *U.S. News & World Report* 138 (April 18, 2005): 70.

36. Michelle Merlo, "Training Program Prepares Future Electricians," *Electric Perspectives* 27 (May/June 2002): 29.

37. Debra K. Rubin and Mary B. Powers, "The Push to Know More and Do More Lifts Industry's Learning Curve," *ENR: Engineering News-Record* 254 (April 11, 2005): 28–31.

38. Margery Weinstein, "What Can a Corporate U Do for You?" *Training* 43 (July 2006): 34–38.

39. Mark Allen, "Beyond Training," *Executive Excellence* 21 (December 2004): 19.

40. Margaret Terry Orr, "Community Colleges and Their Communities: Collaboration for Workforce Development," *New Directions for Community Colleges* 115 (Fall 2001): 39.

41. Jeff Bailey, "Community Colleges Can Help Small Firms with Staffing—Programs with Two-Year Institutions Aid in Developing Skills in Short Supply," *Wall Street Journal* (February 19, 2002): B2.

42. Ibid.

43. "Partial Client Listing," Business & Industry Services Network, Connecticut Community Colleges (April 29, 2003). http://www.commnet.edu/bisn/clients.html.

44. "Is Online Higher Education Right For Corporate Learning?" T+D 59 (September 2005): 44–47.

45. Kimberly Merriman, "Employers Warm Up to Online Education," HR Magazine 51 (January 2006): 79–82.

46. William C. Symonds, "The Bleak Writing on the Blackboard," Business Week (January 12, 2004): 121.

47. Krysten Crawford, "A Degree of Respect for Online MBAs," Business 2.0 6 (December 2005): 102–104.

48. Walter S. Mossberg, "Seeing Is Believing," Smart Money 15 (May 2006): 118–119.

49. Dan Beucke and Robert LaFranco, "The Next Best Thing to Being There," Business Week (September 12, 2005): 14.

50. Doug Bartholomew, "Training Goes High Tech," Industry Week 255 (August 2006): 17.

51. Michael A. Tucker, "E-Learning Evolves," HR Magazine 50 (October 2005): 74–78.

52. Doug Batholomew, "Taking the E-Train," Industry Week 254 (June 2005): 34–37.

53. "Training Cost-Control Measure," HR Focus 82 (May 2005): 9.

54. "E-Learning Evolves into Mature Training Tool," T+D 60 (April 2006): 20.

55. "Is E-learning as Effective as Classroom Learning?" T+D 59 (August 2005): 18.

56. Michael A. Tucker, "E-Learning Evolves," HR Magazine 50 (October 2005): 74–78.

57. Jessica Marquez, "Faced with High Turnover, Retailers Boot Up e-Learning Programs for Quick Training," Workforce Management 84 (August 2005): 74–75.

58. Ralph Kisiel, "Repairs Are a Click Away for Mechanics," Automotive News 78 (July 5, 2004): 24.

59. Ann Pomeroy, "Business Leaders Lack Critical Skills," HR Magazine 51 (January 2006): 14–16.

60. Jacqueline Durett, "Mentors in Short Supply," Training 43 (July 2006): 14.

61. Margaret Heffernan and Joni Saj-Nicole, "Of Protégés and Pitfalls," Fast Company 97 (August 2005): 81–83.

62. "For Success with Corporate Coaching, Begin with Assessment," HR Focus 83 (July 2006): 8.

63. Tamara E. Holmes, "Networking for Success," Black Enterprise 37 (August 2006): 117.

64. Kelley M. Butler, "Today's Working Women Seek Mentors, Motherhood Transition," Employee Benefit News 20 (April 2006): 17–19.

65. Donna N. Owens, "Virtual Mentoring," HR Magazine 51 (March 2006): 105–107.

66. "Career Advancement," Essence 36 (May 2005): 247.

67. Dan Sussman, "A Monstrous Welcome," T+D 59 (April 2005): 40–41.

68. "Money Isn't Everything," The Journal of Business Strategy 21 (March/April 2000): 4.

69. Trish Rintels, "Career Stalled? Get It in Gear with Reverse Mentoring," Selling (March 2005): 6.

70. Ibid.

71. John F. Welch Jr. with John A. Byrne, Jack Straight from the Gut (New York: Warner Books, Inc., 2001): 347.

72. Samuel Greengard, "Moving Forward with Reverse Mentoring," Workforce 81 (March 2002): 15.

73. Brent Schlender, "The Odd Couple," Fortune 141 (May 1, 2000): 106–114.

74. Martin Delahoussaye, "Capital One," Training 38 (March 2001): 70.

75. Barbara Morris, "Why Good Hires Go Bad," Profit 24 (June 2005): 106.

76. "Employee Retention Starts at Orientation," Selling (April 2005): 14.

77. Dan Sussman, "A Monstrous Welcome," T+D 59 (April 2005): 40–41.

78. Ibid.

79. Terence F. Shea, "'Sink-or-Swim' Is Not an Option," HR Magazine 50 (March 2005): 14.

80. Ann Pomeroy, "Better Executive Onboarding Processes Needed," HR Magazine 51 (August 2006): 16.

81. Susan J. Wells, "Diving In," HR Magazine 50 (March 2005): 54–59.

82. Lauren Keller Johnson, "Get Your New Managers Moving," Harvard Management Update 10 (June 2005): 3–5.

83. Ann Fisher, "How You Can Do Better on Diversity," Fortune 150 (November 15, 2004): 60.

84. "Many U.S. Employers Lack Formal Diversity Recruitment Programs," HR Focus 83 (January 2006): 9.

85. Dina Berta, "Language Smarts: Shared Ideas Form ESL Program," Nation's Restaurant News 36 (September 16, 2002): 18.

86. Barry R. Weissman, "English Only Training," Industrial Safety & Hygiene News 39 (October 2005): 37.

87. Kelly Mollica, "Stay Above the Fray," HR Magazine 50 (April 2005): 111.

88. Martin L. Gross, The Conspiracy of Ignorance: The Failure of American Public Schools (New York: HarperCollins, 1999): 6.

89. "Training and Development," HR Magazine 50 (November 2005): 135–136.

90. How One Trainer Developed an Eight-Step Program for ROI," HR Focus 82 (March 2005): 10–13.

91. Jim Kirkpatrick, "Transferring Learning to Behavior," T+D 59 (April 2005): 19–20.

92. Robert W. Rowden, "Exploring Methods to Evaluate the Return-on-Investment from Training," Business Forum 27 (2005): 31–36.

93. Kirkpatrick, "Transferring Learning to Behavior."

94. Rowden, "Exploring Methods to Evaluate the Return-on-Investment from Training."

95. "How One Trainer Developed an Eight-Step Program for ROI."

96. "Finding Competitive Advantage in Self-Managed Work Teams," Business Forum 27 (2005): 20–24.

97. Thomas Capozzoli, "Succeed with Self-directed Work Teams," Supervision 65 (June 2004): 26.

98. Kathryn Tyler, "Take New Employee Orientation off the Back Burner," HR Magazine 43 (May 1998): 49.

99. Howard Prager, "Cooking up Effective Team Building," Training & Development 53 (December 1999): 14–15.

100. Michael Laff, "Effective Team Building: More Than Just Fun at Work," T+D 60 (August 2006): 24–25.

101. Andrew Scott, "China's Growth Sends Businesses to School," Fairfield County Business Journal 44 (April 4, 2005): 12.

102. Ibid.

103. Ibid.

Appendix
CHAPTER 7

Career Planning and Development

Career Planning and Development Defined

A **career** is a general course that a person chooses to pursue throughout his or her working life. Historically, a *career* was a sequence of work-related positions an individual has occupied during a lifetime, although not always with the same company. However, today there are few relatively static jobs. **Career planning** is an ongoing process whereby an individual sets career goals and identifies the means to achieve them. Career planning should not concentrate only on advancement opportunities since the present work environment has reduced many of these opportunities. At some point, career planning should focus on achieving successes that do not necessarily entail promotions.

Organizational career planning is the planned succession of jobs worked out by a firm to develop its employees. With organizational career planning, the organization identifies paths and activities for individual employees as they develop. A **career path** is a flexible line of movement through which an employee may move during employment with a company. Following an established career path, the employee can undertake career development with the firm's assistance. Companies are increasingly using the Web to assist employees in determining their career paths and required competencies.[1] From a worker's perspective, following a career path may involve weaving from company to company and from position to position as he or she obtains greater knowledge and experience.[2]

Career development is a formal approach used by the organization to ensure that people with the proper qualifications and experiences are available when needed. Formal career development is important to maintain a motivated and committed workforce.[3] Career planning and development benefit both the individual and the organization and must therefore be carefully considered by both.

Career Planning

As Alice said in *Through the Looking Glass*, "If you don't know where you're going, any road will get you there." Such is the case with career planning. As one manager stated, "You need to always have a sense of crisis with your career, a sense of emergency. If you don't have a back-up plan, you get caught off guard."[4] Career planning must now accommodate a number of objectives and enable us to prepare for each on a contingency basis.[5] It will need updating to accommodate changes in our own interests as well as in the work environment. Historically, it was thought that career planning was logical, linear, and indeed, planned. That is not the case today, as individuals have experienced or seen downsizing, job creation, and job elimination. Because of the many changes that are occurring, career planning is essential for survival for individuals and organizations.

As previously mentioned, organizational career planning involves the identification of paths and activities for employees as they develop. Career planning at the individual level and organizational career planning are interrelated and interdependent; therefore, success requires parallel planning at both levels.

Individual Career Planning: Self-Assessment

Through career planning, a person continuously evaluates his or her abilities and interests, considers alternative career opportunities, establishes career goals, and plans practical developmental activities. A career plan lets you know where you are and where you are going.[6] Individual career planning must begin with self-understanding or self-assessment.[7] Then, the person is in a position to establish realistic goals and determine what to do to achieve these goals.[8] This action also lets the person know whether his or her goals are realistic.

Self-assessment is the process of learning about oneself.[9] Anything that could affect one's performance in a future job should be considered. It is one of the first things that a person should do in planning a career.[10] Realistic self-assessment may help a person avoid mistakes that could affect his or her entire career progression. Often an individual accepts a job without considering whether it matches his or her interests and abilities. This approach can result in failure. A thorough self-assessment will go a long way toward helping match an individual's specific qualities and goals with the right job or profession.[11] Deborah Warner, founder of Career Development Partners, said, "Applicants should pay attention to the skills they want to use and

---

Career:
General course that a person chooses to pursue throughout his or her working life.

Career planning:
Ongoing process whereby an individual sets career goals and identifies the means to achieve them.

Organizational career planning:
Planned succession of jobs worked out by a firm to develop its employees.

Career path:
Flexible line of progression through which an employee may move during his or her employment with a company.

Career development:
Formal approach used by the organization to ensure that people with the proper qualifications and experiences are available when needed.

Self-assessment:
Process of learning about oneself.

the ones they no longer want to use. When an individual has to frequently use skills [he doesn't] enjoy using, that can lead to job dissatisfaction and burnout."[12] For many people, being fired causes them to take stock of themselves for the first time and to analyze their strengths and weaknesses. Nick Colas, director of research at Rochdale Securities, a person who says he has reinvented his own career on Wall Street several times in the past 10 years, said, "The average American worker isn't going to have one career for his or her lifetime. Think about what your key skills are. You're going to have to change careers."[13]

Some useful tools include a strength/weakness balance sheet and a likes and dislikes survey. However, any reasonable approach that assists self-understanding is helpful.

Strength/Weakness Balance Sheet. A self-evaluation procedure, developed originally by Benjamin Franklin, that assists people in becoming aware of their strengths and weaknesses is the **strength/weakness balance sheet**. Employees who understand their strengths can use them to maximum advantage. By recognizing their weaknesses, they are in a better position to overcome them. This statement sums up that attitude; "If you have a weakness, understand it and make it work for you as a strength; if you have a strength, do not abuse it to the point where it becomes a weakness."

To use a strength/weakness balance sheet, the individual lists strengths and weaknesses as he or she perceives them. This is quite important because believing, for example, that a weakness exists even when it does not can equate to a real weakness. Thus, if you believe that you make a poor first impression when meeting someone, you will probably make a poor impression. The perception of a weakness often becomes a self-fulfilling prophecy.

The mechanics for preparing the balance sheet are quite simple. To begin, draw a line down the middle of a sheet of paper. Label the left side *Strengths* and the right side *Weaknesses*. Record all perceived strengths and weaknesses. You may find it difficult to write about yourself. Remember, however, that no one else need see the results. The primary consideration is complete honesty.

Table A7-1 shows an example of a strength/weakness balance sheet. Obviously, Wayne (the person who wrote the sheet) did a lot of soul-searching in making these evaluations. Typically, a person's weaknesses will outnumber strengths in the first few iterations. However, as the individual repeats the process, some items that first appeared to be weaknesses may eventually be recognized as strengths and should then be moved from one column to the other. A person should devote sufficient time to the project to obtain a fairly clear understanding of his or her strengths and weaknesses. Typically, the process should take a minimum of one week. The balance sheet will not provide all the answers regarding a person's strengths and weaknesses, but many people have gained a better understanding of themselves by completing it. Analyzing oneself should not be just a one-time event. People change and every few years the process should again be undertaken. You can determine means to react to your findings and, perhaps, overcome a weakness after you have conducted the self-assessment.

Likes and Dislikes Survey. An individual should also consider likes and dislikes as part of a self-assessment.[14] A **likes and dislikes survey** assists individuals in recognizing restrictions they place on themselves. You are looking for qualities you want in a job and attributes of a job you do not want.[15] For instance, some people are not willing to live in certain parts of the country, and such feelings should be noted as a constraint. Some positions require a person to spend a considerable amount of time traveling. Thus, an estimate of the amount of time a person is willing to travel would also be helpful. Recognition of such self-imposed restrictions may reduce future career problems. Another limitation is the type of firm an individual will consider working for.

The size of the firm might also be important. Some like a major organization whose products or services are well known; others prefer a smaller organization, believing that the opportunities for advancement may be greater or that the environment is better suited to their tastes. All factors that could affect an individual's work performance should be listed in the likes and dislikes survey. An example of this type of survey is shown in Table A7–2.

A self-assessment such as this one helps a person understand his or her basic motives, and sets the stage for pursuing a career or seeking further technical competence. People who know themselves can more easily make the decisions necessary for successful career planning. Many people get sidetracked because they choose careers based on haphazard plans or the wishes of others, rather than on what they believe to be best for them.

Getting to know yourself is not a singular event. As individuals progress through life, priorities change. Individuals may think that they know themselves quite well at one stage of life and later begin to see themselves quite differently. Therefore, the self-assessment should be viewed as a continuous process. Career-minded individuals must heed the Red Queen's

---

Strength/weakness balance sheet:

A self-evaluation procedure, developed originally by Benjamin Franklin, that assists people in becoming aware of their strengths and weaknesses.

Likes and dislikes survey:

Procedure that helps individuals recognize restrictions they place on themselves.

Table A7-1 **Strength/Weakness Balance Sheet**

Strengths	Weaknesses
Work well with people.	Get very close to few people.
Like to be given a task and get it done in my own way.	Do not like constant supervision.
Good manager of people.	Am extremely high-strung.
Hard worker.	Often say things without realizing consequences.
Lead by example.	Cannot stand to look busy when there is no work to be done.
People respect me as being fair and impartial.	Cannot stand to be inactive. Must be on the go constantly.
Tremendous amount of energy.	Cannot stand to sit at a desk all the time.
Function well in an active environment.	Basically a rebel at heart but have portrayed myself as just the opposite. My conservatism has gotten me jobs that I emotionally did not want.
Relatively open-minded.	
Feel comfortable in dealing with high-level businesspersons.	Am sometimes nervous in an unfamiliar environment.
Like to play politics (This may be a weakness.)	Make very few true friends.
Get the job done when it is defined.	Not a conformist but appear to be.
Excellent at organizing other people's time.	Interest level hits peaks and valleys.
Can get the most out of people who are working for me.	Many people look on me as being unstable. Perhaps I am. Believe not.
Have an outgoing personality—not shy.	Divorced.
Take care of those who take care of me. (This could be a weakness).	Not a tremendous planner for short range. Long-range planning is better.
Have a great amount of empathy.	Impatient—want to have things happen fast.
Work extremely well through other people.	Do not like details.
	Do not work well in an environment where I am the only party involved.

Source: Wayne Sanders.

admonition to Alice: "It takes all the running you can do, to keep in the same place."[16] This admonition is so very true in today's work environment.

Using the Web for Self-Assessment Assistance

The Internet has valuable information to assist in developing a self-assessment. Some sites are free and others charge a modest fee. Some Websites that might be valuable as you conduct your self-assessment include:

- *CareerMaze:* An assessment of vocational interests and weaknesses, interests, and capabilities for every job seeker at every level is provided. There is a charge of $19.95 for the Career Maze report.[17]
- *Career-intelligence:* A career resource site targeted toward women. Career-assessment planning information, exercises, and assessment tools are available in addition to a multitude of other resources.[18]

Table A7-2 **Likes and Dislikes Survey**

Likes	Dislikes
Like to travel.	Do not want to work for a large firm.
Would like to live in the East.	Will not work in a large city.
Enjoy being my own boss.	Do not like to work behind a desk all day.
Would like to live in a medium-sized city.	Do not like to wear suits all the time.
Enjoy watching football and baseball.	
Enjoy playing racquetball.	

Source: Wayne Sanders.

- *Hollands Theory of Career Choice:* The Career Key is based on the theory that people like to be around others who have similar personalities. In choosing a career, it means that people choose jobs where they can be around other people who are like them.[19]
- *International Assessment Network:* An assessment tool available through the Internet that measures an individual's motivation toward specific work areas.[20]
- *Princeton Review Career:* For a free career assessment go to "Learn more about your personal interest and style" to identify potential careers.[21]

Using the Web for Career Planning Assistance

The Web can often be an excellent tool for assisting you in planning your career. Listed below is some advice on how the Web can assist you.

- There is a large amount of free information available on the Web that should prove helpful. Virtually all of the major job boards provide tips for writing a cover letter and résumés. For example, at Monster.com, click the *Career Advice* tab and a large amount of valuable information becomes available.
- The Web can be used to develop and maintain a professional network. It is much easier and more convenient to keep in touch with other professionals through e-mail. This is important since the number-one way people find a job is through some kind of networking or referral.[22] Individuals that you have met at conferences or business meetings may provide useful assistance in a job search. A network should be maintained even though you are satisfied with your present job.
- The Web should be used to investigate specific companies before seeking employment or going for an interview. For instance, with WetFeet.com, a job seeker can research companies, careers, and industries.[23]

Organizational Career Planning

Organizational career planning should begin with a person's job placement and initial orientation. Management then observes the employee's job performance and compares it to job standards. At this stage, strengths and weaknesses will be noted, enabling management to assist the employee in making a tentative career decision. Naturally, this decision can be altered later as the process continues. This tentative career decision is based on a number of factors, including personal needs, abilities, and aspirations, and the organization's needs. Management can then schedule development programs that relate to the employee's specific needs.

Although the primary responsibility for career planning rests with the individual, organizational career planning must closely parallel individual career planning if a firm is to retain its best and brightest workers. Employees must see that the firm's organizational career planning effort is directed toward furthering their specific career objectives. Companies must therefore help their employees obtain their career objectives and, most notably, career security. They must provide them with opportunities to learn and do different things. Performing the same or similar task over and over provides little development. Through effective organizational career planning, a pool of men and women can be developed who can thrive in any number of organizational structures in the future.

Firms should undertake organizational career planning programs only when the programs contribute to achieving current and future organizational goals. Therefore, the rationale and approach to career planning programs vary among firms. This rationale is more important in today's environment. Career planning programs are expected to achieve one or more of the following objectives:

- *Effective development of available talent.* Individuals are more likely to be committed to development that is part of a specific career plan. This way, they can better understand the purpose of development. Career planning and development consistently rank high on employees' *want* lists, and they can often be a less expensive option than pay raises and bonuses.[24]

- *Self-appraisal opportunities for employees considering new or nontraditional career paths.* Some excellent workers do not view traditional upward mobility as a career option since firms today have fewer promotion options available. Other workers see themselves in dead-end jobs and seek relief. Rather than lose these workers, a firm can offer career planning to help them identify new and different career paths.

- *Development of career paths that cut across divisions and geographic locations.* The development should not be limited to a narrow spectrum of one part of a company.

- *A demonstration of a tangible commitment to EEO and affirmative action.* Adverse impact can occur at virtually any level in an organization. Firms that are totally committed to reducing adverse impact often cannot find qualified women and minorities to fill vacant positions. One means of overcoming this problem is an effective career planning and development program.

- *Satisfaction of employees' specific development needs.* Individuals who see their personal development needs being met tend to be more satisfied with their jobs and the organization. They tend to remain with the organization.

- *Improvement of performance.* The job itself is the most important influence on career development. Each job can provide different challenges and experiences.

- *Increased employee loyalty and motivation, leading to decreased turnover.* Individuals who believe that the firm is interested in their career planning are more likely to remain with the organization.

- *A method of determining training and development needs.* If a person desires a certain career path and does not presently have the proper qualifications, this identifies a training and development need.

Successful career planning depends on a firm's ability to satisfy those that it considers most crucial to employee development and the achievement of organizational goals.

Career Paths

Career paths have historically focused on upward mobility within a particular occupation, a choice not nearly as available as in the past. Other career paths include the network, lateral skill, dual-career paths, adding value to your career, and even demotion. By selecting an alternative career path, a person may transfer current skills into a new career, one that was only dreamed about in the past. Typically, these career paths are used in combination and may be more popular at various stages of a person's career.

Traditional Career Path

The following is a quote from a *Fortune* magazine article:

> *Close your eyes and picture an object that embodies the word* career. *If you joined the workforce, say, 15 or 20 or 25 years ago, you're probably hard-wired, as the techies say to visualize your working life as a predictable series of narrow and distinctly separate rungs that lead straight up (or down), in other words, a ladder. Ha! Ha, ha, ha! My friend, the ladder has been chopped up into little pieces and dumped in the garbage pile. A team of sanitation engineers disposed of it at dawn, while you were dreaming.*[25]

Although the traditional career path is not as viable a career path option as it previously was, understanding it furthers one's comprehension of the various career path alternatives.

Traditional career path:
Employee progresses vertically upward in the organization from one specific job to the next.

The **traditional career path** is one in which an employee progresses vertically upward in the organization from one specific job to the next. The assumption is that each preceding job is essential preparation for the next higher-level job. Therefore, an employee must move, step-by-step, from one job to the next to gain needed experience and preparation. One of the biggest advantages of the traditional career path is that it was straightforward. The path was clearly laid out, and the employee knew the specific sequence of jobs through which he or she must progress.

Today, the old model of a career in which an employee worked his way up the ladder in a single company is becoming somewhat rare. Some of the factors that have contributed to this situation include the following:

- A massive reduction in management ranks due to mergers, downsizing, stagnation, growth cycles, and reengineering.
- Extinction of paternalism and job security.
- Erosion of employee loyalty.
- A work environment where new skills must constantly be learned.

The certainties of yesterday's business methods and growth have disappeared in most industries, and neither organizations nor individuals can be assured of ever regaining them. However, the one certainty that still remains is that there will always be top-level managers and individuals who strive to achieve these positions. Unfortunately, it is just more difficult to obtain one.

Network Career Path

The **network career path** contains both a vertical sequence of jobs and a series of horizontal opportunities. The network career path recognizes the interchangeability of experience at certain levels and the need to broaden experience at one level before promotion to a higher level. Often, this approach more realistically represents opportunities for employee development in an organization than does the traditional career path. For instance, a person may work as an inventory manager for a few years and then move to a lateral position of shift manager before being considered for a promotion. The vertical and horizontal options lessen the probability of blockage in one job. One major disadvantage of this type of career path is that it is more difficult to explain to employees the specific route their careers may take for a given line of work.

Lateral Skill Path

Traditionally, a career path was viewed as moving upward to higher levels of management in the organization. The previous two career path methods focused on such an approach. The availability of these two options has diminished considerably in recent years, but this does not mean that an individual has to remain in the same job for life. The **lateral skill path** allows for lateral moves within the firm taken to permit an employee to become revitalized and find new challenges. Neither pay nor promotion may be involved, but by learning a different job, an employee can increase his or her value to the organization and also become revitalized and reenergized. Firms that want to encourage lateral movement may choose to utilize a skill-based pay system that rewards individuals for the type and number of skills they possess (a topic of Chapter 9). Another approach, which was discussed in Chapter 4, is job enrichment. This approach rewards (without promotion) an employee by increasing the challenge of the job, giving the job more meaning, and giving the employee a greater sense of accomplishment.

Dual-Career Path

The dual career path was originally developed to deal with the problem of technically trained employees who had no desire to move into management through the normal upward mobility procedure. The **dual-career path** recognizes that technical specialists can and should be allowed to contribute their expertise to a company without having to become managers. A dual-career approach is often established to encourage and motivate professionals in such fields as engineering, sales, marketing, finance, and human resources. Individuals in these fields can increase their specialized knowledge, make contributions to their firms, and be rewarded without entering management. Whether on the management or technical path, compensation would be comparable at each level.

The dual-career path is becoming increasingly popular at some firms. At AlliedSignal Inc., in Morristown, New Jersey, turnover among the top technical performers traditionally has hovered around 25 percent. Technical people were leaving because they felt they had nowhere to go unless they went into management. Since the company created a dual-career system, no top

---

Network career path:
Method of career progression that contains both a vertical sequence of jobs and a series of horizontal opportunities.

Lateral skill path:
Career path that allows for lateral moves within the firm taken to permit an employee to become revitalized and find new challenges.

Dual-career path:
Career path that recognizes that technical specialists can and should be allowed to contribute their expertise to a company without having to become managers.

talent has been lost.[26] The dual system is also used in higher education, where individuals can move through the ranks of instructor, assistant professor, associate professor, and professor without having to go into administration.

Adding Value to Your Career

Adding value to your career may appear to be totally self-serving, but nevertheless, it is a logical and realistic career path.[27] In this rapidly changing world of today, professional obsolescence can creep up on a person.[28] John Humphrey, CEO of executive-training powerhouse Forum Corporation, talks about adding personal value as if it could be stored in a toolbox that workers carry with them each day. According to Humphrey, "The old {career} ladder was a rigid thing. Now the question is 'what skills have you got in your toolbox so that you can carry them anywhere and ply your craft?' "[29] An individual's toolbox must be ever expanding and continual personal development is a necessity.[30] The better an employee's qualifications, the greater the opportunities he or she has in the job market. A person must discover what companies need, then develop the necessary skills to meet these needs as defined by the marketplace. Individuals should always be doing something that contributes significant, positive change to the organization. If any vestige of job security exists, this is it. Basically, the primary tie that binds a worker to the company, and vice versa, is mutual success resulting in performance that adds value to the organization.

Demotion

Demotions have long been associated with failure, but limited promotional opportunities in the future and the fast pace of technological change may make demotion a legitimate career option. If the stigma of demotion can be removed, more employees, especially older workers, might choose to make such a move. Working long hours for a limited promotional opportunity loses its appeal to some after a while, especially if the worker can financially afford the demotion. In certain instances, this approach might open up a clogged promotional path and at the same time permit a senior employee to escape unwanted stress without being viewed as a failure.

Free Agents (Being Your Own Boss)

Free agents:
People who take charge of all or part of their careers, by being their own bosses or by working for others in ways that fit their particular needs or wants.

Free agents are people who take charge of all or part of their careers by being their own bosses or by working for others in ways that fit their particular needs or wants. Many of these free agents have become so because of company downsizing and have no desire to reenter the corporate environment.[31] Some free agents work full-time; others work part-time. Others work full-time and run a small business in the hope of converting it into their primary work. Free agents come in many shapes and sizes, but what distinguishes them is a commitment to controlling part or all of their careers. They have a variety of talents and are used to dealing with a wide range of audiences and changing their approach on the spot in response to new information or reactions. They also tend to love challenges and spontaneity.[32]

Career Planning and Development Methods

There are numerous methods for career planning and development. Some currently utilized methods, most of which are used in various combinations, are discussed next.

Manager/Employee Self-Service

We discussed manager and employee self-service in Chapter 4. Many companies are providing managers with the online ability to assist employees in planning their career paths and developing required competencies. Through online employee self-service, employees are provided with the ability to update performance goals online and to enroll in training courses.[33]

Discussions with Knowledgeable Individuals

In a formal discussion, the superior and subordinate may jointly agree on what career planning and development activities are best. The resources made available to achieve these objectives may also include developmental programs. In some organizations, human resource professionals are the focal point for providing assistance on the topic. In other instances, psychologists and guidance counselors provide this service. In an academic setting, colleges and universities often provide career planning and development information to students. Students often go to their professors for career advice.

Company Material

Some firms provide material specifically developed to assist their workers in career planning and development. Such material is tailored to the firm's special needs. In addition, job descriptions provide valuable insight for individuals to personally determine if a match exists between their strengths and weaknesses and specific positions.

Performance Appraisal System

The firm's performance appraisal system can also be a valuable tool in career planning and development. Noting and discussing an employee's strengths and weaknesses with his or her supervisor can uncover developmental needs. If overcoming a particular weakness seems difficult or even impossible, an alternate career path may be the solution.

Workshops

Some organizations conduct workshops lasting two or three days for the purpose of helping workers develop careers within the company. Employees define and match their specific career objectives with the needs of the company. At other times, the company may send workers to workshops available in the community or workers may initiate the visit themselves. Consider just two of the developmental activities available for HR professionals:

- *Society for Human Resource Management Seminar Series*—Many HR seminars are available to SHRM members. For instance, the Global Certification Preparation Course is designed to strengthen a person's knowledge base of the entire body of international HR knowledge while preparing for the GPHR exam.[34]
- *American Management Association, Human Resource Seminars*—Human resources seminars offered through the AMA provide the skills, behaviors, and strategies needed to attract and retain a talented and diverse workforce.[35]

Personal Development Plans (PDPs)

Many employees write their own personal development plans, which is a summary of a person's personal development needs and an action plan to achieve them. Workers analyze their strengths and weaknesses, as previously described in this appendix. A PDP could be the nucleus of a wider career plan such as setting out alternative long-term strategies, identifying one's long-term learning needs, and setting out a plan of self-development.[36] It is important that a person not depend on someone else to drive his or her career.

Developing Unique Segments of the Workforce

Career planning and development is essential for the continual evolution of the labor force and the success of organizations, as well as individuals. Never in American history have so many different generations with such different worldviews and attitudes been asked to work together. Certain groups of employees are unique because of the specific characteristics of the work they do or who they are.[37] In previous editions of this text, our discussion began with Generation X, progressed to the new factory worker, and then to Generation Y and Generation I. But, a strange event occurred on the way to Generation I. Up popped the baby boomers again as valued members of the workforce, though many had written them off into retirement. Because of certain differences between these groups, each group must be developed in rather unique ways. Although generalizations about a group are risky, the following are offered to provide additional insight into what some members of each group may require developmentally.

Baby Boomers

Baby boomers:
People born just after World War II through the mid-1960s.

Only a few years ago the discussion of baby boomers in the same topic of developing a unique segment of the workforce would have been unheard of. **Baby boomers** were born just after World War II through the mid-1960s. The 77 million boomers, the oldest of whom were 60 in

2005, do not appear to be ready for retirement. In a recent American Association for Retired Persons (AARP) survey, 80 percent of them stated that they intend to work past age 65.[38] In another study conducted by Merrill Lynch & Company, only 20 percent of baby boomers believe they will stop working altogether as they age.[39]

Corporate downsizing in the 1980s and 1990s cast aside millions of baby boomers.[40] Companies are now again recruiting these retirees. They are realizing that many older workers have skills and experience that are critically needed. Companies today place high value on skill, experience, and a strong work ethic, characteristics that many boomers possess.[41] Training replacement workers for an organization is very expensive. Bringing back retirees reduces training costs. Retirees and laid-off former employees can quickly move into production with little or no training. Many companies have started recruiting knowledgeable retirees as an alternative to adding additional staff or hiring unknown outside contractors. Boomers are also becoming senior entrepreneurs. Americans 55 and older make up one of the fastest-growing groups of self-employed workers. John Challenger, CEO of Challenger, Gray & Christmas, an outplacement consulting firm based in Chicago, said, "There's more and more access to self-employment possibilities as people decide to put off retirement as they get into their 60s and 70s and 80s."[42]

Generation X Employees

Generation X:
Label affixed to the 40 million American workers born between the mid-1960s and late 1970s.

Generation X is the label affixed to the 41 million American workers born between the mid-1960s and late 1970s.[43] Many organizations have a growing cadre of Generation X employees who possess lots of energy and promise. They are one of the most widely misunderstood phenomena facing management today. Generation Xers differ from previous generations in some significant ways, including their natural affinity for technology and their entrepreneurial spirit. In fact, four out of five new enterprises are the work of Xers.[44] Job instability and the breakdown of traditional employer–employee relationships brought a new realization to Generation Xers that it is necessary to approach the world of work differently from past generations.[45]

Managers who understand how circumstances have shaped Generation Xers' outlook on career issues can begin to develop a positive relationship with these workers and harness their unique abilities. Developing Generation X employees requires support for their quest to acquire skills and expertise. Generation Xers recognize that their careers cannot be founded securely on a relationship with any one employer. Today, they are very skeptical, particularly when it comes to the business world and job security.[46] They are disturbed about their jobs being outsourced and how they are going to pay for their children's education when wages are rising so slowly.[47] They think of themselves more as free agents in a mobile workforce and expect to build career security, not job security, by acquiring marketable skills and expertise. They are not afraid of changing jobs quite often.[48] The surest way to gain Xers' loyalty is to help them develop career security. When a company helps them expand their knowledge and skills, in essence, preparing them for the job market, Xers will often want to stay on board to learn those very skills.

New Factory Workers

Today, life on the factory line requires more brains than brawn, so laborers are taking evaluation examinations to identify skill and educational strengths and weaknesses and adaptability. After being evaluated, new factory workers are heading for development in the form of training, classroom lectures, computer-aided learning, organizational development techniques, and so on. Tens of thousands of factory workers across America are going back to school. These days, in an economy where even factory work increasingly is defined by blips on a computer screen, more schooling is the road to success.

Over the past decades, managers have been equipping factory workers with industrial robots and teaching them to use computer controls to operate technologically advanced manufacturing processes. At the same time, managers are funneling information through computers, thereby bringing employees into the data loop. Workers are trained to watch inventories and to know suppliers and customers, as well as be aware of costs and prices. Knowledge that long separated brain workers from brawn workers is now available from computers on the factory floor.[49]

The trend toward high-skills manufacturing began with innovative companies such as Corning, Motorola, and Xerox. They replaced rote assembly-line work with an industrial vision that requires skilled and nimble workers to think while they work. Large, old-line companies have learned that investments in people boost productivity, often at less cost than capital investments. Indeed, the old formula of company loyalty, a strong back, and showing up on time no longer guarantees job security or even a decent paycheck. Today, industrial workers will thrive only if they use their wits and keep adding to their skills base by continual development. Closing the skills gap requires carefully considered career development programs to ensure that workers can compete in the factories of the future.

Generation Y, as Present and Future Employees

Generation Y:
Comprises people born between the late 1970s and early 1990s.

Generation Y comprises people born between the late 1970s and early 1990s.[50] They have never wound a watch, dialed a rotary phone, or plunked the keys of a manual typewriter. But, without a thought, they format disks, download music from the Internet, and set the clock on a DVD player.[51] These individuals are the leading edge of a generation that promises to be the richest, smartest, and savviest ever. These Generation Yers, often referred to as the echo boomers, and nexters,[52] are the coddled, confident offspring of post–World War II baby boomers. Generation Y individuals are a most privileged generation, who came of age during the hottest domestic economy in memory.[53] They want a workplace that is both fun and rewarding.[54] They want jobs that conform to their interests and do not accept the way things have been done in the past. They are the first generation to grow up in the digital world and they know how to use technology to create a life and work environment that supports their lifestyle. Their enthusiasm and experience is seemingly of people much older and they are willing to tackle major challenges and have the technology to back it up. The new workforce will require more team effort and this group is well equipped to work successfully in this environment.

Yers' childhoods have been short-lived, as they have been exposed to some of the worst things in life: schoolyard shootings, drug use, sex scandal, and war. This new wave of young Americans has given early notice of its potential, especially when it comes to leadership and success. One of the predictors is the group's penchant for self-employment. The U.S. Labor Department has charted record levels of part-time employment among Yers', many still too young to officially enter the world of work, and the U.S. Small Business Administration has charted a leap in business ownership among the age group's elder statesmen.[55]

Generation I as Future Employees

Generation I:
Internet-assimilated children born after the mid-1990s.

First it was Generation X, and then came Generation Y. Bill Gates, the chairman of Microsoft Corporation, referred to Internet-assimilated children born after the mid-1990s as **Generation I**. According to Gates, "These kids will be the first generation to grow up with the Internet. The Web will change Generation I's world as much as television transformed our world after World War II. That is why it is so critical to ensure that new teachers understand how to incorporate technology into their instruction and that teachers have the technological training they want and need. We cannot afford to have any teacher locked out of the greatest library on earth, the Internet."[56]

Key Terms

Career, 231
Career planning, 231
Organizational career planning, 231
Career path, 231
Career development, 231
Self-assessment, 231

Strength/weakness balance sheet, 232
Likes and dislikes survey, 232
Traditional career path, 235
Network career path, 236
Lateral skill path, 236
Dual-career path, 236

Free agents, 237
Baby boomers, 238
Generation X, 239
Generation Y, 240
Generation I, 240

Notes

1. "Self-Service Will Star in Staff & Performance Development," *HR Focus* 82 (April 2005): 8.
2. John A. Challenger, "Boomers at a Crossroads," *Vital Speeches of the Day* 70 (April 1, 2004): 360–364.
3. "Retention & Recruitment Now Top HR Professionals' Objectives," *HR Focus* 83 (April 2006): 8.
4. Kevin Voigt, "The New Face of HR," *Far Eastern Economic Review* 165 (September 5, 2002): 61.

5. Alexander Dimitrijevic and M. Aleks Engel, "Climbing the Corporate Ladder," *Supervision* 65 (November 2004): 8–11.

6. Barbara Wirtz, "How to Become the Chief Executive of Your Own Job," *Credit Union Journal* 9 (October 3, 2005): 4.

7. Beverly Kaye, "Build a Culture of Development," *Leadership Excellence* 22 (March 2005): 18.

8. Marie R. Herman, "The 21st Century Professional," *Office Pro* 65 (April 2005): 10–14.

9. The following section is adapted from James R. Young and Robert W. Mondy, *Personal Selling: Function, Theory and Practice* (Hinsdale, IL: The Dryden Press, 1978): 50–55.

10. Henry T. Kasper, "Matching Yourself with the World of Work," *Occupational Outlook Quarterly* 48 (Fall 2004): 2–21.

11. Michael A. Broscio, "It's Time for Your Career Checkup," *Healthcare Executive* 20 (November/December 2005): 42–45.

12. Emily Walls Ray, "Tap-Tap-Tap into Internet Job Research: Good Tool, but Remember Basic Steps in Any Search," *Richmond Times Dispatch* (February 10, 2002): S-5.

13. Amey Stone and Beth Belton, "Musical Chairs in the Job Market," *Business Week Online* (July 28, 2005).

14. Broscio, "It's Time for Your Career Checkup."

15. Charlie Greer, "Do You Know What You Want?" *Air Conditioning, Heating & Refrigeration News* 222 (June 19, 2004): 51.

16. Lewis Carroll, *Through the Looking Glass* (New York: Norton, 1971): 127.

17. http://www.careermaze.com/home.asp?licensee=CareerMaze, September 8, 2006.

18. http://www.career-intelligence.com/, September 8, 2006.

19. http://www.career-resource.net/theory.php, September 8, 2006.

20. http://www.assessment.com/MAPPInfo/FreeAnalysis.asp, September 8, 2006.

21. http://jostens.princetonreview.com/cte/default.asp, September 8, 2006.

22. Linda Stern, "The Tough New Job Hunt," *Newsweek* 145 (January 17, 2005): 73–74.

23. http://www.wetfeet.com/asp/home.asp, September 8, 2006.

24. "How to Maximize a Tight Pay Budget," *Report on Salary Surveys* 5 (November 2005): 1–14.

25. Anne Fisher, "Six Ways to Supercharge Your Career," *Fortune* 135 (January 13, 1997): 46+.

26. Barb Cole-Gomolski, "Dual Career Paths Reduce Turnover Practicing," *Computerworld* 33 (February 22, 1999): 24.

27. "Moving Up the Career Ladder," *AFP Exchange* 22 (September/October 2002): 9, 11+.

28. Patricia Leonard, "Leading the Transformation From Training to Learning," *Chief Learning Officer* 5 (February 2006): 26–29.

29. Fisher, "Six Ways to Supercharge Your Career."

30. Mark Morgan, "Career-Building Strategies," *Strategic Finance* 83 (June 2002): 38–43.

31. Jim Hopkins, "The New Entrepreneurs: Americans Over 50," *USA Today* (January 18, 2005): News, 1a.

32. Barbara Reinhold, "Choosing Free Agency," *T + D* 56 (November 2002): 56–57.

33. Self-Service Will Star in Staff & Performance Development," *HR Focus* 82 (April 2005): 8.

34. http://www.shrm.org/seminars/indexGlobal.asp, April 4, 2006.

35. http://www.amanet.org/index.htm, April 4, 2006.

36. Mark Morgan, "Career-Building Strategies," *Strategic Finance* 83 (June 2002): 38–43.

37. "How Compatible Are Your Multigenerational Workers?" *HR Focus* 83 (July 2006): 9.

38. Stephanie Clifford, "Saying No to Retirement," *Inc.* 27 (September 2005): 27–29.

39. Louise Lee and David Kiley, "Love Those Boomers," *Business Week* (October 24, 2005): 94–102.

40. T. L. Stanley, "Don't Let the Gray Hair Fool You," *Supervision* 62 (July 2001): 7–10.

41. "Keeping Graying Baby Boomers at Work and Productive," *Employee Benefit Plan Review* 60 (October 2005): 9–10.

42. James M. Pethokoukis, "Going Your Own Way," *U.S. News & World Report* 140 (April 3, 2006): 52–55.

43. Peter Francese, "In the Shadow of the Boom," *American Demographics* 26 (May 2004): 40–41.

44. Jean Chatzky, "Gen Xers Aren't Slackers After All," *Time* 159 (April 8, 2002): 87.

45. "Succession Planning: The Art of Transferring Leadership," *Trustee* 58 (September 2005): 14–16.

46. Glenn Withiam, "Today's Young Managers Want Career Planning, Challenges," *Hotel & Motel Management* 220 (March 21, 2005): 10.

47. Francese, "In the Shadow of the Boom."

48. Chatzky, "Gen Xers Aren't Slackers After All."

49. George Weimer, "Manufacturing Is a Job for Knowledge Workers," *Material Handling Management* 57 (June 2002): 20.

50. Joe Jancsurak, "The Value of 'Y' " *Appliance Manufacturer* 50 (June 2002): 13.

51. "Is 'Generation Y' a Cinch to Save Xmas?" *Barron's* 82 (November 25, 2002): 11.

52. Denies Markley, "Here Comes Y," *Successful Meetings* 51 (July 2002): 39–40.

53. Glenn Baker, "Understanding Gen Y," *Digest of Equipment, Materials, & Management* (August 2006): 1.

54. Sommer Kehrli and Trudy Sopp, "Managing Generation Y," *HR Magazine* (May 2006): 113–119.

55. Sharon Linstedt, "Generation Yers Turning Out Take-Charge Entrepreneurs," *Buffalo News* (May 13, 2002): C-1.

56. Bill Leonard, "After Generations X and Y Comes I," *HR Magazine* 45 (January 2000): 21.

CHAPTER OBJECTIVES

After completing this chapter, students should be able to:

1 Define performance management and describe the importance of performance management.

2 Define performance appraisal and identify the uses of performance appraisal.

3 Discuss the performance appraisal environmental factors.

4 Describe the performance appraisal process.

5 Identify the various performance criteria (standards) that can be established.

6 Identify who may be responsible for performance appraisal and the performance period.

7 Identify the various performance appraisal methods used.

8 Describe how computer software is used in performance appraisal.

9 List the problems that have been associated with performance appraisal.

10 Explain the characteristics of an effective appraisal system.

11 Describe the legal implications of performance appraisal.

12 Explain how the appraisal interview should be conducted.

Performance Management and Appraisal

"It's true that you have to identify top performers," says Patrick Moore, executive director of finance for BellSouth, "but we focus so much on the top that the mighty middle is often overlooked." Few companies actively decide to ignore their middle performers. Yet because of time and budget constraints, many focus solely on the top-performing and high-potential employees. "With A-players, you're very interested in what motivates them—is it money, recognition, titles?" says Jose Zeilstra, vice president in JPMorgan Chase & Co.'s auditing department. "You want to keep your B-players and keep them happy, but you don't go the extra mile to figure out the motivation piece, which is unfortunate."[1]

"You need to know who your top people are, but you also have to watch out for the message you're sending, because a disenfranchised middle can be just as damaging to your business as the loss of all of your top talent," says Martin Cozyn, vice president of human resources at Nortel Networks Inc., which has revised its performance-rating system twice in the past five years to be more *middle-friendly*. Rewarding the middle does not necessarily mean paying more. A combination of honest communication, clear standards, and reasonable career mobility will certainly help. "You want to define the middle as a good place to be, because that's where most of your workforce is," says Dan Boccabella, general manager at Gainesville, Florida–based MindSolve Technologies Inc., an employee-performance-management software vendor. He advocates avoiding overly precise numerical grades and words that convey a stigma, like *average* or *meets expectations*, in performance reviews.[2]

Libby Sartain, chief people officer at Yahoo!, would even avoid the common *high-potential* label. "When you segment someone as a 'high-po,' it seems as if you think the other 95 percent of your workforce are 'low-po's' or something, and that's what causes the friction," says Sartain, who helped Yahoo! craft its first-ever pay-for-performance bonus system three years ago. In its performance-review system, Yahoo!'s middle (and most commonly used) category is *performs well*. "They're the workhorses; they get the job done and we want to keep them," says Sartain. At Yahoo!, even people in the middle range get salaries and bonuses above the market averages, with further incentives in stock options. "The people we don't want to retain are in the 'does not meet expectations' group," she says. Since then, the company has broadened performance categories to top, high, core, and low contributors, and eliminated the forced distribution system that allowed only a certain number of employees to be deemed *top*.[3]

Another factor to consider with regard to keeping the middle ranks satisfied is to make the incentive system objective through clearly defined goals and precise definitions of various performance levels. "A lot of the employee reaction to [bonus] differentiation depends on how well you define high performance," says Watson Wyatt's Ilene Gochman. "If you have the goals very clearly outlined and you can objectively measure them, that's motivating. But if they seem murky and bonuses depend on who you know, that can be demotivating."[4]

"The most powerful way to move the middle is through nonfinancial rewards such as career development—rotational assignment, training opportunities, special projects, and more exposure to executives," says Peter LeBlanc, managing partner of Chicago-based Axiom Consulting Partners LLC. "Those are powerful rewards for everybody, but getting the middle trained and developed also helps increase the chance they can return more knowledgeable and more engaged."[5]

This chapter begins by stressing the reasons why identifying those in the middle is also important. Then performance management is defined and its relationship to performance appraisal is studied. Next, we look at the uses made of appraisal data, and the environmental factors affecting the performance appraisal process are explained. The performance appraisal process is then described and the possible criteria used in evaluating performance are discussed. Then the person(s) responsible for appraisal and the appraisal period are described, and the various performance appraisal methods are explained. The use of computer software in performance appraisal, problems associated with performance appraisal, and characteristics of an effective appraisal system are described next, followed by a discussion of the legal aspects of performance appraisal and the appraisal interview. This chapter concludes with a Global Perspective entitled "Two Cultures' Views of Performance Appraisal."

OBJECTIVE

Define performance management and describe the importance of performance management.

Performance management (PM):
Goal-oriented process directed toward ensuring that organizational processes are in place to maximize productivity of employees, teams, and ultimately, the organization.

Performance Management

Performance management (PM) is a goal-oriented process directed toward ensuring that organizational processes are in place to maximize productivity of employees, teams, and ultimately, the organization.

Although every HR function contributes to performance management, training and performance appraisal play a significant role in the process.[6] Whereas performance appraisal is a one-time event each year, performance management is a dynamic, ongoing, continuous process.[7] Every person in the organization is a part of the PM system. Each part of the system, such as training, appraisal, and rewards, is integrated and linked for the purpose of continuous organizational effectiveness.[8] With PM, the effort of each and every worker should be directed toward achieving organizational goals. If a worker's skills need to be improved, training is needed.

HR

Web — *Wisdom*

Performance Management

**http://www.opm.gov/
perform/overview.asp**

Office of Personnel Management Website on performance management.

2   **OBJECTIVE**

Define performance appraisal and identify the uses of performance appraisal.

Performance appraisal (PA):
Formal system of review and evaluation of individual or team task performance.

With PM systems, training has a direct tie-in to achieving organizational effectiveness. In addition, pay and performance are directly related to achieving organizational goals. Workers who best achieve their parts of organization goals are rewarded.[9]

According to a report prepared by Development Dimensions International, organizations with strong performance management systems are nearly 50 percent more likely to outperform their competitors.[10] "Performance management is the single largest contributor to organizational effectiveness," says Robert J. Greene, CEO of Reward Systems Inc. "If you ignore performance management," Greene adds, "you fail."[11] Organizations must take a more strategic approach to the performance appraisal. Instead of using the familiar "check the box, write a comment" ritual, organizations need to integrate the company's mission statement, vision, and values into their performance management systems. However, in a recent survey of 218 HR leaders at companies of 2,500 or more, performance continues to be managed the same as it was in the past, through annual evaluations and paper-based processes.[12]

Performance Appraisal

Performance appraisal (PA) is a formal system of review and evaluation of individual or team task performance.

PA is especially critical to the success of performance management. Although performance appraisal is but one component of performance management, it is vital in that it directly reflects the organization's strategic plan. Although evaluation of team performance is critical when teams exist in an organization, the focus of PA in most firms remains on the individual employee. Regardless of the emphasis, an effective appraisal system evaluates accomplishments and initiates plans for development, goals, and objectives.

Performance appraisal is often a negative, disliked activity and one that seems to elude mastery.[13] If this is so, why not just eliminate it? Actually, some managers might do just that *if* they did not need to provide feedback, encourage performance improvement, make valid decisions, justify terminations, identify training and development needs, and defend personnel decisions.[14] Performance appraisal serves many purposes and improved results and efficiency are increasingly critical in today's globally competitive marketplace. Therefore, abandoning the only program with *performance* in its name and *employees* as its focus would seem to be an ill-advised overreaction. On top of these considerations, managers must be concerned about legal ramifications. Developing an effective performance appraisal system has been and will continue to be a high priority for management. Performance appraisal is not an end in itself, but rather the means to impact performance.

Uses of Performance Appraisal

For many organizations, the primary goal of an appraisal system is to improve individual and organizational performance. There may be other goals, however. A potential problem with PA, and possible cause of much dissatisfaction, is expecting too much from one appraisal plan. For example, a plan that is effective for developing employees may not be the best for determining pay increases. Yet, a properly designed system can help achieve organizational objectives and enhance employee performance. In fact, PA data are potentially valuable for virtually every human resource functional area.

Human Resource Planning

In assessing a firm's human resources, data must be available to identify those who have the potential to be promoted. Through performance appraisal it may be discovered that there is an insufficient number of workers who are prepared to enter management. Plans can then be made for greater emphasis on management development. Management succession planning (discussed in Chapter 4) is a key concern for all firms. A well-designed appraisal system provides a profile of the organization's human resource strengths and weaknesses to support this effort.

Recruitment and Selection

Performance evaluation ratings may be helpful in predicting the performance of job applicants. For example, it may be determined that a firm's successful managers (identified through performance evaluations) exhibit certain behaviors when performing key tasks. These data may then provide benchmarks for evaluating applicant responses obtained through behavioral interviews, which was discussed in Chapter 6. Also, in validating selection tests, employee ratings may be used as the variable against which test scores are compared. In this instance, determination of the selection test's validity would depend on the accuracy of appraisal results.

Training and Development

Performance appraisal should point out an employee's specific needs for training and development. For instance, if Pat Compton's job requires skill in technical writing and her evaluation reveals a deficiency in this factor, she may need additional training in written communication. If a firm finds that a number of first-line supervisors are having difficulty in administering disciplinary action, training sessions addressing this problem may be appropriate. By identifying deficiencies that adversely affect performance, T&D programs can be developed that permit individuals to build on their strengths and minimize their deficiencies. An appraisal system does not guarantee properly trained and developed employees. However, determining T&D needs is more precise when appraisal data are available.

Career Planning and Development

Career planning and development may be viewed from either an individual or organizational viewpoint. In either case, performance appraisal data are essential in assessing an employee's strengths and weaknesses and in determining the person's potential.[15] Managers may use such information to counsel subordinates and assist them in developing and implementing their career plans.

Compensation Programs

Performance appraisal results provide a basis for rational decisions regarding pay adjustments. Most managers believe that you should reward outstanding job performance tangibly with pay increases. They believe that *the behaviors you reward are the behaviors you get*. Rewarding the behaviors necessary for accomplishing organizational objectives is at the heart of a firm's strategic plan. To encourage good performance, a firm should design and implement a reliable performance appraisal system and then reward the most productive workers and teams accordingly. This is especially important since, according to a recent study, two-thirds of the companies use performance reviews to determine pay increases, and almost half use them to calculate bonuses.[16]

Internal Employee Relations

Performance appraisal data are also frequently used for decisions in several areas of internal employee relations, including promotion, demotion, termination, layoff, and transfer.[17] For example, an employee's performance in one job may be useful in determining his or her ability to perform another job on the same level, as is required in the consideration of transfers. When the performance level is unacceptable, demotion or even termination may be appropriate. SAS uses a performance-driven approach to turnover. Jeff Chambers, vice president for human resources at SAS Institute, said, "Involuntary turnover is rising because we are being more aggressive. If employees can't do the job, we cut them loose."[18] When employees work under a labor agreement, seniority is typically the basis for layoffs. However, when management has more flexibility, an employee's performance record is generally a more relevant criterion.

Assessment of Employee Potential

Some organizations attempt to assess employee potential as they appraise their job performance. Although past behaviors may be the best predictors of future behaviors, an employee's past performance in one job may not accurately indicate future performance in a higher-level or different position. The best salesperson in the company may not have what it takes to become a successful district sales manager, where the tasks are distinctly different. Similarly, the best computer programmer may, if promoted, be a disaster as an information technology (IT) manager. Overemphasizing technical skills and ignoring other equally important skills is a common error in promoting employees into management jobs. Recognition of this problem has led some firms to separate the appraisal of performance, which focuses on past behavior, from the assessment of potential, which is future oriented.

OBJECTIVE

Discuss the performance appraisal environmental factors.

Performance Appraisal Environmental Factors

Many external and internal environmental factors can influence the appraisal process. For example, legislation requires that appraisal systems be nondiscriminatory. In the case of *Mistretta v Sandia Corporation* (a subsidiary of Western Electric Company, Inc.), a federal district court judge ruled against the company, stating, "There is sufficient circumstantial evidence to indicate that age bias and age based policies appear throughout the performance rating process to the detriment of the protected age group." The *Albermarle Paper v Moody* case supported validation requirements for performance appraisals, as well as for selection tests. Organizations should avoid using any appraisal method that results in a disproportionately negative impact on a protected group.

The labor union is another external factor that might affect a firm's appraisal process. Unions have traditionally stressed seniority as the basis for promotions and pay increases. They may vigorously oppose the use of a management-designed performance appraisal system used for these purposes.

Factors within the internal environment can also affect the performance appraisal process. For instance, a firm's corporate culture can assist or hinder the process. Today's dynamic organizations, which increasingly utilize teams to perform jobs, recognize overall team results as well as individual contributions. A nontrusting culture does not provide the environment needed to encourage high performance by either individuals or teams. In such an atmosphere, the credibility of an appraisal system will suffer regardless of its merits.

OBJECTIVE

Describe the performance appraisal process.

Performance Appraisal Process

As shown in Figure 8-1, the starting point for the PA process is identifying specific performance goals. An appraisal system probably cannot effectively serve every desired purpose, so management should select those specific goals it believes to be most important and realistically achievable. For example, some firms may want to stress employee development, whereas other organizations may want to focus on administrative decisions, such as pay adjustments. Too many PA systems fail because

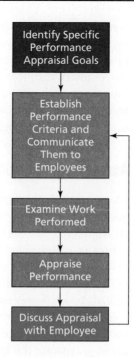

Figure 8-1 Performance Appraisal Process

management expects too much from one method and does not determine specifically what it wants the system to accomplish.

The next step in this ongoing cycle continues with establishing performance criteria (standards) and communicating these performance expectations to those concerned. Then the work is performed and the supervisor appraises the performance. At the end of the appraisal period, the appraiser and the employee together review work performance and evaluate it against established performance standards. This review helps determine how well employees have met these standards, determines reasons for deficiencies, and develops a plan to correct the problems. At this meeting goals are set for the next evaluation period set and the cycle repeats.

5 **OBJECTIVE**

Identify the various performance criteria (standards) that can be established.

Establish Performance Criteria (Standards)

What aspect of a person's performance can be established? The most common appraisal criteria are traits, behaviors, competencies, goal achievement, and improvement potential.

Traits

Certain employee traits such as *attitude*, *appearance*, and *initiative* are the basis for some evaluations. However, many of these commonly used qualities are subjective and may be either unrelated to job performance or difficult to define. In such cases, inaccurate evaluations may occur and create legal problems for the organization as well. In *Wade v Mississippi Cooperative Extension Service* the circuit court ruled that:

> *In a performance appraisal system, general characteristics such as leadership, public acceptance, attitude toward people, appearance and grooming, personal conduct, outlook on life, ethical habits, resourcefulness, capacity for growth, mental alertness, loyalty to organization are susceptible to partiality and to the personal taste, whim, or fancy of the evaluator as well as patently subjective in form and obviously susceptible to completely subjective treatment by those conducting the appraisals.*

At the same time, certain traits may relate to job performance and, if this connection is established, using them may be appropriate. Traits such as adaptability, judgment, appearance, and attitude may be used when shown to be job related.

Behaviors

When an individual's task outcome is difficult to determine, organizations may evaluate the person's task-related behavior or competencies. For example, an appropriate behavior to evaluate for a manager might be *leadership style*. For individuals working in teams, *developing others*, *teamwork and cooperation*, or *customer service orientation* might be appropriate. Desired behaviors may be appropriate as evaluation criteria because if they are recognized and rewarded, employees tend to repeat them. If certain behaviors result in desired outcomes, there is merit in using them in the evaluation process.

Competencies

Competencies:
Broad range of knowledge, skills, traits, and behaviors that may be technical in nature, relate to interpersonal skills, or are business oriented.

Competencies include a broad range of knowledge, skills, traits, and behaviors that may be technical in nature, relate to interpersonal skills, or are business oriented.

Dick Grote, president of Grote Consulting Corporation in Dallas, recommends the inclusion of cultural competencies such as ethics and integrity for all jobs. He adds that there are also competencies that are job specific. For example, analytical thinking and achievement orientation might be essential in professional jobs. In leadership jobs, relevant competencies might include developing talent, delegating authority, and people management skills. The competencies selected for evaluation purposes should be those that are closely associated with job success.[19]

Research conducted by the University of Michigan Business School and sponsored by SHRM and the Global Consulting Alliance determined that success in HR is dependent on competency and specific skills in the following five key areas:

- *Strategic contribution:* Connecting firms to their markets and quickly aligning employee behaviors with organizational needs.
- *Business knowledge:* Knowing how businesses are run and translating this into action.
- *Personal credibility:* Demonstrating measurable value; being part of an executive team.
- *HR delivery:* Providing efficient and effective service to customers in the areas of staffing, performance management, development, and evaluation.
- *HR technology:* Using technology and Web-based means to deliver value to customers.[20]

Goal Achievement

If organizations consider *ends* more important than *means*, goal achievement outcomes become an appropriate factor to evaluate. The outcomes established should be within the control of the individual or team and should be those results that lead to the firm's success. At upper levels, the goals might deal with financial aspects of the firm such as profit or cash flow, and market considerations such as market share or position in the market. At lower organizational levels, the outcomes might be meeting the customer's quality requirements and delivering according to the promised schedule.

To assist the process, the manager needs to provide specific examples of how the employee can further his or her development and achieve specific goals. Both parties should reach an agreement as to the employee's goals for the next evaluation period and the assistance and resources the manager needs to provide. This aspect of employee appraisal should be the most positive element in the entire process and help the employee focus on behavior that will produce positive results for all concerned.

Improvement Potential

When organizations evaluate their employees' performance, many of the criteria used focus on the past. From a performance management viewpoint, the problem is that you cannot change the past. Unless a firm takes further steps, the evaluation data become merely historical documents. Therefore, firms should emphasize the future, including the behaviors and outcomes needed to develop the employee, and, in the process, achieve the firm's goals. This involves an assessment of the employee's potential. Assessment centers were discussed as a method for selecting employees in Chapter 6. They may also be used as an adjunct to a performance appraisal system in assessing potential. Including *potential* in the evaluation process helps to ensure more effective career planning and development.

You should remember that the evaluation criteria presented here are not mutually exclusive. In fact, many appraisal systems are hybrids of these approaches.

OBJECTIVE

Identify who may be responsible for performance appraisal and the performance period.

Responsibility for Appraisal

Often the human resource department is responsible for coordinating the design and implementation of performance appraisal programs. However, it is essential that line managers play a key role from beginning to end. These individuals usually conduct the appraisals, and they must directly participate in the program if it is to succeed. Several possibilities exist as to the person who will actually rate the employee, and these are presented next.

Immediate Supervisor

An employee's immediate supervisor has traditionally been the most common choice for evaluating performance. This continues to be the case, and there are several reasons for this approach. In the first place, the supervisor is usually in an excellent position to observe the employee's job performance. Another reason is that the supervisor has the responsibility for managing a particular unit. When someone else has the task of evaluating subordinates, the supervisor's authority may be undermined. Finally, subordinate training and development is an important element in every manager's job and, as previously mentioned, appraisal programs and employee development are usually closely related.

On the negative side, the immediate supervisor may emphasize certain aspects of employee performance and neglect others. Also, managers have been known to manipulate evaluations to justify pay increases and promotions.

When geography separates subordinates from their supervisors, evaluation becomes increasingly difficult. In other cases, the appraised employee may be more technically knowledgeable than the boss, and this presents another potential problem. One suggestion for overcoming these disadvantages is to bring subordinates into the process more closely. Have them suggest ways to fairly evaluate their performance and then use their suggestions as part of the appraisal criteria.

In most instances, the immediate supervisor will probably continue to be involved in evaluating performance. Organizations will seek alternatives, however, because of the organizational innovations that have occurred and a desire to broaden the perspective of the appraisal.

Subordinates

Historically, our culture has viewed evaluation by subordinates negatively. However, this thinking has changed somewhat. Some firms conclude that evaluation of managers by subordinates is both feasible and needed. They reason that subordinates are in an excellent position to view their superiors' managerial effectiveness. Advocates of this approach believe that supervisors will become especially conscious of the work-group's needs and will do a better job of managing. In the higher education environment, it is a common practice for instructors to be evaluated by students. Critics are concerned that the manager (and instructors) will be caught up in a popularity contest or that employees will be fearful of reprisal. If this approach has a chance for success, one thing is clear: the evaluators must be guaranteed anonymity. Assuring this might be particularly difficult in a small department and especially if demographic data on the appraisal form could identify raters.

Peers and Team Members

A major strength of using peers to appraise performance is that they work closely with the evaluated employee and probably have an undistorted perspective on typical performance, especially in team assignments.[21] Organizations are increasingly using teams, including those that are self-directed. The rationale for evaluations conducted by team members includes the following:

- Team members know each others' performance better than anyone and can, therefore, evaluate performance more accurately.
- Peer pressure is a powerful motivator for team members.
- Members who recognize that peers within the team will be evaluating their work show increased commitment and productivity.
- Peer review involves numerous opinions and is not dependent on one individual.

Problems with peer evaluations include the reluctance of some people who work closely together, especially on teams, to criticize each other. On the other hand, if an employee has been at odds with another, he or she might really *unload* on the *enemy*, resulting in an unfair evaluation. Another problem concerns peers who interact infrequently, who often lack the information needed to make an accurate assessment.

When employees work in teams, and their appraisal system focuses entirely on individual results, it is not surprising that they show little interest in their teams. But, this problem can be corrected. If teamwork is essential, make it a criterion for evaluating employees; rewarding collaboration will encourage teamwork.

Self-Appraisal

If employees understand their objectives and the criteria used for evaluation, they are in a good position to appraise their own performance. Many people know what they do well on the job and what they need to improve. If they have the opportunity, they will criticize their own performance objectively and take action to improve it. Also, because employee development is self-development, employees who appraise their own performance may become more highly motivated. Even if a self-appraisal is not a part of the system, the employee should at least provide a list of his or her most important accomplishments and contributions over the appraisal period. This will prevent the manager from being blindsided when the employee complains, perhaps justifiably, "You didn't even mention the Bandy contract I landed last December!"

As a complement to other approaches, self-appraisal has great appeal to managers who are primarily concerned with employee participation and development. For compensation purposes, however, its value is considerably less. Some individuals are masters at attributing good performance to their own efforts and poor performance to someone else's.

Customer Appraisal

Customer behavior determines a firm's degree of success. Therefore, some organizations believe it is important to obtain performance input from this critical source. Organizations use this approach because it demonstrates a commitment to the customer, holds employees accountable, and fosters change. Customer-related goals for executives generally are of a broad, strategic nature, whereas targets for lower-level employees tend to be more specific. For example, an objective might be to improve the rating for accurate delivery or reduce the number of dissatisfied customers by half. It is important to have employees participate in setting their goals and to include only those factors within the employees' control.

Appraisal Period

Formal performance evaluations are usually prepared at specific intervals. Although there is nothing magical about the period for formal appraisal reviews, in most organizations they occur either annually or semiannually. Even more significant, however, is the continuous interaction (primarily informal), including coaching and other developmental activities, that continues throughout the appraisal period. Performance feedback once a year is just not good enough. Managers should be conditioned to understand that managing performance is a continuous process that is built into their job every day.

In the current business climate, it may be well for all firms to consider monitoring performance more often. According to a recent survey, while 50 percent of the respondents continue to conduct yearly reviews, 40 percent conduct them at least twice a year.[22] Changes occur so fast that employees need to look at objectives and their own roles throughout the year to see if changes are in order. In high-tech organizations, the speed of change mandates that a performance period be shorter, perhaps every three or four months. One source has the opinion that conducting reviews only once or twice a year is like trying to get in shape by working out just once a month; it does not work.[23]

Some organizations use the employee's date of hire to determine the rating period. At times a subordinate's first appraisal may occur at the end of a probationary period, anywhere from 30 to 90 days after his or her start date.[24] However, in the interest of consistency, it may be advisable to perform evaluations on a calendar basis rather than on anniversaries. If firms do not conduct all appraisals at the same time, it may be impossible to make needed comparisons between employees.

OBJECTIVE

Identify the various performance appraisal methods used.

Performance Appraisal Methods

Managers may choose from among a number of appraisal methods. The type of performance appraisal system utilized depends on its purpose. If the major emphasis is on selecting people for promotion, training, and merit pay increases, a traditional method, such as rating scales, may be appropriate. Collaborative methods, including input from the employees themselves, may prove to be more suitable for developing employees.

360-Degree Feedback Evaluation Method

360-degree feedback evaluation method:

Popular performance appraisal method that involves evaluation input from multiple levels within the firm as well as external sources.

The **360-degree feedback evaluation method** is a popular performance appraisal method that involves evaluation input from multiple levels within the firm as well as external sources.[25]

In this method, people all around the rated employee may provide ratings, including senior managers, the employee himself or herself, supervisors, subordinates, peers, team members, and internal or external customers.[26] Businesses using 360-degree feedback include McDonnell-Douglas, AT&T, Allied Signal, Dupont, Honeywell, Boeing, and Intel. These firms use 360-degree feedback to provide evaluations for conventional uses. Many companies use results from 360-degree programs not only for conventional uses but also for succession planning, training, professional development, and performance management.[27]

Unlike traditional approaches, 360-degree feedback focuses on skills needed across organizational boundaries. Also, by shifting the responsibility for evaluation to more than one person, many of the common appraisal errors can be reduced or eliminated. Thanks to computer software, the people who provide the ratings can do so quickly and conveniently since many rating instruments are available online. The 360-degree feedback method may provide a more objective measure of a person's performance. Including the perspective of multiple sources results in a broader view of the employee's performance and may minimize biases that result from limited views of behavior. Personal development, which is essential in the workplace, requires good, honest, well-expressed, and specific feedback.

Having multiple raters also makes the process more legally defensible. However, it is important for all parties to know the evaluation criteria, the methods for

---

Trends & Innovations

720-Degree Review

It was not too long ago that executive coach and trainer Rick Galbreath became dissatisfied with 360-degree reviews. "They had gotten to be a business fad and were being widely misused," says Galbreath, president of Bloomington, Illinois–based Performance Growth Partners Inc. "I saw scars created," he says. "I saw mature professionals reduced to tears, their work relationships hurt."[28]

Galbreath started using what he called the 720-degree review, defined as "a more intense, personalized and, above all, greater review of upper-level managers that brings in the perspective of their customers or investors, as well as subordinates. We still do assessments. We start with a 360-degree review, but then we go out and do interviews," Galbreath says. "We are no longer dealing with the employees. We are dealing with this employee."[29]

Even more importantly, says David Ulrich, a professor of business administration at the University of Michigan's Ross School of Business, the 720-degree review "focuses on what matters most, which is the customer or investor perception of their work." The 720-degree review has three purposes Ulrich says: "First, what customers or investors expect, and what the executive can do to better serve them; second, how customers view an employee's performance; and third, what skills the employee should focus on improving. The reviewee learns to prioritize his time and energy more appropriately for the customer or investor, and where he should focus his own career development."[30]

From an incentive point of view, Galbreath says, "people want to be happy, and most people aren't." The 720-degree review "gives them the opportunity to be more effective on the job and get higher in their careers," he adds. At times the individual being reviewed will have to be made comfortable with having customers included in the process. Ulrich says, "Most customers are happy when firms reach out to them. Customers need suppliers who are responsive and engaged and helpful."[31]

gathering and summarizing the feedback, and the use to which the feedback will be put. An appraisal system involving numerous evaluators will naturally take more time and, therefore, be more costly. Nevertheless, the way firms are being organized and managed may require innovative alternatives to traditional top-down appraisals.

According to some managers, the 360-degree feedback method has problems. Ilene Gochman, director of Watson Wyatt's organization effectiveness practice, says, "We've found that use of the 360 is actually negatively correlated with financial results."[32] GE's former CEO Jack Welch maintains that the 360-degree system in his firm had been *gamed* and that people were saying nice things about one another, resulting in all good ratings.[33] Another critical view with an opposite twist is that input from peers, who may be competitors for raises and promotions, might intentionally distort the data and sabotage the colleague. Yet, since so many firms use 360-degree feedback evaluation, including virtually every *Fortune* 100 company,[34] it seems that many firms have found ways to avoid the pitfalls.

The biggest risk with 360-degree feedback is confidentiality. Many firms outsource the process to make participants feel comfortable that the information they

Web Wisdom
360-Degree Feedback Evaluation

http://humanresources.about.com/od/360feedback/a/360feedback.htm

Information regarding the 360-degree feedback method and other appraisal information is provided.

Name		Job Title	
Supervisor/Manager		Department	
Appraisal Period:	From	To	

Evaluate the performance in each of the following factors on a scale of 1 to 5:
5 = Outstanding, consistently exceeds expectations for this factor.
4 = Above Expectations, consistently meets and occasionally exceeds expectations.
3 = Meets Expectations, consistently meets expectations.
2 = Below Expectations, occasionally fails to meet expectations.
1 = Needs Improvement, consistently fails to meet expectations.

Part 1—Task Outcomes (Weighted 80% of total score)
List mutually agreed-to performance factors from the job description   **Points**
and goals established from the preview performance review.

- _____   ____
- _____   ____
- _____   ____
- _____   ____
- _____   ____
- Quality of work   ____
- Quantity of work   ____
                              Total Points ____
Average Score (Divide total points by number of factors used)   ____ Multiplied by **16** = ____
Comments _____
_____
_____

Part 2—Personal Behaviors (10% of total score)
- Leadership
- Interpersonal skills   ____
- Developing others   ____
- Customer service   ____
- Teamwork   ____
                              Total Points ____
Average Score (Divide total points by number of applicable factors)   ____ Multiplied by **2** = ____
Comments _____
_____
_____

Figure 8-2 Rating Scales Method of Performance Appraisal

share and receive is completely anonymous, but the information is very sensitive and, in the wrong hands, could impact careers.[35]

Rating Scales Method

Rating scales method:

Performance appraisal method that rates employees according to defined factors.

The **rating scales method** is a performance appraisal method that rates employees according to defined factors.

Using this approach, evaluators record their judgments about performance on a scale. The scale includes several categories; normally 5 to 7 in number, defined by adjectives such as *outstanding*, *meets expectations*, or *needs improvement*. Although systems often provide an overall rating, the method generally allows for the use of more than one performance criterion. One reason for the popularity of the rating scales method is its simplicity, which permits quick evaluations of many employees. When you quantify the ratings, the method facilitates comparison of employees' performances.

The factors chosen for evaluation are typically of two types: job-related and personal characteristics. Note that in Figure 8-2, job-related factors include quality and

Part 3—Personal Traits (10% of total score)
- Adaptability _____
- Judgment _____
- Appearance _____
- Attitude _____
- Initiative _____

Total Points _____

Average Score (Divide total points by 5) _____ Multiplied by 2 = _____

Comments _____

_____

_____

Points from Part 1 _____ **+ Part 2** _____ **+ Part 3** _____ **= Total Points** _____

Performance goals for next appraisal period:
- _____
- _____
- _____
- _____
- _____

Self-development activities for this employee

_____

_____

Employee comments

_____

_____

Evaluated By:	Title	Date
Approved	Title	Date
Employee's Signature (Does not necessarily indicate agreement)	Title	Date

Figure 8-2 (*continued*)

quantity of work, whereas personal factors include such behaviors as interpersonal skills and traits, like adaptability. The rater (evaluator) completes the form by indicating the degree of each factor that is most descriptive of the employee and his or her performance. In this illustration, evaluators total and then average the points in each part. They then multiply this average by a factor representing the weight given to each section. The final score (total points) for the employee is the total of each section's points.

Some firms provide space for the rater to comment on the evaluation given for each factor. This practice may be especially encouraged, or even required, when the rater gives an extreme rating, either the highest or lowest. For instance, if an employee is rated *needs improvement* (a 1 on the sample form) on *teamwork*, the rater provides written justification for this low evaluation. The purpose of this requirement is to focus on correcting deficiencies and to discourage arbitrary and hastily made judgments.

In order to receive an *outstanding* rating for a factor such as *quality of work*, a person must consistently go beyond the prescribed work requirements. Although the sample form is deficient in this respect, the more precise the definition of factors and degrees, the more accurately the rater can evaluate worker performance. When the various performance levels are described merely as *above expectations* or *below expectations* without further elaboration, what has the employee really learned? These generalities do not provide the guidance needed for improving performance. It is important that each rater interpret the factors and degrees in the same way. Raters acquire this ability through performance appraisal training. Many rating scale forms also provide for consideration of future behavior. Notice that the form shown as Figure 8-2 has space for performance goals for the next period and self-development activities for the next appraisal period.

Critical Incident Method

Critical incident method:
Performance appraisal method that requires keeping written records of highly favorable and unfavorable employee work actions.

The **critical incident method** is a performance appraisal method which requires keeping written records of highly favorable and unfavorable employee work actions.

When such an action, a *critical incident*, affects the department's effectiveness significantly, either positively or negatively, the manager writes it down. At the end of the appraisal period, the rater uses these records along with other data to evaluate employee performance. With this method, the appraisal is more likely to cover the entire evaluation period and not focus on the last few weeks or months.

Essay Method

Essay method:
Performance appraisal method in which the rater writes a brief narrative describing the employee's performance.

The **essay method** is a performance appraisal method in which the rater writes a brief narrative describing the employee's performance.

This method tends to focus on extreme behavior in the employee's work rather than routine day-to-day performance. Ratings of this type depend heavily on the evaluator's writing ability. Supervisors with excellent writing skills, if so inclined, can make a marginal worker sound like a top performer. Comparing essay evaluations might be difficult because no common criteria exist. However, some managers believe that the essay method is not only the most simple but also an acceptable approach to employee evaluation.

Work Standards Method

Work standards method:
Performance appraisal method which compares each employee's performance to a predetermined standard or expected level of output.

The **work standards method** is a performance appraisal which compares each employee's performance to a predetermined standard or expected level of output.

Standards reflect the normal output of an average worker operating at a normal pace. Firms may apply work standards to virtually all types of jobs, but production jobs generally receive the most attention. Several methods are available to determine work standards, including time study and work sampling. An obvious advantage of using standards as appraisal criteria is objectivity. However, in order for employees to perceive that the standards are objective, they should understand clearly how the standards were set. Management must also explain the rationale for any changes to the standards.

Ranking Method

Ranking method:
Performance appraisal method in which the rater places all employees from a group in order of overall performance.

The **ranking method** is a performance appraisal method where the rater places all employees from a group in order of overall performance.

For example, the best employee in the group is ranked highest, and the poorest is ranked lowest. You follow this procedure until you rank all employees. A difficulty occurs when all individuals have performed at comparable levels (as perceived by the evaluator).

Paired comparison is a variation of the ranking method in which the performance of each employee is compared with that of every other employee in the group. A single criterion, such as overall performance, is often the basis for this comparison. The employee who receives the greatest number of favorable comparisons receives the highest ranking.

Some professionals in the field argue for using a comparative approach, such as ranking, whenever management must make human resource decisions. They believe that employees are promoted or receive the highest pay increases not because they achieve their objectives, but rather because they achieve them better than others in their workgroup. Such decisions go beyond a single individual's performance and, therefore, need consideration on a broader basis.

Forced Distribution Method

Forced distribution method:
Performance appraisal method in which the rater is required to assign individuals in a workgroup to a limited number of categories, similar to a normal frequency distribution.

The **forced distribution method** performance appraisal method requires the rater to assign individuals in a workgroup to a limited number of categories, similar to a normal frequency distribution.

Forced distribution systems have been around for decades and firms such as General Electric, Microsoft, and JPMorgan use them today.[36] Because of an increased focus on pay for performance, more firms are beginning to use forced distribution.[37,38] Proponents of forced distribution believe they facilitate budgeting and guard against weak managers who are too timid to get rid of poor performers. They think that forced rankings require managers to be honest with workers about how they are doing.

The forced distribution systems tend to be based on three levels.[39] In GE's system, all top executives are ranked with the best performers placed in the top 20 percent, the next group in the middle 70 percent, and the poorest performing group winds up in the bottom 10 percent. The underperformers are, after being given a time period to improve their performance, generally let go.[40] If any of the underperformers are able to improve their performance, you might wonder if any in the 70 percent group would get nervous!

Although used by some prestigious firms, the forced distribution system appears to be unpopular with many managers. In a recent survey of HR professionals, 44 percent of respondents felt their firm's forced ranking system damages morale and generates mistrust of leadership.[41] Some believe it fosters cutthroat competition, paranoia, and general ill will, and destroys employee loyalty. A midwestern banker states that his company "recently began a rank-and-yank system that flies directly in the face of the 'teamwork' that senior management says it wants to encourage. Don't tell me I'm supposed to put the good of the team first and then tell me the bottom 10 percent of us are going to lose our jobs because, team be damned, I'm going to make sure I'm not in that bottom 10 percent."[42] Critics of forced distribution contend that they compel managers to penalize a good, although not a great, employee who is part of a superstar team. One reason employees are opposed to forced ranking is that they suspect that the rankings are a way for companies to rationalize firings more easily.

Behaviorally Anchored Rating Scales Method

Behaviorally anchored rating scale (BARS) method:
Performance appraisal method that combines elements of the traditional rating scale and critical incident methods; various performance levels are shown along a scale with each described in terms of an employee's specific job behavior.

Appraisal News

http://www.performance-appraisal.com/home.htm

Performance appraisal news and general PA information is provided.

The **behaviorally anchored rating scale (BARS) method** is a performance appraisal method that combines elements of the traditional rating scales and critical incident methods; various performance levels are shown along a scale with each described in terms of an employee's specific job behavior.

Table 8-1 illustrates a portion of a BARS system that was developed to evaluate college recruiters. Suppose the factor chosen for evaluation is *Ability to Present Positive Company Image*. On the *very positive* end of this factor would be "Makes excellent impression on college recruits. Carefully explains positive aspects of the company. Listens to applicant and answers questions in a very positive manner." On the *very negative* end of this factor would be "Even with repeated instructions continues to make a poor impression. This interviewer could be expected to turn off college applicant from wanting to join the firm." As may be noted, there are several levels in between the very negative and the very positive. The rater is able to determine more objectively how frequently the employee performs in each defined level.

A BARS system differs from rating scales because, instead of using terms such as *high*, *medium*, and *low* at each scale point, it uses behavioral anchors related to the criterion being measured. This modification clarifies the meaning of each point on the scale and reduces rater bias and error by anchoring the rating with specific behavioral examples based on job analysis information. Instead of providing a space for entering a rating figure for a category such as *Above Expectations*, the BARS method provides examples of such behavior. This approach facilitates discussion of the rating because it

Table 8-1　BARS for Factor: Ability to Present Positive Company Image

Clearly Outstanding Performance	Makes excellent impression on college recruits. Carefully explains positive aspects of the company. Listens to applicant and answers questions in a very positive manner.
Excellent Performance	Makes good impression on college recruits. Answers all questions and explains positive aspects of the company. Answers questions in a positive manner.
Good performance	Makes a reasonable impression on college recruits. Listens to applicant and answers questions in knowledgeable manner.
Average Performance	Makes a fair impression on college recruits. Listens to applicant and answers most questions in a knowledgeable manner.
Slightly Below Average Performance	Attempts to make a good impression on college recruits. Listens to applicants but at times could be expected to have to go to other sources to get answers to questions.
Poor Performance	At times makes poor impression on college recruits. Sometimes provides incorrect information to applicant or goes down blind avenues before realizing mistake.
Very Poor Performance	Even with repeated instructions continues to make a poor impression. This interviewer could be expected to turn off college applicant from wanting to join the firm.

addresses specific behaviors, thus overcoming weaknesses in other evaluation methods. Regardless of apparent advantages of the BARS method, reports on its effectiveness are mixed. A specific deficiency is that the behaviors used are *activity* oriented rather than *results* oriented. Also, the method may not be economically feasible since each job category requires its own BARS. Yet, among the various appraisal techniques, the BARS is perhaps the most highly defensible in court because it is based on actual observable job behaviors.[43]

Results-Based System

Results-based system:
Performance appraisal method in which the manager and subordinate jointly agree on objectives for the next appraisal period; in the past a form of *management by objectives*.

The manager and subordinate jointly agree on objectives for the next appraisal period in a **results-based system**, in the past a form of *management by objectives*.

In such a system, one objective might be, for example, to cut waste by 10 percent. At the end of the appraisal period, an evaluation focuses on how well the employee achieved this objective.

 OBJECTIVE

Describe how computer software is used in performance appraisal.

Use of Computer Software

Computer software is available for recording the appraisal data. A big advantage in utilizing the computer is reduction of paperwork. Also, managers have the option of customizing most programs. This is necessary to reflect the goals and values of the organization more accurately and to permit fair evaluations.[44] Listed below are some examples:

- KnowledgePoint's Performance Impact System™ walks managers through documenting performance, providing coaching and feedback, managing goals, writing performance reviews, and creating development plans.[45]

- OneForce/Performance, Workscape's employee performance management solution, automates and streamlines all aspects of performance management while enhancing the quality and frequency of performance-related interactions between employees and managers.[46]

- Halogen eAppraisal offers organizations an employee performance appraisal solution that replaces time-consuming "computerized paper" appraisals with a Web-based system.[47]

 OBJECTIVE

List the problems that have been associated with performance appraisal.

Problems in Performance Appraisal

As indicated at the beginning of this chapter, performance appraisal is constantly under a barrage of criticism. The rating scales method seems to be the most vulnerable target. Yet, in all fairness, many of the problems commonly mentioned are not inherent in this method but, rather, reflect improper implementation. For example, firms may fail to provide adequate rater training; or they may use appraisal criteria that are too subjective and lack job relatedness. The following section highlights some of the more common problem areas.

Appraiser Discomfort

Conducting performance appraisals is often a frustrating human resource management task. One management guru, Edward Lawler, noted the considerable documentation showing that performance appraisal systems neither motivate individuals nor effectively guide their development. Instead, he maintains, they create conflict between supervisors and subordinates and lead to dysfunctional behaviors.[48] This caveat is important. If a performance appraisal system has a faulty design, or improper administration, the employees will dread receiving appraisals and the managers will despise giving them. In fact, some managers have always loathed the time, paperwork, difficult choices, and discomfort that often accompanies the appraisal process. Going through the procedure cuts into a manager's high-priority workload and the experience can be especially unpleasant when the employee in question has not performed well. According to a British source, one in eight managers would actually prefer to visit the dentist than carry out a performance appraisal.[49]

Lack of Objectivity

A potential weakness of traditional performance appraisal methods is that they lack objectivity. In the rating scales method, for example, commonly used factors such as attitude, appearance, and personality are difficult to measure. In addition, these factors may have little to do with an employee's job performance. Although subjectivity will always exist in appraisal methods, employee appraisal based primarily on personal characteristics may place the evaluator and the company in untenable positions with the employee and equal employment opportunity guidelines. The firm may be hard-pressed to show that these factors are job related.

Halo/Horn Error

Halo error:
Evaluation error that occurs when a manager generalizes one *positive* performance feature or incident to all aspects of employee performance, resulting in a higher rating.

Halo error occurs when a manager generalizes one *positive* performance feature or incident to all aspects of employee performance, resulting in a higher rating.

For example, Rodney Pirkle, accounting supervisor, placed a high value on *neatness*, a factor used in the company's performance appraisal system. As Rodney was evaluating the performance of his senior accounting clerk, Jack Hicks, he noted that Jack was a very neat individual and gave him a high ranking on this factor. Also, consciously or unconsciously, Rodney permitted the high ranking on neatness to carry over to other factors, giving Jack undeserved high ratings on all factors. Of course, if Jack had not been neat, the opposite could have occurred. This phenomenon is known as the **horn error**, evaluation error that occurs when a manager generalizes one *negative* performance feature or incident to all aspects of employee performance, resulting in a lower rating.

Horn error:
Evaluation error that occurs when a manager generalizes one *negative* performance feature or incident to all aspects of employee performance, resulting in a lower rating.

Leniency/Strictness

Leniency:
Giving an undeserved high performance appraisal rating to an employee.

Giving undeserved high ratings is referred to as **leniency**.

This behavior is often motivated by a desire to avoid controversy over the appraisal. It is most prevalent when highly subjective (and difficult to defend) performance criteria are used, and the rater is required to discuss evaluation results with employees. One research study found that when managers know they are evaluating employees for administrative purposes, such as pay increases, they are likely to be more lenient than when evaluating performance to achieve employee development.[50] Leniency, however, may result in failure to recognize correctable deficiencies. The practice may also deplete the merit budget and reduce the rewards available for superior employees. In addition, an organization will find it difficult to terminate poor-performing employees who continuously receive positive evaluations.

Being unduly critical of an employee's work performance is referred to as **strictness**.

Strictness:
Being unduly critical of an employee's work performance.

Although leniency is usually more prevalent than strictness, some managers, on their own initiative, apply an evaluation more rigorously than the company standard. This behavior may be due to a lack of understanding of various evaluation factors.

The worst situation is when a firm has both lenient and strict managers and does nothing to level the inequities. Here, the weak performers get relatively high pay increases and promotions from a lenient boss, whereas the strict manager short-changes the stronger employees. This can have a demoralizing effect on the morale and motivation of the top-performing people.

Central Tendency Error

Central tendency error:
Evaluation appraisal error that occurs when employees are incorrectly rated near the average or middle of a scale.

Central tendency error is an evaluation appraisal error that occurs when employees are incorrectly rated near the average or middle of a scale.

This practice may be encouraged by some rating scale systems that require the evaluator to justify in writing extremely high or extremely low ratings. With such a system, the rater may avoid possible controversy or criticism by giving only average ratings. However, since these ratings tend to cluster in the *fully satisfactory* range, employees do not often complain about this. Nevertheless, this error does exist and it influences the accuracy of evaluations.

Recent Behavior Bias

Anyone who has observed the behavior of young children several weeks before Christmas can readily identify with the problem of recent behavior bias. Suddenly, the wildest kids in the neighborhood develop angelic personalities in anticipation of the rewards they hope to receive from Old Saint Nick. Individuals in the workforce are not children, but they are human. Virtually every employee knows precisely when a performance review is scheduled. Although his or her actions may not be conscious, an employee's behavior often improves and productivity tends to rise several days or weeks before the scheduled evaluation. It is only natural for a rater to remember recent behavior more clearly than actions from the more distant past. However, formal performance appraisals generally cover a specified time, and an individual's performance over the entire period should be considered.[51] Maintaining records of performance throughout the appraisal period helps avoid this problem.

Personal Bias (Stereotyping)

This pitfall occurs when managers allow individual differences such as gender, race, or age to affect the ratings they give.[52] Not only is this problem detrimental to employee morale, but it is blatantly illegal and can result in costly litigation. The effects of cultural bias, or stereotyping, can definitely influence appraisals. Managers establish mental pictures of what are considered ideal typical workers and employees who do not match this picture may be unfairly judged.[53]

Discrimination in appraisal can be based on other factors as well. For example, mild-mannered employees may be appraised more harshly because they do not seriously object to the results. This type of behavior is in sharp contrast to the more outspoken employee, who often confirms the adage: *the squeaky wheel gets the grease.* In another example, one study concluded that people perceived to be smokers received lower performance evaluations than nonsmokers, the implication being that if they stopped smoking, they would get higher ratings.[54]

Manipulating the Evaluation

In some instances, managers control virtually every aspect of the appraisal process and are therefore in a position to manipulate the system. For example, a supervisor may want to give a pay raise to a certain employee. In order to justify this action, the supervisor may give the employee an undeserved high performance evaluation. Or, the

Table 8-2 Reasons for Intentionally Inflating or Lowering Ratings

Inflated Ratings

- The belief that accurate ratings would have a damaging effect on the subordinate's motivation and performance
- The desire to improve an employee's eligibility for merit raises
- The desire to avoid airing the department's dirty laundry
- The wish to avoid creating a negative permanent record of poor performance that might hound the employee in the future
- The need to protect good performers whose performance was suffering because of personal problems
- The wish to reward employees displaying great effort even results are relatively low
- The need to avoid confrontation with certain hard-to-manage employees
- The desire to promote a poor or disliked employee up and out of the department

Lowered Ratings

- To scare better performance out of an employee
- To punish a difficult or rebellious employee
- To encourage a problem employee to quit
- To create a strong record to justify a planned firing
- To minimize the amount of the merit increase a subordinate receives
- To comply with an organization edict that discourages managers from giving high ratings

Source: Clinton Longenecker and Dean Ludwig, "Ethical Dilemmas in Performance Appraisal Revisited," *Journal of Business Ethics* 9 (December 1990): 963. Reprinted by permission of Kluwer Academic Publishers.

supervisor may want to get rid of an employee and so may give the individual an undeserved low rating. In either instance, the system is distorted and the goals of performance appraisal cannot be achieved. Additionally, in the latter example, if the employee is a member of a protected group, the firm may wind up in court. If the organization cannot adequately support the evaluation, it may suffer significant financial loss.

One study revealed that over 70 percent of responding managers believe that inflated and lowered ratings are given *intentionally*. Table 8-2 shows these managers' explanations for their rationale. The results suggest that the validity of many performance appraisal systems is flawed, although another study indicated that appraisal data are valid 75 percent of the time.[55] Yet, having invalid appraisal data 25 percent of the time would be nothing to brag about. It seems obvious that evaluator training emphasizing the negative consequences of rater errors would pay for itself many times over.

Ethical Dilemma

Abdication of Responsibility

You are the new vice president for human resources of a company that has not been performing well, and everyone, including yourself, has a mandate to deliver results. The pressure has never been heavier. Shareholders are angry after 31 months of a *tough* market that has left their stock *underwater*. Many shareholders desperately need stock performance to pay for their retirement. Working for you is a 52-year-old manager with two kids in college. In previous evaluations, spineless executives told him he was doing fine, when he clearly was not, and his performance is still far below par.

If you are to show others in the company that you are willing to make tough decisions, you feel you must fire this individual. The question is, Who's going to suffer: the firm and ultimately shareholders whose retirement is in jeopardy, or a nice guy who's been lied to for 20 years, through no fault of his?

What would you do?[56]

Employee Anxiety

The evaluation process may also create anxiety for the appraised employee. Opportunities for promotion, better work assignments, and increased compensation may hinge on the results. This could cause not only apprehension, but also outright resistance. One opinion is that if you surveyed typical employees, they would tell you performance appraisal is management's way of highlighting all the bad things they did all year.[57]

10 OBJECTIVE

Explain the characteristics of an effective appraisal system.

Characteristics of an Effective Appraisal System

The basic purpose of a performance appraisal system is to improve performance of individuals, teams, and the entire organization. The system may also serve to assist in making administrative decisions concerning pay increases, transfers, or terminations. In addition, the appraisal system must be legally defensible. Although a perfect system does not exist, every system should possess certain characteristics. Organizations should seek an accurate assessment of performance that permits the development of a plan to improve individual and group performance. The system must honestly inform people of how they stand with the organization. The following factors assist in accomplishing these purposes.

Job-Related Criteria

Job relatedness is perhaps the most basic criterion needed in employee performance appraisals. The *Uniform Guidelines* and court decisions are quite clear on this point. More specifically, evaluation criteria should be determined through job analysis. Subjective factors, such as initiative, enthusiasm, loyalty, and cooperation are obviously important; however, unless clearly shown to be job related, they should not be used.

Performance Expectations

Managers and subordinates must agree on performance expectations in advance of the appraisal period. How can employees function effectively if they do not know what they are being measured against? On the other hand, if employees clearly understand the expectations, they can evaluate their own performance and make timely adjustments as they perform their jobs without having to wait for the formal evaluation review. The establishment of highly objective work standards is relatively simple in many areas, such as manufacturing, assembly, and sales. For numerous other types of jobs, however, this task is more difficult. Still, evaluation must take place based on clearly understood performance expectations.

Standardization

Firms should use the same evaluation instrument for all employees in the same job category who work for the same supervisor. Supervisors should also conduct appraisals covering similar periods for these employees. Although annual evaluations are most common, many successful firms evaluate their employees more frequently. Regularly scheduled feedback sessions and appraisal interviews for all employees are essential.

Formal documentation of appraisal data serves several purposes including protection against possible legal action. Employees should sign their evaluations. If the employee refuses to sign, the manager should document this behavior. Records should also include a description of employee responsibilities, expected performance results, and the role these data play in making appraisal decisions. Although performance appraisal is important for small firms, they are not expected to maintain performance appraisal systems that are as formal as those used by large organizations. Courts have reasoned that objective criteria are not as important in firms with only a few employees because smaller firms' top managers are more intimately acquainted with their employees' work.

Trained Appraisers

The individual or individuals who observe at least a representative sample of job performance *normally* have the responsibility for evaluating employee performance. This person is often the employee's immediate supervisor. However, as previously discussed, other approaches are gaining in popularity.

A common deficiency in appraisal systems is that the evaluators seldom receive training on how to conduct effective evaluations.[58] Unless everyone evaluating performance receives training in the art of giving and receiving feedback, the process can lead to uncertainty and conflict. The training should be an ongoing process in order to ensure accuracy and consistency. The training should cover how to rate employees and how to conduct appraisal interviews. Instructions should be rather detailed and the importance of making objective and unbiased ratings should be emphasized. A training module on the Internet or company intranet may serve to provide information for managers as needed.

Continuous Open Communication

Most employees have a strong need to know how well they are performing. A good appraisal system provides highly desired feedback on a continuing basis. There should be few surprises in the performance review. Managers should handle daily performance problems as they occur and not allow them to pile up for six months or a year and then address them during the performance appraisal interview. When something new surfaces, the manager probably did not do a good enough job communicating with the employee throughout the appraisal period. Even though the interview presents an excellent opportunity for both parties to exchange ideas, it should never serve as a substitute for the day-to-day communication and coaching required by performance management.

Conduct Performance Reviews

In addition to the need for continuous communication between managers and their employees, a special time should be set for a formal discussion of an employee's performance. Since improved performance is a common goal of appraisal systems, withholding appraisal results is absurd. Employees are severely handicapped in their developmental efforts if denied access to this information. A performance review allows them to detect any errors or omissions in the appraisal, or an employee may disagree with the evaluation and want to challenge it.

Constant employee performance documentation is vitally important for accurate performance appraisals. Although the task can be tedious and boring for managers, maintaining a continuous record of observed and reported incidents is essential in building a useful appraisal. The appraisal interview will be discussed in a later section.

Due Process

Ensuring due process is vital. If the company does not have a formal grievance procedure, it should develop one to provide employees an opportunity to appeal appraisal results that they consider inaccurate or unfair. They must have a procedure for pursuing their grievances and having them addressed objectively.

OBJECTIVE

Describe the legal implications of performance appraisal.

Legal Implications

Employee lawsuits may result from negative evaluations. Employees often win these cases, thanks in part to the employer's own performance appraisal procedures.[59] A review of court cases makes it clear that legally defensible performance appraisal systems should be in place. Perfect systems are not expected, and the law does not preclude supervisory discretion in the process. However, the courts normally require these conditions:

- Either the absence of adverse impact on members of protected classes or validation of the process.
- A system that prevents one manager from directing or controlling a subordinate's career.
- The appraisal should be reviewed and approved by someone or some group in the organization.
- The rater, or raters, must have personal knowledge of the employee's job performance.
- The appraisal systems must use predetermined criteria that limit the manager's discretion.

Mistakes in appraising performance and decisions based on invalid results can have serious repercussions.[60] For example, discriminatory allocation of money for merit pay increases can result in costly legal action. In settling cases, courts have held employers liable for back pay, court costs, and other costs related to training and promoting certain employees in protected classes. For example, a female employee who was due for promotion sued the firm when her promotion was denied. She claimed she was the victim of sex discrimination under the Civil Rights Act. Her supervisor had noted in her appraisal that she needed to "take a course in a charm school, walk more femininely, talk more femininely, dress more femininely, wear makeup and wear jewelry."[61] Although these remarks are inexcusable, the firm would have been in a much better position to defend itself if the appraisal had read differently, perhaps stating that the employee lacked interpersonal skills rather than implying gender in the remarks.

An employer may also be vulnerable to a *negligent retention* claim if an employee who continually receives unsatisfactory ratings in safety practices, for example, is kept on the payroll and he or she causes injury to a third party. In these instances, firms might reduce their liability if they provide substandard performers with training designed to overcome the deficiencies.

It is unlikely that any appraisal system will be immune to legal challenge. However, systems that possess the characteristics previously discussed are apparently more legally defensible. At the same time, they can provide a more effective means for achieving performance management goals.

OBJECTIVE

Explain how the appraisal interview should be conducted.

Appraisal Interview

The appraisal interview is the *Achilles' heel* of the entire evaluation process. In fact, appraisal review sessions often create hostility and can do more harm than good to the employee–manager relationship. To minimize the possibility of hard feelings, the face-to-face meeting and the written review must have performance improvement, not criticism, as their goal. The reviewing manager must utilize all the tact he or she can muster in discussing areas needing improvement. Managers should help employees understand that they are not the only ones *under the gun*. Rating managers should emphasize their own responsibility for the employee's development and commitment for support.

The appraisal interview definitely has the potential for confrontation and undermining the goal of motivating employees. The situation improves considerably when several sources provide input, including perhaps the employee's own self-appraisal. Regardless of the system used, employees will not trust a system they do not understand.

Scheduling the Interview

Supervisors usually conduct a formal appraisal interview at the end of an employee's appraisal period. Employees typically know when their interview should take place, and their anxiety tends to increase if their supervisor delays the meeting. Interviews with top performers are often pleasant experiences for all concerned. However, supervisors may be reluctant to meet face-to-face with poor performers. They tend to postpone these anxiety-provoking interviews.

Interview Structure

A successful appraisal interview should be structured in a way that allows both the supervisor and the subordinate to view it as a problem-solving rather than a fault-finding session. The manager should consider three basic purposes when planning an appraisal interview:

1. Discuss the employee's performance.
2. Assist the employee in setting goals and personal development plans for the next appraisal period.
3. Suggest means for achieving established goals, including support from the manager and firm.

For instance, a worker may receive an average rating on a factor such as *quality of production*. In the interview, both parties should agree to the *specific* improvement needed during the next appraisal period and *specific* actions that each should take.

During performance reviews, managers might ask employees if their current duties and roles are effective in achieving their goals. In addition to reviewing job-related performance, they might also discuss subjective topics, such as career ambitions. For example, in working on a project, perhaps an employee discovered an unrealized aptitude. This awareness could result in a new goal or serve as a springboard to an expanded role in the organization.[62]

The amount of time devoted to an appraisal interview varies considerably with company policy and the position of the evaluated employee. Although costs are a consideration, there is merit in conducting separate interviews for discussing (1) employee performance and development and (2) pay.[63] Many managers have learned that as soon as the topic of pay emerges in an interview, it tends to dominate the conversation with performance improvement taking a back seat.[64] For this reason, if pay increases or bonuses are involved in the appraisal, it might be advisable to defer those discussions for one to several weeks after the appraisal interview.

Use of Praise and Criticism

As suggested at the beginning of this section, conducting an appraisal interview requires tact and patience on the part of the evaluator. Praise is appropriate when warranted, but it can have limited value if not clearly deserved. Criticism, even if warranted, is especially difficult to give. The employee may not perceive it as being *constructive*. It is important that discussions of these sensitive issues focus on the deficiency, not the person. Effective managers minimize threats to the employee's self-esteem whenever possible. When giving criticism, managers should emphasize the positive aspects of performance; criticize actions, not the person; and ask the employee how he or she would change things to improve the situation. Also, the manager should avoid supplying all the answers and try to turn the interview into a win-win situation so that all concerned gain.

Employees' Role

From the employees' side, two weeks or so before the review, they should go through their diaries or files and make a note of all projects worked on, regardless of whether they were successful or not. The best recourse for employees in preparing for an appraisal review is to prepare a list of creative ways they have solved problems with limited resources. They will look especially good if they can show how their work bolstered the bottom line.[65] This information should be on the appraising manager's desk well before the review. Reminding managers of information they may have missed should help in developing a more objective and accurate appraisal.

Concluding the Interview

Ideally, employees will leave the interview with positive feelings about management, the company, the job, and themselves. If the meeting results in a deflated ego, the prospects for improved performance will be bleak. Although you cannot change past behavior, future performance is another matter.[66] The interview should end with specific and mutually agreed-upon plans for the employee's development. Managers should assure employees who require additional training that it will be forthcoming and that they will have the full support of their supervisor. When management does its part in employee development, it is up to the individual to perform in an acceptable manner.

Conducting performance appraisal in the United States presents significant challenges to domestic managers. But, the technique offers even greater problems in the global human resources arena, as the following Global Perspective illustrates.

A Global Perspective

Two Cultures' View of Performance Appraisal

Performance appraisal is an area of human resource management that has special problems when translated into different cultural environments. Chinese managers often have a different idea about what performance is than do Western managers, as Chinese companies tend to focus appraisals on different criteria. Chinese managers appear to define performance in terms of personal characteristics, such as loyalty and obedience, rather than outcome measurement. Chinese performance appraisals place great emphasis upon *moral* characteristics. Western performance appraisal seeks to help achieve organizational objectives, and this is best obtained by concentrating on individual outcomes and behaviors that are related to the attainment of those objectives.[67]

Chinese organizational objectives often differ widely from the objectives of Western firms. Chinese firms have had to fulfill state political objectives such as maximizing employment, and internal HRM practices are oriented to serve these objectives. Many overseas Chinese business practices are grounded in the traditions of Chinese family business, where a primary objective is to maintain family control of the business. Even when the business is incorporated and publicly traded, the family often maintains majority control and this is a major organizational objective. The organization may tolerate less-than-optimal performance because maintaining family control is so important. One implication of this is that performance appraisals would tend to favor workers that supported the family over workers that challenged family authority. These differing objectives will influence the way in which appraisal judgments are made.[68]

There are other well-known characteristics of the Chinese that also have a direct bearing on the practice of performance appraisal. Three such characteristics are face (*mianzi*), fatalism, and the somewhat broad term *Confucianism*. *Mianzi* is the social status that one has, and a person's *mianzi* will have an effect on that person's ability to influence others. It is particularly important that performance reviews be held in private, since a poor review in public will cause a subordinate to lose *mianzi*. It is for this reason that the Chinese tend to avoid the possibility of confrontation and loss of face that could result from a formal appraisal process. This concern with *mianzi* also makes it difficult to publicly act on performance problems.[69]

Fatalism also has a direct impact on performance appraisal. Research has indicated that Chinese individuals are more likely to blame their own problems on external factors, and since the outcome is due to things outside the individual's control, the poor achievement will not lead to a loss of face. Such a defensive reaction is natural and occurs in all cultures, but appears to be stronger and more formally ritualized in mainland China.[70]

One legacy of Confucianism is an emphasis upon morality as a basis for evaluation. Under the Confucian view, the most important characteristic of an individual was the moral basis of his or her character. A quotation from the Confucian classic *Da Xue* (Great Wisdom) says, "Cultivate oneself, bring order to the family, rule the country, and bring peace to the world." Thus, peace, harmony, and success all start with cultivating oneself, including the cultivation of one's moral character. In the view of the Chinese, a *moral* worker will also be an effective worker. Therefore, evaluation of performance and achievement carries strong elements of judgments of the employee's moral character.[71]

Summary

1. Define performance management and describe the importance of performance management.

Performance management is a goal-oriented process that is directed toward ensuring that organizational processes are in place to maximize productivity of employees, teams, and ultimately, the organization. Whereas performance appraisal is a one-time event each year, performance management is a dynamic, ongoing, continuous process.

2. Define performance appraisal and identify the uses of performance appraisal.

Performance appraisal is a system of review and evaluation of an individual's or team's job performance.

Performance appraisal data are potentially valuable for use in numerous human resource functional areas including human resource planning, recruitment and selection, training and development, career planning and development, compensation programs, internal employee relations, and assessment of employee potential.

3. Discuss the performance appraisal environmental factors.

Many of the external and internal environmental factors discussed in Chapter 1 can influence the appraisal process. For example, legislation requires that appraisal systems be nondiscriminatory.

4. Describe the performance appraisal process.

The identification of specific goals is the starting point for the PA process and the beginning of a continuous cycle. Then job expectations are established with the help of job analysis. The next step involves examining the actual work performed. Performance is then appraised. The final step involves discussing the appraisal with the employee.

5. Identify the various performance criteria (standards) that can be established.

The aspects of a person's performance that an organization can be established include traits, behaviors, task outcomes, goal achievement, and improvement potential.

6. Identify who may be responsible for performance appraisal and the performance period.

People who are usually responsible for performance appraisal include immediate supervisors, subordinates, peers, groups, the employee, customers; and for the 360-degree feedback evaluation method, perhaps all of the above.

7. Identify the various performance appraisal methods used.

Performance appraisal methods include 360-degree feedback evaluation, rating scales, critical incidents, essay, work standards, ranking, forced ranking, forced distribution, behaviorally anchored rating scales, and results-oriented approaches.

8. Describe how computer software is used in performance appraisal.

Computer software is available for recording the appraisal data. A big advantage in utilizing the computer is the reduction of paperwork required. Also, managers have the option of customizing most programs.

9. List the problems that have been associated with performance appraisal.

The problems associated with performance appraisals include appraiser discomfort, lack of objectivity, halo/horn error, leniency/strictness, central tendency error, recent behavior bias, personal bias (stereotyping), manipulating the evaluation, and employee anxiety.

10. Explain the characteristics of an effective appraisal system.

Characteristics include job-related criteria, performance expectations, standardization, trained appraisers, continuous open communication, performance reviews, and due process.

11. Describe the legal implications of performance appraisal.

It is unlikely that any appraisal system will be totally immune to legal challenge. However, systems that possess certain characteristics are more legally defensible.

12. Explain how the appraisal interview should be conducted.

A successful appraisal interview should be structured in a way that allows both the supervisor and the subordinate to view it as a problem-solving rather than a fault-finding session.

Key Terms

- Performance management (PM), 244
- Performance appraisal (PA), 245
- Competencies, 249
- 360-degree feedback evaluation method, 253
- Rating scales method, 255
- Critical incident method, 256

- Essay method, 256
- Work standards method, 256
- Ranking method, 257
- Forced distribution method, 257
- Behaviorally anchored rating scale (BARS) method, 258
- Results-based system, 259

- Halo error, 260
- Horn error, 260
- Leniency, 260
- Strictness, 260
- Central tendency error, 261

Questions for Review

1. Define performance management and performance appraisal.
2. What are the uses of performance appraisal?
3. What are the steps in the performance appraisal process?
4. What aspects of a person's performance might an organization evaluate?
5. Many different people can conduct performance appraisals. What are the various alternatives?
6. Briefly describe each of the following methods of performance appraisal:
   a. 360-degree feedback evaluation
   b. Rating scales
   c. Critical incidents
   d. Essay
   e. Work standards
   f. Ranking
   g. Forced distribution
   h. Behaviorally anchored rating scales
   i. Results-based systems
7. What are the various problems associated with performance appraisal? Briefly describe each.
8. What are the characteristics of an effective appraisal system?
9. What are the legal implications of performance appraisal?
10. Explain why the following statement is often true: "The *Achilles' heel* of the entire evaluation process is the appraisal interview itself."

HRM Incident 1

These Things Are a Pain

"There, at last it's finished," thought Rajiv Chaudhry, as he laid aside the last of 12 performance appraisal forms. It had been a busy week for Rajiv, who supervises a road maintenance crew for the Georgia Department of Highways.

In passing through Rajiv's district a few days earlier, the governor had complained to the area superintendent that repairs were needed on several of the highways. Because of this, the superintendent assigned Rajiv's crew an unusually heavy workload. In addition, Rajiv received a call from the human resource office that week reminding him that the performance appraisals were late. Rajiv explained his predicament, but the HR specialist insisted that the forms be completed right away.

Looking over the appraisals again, Rajiv thought about several of the workers. The performance appraisal form had places for marking *quantity of work*, *quality of work*, and *cooperativeness*. For each characteristic, the worker could be graded *outstanding*, *good*, *average*, *below average*, or *unsatisfactory*. As Rajiv's crew had completed all of the extra work assigned for that week, he marked every worker *outstanding* in *quantity of work*. He marked Joe Blum *average* in *cooperativeness* because Joe had questioned one of his decisions that week. Rajiv had decided to patch a pothole in one of the roads, and Joe thought the small section of road surface ought to be broken out and replaced. Rajiv didn't include this in the remarks section of the form, though. As a matter of fact, he wrote no remarks on any of the forms.

Rajiv felt a twinge of guilt as he thought about Roger Short. He knew that Roger had been sloughing off, and the other workers had been carrying him for quite some time. He also knew that Roger would be upset if he found that he had been marked lower than the other workers. Consequently, he marked Roger the same to avoid a confrontation. "Anyway," Rajiv thought, "these things are a pain, and I really shouldn't have to bother with them."

As Rajiv folded up the performance appraisals and put them in the envelope for mailing, he smiled. He was glad he would not have to think about performance appraisals for another six months.

Question

1. What weaknesses do you see in Rajiv's performance appraisals?

HRM Incident 2

Performance Appraisal?

As the production supervisor for Sweeny Electronics, Nakeisha Joseph was generally well regarded by most of her subordinates. Nakeisha was an easygoing individual who tried to help her employees in any way she could. If a worker needed a small loan until payday, she would dig into her pocket with no questions asked. Should an employee need some time off to attend to a personal problem, Nakeisha would not dock the individual's pay; rather, she would take up the slack herself until the worker returned.

Everything had been going smoothly, at least until the last performance appraisal period. One of Nakeisha's workers, Bill Overstreet, had been experiencing a large number of personal problems for the past year. Bill's wife had been sick much of the time and her medical expenses were high. Bill's son had a speech impediment and the doctors had recommended a special clinic. Bill, who had already borrowed the limit the bank would loan, had become upset and despondent over his circumstances.

When it was time for Bill's annual performance appraisal, Nakeisha decided she was going to do as much as possible to help him. Although Bill could not be considered more than an average worker, Nakeisha rated him outstanding in virtually every category. Because the firm's compensation system was heavily tied to performance appraisal, Bill would be eligible for a merit increase of 10 percent in addition to a regular cost-of-living raise.

Nakeisha explained to Bill why she was giving him such high ratings, and Bill acknowledged that his performance had really been no better than average. Bill was very grateful and expressed this to Nakeisha. As Bill left the office, he was excitedly looking forward to telling his friends about what a wonderful boss he had. Seeing Bill smile as he left gave Nakeisha a warm feeling.

Questions

1. From Sweeny Electronics' standpoint, what difficulties might Nakeisha's performance appraisal practices create?

2. What can Nakeisha do now to diminish the negative impact of her evaluation of Bill?

Notes

1. Alix Nyberg Stuart, "Motivating the Middle," *CFO* 21 (October 2005): 62.
2. Ibid.
3. Ibid.
4. Ibid.
5. Ibid.
6. Elaine D. Pulakos, "Performance Management: A Roadmap for Developing, Implementing and Evaluating Performance Management Systems," *SHRM Foundation* (2004): 1.
7. "HR Drives More Training, Appraisals, and Other Updated Review Practices," *HR Focus* 83 (April 2006): S1–S4.
8. Steve Arneson, "Continuous Learning and Workforce Engagement," *Chief Learning Officer* 5 (January 2006): 24–27.

9. "Performance Management: Getting It Right from the Start," *HR Magazine* 49 (March 2004): Special Section 2–10.

10. "Parallels between Performance Management Quality and Organizational Performance," *Supervision* 66 (August 2005): 19–20.

11. Kathryn Tyler, "Performance Art," *HR Magazine* 50 (August 2005): 58–63.

12. Gina Ruiz, "Performance Management Underperforms," *Workforce Management* (June 26, 2006): 47–49.

13. "Are Performance Appraisals Worth the Hassle?" *Across the Board* 43 (July/August 2006): 39–44.

14. Dick Grote, "Performance Appraisal," *Executive Excellence* 19 (December 2002): 12.

15. Vandana Allman and Barry Conchie, with Jerry Hadd, "Start Finding Tomorrow's Leaders Now," *Gallup Management Journal Online* (February 9, 2006): 1–7.

16. Tyler, "Performance Art."

17. "Why a Well-honed Performance Management System Is Now Key," *Compensation & Benefits for Law Offices* 6 (April 2006): 1–10.

18. Fay Hansen, "The Turnover Myth," *Workforce Management* 84 (June 2005): 34–40.

19. Dick Grote, "Public Sector Organizations: Today's Innovative Leaders in Performance Management," *Public Personnel Management* 29 (Spring 2000): 2.

20. Susan Meisinger, "Adding Competencies, Adding Value," *HR Magazine* 48 (July 2003): 8.

21. George T. Milkovich and Jerry M. Newman, with the assistance of Carolyn Milkovich, *Compensation*, 7th ed. (Boston: McGraw-Hill, 2002): 368.

22. "Parallels Between Performance Management Quality and Organizational Performance," *Supervision* 66 (August 2005): 19–20.

23. Ellyn Spragins, "Destructive Criticism," *Fortune Small Business* 12 (December 2002/January 2003): 92.

24. David K. Lindo, "Can You Answer Their Questions," *Supervision* 64 (January 2003): 20.

25. Robert W. Rowden, "Exploring Methods to Evaluate the Return-on-Investment from Training," *Business Forum* 27 (2005): 31–36.

26. Sue Bowness, "Full-circle Feedback," *Profit* 25 (May 2006): 77.

27. "Survey Says: 360 Degree Feedback," *T+D* 58 (September 2004): 14.

28. Leo Jakobson, "Ask the Customer," *Incentive* 179 (August 2005): 8.

29. Ibid.

30. Ibid.

31. Ibid.

32. Patrick J. Kiger, "When People Practices Damage Market Value," *Workforce Management* (June 26, 2006): 42.

33. John F. Welch Jr. *Jack: Straight from the Gut* (New York: Warner Business Books, 2001): 157–158.

34. Evelyn Rogers, Charles W. Rogers, and William Metley, "Improving the Payoff from 360-Degree Feedback," *Human Resource Planning* 25 (2002): 44.

35. Paddy Kamen, "The Way That You Use It," *CMA Management* 77 (April 2003): 10.

36. Stuart, "Motivating the Middle."

37. "Parallels Between Performance Management Quality and Organizational Performance."

38. "'Rank and Yank' Systems May Improve Workforce Performance, Study Finds," *Community Banker* 14 (April 2005): 64.

39. "Getting to the Most Productive Results," *HR Focus* 82 (January 2005): 6–10.

40. Welch Jr., *Jack: Straight from the Gut.*

41. "Why HR Professionals Are Worried About Forced Rankings," *HR Focus* 81 (October 2004): 8–9.

42. Anne Fisher, "I'm Not Shedding Tears for Dot-Commers Facing Reality," *Fortune* 146 (December 9, 2002): 244.

43. Joseph J. Martocchio, *Strategic Compensation*, 2nd ed. (Upper Saddle River, NJ: Prentice Hall, 2001): 77.

44. Gail Dutton, "Making Reviews More Efficient and Fair," *Workforce* 80 (April 2001): 76.

45. http://www.knowledgepoint.com/, January 2, 2006.

46. http://www.workscape.com/content_page.asp?content_id=products/OneForcePerformance.htm, January 2, 2006.

47. http://www.halogensoftware.com/about/index.php, January 2, 2006.

48. Edward E. Lawler III, "Performance Management: The Next Generation," *Compensation & Benefits Review* 26 (May/June 1994): 16.

49. David Butcher, "It Takes Two to Review," *Management Today* (November 2002): 54.

50. "Research on Performance Appraisals Wins Award," *HR News* 16 (July 1997): 13.

51. Scott Leibs, "Building a Better Workforce," *CFO* 21 (Fall 2005): 20–25.

52. Desda Moss, "Bias? What Bias?" *HR Magazine* 51 (February 2006): 14.

53. Peter W. Kennedy and Sandy Gorgan Dresser, "Appraising and Paying for Performance: Another Look at an Age-Old Problem," *Employee Benefits Journal* 26 (December 2001): 8–14.

54. G. Ronald Gilbert, Edward L. Hannan, and Kevin B. Lowe, "Is Smoking Stigma Clouding the Objectivity of Employee Performance Appraisal?" *Public Personnel Management* 27 (Fall 1998): 285.

55. Iris Randall, "Performance Appraisal Anxiety," *Black Enterprise* 25 (January 1995): 60.

56. Adapted from story presented in Geoffrey Colvin, "Between Right and Right," *Fortune* 146 (November 11, 2002): 66.

57. Skip Waugh, "Delivering Solid Performance Reviews," *Supervision* (August 2002): 16.

58. Tyler, "Performance Art."

59. Patricia S. Eyres, "Performance Management Without Pain—And Without Lawsuits," *Agency Sales* 33 (March 2003): 49.

60. "Train Managers and Executive to Avoid Legal 'Danger Zones'," *HR Focus* 83 (August 2006): 4–7.

61. William E. Lissy, "Performance Appraisals Can Be a Weapon for Employees," *Supervision* 58 (March 1997): 17.

62. Liz Hughes, "Motivating Your Employees," *Women in Business* (March 1, 2003): 17.

63. T. Allen Rose, "Separating Performance Appraisals from Salary Reviews Enhances Staff Progress," *NPA Magazine* 5 (August/September 2006): 14.

64. Diane Domeyer, "Planning for Performance Reviews," *Women in Business* 57 (January/February 2005): 34.

65. Susan Scherreik, "Your Career: Your Performance Review: Make it Perform," *Business Week* (December 17, 2001): 139.

66. "How to . . . Conduct a Performance Review," *Contract Journal* 432 (March 1, 2006): 51.

67. Paul S. Hempel, "Differences Between Chinese and Western Managerial Views of Performance," *Personnel Review* 30 (2001): 203–226.

68. Ibid.

69. Ibid.

70. Ibid.

71. Ibid.

CHAPTER OBJECTIVES

After completing this chapter, students should be able to:

1 Define compensation and describe the various forms of compensation.

2 Define financial equity and explain the concept of equity in direct financial compensation.

3 Identify the determinants of direct financial compensation.

4 Describe the organization as a determinant of direct financial compensation.

5 Describe the labor market as a determinant of direct financial compensation.

6 Explain how the job is a determinant of direct financial compensation.

7 Define job evaluation and describe the four traditional job evaluation methods.

8 Describe job pricing.

9 Identify factors related to the employee that are essential in determining direct financial compensation.

10 Describe team-based pay, company-wide pay plans, professional employee compensation, sales representative compensation, and contingency worker compensation.

11 Explain the various elements of executive compensation.

Direct Financial Compensation

HRM IN *Action:*

Are Top Executives Paid Too Much?

Over the past decade, the rise of executive compensation has truly been thought of by many as out of control.[1] Peter Drucker, the famous management author, once said, "I have often advised managers that a 20-to-1 salary ratio between senior executives and rank-and-file white-collar workers is the limit beyond which they cannot go if they don't want resentment and falling morale to hit their companies."[2] Evidently Drucker's advice has not been followed, because in 2004, the ratio of chief executives' compensation to the pay of the average production worker jumped to 431-to-one from 301-to-one in 2003.[3] If wages overall had risen at the same pace as that of CEOs since the 1980s, the average worker today would be earning more than $184,000 a year rather than today's not quite $27,000, and the minimum wage would now be almost $45 an hour.[4] And, the trend appears to be continuing. The 2006 Total Cash Compensation Report released by ERI Economic Research Institute and the *Wall Street Journal*'s CareerJournal.com revealed that the total cash compensation received by America's highest-paid executives exceeds 2005 levels by 41.3 percent.[5]

A recent Watson Wyatt Worldwide survey of 55 institutional investors managing a total of $800 billion in assets shows 90 percent of investors think executives are overpaid. Further, 64 percent believe that executive compensation is not fully disclosed.[6] The need for rational compensation decisions seems imperative, especially since the collapse of Enron and other firms, in which top executives pocketed enormous sums in shady deals.

Michael Eisner, Disney's former CEO, was paid $800 million over a 13-year period during which the company's shareholders would have done better by investing in treasury bonds.[7] He was paid $38 million above the industry average and for three out of six years the company's performance actually declined relative to competitors.[8] The business and regulatory environment has changed and many organizations are rethinking executive compensation practices, including pay, bonuses, and severance pay.[9] Performance assessment and accountability are the leading trends. As a result of the Sarbanes-Oxley Act and the recent outcry over large compensation packages for top executives at public companies, boards of directors are re-evaluating the way they determine executive pay.[10] The trend toward pay for performance is gaining ground.[11] Usually, shareholders do not object to high compensation for top executives when their firm is profitable. In fact, they generally feel it is essential to reward them highly to retain them.[12] Bruce Ellig, an executive compensation expert and author of *The Complete Guide to Executive Compensation,* said, "Compensation committees should be focused on pay-for-performance plans. Perks are pay-for-position, and do nothing to create shareholder value."[13]

As Jeff Miller, a partner at Redpoint Ventures who has served on several corporate boards, said, "If you think your CEO is doing a good job, pay him accordingly. If not, get a new one."[14] For the Securities and Exchange Commission chairman, Christopher Cox, executive pay and perks are emerging on top of his corporate reform *to-do list.*[15] "Management and corporate boards have heard and responded to the calls for change in executive compensation," says Peter Chingos, a senior executive with Mercer in New York. "For the last few years, we've seen boards revising compensation programs, adopting new performance metrics, and enacting tougher performance standards—all designed to strengthen the connection between executive pay and company performance."[16] The idea of pay-for-performance compensation packages for top executives is gaining momentum but has yet to be fulfilled.[17]

This chapter begins by considering the question of whether top executives are paid too much; the various forms of compensation are described and the concept of equity in financial compensation is explained. Then we explain the determinants of individual financial compensation and look at how the organization influences financial compensation. This is followed by discussions of how both the labor market and the job are factors in determining financial compensation. Then, topics related to job evaluation and job pricing are studied, and factors related to the employee that are essential in determining financial compensation are described. Team-based pay and company-wide plans are then discussed, and compensation for professionals, sales employees, contingent workers, and executives is studied. The chapter concludes with a Global Perspective entitled "Costs of Expatriates."

1 OBJECTIVE

Define compensation and describe the various forms of compensation.

Compensation:
Total of all rewards provided employees in return for their services.

Direct financial compensation:
Pay that a person receives in the form of wages, salary, commissions, and bonuses.

Compensation: An Overview

Compensation administration is one of management's most difficult and challenging human resource areas because it contains many elements and has a far-reaching impact on an organization's strategic goals. **Compensation** is the total of all rewards provided employees in return for their services. The overall purposes of providing compensation are to attract, retain, and motivate employees. The components of a total compensation program are shown in Figure 9-1. **Direct financial compensation** consists of the pay that a person receives in the form of wages, salaries, commissions, and bonuses.

EXTERNAL ENVIRONMENT			
INTERNAL ENVIRONMENT			
Compensation			
Financial		**Nonfinancial**	
Direct	**Indirect (Benefits)**	**The Job**	**Job Environment**
Wages	**Legally Required Benefits**	Skill Variety	Sound Policies
Salaries	Social Security	Task Identity	Capable Managers
Commissions	Unemployment Compensation	Task Significance	Competent Employees
Bonuses	Workers' Compensation	Autonomy	Congenial Co-workers
	Family & Medical Leave	Feedback	Appropriate Status Symbols
			Working Conditions
	Voluntary Benefits		
	Payment for Time Not Worked		**Workplace Flexibility**
	Health Care		Flextime
	Life Insurance		Compressed Workweek
	Retirement Plans		Job Sharing
	Employee Stock Option Plans		Telecommuting
	Supplemental Unemployment Benefits		Part-Time Work
	Employee Services		More Work, Fewer Hours
	Premium Pay		
	Customized Benefit Plans		

Figure 9-1 Components of a Total Compensation Program

Indirect financial compensation:

All financial rewards that are not included in direct financial compensation.

Nonfinancial compensation:

Satisfaction that a person receives from the job itself or from the psychological and/or physical environment in which the person works.

2 OBJECTIVE

Define financial equity and explain the concept of equity in direct financial compensation.

Equity theory:

Motivation theory that people assess their performance and attitudes by comparing both their contribution to work and the benefits they derive from it to the contributions and benefits of *comparison others* whom they select—and who in reality may or may not be like them.

In a recent survey by the Society for Human Resource Management, the top driver for employee satisfaction was pay.[18] **Indirect financial compensation** (benefits) consists of all financial rewards that are not included in direct financial compensation. This form of compensation includes a wide variety of rewards normally received indirectly by the employee. **Nonfinancial compensation** consists of the satisfaction that a person receives from the job itself or from the psychological and/or physical environment in which the person works. This aspect of nonfinancial compensation involves both psychological and physical factors within the firm's working environment.

The various rewards described comprise a *total compensation system*. Historically, compensation practitioners focused primarily on direct financial compensation and indirect financial compensation (benefits).[19] However, this has changed over time and the expanded emphasis is reflected in the name change of compensation's professional organization. The American Compensation Association, as noted in Chapter 2, is now WorldatWork, the Professional Association for Compensation, Benefits, and *Total Rewards*. With Total Rewards, the idea of a three-legged stool is used to balance workforce compensation.[20] These legs are direct financial compensation, indirect financial compensation, and nonfinancial compensation. If one leg breaks or is shorter than the others, the pieces of the compensation package will also experience problems. Such would be the case with a person attempting to sit on a stool where one or two legs were a little short.

Equity in Financial Compensation

Equity theory is the motivation theory that people assess their performance and attitudes by comparing both their contribution to work and the benefits they derive from it to the contributions and benefits of *comparison others* whom they select—and who in reality may or may not be like them. It evolved from social comparison theory—the theory that individuals must assess and know their degree of performance and the *correctness* of their attitudes in a situation. Lacking objective measures of performance or correct attitudes, they compare their performance and attitudes to those of others.[21] Equity theory further states that a person is motivated in proportion to the perceived fairness of the rewards received for a certain amount of effort as compared to what others receive. Someone might say, "I'm going to stop working so hard. I work harder

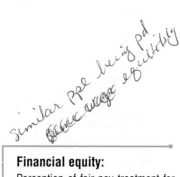

similar ppl being pd
before average equitably

than Susan and she gets all the bonuses." This individual has compared his effort and the rewards he received to the effort exerted and the rewards received by Susan. In fact, no actual inequity may exist, but the perception of inequity influences subsequent actions. According to equity theory, individuals are motivated to reduce any perceived inequity. They strive to make the ratios of outcomes to inputs equal. When inequity exists, the person making the comparison strives to make the ratios equal by changing either the outcomes or the inputs.

Understanding equity theory is very important as it pertains to compensations. Organizations must attract, motivate, and retain competent employees. Because a firm's financial compensation system plays a huge role in achieving these goals, organizations ought to strive for equity. **Financial equity** means a perception of fair pay treatment for employees. As will be seen, firms and individuals view fairness from several perspectives. Ideally, compensation will be evenhanded to all parties concerned and employees will perceive it as such. However, this is a very elusive goal. As you read this section, remember also that nonfinancial factors can alter one's perception of equity.

External equity exists when a firm's employees receive pay comparable to workers who perform similar *jobs in other firms*. Compensation surveys help organizations determine the extent to which external equity is present. **Internal equity** exists when employees receive pay according to the relative value of their jobs within the same organization. Job evaluation is a primary means for determining internal equity. Most workers are concerned with both internal and external pay equity. From an employee relations perspective, internal pay equity may be more important because employees have more information about pay matters within their own organizations, and they use this information to form perceptions of equity. On the other hand, an organization must be competitive in the labor market to remain viable. In a competitive environment, and especially for high-demand employees, it becomes clear that the market is of primary importance (external equity).

Employee equity exists when individuals performing similar jobs for the same firm receive pay according to factors unique to the employee, such as performance level or seniority. Suppose that two accountants in the same firm are performing similar jobs, and one is clearly the better performer. If both workers receive equal pay increases, employee equity does not exist, and the more productive employee is likely to be unhappy. **Team equity** is achieved when teams are rewarded based on their group's productivity. However, achieving equity may be a problem when it comes to team incentives. If all team members contributed equally, there would not likely be a problem. But, that is usually not the case as more enthusiastic team members may cover for loafers. Performance levels for teams, as well as individuals, may be determined through performance appraisal systems, discussed in Chapter 8.

Inequity in any category can result in morale problems. If employees feel that their compensation is unfair, they may leave the firm. Even greater damage may result for the firm if the employees choose not to leave but stay and restrict their efforts. In either event, the organization's overall performance is damaged.

Financial equity:
Perception of fair pay treatment for employees.

External equity:
Equity that exists when a firm's employees receive pay comparable to workers who perform similar jobs in other firms.

Internal equity:
Equity that exists when employees receive pay according to the relative value of their jobs within the same organization.

Employee equity:
Equity that exists when individuals performing similar jobs for the same firm receive pay according to factors unique to the employee, such as performance level or seniority.

Team equity:
Equity that is achieved when teams are rewarded based on their group's productivity.

 OBJECTIVE

Identify the determinants of direct financial compensation.

Determinants of Direct Financial Compensation

"Influences"

Compensation theory has never been able to provide a completely satisfactory answer to what an individual's service for performing a job is worth. Although no scientific approach is available, organizations typically use a number of relevant factors to determine individual pay. These determinants appear in Figure 9-2. Historically, the *organization*, the *labor market*, the *job*, and the *employee* all have influenced job pricing and the ultimate determination of an individual's financial compensation. These factors continue to play an important role.

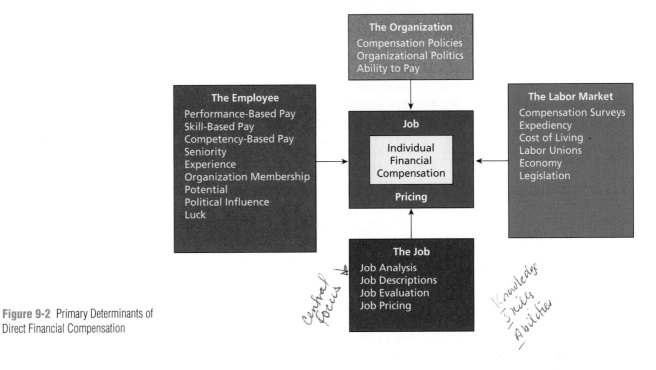

Figure 9-2 Primary Determinants of Direct Financial Compensation

 OBJECTIVE

Describe the organization as a determinant of direct financial compensation.

Organization as a Determinant of Direct Financial Compensation

Managers tend to view financial compensation as both an expense and an asset. It is an expense in the sense that it reflects the cost of labor. However, financial compensation is clearly an asset when it is instrumental in recruiting and hiring good people, encouraging them to put forth their best efforts and remain in their jobs. A firm that pays well attracts many applicants, enabling management to pick and choose the skills and traits it values. It holds on to these quality hires by equitably sharing the fruits of its financial success, not only among the management team but also with the rank-and-file. Compensation programs have top management's attention because they have the potential to influence employee work attitudes and behavior that lead to improved organizational performance and implementation of the firm's strategic plan.

Compensation Policies

Compensation policy:
Policy that provides general guidelines for making compensation decisions.

A **compensation policy** provides general guidelines for making compensation decisions. Some employees may perceive their firm's compensation policies as being fair and unbiased and others may have different opinions. The result of these perceptions may well have an effect on employees' perceptions of fairness and result in lower productivity or turnover. An organization often, formally or informally, establishes compensation policies that determine whether it will be a pay leader, a pay follower, or strive for an average position in the labor market.

Pay leaders:
Organizations that pay higher wages and salaries than competing firms.

Pay Leaders. **Pay leaders** are organizations that pay higher wages and salaries than competing firms. Using this strategy, they feel that they will be able to attract high-quality, productive employees and thus achieve lower per-unit labor costs. Higher-paying firms usually attract more highly qualified applicants than lower-paying companies in the same labor market.

Market rate (going rate):
Average pay that most employers provide for a similar job in a particular area or industry.

Market Rate. The **market rate (going rate)** is the average pay that most employers provide for a similar job in a particular area or industry. Many organizations have a policy that calls for paying the market rate. In such firms, management believes that it can employ qualified people and yet remain competitive by not having to raise the price of its goods or services.

Pay Followers. Companies that choose to pay below the market rate because of poor financial conditions or a belief that they do not require highly capable employees are **pay followers**. When organizations follow this policy, difficulties often occur. Consider the case of Trig Ekeland.

> *Trig managed a large, but financially strapped farming operation in South Dakota. Although no formal policies were established, Trig had a practice of paying the lowest wage possible. One of his farmhands, Charlie Roberts, was paid minimum wage. During a period of three weeks, Charlie wrecked a tractor, severely damaged a combine, and tore out the transmission in a new pickup truck. Charlie's actions prompted Trig to remark, "Charlie is the most expensive darned employee I've ever had."*

As Trig discovered, paying the lowest wage possible did not save money; actually, the practice was quite expensive. In addition to hiring unproductive workers, organizations that are pay followers may have a high turnover rate as their most qualified employees leave to join higher-paying organizations. Equally important, in situations where incompetent or disgruntled employees make contact with customers, they may not provide the kind of customer service management desires. If management does not give its employees first-class treatment, customers may also suffer, and this is not a formula for success in anyone's business.

Organizational Level

The organizational level in which compensation decisions are made can also have an impact on pay. Upper management often makes these decisions to ensure consistency. However, in some cases, there may be advantages to making pay decisions at lower levels where better information may exist regarding employee performance. In addition, extreme pressure to retain top performers may override the desire to maintain consistency in the pay structure. Organizations increasingly make exceptions for just this reason.

Ability to Pay

An organization's assessment of its ability to pay is also an important factor in determining pay levels. Financially successful firms tend to provide higher-than-average compensation. However, an organization's financial strength establishes only the upper limit of what it will pay. To arrive at a specific pay level, management must consider other factors.

Labor Market as a Determinant of Direct Financial Compensation

Potential employees located within the geographic area from which employees are recruited comprise the **labor market**. Labor markets for some jobs extend far beyond the location of a firm's operations. An aerospace firm in St. Louis, for example, may be concerned about the labor market for engineers in Fort Worth or Orlando, where competitive firms are located. Managerial and professional employees are often recruited from a wide geographic area. For more and more business firms, the world has become the labor market. As global economics increasingly sets the cost of labor, the global labor market grows in importance as a determinant of financial compensation for individuals.

Pay followers:
Companies that choose to pay below the going rate because of a poor financial condition or a belief that they do not require highly capable employees.

Wage and Salary Information

http://www.lir.msu.edu/
hotlinks/HR.php#03

Numerous Websites related to wage and salary information are provided.

  OBJECTIVE

Describe the labor market as a determinant of direct financial compensation.

Labor market:
Potential employees located within the geographic area from which employees are recruited.

Pay for the same jobs in different labor markets may vary considerably. Administrative assistant jobs, for example, may carry an average salary of over $40,000 per year in a large, urban community but only $18,000 or less in a smaller town. Compensation managers must be aware of these differences in order to compete successfully for employees. The market rate is an important guide in determining pay. Many employees view it as the standard for judging the fairness of their firm's compensation practices.

Compensation Surveys

> **Compensation survey:**
> A means of obtaining data regarding what other firms are paying for specific jobs or job classes within a given labor market.

A **compensation survey** is a means of obtaining data regarding what other firms are paying for specific jobs or job classes within a given labor market. Virtually all compensation professionals use compensation surveys either directly or indirectly.[22] The surveys may be purchased, outsourced to a consulting firm, or conducted by the organization itself. Organizations use surveys for two basic reasons: to identify their relative position with respect to the chosen competition in the labor market, and to provide input in developing a budget and compensation structure. Of all the wage criteria, market rates remain the most important standard for determining pay. In a competitive environment, the marketplace determines economic worth, and this is *the* critical factor.

Large organizations routinely conduct compensation surveys that typically provide the low, high, and average salaries for a given position. Sometimes the market rate, or going rate, is defined as the 25th to 75th percentile range of pay for jobs rather than a single, specific pay point. They give a sense of what other companies are paying employees in various jobs.

A primary difficulty in conducting a compensation survey involves determining comparable jobs. Surveys that utilize brief job descriptions are far less helpful than surveys that provide detailed and comprehensive descriptions. As the scope of jobs becomes broader, this difficulty grows. Increasingly, employees receive pay for skills and competencies they bring to the job, rather than for the specific work they perform. Therefore, compensation levels must be matched to these broader roles.

> **Benchmark job:**
> Well-known job in the company and industry and one performed by a large number of employees.

The geographic area in the survey is often determined from employment records. Data from this source may indicate maximum distance or time that employees are willing to travel to work. Also, the firms to be contacted in the survey may be product-line competitors or competitors for certain skilled employees. However, not all firms may be willing to share data. Because obtaining data on all jobs in the organization may not be feasible, compensation surveys often include only benchmark jobs. A **benchmark job** is one well known in the company and industry and one performed by a large number of employees.

In addition to surveys, there are other ways to obtain compensation data. Some professional organizations, such as WorldatWork and the Society for Human Resource Management, periodically conduct surveys, as do several industry associations. Consulting firms including Hewett Associates, Towers Perrin, Hay & Associates, and Mercer Human Resource Consulting also conduct surveys. The U.S. Bureau of Labor Statistics conducts the following four surveys that may be valuable:

- National Compensation Survey
- Employee Benefits in Small Private Establishments
- Employee Benefits in Medium and Large Private Establishments
- Employee Benefits in State and Local Governments

The National Compensation Survey contains pay and benefits information. Compensation data are presented by worker traits and by characteristics of the establishment. The survey attempts to respond to common questions from employers such as: What is the average salary for administrative assistants in my area? How have wage costs changed over the past year? How have benefit costs, and specifically health care costs changed over the past year? What is the average employer cost for a defined benefit plan as opposed to a defined contribution plan? The goal of the National Compensation Survey is to be able to answer these questions and more.[23]

Expediency

Although standard compensation surveys are generally useful, managers in highly technical and specialized areas occasionally need to utilize nontraditional means to determine what constitutes competitive compensation for scarce talent and niche positions. They need real-time information and must rely on recruiters and hiring managers on the front lines to let them know what is happening in the job market.

Cost of Living

Although not a problem in recent years, the logic for using cost of living as a pay determinant is both simple and sound: when prices rise over time and pay does not, *real pay* is actually lowered. A pay increase must be roughly equivalent to the increased cost of living if a person is to maintain his or her previous level of real wages. For instance, if someone earns $42,000 during a year in which the average rate of inflation is 4 percent, a $140-per-month pay increase will be necessary merely to maintain the purchasing ability of that employee.

People living on fixed incomes (primarily the elderly and the poor) are hit hard by inflation, but they are not alone, as most employees also suffer financially. In recognition of this problem some firms index pay increases to the inflation rate. In fact, in a questionable practice, some organizations sacrifice *merit pay* to provide across-the-board increases designed to offset the results of inflation.

Inflation is not the only factor affecting cost of living; location also comes into play. For example, according to a comparative salary calculator, an income of $100,000 in Sioux Falls, South Dakota, would be equivalent to $189,962 in Chicago.[24]

Official measures of inflation such as the *Consumer Price Index* (CPI) are market oriented, measuring only the decrease in our money's power to purchase products currently available for sale. An interesting alternative way to view cost of living includes nonmarket elements of our existence, such as the rising costs from crime, lawsuits, pollution, and family breakdown. To this list of factors comprising *hidden inflation*, after 9/11, the threat of terrorism could be included.

Labor Unions

The National Labor Relations Act (Wagner Act) declared legislative support, on a broad scale, for the right of employees to organize and engage in collective bargaining. Unions normally prefer to determine compensation through the process of collective bargaining, a topic covered in Chapter 12. An excerpt from the Wagner Act prescribes the areas of mandatory collective bargaining between management and unions as "wages, hours, and other terms and conditions of employment." These broad bargaining areas obviously have great potential impact on compensation decisions. When a union uses comparable pay as a standard in making compensation demands, the employer needs accurate labor market data. When a union emphasizes cost of living, it may pressure management into including a cost-of-living allowance. A **cost-of-living allowance (COLA)** is an escalator clause in the labor agreement that automatically increases wages as the U.S. Bureau of Labor Statistics' cost-of-living index rises. Cost-of-living allowances in union contracts have been disappearing because the power of the union has been reduced.

Web Wisdom

Calculates Salary Differences from City to City

http://www.homefair.com/

Homepage to determine numerous costs of a move to another city.

Cost-of-living allowance (COLA):

Escalator clause in a labor agreement that automatically increases wages as the U.S. Bureau of Labor Statistics' cost-of-living index rises.

Economy

The economy definitely affects financial compensation decisions. For example, a depressed economy generally increases the labor supply and this serves to lower the market rate. A booming economy, on the other hand, results in greater competition for workers and the price of labor is driven upward. In addition, the cost of living typically rises as the economy expands.

Legislation

Federal and state laws can also affect the amount of compensation a person receives. The Equal Pay Act prohibits an employer from paying an employee of one gender less money than an employee of the opposite gender, if both employees do work that is substantially the same. Equal employment legislation, including the Civil Rights Act, the Age Discrimination in Employment Act, and the Americans with Disabilities Act, prohibits discrimination against specified groups in employment matters, including compensation.[25] The same is true for federal government contractors or subcontractors covered by Executive Order 11246 and the Rehabilitation Act. States and municipal governments also have laws that affect compensation practices. Our focus in the next section, however, is on the federal legislation that provides broad coverage and specifically deals with compensation issues.

Davis-Bacon Act of 1931. The Davis-Bacon Act of 1931 was the first national law to deal with minimum wages. It mandates a prevailing wage for all federally financed or assisted construction projects exceeding $2,000. The Secretary of Labor sets the prevailing wage at the union wage, regardless of what the average wage is in the affected locality.[26]

Walsh-Healy Act of 1936. The Walsh-Healy Act of 1936 requires companies with federal supply contracts exceeding $10,000 to pay prevailing wages. This legislation also requires one-and-a-half times the regular pay rate for hours over eight per day or 40 per week.

Fair Labor Standards Act of 1938, as Amended (FLSA). The most significant law affecting compensation is the Fair Labor Standards Act of 1938. The purpose of the FLSA is to establish minimum labor standards on a national basis and to eliminate low wages and long working hours. The FLSA attempts to eliminate low wages by setting a minimum wage, and to make long hours expensive by requiring a higher pay rate, overtime, for excessive hours. It also requires record keeping, and provides standards for child labor. The Wage and Hour Division of the U.S. Department of Labor (DOL) administers this Act. The amount of the minimum wage has changed several times since it was first introduced in 1938. It also requires overtime payment at the rate of one-and-one-half times the employee's regular rate after 40 hours of work in a 168-hour period. Although the Act covers most organizations and employees, certain classes of employees are specifically exempt from overtime provisions. **Exempt employees** are categorized as executive, administrative, professional, or outside salespersons.

Exempt employees:
Employees categorized as executive, administrative, professional, or outside salespersons.

An *executive employee* is essentially a manager (such as a production manager) with broad authority over subordinates. An *administrative employee*, although not a manager, occupies an important staff position in an organization and might have a title such as account executive or market researcher. A *professional employee* performs work requiring advanced knowledge in a field of learning, normally acquired through a prolonged course of specialized instruction. This type of employee might have a title such as company physician, legal counsel, or senior statistician. *Outside salespeople* sell tangible or intangible items away from the employer's place of business. *Nonexempt employees* are those in jobs not conforming to the above definitions. However, nonexempt employees, many of whom are paid salaries, must receive overtime pay. Also, under new regulations, most employees who earn less than $23,660 will be considered nonexempt no matter what their duties are. [27]

OBJECTIVE

Explain how the job is a determinant of direct financial compensation.

Job as a Determinant of Direct Financial Compensation

The individual employee and market forces are most prominent as wage criteria. However, the job itself continues to be a factor, especially in those firms that have internal pay equity as an important consideration. These organizations pay for the value they attach to certain duties, responsibilities, and other job-related factors such as working conditions. Management techniques utilized for determining a job's relative worth include job analysis, job descriptions, and job evaluation.

Before an organization can determine the relative difficulty or value of its jobs, it must first define their content. Normally, it does so by analyzing jobs. Recall from Chapter 4 that job analysis is the systematic process of determining the skills and knowledge required for performing jobs. Remember also that the primary by-product of job analysis is the job description, a written document that describes job duties or functions and responsibilities.

Job descriptions serve many different purposes, including data for evaluating jobs. They are essential to all *job evaluation* methods that depend heavily on their accuracy and clarity for success.

OBJECTIVE

Define job evaluation and describe the four traditional job evaluation methods.

Job evaluation:
Process that determines the relative value of one job in relation to another.

Job Evaluation

Job evaluation is a process that determines the relative value of one job in relation to another. The basic purpose of job evaluation is to eliminate internal pay inequities that exist because of illogical pay structures. For example, pay inequity probably exists if the mailroom supervisor earns more money than the chief accountant. For obvious reasons, organizations prefer internal pay equity. However, when a job's pay rate is ultimately determined to conflict with the market rate, the latter is almost sure to take precedence. Job evaluation measures job worth in an administrative rather than an economic sense. The latter can be determined only by the marketplace and revealed through compensation surveys. Nevertheless, many firms continue to use job evaluation for the following purposes:

- To identify the organization's job structure.
- To eliminate pay inequities and bring order to the relationships among jobs.
- To develop a hierarchy of job value for creating a pay structure.

The human resource department may be responsible for administering job evaluation programs. However, committees made up of individuals familiar with the specific jobs to be evaluated often perform the actual evaluations. A typical committee might include the human resource executive and representatives from other functional areas such as finance, production, information technology, and marketing. The composition of the committee usually depends on the type and level of the jobs being evaluated. In all instances, it is important for the committee to keep personalities out of the evaluation process and to remember it is evaluating the *job*, not the person(s) performing the job. Some people have a difficult time making this distinction. This is understandable since some job evaluation systems are very similar to some performance appraisal methods. In addition, the duties of a job may, on an informal basis, expand, contract, or change depending on the person holding the job.

Small and medium-sized organizations often lack job evaluation expertise and may elect to use an outside consultant. When employing a qualified consultant, management should require that the consultant not only develop the job evaluation system, but also train company employees to administer it properly.

The four traditional job evaluation methods are the *ranking, classification, factor comparison*, and *point*. There are innumerable versions of these methods, and a firm may choose one and modify it to fit its particular purposes. Another option is to purchase a proprietary method such as the Hay Plan. This system, a variation of the point method, will be discussed later in this section. The ranking and classification methods are nonquantitative, whereas the factor comparison and point methods are quantitative approaches.

Ranking Method

Job evaluation ranking method:
Job evaluation method in which the raters examine the description of each job being evaluated and arrange the jobs in order according to their value to the company.

The ranking method is the simplest of the four job evaluation methods. In the **job evaluation ranking method**, the raters examine the description of each job being evaluated and arrange the jobs in order according to their value to the company. The procedure is essentially the same as that discussed in Chapter 8 regarding the ranking method for evaluating employee performance. The only difference is that you evaluate jobs, not people. The first step in this method, as with all the methods, is conducting job analysis and writing job descriptions.

Classification Method

Classification method:
Job evaluation method in which classes or grades are defined to describe a group of jobs.

The **classification method** involves defining a number of classes or grades to describe a group of jobs. In evaluating jobs by this method, the raters compare the job description with the class description. Class descriptions reflect the differences between groups of jobs at various difficulty levels. The class description that most closely agrees with the job description determines the classification for that job. For example, in evaluating the job of word-processing clerk, the description might include these duties:

1. Data-enter letters from prepared drafts.
2. Print envelopes.
3. Deliver completed correspondence to unit supervisor.

Assuming that the remainder of the job description includes similar routine work, this job would probably be placed in the lowest job class.

Each class is described in such a way that it captures sufficient work detail, yet is general enough to cause little difficulty in slotting a job description into its appropriate class. Probably the best-known illustration of the classification method is the federal government's 18-class evaluation system.

Factor Comparison Method

Factor comparison method:
Job evaluation method that assumes there are five universal factors consisting of mental requirements, skills, physical requirements, responsibilities, and working conditions and the evaluator makes decisions on these factors independently.

The factor comparison method is somewhat more involved than the two previously discussed qualitative methods. The **factor comparison method** of job evaluation assumes that there are five universal factors consisting of mental requirements, skills, physical requirements, responsibilities, and working conditions, and the evaluator makes decisions on these factors independently.

The five universal job factors are:

- Mental requirements, which reflect mental traits such as intelligence, reasoning, and imagination.
- Skills, which pertain to facility in muscular coordination and training in the interpretation of sensory impressions.
- Physical requirements, which involve sitting, standing, walking, lifting, and so on.
- Responsibilities, which cover areas such as raw materials, money, records, and supervision.
- Working conditions, which reflect the environmental influences of noise, illumination, ventilation, hazards, and hours.

In this method, the evaluation committee creates a monetary scale, containing each of the five universal factors, and ranks jobs according to their value for each factor. Unlike most other job evaluation methods that produce relative job worth only, the factor comparison method determines the absolute value as well.

Point Method

Point method:
Job evaluation method where the raters assign numerical values to specific job factors, such as knowledge required, and the sum of these values provides a quantitative assessment of a job's relative worth.

In the **point method**, raters assign numerical values to specific job factors, such as knowledge required, and the sum of these values provides a quantitative assessment of a job's relative worth. Historically, some variation of the point plan has been the most popular option. The procedure for establishing a point method is illustrated in Figure 9-3.[28] The following tasks take place with the point method of job evaluation.

The point method requires selection of job factors according to the nature of the specific group of jobs being evaluated. Normally, organizations develop a separate plan for each group of similar jobs (job clusters) in the company. Production jobs,

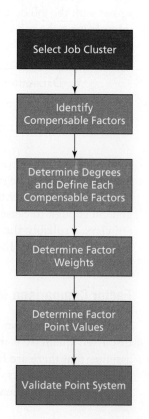

Figure 9-3 Procedure for Establishing the Point Method of Job Evaluation

administrative jobs, and sales jobs are examples of job clusters. After determining the cluster to be studied, analysts (or supervisors in smaller firms) conduct job analyses and write job descriptions if current descriptions are not available. The job evaluation committee will later use these descriptions to make evaluation decisions.

Point Method Example

We will walk through an example of how the point method works.

Select Job Cluster. Let us assume that we are going to develop a point system for an administrative job cluster.

Identify Compensable Factors. The committee next selects the factors for measuring job value. These factors become the standards used for the evaluation of jobs. Individuals who are thoroughly familiar with the content of the jobs under consideration are best qualified to identify the factors. In our example, let us assume that the compensable factors identified are education, job knowledge, contacts, complexity of duties, and initiative.

Determine Degrees and Define Each Compensable Factors. The next consideration is to determine the number of degrees for each compensable job factor. Degrees represent the number of distinct levels associated with a particular factor. The number of degrees needed for each factor depends on job requirements. If a particular cluster required virtually the same level of formal education (a high school diploma or a two-year degree, for example) fewer degrees would be appropriate than if some jobs in the cluster required advanced degrees. Evaluators must divide each factor into number of degrees. These detail definitions for each degree will ultimately permit committee members to more accurately determine the appropriate points for each factor.

In our illustration of the administrative job cluster, Education, Job Knowledge, and Initiative have been determined to have five degrees; Contacts has four; and Complexity of Duties has three. Degree 1 under Education, for example, might indicate the need for a high school education to perform the job. Degree 5 might mean that a master's degree is required. As may be seen in Figure 9-4, the degrees for two of the compensable factors in our example, contacts and complexity of duties, are described. Notice that the factor *Contacts* has four degrees and that the factor of *Complexity of Duties* has three degrees.

Determine Factor Weights. The committee must then establish factor weights according to their relative importance in the jobs to be evaluated. In our example let us assume that the committee believes that education is quite important for the administrative job cluster and sets the weight for education at 35 percent. The weights of the other four factors were determined by the committee: Job Knowledge—25; Contacts—18; Complexity of Duties—17; and Initiative—5. The percent total is 100 percent.

Determine Factor Point Values. The committee then determines the total number of points for the plan. The number may vary, but 500 or 1,000 points may work well. Our committee has determined that a 500-point system will work fine.

You can calculate the maximum points for each factor by multiplying the total points in the system by the assigned weights. In our example, the maximum points any job could receive for Education would be 175 (35 percent weight multiplied by 500 points). If the interval between factors is to be a constant number, points for the minimum degree may take the value of the percentage weight assigned to the factor. For instance, the percentage weight for education is 35 percent, so the minimum number of points would also be 35. You can figure the degree interval by subtracting

FACTOR: CONTACTS
This factor considers the responsibility for working with other people to get results, either interdepartmentally or outside the plant. In the lower degrees, it is largely a matter of giving or getting information or instructions. In the higher degrees, the factor involves dealing with or influencing other persons. In rating this factor, consider how the contacts are made, the duration of the contacts, and their purposes.

Level (Degrees)		Points
IV	Usual purposes of the contacts are to discuss problems and possible solutions, to secure cooperation or coordination of efforts, and to get agreement and action; more than ordinary tact and persuasiveness required.	90
III	Usual purposes of the contacts are to exchange information and settle specific problems encountered in the course of daily work.	66
II	Contacts may be repetitive but usually are brief and with little or no continuity.	42
I	Contacts normally extend to persons in the immediate work unit only.	18

FACTOR: COMPLEXITY OF DUTIES

III	Performs work where only general methods are available. Independent action and judgment are required regularly to analyze facts, evaluate situations, draw conclusions, make decisions, and take or recommend action.	85
II	Performs duties working from standard procedures or generally understood methods. Some independent action and judgment are required to decide what to do, determine permissible variations from standard procedures, review facts in situations, and determine action to be taken, within limits prescribed.	51
I	Little or no independent action or judgment. Duties are so standardized and simple as to involve little choice as to how to do them.	17

Figure 9-4 Degrees for the Factors of "Contacts" and "Complexity of Duties"

the minimum number of points from the maximum number and dividing by the number of degrees used minus 1. For example, the interval for factor 1 (Education) is:

$$\text{Interval} = \frac{175 - 35}{5 - 1} = 35$$

Therefore, the interval between each degree for Education is 35 (see Table 9-1). Notice that the intervals for the other factors are: Job Knowledge—25; Contacts—18; Complexity of Duties—17; and Initiative—5.

Validate Point System. It is now time to determine the reliability of the system. Each committee member should take a random sample of jobs within the chosen job cluster and calculate the weights for each job selected. As may be seen in Table 9-2, the point total for the Administrative 2 job is determined to be 239 points. Committee members should array their jobs with the point total of each to check out the reliability of the point assignment. Only when the hierarchy arrangement appears to be logical for this job cluster is the work of the committee completed. Ultimately all jobs in the company can be evaluated in this manner.

The approach just mentioned to determine the number of points for each degree is called an *arithmetic progression*. An arithmetic progression is simple to understand and explain to employees. In the example, it is assumed that the intervals between the

Table 9-1 **Job Evaluation Worksheet (500-Point System)**

Job Factor	Weight	Degree of Factor				
		1	2	3	4	5
Education	35%	35	70	105	140	175
Job Knowledge	25%	25	50	75	100	125
Contacts	18%	18	42	66	90	
Complexity of Duties	17%	17	51	85		
Initiative	5%	5	10	15	20	25

Table 9-2 Job Evaluation Worksheet for Job Title: Administrative 2 Position

Job Factor	Weight	Degree of Factor 1	2	3	4	5
Education	35%	35	70	**105**	140	175
Job Knowledge	25%	25	**50**	75	100	125
Contacts	18%	**18**	42	66	90	
Complexity of Duties	17%	17	**51**	85		
Initiative	5%	5	10	**15**	20	25
Total Job Value						**239**

degrees are equal. However, if this is not the case, another method, such as a geometric progression where each successive factor is multiplied by a fixed number, may be more appropriate. In this example, the fixed number is two, resulting in the fourth degree being eight years (see Figure 9-5).

Point plans require time and effort to design. Historically, a redeeming feature of the method has been that, once developed, the plan was useful over a long time. In today's environment, the shelf life may be considerably less. In any event, as new jobs are created and old jobs substantially changed, job analysis must be conducted and job descriptions rewritten on an ongoing basis. The job evaluation committee then evaluates the jobs. Only when job factors change, or for some reason the weights assigned become inappropriate, does the plan become obsolete.

Hay Guide Chart-Profile Method (Hay Plan)

Hay guide chart-profile method (Hay Plan):
Refined version of the point method used by approximately 8,000 public and private sector organizations worldwide to evaluate clerical, trade, technical, professional, managerial, and/or executive-level jobs.

The **Hay guide chart-profile method (Hay Plan)** is a widely used refined version of the point method used by approximately 8,000 public and private-sector organizations worldwide to evaluate clerical, trade, technical, professional, managerial, and/or executive-level jobs.[29] It utilizes the compensable factors of know-how, problem solving, accountability, and additional compensable elements. Point values are assigned to these factors to determine the final point profile for any job.

Know-how is the total of all knowledge and skills needed for satisfactory job performance. It has three dimensions including the amount of practical, specialized, or scientific knowledge required; the ability to coordinate many functions; and the ability to deal with and motivate people effectively.

Problem solving is the degree of original thinking required by the job for analyzing, evaluating, creating, reasoning, and making conclusions. Problem solving has two dimensions: the thinking environment in which problems are solved (from strict routine to abstractly defined), and the thinking challenge presented by the problems (from repetitive to uncharted). Problem solving is expressed as a percentage of know-how, since people use what they know to think and make decisions.

Job Factor	Degree of Factor 1	2	3	4
Experience Required	1 year	3 years	5 years	7 years
	(---------------Arithmetic Progression---------------)			

Job Factor	Degree of Factor 1	2	3	4
Experience Required	1 year	2 years	4 years	8 years
	(---------------Geometric Progression---------------)			

Figure 9-5 Illustration of Arithmetic and Geometric Progression

The Hay Guide Chart-Profile Method

http://www.haygroup.com

Homepage of the Hay Method, the most widely used job measurement system in the world, is provided.

OBJECTIVE

Describe job pricing.

Job pricing:
Placing a dollar value on the job's worth.

Pay grade:
Grouping of similar jobs to simplify pricing jobs.

Wage curve:
Fitting of plotted points to create a smooth progression between pay grades (also known as the pay curve).

Pay range:
Minimum and maximum pay rate with enough variance between the two to allow for a significant pay difference.

Accountability is the responsibility for action and accompanying consequences. Accountability has three dimensions including the degree of freedom the job incumbent has to act, the job impact on results, and the extent of the monetary impact of the job.

The fourth factor, *additional compensable elements*, addresses exceptional conditions in the job's environment. Because the Hay Plan is a job evaluation method used by employers worldwide, it facilitates job comparison among firms. Thus, the method serves to determine both internal and external equity.

Most job evaluation plans determine the relative value of jobs resulting in a job hierarchy. The next step is to determine the actual price of each job. Job pricing, and the details involved, is the topic of the next section.

Job Pricing

The process of job evaluation results in a job hierarchy. It might reveal, for example, that the job of senior accountant is more valuable than the job of computer operator, which, in turn, is more valuable than the job of data entry clerk. At this point, you know the *relative* value of these jobs to the company, but not their *absolute* value. **Job pricing** results in placing a dollar value on the job's worth. It takes place after evaluation of the job and the relative value of each job in the organization have been determined. Firms often use pay grades and pay ranges in the job-pricing process.

Pay Grades

A **pay grade** is the grouping of similar jobs to simplify pricing jobs. For example, it is much more convenient for organizations to price 15 pay grades than 200 separate jobs. The simplicity of this approach is similar to a college or university's practice of grouping grades of 90 to 100 into an *A* category, grades of 80 to 89 into a *B*, and so on. In following this approach, you also avoid a false implication of preciseness. Although job evaluation plans may be systematic, none is scientific.

Plotting jobs on a scatter diagram is often useful to managers in determining the appropriate number of pay grades for a company. Looking at Figure 9-6, notice that each dot on the scatter diagram represents one job. The location of the dot reflects the job's relationship to pay and evaluated points, which reflect its worth. When this procedure is used, a certain point spread determines the width of the pay grade (100 points in this illustration). Although each dot represents one job, it may involve dozens of individuals who have *positions* in that one job. The large dot at the lower left represents the job of data entry clerk, evaluated at 75 points. The data entry clerk's hourly rate of $12.90 represents either the average wage currently paid for the job or its market rate. This decision depends on how management wants to price its jobs.

A **wage curve** (or pay curve) is the fitting of plotted points to create a smooth progression between pay grades. The line drawn minimizes the distance between all dots and the line; a line of best fit may be straight or curved. However, when the point system is used, a straight line is often the result, as in Figure 9-6. You can draw this wage line either freehand or by using a statistical method.

Pay Ranges

After pay grades have been determined, the next decision is whether all individuals performing the same job will receive equal pay or whether you should use pay ranges. A **pay range** includes a minimum and maximum pay rate with enough variance between the two to allow for a significant pay difference. Pay ranges are generally

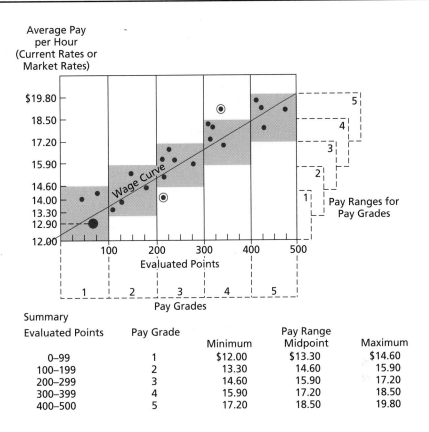

Figure 9-6 Scatter Diagram of Evaluated Jobs Illustrating the Wage Curve, Pay Grades, and Rating Ranges

Summary

Evaluated Points	Pay Grade	Minimum	Pay Range Midpoint	Maximum
0–99	1	$12.00	$13.30	$14.60
100–199	2	13.30	14.60	15.90
200–299	3	14.60	15.90	17.20
300–399	4	15.90	17.20	18.50
400–500	5	17.20	18.50	19.80

preferred over single pay rates because they allow a firm to compensate employees according to performance and length of service. Pay then serves as a positive incentive. When pay ranges are used, a firm must develop a method to advance individuals through the range. Companies typically use different range spreads for jobs that are more valuable to the company.

Points along the Range. Referring again to Figure 9-6, note that anyone can readily determine the minimum, midpoint, and maximum pay rates per hour for each of the five pay grades. For example, for pay grade 5, the minimum rate is $17.20, the midpoint is $18.50, and the maximum is $19.80. The minimum rate may be the *hiring in* rate that a person receives when joining the firm, although in practice, new employees often receive pay that starts above this level. The maximum pay rate represents the maximum that an employee can receive for that job regardless of how well he or she performs the job.

Problem of Topping Out. A person at the top of a pay grade will have to be promoted to a job in a higher pay grade in order to receive a pay increase unless (1) an across-the-board adjustment is made or (2) the job is reevaluated and placed in a higher pay grade. This situation has caused numerous managers some anguish as they attempt to explain the pay system to an employee who is doing a tremendous job but is at the top of a pay grade. Consider this situation:

> *Everyone in the department realized that Beth Smithers was the best administrative assistant in the company. At times, she appeared to do the job of three people. Bob Marshall, Beth's supervisor, was especially impressed. Recently, he had had a discussion with the human resource manager to see what he could do to get a raise for Beth. After Bob described the situation, the human resource manager's only reply was, "Sorry, Bob. Beth is already at the top of her pay grade. There is nothing you can do except have her job upgraded or promote her to another position."*

Situations like Beth's present managers with a perplexing problem. Many would be inclined to make an exception to the system and give Beth a salary increase. However, this action would violate a traditional principle, which holds that every job in the organization has a maximum value, regardless of how well an employee performs the job. The rationale is that making exceptions to the compensation plan would result in widespread pay inequities. Having stated this, today many organizations are challenging traditional concepts as they strive to retain top-performing employees. For example, if Beth Smithers worked for Microsoft or Southwest Airlines, she might get a raise.

Rate Ranges at Higher Levels. The rate ranges established should be large enough to provide an incentive to do a better job. At higher levels, pay differentials may need to be greater to be meaningful. There may be logic in having the rate range become increasingly wide at each consecutive level. Consider, for example, what a $200-per-month salary increase would mean to a file clerk earning $2,000 per month (a 10 percent increase) and to a senior cost accountant earning $5,000 per month (a 4 percent increase). Assuming an inflation rate of 4 percent, the accountant's *real pay* would remain unchanged.

Broadbanding

Broadbanding:
Compensation technique that collapses many pay grades (salary grades) into a few wide bands in order to improve organizational effectiveness.

The pressure on U.S. business firms to do things better, faster, and less expensively has caused management to scrutinize all internal systems. Compensation in particular has received attention because of its ability to affect job behavior. Responding to this need is the concept of **broadbanding**, a technique that collapses many pay grades (salary grades) into a few wide bands to improve organizational effectiveness.

Organizational downsizing and restructuring of jobs create broader job descriptions, with the result that employees perform more diverse tasks than they previously did. Broadbanding creates the basis for a simpler compensation system that de-emphasizes structure and control and places greater importance on judgment and flexible decision making. Broadbanding may add flexibility to the compensation system and require less time having to make fine distinctions among jobs. Bands may also promote lateral development of employees and direct attention away from vertical promotional opportunities. The decreased emphasis on job levels should encourage employees to make cross-functional moves to jobs that are on the same or even lower level because their pay rate would remain unchanged.

Broadbanding also minimizes the problem previously mentioned concerning employees at the top of their pay grade. Moving an employee's job to a higher band would occur only when there was a significant increase in accountability. However, considerable advancement in pay is possible within each band. For example, even massive General Electric has managed to place all its exempt jobs into five bands. This is particularly important in firms with flatter organizational structures that offer fewer promotional opportunities. Figure 9-7 illustrates broadbanding as it relates to pay grades and rate ranges.

Although broadbanding is successful in some organizations, the practice is not without pitfalls. Since each band consists of a broad range of jobs, the market value of these jobs may also vary considerably. Unless carefully monitored, employees in jobs at the lower end of the band could progress to the top of the range and become overpaid.

Single-Rate System

Pay ranges are not appropriate for some workplace conditions such as assembly-line operations. For instance, when all jobs within a unit are routine, with little opportunity for employees to vary their productivity, a single-rate system (or fixed-rate system) may be more appropriate. When single rates are used, everyone in the same job receives the same base pay, regardless of productivity. This rate may correspond to the midpoint of a range determined by a compensation survey.

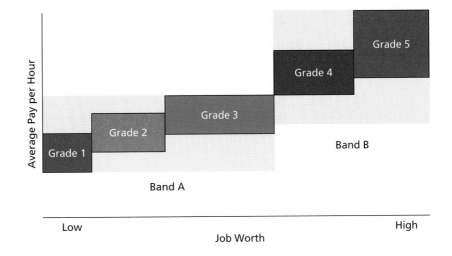

Figure 9-7 Broadbanding and Its Relationship to Traditional Pay Grades and Ranges
Source: Adapted from Joseph J. Martocchio, *Strategic Compensation*, 2nd ed. (Upper Saddle River, NJ: Prentice Hall, 2001), p. 218.

Adjusting Pay Rates

When pay ranges have been determined and jobs assigned to pay grades, it may become obvious that some jobs are overpaid and others underpaid. You normally bring underpaid jobs up to the minimum of the pay range as soon as possible. Referring again to Figure 9-6, you can see that a job evaluated at about 225 points and having a rate of $14.00 per hour is represented by a circled dot immediately below pay grade 3. The job was determined to be difficult enough to fall in pay grade 3 (200–299 points). However, employees working in the job are being paid 60 cents per hour less than the minimum for the pay grade ($14.60 per hour). If one or more female employees should be in this circled job, the employer might soon learn more than desired about the Equal Pay Act. Good management practice would be to correct this inequity as rapidly as possible by placing the job in the proper pay grade and increasing the pay of those in that job.

Overpaid jobs present a different problem. Figure 9-4 illustrates an overpaid job for pay grade 4 (note the circled dot above pay grade 4). Employees in this job earn $19.00 per hour, or 50 cents more than the maximum for the pay grade. This type of overpayment, as well as the kind of underpayment discussed earlier, is called a *red circle rate*.

An ideal solution to the problem of an overpaid job is to promote the employee to a job in a higher pay grade. This is a great idea if the employee is qualified for a higher-rated job and a job opening is available. Another possibility would be to bring the job rate and employee pay into line through a pay cut. Although this decision may appear logical, it is generally not a good management practice, as this action would punish employees for a situation they did not create. Somewhere in between these two possible solutions is a third: to freeze the rate until across-the-board pay increases bring the job into line. In an era where this type of increase is declining in popularity, it might take a long time for this to occur.

Pricing jobs is not an easy task. It requires effort that never ends. It is one of those tasks that managers may dislike but must do anyway.

OBJECTIVE

Identify factors related to the employee that are essential in determining direct financial compensation.

Employee as a Determinant of Direct Financial Compensation

In addition to the organization, the labor market, and the job, factors related to the employee are also essential in determining pay equity. These factors include performance, skills, competencies, seniority, experience, membership in the organization, and potential. Other factors, less controlled by the employee, are political influence and luck.

Job Performance—Performance-Based Pay

A compensation feature generally controllable by employees is their job performance. The objective of performance-based pay is to improve productivity. The typical large firm spends an average of more than $30 million a year on performance-based compensation.[30] An effective performance appraisal program is a prerequisite for any pay system tied to performance.[31] Appraisal data provide input for such approaches as merit pay, bonuses, and piecework. Each of these approaches to compensation management will be discussed in the following sections.

Merit pay:

Pay increase added to employees' base pay based on their level of performance.

Merit Pay. **Merit pay** is a pay increase added to employees' base pay based on their level of performance. In practice, however, it is often merely a cost-of-living increase in disguise. Past studies by compensation professionals have determined that merit pay is *marginally successful* in influencing pay satisfaction and performance. Even if merit increases are small, giving them to all employees regardless of their results sends the wrong message—both to poor performers who are being rewarded for less-than-stellar achievement and to top performers who get a smaller piece of the salary-budget pie.[32]

From the employer's viewpoint, a distinct disadvantage to the typical merit pay increase is that it increases the employee's base pay. Therefore, employees receive the added amount each year they are on the payroll regardless of later performance levels. Some firms find it difficult to justify merit pay increases based on a previous employment period but added perpetually to base pay. Although many companies continue with merit pay plans, others seek to control fixed costs by using variable pay. Actually, the two approaches are not mutually exclusive; in fact, firms often use them together. Merit pay, which increases base salary, recognizes long-term contributions of employees; variable pay, including bonuses, recognizes current accomplishments.

Bonus:

One-time annual financial award based on productivity that is not added to base pay.

Variable Pay (Bonus). Companies are increasingly placing a higher percentage of their compensation budget in variable pay as more and more companies embrace the concept of *pay for performance*.[33] The most common type of variable pay for performance is the **bonus**, a one-time annual financial award, based on productivity, that is not added to base pay.

According to a recent survey, 85 percent of private-sector organizations pay bonuses, which are up from 69 percent the previous year.[34] In a recent study, all companies with double-digit growth said their variable pay programs proved beneficial and contributed to business results.[35] Leon Potgieter, principal and head of Towers Perrin's Global Consulting Group, said, "In the last two years, the use of variable pay has grown worldwide as companies recognized the value of tying pay to performance and results. The use of variable pay has helped employers manage their cash outlay in a tough business environment while laying the foundation to share success with employees when the business results are there."[36]

Managers commonly contend that performance-based pay is a win-win situation because it boosts production and efficiency and gives employees some control over their earning power. With the bonus, there is no carryover into subsequent periods unless employees maintain their performance. According to a study of financial executives, cash bonuses are the best way to acknowledge a job well done.[37] Although they were once reserved for high-ranking executives, firms are pushing these forms of pay down through the ranks.[38]

Spot bonus:

Relatively small monetary gifts provided to employees for outstanding work or effort during a reasonably short period of time.

Many organizations today are providing *spot bonuses* for critical areas and talents. **Spot bonuses** are relatively small monetary gifts provided to employees for outstanding work or effort during a reasonably short period of time. If an employee's performance has been exceptional, the employer may reward the worker with a one-time bonus of $50, $100, or $500 shortly after the noteworthy actions.[39] For example, in a recent study, 82 percent of firms reported granting spot cash rewards to IT personnel.[40]

Piecework:

Incentive pay plan in which employees are paid for each unit they produce.

Piecework. **Piecework** is an incentive pay plan where employees are paid for each unit they produce. For example, if a worker is paid $8 a unit and produces 10 units a day, the worker earns $80. Sometimes a guaranteed base is included in a piece-rate plan where a worker would receive this base amount no matter what the output. Piecework is especially prevalent in the production/operations area. Requirements for the plan include developing output standards for the job and being able to measure the output of a single employee. Obviously, a piecework plan would not be feasible for many jobs.

A basic question that should precede the introduction of any performance-based pay plan is this: "What effect will it have on productivity and quality?" Although advocates of incentive plans cannot guarantee success, results are often positive.

Skills—Skill-Based Pay

Skill-based pay:

System that compensates employees for their job-related skills and knowledge, not for their job titles.

Skill-based pay is a system that compensates employees for their job-related *skills* and *knowledge*, not for their job titles. The system assumes that employees who know more are more valuable to the firm and, therefore, they deserve a reward for their efforts in acquiring new skills. When employees obtain additional job-relevant skills, both individuals and the departments they serve benefit. For example, in a department there may be six different types of machines, each requiring different skills to operate. Under a skill-based pay system, the worker would increase his or her pay as additional machines are learned. Employees may receive both tangible and intangible rewards: pay increases, job security, greater mobility, and the satisfaction of being more valuable. Acquiring additional skills also allows employees the opportunity to increase their earnings without the necessity of moving permanently to a higher-level job. This factor has additional importance in a highly competitive environment in which promotional opportunities are more limited than in the past. Employees with a broader range of skills provide organizational units with a greater degree of versatility in dealing with absenteeism and turnover.

Typically, skill pay is most appropriate in settings where the work tends to be routine and less varied, such as skills of assembly or responding to customer service questions. Skill-based pay is also popular with autonomous workgroups or other job-enrichment programs. A high commitment to human resource development is necessary to implement such a program successfully. In addition, employees involved in skill-based pay programs must have the desire to grow and increase their knowledge and skills.

Although skill-based pay appears to have advantages for both employer and employee, there are some challenges for management. The firm must provide adequate training opportunities or else the system can become a demotivator. Since research has revealed that it takes an average of only three years for a worker to reach a maximum level in a skill-based pay system, what will keep employees motivated? One answer has been coupling the plan with a pay-for-performance system. An additional challenge associated with skill-based pay is that payroll costs will escalate. It is conceivable that a firm could have, in addition to high training and development costs, a very expensive workforce possessing an excess of skills. In spite of these negative possibilities, a number of firms have achieved lower operating costs and other benefits with their pay-for-skills programs.

Competencies—Competency-Based Pay

Competency-based pay:

Compensation plan that rewards employees for the capabilities they attain.

Competency-based pay is a compensation plan that rewards employees for the capabilities they attain. Competencies include skills but also involve other factors such as motives, values, attitudes, and self-concepts that can be linked to better performance. Often considerable time must be spent determining the specific competencies needed for the different jobs. Blocks of competencies are then priced. Often management must invest considerable time in developing, implementing, and continuing such a system. Although core competencies may be unique to each company, one service firm identified the following:

- *Team-centered.* Builds productive working relationships at levels within and outside the organization.
- *Results-driven.* Is focused on achieving key objectives.
- *Client-dedicated.* Works as a partner with internal and external clients.
- *Innovative.* Generates and implements new ideas, products, services, and solutions to problems.
- *Fast cycle.* Displays a bias for action and decisiveness.[41]

Pay for performance focuses on end results; competency-based pay examines how an employee accomplishes the objectives. Although competencies may relate to performance, it appears that they would be more difficult to evaluate than results.

Seniority

Seniority:
Length of time an employee has been associated with the company, division, department, or job.

Seniority is the length of time an employee has been associated with the company, division, department, or job. Although management generally prefers performance as the primary basis for compensation changes, unions tend to favor seniority. They believe the use of seniority provides an objective and fair basis for pay increases. Many union leaders consider performance evaluation systems to be too subjective, permitting management to reward favorite employees arbitrarily.

Experience

Regardless of the nature of the task, experience has the potential for enhancing a person's ability to perform. However, this possibility materializes only if the experience acquired is positive. Knowledge of the basics is usually a prerequisite for effective use of a person's experience. This is true for a person starting to play golf, learn a foreign language, or manage people in organizations. People who express pride in their many years of managerial experience may be justified in their sentiments, but only if their experience has been beneficial. Those who have been autocratic managers for a number of years would likely not find their experience highly valued by a *Fortune* 100 firm. Nevertheless, experience is often indispensable for gaining the insights necessary for performing many tasks.

A relatively new aspect of experience relating to organizational value stems from the creation of a new economy. Today, it is possible that *experience* is becoming somewhat irrelevant. How do you best do things in a dot-com world as opposed to the old economy? Still, employees receive compensation for their experience and the practice is justified if the experience is positive and relevant to the work.

Organization Membership

Employees receive some compensation components without regard to the particular job they perform or their level of productivity. They receive them because they are members of the organization. For example, an average performer occupying a job in pay grade 1 may receive the same number of vacation days, the same amount of group life insurance, and the same reimbursement for educational expenses as a superior employee working in a job classified in pay grade 10. In fact, the worker in pay grade 1 may get more vacation time if he or she has been with the firm longer. The purpose of rewards based on organizational membership is to maintain a high degree of stability in the workforce and to recognize loyalty.

Potential

Potential is useless if it is never realized. However, organizations do pay some individuals based on their potential. In order to attract talented young people to the firm, for example, the overall compensation program must appeal to those with no experience or any immediate ability to perform difficult tasks. Many young employees are paid well, perhaps not because of their ability to make an immediate contribution, but because they have the *potential* to add value to the firm as a professional, first-line supervisor, manager of compensation, vice president of marketing, or possibly even chief executive officer.

Political Influence

Firms should obviously not permit political influence to be a factor in determining financial compensation. However, to deny its existence would be unrealistic. There is an unfortunate element of truth in the statement, "It's not *what* you know, it's *who* you know." To varying degrees in business, government, and not-for-profit organizations, a person's *pull* or political influence may sway pay and promotion decisions. It may be natural for a manager to favor a friend or relative in granting a pay increase or promotion. Nevertheless, if the person receiving the reward is not deserving of it, the workgroup will soon know about it. The result will probably be devastating to employee morale.

Luck

You have undoubtedly heard the expression, "It helps to be in the right place at the right time." There is more than a little truth in this statement as it relates to compensation. Opportunities are continually presenting themselves in firms. Realistically, there is no way for managers to foresee many of the changes that occur. For instance, who could have known that the purchasing agent, Joe Flynn, a seemingly healthy middle-aged man, would suddenly die of a heart attack? Although the company may have been grooming several managers for Joe's position, none may be capable of immediately assuming the increased responsibility. The most experienced person, Tommy Loy, has been with the company only six months. Tommy had been an assistant buyer for a competitor for four years. Because of his experience, Tommy receives the promotion and the increased financial compensation. Tommy Loy was lucky; he was in the right place at the right time.

When asked to explain their most important reasons for success and effectiveness as managers, two chief executives responded candidly. One said, "Success is being at the right place at the right time and being recognized as having the ability to make timely decisions. It also depends on having good rapport with people, a good operating background, and the knowledge of how to develop people." The other replied, "My present position was attained by being in the right place at the right time with a history of getting the job done." Both executives recognize the significance of luck combined with the ability to perform. Their experiences lend support to the idea that luck works primarily for the efficient.

Describe team-based pay, company-wide pay plans, professional employee compensation, sales representative compensation, and contingency worker compensation.

Team-Based Pay

Since team performance consists of individual efforts, individual employees should be recognized and rewarded for their contributions. However, if a team is to function effectively, firms should provide a reward based on the overall team performance as well. Changing a firm's compensation structure from an individual-based system to one that involves team-based pay can have powerful results. By so doing, a firm can improve efficiency, productivity, and profitability.

Team incentives have both advantages and disadvantages. On the positive side, firms find it easier to develop performance standards for groups than for individuals. For one thing, there are fewer standards to determine. Also, the output of a team is more likely to reflect a complete product or service. Another advantage is that employees may be more inclined to assist others and work collaboratively if the organization bases rewards on the team's output. A potential disadvantage for team incentives relates to exemplary performers. If individuals in this category perceive that they contribute more than other employees in the group, they may become disgruntled and leave.

Unisys provides an example of team-based pay. This firm has made dramatic changes in the way people work. In the company, there are more than 140 people organized into 10 teams at their Bismarck, North Dakota, office. These teams handle various accounting functions, such as the firm's accounts payable and employees' business travel reimbursements. Each team takes care of an entire process, from opening mail to issuing checks, and seeks solutions internally to any problems it encounters. All employees receive a base wage in addition to payment for the performance of their team.[42]

Company-Wide Pay Plans

In baseball, you do not judge the team based on its ace pitcher or great outfield. The criterion for success is overall team performance, its win–loss record. In business, company-wide plans offer a possible alternative to the incentive plans previously discussed. Organizations normally base company-wide plans on the firm's productivity, cost savings, or profitability. To illustrate the concept of company-wide plans, profit sharing will be discussed and then, a gainsharing plan known as the Scanlon plan, will be presented.

Profit Sharing

Profit sharing:
Compensation plans that result in the distribution of a predetermined percentage of the firm's profits to employees.

Profit sharing is a compensation plan that results in the distribution of a predetermined percentage of the firm's profits to employees. Many firms use this type of plan to integrate the employees' interests with those of the company. Profit-sharing plans can aid in recruiting, motivating, and retaining employees, which usually enhances productivity.

There are several variations of profit-sharing plans, but three basic kinds of plans are used today: current profit sharing, deferred profit sharing, and combination plans.[43]

- *Current plans* provide payment to employees in cash or stock as soon as profits have been determined.
- *Deferred plans* involve placing company contributions in an irrevocable trust, credited to individual employees' accounts. The funds are normally invested in securities and become available to the employee (or his or her survivors) at retirement, termination, or death.

- *Combination plans* permit employees to receive payment of part of their share of profits on a current basis, while deferring payment of part of their share.

Normally, most full-time employees are included in a company's profit-sharing plan after a specified waiting period. *Vesting* determines the amount of *profit* an employee owns in his or her account. Firms often determine this sum on a graduated basis. For example, an employee may become 25 percent vested after being in the plan for two years; 50 percent vested after three years; 75 percent vested after four years; and 100 percent vested after five years. This gradual approach to vesting encourages employees to remain with the firm, thereby reducing turnover.

The results of profit sharing include increased efficiency and lower costs. In recent years, however, the increased popularity of defined contribution plans (discussed in the next chapter) has slowed the growth of profit-sharing plans. Also, variations in profits may present a special problem. When employees have become accustomed to receiving added compensation from profit sharing, and then there is no profit to share, they may become disgruntled.

A basic problem with a profit-sharing plan stems from the recipients' seldom knowing precisely how they helped generate the profits, beyond just doing their jobs. And, if employees continue to receive a payment, they will come to expect it and depend on it. If they do not know what they have done to deserve it, they may view it as an entitlement program and the intended *ownership* attitude may not materialize.

Gainsharing

Gainsharing:
Plans designed to bind employees to the firm's productivity and provide an incentive payment based on improved company performance.

Gainsharing plans are designed to bind employees to the firm's productivity and provide an incentive payment based on improved company performance. Gainsharing programs, such as the Scanlon, Multicost Scanlon, Rucker, and Improshare plans, are the most popular company-wide plans and they have been increasingly adopted by American corporations.[44] The goal of gainsharing is to focus on improving cost-efficiency, reducing costs, improving throughput, and improving profitability. Gainsharing helps align an organization's people strategy with its business strategy.[45] Gainsharing plans (also known as *productivity incentives*, *team incentives*, and *performance sharing incentives*) generally refer to incentive plans that involve many or all employees in a common effort to achieve a firm's performance objectives.

Joseph Scanlon, after whom the Scanlon plan was named, developed the first gainsharing plan during the Great Depression, and it continues to be a successful approach to group incentive. The **Scanlon plan** provides a financial reward to employees for savings in labor costs resulting from their suggestions. Employee-management committees evaluate these suggestions. Participants in these plans calculate savings as a ratio of payroll costs to the sales value of what that payroll produces. If the company is able to reduce payroll costs through increased operating efficiency, it shares the savings with its employees.

Scanlon plan:
Gainsharing plan that provides a financial reward to employees for savings in labor costs resulting from their suggestions.

Scanlon plans are not only financial incentive systems, but also systems for participative management. The Scanlon plan embodies management/labor cooperation, collaborative problem solving, teamwork, trust, gainsharing, open-book management, and servant leadership. The four basic principles emphasized are the following:[46]

1. *Identity.* To focus on employee involvement, the firm's mission or purpose must be clearly articulated.

2. *Competence.* The plan requires the highest standards of work behavior and a continual commitment to excellence.

3. *Participation.* The plan provides a mechanism for using the ideas of knowledgeable employees and translating these into productivity improvements.

4. *Equity.* Equity is achieved when three primary stakeholders, employees, customers, and investors, share financially in the productivity increases resulting from the program.

Such firms as Herman Miller, Ameritech, Martin Marietta, Donnelly Mirrors, Motorola, and Boston's Beth Israel Hospital are realizing benefits from the Scanlon plan. They have created formal participative means for soliciting suggestions and are sharing the revenue resulting from increases in productivity. Gainsharing studies indicate that firms using these plans increase their productivity from 10 to 12 percent a year.[47] Scott Abel, plant manager at Zircoa, a manufacturer of ceramic and refractory products, said productivity is on the upswing as reflected in the company's gainsharing program, which outlines that any increased revenues tied to operating improvements are set aside and the money is split between workers and the company. Recently, each of Zircoa's 130 employees earned $4,700 in gainsharing money.[48]

New Jersey–based NYF, a privately owned distributor of electronic hardware, found that its performance management program released the firm's creativity and allowed it to utilize the knowledge, skills, flexibility, and drive of its employees. The centerpiece of NYF's performance management system is gainsharing, which includes a financial measurement and feedback process, monitors company performance, and then distributes gains in the form of bonuses when appropriate. Due to the program, employees think like entrepreneurs and make daily decisions affecting company performance. They understand how their decisions affect company performance and are confident management will honor these decisions.[49]

Professional Employee Compensation

As previously mentioned, a *professional employee* performs work requiring advanced knowledge in a field of learning, normally acquired through a prolonged course of specialized instruction. Examples of exempt professionals often employed in industry include scientists, engineers, and accountants. Their pay, initially, is for the knowledge they bring to the organization. Gradually, however, some of this knowledge becomes obsolete, and their salaries reflect this. At times, this encourages professionals to enter management to make more money. A problem with this move is that they may not be suited for management. To deal with this potential dilemma, some organizations have created *dual-career paths* (discussed further in the appendix of Chapter 7). This approach provides a separate pay structure for professionals, which overlaps the managerial pay structure. With this system, high-performing professionals are not required to enter management to obtain greater pay.

The unstable nature of professional jobs and their salaries results in a heavy emphasis on market data for job pricing. This has resulted in the use of maturity curves that reflect the relationship between professional compensation and years of experience. These curves are used primarily to establish rates of pay for scientists and engineers involved in technical work at the professional level. Such maturity curves reveal a rapid increase in pay for roughly five to seven years, and then a more gradual rise as technical obsolescence erodes the value of these jobs.[50]

Sales Representative Compensation

Designing compensation programs for sales employees involves unique considerations. For this reason, this task may belong to the sales staff rather than to human resources. Nevertheless, many general compensation practices apply to sales jobs.

For example, job content, relative job worth, and job market value are all relevant factors.

The *straight salary* approach is one extreme in sales compensation. In this method, salespersons receive a fixed salary regardless of their sales levels. Organizations use straight salary primarily to emphasize continued product service after the sale. For instance, sales representatives who deal largely with the federal government often receive this form of compensation.

At the other extreme is *straight commission* where the person's pay is totally determined as a percentage of sales. If the salesperson makes no sales, the individual working on straight commission receives no pay. On the other hand, highly productive sales representatives can earn a great deal of money under this plan.

Between these extremes are the endless varieties of *part-salary, part-commission* combinations. The possibilities increase when a firm adds various types of *bonuses* to the basic compensation package. The emphasis given to either commission or salary depends on several factors, including the organization's philosophy toward service, the nature of the product, and the amount of time required to close a sale.

In addition to salary, commissions, and bonuses, salespersons often receive other forms of compensation that are intended to serve as added incentives. Sales contests that offer products such as DVD players, notebook computers, or expense-paid vacations to exotic locations are common. If any one feature sets sales compensation apart from other programs, it is the emphasis on incentives. You can usually identify specific sales representatives as the cause for sales increases, a situation that encourages payment of incentive compensation. Experience in sales compensation practices over the years has supported the concept of directly relating rewards to performance.

Contingent Worker Compensation

Contingent workers who are employed through an employment agency or on an on-call basis often earn less than traditional employees. Contingent workers who are independent contract workers typically earn more. However, both classes of contingency workers receive fewer benefits, if they receive them at all. As discussed in Chapter 5, flexibility and lower costs for the employer are key reasons for the growth in the use of contingent workers. An inherent compensation problem relates to internal equity. You may have two employees working side by side, one a temporary employee (temp) and the other a regular employee, performing same or near identical tasks, and one makes more money than the other. In most cases, contingents earn less pay and are far less likely to receive health or retirement benefits than their permanent counterparts.

11   OBJECTIVE

Explain the various elements of executive compensation.

Executive Compensation

Executive skill largely determines whether a firm will prosper, survive, or fail. A company's program for compensating executives is a critical factor in attracting and retaining the best available talent. Therefore, in spite of the criticism of excessive executive pay mentioned in the HRM in Action at the beginning of this chapter, providing adequate compensation for these managers is vital. Designing an executive compensation package begins with determining the organization's goals, its objectives, and the anticipated time for achieving them. It is advisable to obtain advice on tax and accounting implications for both the executive and the company. The executive package depends on the magnitude of the responsibility, risk, and effort shouldered by the chief executive as a function of the firm's scale.[51] Organizations typically prefer to relate salary growth for the highest-level managers to market rates and overall corporate performance, including the firm's market value. For the next management tier, they tend to integrate overall corporate performance with market rates and internal considerations to come up with appropriate pay. For lower-level managers, market rates, internal pay relationships, and individual performance are critical factors.

In general, the higher the managerial position, the more difficult it is to define job tasks. The descriptions focus on anticipated results rather than tasks or how the work is accomplished. Thus, market pricing may be the best general approach to use in determining executive compensation. Even though the market may support a high salary for managers, the amount may still seem extremely large. However, managers at the executive level represent a relatively small percentage of the total workforce, and the overall impact on total labor costs is small.

In using market pricing, organizations utilize compensation survey data to determine pay levels for a representative group of jobs. These data are available from such sources as William M. Mercer, WorldatWork, Towers Perrin, Hay Associates, and Hewitt Associates. Various elements of executive compensation will next be discussed.

Base Salary

Although it may not represent the largest portion of the executive's compensation package, the base salary provided is obviously important. It is a factor in determining the executive's standard of living. Salary also provides the basis for other forms of compensation; for example, it may determine the amount of bonuses and certain benefits. The U.S. tax law does not allow companies to deduct more than $1 million of an executive's salary; therefore, most firms keep it below that amount.[52]

Stock Option Plans

Stock option plan:
Incentive plan in which executives can buy a specified amount of stock in their company in the future at or below the current market price.

Stock option plans give the executive the option to buy a specified amount of stock in the future at or below the current market price. The stock option is a long-term incentive designed to integrate the interests of management with those of the organization. To ensure this integration, some boards of directors require their top executives to hold some of the firm's stock. Although the motivational value of stock ownership seems logical, research on the subject has not been conclusive. One view is that option grants do not succeed in making executives think and act like shareholders. It makes them think and act like option holders, with a shorter-term perspective than shareholders. A recommended alternative is to provide packages that include long-term cash and stock incentives tied to core organizational goals, with the options being more performance based. Also, as of 2006, the Financial Accounting Standards Board (FASB) requires companies to expense stock options, thereby making them less attractive.[53]

In general, more mature companies are expected to move away from options, whereas growth companies are more likely to continue using options.[54] Stock option plans are advantageous when stock prices are rising. However, in a declining stock market, when the market price of many stocks is well below the exercise price, this form of compensation is not nearly as attractive, at least in the short run.[55] There are potential disadvantages to stock option plans. A manager may feel uncomfortable investing money in the same organization in which he or she is building a career. As with profit sharing, this method of compensation is popular when a firm is successful, but during periods of decline when stock prices fall, the participants may become disenchanted. Nevertheless, there are several bona fide reasons for including stock ownership in executive compensation plans. In addition to potentially aligning employees' interests with those of shareholders, *retention* of top executives is also a factor.

Short-Term Incentives or Bonuses

Payment of bonuses reflects a managerial belief in their incentive value. The popularity of this compensation component has risen rapidly in recent years since stock options now have to be expensed.[56]

Performance-Based Pay

There is a trend toward more performance-based compensation packages for executives. According to John Challenger, the chief executive of the Chicago outplacement firm Challenger, Gray & Christmas Inc., "There is certainly a strong long-term trend toward performance-based pay . . . and they are leading by example. It's the way that corporate America is heading."[57] At Bank of America, Kenneth D. Lewis, the chairman, president, and chief executive, gave up some guaranteed pay in return for compensation tied to performance measures. He receives a fixed salary but also gets cash incentives, restricted stock, and stock options if the company hits certain financial and stock performance targets.[58] Ask yourself this question: "If pay for performance is appropriate for lower-level employees, should top executives be exempt from the same practice?" The true superstars can still have huge earnings if their certain targets are met. That is precisely what happened at Goldman Sachs, Merrill Lynch, Lehman Brothers, Bear Stearns, Morgan Stanley, Citigroup, and JPMorgan as their CEOs received substantial pay increases.[59] As shareholders become increasingly disenchanted with high levels of executive compensation, as suggested at the beginning of this chapter, performance-based pay may gain in popularity.

As another example, Mellon Financial Corporation's new chairman, president, and chief executive, Robert P. Kelly, has a performance-based pay agreement that could earn him nearly $10 million a year in total compensation. At Mellon, he is paid a base salary of $975,000 but could earn up to $4.87 million a year in performance-based bonuses. He can earn about another $5.1 million, depending on the company's performance. The long-term program consists of 40 percent stock options, 20 percent time-based restricted stock awards, and 40 percent performance shares. The plan takes three years to vest. Mr. Kelly also receives an initial grant of 280,000 stock options, 34,000 restricted shares, and 69,000 performance shares.[60]

Executive Benefits (Perquisites)

Perquisites (perks):
Special benefits provided by a firm to a small group of key executives and designed to give the executives something extra.

Executive benefits are similar to but usually more generous than benefits received by other employees because they relate to managers' higher salaries. However, current legislation (ERISA) does restrict the value of executive benefits to a certain level above that of other workers. **Perquisites (perks)** are any special benefits provided by a firm to a small group of key executives and designed to give the executives something extra. In addition to conveying status, these rewards are either not considered as earned income or else the government taxes them at a lower level than ordinary income. An executive's perks may include some of the following:

- A company-provided car
- Accessible, no-cost parking
- Limousine service; the chauffeur may also serve as a bodyguard
- Kidnapping and ransom protection
- Counseling service, including financial and legal services
- Professional meetings and conferences
- Spouse travel
- Use of company plane and yacht
- Home entertainment allowance
- Special living accommodations away from home
- Club memberships
- Special dining privileges
- Season tickets to entertainment events

- Special relocation allowances
- Use of company credit cards
- Medical expense reimbursement; coverage for all medical costs
- Reimbursement for children's college expenses
- No- and low-interest loans.[61]

Today, personal use of corporate jets is soaring among corporate America's elite as an executive perk. Recently, more than 250 CEOs had personal flight time worth at least $50,000; more than 100 CEOs and senior managers had a flight time cost of $100,000 or more.[62] Today, when companies give perks worth more than $50,000 or 10 percent of salary and bonus, they are required to disclose the entire amount. Plans are for the threshold to be lowered to $10,000.[63] Once-hidden information regarding pay and perks must now be disclosed.[64]

Golden Parachutes

Golden parachute contract:
Perquisite that protects executives in the event that another company acquires their firm or the executive is forced to leave the firm for other reasons.

A **golden parachute contract** is a perquisite that protects executives in the event that another company acquires their firm or if the executive is forced to leave the firm for other reasons. When SunGard Data Systems Inc. of Wayne, Pennsylvania, spun off much of its business, it promised golden parachutes as large as three times their pay to 35 top executives. The golden parachute agreements would give chief executive Cristobal Conde and 13 others three times their pay if they lost their jobs as late as one year plus 30 days after SunGard Data Systems changed hands. Twenty-one others would get as much as much as 2.5 times their pay, under different terms.[65]

State regulators are becoming significantly more aggressive in their attempts to rein in *obscene* golden parachute plans. For instance, California insurance commissioner John Garamendi recently negotiated $265 million in givebacks from Anthem Inc., the fifth-largest publicly traded health insurance company in the country, as a condition of his approval of its merger with WellPoint Health Networks Inc.[66] Some executives are giving up their rights to severance payments that are provided in case the company is bought or he or she is terminated. G. Kennedy Thompson, chairman, president, and chief executive at Wachovia Corporation gave up rights to a severance payment. Also, CEO Richard Kovacevich terminated a similar agreement with Wells Fargo & Co.[67]

Trends & Innovations

Outrageous Severance Pay Examples?

Today's severance package for CEOs is typically several times annual salary and bonus, and accelerated vesting of options. Because the competition for top executives is fierce, in many cases CEOs have to commit a serious crime to be ineligible for severance. In a recent article entitled "Good News: You're Fired," a list of executive firings and their severance pay was provided. Many execs walk away from troubles with big payouts, pensions, and consulting jobs. Some of these would appear to most to be excessive:

- Philip Purcell, **Morgan Stanley**, $113 million. In addition, the company will pay $1.9 million to provide Purcell with a secretary for the rest of his life.[68]
- Stephen Crawford, **Morgan Stanley**, $32 million.
- Harry Stonecipher, **Boeing**, $600,000/year.

- Carly Fiorina, **Hewlett-Packard**, $21 million. However, in a suit brought by the Service Employees International Union, they claimed that HP paid Fiorina $21.4 million in severance, plus stock options and other benefits that increased her total compensation to $42 million.[69]

- Franklin Raines, **Fannie Mae**, $1.4 million/year.

- Scott Livengood, **Krispy Kreme**, $46,000/month.

- James Kilts, **Gillette**, $100 million.[70]

- Jack Welch, once a business school and GE corporate icon, now presents an example for corporate excess. His former wife revealed his $9 million annual pension plan payout, plus outrageous perks such as lifetime use of GE's $80,000-per-month Manhattan apartment with free food and free maid service; lifetime use of the GE fleet of corporate jets, including a Boeing 737 business jet; a new Mercedes plus a limousine and driver; and assorted free sports and opera box tickets.[71]

What most people may not understand is that those massive severance payments are not set up by a board of directors after a CEO has quit or been fired. In virtually every case those payments were negotiated prior to being hired. As these examples suggest, not only should CEO pay be considered but CEO pay contracts should also be examined.[72]

Ethical Dilemma

Creative Accounting?

You and your best friend Sam work for the same company. You are vice president for human resources and Sam is an accountant. Sam said, "I don't know if I should tell you this, but there's something going on at work you should know about." Sam then told you, in strict confidence, that the company's chief financial officer was planning to take an aggressive stance on sales revenue reporting, that in Sam's view, would stretch the boundaries of acceptable accounting practices. Sam's accounting expertise and responsibilities center on the company's real estate holdings and he does not deal with sales revenue. But he has a pretty good understanding of what's happening in other areas of the company's financial activities, and he was clearly concerned about what the CFO wanted to do.

The CFO's accounting method would increase your firm's earnings outlook and probably help its stock price. "But it could be risky," Sam said. It could "raise questions" about the firm's methods and even its integrity. What's more, Sam said, he wasn't sure the CEO clearly understands the CFO's approach. He might just go along with the CFO since they were college buddies and the CEO personally hired him four years ago. The CEO is 48 and has been with the company for five years. He has boosted sales to double-digit rates every year, but his streak may end soon. Sales gains so far this year have been the lowest in more than six years, and there is no help in the immediate horizon. Your chairman, the son of the founder, is 64 and has been with the company for 35 years. He has spent his career keeping his company on a steady growth path, and he considers the company's reputation and integrity a reflection of his own.[73]

What would you do?

A Global Perspective

Costs of Expatriates

Employers today know that it is more expensive to send workers abroad. Tokyo, for example, ranks as the most expensive city for expatriates, followed by London, Moscow, and Osaka, Japan, according to a survey by Mercer Human Resource Consulting. In Tokyo, an expat can expect to spend $4,501 per month on a luxury two-bedroom apartment rental, $4.73 on a cup of coffee, and $5.48 on a fast-food hamburger dinner.[74]

During the past few years Agilent Technologies, the world's largest maker of scientific-testing equipment, cut 16,000 jobs during a major restructuring. It had become obvious that its multimillion-dollar expatriate program needed serious trimming. The company did not know what it was spending on its employees in foreign countries. It did know that, in general, the cost of an expatriate is three times the expat's annual salary for every year of the assignment. But with spending spread across 21 different countries, such as Germany, Singapore, and China, and across business areas, from compensation to taxation, it was nearly impossible to determine the total cost of relocation. "If you don't know how much you're spending, how do you get started on how to save?" says Lin Contino, global relocation manager at Agilent, which has 28,000 employees. "We couldn't get a grip on it. We had 422 different suppliers globally that provided relocation services. I could tell the cost for the United States, but I couldn't tell for other countries. I couldn't pull it all together."[75]

"A lot of companies are trying to come to grips with the fact that they don't know what the [total] costs are for international relocation," says Rick Schwartz, CEO of GMAC Global Relocation Services, in Oak Brook, Illinois. "It's kind of scary. I've heard it so many times, from large, prestigious, well-run organizations. But the need to do business around the world is increasing significantly. The question facing many organizations is: How can I move more, but in a cost-effective way?"[76]

Employers have had to face the fact that it is more expensive to send workers abroad. To rein in spending, employers are using a variety of strategies. They are sending fewer workers overseas, replacing traditional three-year stints with short-term assignments, localizing expats, offering less generous perks, and hiring third-country nationals or local talent instead of sending a U.S. employee overseas.[77] Today, the trend is toward temporary relocation in which the family remains at home. Recently, 70 percent of global assignments were scheduled for one year or less, a major change from the historical average of 13 percent.[78] The decrease in the number of long-term assignments has been accompanied by the growth in the number of short-term assignments ranging from 2 to 12 months.[79] The short-term assignment uses reimbursement-based allowances and fewer or no family allowances such as schooling.[80] Cost savings are not the only advantage for short-term assignment. Tim Runnion, CEO of Mobility Services International, said, "In recent years, companies have faced reductions in available talent, so they have to move it around on short-term assignments to bring expertise to local situations."[81]

Summary

1. Define compensation and describe the various forms of compensation.

Compensation is the total of all rewards provided employees in return for their services. Forms of compensation include direct financial compensation, indirect financial compensation (benefits), and nonfinancial compensation.

2. Define financial equity and explain the concept of equity in direct financial compensation.

Financial equity is workers' perceptions that they are being treated fairly. Forms of compensation equity include external equity, internal equity, employee equity, and team equity.

3. Identify the determinants of direct financial compensation.

The organization, the labor market, the job, and the employee all have an impact on job pricing and the ultimate determination of an individual's financial compensation.

4. Describe the organization as a determinant of direct financial compensation.

Compensation policies and ability to pay are organizational factors to be considered.

5. Describe the labor market as a determinant of direct financial compensation.

Factors that should be considered include compensation surveys, expediency, cost-of-living increases, labor unions, the economy, and certain federal and state legislation.

6. Explain how the job is a determinant of direct financial compensation.

Management techniques utilized for determining a job's relative worth include job analysis, job descriptions, and job evaluation.

7. Define job evaluation and describe the four traditional job evaluation methods.

Job evaluation is a process that determines the relative value of one job in relation to another. In the job evaluation ranking method, the raters examine the description of each job being evaluated and arrange the jobs in order according to their value to the company. The classification method involves defining a number of classes or grades to describe a group of jobs. In the factor comparison method, raters need not keep the entire job in mind as they evaluate; instead, they make decisions on separate aspects or factors of the job. In the point method, raters assign numerical values to specific job factors, such as knowledge required, and the sum of these values provides a quantitative assessment of a job's relative worth.

8. Describe job pricing.

Placing a dollar value on the worth of a job is job pricing.

9. Identify factors related to the employee that are essential in determining direct financial compensation.

The factors include pay for performance, seniority, experience, membership in the organization, potential, political influence, and luck.

10. Describe team-based pay, company-wide pay plans, professional employee compensation, sales representative compensation, and contingency worker compensation.

If a team is to function effectively, firms should provide a reward based on the overall team performance. Organizations normally base company-wide plans on the firm's productivity, cost savings, or profitability. Compensation for professionals is for the knowledge they bring to the organization. The unstable nature of professional jobs and their salaries results in a heavy emphasis on market data for job pricing. Designing compensation programs for sales employees involves unique considerations. Contingency workers who are employed through an employment agency or on an on-call basis often earn less than traditional employees. Contingency workers who are independent contract workers typically earn more.

11. Explain the various elements of executive compensation.
In determining executive compensation, firms typically prefer to relate salary growth for the highest-level managers to overall corporate performance. Executive compensation often has five basic elements: (1) base salary, (2) short-term incentives or bonuses, (3) stock option plans, (4) executive performance-based pay, and (5) perquisites.

Key Terms

- Compensation, 276
- Direct financial compensation, 276
- Indirect financial compensation, 277
- Nonfinancial compensation, 277
- Equity theory, 277
- Financial equity, 278
- External equity, 278
- Internal equity, 278
- Employee equity, 278
- Team equity, 278
- Compensation policy, 279
- Pay leaders, 279
- Market (going) rate, 279
- Pay followers, 280
- Labor market, 280

- Compensation survey, 281
- Benchmark job, 281
- Cost-of-living allowance (COLA), 282
- Exempt employees, 283
- Job evaluation, 284
- Job evaluation ranking method, 285
- Classification method, 285
- Factor comparison method, 285
- Point method, 286
- Hay guide chart-profile method (Hay plan), 289
- Job pricing, 290
- Pay grade, 290
- Wage curve, 290

- Pay range, 290
- Broadbanding, 292
- Merit pay, 294
- Bonus, 294
- Spot bonus, 294
- Piecework, 295
- Skill-based pay, 295
- Competency-based pay, 295
- Seniority, 296
- Profit sharing, 298
- Gainsharing, 299
- Scanlon plan, 299
- Stock option plan, 302
- Perquisites (perks), 303
- Golden parachute contract, 304

Questions for Review

1. Define each of the following terms:
   a. compensation
   b. direct financial compensation
   c. indirect financial compensation
   d. nonfinancial compensation
2. What are the differences among external equity, internal equity, employee equity, and team equity?
3. Why might a firm want to be a pay leader as opposed to paying market rate?
4. What are the primary determinants of direct financial compensation? Briefly describe each.
5. What organizational factors should be considered as determinants of direct financial compensation?
6. What factors should be considered when the labor market is a determinant of direct financial compensation?
7. How has government legislation affected compensation?
8. What is the difference between an exempt and a nonexempt employee?
9. What factors should be considered when the job is a determinant of direct financial compensation?
10. Give the primary purpose of job evaluation.
11. Distinguish between the following job evaluation methods:
    a. ranking
    b. classification
    c. factor comparison
    d. point method
12. Describe the Hay guide chart-profile method of job evaluation.
13. What is the purpose of job pricing? Discuss briefly.

14. State the basic procedure for determining pay grades.

15. What is the purpose of establishing pay ranges?

16. Define broadbanding.

17. Distinguish between merit pay, bonus, and piecework.

18. Describe factors related to the employee as a determinant of direct financial compensation.

19. What are some company-wide, team-based pay plans?

20. How is the compensation for professionals determined?

21. How is the compensation for sales representatives determined?

22. What are the various types of executive compensation?

HRM Incident 1

A Motivated Worker!

Bob Rosen could hardly wait to get back to work Monday morning. He was excited about his chance of getting a large bonus. Bob is a machine operator with Ram Manufacturing Company, a Wichita, Kansas, maker of electric motors. He operates an armature-winding machine. The machine winds copper wire onto metal cores to make the rotating elements for electric motors.

Ram pays machine operators on a graduated piece-rate basis. Operators are paid a certain amount for each part made, plus a bonus. A worker who produces 10 percent above standard for a certain month receives a 10 percent additional bonus. For 20 percent above standard, the bonus is 20 percent. Bob realized that he had a good chance of earning a 20 percent bonus that month. That would be $787.

Bob had a special use for the extra money. His wife's birthday was just three weeks away. He was hoping to get her a car. He had already saved $2,000, but the down payment on the car was $2,500. The bonus would enable him to buy the car.

Bob arrived at work at seven o'clock that morning, although his shift did not begin until eight. He went to his workstation and checked the supply of blank cores and copper wire. Finding that only one spool of wire was on hand, he asked the forklift truck driver to bring another. Then, he asked the operator who was working the graveyard shift, "Sam, do you mind if I grease the machine while you work?"

"No," Sam said, "that won't bother me a bit."

After greasing the machine, Bob stood and watched Sam work. He thought of ways to simplify the motions involved in loading, winding, and unloading the armatures. As Bob took over the machine after the eight o'clock whistle, he thought, "I hope I can pull this off. I know the car will make Kathy happy. She won't be stuck at home while I'm at work."

Question

1. Explain the advantages and disadvantages of a piecework pay system such as that at Ram.

HRM Incident 2

The Controversial Job

David Rhine, compensation manager for Farrington Lingerie Company, was generally relaxed and good-natured. Although he was a no-nonsense, competent executive, David was one of the most popular managers in the company. This Friday morning, however, David was not his usual self. As chairperson of the company's job evaluation committee, he had called a late-morning meeting at which several jobs were to be considered for reevaluation. The jobs had already been rated and assigned to pay grade 3. But the office manager, Ben Butler, was upset that one was not rated higher. To press the issue, Ben had taken his case to two executives who were also members of the job evaluation committee. The two executives (production manager Bill Nelson and general marketing manager Betty Anderson) then requested that the job ratings be reviewed. Bill and Betty supported Ben's side of the dispute, and David was not looking forward to the confrontation that was almost certain to occur.

The controversial job was that of receptionist. Only one receptionist position existed in the company, and Marianne Sanders held it. Marianne had been with the firm 12 years, longer than any of the committee members. She was extremely efficient, and virtually all the executives in the company, including the president, had noticed and commented on her outstanding work. Bill Nelson and Betty Anderson were particularly pleased with Marianne because of the cordial manner in which she greeted and accommodated Farrington's customers and vendors, who frequently visited the plant. They felt that Marianne projected a positive image of the company.

When the meeting began, David said, "Good morning. I know that you're busy, so let's get the show on the road. We have several jobs to evaluate this morning and I suggest we begin . . . " Before he could finish his sentence, Bill interrupted, "I suggest we start with Marianne." Betty nodded in agreement. When David regained his composure, he quietly but firmly asserted, "Bill, we are not here today to evaluate Marianne. Her supervisor does that at performance appraisal time. We're meeting to evaluate jobs based on job content. In order to do this fairly, with regard to other jobs in the company, we must leave personalities out of our evaluation." David then proceeded to pass out copies of the receptionist job description to Bill and Betty, who were obviously very irritated.

Questions

1. Do you feel that David was justified in insisting that the job, not the person, be evaluated? Discuss.

2. Do you believe that there is a maximum rate of pay for every job in an organization, regardless of how well the job is being performed? Justify your position.

3. Assume that Marianne is earning the maximum of the range for her pay grade. In what ways could she obtain a salary increase?

Notes

1. Rik Kirkland and Doris Burke, "The Real CEO Pay Problem," *Fortune* 154 (July 10, 2006): 78–86.
2. Peter Drucker, "Beyond Capitalism," *Across the Board* 42 (November/December 2005): 14.
3. "Too Many Turkeys," *Economist* 337 (November 26, 2005): 75–76.
4. James Krohe Jr., "The Revolution That Never Was," *Across the Board* 42 (September/October 2005): 28–35.
5. Ann Pomeroy, "Executive Compensation Soars," *HR Magazine* 51 (July 2006): 16.
6. Jesica Marquez, "Exec Pay Under Pressure from Many Quarters," *Workforce Management* 85 (January 16, 2006): 8–9.
7. "Too Many Turkeys."
8. Ann Pomeroy, "Are You Getting What You Pay For?" *HR Magazine* 50 (April 2005): 16–20.
9. "Performance Leads Today's Executive Rewards Programs," *HR Focus* 82 (October 2005): S1–S4.
10. Jessica Marquez, "Consultants Tapped to Review Executive Pay," *Workforce Management* 84 (May 2005): 22.
11. Shawn Tully, "Five Commandments for Paying the Boss," *Fortune* 154 (July 10, 2006): 89–92.
12. Edgar Woolard Jr., "CEOs Are Being Paid Too Much," *Across the Board* 43 (January/February 2006): 28–30.
13. "Compensation Expert: More Action Needed," *Financial Executive* 18 (November 2002): 10.
14. Jeffrey Pfeffer, "The Pay-for-Performance Fallacy," *Business 2.0* 6 (July 2005): 64.
15. Karen Krebsbach, "Executive Compensation & the Boardroom Dilemma," *U.S. Banker* 115 (November 2005): 32–38.
16. "CEO Pay Links to Performance Are Growing Stronger," *Corporate Board* 26 (July/August 2005): 27–28.
17. Marquez, "Exec Pay Under Pressure from Many Quarters."
18. "Pay Ranked Higher than Benefits," *Employee Benefit News* 20 (August 2006): 3.
19. Stacey L. Kaplan, "Total Rewards in Action: Developing a Total Rewards Strategy," *Benefits & Compensation Digest* 42 (August 2005): 32–37.
20. Brent M. Longnecker and Nicole Shanklin, "Total Rewards: A Three-Legged Platform Toward Improved Productivity," *Employee Benefit Plan Review* 59 (July 2004): 8–10.
21. R. Wayne Mondy and Shane R. Premeaux, *Management: Concept, Practices, and Skills* (Englewood Cliffs, NJ: Prentice Hall, 1995): 23.
22. "Getting the Most Out of Salary Surveys," *HR Focus* 82 (April 2005): 6–7.
23. http://www.bls.gov/ncs/home.htm, January 6, 2006.
24. http://www.homefair.com/homefair/servlet/ActionServlet?pid=200&tool=salarycalculator&previousPage=116&cid=homestoregates&gate=homestore&fromState=SD&toState=IL&salary=100000&fromCity=4659020&toCity=1714000&ownrent=own, March 9, 2006.
25. Desda Moss, "Bias? What Bias?" *HR Magazine* 51 (February 2006): 14.
26. Walter Williams, "Congress' Insidious Discrimination," *Augusta Constitution* (March 14, 2003): A05.
27. Karen Giffen and Karen L. Giffen, "Employers Wise to Review Overtime Rules," *Crain's Cleveland Business* 26 (January 10, 2005): 13.
28. The following discussion of the point method was adapted from Joseph J. Martocchio *Strategic Compensation: A Human Resource Management Approach* (Upper Saddle River, NJ: Prentice Hall, 2006): 233–237.
29. http://www.haygroup.ca/services/job_evaluation_chart.html, August 9, 2006.
30. Andy Cohen and Maggie Rauch, "Companies Favor Bonuses Over Pay Raises in 2005," *Incentive* 179 (February 2005): 9.
31. Julia Vowler, "Reaping the Benefits of Bonus Plans," *Computer Weekly* (July 28, 2005): 16.
32. Susan J. Wells, "No Results, No Raise," *HR Magazine* 50 (May 2005): 76–80.
33. "Bonus Planning," *Controller's Report* 2005 (December 2005): 8–9.
34. Jamin Robertson, "Take the Money and Run," *Employee Benefits* (February 2006): 53–54.

CHAPTER 10

Benefits, Nonfinancial Compensation, and Other Compensation Issues

HRM IN *Action:*

Nontraditional Benefits

Regardless of economic conditions, it seems organizations are continually competing for top caliber employees. Although benefits may not serve as strong motivators of performance, they are obviously important in attracting and retaining these desired individuals. Among numerous unique benefits offered by some firms are the following:

- Lake Zurich–based New Age Transportation, Distribution and Warehousing Inc., handed out pedometers and promised to pay a dollar for every mile employees walked, plus more for losing weight. One employee received a check for $1,200.[1]
- Chicago branding agency Bamboo Worldwide Inc., gives employees *working vacation days*, when they can be out of the office but must check e-mail and voice mail twice during the day.[2]
- At Goldman Sachs, employees get 52 hours of paid volunteer time each year.
- At Fannie Mae, employees receive a healthy-living day off and a day of home-purchase leave.
- At Starbucks, even part-timers get health insurance, stock options, and tuition reimbursement as well as a free pound of coffee weekly.
- At AFLAC, the firm's 32-acre campus has a YMCA fitness center, acute-care clinic, walking trails, child-care center, and a duck pond. Twelve weeks of paid maternity/paternity leave are available for eligible staff.
- At Colgate-Palmolive, new parents get a three-week paid leave on top of regular disability time off. On-site banking, a travel agent, and a film-processing center make errands easier and intramural sports leagues contribute to the fun.
- At Ernst & Young, the company provides a concierge service.[3]
- At Communicorp, in Columbus, Georgia, the company has two on-site child-care centers offering infant care, kindergarten programs, after-school programs, and evening services on Saturdays.[4]

- At SRP in Arizona, the nation's third-largest public power and water utility, the company offers its employees identity theft services to educate them about protecting their identity and help them restore their identity and credit after a theft. SRP recently began offering services to its 4,500 employees after noticing workers were contacting its security services weekly for help in dealing with stolen credit cards and lost wallets. Identity theft services cut down on lost productivity and gave employees peace of mind.[5]

This chapter begins by describing some nontraditional benefits, and benefits as indirect financial compensation. A discussion of mandated and voluntary benefits follows. Topics related to health care, life insurance, retirement plans, disability protection, employee stock option plans, supplemental unemployment benefits, and employee services are then discussed. Premium pay and legislation concerning benefits are presented next, and the factors involved in nonfinancial compensation are then described. Topics related to the job itself as a total compensation factor, job characteristics theory, and the job environment as a total compensation factor are then presented, followed by a discussion of factors that are involved in workplace flexibility (work-life balance) and concepts regarding severance pay, comparable worth, pay secrecy, and pay compression. This chapter concludes with a Global Perspective entitled "China's Work Week."

1 OBJECTIVE

Define benefits.

Benefits:
All financial rewards that are not included in direct financial compensation (indirect financial compensation).

Benefits (Indirect Financial Compensation)

Most organizations recognize that they have a responsibility to their employees to provide insurance and other programs for their health, safety, security, and general welfare (see Figure 10-1). These programs, called **benefits**, include all financial rewards not included in direct financial compensation. Benefits generally cost the firm money, but employees usually receive them indirectly. For example, an organization may spend several thousand dollars a year as a contribution to the health insurance premiums for each employee. The employee does not receive the money but does obtain the benefit of health insurance coverage. This type of compensation has two distinct advantages: (1) it is generally nontaxable to the employee and (2) the cost of some benefits may be much less for large groups of employees than for individuals.

As a rule, employees receive benefits because of their membership in the organization. Benefits are typically unrelated to employee productivity; therefore, although they may be valuable in recruiting and retaining employees, they do not generally serve as motivation for improved performance. Legislation mandates some benefits, and employers voluntarily provide others.

According to the U.S. Bureau of Labor Statistics, benefits account for nearly 30 percent of employers' total compensation costs, but over the past decade, the change in benefits costs has outpaced the change in the cost of wages and salaries.[6] U.S. businesses are paying an average of $7.40 in benefits for each hour their employees work.[7] The cost of the health care benefit alone is estimated at $8,424 annually per

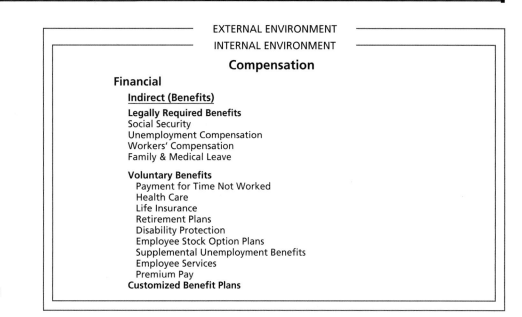

Figure 10-1 Benefits in a Total Compensation Program

person.[8] The magnitude of this expenditure no doubt accounts for the less frequent use of the term *fringe benefits*. In fact, the benefits that employees receive today are significantly different from those of just a few years ago. As benefit dollars compete with financial compensation, some employers are moving away from paternalistic benefits programs. They are shifting more responsibilities to employees as with 401(k) retirement plans (discussed later). However, in a competitive labor market, many firms are careful to provide desired benefits to attract and retain employees with critical skills.

2 OBJECTIVE

Describe mandated (legally required) benefits.

Mandated (Legally Required) Benefits

Employers provide most benefits voluntarily, but the law requires others. These required benefits currently account for about 10 percent of total compensation costs. They include Social Security, workers' compensation, unemployment insurance, and family and medical leave. The future comparative importance of these benefits will depend on how the United States deals with rising health care costs and with long-term custodial care for elderly citizens.

Ethical Dilemma

A Poor Bid

You are vice president of human resources for a large construction company, and your company is bidding on an estimated $2.5 million public housing project. A local electrical subcontractor submitted a bid that you realize is 20 percent too low because labor costs have been incorrectly calculated. It is obvious to you that compensation benefits amounting to over 30 percent of labor costs have not been included. In fact, the bid was some $30,000 below those of the other four subcontractors. But, accepting it will improve your chance of winning the contract for the big housing project.

What would you do?

Social Security

The Social Security Act of 1935 created a system of retirement benefits. The Act established a federal payroll tax to fund unemployment and retirement benefits. It also established the Social Security Administration. Employers are required to share equally with employees the cost of old age, survivors', and disability insurance. Employers are required to pay the full cost of unemployment insurance.

Subsequent amendments to the Act added other forms of protection, such as disability insurance, survivors' benefits, and, more recently, Medicare. Medicare spending per beneficiary has doubled in real terms in the past two decades and as baby boomers become eligible, the costs will really escalate. Increased costs have resulted from greater use of post–acute care services such as skilled nursing, home health care, and rehabilitation facilities. Medicare's financial outlook has deteriorated dramatically over the past five years and is now much worse than Social Security's.[9]

Disability insurance protects employees against loss of earnings resulting from total incapacity. *Survivors' benefits* are provided to certain members of an employee's family when the employee dies. These benefits are paid to the widow or widower and unmarried children. Unmarried children may be eligible for survivors' benefits until they are 18 years old. In some cases, students retain eligibility until they are 19. *Medicare* provides hospital and medical insurance protection for individuals 65 years of age and older and for those who have become disabled.

Although employees must pay a portion of the cost of Social Security coverage, the employer makes an equal contribution and considers this cost to be a benefit. The present tax rate is 6.2 percent for the Social Security portion and 1.45 percent for Medicare. The total tax rate of 7.65 percent is applied to a maximum taxable wage of $90,000. The rate for Medicare applies to all earnings. Approximately 95 percent of the workers in this country pay into and may draw Social Security benefits. The Social Security program currently is running a surplus but the retirement of the 77-million-member baby-boom generation is looming. Unless Congress makes changes by 2041, the program will have used up its surplus and will no longer be able to pay full benefits.[10]

Beginning with employees who reached age 62 in 2000, the retirement age increases gradually until 2009, when it reaches age 66. After stabilizing at this age for a time, it will again increase in 2027, when it reaches age 67. These changes will not affect Medicare, with full eligibility under this program holding at age 65.

Unemployment Compensation

Unemployment insurance provides workers whose jobs have been terminated through no fault of their own monetary payments for up to 26 weeks or until they find a new job. The intent of unemployment payments is to provide an unemployed worker time to find a new job equivalent to the one lost without suffering financial distress. Without this benefit, workers might have to take jobs for which they are overqualified or end up on welfare. Unemployment compensation also serves to sustain consumer spending during periods of economic adjustment. In the United States, unemployment insurance is based on both federal and state statutes and, although the federal government provides guidelines, the programs are administered by the states and therefore benefits vary by state. A payroll tax paid solely by employers funds the unemployment compensation program.

Workers' Compensation

Workers' compensation benefits provide a degree of financial protection for employees who incur expenses resulting from job-related accidents or illnesses. As with unemployment compensation, the various states administer individual programs, which are subject to federal regulations. Employers pay the entire cost of workers' compensation insurance, and their past experience with job-related accidents and illnesses largely determines their premium expense. These circumstances should provide further encouragement to employers to be proactive with health and safety programs, topics discussed in Chapter 11.

Family and Medical Leave Act of 1993 (FMLA)

The Family and Medical Leave Act applies to private employers with 50 or more employees and to all governmental employers regardless of number. The FMLA provides employees up to 12 weeks a year of unpaid leave in specified situations. The overall intent of the Act was to help employees balance work demands without hindering their ability to attend to personal and family needs. FMLA rights apply only to employees who have worked for the employer for at least 12 months and who have at least 1,250 hours of service during the 12 months immediately preceding the start of the leave. The FMLA guarantees that health insurance coverage is maintained during the leave and also that the employee has the right to return to the same or an equivalent position after a leave.

OBJECTIVE

Explain the various discretionary benefits.

Discretionary (Voluntary) Benefits

Although the law requires some benefits, organizations voluntarily provide numerous other benefits.[11] These benefits usually result from unilateral management decisions in some firms and from labor/management negotiations in others. Further, an employee's desire for a specific benefit may change. For instance, with the soaring gas prices has come a desire for commuter benefits, such as employers paying for employees to use public transit and van pools.[12] Major categories of discretionary benefits include payment for time not worked, health care, life insurance, retirement plans, employee stock option plans, supplemental unemployment benefits, and employee services. An example of the wide range of discretionary corporate benefits may be seen in Figure 10-2.

Payment for Time Not Worked

In providing payment for time not worked, employers recognize that employees need time away from the job for many purposes. Discussed below are paid vacations, sick pay and paid time off, sabbaticals, and other forms of payment for time not worked.

Paid Vacations

In a recent Employee Benefits Trend Study, 64 percent of full-time employees identified paid vacation days as the most important benefit they receive.[13] Payment for time not worked serves important compensation goals. For instance, paid vacations provide workers with an opportunity to rest, become rejuvenated, and thus more productive. They may also encourage employees to remain with the firm. Paid vacation time typically increases with seniority. For example, employees with six months' service might receive one week of vacation; employees with one year of service, two weeks; ten years' service, three weeks; and fifteen years' service, four weeks.

But, some workers are apparently choosing to not take all their vacation. According to a recent survey, American workers are giving back 415 million vacation days a year.[14] In a climate of increased outsourcing and job insecurity, it is not surprising that many Americans do not take full advantage of their vacation benefits. Further, 35 percent of U.S. workers feel stressed about work even while on vacation;

Personal Benefits:

Medical Plans: Two options as well as various HMOs are available.

Dental Plans: Two options as well as various Dental Maintenance Alternatives (DMAs) and the MetLife Preferred Dentist Program (PDP) are available.

Work and Personal Life Balancing:

Vacation: 1 to 4 years service—10 days per year
5 to 9 years service (or age 50–59)—15 days
10 to 19 years service or age 60 and over—20 days
20 years or more—25 days

Holidays: 12 days per year (6 observed nationally; other 6 vary with at least one personal choice).

Life Planning Account: $250 of taxable financial assistance each year, with certain conditions.

Flexible Work Schedules, Telecommuting, and Work Week Balancing: (with local management approval).

Capital Accumulation, Stock Purchase, and Retirement:

401(k) Plan: Employees may contribute up to 12 percent of eligible compensation, which is matched 50 percent on the first 6 percent.

Stock Purchase Plan: Employees may contribute up to 10 percent of eligible compensation each pay period for the purchase of company stock (pay 85 percent of average market price per share on date of purchase).

Retirement Plan: Competitive, company-paid retirement benefit plan with vesting after 5 years of continuous service.

Income and Asset Protection: Some of the plans offered include:

Sickness and Accident Income Plans
Long-Term Disability Plan
Group Life Insurance
Travel Accident Insurance
Long-Term Care Insurance

Skills Development:

Tuition Refund: If aligned with business needs and approved.

Educational Leaves of Absence: Under appropriate circumstance and approved by management.

Additional Employee Programs:

Site Offerings: Many sites offer programs including:
Fitness Centers
Educational Courses
Award Programs
Career Planning Centers

Clubs: These clubs organize recreational leagues, company-sponsored trips, and a variety of classes and programs.

Figure 10-2 An Example of a Corporation's Benefit Program

CareerBuilder.com found that 39 percent return to work as stressed or more stressed than when they left.[15]

Vacation time may vary with organizational rank. For instance, an executive, regardless of time with the firm, may be given a month of vacation. With an annual salary of $120,000, this manager would receive a benefit worth approximately $10,000 each year while not working. A junior accountant earning $36,000 a year might receive two weeks of vacation time worth about $1,500.

Sick Pay and Paid Time Off

Each year many firms allocate to each employee a certain number of days of sick leave that they may use when ill. Employees who are too sick to report to work continue to receive their pay up to the maximum number of days accumulated. As with vacation pay, the number of sick leave days often depends on seniority.

Some managers are very critical of sick leave programs. At times, individuals have abused the system by calling in sick when all they really wanted was additional paid

Paid time off (PTO):
Means of dealing with the problem of unscheduled absences by providing a certain number of days each year that employees can use for any purpose.

vacation. One approach in dealing with the problem of unscheduled absences is to provide more flexibility. In lieu of sick leave, vacation time, and a personal day or two, a growing number of companies are providing **paid time off (PTO)**, a certain number of days off provided each year that employees can use for any purpose. With a PTO plan, all the reasons for time off—sick, vacation, and personal days—are grouped together and no one has to lie.[16] "We had four different time-off programs," said Paula Mutch, manager of compensation and benefits with Mount Clemens General Hospital in Michigan. "The PTO bank folded them together, and it's not only much easier for us to administer, it's easier for employees to understand."[17]

According to one survey, up to 27 percent of American firms now have such plans. Maureen Brookband, benefits vice president at Marriott, which has such a plan, says that employees tell her, "It's very nice, there's no guilt. You don't have to use a sick day when you aren't really sick."[18] Some critics of the plan feel there is still a need for sick leave. But, as one expert pointed out, a prominent reason for taking sick days is stress, and this factor is not really dealt with. The impact of stress will be discussed in the next chapter.

Sabbaticals

Sabbaticals:
Temporary leaves of absence from an organization, usually at reduced pay.

Sabbaticals are temporary leaves of absence from an organization, usually at reduced pay. Although sabbaticals have been used for years in the academic community, they have only recently entered the private sector. According to a recent survey, only 5 percent of companies provide paid sabbaticals but another 18 percent provide unpaid sabbaticals.[19] Often sabbaticals help to reduce turnover and keep workers from burning out; hopefully they will return revitalized and more committed to their work.[20] UPS and Xerox are among the growing number of companies who pay employees' expenses to participate in extended volunteer sabbaticals. Since 1971, Xerox has maintained its Social Service Leave program, which allows employees to take fully paid leaves from their jobs, ranging from three months to a year, to work full-time on volunteer projects of their own design and choosing. Their jobs are waiting for them upon return.[21] Remember the concept of sequencing moms discussed in Chapter 3.

At Fleishman-Hillard, a global public relations firm, employees with four or more years of service can take a six-week sabbatical. Benefits, such as health insurance, continue throughout. The firm pays for two weeks; the employee uses two weeks of vacation, and then takes more weeks without pay. Or employees can take up to one year of unpaid leave and can pay their share of health insurance. They retain the benefit of lower rates from being in the company's pool. "We were looking for ways to attract and retain employees," said Agnes Gioconda, Fleishman-Hillard's chief talent officer. "We find that it reduces employee burnout. They need new ideas for their clients. And it gives us cross-training and career development for others who are out (on leave)."[22]

As another example, every employee who has worked at Arrow Electronics, a New York–based distributor of computer products and electronic components, for seven years is eligible for an 8- to 10-week sabbatical. "Employees can use the time off as they wish," says Kathy Bernhard, director of management development. "We tend to run people really hard," she explains. "There's a lot of travel associated with many of these jobs, and it's a high-stress, high-change industry, so it's really just a chance for people to get recharged." Another benefit of the sabbatical program is that of employee development. Employees showing promise and a willingness to learn are assigned to the vacant positions. The opportunity enhances their careers and increases their understanding of the business.[23]

Sabbaticals also help to accommodate workplace needs of the baby boomers. According to a recent survey, boomers are likely to continue working, either part-time or full-time, as consultants or by setting up their own companies. They want a *flexible* workplace that lets them take extended sabbaticals and then work intensely for shorter periods of time. They want to *phase-in* retirement by working fewer hours as they near 65, or after.

Other Types of Payment for Time Not Worked

Although paid vacations and sick pay comprise the largest portion of payment for time not worked, there are numerous other types that companies use. It is common for organizations to provide payments to assist employees in performing civic duties. For example, companies often give workers time off to work with the United Way. At times an executive may be on loan to work virtually full-time on such an endeavor.

Some companies routinely permit employees to take off during work hours to handle personal affairs without taking vacation time. When a worker is called for jury duty, some organizations continue to pay their salary; others pay the difference between jury pay and their salary. When the National Guard or military reserve are called to duty, as has been the case in Afghanistan and Iraq, some companies pay their employees a portion of their salary while on active duty. Further, during an election, many companies permit employees voting time. Still other firms permit bereavement time for the death of a close relative. Finally, there is the payment for time not worked while at the company such as rest periods, coffee breaks, lunch periods, cleanup time, and travel time.

Health Care

Benefits for health care represent the most expensive item in the area of indirect financial compensation. In a recent survey of HR professionals, rising health care costs were listed as number one.[24] Currently, employers spend $300 billion annually on health insurance for employees, dependents, and retirees. When provided, health insurance typically constitutes 25 percent of an employer's benefit costs. Health insurance premiums have outpaced inflation and wage growth by wide margins. According to a recent study issued by The Kaiser Family Foundation, premiums in the past five years have grown by 73 percent, compared with cumulative inflation (14 percent) and wage rates (up 15 percent) during that same time. Premiums for an average family of four now cost about $11,000 a year.[25]

A number of factors have combined to create the high cost of health care:

- An aging population
- A growing demand for medical care
- Increasingly expensive medical technology
- Inefficient administrative processes

In 2004, the Canadian province of Ontario surpassed Michigan in car production. However, most of the cars made in Ontario are manufactured by General Motors, Ford, and DaimlerChrysler. These companies are shifting production out of the United States because of enormous health care costs. In Canada, which has a government-funded and government-run health care system, the cost to the employer per worker is just $800.[26] Recently, General Motors and the United Auto Workers agreed to a substantial cut in the medical benefits GM gives its UAW retirees. That deal saves the company an estimated $1 billion a year after taxes and reduces its total medical cost liability by about $15 billion, which is about GM's total market value.[27]

Managed-Care Health Organizations

In addition to self-insurance (in which firms provide benefits directly from their own assets) and traditional commercial insurers (which supply indemnity insurance covering bills from any health care provider), employers may utilize one of several managed-care options. Managed-care systems have been the general response to increased

**Health maintenance organiza-
tion (HMO):**
Managed-care health organization that covers all services for a fixed fee but control is exercised over which doctors and health facilities a member may use.

**Preferred provider organiza-
tion (PPO):**
Managed-care health organization in which incentives are provided to members to use services within the system; out-of-network providers may be utilized at greater cost.

Point-of-service (POS):
Managed-care health organization that requires a primary care physician and referrals to see specialists, as with HMOs, but permits out-of-network health care access.

**Exclusive provider organiza-
tion (EPO):**
Managed-care health organization that offers a smaller preferred provider network and usually provides few, if any, benefits when an out-of-network provider is used.

medical costs. These networks are comprised of doctors and hospitals that agree to accept negotiated prices for treating patients. Employees receive financial incentives to use the facilities within the network. Today, many insured American employees participate in some kind of managed-care plan. Approximately 90 percent of the 178 million Americans insured are covered by group plans from employers.[28] However, some believe that health savings accounts (discussed later) will eventually replace managed-care plans.[29] The following are various forms of managed-care health organizations:

- **Health maintenance organizations (HMOs)** cover all services for a fixed fee but control is exercised over which doctors and health facilities a member may use.
- **Preferred provider organizations (PPO)** are managed-care health organizations in which incentives are provided to members to use services within the system; out-of-network providers may be utilized at greater cost. Recent HMO data indicate an enrollment shift to PPOs.[30]
- **Point-of-service (POS)** requires a primary care physician and referrals to see specialists, as with HMOs, but permits out-of-network health care access.
- **Exclusive provider organizations (EPOs)** offer a smaller PPO provider network and usually provides little, if any, benefits when an out-of-network provider is used.

Each of these managed-care systems appears to be losing its uniqueness. For example, HMOs are developing products that are more flexible and many offer POS and PPOs. Large, independent PPO companies are providing programs that resemble HMOs. Regardless of the precise form, managed-care systems strive to control health care costs.

Consumer-Driven Health Care Plans

Companies are increasingly placing the responsibility for health care on employees. A recent study revealed that consumer-driven plans also reduce total health care costs.[31] The assumption is made that they are in the best position to know what is best for their families. Some of these will be discussed next.

**Defined contribution health
care plan:**
System where companies give each employee a set amount of money annually with which to purchase health care coverage.

Defined Contribution Health Care Plan. In a **defined contribution health care plan**, companies give each employee a set amount of money annually with which to purchase health care coverage. In this health care system, employees could shop around, probably using online services, for plans that meet their individual needs. Employees may spend the funds on any medical expense they choose and on any doctor they choose. That is why the plan is often referred to as consumer-driven.[32] The defined contribution health care plan is based on the belief that consumers are in the best position to know what kind of health care they need and how much they want to spend for it. They could also add personal funds to the employers' contribution and purchase more deluxe coverage.

Health savings account (HSA):
A tax-sheltered savings account similar to an IRA, but earmarked for medical expenses with high-deductible health plans that have annual deductibles of at least $1,050 for individuals and $2,100 for families.

Health Savings Account. Congress authorized health savings accounts to replace medical savings accounts in 2004. At least 3 million consumers were covered by an HSA in 2006, up from 1 million in 2005.[33] Created by a provision of the Medicare Prescription Drug Improvement and Modernization Act of 2003, the **health savings account (HSA)** is a tax-sheltered savings account similar to an IRA, but earmarked for medical expenses with high-deductible health plans that have annual deductibles of at least $1,050 for individuals and $2,100 for families.

Individuals can save up to $2,650 a year ($5,250 for families) and withdraw the money tax free for health care expenses, or let it keep growing. Workers do not owe taxes on contributions and if they leave their job, the HSA goes with them. Tax-free money may be used for expected medical costs, such as buying new eyeglasses once a year.[34] Money deposited into HSAs is not owned by an employer and can roll over into the next year. A HSA offers attractive tax breaks, but the HSA program law requires employers who want to offer HSAs to buy high-deductible health insurance and give employees control over the assets in their HSAs. A family's insurance plan would be used for major medical expenses, whereas the cash in their HSA would go toward out-of-pocket costs, such as prescriptions, co-payments, or special treatments like a CAT scan.

Ted Shannon, equity research analyst for Janus Capital Management, predicts that HSAs will dominate the health care market within 5 to 10 years, eventually replacing managed-care plans. He says HSAs will be 40 percent to 50 percent of the private insurance market by 2010. The reason HSAs will catch on so strongly is that employers will seek to give workers more power over health care choices as they continue to try to lower their costs. The number of employers offering health savings accounts (HSAs) was expected to more than quadruple in 2006, says a Mellon Human Resources & Investor Solutions (HR&IS) survey.[35]

Flexible spending account (FSA):

Benefit plan established by employers that allows employees to deposit a certain portion of their salary into an account (before paying income taxes) to be used for eligible expenses.

Flexible Spending Account. A **flexible spending account (FSA)** is a benefit plan established by employers that allows employees to deposit a certain portion of their salary into an account (before paying income taxes) to be used for eligible expenses. The employee consents to a reduced salary by allowing the employer to contribute a salary portion to an FSA. There are two categories of FSAs. The first is a medical FSA for expenses not reimbursed by a medical, dental, or vision care plan. The second is a dependent care FSA for dependent care expenses for necessary child or adult day-care services. Until recently, employees who funded the plans faced the possibility that they might lose their share of plan assets at the end of the year. However, the IRS now allows companies to amend their plans to permit a grace period of up to two-and-one-half months immediately following the end of each plan year. Unused benefits or contributions may be paid or reimbursed to plan participants for qualified benefit expenses incurred during the grace period.[36]

On-Site Health Care

One way of curbing in health care costs and also providing an employee benefit is the use of on-site health care. Businesses are increasingly using an old approach to employer-sponsored health benefits. Today's trend of providing on-site medical care is growing because it permits employers to better manage and at times reduce the growth of health care costs. On-site health care assists in treating minor illnesses and injuries and provides follow-up care; employers can reduce the number of visits employees make to more costly facilities, such as physicians' offices and hospital emergency rooms. "I think it's a modern model that is indeed proving to be cost-effective" says Sean Sullivan, president, CEO, and co-founder of the Institute for Health and Productivity Management, a nonprofit corporation in Scottsdale, Arizona, that works to link employee health to corporate performance. "Not only does it pick up health issues earlier, but it doesn't require time away from work and at the same time creates a culture of caring." The approach reduces time spent on doctors' visits and recovery, and encourages employees to adopt healthier lifestyles.[37] Raymond Fabius, president and chief medical officer of I-trax Inc., a workplace health and productivity consulting company, said, "On-site clinics normally produce health care savings in the range of 5 percent to 20 percent."[38]

Major Medical Benefits

Many plans provide for major medical benefits to cover extraordinary expenses that result from long-term or serious health problems. The use of *deductibles* is a common feature of medical benefits. For example, the employee may have to pay the first $500 of medical bills before the insurance takes over payment.

Dental and Vision Care

Dental and vision care are popular benefits in the health care area. Employers typically pay the entire costs for both types of plans except for a deductible, which may amount to $50 or more per year. Dental plans may cover, for example, 70 to 100 percent of the cost of preventive procedures (including semiannual examinations) and 50 to 80 percent of restorative procedures (including crowns, bridgework, etc.). Some plans also include orthodontic care. Vision care plans may cover all or part of the cost of eye examinations and glasses.

Long-Term Care Insurance

Recently, national spending on long-term care totaled $183 billion, and nearly half of that was paid for by the Medicaid program. Private insurance paid a small portion of long-term care expenditures, about $16 billion or 9 percent.[39] The increasing costs of 24-hour home health care for elderly relatives have given rise to LTC programs.[40] LTC insurance picks up most or all of the expenses for skilled and custodial care for people in their own homes, in adult day-care centers, in assisted-living facilities, and in nursing homes. It typically covers medically prescribed diagnostic, preventive, therapeutic, and rehabilitative services for patients who are chronically ill or who have severe mental impairment, such as Alzheimer's disease. Employers' role in LTC typically involves establishing and maintaining a payroll deduction program. Employees pay all the costs in most employer-sponsored group policies. Employers that contribute to premiums generally offer a basic plan that employees can enrich by paying more.

Life Insurance

Group life insurance is a benefit provided by virtually all firms to protect the employee's family in the event of his or her death. Although the cost of group life insurance is relatively low, some plans call for the employee to pay part of the premium. Coverage may be a flat amount (for instance, $50,000) or based on the employee's annual earnings. For example, workers earning $40,000 per year may have $80,000, twice their annual earnings, worth of group life coverage.

Web Wisdom

Types of Retirement Plans

http://www.dol.gov/dol/topic/retirement/typesofplans.htm

Retirement information from the U.S. Department of Labor.

Defined benefit plan:
Retirement plan that provides the participant with a fixed benefit upon retirement.

Retirement Plans

Retirement is currently a hot topic because of the aging baby-boomer generation. Employers are in the middle of this challenge since they are one of our society's primary providers of retirement income. Various types of retirement plans will be discussed next.

Defined Benefit Plans

Retirement plans are generally either *defined benefit* or *defined contribution*. A **defined benefit plan** is a formal retirement plan that provides the participant with a *fixed* benefit upon retirement. Although benefit formulas vary, they are typically based on the participant's final years' average salary and years of service. Plans that are considered generous provide pensions equivalent to 50 to 80 percent of an employee's final earnings. This type of retirement plan has declined in recent years although older workers tend to prefer them. What do Verizon, Lockheed Martin, Motorola, and IBM have in common?[41] They have all decided to eliminate the defined benefit form of retirement plan. Verizon Communications froze its $39 billion cash balance plan for management employees. This action was described as "the latest nail in the coffin" for defined benefit plans.[42]

Defined Contribution Plans

Defined contribution plan:
Retirement plan that requires specific contributions by an employer to a retirement or savings fund established for the employee.

A **defined contribution plan** is a retirement plan that requires specific contributions by an employer to a retirement or savings fund established for the employee. One of the most significant changes in the composition of individual household retirement savings over the past 25 years has been the shift from defined *benefits* to defined *contribution* pension plans.[43] Although employees will know in advance how much their retirement income will be under a defined benefit plan, the amount of retirement income from a defined contribution plan will depend upon the investment success of the pension fund.

401(k) plan:
Defined contribution plan in which employees may defer income up to a maximum amount allowed.

A **401(k) plan** is a defined contribution plan in which employees may defer income up to a maximum amount allowed. Some employers match employee contributions 50 cents for each dollar deferred. Although employers typically pay the expenses for their defined benefit pension plans, there is a wide variety of payment arrangements for 401(k) plans. Some plan sponsors pay for everything, including investment fees and costs. Others pay for virtually nothing with the result that nearly all fees are paid out of the plan's assets. In the middle are those plans where the sponsor and participants share the expenses.

As 401(k)s become the primary retirement plans, sponsoring firms are making them more flexible by permitting employees to make more frequent transfers between investment accounts. They are also providing more investment choices for employees. In addition, more firms are starting to provide financial planning for all their employees, not just their top executives. The explosion of 401(k) retirement plans has required about 42 million employees to become investment managers, shifting the burden of retirement planning from employers to employees. Employees then often look to their employers for help. Federal law requires employers to give guidance on these plans but forbids their recommending specific investments. The employers' role is to get financial planners from firms such as Fidelity and Charles Schwab to provide this advice.

Many Americans are not saving enough for retirement. A recent survey found that 32 percent of respondents believe that between half and nearly three-quarters of their employees will not have sufficient income to retire between ages 62 and 65.[44] The percentage of salary that participants are deferring into their defined contribution plans declined by 20 percent from 1999 to 2005.[45] Additionally, employers are skeptical about whether employees adequately understand how to invest 401(k) savings plan assets. This problem becomes a critical issue as Americans are living longer and as confidence in Social Security wanes. If the trend continues, workers will either have to work longer, live on less in retirement, or significantly boost their savings in their later years to catch up. However, the recently passed Pension Protection Act (discussed later) is designed to get more workers enrolled in 401(k) savings plans because companies can now automatically enroll them.

Cash Balance Plans

In designing an appropriate retirement system, some sources suggest ignoring the terms *defined benefit* and *defined contribution*. Instead, they maintain that the focus should be on a plan that meets specific objectives. In other words, for some organizations, a hybrid fund may be the desired approach to retirement plans. A **cash balance plan** is such a plan, with elements of both defined benefit and defined contribution plans.

Cash balance plan:

Retirement plan with elements of both defined benefit and defined contribution plans.

It resembles a defined contribution plan in that it uses an account balance to communicate the benefit amount.[46] However, it is closer to being a defined benefit plan because the employer normally bears the responsibility for and the risks of managing the assets. Also, in contrast to defined contribution plans, the Pension Benefit Guaranty Corporation usually insures cash balance plans. Normally, the employer contributes to each participant's account annually, and investment earnings are at a set amount. If the fund's investment earnings exceed this set amount, the plan sponsor benefits from the performance. If the trust fund does not perform well, the plan sponsor funds the shortfall. A survey by the U.S. General Accounting Office indicated that 19 percent of *Fortune* 1000 firms sponsored cash balance plans at the end of the last decade.[47]

Disability Protection

Workers' compensation protects employees from job-related accidents and illnesses. Some firms, however, provide additional protection that is more comprehensive. A firm's sick leave policy may provide full salary for short-term health problems; when these benefits expire, a short-term disability plan may provide pay equivalent to 50 to 100 percent of pretax pay. Short-term disability plans may cover periods of up to six months.

When the short-term plan runs out, a firm's long-term plan may become active; such a plan may provide 50 to 70 percent of an employee's pretax pay. Long-term disability provides a monthly benefit to employees who due to illness or injury are unable to work for an extended period. Payments of long-term disability benefits usually begin after three to six months of disability and continue until retirement or for a specified number of months.

Employee Stock Option Plan (ESOP)

Employee stock option plan (ESOP):

Defined contribution plan in which a firm contributes stock shares to a trust.

An **employee stock option plan (ESOP)** is a plan in which a firm contributes stock shares to a trust. The trust then allocates the stock to participating employee accounts according to employee earnings. ESOP advocates have promoted employee ownership plans as a means to align the interests of workers and their companies to stimulate productivity. This practice, long reserved for executives, now often includes employees working at lower levels in the firm.[48]

Although the potential benefits of ESOPs are attractive, some employees want the ability to sell their shares prior to retirement, which ESOPs do not allow. Many people do not want to take the chance that the stock is going to be less valuable when they retire. Periods of wild rides in the stock market also dampen worker enthusiasm for ESOPs. Although the potential advantages of ESOPs are impressive, the other side of the coin is the danger of having all your eggs in one basket. The Enron experience makes this point only too well.

Supplemental Unemployment Benefits (SUB)

Supplemental unemployment benefits:

Provide additional income for employees receiving unemployment insurance benefits.

Supplemental unemployment benefits provide additional income for employees receiving unemployment insurance benefits. They first appeared in auto industry labor agreements in 1955 and have spread to many industries; they are usually financed by the company. They tend to benefit newer employees since seniority normally determines layoffs. For this reason, employees with considerable seniority are often not enthusiastic about these benefits.

Employee Services

Organizations offer a variety of benefits that can be termed *employee services*. These benefits encompass a number of areas including relocation benefits, child care, educational assistance, food services/subsidized cafeterias, financial services, legal services, and scholarships for dependents.

Relocation

Relocation benefits:

Company-paid shipments of household goods and temporary living expenses, covering all or a portion of the real estate costs associated with buying a new home and selling the previously occupied home.

Relocation benefits are company-paid shipments of household goods and temporary living expenses, covering all or a portion of the real estate costs associated with buying a new home and selling the previously occupied home. Although employees once viewed a transfer as a step up, they are now taking a closer look at not only the economic impact of the move, but also what it does to quality of life. This concern has broadened the scope of relocation services to include providing information about crime statistics, children's sports teams, tutors, churches, and doctors. Relocation can be as stressful for employees as a death in the family, divorce, or loss of a job. Not only are job-related factors considered, but also the disruption of the familiar patterns of daily life, such as commuting, cultural and recreational opportunities, and school and church affiliations.[49]

Child Care

Another benefit offered by some firms is subsidized child care. According to the National Conference of State Legislatures, an estimated 80 percent of employees miss work due to unexpected child-care coverage issues. It is estimated that every $1 invested in backup child care yields $3 to $4 in returned productivity and benefit.[50] At Abbott Laboratories headquarters campus 30 miles north of Chicago, the company has built a $10 million state-of-the-art child-care center for more than 400 preschool children of Abbott workers. For parents who prefer a different arrangement if an employee's babysitter is sick, Abbott provides emergency backup service.[51] Company child-care arrangements tend to reduce absenteeism, protect employee productivity, enhance retention and recruiting, promote the advancement of women, and make the firm an employer of choice.[52] Remember that in Chapter 3, the importance of child care for single parents and working mothers was discussed.

Educational Assistance

Some companies reimburse employees after they have completed a course with a grade of "C" or above whereas others provide for advance payment of these expenses. Other employers provide half the reimbursement up front and the rest upon satisfactory completion of the course. United Technologies Corporation pays for an employee's entire tuition and books up front. It also offers paid time off—as much as three hours a week, depending on the course load—to study.[53] Internal Revenue Service regulations allow for educational assistance benefits to be nontaxable up to $5,250 per year, although the average educational reimbursement by employers is $1,600 per year.

Food Services/Subsidized Cafeterias

There is generally no such thing as a free lunch. However, firms that supply food services or subsidized cafeterias provide an exception to this rule. What they hope to gain in return is increased productivity, less wasted time, enhanced employee morale, and, in some instances, a healthier workforce. Most firms that offer free or subsidized lunches feel that they get a high payback in terms of employee relations. Northwestern Mutual is one such company. Free lunches are available in its cafeterias, where the menus list calories instead of prices.[54] Keeping the lunch hour to a minimum is an obvious advantage, but employees also appreciate the opportunity to meet and mix with people they work with. Making one entree a heart-healthy choice and listing the calories, fat, cholesterol, and sodium content in food is also appealing to a large number of employees.

Financial Services

Some firms offer various types of financial services. One financial benefit that is growing in popularity permits employees to purchase different types of insurance policies through payroll deduction. Using this approach, the employer can offer a benefit at almost no cost and employees can save money by receiving a deeply discounted rate. Firms can offer discounts to employers because the plans usually eliminate the middlemen. Administrative costs are also drastically reduced. For example, the insurance company sends one statement to the business and receives one premium check. Otherwise, this business might involve dozens or even hundreds of individual transactions. It is also possible for employers to offer employees discounted policies on automobile or homeowner's insurance. In fact, a company may offer many other benefits through payroll deduction plans.

Legal Services

A recent survey found that the number of Americans covered by some type of legal services plan has increased by almost 20 percent since 2000. An estimated 3 million employees are currently enrolled in plans sponsored by employers and funded through employee payroll deductions.[55]

Scholarships for Dependents

According to the 2005 Benefits Survey Report by the Society for Human Resource Management, about 27 percent of companies provide scholarships for dependents. Moreover, 50 percent of all companies with more than 500 employees offer scholarships for employees' dependents. Scholarship programs can help boost employee recruitment and retention. Franciscan Health Systems, a nonprofit health care provider in Tacoma, Washington, targets its awards primarily to employees' children who are interested in entering the health care field, although it also awards scholarships for study in other areas.[56]

OBJECTIVE

Describe customized benefit plans.

Customized benefit plan:
Benefit plan that permits employees to make yearly selections to largely determine their benefit package by choosing between taxable cash and numerous benefits.

Customized Benefit Plans (Cafeteria Compensation)

An emerging trend in the area of benefits is *customization*, whereby employees are permitted to tailor their benefits to fit their individual needs. **Customized benefit plans** permit employees to make yearly selections to largely determine their benefit package by choosing between taxable cash and numerous benefits.

Twenty years ago or so firms offered a uniform package that generally reflected a typical employee. Today, the workforce has become considerably more heterogeneous, and this prototype is no longer representative. According to the Society for Human Resources Management, 38 percent of companies are offering customized benefits packages.[57] Workers have considerable latitude in determining how much they will take in the form of salary, life insurance, pension contributions, and other benefits. Customized plans permit flexibility in allowing each employee to determine the compensation components that best satisfy his or her particular needs.

Table 10-1 **Possible Alternatives Available in a Customized Approach**

Accidental death, dismemberment insurance	Health maintenance organization fees
Birthdays (vacation)	Home health care
Bonus eligibility	Hospital-surgical-medical insurance
Business and professional membership	Incentive growth fund
Cash profit sharing	Interest-free loans
Club memberships	Long-term disability benefit
Commissions	Matching educational donations
Company medical assistance	Nurseries
Company-provided automobile	Nursing home care
Company-provided housing	Outside medical services
Company-provided or -subsidized travel	Personal accident insurance
Day-care centers	Price discount plan
Deferred bonus	Recreation facilities
Deferred compensation plan	Resort facilities
Dental and eye care insurance	Sabbatical leaves
Discount on company products	Salary continuation
Educational activities (time off)	Scholarships for dependents
Free checking account	Severance pay
Free or subsidized lunches	Sickness and accident insurance
Group automobile insurance	Stock appreciation rights
Group homeowners' insurance	Stock bonus plan
Group life insurance	Stock purchase plan

The rationale behind customized plans is that employees have individual needs and preferences. A 60-year-old woman would not need maternity benefits in an insurance plan. At the same time, a 25-year-old single man would not likely place a high value on home health care. Some of the possible alternatives available in a customized approach are shown in Table 10-1.

Obviously, organizations cannot permit employees to select all their benefits. For one thing, firms must provide the benefits required by law. In addition, it is probably wise to require that each employee have core benefits, especially in areas such as retirement and medical insurance. Some guidelines would likely be helpful for most employees in the long run. However, the freedom to select highly desired benefits would seem to maximize the value of an individual's compensation. Employees' involvement in designing their own benefit plans would also effectively communicate to them the cost of their benefits.

The downside to customized compensation plans is that they are costly. Development and administrative costs for these plans exceed those for traditional plans. Even though customized benefit plans add to the organization's administrative burden, some firms apparently find that the advantages outweigh shortcomings.

 **OBJECTIVE**

Explain premium pay.

Premium pay:
Compensation paid to employees for working long periods of time or working under dangerous or undesirable conditions.

Hazard pay:
Additional pay provided to employees who work under extremely dangerous conditions.

Premium Pay

Premium pay is compensation paid to employees for working long periods of time or working under dangerous or undesirable conditions. As mentioned in Chapter 9, payment for overtime is legally required for nonexempt employees who work more than 40 hours in a given week. However, some firms voluntarily pay overtime for hours worked beyond eight in a given day and pay double time, or even more, for work on Sundays and holidays.

Additional pay provided to employees who work under extremely dangerous conditions is called **hazard pay**. A window washer for skyscrapers in New York City might receive extra compensation because of precarious working conditions. Military pilots collect extra money in the form of *flight pay* because of the risks involved in the job.

Shift differential:
Additional money paid to employees for the inconvenience of working less-desirable hours.

Some employees receive **shift differential** pay for the inconvenience of working less-desirable hours. This type of pay may be provided as additional cents per hour. For example, employees who work the second shift (swing shift), from 4:00 p.m. until midnight, might receive $2.00 per hour above the base rate for that job. The third shift (graveyard shift) often warrants an even greater differential; for example, an extra $3.00 per hour may be paid for the same job. Shift differentials are sometimes based on a percentage of the employee's base rate.

 **OBJECTIVE**

Explain health care legislation.

Health Care Legislation

Five pieces of federal legislation related to health care are discussed in the next sections.

Consolidated Omnibus Budget Reconciliation Act

With the high cost of medical care, an individual without health care insurance is vulnerable. The Consolidated Omnibus Budget Reconciliation Act (COBRA) of 1985 was enacted to give employees the opportunity to temporarily continue their coverage, which they would otherwise lose because of termination, layoff, or other changes in employment status. The Act applies to employers with 20 or more employees. Under COBRA, individuals may keep their coverage, as well as coverage for their spouses and dependents, for up to 18 months after their employment ceases. Certain qualifying events can extend this coverage for up to 36 months. The individual, however, must pay for this health insurance and it is expensive.

Health Insurance Portability and Accountability Act

The Health Insurance Portability and Accountability Act (HIPAA) of 1996 provides protection for approximately 25 million Americans who move from one job to another, who are self-employed, or who have pre-existing medical conditions. The prime objective of this legislation is to make health insurance portable and continuous for employees, and to eliminate the ability of insurance companies to reject coverage for individuals because of a pre-existing condition. As an element of HIPAA, there is now a regulation designed to protect the privacy of personal health information.

Employee Retirement Income Security Act

The Employee Retirement Income Security Act (ERISA) of 1974 strengthens existing and future retirement programs. Mismanagement of retirement funds was the primary spur for this legislation. Many employees were entering retirement only to find that the retirement income they had counted on was not available. The Act's intent was to ensure that when employees retire, they receive deserved pensions. The purpose of the Act is described here:

> *It is hereby declared to be the policy of this Act to protect . . . the interests of participants in employee benefit plans and their beneficiaries . . . by establishing standards of conduct, responsibility and obligations for fiduciaries of employee benefit plans, and by providing for appropriate remedies, sanctions, and ready access to the federal courts.*[58]

Note that the word *protect* is used here because the Act does not force employers to create employee retirement plans. It does set standards in the areas of participation, vesting of benefits, and funding for existing and new plans. Numerous existing retirement plans have been altered in order to conform to this legislation.

Older Workers Benefit Protection Act

The Older Workers Benefit Protection Act of 1990 (OWBPA), an amendment to the Age Discrimination in Employment Act, prohibits discrimination in the administration of benefits on the basis of age, but also permits early retirement incentive plans as long as they are voluntary. Employers must offer benefits to older workers that are equal to or greater than the benefits given to younger workers, with one exception. The Act does not require employers to provide equal or greater benefits to older workers when the cost to do so is greater than for younger workers. The Act establishes wrongful termination waiver requirements as a means of protecting older employees by ensuring that fully informed and willful personnel make that waiver acceptance.[59] In a recent decision, the Supreme Court, in *General Dynamics Land Systems, Inc. v Cline*, permitted an employer to establish minimum age requirements for some employee benefits, and to treat older members of a protected class more favorably with respect to the provision of certain benefits.[60]

Pension Protection Act (PPA)

Web Wisdom
Pension Protection Act
http://www.whitehouse.
gov/news/releases/2006/
08/20060817-1.html
President Bush signing ceremony for the Pension Protection Act.

Some say that the Pension Protection Act (PPA) of 2006 is the most sweeping reform of America's pension laws in over 30 years. The bill contains a variety of provisions designed to strengthen the funding rules for defined benefit pension plans. The bill seeks to ensure that employers make greater contributions to their pension funds, ensuring their solvency, and avoiding a potential multibillion-dollar taxpayer bailout of the Pension Benefit Guaranty Corporation (PBGC), which already has a $23 billion deficit because more than 300 companies have dumped their defined benefit pension plans on the federal insurer. Companies such as US Airways and United Airlines have terminated their pension plans and turned them over to the PBGC. The bill establishes increased liabilities for plans that are defined as "at risk." The legislation makes it easier for employers to automatically enroll workers in their 401(k). The new rules generally apply to plan years beginning after 2007.[61]

Communicating Information about the Benefits Package

Employee benefits can help a firm recruit and retain a top-quality workforce. In keeping the program current, management depends on an upward flow of information from employees to determine when benefit changes are needed. In addition, because employee awareness of benefits is often limited, the program information must be communicated downward. Many times organizations do not have to improve benefits to keep their best employees; rather, workers need to fully understand the benefits that are provided them. For example, a survey of 22,000 MedStar employees found that only 30 percent were satisfied with the firm's compensation and benefits program and they did not believe them to be competitive. However, research indicated otherwise. Marjory Zylich, assistant vice president of operational communications and special projects, said, "That's discouraging when half our expenses are on pay and benefits. For a health system our size, that's more than a billion dollars on total compensation." Based on the survey, MedStar began a campaign to educate the workforce regarding their compensation and benefits, resulting in much greater satisfaction in the firm's total compensation program.[62]

The Employee Retirement Income Security Act (previously discussed) provides still another reason for communicating information about a firm's benefits program.

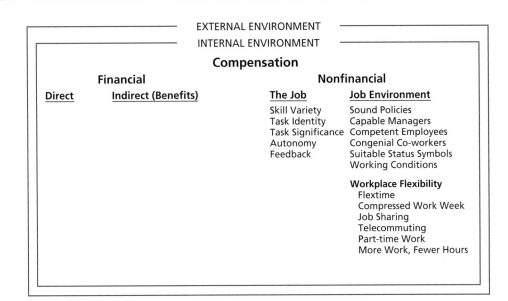

Figure 10-3 Nonfinancial Compensation in a Total Compensation Program

This Act requires organizations with a pension or profit-sharing plan to provide employees with specific data at specified times. The Act further mandates that the information be presented in an understandable manner. With the advent of the Internet and individual intranets, many firms will have little difficulty in achieving the desired communication with employees about anything, including their benefits.

 OBJECTIVE

Describe the components of nonfinancial compensation.

Nonfinancial Compensation

Historically, compensation departments in organizations have not dealt with nonfinancial factors. However, as indicated in the previous chapter, the new model of WorldatWork indicates that this is changing. The components of nonfinancial compensation consist of the job itself and the job environment (see Figure 10-3). A number of work arrangements are included in this environment. These arrangements provide for greater work-life balance resulting in a more desirable life for employees.

OBJECTIVE

Describe the job itself as a nonfinancial compensation factor and job characteristics theory.

Job Itself as a Nonfinancial Compensation Factor

The job itself can be a very powerful factor in the compensation equation. Answering the following questions can provide considerable insight into the value of the job itself:

1. Is the job meaningful and challenging?
2. Is there recognition for accomplishment?
3. Do I get a feeling of achievement from doing the job?
4. Is there a possibility for increased responsibility?
5. Is there an opportunity for growth and advancement?
6. Do I enjoy doing the job itself?[63]

Consider this situation:

The workplace atmosphere is highly invigorating. Roy, Ann, Jack, Sandra, Britt, and Patsy are excited as they try to keep up with double-digit growth in sales orders. They do whatever it takes to get the job done, wearing multiple

*hats that would be difficult to cover in a job description. Their jobs have no
salary grades, and no one ever formally reviews their performance. This
doesn't worry them, however, because they enjoy the camaraderie and
teamwork at their firm. They have complete trust in the firm's highly visible
management, and they have total confidence their leaders will do what's
right for them and the company. Believe it or not, it is a real-life scene from a
real-life company.[64]*

As the situation above suggests, some jobs can be so stimulating that the incumbent is anxious to get to work each day. At the evening meal, details of what happened on the job may be shared with family or friends. Given the prospect of getting a generous raise by leaving this job, this worker may quickly say "No" to the opportunity. Unwillingness to change jobs for additional financial compensation suggests that the job itself is indeed an important reward. Such jobs are often meaningful and challenging, workers are recognized for their accomplishments, there is a feeling of achievement, and there is the opportunity for growth and development.

On the other hand, a job may be so boring or distasteful that an individual dreads going to work. This condition is sad considering the time a person devotes to his or her job. Most of us spend a large part of our lives working. When work is a drag, life may not be very pleasant and, as discussed in Chapter 11, if a boring job creates excessive and prolonged stress, the person involved may eventually become emotionally or physically ill. The job itself is a central issue in many theories of motivation. It is also a vital component in a total compensation program. Job characteristics theory goes a long way in explaining the importance of the job itself in determining compensation. As long as employees exist in organizations, a major management challenge will be to match job requirements with employee abilities and aspirations. Without question, as the scope of many jobs expands and they become more complex, this challenge will also increase in difficulty.

Job Characteristics Theory

Job characteristics theory:
Employees experience intrinsic compensation when their jobs rate high on five core job dimensions: skill variety, task identity, task significance, autonomy, and feedback.

Developed by J. Richard Hackman and Greg Oldham, job characteristics theory provides a comprehensive approach to work redesign and how the job itself is a part of the total compensation factor. The model has three basic components, which include core job characteristics, critical psychological stages, and expected outcomes.[65] According to **job characteristics theory**, employees experience intrinsic compensation when their jobs rate high on five core job dimensions: skill variety, task identity, task significance, autonomy, and feedback. These characteristics create the potential for increased performance, lower absenteeism and turnover, and higher employee satisfaction.

Skill Variety

Skill variety:
Extent to which work requires a number of different activities for successful completion.

Skill variety is the extent to which work requires a number of different activities for successful completion. This factor is similar to the concept of job enlargement discussed previously in Chapter 4. Some workers enjoy variety in their jobs, and if so, it serves as compensation. One only has to visualize work on an assembly line, where an individual is more like a machine, to realize the importance of skill variety. Expanding the number of job activities is quite important to some workers. When this is the case, skill variety becomes a form of compensation.

Task Identity

Task identity:
Extent to which the job includes an identifiable unit of work performed from start to finish.

Task identity is the extent to which the job includes an identifiable unit of work performed from start to finish. As a product rolls off the assembly line, the worker might say, "I made that widget." Some individuals enjoy the added responsibility provided by a project that permits involvement to its completion. For example, an author reviewing her recently published book and recognizing the sentences and paragraphs she wrote as her own, provides an example of task identity. No one else can claim responsibility, or take the blame, for the content of the book. Task identity is an element of job enrichment, also previously discussed.

Task Significance

Task significance:
Impact that the job has on other people.

The impact that the job has on other people constitutes **task significance**, another component of job enrichment. When performance of a person's job influences the life of others, the employee often realizes a real sense of achievement. Jim Stahl, director of wellness for a regional university, designed hundreds of exercise and diet regimens for clients over several decades. When these clients later achieved their personal goals, such as weight loss or a reduction in cholesterol level, they were grateful and Jim knew he had performed important work. His success in changing lifestyles for the better emphasized that his job was truly significant.

Autonomy

Autonomy:
Extent of individual freedom and discretion employees have in performing their jobs.

Autonomy is the extent of individual freedom and discretion employees have in performing their jobs. Jobs that provide autonomy often lead employees to feel responsible for outcomes of work. Most workers do not want someone standing over their shoulders all day long just waiting for them to make the slightest error. These individuals know what needs to be done and, within reason, want the freedom to get the job done their way. Autonomy is at the very heart of self-directed work teams, discussed in Chapter 7. Some of these groups have the authority to make decisions such as whom to hire and promote, work scheduling, and methods to follow. This freedom of action creates a sense of responsibility that is probably unachievable in any other manner.

Feedback

Feedback:
Information employees receive about how well they have performed the job.

Feedback is the information employees receive about how well they have performed the job. For some, it is exhilarating to hear the boss or a respected co-worker say, "You did an excellent job." In fact, most people have a strong need to know how they are doing in their jobs. Top salespersons, for example, want and obtain rapid feedback from securing a sale. When they make a sale, one way they get tangible feedback is in the form of a commission check.

 OBJECTIVE

Describe the job environment as a nonfinancial compensation factor.

Job Environment as a Nonfinancial Compensation Factor

Performing a challenging, responsible job in a pigsty would not be rewarding to most people. The physical environment of the job must also be satisfactory. Employees can draw satisfaction from their work through several nonfinancial factors, discussed next.

Sound Policies

A *policy* is a predetermined guide established to provide direction in decision making. Human resource policies and practices reflecting management's concern for its employees can serve as positive rewards. Consider how the following policies would contribute to the satisfaction of a worker.

- To provide realistic and practical incentives as a means of encouraging the highest standard of individual performance and to assure increased quality and quantity of performance.
- To create and maintain good working conditions, to provide the best possible equipment and facilities, and plants and offices that are clean, orderly, and safe.
- To employ people without regard to race, sex, color, national origin, or age. To encourage employees to improve their skills by participating in available educational or training programs. To provide every possible opportunity for advancement so that each individual may reach his or her highest potential.

If a firm's policies show consideration rather than disrespect, fear, doubt, or lack of confidence, the result can be rewarding to both the employees and the organization. Policies that are arbitrary and too restrictive turn people off.

Capable Managers

Anyone who has worked under a manager who does not possess the managerial skills needed to successfully lead the unit understands the importance of having a capable individual in charge. Many workers quit their jobs because of the way the unit is being managed. Just being around an incompetent boss every day may provide the motivation to call in sick when you are not ill. There may be the bull-of-the-woods manager who only wants it done his or her way. Then, there is the manager who can seemingly never make a decision. There are endless examples of supervisors who are incapable of performing their jobs, thus making the job environment of their employees less than desirable

Competent Employees

Working with individuals who are capable and knowledgeable can often create a synergistic environment. *Synergism* is the cooperative action of two or more persons working together to accomplish more than they could working separately. Synergy implies the possibility of accomplishing tasks that could not even be done by people working separately. Solving problems together is often exhilarating when a co-worker is also competent. Successful organizations emphasize continuous development and assure employment of competent managers and nonmanagers. Competitive environments and the requirement for teamwork will not permit otherwise. *Bad apples* can disrupt any organization.

Congenial Co-workers

Although a few individuals in this world may be quite self-sufficient and prefer to be left alone, they will likely be unsuccessful in the team-oriented organizations that exist today. The American culture has historically embraced individualism, yet most people possess, in varying degrees, a desire for acceptance by their workgroup. It is very important that management develop and maintain congenial workgroups. A workgroup's need for creativity may require individuals with diverse backgrounds. However, to be effective, they must be compatible in terms of sharing common values and goals.

Appropriate Status Symbols

Status symbols are organizational rewards that take many forms such as office size and location, desk size and quality, how close one's private parking space is to the office, floor covering, and job title. Status symbols vary from company to company and sometimes are understood only by persons within the company. Some firms make liberal use of these types of rewards; others tend to minimize them. This latter approach reflects a concern about the adverse effect they may have on creating and maintaining a team spirit among members at various levels in the firm. This is true within many workplaces where the corner office and private washroom have given way to more democratic arrangements.

Working Conditions

The definition of working conditions has broadened considerably over the years. Today, an air-conditioned and reasonably safe and healthy workplace is considered necessary. Another factor of increasing importance is the flexibility or work-life balance employees have in their work situations. These factors will be discussed in the following sections.

OBJECTIVE

Describe workplace flexibility (work-life balance) factors.

Workplace Flexibility (Work-Life Balance)

According to Maria Morris, MetLife executive vice president for institutional business, "To retain top talent in today's competitive job market, employers need to do more than loosen their purse strings. They must create a work environment that reflects their employees' life-stage needs and values."[66] The primary purpose of achieving work-life balance is to minimize stress. For stressed employees (both men and women)[67] seeking to balance work and personal lives, time is nearly as important as money; more important for some. A report by the Families and Work Institute found that 45 percent of employees say work and family responsibilities interfere with each other, and 67 percent of working parents say they do not have enough time with their children.[68] That is why more employees are requesting workplace flexible benefits to achieve a better work and life balance.[69] Ellen Galinsky, president of the New York City–based Families and Work Institute, said, "Employers used to think, if you gave employees an inch they'd take a mile. But in fact, if people have some say in how they do their work, it's more likely that the work will get done." Flexible work arrangements comprise an aspect of nonfinancial compensation that allows families to manage a stressful work/home-juggling act. CEO Roy Krause of Sphericon Corporation, a staffing and recruiting firm, said, "Employers that choose to ignore or discount [the importance to employees of work/life balance] expose themselves to a greater chance of employee burnout, lower productivity and eventual turnover."[70] But that is exactly what may be occurring. A recent *Emerging Workforce Study* found a gap between what employers and employees find important. The survey found that 60 percent of the workers but only 35 percent of employers rate time and flexibility as very important in retention.[71]

For employers, creating a balanced work-life environment can be a key strategic factor in attracting and retaining the most talented employees.[72] By providing such an environment, employees are better able to fit family, community, and social commitments into their schedules and they appreciate that.[73] Some of the key programs that provide a work-life balance are discussed in the following sections.

Flextime

Flextime is the practice of permitting employees to choose their own working hours, within certain limitations. For many old economy managers who think they must see their employees every minute to make sure they are working, this may be difficult. However, today, approximately 27.4 million employees have a flextime schedule.[74] According to the annual survey conducted by the Society of Human Resource Management, 57 percent of companies now offer flextime to some of their employees.[75] If you wonder why this is such an important benefit, consider the recent Harvard study that asked employees to list their most important job components. Number one on the list was, "having a work schedule that allows me to spend time with my family."[76]

In a flextime system, employees work the same number of hours per day as they would on a standard schedule. However, they work these hours within what is called a bandwidth, which is the maximum length of the workday (see Figure 10-4). Core time is that part of the day when all employees must be present. *Flexible time* is the period within which employees may vary their schedules. A typical schedule permits employees to begin work between 6:00 a.m. and 9:00 a.m. and to complete their workday between 3:00 p.m. and 6:00 p.m. Andy Brimble, head of IT at the Adult Learning Inspectorate, which won Best Place to Work in the central and local government sector, said, "We ensure that we have generous flexible hours, so staff work their 37 hours within a daily core. It has panned out well—for every person who needs to come in late after school drop-off, there is someone who wants to get in early to beat the traffic."[77]

Because flexible hours are highly valued in today's society, a flexible work schedule gives employers an edge in recruiting new employees and retaining highly qualified employees. Also, flextime allows employees to expand their opportunities. For example, it may be easier for them to continue their education than if they were on a traditional work schedule. The public also seems to reap benefits from flextime. Transportation services, recreational facilities, medical clinics, and other services can be better utilized by reducing competition for service at conventional peak times. Yet, flextime is not suitable for all types of organizations. For example, its use may be severely limited in assembly-line operations and companies utilizing multiple shifts.

Compressed Work Week

The **compressed work week** is an arrangement of work hours that permits employees to fulfill their work obligation in fewer days than the typical five-day work week. A common compressed work week is four 10-hour days. Of the 100 Best Companies to Work For, 81 used this form of the compressed work week, which is up from 25 in 1999.[78] Another form of the compressed work week is four nine-hour days and a half day on Friday. Some hospitals permit their registered nurses to work three 12-hour days.

Working under this arrangement, employees have reported greater job satisfaction. In addition, the compressed work week offers the potential for better use of leisure time for family life, personal business, and recreation. Employers in some instances have cited advantages such as increased productivity and reduced turnover and absenteeism. Other firms, however, have encountered difficulty in scheduling worker's hours and at times employees become fatigued from working longer hours. In some cases, these problems have resulted in lower product quality and reduced customer service.

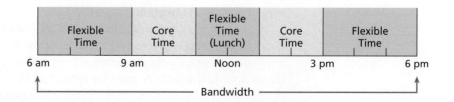

Figure 10-4 Illustration of Flextime

Job Sharing

Job sharing is an approach to work that is attractive to people who want to work fewer than 40 hours per week. It can also assist with child-care responsibilities. In **job sharing**, two part-time people split the duties of one job in some agreed-on manner and are paid according to their contributions.

Some have equated job sharing to running a marathon. Given an equal athletic ability, two runners running half a marathon back to back will invariably outrun one runner going the entire distance alone.[79] Today, job sharing is offered by 19 percent of employers, according to the Society for Human Resource Management's Benefits Survey Report.[80] Pat Katepoo, founder of WorkOptions.com, an online resource that helps professionals arrange flexible work schedules, says that "although the arrangements vary, the outcome is the same: Job sharing provides the flexibility to enjoy life."[81] As a means of encouraging older workers to remain on the job past retirement age, many companies are offering job sharing.[82] Sharing jobs has potential benefits that include the broader range of skills the partners bring to the job. For job sharing to work, however, the partners must be compatible, have good communication skills, and have a bond of trust with their manager. Job sharing also can pose challenges, including the need for additional oversight—such as conducting administrative tasks and performance reviews for two employees rather than one.[83]

Trends & Innovations

Two in a Box

Companies such as Intel Corporation and Goldman Sachs Group Inc., are giving two managers the same responsibilities and the same title and letting them decide how the work is to be divided (Two in a Box). Unlike job sharing, it is a full-time job for both managers. It certainly has some risk, as in the case of the 1998 DaimlerChrysler Corporation disaster of executive job sharing when one executives was unwilling to share authority resulting in the resignation of the other executive. A major advantage of this approach is that it can ease transition, permitting a manager to learn from a more experienced manager. It is also useful as managers confront the requirement of global traveling. One manager could be at the home office taking care of regular business while the other is traveling. Problems certainly can occur as the egos of two executives meet, but it has proven successful in certain instances; for example with Cisco Inc., a computer network equipment manufacturer. For two-and-a-half years, two executives shared a job as heads of Cisco's routing group. The two had complementary skills and each gained experience from the other. Intel typically combines a technically oriented manager with a business-oriented one. Certainly, the Two in a Box approach requires work and constant communication, but for the right two executives, the benefits derived are worth it.[84]

Another Two in a Box example occurred when Peter Chernin, the president of NewsCorp., and head of its Fox subsidiary, appointed Gary Newman and Dana Walden as presidents of 20th Century Fox Television. Both are responsible for the performance of the entire company. "What I was really thinking was where to find the skill set to manage these businesses," Chernin says. "I came to believe that, because of the complexity, if I could find two people with complementary skills, it would probably be better." Gary Newman said, "Because there are two of us, we're capable of getting involved in many more things. There's more productivity here than at any other company like this where there's only one person in charge," The arrangement has been great for their family lives. "There's no meeting that I can't cover or that Gary can't cover," Walden says.[85]

Examples of Executive Job Sharing

Job sharing normally occurs below executive ranks. However, this is not always the case. If job sharing were a category in the collection of *Guinness World Records*, top honors might go to Charlotte Schutzman and Sue Manix. The two women have shared many jobs during 16 years, surviving two corporate mergers and a relocation while earning two promotions in the process. Currently, Schutzman and Manix share the post of vice president of public affairs and communications at New York–based Verizon Communications Inc. Each works two days a week and on alternate Wednesdays. They talk by phone at least twice a week, and their close partnership has enabled them to stay on track professionally while raising their children—Manix has three, Schutzman has two. "It's been good for us, it's been good for the company," says Schutzman. "If we didn't job-share," she says, "we might have left."[86]

As another example, Sue Osborn and Susan Williams share the chief executive role at the National Patient Safety Agency (NPSA). They have been there since 2001, but they have been job-share partners since 1986. Before joining the NPSA, they were joint chief executives at Barking and Havering Authority. Each of them works three days a week, including Wednesdays, when they overlap. They talk to each other on the phone quite a lot and also leave detailed notes for each other.[87]

Telecommuting

Telecommuting:
Work arrangement whereby employees, called teleworkers or telecommuters, are able to remain at home (or otherwise away from the office) and perform their work using computers and other electronic devices that connect them with their offices.

Telecommuting is a work arrangement whereby employees, called teleworkers or telecommuters, are able to remain at home (or otherwise away from the office) and perform their work using computers and other electronic devices that connect them with their offices.

For self-motivated workers telecommuting can increase worker productivity and improve job satisfaction and loyalty.[88] Of the 100 Best Companies to Work For, 79 allow employees to telecommute or work at home on a regular basis at least 20 percent of their time. Only 18 companies on the list permitted telecommuting in 1999.[89] Modern communications and information technologies permit people to work just about anywhere. According to Kevin Shannon, executive director of the Association of Commuter Transportation in Atlanta, telecommuting has become more popular in recent years, thanks to traffic congestion, frustration with commuting, and more sophisticated broadband Internet and cell phone communication.[90] It is estimated that about 45 million American workers telecommute regularly, with about half working at home at least one day.[91]

Some companies have made parts of their workforce virtual. JetBlue broke new ground with its call center made up primarily of stay-at-home mothers. According to a case study by Blue Pumpkin, a workforce optimization supplier, JetBlue saw performance improvements that resulted in $1.2 million in benefits the first year.[92]

Telecommuters generally are information workers. They accomplish jobs that require, for example, analysis, research, writing, budgeting, data entry, or computer programming. Teleworkers also include illustrators, loan executives, architects, attorneys, and publishers. Employees can accomplish both training and job duties without losing either efficiency or quality by using the Internet. Thanks largely to telecommuting, when the New York City transit union went on strike in 2005, knowledge workers were able to work from home, which greatly lessened the effect of the strike.[93]

Another advantage of telecommuting is that it eliminates the need for office space. As one manager put it, "The expense of an employee is not just the person, it's also the fact that I pay $90,000 a year for the office that person sits in." Also, commuting distances are not a factor for teleworkers. The average time it takes to get to work continues to increase, which often contributes to tardiness and lost work hours.[94] Therefore, firms may hire the best available employees located virtually anywhere in the world for many jobs. The ability to utilize disabled workers and workers with small children further broadens the labor market.

Although telecommuting has many advantages, it also has some potential pitfalls. For example, it may weaken the ties between employees and their firms. In one survey, telecommuters reported feeling a time crunch and believed that the best assignments went to regular employees who were able to collaborate with colleagues face-to-face.[95] In addition, managers have to learn how to manage remotely, which is at times resisted. Also, some workers may be taking advantage of being out of sight to the boss. In a recent survey conducted by CareerBuilder.com, a large number confessed to working less than the normal eight-hour day; 25 percent disclosed that they spend less than one hour on company work with telecommuting.[96]

Firms considering telecommuting will need to think about changes in other policy areas as well. Questions such as the following should be addressed:

Telecommuting

http://www.telework.gov/

Governmental Website for employees who think they might like to telecommute (or are already doing so), for managers and supervisors who supervise teleworkers, and for agency telework coordinators.

- Will compensation and benefits be affected? If so, how?
- Who will be responsible for workers injured at home?
- What about the responsibility for purchasing and providing insurance coverage for equipment?
- How will taxes be affected by telecommuting?
- Will overtime be allowed?
- Will security be provided for the telecommuter's work? How?
- Will the firm have safety requirements for the home? Will OSHA be involved?

These kinds of questions seem to suggest that telecommuting poses insurmountable problems. Yet, there are sufficient examples of successful telecommuting to suggest that it can work effectively in certain environments.

Part-Time Work

In an *HRFocus* study, part-time work was listed as the most important flexible work option.[97] Part-time employees currently comprise 13.6 percent of the workforce, or about 19 million people. Workers in part-time jobs often receive substantially lower wages and benefits than workers in full-time jobs.[98] For example, Labor Department statistics show that part-time employees earn, on average, a 45 percent lower rate of pay than their equivalent full-time counterparts.[99] For some, however, the lower pay does not matter. In a recent survey, 89 percent of current workers said they expected to work part-time after they retire. Having a part-time job helps workers to make the transition from full-time employment, and part-time employment adds many highly qualified individuals to the labor market by permitting employees to address both job and personal needs.

For some organizations, the availability of part-time work provides a plus. According to research by the University of Chicago's Sloan Center on Parents, Children and Work, two-thirds of mothers who work full-time would prefer part-time employment, and about half of at-home mothers would prefer to be working part-time rather than staying out of the workforce. Both parties benefit when part-time employment does work out. Companies that offer part-time employment show increased rates of productivity and less employee turnover than other companies.[100]

KPMG and Ernst & Young are two companies with successful reduced workload models. Their programs are designed to take the stigma out of part-time work. At KPMG, the program ensures that part-time employees have the same opportunities for pay and career progression as their full-time counterparts. At Ernst & Young, all employees receive a laptop computer with 24/7 technical support so they can work whenever or wherever.[101]

Liza Warner, a financial advisor with Jefferson Wells International, works 30 hours a week in order to spend time with her two young sons. Of Wells's 2,000 employees, 10 percent work a flexible schedule, with benefits, like Warner. A further 20 percent work even fewer hours, project by project, without benefits. The remaining 70 percent are full-time, but still have a lot more control over their lives.[102]

A variation of part-time work is where companies permit selected workers who are typically older to split their work locations. Often professionals want to spend time in a better climate, or perhaps have a second home in Florida where they spend six months of the year. Rather than lose a valuable employee who has made a decision to relocate for the winter, companies are finding places for them at both locations. For example, a pharmacist working for a major company might work for six months in New York and six months in Cocoa Beach. Stephen Wing, who oversees the CVS stores, said, "Our older workers tend to be great at customer service and at teaching our younger folks. So it makes sense for us to be flexible and keep them on the job. Home Depot has set up "snowbird" employment programs to retain valuable employees.[103]

More Work, Fewer Hours

A variation of part-time work is where employees receive full-time pay and get more done in fewer hours. Sandy Burud, author of the book *Leveraging the New Human Capital*, did a case study of a Tennessee bank. The bank had an innovative arrangement where the employees got to set their own hours. By working more at busy times of the month, and less during the off periods, "they generated twice as much work with the same number of employees," she says. Plus, employees got extra days off during the down time—which, understandably, markedly increased their job satisfaction. That bank is a prime example of what is called the *corporate athlete paradigm*. One training habit of world-class athletes is that they have short periods of very demanding work, but "when they rest, they really rest."[104]

A Exemplary Work-Life Balance Program

Software giant SAS Institute Inc., has a culture that gives it a powerful competitive edge. The environment and benefits provided for employees are outstanding. To begin, the company's main campus offers day care as inexpensively as $250 per month; free access to a 36,000-square-foot gym; a putting green; sky-lit meditation rooms; and the services of a full-time, in-house elder-care consultant. The café also has a pianist at noon and baby seats so children in day care can lunch with their parents. Also available is free juice and soda for employees. There are subsidized cafeterias, casual dress every day, profit sharing (which has been 15 percent every year for 23 years), domestic partner benefits, unlimited sick days, free health insurance, an on-site medical clinic staffed by doctors and nurse practitioners, and free laundering of sweaty gym clothes overnight. There are soccer fields, baseball diamonds, co-ed workout areas, separate workout areas for men and women, and pool tables. Every white-collar employee has a private office and flexible work schedule with a standard 35-hour work week. All employees have three weeks' paid vacation plus the week off from Christmas to New Year's Day. After 10 years with the firm, employees get an additional week of paid vacation. What does all this amount to? SAS has a turnover rate that is never more than 5 percent a year compared to the industry average of over 20 percent. *Harvard Business Review* figured that SAS's low turnover saves the company $75 million a year.[105]

11 OBJECTIVE

Describe the concepts of severance pay, comparable worth, pay secrecy, and pay compression.

Other Compensation Issues

Several issues related to compensation deserve mention. These topics are examined next.

Severance Pay

Severance pay:
Compensation designed to assist laid-off employees as they search for new employment.

Severance pay is compensation designed to assist laid-off employees as they search for new employment. This factor is especially prominent during periods of downsizing. Although some firms are trimming the amount of severance pay offered, they typically offer one to two weeks of severance pay for every year of service, up to some predetermined maximum. The employee's organizational level generally determines the amount of severance pay. For example, nonmanagers may get eight or nine weeks of pay even if their length of service is greater than eight or nine years. Middle managers may receive 12 to 16 weeks.[106]

In spite of headlines describing executives leaving corporations with multimillion-dollar payouts, most companies send departing CEOs out the door with far less. For example, a recent survey found that most severance calculations still use the traditional measure of years of service. A little more than half (54 percent) of U.S. companies give two or more weeks of severance pay per year of service for senior executives.[107]

Comparable Worth

The comparable worth, or pay equity, theory extends the concept of the Equal Pay Act. While the Act requires equal pay for equal work, comparable worth advocates prefer a broader interpretation of requiring equal pay for comparable worth, even if market rates vary and job duties are considerably different. **Comparable worth** requires determination of the values of dissimilar jobs (such as company nurse and welder) by comparing them under some form of job evaluation, and the assignment of pay rates according to their evaluated worth. Although the Supreme Court has ruled the law does not require comparable worth, a number of state and local governments, along with some jurisdictions in Canada, have passed legislation mandating this version of pay fairness.

Comparable worth:
Determination of the values of dissimilar jobs (such as company nurse and welder) by comparing them under some form of job evaluation, and the assignment of pay rates according to their evaluated worth.

Comparable worth advocates argue the gap between male and female pay is the result of gender bias. Historically, they claim, employers set wages in various occupations based on mistaken stereotypes about women that have stuck over time, leaving the 60 percent of women who work in female-dominated occupations at a disadvantage.[108] Former Congressional Budget Office Director June O'Neill rebuts this notion because, she says, "it conveys the message that women cannot compete in nontraditional jobs and can only be helped through the patronage of a job evaluation."[109]

In the business world, comparable worth would create numerous difficulties. To implement such a system, it would require a reliable way to determine when completely different jobs have a comparable value. Experts cannot agree on any system that would intelligently do this. Remember that in the point system of job evaluation, separate job clusters were considered necessary because of the difficulty in relating dissimilar jobs in the same company. Comparable worth advocates envision comparing dissimilar jobs not only between job clusters in one firm but jobs between industries.

In addition, the concept of comparable worth is antithetical to our nation's free-market economic system. In this system, the market allocates scarce resources according to supply and demand. To implement comparable worth, a bureaucratic government would artificially establish pay levels for jobs it deems comparable. If the wages for scarce male-dominated jobs were artificially set below the level that the market would demand, labor shortages would result.

The goal of nondiscriminatory pay practices is one that every organization should seek to achieve for ethical and legal reasons. Whether comparable worth is an appropriate solution remains to be seen. If the past is any indication, the debate will continue as long as there is a disparity between the compensation of men and women.

Pay Secrecy

Approximately one-third of organizations in the private sector have specific rules prohibiting employees from discussing their wages with co-workers, known as pay secrecy/confidentiality rules (PSC).[110] The legal use of such rules is questionable, however, since the National Labor Relations Act protects workers' rights to engage in "concerted activity for the purpose of . . . mutual aid or protection." The NLRB has routinely found PSC rules unlawful.[111] If a firm's compensation plan is illogical, secrecy may indeed be appropriate because only a well-designed system can stand careful scrutiny. An open system would almost certainly require managers to explain the rationale for pay decisions to subordinates. Secrecy, however, can have some negative side effects, including a distortion of the actual rewards people receive. Secrecy also spawns a low-trust environment in which people have trouble understanding the relationship between pay and performance. In such an environment, an otherwise sound program loses its effectiveness.

Pay Compression

Pay compression:

Situation that occurs when less experienced employees are paid as much as or more than employees who have been with the organization a long time; this is due to a gradual increase in starting salaries and limited salary adjustment for long-term employees.

Pay compression occurs when less experienced employees are paid as much as or more than employees who have been with the organization a long time; this is due to a gradual increase in starting salaries and limited salary adjustment for long-term employees.[112]

This situation most likely occurs when labor market pay levels increase more rapidly than current employees' pay raises. Pay compression may also take place when firms make pay adjustments at the lower end of the job hierarchy without commensurate adjustments at the top. The explanation for this action may be the firm's need to meet market prices in retaining or hiring people with scarce skills and an inability to make needed adjustments elsewhere in the pay structure. There are numerous problems associated with pay compression. First, those who end up with less because of compression often feel that their tenure, experience, historical knowledge, and contributions have not been taken into account by the organization. Second, the old-timers may resent and refuse to help newcomers who are paid more, taking the attitude that if you pay them more, "let them earn their money." Finally, existing employees are more likely to leave if they feel unappreciated.[113] Unfortunately, no easy solution is available if a firm lacks the resources to maintain internal equity or believes that external equity should be of primary concern.

A Global Perspective

China's Work Week

The average worker in China does not have the same average work week as in the United States. Dong Ziaobo is a senior manager at a small, private provider of telecom software services in Beijing whose main client is China Mobile Ltd., the national carrier. Dong, 30 and unmarried, earns almost $2,000 a month, which is nearly twice what the average city worker earns. However, he works 60-hour, six-day weeks and he receives no overtime pay. "I have no choice but to work overtime," says Dong. "Anyway, it's my duty to work hard at my job."[114]

Liu Bo, a 31-year-old, has a very different work week. As one of 120 teachers at the Taiyuan Middle School, he works 40 hours over five days a week teaching history. He never works overtime. For this, the married Liu earns just under $200 a month. But he's happy with his employment. "I just want to keep teaching my students," says Liu, who adds that as a government-employed teacher he is assured of social welfare benefits such as medical care. "I like my job because I face little stress and can fully enjoy my free time," he says.[115]

According to a study by the International Labor Organization, the Chinese work week averages 44.6 hours. It makes a difference if a person is employed by the state with shorter hours, or in the private sector, where the average work week exceeds 46 hours. "Chinese, especially young people, are facing ever more pressure in their jobs," says Ma Mingjie, director of the Beijing-based China Youth Daily's Social Research Center. According to a survey by the center, 65.6 percent are working longer than eight-hour days, with 20 percent putting in more than 10 hours.[116]

One study found that over 50 percent of Chinese workers, unlike those in Japan and South Korea, do not get paid for overtime, according to Zeng Xiangquan, dean of the School of Labor & Human Resources at People's University and one of the authors of the study. "While blue-collar workers work long hours to earn more money, white-collars do so for less tangible goals such as promotion or personal satisfaction," says Zeng.[117]

Constance Thomas, director of the ILO Office for China and Mongolia in Beijing, said, "China's labor regulations are actually good—and pretty much in keeping with international norms." The laws mandate a 44-hour, five-day work week; two weeks of annual leave; regular holidays; and a minimum of one-and-a-half times pay for overtime. The mandated work hours are down from close to 50 hours in a six-day week before 1995. However, the law may not always be followed. "It's a big country with a lot of regions that still need to develop," Thomas says. "We see differences in how the labor law is applied."[118]

Summary

1. Define benefits.

Benefits include all financial rewards that generally are not paid directly to the employee.

2. Describe mandated (legally required) benefits.

Legally required benefits include Social Security retirement benefits, disability insurance, and survivors' benefits; Medicare; workers' compensation benefits; and unpaid leave, mandated by the Family and Medical Leave Act.

3. Explain the various discretionary benefits.

Categories of discretionary benefits include: payment for time not worked, health care, life insurance, retirement plans, disability protection, employee stock option plans (ESOPs), supplemental unemployment benefits (SUB), and employee services.

4. Describe customized benefit plans.

Customized benefit plans permit employees to make yearly elections to largely determine their benefit package by choosing between taxable cash and numerous benefits.

5. Explain premium pay.

Premium pay is compensation paid to employees for working long periods of time or working under dangerous or undesirable conditions.

6. Explain health care legislation.

The Consolidated Omnibus Budget Reconciliation Act was enacted to give employees the opportunity to temporarily continue their coverage, which they would otherwise lose because of termination, layoff, or other change in employment status. The Health Insurance Portability and Accountability Act provides protection for Americans who move from one job to another, who are self-employed, or who have pre-existing medical conditions. The Employee Retirement Income Security Act was passed to strengthen existing and future retirement programs. The Older Workers Benefit Protection Act is an amendment to the Age Discrimination in Employment Act and extends its coverage to all employee benefits. The Pension Protection Act (PPA) of 2006 is the most sweeping reform of America's pension laws in over 30 years.

7. Describe the components of nonfinancial compensation.

The components of nonfinancial compensation consist of the job itself and the job environment.

8. Describe the job itself as a nonfinancial compensation factor and job characteristics theory.

The job itself can be a very powerful factor in the compensation equation. Some jobs can be so stimulating that the incumbent is anxious to get to work each day. On the other hand, a job may be so boring or distasteful that an individual dreads going to work.

According to job characteristics theory, employees experience intrinsic compensation when their jobs rate high on five core job dimensions: skill variety, task identity, task significance, autonomy, and feedback. These characteristics create the potential for increased performance, lower absenteeism and turnover, and higher employee satisfaction.

9. Describe the job environment as a nonfinancial compensation factor.

The physical environment and the psychological climate are important factors. Employees can draw satisfaction from their work through several nonfinancial factors. Sound policies, capable managers, competent employees, congenial co-workers, appropriate status symbols, and working conditions are all important features.

10. Describe workplace flexibility (work-life balance) factors.

Workplace flexibility factors such as flextime; the compressed work week; job sharing; flexible compensation plans; telecommuting; part-time work; and more work, fewer hours are components of nonfinancial compensation.

11. Describe the concepts of severance pay, comparable worth, pay secrecy, and pay compression.

Compensation designed to assist laid-off employees as they search for new employment is referred to as severance pay. Comparable worth requires the value for dissimilar jobs, such as company nurse and welder, to be compared under some form of job evaluation, and pay rates for both jobs to be assigned according to their evaluated worth. With pay secrecy, organizations tend to keep their pay rates secret for various reasons. Pay compression occurs when less experienced employees are paid as much as or more than employees who have been with the organization a long time due to a gradual increase in starting salaries and limited salary adjustment for long-term employees.

Key Terms

- Benefits, 314
- Paid time off (PTO), 319
- Sabbaticals, 319
- Health maintenance organization (HMO), 321
- Preferred provider organization (PPO), 321
- Point-of-service (POS), 321
- Exclusive provider organization (EPO), 321
- Defined contribution health care plan, 321
- Health savings account (HSA), 321

- Flexible spending account (FSA), 322
- Defined benefit plan, 323
- Defined contribution plan, 324
- 401(k) plan, 324
- Cash balance plan, 325
- Employee stock option plan (ESOP), 325
- Supplemental unemployment benefits, 325
- Relocation benefits, 326
- Customized benefit plan, 327
- Premium pay, 328
- Hazard pay, 328
- Shift differential, 329

- Job characteristics theory, 332
- Skill variety, 332
- Task identity, 333
- Task significance, 333
- Autonomy, 333
- Feedback, 333
- Flextime, 336
- Compressed work week, 336
- Job sharing, 337
- Telecommuting, 338
- Severance pay, 341
- Comparable worth, 341
- Pay compression, 342

Questions for Review

1. Define benefits.
2. What are the legally required benefits? Briefly describe each.
3. What are the basic categories of voluntary benefits? Describe each.
4. What items are included in the voluntary benefit of payment for time not worked?
5. Define each of the following:
   a. Health maintenance organization (HMO)
   b. Preferred provider organization (PPO)
   c. Point-of-service (POS)
   d. Exclusive provider organization (EPO)
   e. Defined contribution health care system
   f. Health savings account (HSA)
   g. Flexible spending account (FSA)
6. There are numerous forms of retirement plans. Describe each of the following:
   a. Defined benefit plan
   b. Defined contribution plan
   c. 401(k) plan
   d. Cash balance plan
7. What is an employee stock option plan?
8. Distinguish among premium pay, hazard pay, and shift differential pay.
9. Define each of the following benefit laws:
   a. Consolidated Omnibus Budget Reconciliation Act of 1985
   b. Health Insurance Portability and Accountability Act of 1996

    c. Employee Retirement Income Security Act of 1974

    d. Older Workers Benefit Protection Act

10. What is job characteristics theory? What are the components of job characteristics theory?

11. What nonfinancial compensation factors are related to the job environment?

12. Define each the following workplace flexibility factors:

    a. Flextime

    b. Compressed work week

    c. Job sharing

    d. Telecommuting

13. Define each of the following:

    a. Severance pay

    b. Comparable worth

    c. Pay compression

HRM Incident 1

You're Doing a Great Job, Though

During a Saturday afternoon golf game with her friend Randy Dean, Ashley Aubert discovered that her department had hired a recent university graduate as a systems analyst at a starting salary almost as high as Ashley's. Although Ashley was good-natured, she was bewildered and upset. It had taken her five years to become a senior systems analyst and attain her current salary level at Trimark Data Systems. She had been generally pleased with the company and thoroughly enjoyed her job.

    The following Monday morning, Ashley confronted Dave Edwards, the human resource director, and asked if what she had heard was true. Dave apologetically admitted that it was and attempted to explain the company's situation "Ashley, the market for systems analysts is very tight, and in order for the company to attract qualified prospects, we have to offer a premium starting salary. We desperately needed another analyst, and this was the only way we could get one."

    Ashley asked Dave if her salary would be adjusted accordingly. Dave answered, "Your salary will be reevaluated at the regular time. You're doing a great job, though, and I'm sure the boss will recommend a raise." Ashley thanked Dave for his time, but left the office shaking her head and wondering about her future.

Questions

1. Do you think Dave's explanation was satisfactory? Discuss.

2. What action do you believe the company should have taken with regard to Ashley?

HRM Incident 2

A Benefits Package Designed for Whom?

Wayne McGraw greeted Robert Peters, his next interviewee, warmly. Robert had an excellent academic record and appeared to be just the kind of person Wayne's company, Beco Electric, was seeking. Wayne is the university recruiter for Beco and had already interviewed six graduating seniors at Centenary College.

    Based on the application form, Robert appeared to be the most promising candidate to be interviewed that day. He was 22 years old and had a 3.6 grade point average with a 4.0 in his major field, industrial management. Not only was Robert the vice president of the Student Government Association, but he was also activities chairman for Kappa Alpha Psi, a social fraternity. The reference letters in Robert's file revealed that he was both very active socially and a rather intense and serious student. One of the letters from Robert's employer during the previous summer expressed satisfaction with Robert's work habits.

    Wayne knew that discussion of benefits could be an important part of the recruiting interview. But he did not know which aspects of Beco's benefits program would appeal most to Robert. The company has an excellent profit-sharing plan, although 80 percent of profit distributions are deferred and included in each employee's retirement account. Health benefits are also good. It also has long-term care insurance. The company's medical and dental plan pays a significant portion of costs. A company lunchroom provides meals at about 70 percent of outside prices, although few managers take advantage of this. Employees get one week of paid vacation after the first year and two weeks after two years with the company. Two weeks are provided each year for sick leave. In addition, there are 12 paid holidays each year. Finally, the company encourages advanced education, paying for tuition and books in full, and, under certain circumstances, allowing time off to attend classes during the day. It also provides scholarships for dependents.

Questions

1. What aspects of Beco's benefits program are likely to appeal to Robert? Explain.

2. In today's work environment, what additional benefits might be more attractive to Robert? Explain.

Notes

1. Sandra Swanson, "Sound Hokey? Employers Trout Out Quirky Perks," *Crain's Chicago Business* 28 (February 14, 2005): 32–33.

2. Ibid.

3. Ron Scherer, "Now Hiring: The Hot Jobs of the Moment," *Christian Science Monitor* 97 (May 19, 2005): 1–2.

4. "Juggling Work with Life," *Graphic Arts Monthly* (February 2005): S14–S15.

5. Kathy Gurchiek, "ID Theft Services Emerge as New Employee Benefit," *HR Magazine* 50 (October 2005): 29–32.

6. Elka Jones, "An Overview of Employee Benefits," *Occupational Outlook Quarterly* 49 (Summer 2005): 12–21.

7. Mary Slepicka, "What Employee Benefits Cost You," *Dealernews* 41 (October 2005): 46–54.

8. "Towers Predicts 2006 Health Benefits Costs at $8,424 per Staffer," *Controller's Report* 2006 (January 2006): 1–3.

9. "The 2005 Annual Social Security and Medicare Trust Fund Reports," *Pension Benefits* 14 (May 2005): 2–4.

10. Ibid.

11. Carolyn Hirchman, "Employees' Choice," *HR Magazine* 51 (February 2006): 95–100.

12. "Transportation: The Latest 'Hot' Benefit," *HR Focus* 83 (July 2006): 12.

13. "Employees Value Paid Vacation Time More Than Other Benefits, Data Show," *Compensation & Benefits for Law Offices* 5 (May 2005): 7.

14. Lynn Gresham, "When Employees Give Too Much," *Employee Benefit News* 18 (July 2004): 9.

15. Kathy Gurchiek, "Workers Find It Hard to Let Go," *HR Magazine* 50 (August 2005): 30–34.

16. "Recruitment & Retention Strategy: Give Employees the Benefits They Want," *Contractors Business Management Report* 2006 (January 2006): 1–12.

17. Diane Cadrain, "Employers Find Smooth Sailing in PTO Waters," *HR Magazine* 50 (September 2005): 29–41.

18. *Ibid.*

19. Stephanie Overman, "Sabbaticals Benefit Companies as Well as Employees," *Employee Benefit News* 20 (April 2006): 56–58.

20. Michael Arndt, "Nice Work If You Can Get It," *Business Week* (January 9, 2006): 56–57.

21. Kelly M. Butler, "Faced with Worker Burnout Employers Pay Employees to Get Away," *Employee Benefit News* 19 (June 1, 2005): 55–56.

22. Repps Hudson, "Leaves of Absence Can Recharge a Worker or Drain a Career," *St. Louis Post-Dispatch* (February 19, 2002): 1.

23. Ibid.

24. "Top Trends Cited by HR Pros: Competition, Health Care, Staffing," *HR Focus* 83 (August 2006): 8.

25. Slepicka, "What Employee Benefits Cost You."

26. Fareed Zakaria, "How We Drive Our Jobs Away," *Newsweek* 145 (April 18, 2005): 43.

27. Geoffrey Colvin, "The Doctor Is Out," *Fortune (Europe)* 152 (October 14, 2005): 44.

28. Gina Ruiz, "AOL Founder Champions a Revolution in Health Care,"*Workforce Management* 85 (February 13, 2006): 51–53.

29. "HSA Update: What's Working, What's the Prognosis," *HR Focus* 82 (October 2005): 5–6.

30. Joanne Wojcik, "Enrollment Changes Seen as Undermining NCQA Quality Effort," *Business Insurance* 39 (October 10, 2005): 1–41.

31. "Good News About Consumer-Directed Health Plans," *HR Focus* 83 (June 2006): 6–7.

32. Gina Ruiz, "AOL Founder Champions a Revolution in Health Care," *Workforce Management* 85 (February 13, 2006): 51–53.

33. Leah Carlson Shepherd, "As HSAs Grow, Leaders Debate Accounts' Effectiveness," *Employee Benefit News* 20 (April 2006): 30.

34. Dave Willis, "Trends in Health Insurance," *Advisor Today* 101 (March 2006): 49–51.

35. Kathy Gurchiek, "Explosion of HSAs Foreseen in 2006," *HR Magazine* 50 (July 2005): 30.

36. Jennifer Pellet, "Savings Grace," *Entrepreneur* 34 (January 2006): 56.

37. Susan J. Wells, "The Doctor Is In-House," *HR Magazine* 51 (April 2006): 48–54.

38. Ibid.

39. John E. Dicken, "Overview of the Long-Term Care Partnership Program: GAO-05-1021," *GAO Reports* (October 11, 2005): 1, 37.

40. Kimberly Lankford, "A Fresh Look at Long Term Care," *Kiplinger's Personal Finance* 60 (May 2006): 92–93.

41. "IBM Pensions Are the Latest Defined Benefits Plans Casualties," *HR Focus* 83 (April 2006): 12.

42. Jenna Gottlieb, "Verizon Move Seen as New Blow to DB Funds," *Pensions & Investments* 33 (December 12, 2005): 6–41.

43. Alan Glickstein and Kevin Wagner, "Reassessing Retirement Plans: Five Aspects to Consider," *Employee Benefit News* 20 (August 2006): 56–57.

44. Jerry Geisel, "Employers Fear Retiree Funds Lacking," *Business Insurance* 40 (April 3, 2006): 16.

45. "Workers Contributing Less to 401(k) Plans, Six-Year Study on Participation Rates Show," *Managing 401(k) Plans* 2006 (April 2006): 9.

46. Eugene C. Gordon and Lance Wallach, "Cash Balance Plans Might Enhance Clients' Retirement," *Accounting Today* 21 (April 3, 2006): 18–19.

47. John A. Turner, "Are Cash Balance Plans Defined Benefit or Defined Contribution Plans?" *Benefits Quarterly* 19 (Second Quarter 2003): 71.

48. Ann Pomeroy, "Money Talks," *HR Magazine* 50 (July 2005): 46–51.

49. "Smooth Moves," *Workforce Management* 85 (February 13, 2006): 33–34.

50. John Marvin, "Dollars and Sense of Backup Child Care: When Is It the Right Choice?" *Employee Benefit News* 19 (April 15, 2005): 46–48.

51. Patrick J. Kiger, "A Case for Child Care," *Workforce Management* 83 (April 2004): 34–40.

52. Marvin, "Dollars and Sense of Backup Child Care: When Is It the Right Choice?"

53. Matt Bloch, "Bearing Fruit," *HR Magazine* 51 (March 2006): 56–60.

54. Robert Levering and Milton Moskowitz, "100 Best Companies to Work For," *Fortune* 147 (January 20, 2003): 140.

55. Charlotte Garvey, "Access to the Law," *HR Magazine* 47 (September 2002): 83.

56. Nancy Hatch Woodward, "Helping Workers Pay College Costs," *HR Magazine* 50 (August 2005): 74–82.

57. Ibid.

58. *U.S. Statutes at Large* 88, Part I, 93rd Congress, 2nd Session, 1974: 833.

59. Maria Greco Danaher, "Legalese May Nullify a Release of ADEA Claims," *HR Magazine* 50 (August 2005): 117–118.

60. Jerry Kinard and Brian R. Kinard, "Who's Rights Were Trampled?" *Supervision* 66 (June 2005): 3–5.

61. http://hr.cch.com/pension/protection-act/default.asp?cID=Y5230, August 17, 2006.

62. Dagmara Scalise, "Happy Workers," *H&HN: Hospitals & Health Networks* 80 (March 2006): 28–30.

63. Adapted from Frederick Herzberg, *Work and the Nature of Man* (Cleveland: World, 1966): 91–106.

64. Adapted from Craig J. Cantoni, "Learn to Manage Pay and Performance Like an Entrepreneur," *Compensation & Benefits Review* 29 (January/February 1997): 52–58.

65. J. R. Hackman and G. R. Oldham, *Work Redesign* (Reading, MA: Addison-Wesley, 1980).

66. Ed Frauenheim, "Studies: More Workers Look to Switch Jobs," *Workforce Management* 85 (February 13, 2006): 12.

67. "No Surprises, Work/Life Balance Is Not Just a Woman's Issue," *Compensation & Benefits for Law Offices* 6 (May 2006): 4–6.

68. Karen Kornbluh, "The Joy of Flex," *Washington Monthly* 37 (December 2005): 30–31.

69. Nichole L. Torres, "Perking Up," *Entrepreneur* 34 (April 2006): 30.

70. "'Emergent' Workers Make Up One-Third of Workforce," *HR Magazine* 51 (January 2006): 16.

71. "Employers Work to Retain Staff, Despite Rise in Job Seeking," *HR Focus* 84 (January 2006): 8.

72. "Retention Takes Center Stage Again as More Employees Plot a Move," *Compensation & Benefits for Law Offices* 6 (January 2006): 7.

73. Laura Demars, "Finders Keepers," *CFO* 22 (February 2006): 8–9.

74. Kathy Gurchiek, "Fewer Workers Use Flexible Schedules," *HR Magazine* 50 (September 2005): 30–36.

75. Chris Taylor, "Life in the Balance," *Incentive* 179 (January 2005): 16–19.

76. Joel Schettler, "A New Social Contract," *Training* 39 (April 2002): 62.

77. Julia Vowler, "Flexible Working Makes Everyone a Winner," *Computer Weekly* (March 29, 2005): 22.

78. "Live a Little!" *Fortune* 153 (January 23, 2006): 102.

79. Steve Davolt, "Lightening Workload Heightens Job Satisfaction, Productivity," *Employee Benefit News* 20 (April 2006): 19.

80. Carolyn Hirschman, "Share and Share Alike," *HR Magazine* 50 (September 2005): 52–57.

81. Marcia A. Reed-Woodward, "Share and Share Alike," *Black Enterprise* 36 (April 2006): 63.

82. Melissa Hennessy, "The Retirement Age," *CFO* 20 (February 2006): 42–45.

83. Ibid.

84. Scott Thurm, "Power-Sharing Prepares Managers," *Wall Street Journal* (December 5, 2005): B4.

85. Jody Miller and Matt Miller, "Get a Life," *Fortune* 152 (November 28, 2005): 109–124.

86. Ibid.

87. Jane Simms, "Who Job Shares Wins? *Director* 59 (January 2006): 48–52.

88. Barbara Gomolski, "Confessions of a Full-Time Telecommuter," *Computerworld* 40 (February 27, 2006): 46.

89. "Live a Little!"

90. "Telework Seen as Helpful to Employers, Yet Full-Time," *HR Focus* 82 (June 2005): 8–9.

91. Ed Frauenheim, "Telecommuting Cutbacks at HP Represent Shift," *Workforce Management* 85 (June 26, 2006): 4–6.

92. "Virtual Work: It's Not Just for Members of the Jedi Council," *T+D* 59 (August 2005): 12–13.

93. Coreen Bailor, "NYC Rides with Telecommuting," *CRM Magazine* 10 (March 2006): 11–12.

94. "Employers That Offer Commuting Options Can Reap Many Benefits," *HR Focus* 82 (February 2005): 9.

95. Edward Prewitt, "Flextime and Telecommuting," *CIO* (April 15, 2002): 130.

96. Kelley M. Butler, "Survey Results Report Productivity Lag Among Teleworkers," *Employee Benefit News* 20 (March 2006): 56.

97. "Flexible Work Grows as a Work/Life Solution," *HR Focus* 81 (October 2004): S1–S4.

98. Barry T. Hirsch, "Why Do Part-Time Workers Earn Less? The Role of Workers and Job Skills," *Industrial & Labor Relations Review* 58 (July 2005): 525–551.

99. Beth Joyner Waldron, "Help Mothers by Removing Obstacles to Part-Time Work," *USA Today* (February 29, 2004): News, 13a.

100. Ibid.

101. Ibid.

102. Nanette Byrnes, "Treating Part-Timers like Royalty," *Business Week* (October 10, 2005): 78.

103. "For Some Folks, Where to Work Is a Split Decision," *AARP Bulletin* 47 (June 2006): 4.

104. Taylor, "Life in the Balance."

105. Charles Fishman, "Moving Toward a Balanced Work Life," *Workforce* 79 (March 2000): 39–40.

106. Louis Kickhofel "How to Land on Your Own Two Feet," *Money* 34 (September 2005): 96.

107. "Severance Is Lower Yet Still Exceeds Mid-1990s," *HR Focus* 82 (November 2005): 12.

108. Amy Gluckman, "Comparable Worth," *Dollars & Sense* (September 1, 2002): 42.

109. Diana Furchtgoff-Roth, "Comparable Worth Is Back," *The American Spectator* 33 (September 2000): 38.

110. Leonard Bierman and Rafael Gely, "'Love, Sex and Politics? Sure. Salary? No Way': Workplace Social Norms and the Law," *Berkeley Journal of Employment & Labor Law* 25 (2004): 168.

111. Ibid., 169.

112. Susan Ladika, "Decompressing Pay," *HR Magazine* (December 2005): 79–81.

113. "How to Avoid 'Fallout' from Pay Compression," *HR Focus* 81 (November 2004): 3–4.

114. Dexter Roberts, "A Long March for Workers," *Business Week* (October 10, 2005): 66–67.

115. Ibid.

116. Ibid.

117. Ibid.

118. Ibid.

PART SIX

Safety and Health

CHAPTER OBJECTIVES

After completing this chapter, students should be able to:

1 Describe the nature and role of safety and health.

2 Explain the role of the Occupational Safety and Health Administration.

3 Describe the economic impact of safety and explain the focus of safety programs in business operations.

4 Describe the consequences of repetitive stress injuries.

5 Explain the purpose of ergonomics.

6 Explain the effects of workplace and domestic violence on businesses.

7 Describe the nature of stress and means of managing stress.

8 Explain burnout.

9 Describe the purposes of wellness programs.

10 Describe the importance of physical fitness programs.

11 Explain substance abuse and describe substance-abuse-free workplaces.

12 Describe employee assistance programs.

13 Describe the impact of smoke-free workplaces.

A Safe and Healthy Work Environment

A New Security Threat: Identity Theft

Identity theft has become a harsh reality for today's employers, especially human resources professionals, since employment records contain just about everything an identity thief could want to know about an individual.[1] Identity fraud has emerged as the dominant crime of the twenty-first century with losses totaling $52.6 billion and affecting 9.3 million people each year.[2] A large percentage of identity theft occurs at work. For example, trouble began at Ligand Pharmaceuticals, Inc., in San Diego, when an employee stumbled across a box in a storage closet. Inside she found the personnel records of 38 former employees of a firm that Ligand had acquired a few years earlier. Using the information from these files, including names, addresses, Social Security numbers, birth dates, and other information, the employee and her partners in crime fraudulently rented three apartments, operated 20 cellular telephone accounts, and established more than 25 credit card accounts. Then they proceeded to buy $100,000 in goods.[3]

Identity theft artists are now contacting job hunters who have posted résumés on Websites. They make a fake job offer and then ask for a Social Security number and birth date, saying that they need it to conduct a background check. Consider the case of Bob Knoe, a senior marketing executive with 22 years' experience, who had spent several months looking for a new position. He posted his résumé on the Web and one day he received a call from a person who said he was an HR director with a well-known company. The person said he was impressed with the résumé Bob had posted and wanted to meet with him as soon as possible since there appeared to be a perfect match. The HR person said that they needed to get the background check done as soon as possible. A very detailed form was e-mailed to Bob with requests for Social Security number, date of birth, mother's maiden name, even a bank account number. Bob completed the form but did not hear back from the person and became nervous. He tried to get in touch with the individual and could not. Then he tried to use one of his credit cards and discovered that not only was the account maxed out, but several new accounts had been opened in his name and emptied.[4] Certainly, Bob should not have given out this personal information until he was sure that he was dealing with a legitimate company.[5]

Identity theft impacts approximately one out of every eight adults living in the United States today. In some states it is even higher, for example, in Arizona where identity theft impacts one in six adults.[6] The crime has become so widespread that consumer protection agencies and the financial industry have created a standard checklist of steps victims can take to clear their name. In addition to injuring victims psychologically, identity theft is also expensive. Victims spend an average of 81 hours trying to undo the damage, according to Nationwide Mutual Insurance, and 28 percent of those polled had been unable to restore their identity, even after trying for more than a year.[7]

Congress passed the Identity Theft and Assumption Deterrence Act in 1988 that makes it a federal crime when anyone knowingly transfers or uses, without lawful authority, a means of identification of another person with the intent to commit, or to aid or abet, any unlawful activity that constitutes a violation of federal law. In 2005, the FTC's Disposal Rule, the outcome of the Fair and Accurate Credit Transactions Act (FACTA) of 2003, went into effect, requiring businesses and individuals to take appropriate measures to dispose of sensitive information derived from consumer reports. FACTA is specifically directed at information used to establish eligibility for employment, credit, or insurance, among other uses.[8] But, identity theft crimes continue to occur.

This chapter begins by discussing the problems associated with identity theft. Next, the nature and role of safety and health and the role of the Occupational Safety and Health Administration are discussed. The economic impact of safety and the focus of safety programs in business operations are presented next, and the consequences of repetitive stress injuries and the purpose of ergonomics are discussed. An explanation of the effect of workplace and domestic violence on businesses follows. The nature of stress and burnout is then described, as are the sources and means of coping with stress. Following this, the purposes of wellness programs and the importance of physical fitness programs are described, and substance abuse, substance-abuse-free workplaces, the rationale for employee assistance programs, and the impact of smoking in the workplace are discussed. This chapter concludes with a Global Perspective entitled "Global Safety Programs."

1 OBJECTIVE

Describe the nature and role of safety and health.

Safety:
Protection of employees from injuries caused by work-related accidents.

Health:
Employees' freedom from physical or emotional illness.

Nature and Role of Safety and Health

In our discussion, **safety** involves protecting employees from injuries caused by work-related accidents. Included within the umbrella definition of safety are factors related to repetitive stress injuries and workplace and domestic violence. **Health** refers to employees' freedom from physical or emotional illness. Problems in these areas can seriously affect a worker's productivity and quality of work life. They can dramatically lower a firm's effectiveness and employee morale. In fact, job-related injuries and illnesses are more common than most people realize.

Occupational Safety and Health Administration

The Occupational Safety and Health Act of 1970 created the Occupational Safety and Health Administration (OSHA). OSHA aims to ensure worker safety and health in the United States by working with employers and employees to create better working environments. The Act requires employers to provide employees a safe and healthy place to work and this responsibility extends to providing *safe employees*. The courts have reasoned that a dangerous worker is comparable to a defective machine. Specifically, employers have a responsibility under the *general duty clause* of the Occupational Safety and Health Act to furnish a workplace free from recognized hazards that are causing or are likely to cause death or serious physical harm.

Since its inception, OSHA has helped to cut workplace fatalities by more than 60 percent and occupational injury and illness rates by 40 percent. At the same time, U.S. employment has more than doubled from 56 million workers at 3.5 million work sites to 147 million workers at 7.2 million sites. To handle this workload, OSHA has more than 2,220 employees, including 1,100 inspectors.[9]

The current stated mission of OSHA is to promote and assure workplace safety and health and reduce workplace fatalities, injuries, and illnesses.[10] According to its five-year strategic management plan, OSHA is committed to focusing its resources on achieving three goals: (1) reduce occupational hazards through direct intervention; (2) promote a safety and health culture through compliance assistance, cooperative programs, and strong leadership; and (3) maximize OSHA's effectiveness and efficiency by strengthening its capabilities and infrastructure.[11] Specifically, during the five-year span from 2003 to 2008, OSHA is committed to reducing the rate of workplace fatalities by at least 15 percent and reducing the rate of workplace injuries and illnesses by at least 20 percent.[12] To achieve these goals, OSHA is focusing on specific, incremental improvements each year. Recently, the target was a 3 percent drop in construction fatalities and a 1 percent drop in general industry fatalities. With respect to injuries and illnesses, the agency is seeking a 4 percent drop in construction, general industry, and the following industries with high hazard rates: landscaping/horticultural services; oil and gas field services; fruit and vegetable processing; concrete and concrete products; blast furnace and basic steel products; ship- and boat-building and repair; and public warehousing and storage.[13]

OSHA's current thrust is to give employers a choice between partnership and traditional enforcement, to inject common sense into regulation and enforcement, and to eliminate red tape. The overall purpose, of course, is to reduce injuries, illnesses, and fatalities. To help small businesses, OSHA is expanding its assistance, reducing penalties, and putting more of its informational materials in electronic formats such as DVDs and Internet sites. OSHA has emphasized that these firms will not be punished for violations if they seek OSHA's assistance in correcting problems.[14] OSHA has formed agreements with a number of companies to promote increased safety education and outreach.

Even though OSHA would like a successful partnership relationship to exist, at times penalties must be given. Financial penalties serve as reminders to industry of the benefits of maintaining safe and healthy working conditions. A serious hazard citation has a maximum penalty of $7,000. A willful citation might have a maximum amount of $70,000 per violation. Calculated instance-by-instance, if 10 employees were exposed to one hazard the employer intentionally did not eliminate, the penalty amount would immediately jump to $700,000. Repeat citations also have a maximum penalty amount of $70,000 per violation. Significant costs for workers' compensation insurance, the expense of training new workers, and the fact that risky jobs command higher pay also keep safety and health issues on managers' minds.

OSHA has authorized stricter enforcement measures for manufacturers and other employers that repeatedly violate health and safety standards. This policy will increase oversight of firms that have received *high gravity* citations, which may include charges of willful violations and a failure to correct previously noted hazards. OSHA is increasingly cooperating with the EPA's more robust enforcement program to mount criminal prosecutions against employers where fatalities are involved.[15] This policy will put more teeth in enforcement practices but it will not change the emphasis on improving compliance assistance and reducing reliance on OSHA fines.

The average employer will not likely see an OSHA inspector unless an employee instigates an inspection. About 70 percent of OSHA inspections have resulted from employee complaints. When OSHA inspectors come to a site, the employer has the option of denying the inspector access to the work site. In such cases, OSHA would be required to get a warrant to proceed with the inspection. If the employer refuses access to view certain documents, OSHA must obtain an administrative subpoena.

Under the Occupational Safety and Health Act, an employee can legally refuse to work when the following conditions exist:

- The employee reasonably fears death, disease, or serious physical harm.
- The harm is imminent.
- There is too little time to file an OSHA complaint and get the problem corrected.
- The worker has notified the employer about the condition and requested correction of the problem, but the employer has not taken action.

General perceptions of OSHA have not always been positive. However, it appears that OSHA has overcome most of the past criticisms. A Gallup survey of nearly 2,500 workers found they were very satisfied or satisfied with their dealings with the agency. More than 87 percent of workers and employers rated OSHA staff professionalism, competence, and knowledge as satisfactory.[16] Janice Ochenkowski, vice president of external affairs for the Risk & Insurance Management Society, Inc., said, "We're very pleased with the direction that OSHA is taking . . . it's great that OSHA continues to strive to work with American businesses to make workplaces safer."[17] Older HR types can remember a time when few people representing industry would have made such a statement.

<table>
<tr><td>**3**   **OBJECTIVE**</td></tr>
</table>

Describe the economic impact of safety and explain the focus of safety programs in business operations.

Safety: The Economic Impact

Job-related deaths and injuries of all types extract a high toll not only in terms of human misery, but also in economic loss. The significant financial costs are often passed along to the consumer in the form of higher prices. Thus, job-related deaths and injuries affect everyone, directly or indirectly. Safety risks can be significant for employers. In addition to workers' compensation costs, OSHA can levy major fines. Indirect costs related to turnover and lost productivity add to the expense. The rate of growth in the cost of workplace injuries has slowed significantly. However, the cost remains high. Recently, employers spent $50.8 billion on wage payments and medical care for workers hurt on the job.[18] The top leading causes of workplace injuries and their associated costs include: overexertion ($13.4 billion), falls on the same level ($6.9 billion), bodily reaction (injuries from bending, climbing, slipping, or tripping without falling) ($5.1 billion), falls to lower level ($4.6 billion), and struck by object ($4.3 billion).[19]

Companies have come a long way in recognizing the importance and cost benefits of safety. Workplaces are safer, thanks to efforts of employers, insurance companies, unions, and state and federal agencies. Safety professionals strive for lower workers' compensation costs as do insurance companies, who work to keep both their clients' and their own costs down. In a recent survey of senior financial executives, more than

60 percent report that for each $1 invested in injury prevention, returns are $2 or more.[20]

According to the Bureau of Labor Statistics' Census of Fatal Occupational Injuries (CFOI), both workplace fatalities and fatality rates increased slightly in 2004 (the latest date that figures are available). Workplace fatalities increased to 5,703 in 2004 from 5,575 reported in 2003. Fatal workplace injury rates also increased slightly to 4.1 deaths per 100,000 workers from 4.0 in 2003, the first increase since 1994.[21] Some people may be surprised to discover that motor vehicle accidents are the number-one cause of death on the job. Of the preventable deaths occurring on the job, 2,000 of these were the result of a motor vehicle collision.[22]

Focus of Safety Programs

Faulty management safety policies and decisions, personal factors, and environmental factors are the basic causes of accidents. These factors result in unsafe working conditions and/or unsafe employee actions. Every employer needs to have a comprehensive safety program in place regardless of the degree of danger involved. Safety programs may accomplish their purposes in two primary ways: one focusing on *unsafe employee actions* and the other on *unsafe working conditions*.

Unsafe Employee Actions

Training and orientation of new employees emphasizing safety is especially important. The early months of employment are often critical because work injuries decrease with length of service. The first approach in a safety program is to create a psychological environment and employee attitudes that promote safety. When workers consciously or subconsciously think about safety, accidents decline. This attitude must permeate the firm's operations, and a strong company policy emphasizing safety and health is crucial. For example, a major chemical firm's policy states: "It is the policy of the company that every employee be assigned to a safe and healthful place to work. We strongly desire accident prevention in all phases of our operations. Toward this end, the full cooperation of all employees will be required." As the policy infers, no individual employee has the task of making the workplace safe. Although there is danger that everyone's responsibility will become no one's responsibility, a truly safe environment takes the effort of everyone from top management to the lowest-level employee. Although every individual in a firm should be encouraged to come up with solutions to potential safety problems, the firm's managers must take the lead. Management's unique role is clear since OSHA places primary responsibility for employee safety on the employer.

Ethical Dilemma

Illegal Dumping

You have just become aware that the company that disposes of your plant waste is not following Environmental Protection Agency guidelines. The firm is dumping toxic waste at night in a closed landfill six miles from the plant. To make matters worse, your brother-in-law operates the waste disposal company. You have already warned him once, and you have just learned that he is still illegally dumping. You confront him, telling him that you are going to use the hotline to report him if he illegally dumps waste one more time, but he threatens to implicate you if you blow the whistle.

What would you do?

Unsafe Working Conditions

The second approach to safety program design is to develop and maintain a safe physical working environment. Here, altering the environment becomes the focus for preventing accidents. Even if Joe, a machine operator, has been awake all night with a sick child and can barely keep his eyes open, the safety devices on his machine will help protect him. Management should create a physical environment in which accidents cannot occur. It is in this area that OSHA has had its greatest influence.

Developing Safety Programs

Workplace accident prevention requires safety program planning. Plans may be relatively simple, as for a small retail store, or more complex and highly sophisticated, as for a large automobile assembly plant. Regardless of the organization's size, the support of top management is essential if safety programs are to be effective. Top executives in a firm must be aware of the tremendous human suffering and economic losses that can result from accidents.

Table 11-1 shows some of the reasons for top management's support of a safety program. This information suggests that the lost productivity of a single injured worker is not the only factor to consider. Every phase of human resource management is involved. For instance, the firm may have difficulty in recruitment if it gains a reputation for being an unsafe place to work. Employee relations erode if workers believe that management does not care enough about them to provide a safe workplace. Firms will see an increase in compensation costs when they must pay a premium to attract qualified applicants and retain valued employees. Maintaining a stable workforce may become very difficult if employees perceive their workplace as hazardous.

Job hazard analysis (JHA):
Multistep process designed to study and analyze a task or job and then break down that task into steps that provide a means of eliminating associated hazards.

Job Hazard Analysis. The main goal of safety and health professionals is to prevent job-related injuries and illnesses. Firms achieve this goal in several ways: by educating workers in the hazards associated with their work, installing engineering controls, defining safe work procedures, and prescribing appropriate personal protective equipment. **Job hazard analysis (JHA)** is a multistep process designed to study and analyze a task or job and then break down that task into steps that provide a means of eliminating associated hazards.

Table 11-1 Reasons for Management Support of a Safety Program

- **Personal loss.** The physical pain and mental anguish associated with injuries are always unpleasant and may even be traumatic for an injured worker. Of still greater concern is the possibility of permanent disability or even death.
- **Financial loss to injured employees.** Most employees are covered by company insurance plans or personal accident insurance. However, an injury may result in financial losses not covered by insurance.
- **Lost productivity.** When an employee is injured, there will be a loss of productivity for the firm. In addition to obvious losses, there are often hidden costs. For example, a substitute worker may need additional training to replace the injured employee. Even when another worker is available to move into the injured employee's position, efficiency may suffer.
- **Higher insurance premiums.** Workers' compensation insurance premiums are based on the employer's history of insurance claims. The potential for savings related to employee safety provides a degree of incentive to establish formal programs.
- **Possibility of fines imprisonment.** Since the enactment of the Occupational Safety and Health Act, a willful and repeated violation of its provisions may result in serious penalties for the employer.
- **Social responsibility.** Many executives feel responsible for the safety and health of their employees. A number of firms had excellent safety programs years before OSHA existed. They understand that a safe work environment is not only in the best interests of the firm; providing one is the right thing to do.

JHA can have a major impact on safety performance. It results in a detailed written procedure for safely completing many tasks within a plant. A successful JHA program features several key components: management support, supervisor and employee training, written program, and management oversight. OSHA publication 3071 (2002 Revised), *Job Safety Hazard Analysis*, is a good primer on performing a JHA.

Superfund Amendments Reauthorization Act, Title III (SARA). SARA requires businesses to communicate more openly about the hazards associated with the materials they use and produce and the wastes they generate.[23] Although SARA has been around for several years, some firms do not yet have a satisfactory program for it in place. The hazard communication standard often leads the list of OSHA violations since the top category for OSHA citations is for no written hazard communication program. Dealing with this standard appears to be relatively simple and inexpensive, except when organizations ignore its provisions.

Employee Involvement. One way to strengthen a safety program is to include employee input, which provides workers with a sense of accomplishment. To prevent accidents, each worker must make a personal commitment to safe work practices. A team concept, where employees watch out for each other as a moral obligation, is a worthy goal. Supervisors can show support for the safety program by conscientiously enforcing safety rules and by closely conforming to the rules themselves. Participation in such teams helps form positive attitudes, and employees develop a sense of ownership of the program. Involved employees may become concerned with not only safety issues but also ways to improve productivity.

Safety Engineer. In many companies, one staff member coordinates the overall safety program. Such titles as *safety engineer* and *safety director* are common. One of the safety engineer's primary tasks is to provide safety training for company employees. This involves educating line managers about the merits of safety, and recognizing and eliminating unsafe situations. Although the safety engineer operates essentially in an advisory capacity, a well-informed and assertive person in this capacity may exercise considerable influence in the organization. Some major corporations also have *risk management departments* that anticipate losses associated with safety factors and prepare legal defenses in the event of lawsuits.

Accident Investigation

Accidents can happen even in the most safety-conscious firms. Whether or not an accident results in an injury, an organization should carefully evaluate each occurrence to determine its cause and to ensure that it does not recur. The safety engineer and the line supervisor jointly investigate accidents. One of the responsibilities of any supervisor is to prevent accidents. To do so, the supervisor must learn, through active participation in the safety program, why accidents occur, how they occur, where they occur, and who is involved. Supervisors gain a great deal of knowledge about accident prevention by helping to prepare accident reports. Most employers will mail or electronically transmit records of occupational injuries and illnesses directly to OSHA. The OSHA Form 300 is a log of work-related injuries and illnesses[24] (see Figure 11-1).

Evaluation of Safety Programs

Perhaps the best indicator of a successful safety program is a reduction in the *frequency* and *severity* of injuries and illnesses. Therefore, statistics including the number of injuries and illnesses (frequency rate) and the amount of work time lost (severity rate) are often used in program evaluation. OSHA metrics currently in use are: total cases; nonfatal cases without lost workdays; total lost workday cases; cases with days away

OSHA's Form 300

Log of Work-Related Injuries and Illnesses

Attention: This form contains information relating to employee health and must be used in a manner that protects the confidentiality of employees to the extent possible while the information is being used for occupational safety and health purposes.

Year _____

U.S. Department of Labor
Occupational Safety and Health Administration

Form approved OMB no. 1218-0176

You must record information about every work-related injury or illness that involves loss of consciousness, restricted work activity or job transfer, days away from work, or medical treatment beyond first aid. You must also record significant work-related injuries and illnesses that are diagnosed by a physician or licensed health care professional. You must also record work-related injuries and illnesses that meet any of the specific recording criteria listed in 29 CFR 1904.8 through 1904.12. Feel free to use two lines for a single case if you need to. You must complete an injury and illness incident report (OSHA Form 301) or equivalent form for each injury or illness recorded on this form. If you're not sure whether a case is recordable, call your local OSHA office for help.

Establishment name _____

City _____   **State** _____

(A) Case No.	(B) Employee's Name	(C) Job Title (e.g., Welder)	(D) Date of injury or onset of illness (mo./day)	(E) Where the event occurred (e.g., Loading dock north end)	(F) Describe injury or illness, parts of body affected, and object/substance that directly injured or made person ill (e.g. Second degree burns on right forearm from acetylene torch)	Classify the case									
	Identify the person			Describe the case		Using these categories, check ONLY the most serious result for each case:		Enter the number of days the injured or ill worker was:		Check the "injury" column or choose one type of illness: (M)					
						Death (G)	Days away from work (H)	Remained at work		On job transfer or restriction (days) (K)	Away from work (days) (L)	Injury (1)	Skin Disorder (2)	Respiratory Condition (3)	Poisoning (4)	All other illnesses (5)
								Job transfer or restriction (I)	Other recordable cases (J)							
					Page totals	0	0	0	0	0	0	0	0	0	0	0

Be sure to transfer these totals to the Summary page (Form 300A) before you post it.

Injury (1)   Skin Disorder (2)   Respiratory Condition (3)   Poisoning (4)   All other illnesses (5)

Page 1 of 1

Public reporting burden for this collection of information is estimated to average 14 minutes per response, including time to review the instruction, search and gather the data needed, and complete and review the collection of information. Persons are not required to respond to the collection of information unless it displays a currently valid OMB control number. If you have any comments about these estimates or any aspects of this data collection, contact: US Department of Labor, OSHA Office of Statistics, Room N-3644, 200 Constitution Ave, NW, Washington, DC 20210. Do not send the completed forms to this office.

Figure 11-1 OSHA's Form 300, Log of Work-Related Injuries and Illnesses

**Workplace Safety
and Health**

**http://www.lir.msu.edu/
hotlinks/Safety.php**

Numerous sites related to workplace safety and health are provided.

 **OBJECTIVE**

Describe the consequences of repetitive stress injuries.

Repetitive stress injuries:
Group of conditions caused by placing too much stress on a joint when the same action is performed repeatedly.

Carpal tunnel syndrome (CTS):
Caused by pressure on the median nerve that occurs as a result of a narrowing of the passageway that houses the nerve.

from work; and measure of fatalities.[25] Each of these measures is per 100 full-time 200,000 work hours. In addition to program evaluation criteria, an effective reporting system helps to ensure that accidents are reported and receive attention. With the start of a new safety program, the number of accidents may decline significantly. However, some supervisors may fail to report certain accidents to make the statistics for their units look better. Proper evaluation of a safety program depends on the accurate reporting and recording of data.

Organizations must use the conclusions derived from an evaluation for them to be of any value in improving the safety program. Gathering data and permitting this information to collect dust on the safety director's desk will not solve problems or prevent accidents. Accident investigators must transmit evaluation results upward to top management and downward to line managers in order to generate improvements.

Repetitive stress injury, another significant problem in industry, is discussed next.

Repetitive Stress Injuries (RSIs)

Repetitive stress injuries refer to a group of conditions caused by placing too much stress on a joint when the same action is performed repeatedly. The U.S. Bureau of Labor Statistics reports that repetitive stress injuries account for 25 percent of cases involving days away from work and that disorders associated with repetitive stress are responsible for nearly 60 percent of all work-related illness. Further, RSI now represents 62 percent of all North American workers' compensation claims and results in between $15 and $20 billion in lost work time and compensation claims each year.[26]

Carpal tunnel syndrome (CTS) is caused by pressure on the median nerve that occurs as a result of a narrowing of the passageway that houses the nerve.[27] People developing CTS may experience pain, numbness or tingling in the hands or wrist, a weak grip, the tendency to drop objects, sensitivity to cold, and in later stages, muscle deterioration, especially in the thumb. The syndrome affects approximately 3 percent of the adults in the United States.[28]

People who use their hands and wrists repeatedly in the same way tend to develop carpal tunnel syndrome. Illustrators, carpenters, assembly-line workers, and people whose jobs involve work on personal computers are the ones most commonly affected. CTS sufferers spend an average of 30 days away from work, compared to 29 days for fracture victims, and 26 days for amputees.[29] Also related to the large number of workers' compensation claims is the increased recognition that such injuries are compensable. According to the National Council on Compensation Insurance, claims for carpal tunnel syndrome accounted for just 2 percent of all lost-time workplace injuries, but such injuries accounted for $1 billion in workers' compensation claim benefits, or about an average of $20,000 each.[30]

Carpal tunnel syndrome is preventable, or at least the severity can be reduced. Managers can provide ergonomic furniture, especially chairs, and ensure that computer monitors are positioned at eye level and keyboards at elbow level. Employees can also cooperate by reporting early symptoms of CTS RSI and by taking the following actions:

- Rest the hand and wrist in a neutral position.
- Do not perform the exact activities that caused the syndrome.
- Take nonsteroidal anti-inflammatory drugs.
- Avoid any physical therapy aimed at exercising the hand muscle-tendon units until after symptoms have disappeared.

Other suggested actions include: keep wrists straight, take exercise breaks, alternate tasks, shift positions periodically, adjust chair height, work with feet flat on the floor, and be conscious of posture. Many of these actions suggest the need for ergonomics, the next topic.

5 OBJECTIVE

Explain the purpose of ergonomics.

Ergonomics:
Study of human interaction with tasks, equipment, tools, and the physical environment.

Ergonomics

A specific approach to dealing with health problems such as repetitive stress injuries and enhancing performance is ergonomics. **Ergonomics** is the study of human interaction with tasks, equipment, tools, and the physical environment. Through ergonomics, the goal is to fit the machine and work environment to the person, rather than require the person to make the adjustment. Ergonomics includes all attempts to structure work conditions so that they maximize energy conservation, promote good posture, and allow workers to function without pain or impairment. Failure to address ergonomics issues results in fatigue, poor performance, and repetitive stress injuries.

Congress and OSHA

Congress rescinded OSHA's controversial ergonomics standards in 2001 in accordance with the Congressional Review Act. OSHA responded to this Act by releasing a public notice that it would develop new guidelines addressing ergonomics hazards.[31] The ergonomics guidelines, however, are not mandatory and do not carry the force of law. The guidelines interpret agency policy at a given point in time. Until ergonomics standards are set forth in legislation, it appears that OSHA will lack authority to enforce ergonomics standards at companies. Meanwhile, OSHA continues to work closely with stakeholders to develop industry- and task-specific guidelines to protect workers from ergonomic-related injuries and illnesses.

Many firms have an ergonomics problem that needs to be fixed. The question is whether they need federal legislation or whether the private sector is up to the task. California has been a leader in ergonomics regulation and has a standard that became effective in 1999. If many other states follow this lead, some experts believe that the burden caused by uneven and inconsistent standards in the states will eventually lead to federal regulation.

Ergonomics Payoff

It is clear that there is an economic payoff in using ergonomics. Firms like Allied Signal have discovered that an ergonomic working environment not only helps employees, but also makes good business sense. Reports show that the company saves about $2 million per year in worker compensation costs.[32] The ergonomic initiatives of Schneider National, a provider of transportation, logistics, and related services, helped reduce workers' compensation costs by more than 9 percent. The injury reduction strategy helps prevent the stress and discomforts of driving, reduces in-cab injuries, reduces back injuries outside of the cab, and lessens fatigue. After only six months, the percentage of drivers reporting discomfort dropped by more than 47 percent and the carrier also experienced 114 fewer lost-time injuries.[33] Other companies have also discovered that improving the work environment boosts morale, lowers injury rates, and yields a positive return on investment. Employee input in the design and implementation of safety and health programs may well increase the chances for success of such programs.

Another threat to the safety and security of people on the job is workplace violence. The various ramifications of this phenomenon are discussed in the next section.

6   OBJECTIVE

Explain the effects of
workplace and domestic
violence on businesses.

Workplace violence:
Violent acts, including physical assaults
and threats of assault, directed toward
employees at work or on duty.

Workplace Violence

According to the National Institute for Occupational Safety and Health (NIOSH), **workplace violence** is defined as violent acts, including physical assaults and threats of assault, directed toward employees at work or on duty.[34] In a survey of employers with between 300 and 900 employees, 82 percent of managers responsible for HR or security said violence has increased in their workplace in the last two years.[35] Costs related to business interruption, product tampering, security consulting, employee consulting, legal liability, and brand erosion add up. Costs linked to workplace violence rose from $4.2 billion in 1992 to $36 billion in 1995 and to $121 billion recently.[36] The Bureau of Labor Statistics reports that U.S. employees at work were the victims of 18,104 injuries from assault and 609 homicides.[37] Because workplace violence is a growing threat, some employers are seeking insurance coverage for the financial impact of workplace violence incidents, a threat previously viewed as a self-insured risk.

Murder is the number-one workplace killer of women and the third-leading cause of death for men, after motor vehicle accidents and machine-related fatalities, according to NIOSH. In total, workplace violence accounted for 18 percent of all violent crime in this country.[38] Regardless of who commits the crime, consider the horror of random workplace violence:

> *Michael McDermott was a 42 year-old software programmer at Edgewater Technology in Wakefield, Massachusetts. He chose the day after Christmas 2000 for workforce catastrophe. After chatting with other employees until 11 a.m., he strolled through the high-tech firm's lobby with an AK-47 assault rifle, a shotgun, and a semiautomatic handgun. Bypassing the receptionist, he entered the Human Resources office, shot and killed three people; he then headed to accounting, where three employees had barricaded the door. Barging through, he shot and killed two accountants; the third escaped, hidden under her desk. What triggered McDermott's ire? The accounting department had garnished his wages to pay overdue taxes to the IRS.[39]*

Homicide, as terrible as it is, accounts for only a small percentage of the overall incidence of workplace violence. There is no way to estimate the physical and psychological damage to other employees, who are only onlookers to the violent behavior. A survey of 1,000 U.S. adults found that more than 25 percent of those polled believe their employers are not prepared to deal with workplace violence. Since one in 10 employees has personally experienced violence, the issue facing most large employers is not *if* they will ever deal with an act of workplace violence, but *when*.[40]

Although employers must take steps to reduce the potential for employee homicides, they must also take action against more pervasive problems that can inflict havoc day in and day out. These include bullying, verbal threats, harassment, intimidation, pushing, shoving, slapping, kicking, and fistfights. The vast majority of these types of assaults and other forms of aggression do not show up in the statistics, as they go unreported.

Vulnerable Employees

Employees at gas stations and liquor stores, taxi drivers, and police officers working night shifts face the greatest danger from workplace violence. Ninety percent of the time, armed criminals threaten these workers, not disgruntled co-workers. Taxi and delivery drivers are 60 times more likely than other workers to be murdered while on the job. NIOSH identified the following factors that put drivers at risk:

- Working with the public
- Working with cash
- Working alone
- Working at night
- Working in high-crime areas

Although these factors increase risk, no workplace is immune from violence. Hospital managers overwhelmingly say the biggest threat that emergency room workers face is patient violence. Most hospitals now have security guards stationed in their emergency rooms, particularly at times such as Saturday nights, when violence seems to escalate.

Vulnerable Organizations

It is clear that certain businesses are more susceptible to workplace violence. The characteristics of a high-risk workplace, according to the National Safe Workplace Institute, include the following:

- Chronic labor/management disputes
- Frequent grievances filed by employees
- A large number of workers' compensation injury claims, especially for psychological injury
- Understaffing and excessive demands for overtime in an authoritarian management style[41]

There are numerous reasons for violent acts committed by employees or former employees. Among the most common are personality conflicts, marital or family problems, drug or alcohol abuse, and firings or layoffs.

Legal Consequences of Workplace Violence

In addition to the horror of workplace violence, there is also the ever-present threat of legal action. Civil lawsuits claiming *negligent hiring* or *negligent retention* account for more than half of the estimated $36 billion a year in costs to businesses.[42] Remember from Chapter 6 that negligent hiring is the liability an employer incurs when it fails to conduct a reasonable investigation of an applicant's background, and then assigns a potentially dangerous person to a position where he or she can inflict harm. **Negligent retention** is the liability an employer may incur when a company keeps persons on the payroll whose records indicate strong potential for wrongdoing and fails to take steps to defuse a possible violent situation. If an employer ignores warning signs leading up to a violent incident, it could be held legally liable.[43] Perhaps many of the previously discussed forms of workplace violence could have been prevented if managers had paid more attention to potential problem employees.

Other legal consequences of workplace violence include discrimination lawsuits, workers' compensation claims, third-party claims for damages, invasion of privacy actions, and OSHA violation charges. As previously mentioned, under OSHA's *general duty clause*, employers are required to furnish, to each employee, employment and a place of employment that is free from recognizable hazards that are causing, or likely to cause, death or serious harm to the employee.

Negligent retention:
Liability an employer may incur when a company keeps persons on the payroll whose records indicate strong potential for wrongdoing and fails to take steps to defuse a possible violent situation.

Individual and Organizational Characteristics to Monitor

Some firms that have had extensive experience with workplace violence are trying an alternative approach. Instead of trying to screen out violent people, they are attempting to detect employees who commit minor aggressive acts and exhibit certain behaviors. These individuals often go on to engage in more serious behaviors. Once identified, these people are required to meet with trained staff members for counseling as long as needed. This approach may require more commitment on the part of the firm, but the alternative cost of violence may make this expenditure reasonable in the long run.

There are usually preceding signs to workplace violence.[44] "We've never seen a case where someone just snapped," says Marc McElhaney, a psychologist and director of Critical Response Associates in Atlanta. "In every single one, there are a series of events that either someone ignored or did not respond to adequately."[45] One study found that workers who shoot and kill their co-workers are likely to be employees who have recently experienced a negative change in employment status, including those who have been fired, whose contracts have not been renewed, or who have been suspended because of a dispute with management.[46] Remember the incident of Michael McDermott, previously mentioned. Payroll had garnished his wages to pay overdue taxes to the IRS.

Some behavioral warning signs for employers to watch for are:

- Screaming
- Explosive outbursts over minor disagreements
- Making off-color remarks
- Crying
- Decreased energy or focus
- Deteriorating work performance and personal appearance
- Becoming reclusive

Preventive Actions

There is no way an employer can completely avoid risk when it comes to violence. Incidences of some unbalanced person coming in and shooting people happen randomly and organizations can do little to anticipate or prevent them. However, there are things that can be done to reduce the risk. There are basically two parts to violence prevention. First, there must be a process in place to help with early detection of worker anger. Second, supervisors and HR staff need to be trained in how to skillfully handle difficult employment issues. Firms should consider the following actions to minimize violent acts and to avoid lawsuits:

- Implement policies that ban weapons on company property, including parking lots.[47]
- Under suspicious circumstances, require employees to submit to searches for weapons or examinations to determine their mental fitness for work.
- Have a policy stating that the organization will not tolerate any incidents of violence or even threats of violence.
- Have a policy that encourages employees to report all suspicious or violent activity to management.
- Develop relationships with mental health experts who will be available when emergencies arise.

- Equip receptionists with panic buttons to enable them to alert security officers instantly.
- Train managers and receptionists to recognize the warning signs of violence and techniques to diffuse violent situations.

In spite of the human and financial costs of violence in the workplace, employers generally have not adequately trained employees in how to deal with potentially violent individuals. This is unfortunate, since research shows that providing workplace violence training to all employees, not just supervisors, may make a difference.

Can the selection process predict applicants who will be prone to violence? The answer is "No." On the other hand, the profiles of individuals *not* prone to violence tend to have certain things in common. The most important markers for these people include:[48]

- No substance abuse (one of the highest correlating factors).
- Being outwardly focused; having outside interests and friendships rather than being mainly self-involved.
- A good work history.

In order to confirm these characteristics, the firm must conduct a thorough background investigation.

Domestic violence occurs away from the workplace. Nevertheless, this type of violence often spills into the business world and therefore becomes a workplace issue; it is discussed next.

Domestic Violence

Spillover from domestic violence is a threat to both women and their companies.[49] Domestic violence has become an epidemic in this country. Robin Runge, director of the American Bar Association's Commission on Domestic Violence, said, "Beyond affecting the victim, domestic violence affects the victim's family members and co-workers—and that involves the workplace."[50] Domestic violence can have an impact on firms' bottom lines, costing about $5.8 billion each year in absenteeism, lower productivity, and turnover.[51]

The Office of Criminal Justice calculates that 3 to 4 million women are battered each year. Employees miss an estimated 175,000 days of work each year because of domestic violence, according to the Family Violence Prevention Fund, a national nonprofit group. The U.S. Surgeon General's office reports that domestic violence is the most widespread cause of injury for women between 15 and 44 years of age. Business organizations have a huge stake in the problem of violence. The courts apparently agree as they have ruled that employers owe a duty of care for their employees, customers, and business associates to take reasonable steps to prevent violence on their premises.

 OBJECTIVE

Describe the nature of stress and means of managing stress.

Stress:
Body's nonspecific reaction to any demand made on it.

Nature of Stress

Stress is the body's nonspecific reaction to any demand made on it. It affects people in different ways and is therefore a highly individualized condition. Certain events may be quite stressful to one person but not to another. Moreover, the effect of stress is not always negative.[52] For example, mild stress actually improves productivity, and it can be helpful in developing creative ideas.

Stress in the workplace is nothing new. However, a number of studies have shown that in the twenty-first century, it is skyrocketing. About one-third of the 40.2 million workdays lost annually due to illness and injury result from stress, anxiety, and

Web Wisdom

Stress Busters

http://www.stressrelease
.com

This site offers thoughts for reducing work stress as well as stress-building concepts.

depression.[53] The annual price tag of stress in corporate America is more than $150 billion.[54] Several factors account for this rise, including increased workloads, terrorism, corporate scandals, and economic conditions. Although much of the world has reduced the number of hours worked each year per person over the past decade, Americans have done just the opposite. Remember from the previous chapter that on average, every employed American missed out on three days of vacation in 2004, which is up 50 percent from the two days they each forfeited in 2003.[55] If people work longer hours, they often do not have time to refresh.

Potential Consequences of Stress

Although everyone lives under a certain amount of stress, if it is severe enough and persists long enough, it can be harmful. In fact, stress can be as disruptive to an individual as any accident. It can result in poor attendance, excessive use of alcohol or other drugs, poor job performance, or even overall poor health. There is increasing evidence indicating that severe, prolonged stress is related to the diseases that are the leading causes of death, including cardiovascular disease, depression, immune system disorders, alcoholism, and drug addiction; plus the everyday headaches, back spasms, overeating, and other annoying ailments the body has developed in response.[56] To further illustrate the problem, according a recent survey, 67 percent of employees polled report having high levels of stress.[57] Stress tops the list of changeable health risks that contribute to health care costs, ahead of other top risks including current and past tobacco use, obesity, lack of exercise, high blood-glucose levels, depression, and high blood pressure.

Stressful Jobs

The National Institute for Occupational Safety and Health has studied stress as it relates to work. This organization's research indicates that some jobs are generally perceived as being more stressful than other jobs. The 12 most stressful jobs are listed in Table 11-2. The common factor among these jobs is lack of employee control over work. Workers in such jobs may feel that they are trapped, treated more like machines than people. Workers who have more control over their jobs, such as college professors and master craftpersons, hold some of the less stressful jobs.

The fact that certain jobs are identified as more stressful than others has important managerial implications. Managers are responsible for recognizing significantly deviant behavior and referring employees to health professionals for diagnosis and treatment. Telling signs include irritability, forgetfulness, social isolation, and sudden changes in appearance such as untidy clothing and weight change. Under excessive stress, a person's dominant trait may become even more obvious. For example, if the individual is a private person, he or she withdraws from colleagues; if the person is upbeat, he or she becomes hyperactive. Ideally, stress is dealt with before it occurs. To do this, managers must be aware of potential sources of stress. These sources exist both within and outside the organization. Regardless of its origin, stress possesses devastating potential.

Organizational Factors

Many aspects associated with a person's employment can be potentially stressful. In fact, in a recent survey, work was identified by 45 percent of the respondents as the leading cause of stress.[58] These include the firm's culture, the individual's job, and general working conditions.

Corporate Culture. Corporate culture has a lot to do with stress. The CEO's leadership style often sets the tone. An autocratic CEO who permits little input from subordinates may create a stressful environment. At the other extreme, a weak CEO may

Table 11-2 Stressful Jobs

The 12 Jobs with the Most Stress

1. Laborer	7. Manager/administrator
2. Secretary	8. Waitress/waiter
3. Inspector	9. Machine operator
4. Clinical lab technician	10. Farm owner
5. Office manager	11. Miner
6. Supervisor	12. Painter

Other High-Stress Jobs (in Alphabetical Order)

Bank teller	Nurse's aide
Clergy member	Plumber
Computer programmer	Police officer
Dental assistant	Practical nurse
Electrician	Public relations worker
Firefighter	Railroad switchperson
Guard	Registered nurse
Hairdresser	Sales manager
Health aide	Sales representative
Health technician	Social worker
Machinist	Structural-mental worker
Meat cutter	Teacher's aide
Mechanic	Telephone operator
Musician	Warehouse worker

Source: From a ranking of 130 occupations by the federal government's National Institute for Occupational Safety and Health.

encourage subordinates to compete for power, resulting in internal conflicts. Policies that originate from the top of the organization may also have a negative effect when it comes to stress. Policies and rules that discourage workplace flexibility may create situations that put employees in personal binds. For example, important personal business may be impossible to conduct because of an unyielding work schedule. Also, competition encouraged by the organization's reward system for promotion, pay increases, and status may add to the problem. Even in the healthiest corporate culture, stressful relationships among employees can occur.

Job Itself. A number of factors related to the jobs people perform may produce excessive stress. As previously stated, some jobs are generally perceived as being more stressful than others due to the nature of the tasks involved and the degree of responsibility and control the job permits. Managerial work may itself be a source of stress. Responsibility for people, conducting performance appraisals, coordinating and communicating layoffs, and conducting outplacement counseling can create a great deal of stress for some people.

Working Conditions. Working conditions, including the physical characteristics of the workplace and the machines and tools used, can also create stress. Overcrowding, excessive noise, poor lighting, poorly maintained workstations, and faulty equipment can all adversely affect employee morale and increase stress.

Personal Factors

Stress factors outside the job and job environment also may affect job performance. Although these are often beyond the control of management, managers should recognize that they do exist and may have implications for job performance. Factors in this category include the family and financial problems.

Family. Although a frequent source of happiness and security, the family can also be a significant stressor. As noted in Chapter 3, approximately one-half of all marriages end in divorce, which in itself is generally quite stressful. When divorce leads to single parenthood, the difficulties may be compounded. Contrary to conventional wisdom, women feel no more anxiety on the job because they are mothers than do men because they are fathers. However, concern about their children can cause either parent to suffer stress-related health problems. When trouble exists both at home and at work, a double dose of stress exists. On the positive side, a healthy home life provides a protective buffer against work-related stressors such as an overbearing boss.

An increasingly common circumstance involving a change in traditional roles is the dual-career family, discussed in Chapter 3, in which both husband and wife have jobs and family responsibilities. What happens when one partner is completely content with a job, and the other is offered a desired promotion requiring relocation to a distant city? At best, these circumstances are beset with difficulties. Another emerging problem employees face is the emotional, physical, and financial burden of caring for an aging family member. Research by the National Alliance for Caregiving and Metropolitan Life Insurance Co., estimated that productivity losses due to elder-care issues range from $11 billion to $29 billion per year.[59]

Financial Problems. Problems with finances may place an unbearable strain on the employee. For some, these problems are persistent and never quite resolved. Unpaid bills and bill collectors can create great tension and play a role in divorce or poor work performance. Financial problems are not limited to individuals who are low-wage earners; people at any economic level can wind up with heavy debt due to many factors, including poor personal financial management.

General Environment

Stress is a part of everyone's everyday life; its potential lurks not only in the workplace and the home, but also in our general environment. Economic uncertainties, war or the threat of war, the threat of terrorism, long commutes in rush hour traffic, unrelenting rain, oppressive heat or chilling cold all can create stress. Excessive noise can also create extreme stress in some people. Although stress is seemingly everywhere, there are ways to deal with it. Some suggestions that may be helpful in dealing with stress are discussed in the following sections.

Managing Stress

Only dead people are totally without stress and experts emphasize that some stress is healthy. In fact, moderate stress is the key to survival. Yet, excessive, prolonged stress must be dealt with, and both the individual and organizations have a responsibility to take appropriate measures. There are a number of ways that individuals may control excessive stress. The following approaches are recommended:

- **Exercise**—One of the most effective means of dealing with stress is physical exercise. Stress results in chemical changes in the body, and exercise provides a means of returning the body to its normal state. Most people have a favorite form of exercise; it may be jogging, tennis, golf, racquetball, or walking.

- **Follow good diet habits**—A person under stress is burning up energy at a faster pace than normal. Proper eating habits are extremely important, but unfortunately junk food often becomes the order of the day. Individuals must establish dietary goals that limit junk food and allow the maintenance of normal weight.

- **Know when to pull back**—Relaxation is essential to temper stress. Some people hold up well under stress for extended periods; others do not. But everyone should find time to pull back.

- **Put the stressful situation into perspective**—Some people tend to treat virtually all situations as a matter of life and death. Such an attitude can build up a tremendous amount of stress.

- **Find someone who will listen**—Finding someone who will listen can keep you from bottling up a problem that seems to eat away at your inner self.

- **Establish some structure to your life**—Stress often occurs when a person does not have control over a situation. In many instances, planning ahead is all that is needed to keep a person out of a stressful situation. Establishing structure may also mean leaving the job at the office. Most people need time away from the job to reduce stress levels.

- **Recognize your own limitations**—Probably among the most stressful conditions you can encounter is being placed in a situation where your limitations and inability to cope become quickly evident.

- **Be tolerant**—Learn to tolerate people for what they are. Being tolerant of others tends to keep you in touch with reality.

- **Pursue outside diversions**—Individuals need to establish a reasonable balance between work and family commitments and leisure.

- **Avoid artificial control**—It is true that loss or lack of control directly contributes to feelings of stress. However, the worst possible solution is to use artificial means to regain that sense of control.

To deal with stress associated with your job, isolate what is and is not important and do not worry about unimportant issues or issues beyond your control.[60]

 8 OBJECTIVE

Explain burnout.

Burnout:
Incapacitating condition in which individuals lose a sense of the basic purpose and fulfillment of their work.

Burnout

Burnout, while rarely fatal, is an incapacitating condition in which individuals lose a sense of the basic purpose and fulfillment of their work. A recent survey by CareerBuilders.com found that three out of four reported job burnout.[61] Burnout differs from stress in that it causes people who have previously been highly committed to their work to become disillusioned and lose interest and motivation. Burnout is often associated with a midlife or mid-career crisis, but it can happen at different times to different people. When this occurs, they may lose their motivation to perform. Burnout is the most common factor leading to the decision to *check out* temporarily.[62]

Individuals in the helping professions, such as teachers and counselors, seem to be susceptible to burnout because of their jobs; others may be vulnerable because of their upbringing, expectations, or personalities. Burnout is frequently associated with people whose jobs require them to work closely with others under stressful and tension-filled conditions, such as in the information technology field. However, any employee may experience burnout, and no one is exempt. The dangerous part of burnout is that it is contagious. A highly cynical and pessimistic burnout victim can quickly transform an entire group into burnouts. A recent survey found that virtual teams that exist over the long term (more than a year) run a strong risk of declining performance due to team burnout.[63]

Burnout's price tag is high: it results in reduced productivity, higher turnover, and generally lousy performance. People often become physically and psychologically weakened from trying to combat it. Although some employees try to hide their problems, shifts in their behavior may indicate dissatisfaction. They may start procrastinating or go to the opposite extreme of taking on too many assignments. They may lose things and become increasingly disorganized. Good-natured individuals may turn irritable. They may become cynical, disagreeable, pompous, or even paranoid. Their motivation toward a project may not be like it used to be and they dread doing work that they used to enjoy.[64] It is very important that the problem be dealt with quickly. Some means of dealing with burnout include keeping expectations realistic, reducing your workload, finding means to relax at work, and developing and maintaining interests outside work.

9 OBJECTIVE

Describe the purposes of wellness programs.

Wellness Programs

The traditional view that health is dependent on medical care and is the absence of disease is changing. Today, it is clear that optimal well-being is often achieved through environmental safety, organizational changes, and healthy lifestyles. Infectious diseases, over which a person has little control, are not the problem they once were. From 1900 to 1970, the death rate from major infectious diseases dropped dramatically. However, the death rate from major chronic diseases, such as heart disease, cancer, and stroke, has significantly increased. Today, heart disease and stroke are the

---

Trends & Innovations

Paying You to Be Healthy

Health insurance costs appear to be out of control. Recently, the average increase in premiums has been over 11 percent and few expect the number to do anything but continue to go up. To deal with these forecasts businesses have become creative in the way they meet the rising costs of health insurance. With nearly 400 salaried employees qualifying for coverage, Noodles & Co., found a unique way of addressing the issue.[65]

The Boulder, Colorado–based company set up a program that gives employees cash incentives for staying healthy. It introduced *Fitness Bucks*, which rewards employees $100 for each of the three basic wellness goals they meet. Participating workers pledge to meet the goals pertaining to doctor visits, exercise, and smoking at the start of the year, and then revisit them in November. If they claim to have met the goals, they get the cash.[66] This claim is based on the honor system.

If they have gotten a physical and dental exam, which are both are covered in full by insurance, they get $100. If they have followed a regular exercise program such as walking, running, weightlifting, or yoga, they get another $100. And if they quit smoking (cessation programs are covered in their insurance too), it is another $100. Employees who do not smoke get the $100 anyway.[67] Noodles human resource vice president John Puterbaugh says, "The program serves many purposes. Healthier employees mean better attendance and productivity. It also means fewer insurance claims. Claims have been merely marginal during the two years of the program. This should lead to reduced premiums although it has not happened yet." Puterbaugh believes the program sends the right message about staying healthy. "It lets employees know they've got to take care of themselves. It's the only surefire strategy for fighting health insurance costs."[68]

top two killers worldwide. Chronic obstructive pulmonary disease and lung cancer are also growing threats to life. Healthy lifestyle measures such as not smoking, eating healthy foods, and exercising more may help prevent these diseases. According to a survey by the International Foundation of Employee Benefit Plans, 62 percent of employers now offer wellness programs.[69]

Chronic lifestyle diseases are much more prevalent today than ever before. The good news is that people have a great deal of control over many of them.[70] These are diseases related to smoking, excessive stress, lack of exercise, obesity, and alcohol and drug abuse. Increased recognition of this has prompted employers to become actively involved with their employees' health and to establish wellness programs. As one wellness director stated, "Focusing on health care is inherently reactive; focusing on health is proactive and, potentially, a game changer."[71] There has been a shift toward an approach to improving health that includes involving workers in identifying problems and developing solutions. David Beech, a senior consultant at Watson Wyatt Worldwide, said, "A comprehensive, integrated solution really targeted on health and health improvement really can be an important engine for driving this transformation from managing benefits to managing health."[72] When Moen Inc., a home-care center supplier opened its wellness center over a decade ago, it was viewed primarily as a "soft benefit." Today, it definitely impacts the bottom line. A formal study conducted by Moen concluded that for every dollar spent on wellness initiatives, Moen trims $3 to $4 from the bottom line. Also, for every $100 spent on health care over the course of a year, nonmembers spent $46.30 on inpatient medical services while members spent $4.76.[73] Wellness programs often expand their focus to include other health issues such as diet, stress, substance abuse, employee assistance programs, and smoking cessation.

In developing a wellness program, firms should first conduct a *health risk assessment* by surveying their employees and determining which employees are at elevated risk for chronic diseases, before implementing a wellness program to address appropriate employee health needs. Sometimes getting everyone on board to take a health risk assessment is difficult. Sprint Corporation found a way to overcome this difficulty. At Sprint, employees could take health risk assessments, either online or on paper, and would receive follow-up calls discussing any conditions or potential risks found. To increase participation, Sprint gave every employee $45 to take the assessment and the company raffled off twenty-five $500 American Express gift cards to employees and dependents who took the assessment.[74] Some companies use a more direct approach to health care screening. Cadmus Communications, a publishing services company, actually required employees to take a health risk assessment that involved blood pressure and cholesterol screening. Seventeen employees lost their health coverage because they did not cooperate. Cadmus found high levels of hypertension and high cholesterol among its staffers. Although 23 percent of employees thought they were overweight, 78 percent actually were. Health care professionals followed up to ensure that workers received appropriate treatments.[75]

Data such as the following are needed for each employee:

- Medical records such as blood pressure checks, height-to-weight ratios, and cholesterol levels.

- Absenteeism rates.

- Health risk appraisals, including employee health habits and family histories.

Once companies have identified high-risk employees and the health issues they face, they can determine what programs are needed and again offer incentives for participation in activities such as smoking cessation classes or joining Weight Watchers.[76] Although these data will indicate possible areas of health needs, it is also important to measure employee interests. At Lincoln Plating, everyone gets quarterly health risk appraisals that include blood pressure screening and body weight, and body fat and flexibility measurements. Each employee reviews the quarterly results with the wellness manager or occupational nurse and sets individual wellness objectives. These objectives influence everyone's merit increase. For supervisor-level and above, it is also tied in with employees' compensation. Dan Krick, Lincoln Plating's vice president of human resources, said, "Last year, it cost me between $500 and a thousand dollars for missing my wellness objective, but I am working harder to meet my goals."[77]

Over 200 large companies, which together provide health insurance for more than 45 million Americans, have joined together to create a nonprofit organization called the National Business Group on Health. It advises large employers on health care and benefits issues and has started bestowing a new honor—the Best Employers for Healthy Lifestyles award—on companies that are investing in making their workers healthier.[78] Some of the winners approached were installing walking routes and hiking paths around workplaces and stocking cafeterias and vending machines with more fruit and other foods containing less fat and salt. Other awards included:

- Employees at Aetna can earn financial incentives of up to $345 a year for participating in weight-management and fitness courses. Aetna saw a 66 percent increase in workouts from the year before the program was instated to the end of its wellness program's first year.[79]

- Union Pacific Railroad has an online system called HealthTrack that can create a customized health plan for each of its 48,000 employees. The program identifies risks and offers employees personalized risk reduction programs. Union Pacific Railroad's HealthTrack targets 10 risk factors: asthma, blood pressure, cholesterol, depression, diabetes, fatigue, inactivity, excess weight, smoking, and stress.[80]

- GE Energy's Health by Numbers program is available in seven languages at all GE Energy locations worldwide. Based on a formula of 0-5-10-25—zero tobacco use, five daily servings of fruits and vegetables, 10,000 steps (or 30 minutes of moderate exercise) daily, and striving to maintain a body mass index of less than 25— the program includes motivational tools and personal coaching.[81]

10 **OBJECTIVE**

Describe the importance of physical fitness programs.

Physical Fitness Programs

According to a survey by executive search firm TheLadders.com, most executives say physical fitness is critical to career success and employers should be involved in promoting it.[82] The most commonly offered in-house corporate wellness programs involve efforts to promote exercise and fitness, according to a survey by the American Management Association.[83] To understand the interest in such programs, consider the results of physical inactivity. They can include obesity, hypertension, heart disease, diabetes, anxiety, depression, and certain types of cancer.

From management's viewpoint, physical fitness programs make a lot of sense. Loss of productivity resulting from coronary disease alone costs U.S. businesses billions of dollars annually. Company-sponsored fitness programs often reduce absenteeism, accidents, and sick pay. There is increasing evidence that if employees stick to company fitness programs, they will experience better health, and the firm will have lower health costs. A study at Steelcase, an office equipment manufacturer, found that participants in a corporate fitness program had 55 percent lower medical claims costs over a six-year period than did nonparticipants.[84] Of interest, one of the primary benefits that baby boomers desire is health club or gym memberships.[85]

The late Kenneth Cooper, who coined the term *aerobics* (which literally means *with oxygen*) had advice for those with or without access to fitness centers. To begin, he feels that moderate exercise is king. The basic recommendation is 30 minutes of exercise four to five days a week. He adds, "If you walk fast enough (12 minutes per mile) you can get the same benefits as running a 9-minute mile, without the strain on the joints." His studies also show that cardiovascular training is not enough. He advocated a heart-healthy diet and vitamin supplements like antioxidants. He felt that eliminating tobacco products and habit-forming drugs, controlling alcohol, keeping stress levels down, and getting periodic health exams round out everyone's fitness picture.[86]

Substance Abuse

OBJECTIVE 11

Explain substance abuse and describe substance-abuse-free workplaces.

Substance abuse:
Use of illegal substances or the misuse of controlled substances such as alcohol and drugs.

Substance abuse involves the use of illegal substances or the misuse of controlled substances such as alcohol and drugs. The U.S. Department of Labor says that alcohol and drug abuse costs American businesses roughly $81 billion a year in lost productivity—$37 billion attributable to premature death and $44 billion attributable to illness. There are also the hidden costs related to tardiness, absenteeism, benefits, and turnover.[87] Even so, few issues generate more controversy today than substance-abuse testing. Yet, drug and alcohol abuse are definitely workplace issues. According to the federal government, about 71 percent of alcohol and drug abusers have jobs.[88] Studies show that more than 60 percent of adults know people who have gone to work under the influence of drugs or alcohol.

Alcohol Abuse

Alcoholism:
Medical disease characterized by uncontrolled and compulsive drinking that interferes with normal living patterns.

Alcoholism is a medical disease characterized by uncontrolled and compulsive drinking that interferes with normal living patterns. The National Council on Alcoholism & Drug Dependence (NCADD) reports that 40 percent of workplace fatalities and 47 percent of workplace injuries are related to alcohol consumption. Stress plays an important role in a person becoming an alcoholic. However, alcoholism tends to run in families in which there is a chemical imbalance in the brain's neurotransmitters and is therefore a hereditary trait. Sons of alcoholics are four times more likely to become alcoholics themselves, even if they are raised in foster homes by nonalcoholic parents.[89] It is a significant problem that affects people at every level of society, and it can both result from and cause excessive stress. As a person starts to drink excessively, the drinking itself produces greater stress. A vicious cycle is created as this increased stress is dealt with by more drinking. Early signs of alcohol abuse are especially difficult to identify. Often the symptoms are nothing more than an increasing number of absences from work. Although our society attaches a stigma to alcoholism, in 1956, the American Medical Association described it as a treatable disease.

Drug Abuse

The NCADD reports that about half of those who test positive for drugs in the workplace report using drugs on a daily basis. Government studies reveal that 70 percent of illicit drug users aged 18 to 49 work full-time.[90] Drug-using employees are 3.5 times more likely to be involved in a workplace accident and five times more likely to file a workers' compensation claim. Absenteeism among illegal drug users is up to 16 times greater than among other workers; illegal drug users use three times as many sick day benefits as other workers and are five times as likely to file workers' compensation claims. Drug users are increasingly gravitating to the workplace, which is an ideal place to sell drugs. Since 95 percent of *Fortune* 500 companies conduct pre-employment drug screening, 60 percent of employed drug users work for smaller businesses, many of which do not use drug testing.

All illegal drugs have some adverse effects. Although some claim that marijuana is harmless, if people use marijuana regularly, the drug can damage and destroy cells in the brain. People may have difficulty learning things. Pot also contains cancer-causing chemicals and when a smoker inhales marijuana, it can lead to lung cancer. But, lung cancer is not the only danger. Smoking marijuana may increase the risk of developing head and neck cancers. Prescription drugs can also be as addictive, impairing, and destructive as common street drugs. According to drug enforcement agencies, at least 25 to 30 percent of drug abuse in the workplace involves prescription drugs. And, standard drug screens do not always detect these drugs.

Chemically dependent employees exhibit behaviors that distinguish them from drug-free workers. One study showed that employees who had a positive drug test but were hired anyway missed 50 percent more time from work than other employees. They also had a 47 percent higher chance of being fired. According to the National Institute on Drug Abuse (NIDA), one Utah power company found that drug-positive employees were five times more likely than other employees to cause an on-the-job accident. Substance abuse involving either alcohol or drugs increases employee theft, lowers morale, and reduces productivity. Some good news may be in order; workplace drug use was down recently, having fallen to its lowest level since 1988.[91]

Substance-Abuse-Free Workplace

The Drug-Free Workplace Act of 1988 requires some federal contractors and all federal grantees to agree that they will provide drug-free workplaces as a condition of receiving a contract or grant from a federal agency (details of the Act may be seen in Table 11-3). Many organizations that do not fall under the Act have opted for an alcohol- and drug-free policy. Drug testing as a component in an organization's selection process is one means of achieving this goal. However, since a large percentage of substance abusers are employed, this is obviously not the only solution to the problem. Many firms have tackled the drug abuse problem head-on by establishing a drug-free workplace program. But, some cautions should be taken. Some philosophies and

Table 11-3 Drug-Free Workplace Act of 1988

The Drug-Free Workplace Act of 1988 requires some Federal Contractors and all Federal grantees to agree that they will provide drug-free workplaces as a condition of receiving a contract or grant from a Federal agency.

Organizations, with contracts from any U.S. Federal agency, must comply with the provisions of the Act if the contract is in the amount of $100,000 or more. Organizations must do the following:

(A) publish a statement notifying employees that the unlawful manufacture, distribution, dispensation, possession, or use of a controlled substance is prohibited in the person's workplace. The statement should also notify employees of any punitive actions that will be taken.

(B) establish a drug-free awareness program to inform employees about

    (i)   the dangers of drug abuse in the workplace;

    (ii)   the policy of maintaining a drug-free workplace;

    (iii) any available drug counseling, rehabilitation, and employee assistance programs; and

    (iv) and the penalties that many be imposed upon employees for drug abuse violations.

(C) make it a requirement that each employee be given a copy of the workplace substance abuse policy.

If a contractor is found not to have a drug-free workplace, each contract awarded by any federal agency shall be subject to suspension of payments under the contract or termination of the contract, or both. The contractor may also be ineligible for award of any contract by any federal agency, and for participation in any future procurement by any federal agency, for a period not to exceed 5years.

Source: http://workplace.samhsa.gov/FedPrograms/FedCntrsGrantee/DTWAct1988.htm, January 8, 2006.

Table 11-4 Philosophies and Practices That Can Undermine the Effectiveness of Drug-free Workplace Programs

- Focusing only on illicit drug use and failing to include alcohol—the number one drug of abuse in our society
- Accepting drug use and alcohol abuse as part of modern life and a cost of doing business
- Overreliance on drug testing
- Focusing on termination of users rather than rehabilitation
- Reluctance of supervisors to confront employees on the basis of poor performance
- Reinforcing an individual's denial regarding the impact of his/her alcohol and drug use
- Restricting benefits and/or access to treatment of alcoholism and addiction
- Allowing insurers to restrict access to treatment programs

Source: http://www.dol.gov/elaws/asp/drugfree/drugs/screen5.asp?selection_list=, January 3, 2006.

practices that can undermine the effectiveness of drug-free workplace programs may be seen in Table 11-4.

The steps for establishing a substance-abuse-free workplace may be seen in Figure 11-2. Note that the first step is to establish a drug- and alcohol-free policy. The U.S. Department of Labor offers a Drug-Free Workplace Advisor that offers guidance on how to develop a drug- and alcohol-free workplace.[92] At Texas Instruments, the policy is simple and straightforward: "There will be no use of any illegal drug."

The second step is to provide education and training for supervisors and workers. At a minimum, supervisor training should include a review of the drug-free workplace policy, the supervisor's specific responsibilities in implementing the policy, and ways to recognize and deal with employees who have job performance problems that could be related to alcohol and other drugs. Managers must learn to recognize impaired or intoxicated employees and those who may be addicted. Table 11-5 lists signs that *suggest* an employee may be a substance abuser. Many indicators of poor performance also may be signs of medical or mental health problems. The existence of these indicators alone is not adequate to determine the presence or absence of any condition. The supervisor should never try to diagnose, make accusations, or treat such problems. The indicators provide the supervisor a basis for making a referral to a person who can help the employee, such as an Employee Assistance Program (EAP) professional.

Employees should also be educated as to the purpose and ramifications of the drug- and alcohol-free environment.[93] The purpose of this training is to familiarize employees with the drug-free workplace program and provide general awareness education about the dangers of alcohol and drug abuse. Employees should be informed about: the requirements of the organization's drug-free workplace policy, the prevalence of alcohol and drug abuse and their impact on the workplace, how to recognize the connection between poor performance and alcohol and/or drug abuse, the progression of the disease of alcohol and drug addiction, and what types of assistance may be available. The program should send a clear message that use of alcohol and

Figure 11-2 Developing a Substance-Abuse-Free Workplace

Table 11-5 Signs of Possible Substance Abuse

- Excessive absenteeism
- Radical mood swings
- Decline in personal appearance
- Smell of alcohol or other physical evidence of substance abuse
- Accident proneness and multiple workers' compensation claims
- Lack of coordination
- Psychomotor agitation or retardation. Alcohol, marijuana, and opioids can all cause fatigue. Cocaine, amphetamines, and hallucinogens can cause anxiety.
- Thought disturbances. Cocaine, alcohol, PCP, amphetamines, and inhalants often cause grandiosity or a subject sense of profound thought.
- Other indicators. Cocaine, PCP, and inhalants can all cause aggressive or violent behavior. Alcohol and other sedatives reduce inhibition. Marijuana increases appetite, whereas stimulants decrease it. Both types of drugs cause excessive thirst.

Sources: "Are You Prepared?" *Safety Management* (January 2003): 7; Deanna Kelemen, "How to Recognize Substance Abuse in the Workplace," *Supervision* 56 (September 1995): 4.

drugs in the workplace is prohibited. Employees are encouraged to voluntarily seek help with alcohol and drug problems.[94]

The third step is to implement a drug-testing program. A drug-free workplace program should: balance the rights of employees and the rights of employers, balance the need to know and rights to privacy, balance detection and rehabilitation, and balance the respect for employees and the safety of all. The difficulty is not in formulating the policy, but rather in implementing it. Also, remember that the Americans with Disabilities Act protects an employee in a substance-abuse rehabilitation program.[95] Drug testing was discussed in Chapter 6.

The final step in obtaining a substance-abuse-free workplace is the creation of an employee assistance program, discussed next.

 OBJECTIVE

Describe employee assistance programs.

Employee assistance program (EAP):

Comprehensive approach that many organizations have taken to deal with burnout, alcohol and drug abuse, and other emotional disturbances.

Employee Assistance Programs (EAPs)

The Drug-Free Workplace Act mentioned earlier also requires federal employees and employees of firms under government contract to have access to employee assistance program services. An **employee assistance program (EAP)** is a comprehensive approach that many organizations have taken to deal with numerous problem areas such as burnout, alcohol and drug abuse, and other emotional disturbances.

As you would imagine, EAPs grew rapidly in number following that Act and their use is still growing. Carrie Reuter, manager of business development for NEAS, a Waukesha, Wisconsin–based EAP provider, said, "We really don't even define it anymore. Anything that someone is experiencing as a roadblock in their life, we can provide assistance for, either with a referral or with counseling."[96] Returns on investment in EAPs will vary but one estimate is that a mature, well-run program will return a minimum of three dollars for every dollar spent on it. Advantages claimed for EAPs include lower absenteeism, decreases in workers' compensation claims, and fewer accidents.

Whether managed in-house or outsourced, EAPs have traditionally focused first on mental health, including substance-abuse counseling. Many have expanded to include financial and legal advice, referrals for day care and elder care and a host of other services, including assistance with marital or family difficulties, job performance problems, stress, and grief.[97] In an EAP, most or all of the costs (up to a predetermined amount) are borne by the employer. The EAP concept includes a response to personal psychological problems that interfere with both an employee's well-being and overall productivity. The purpose of assistance programs is to provide emotionally troubled employees with the same consideration and assistance given employees with physical illnesses. Just having an EAP sends a message that the employer cares and this can provide considerable encouragement for employees. Comcast, a leading communication company with 80,000 workers nationwide, offers a full-service EAP. Workers can obtain expert financial advice on such subjects as budgeting, credit problems, taxes, estate planning, investment options, insurance, and retirement. Workers can use EAP-retained attorneys for guidance on divorce, estate planning, lawsuits, bankruptcy, adoptions, and personal injury. The EAP also provides child-care, elder-care, and pet-care assistance. Further, counselors offer advice on time management and stress reduction. EAP advisors even provide guidance on buying a car, home improvement, relocation, and travel plans.[98]

A primary concern is getting employees to use the program. Some employees perceive that there is a stigma attached to *needing help*. Supervisors must receive training designed to provide specialized interpersonal skills for recognizing troubled employees and encouraging them to utilize the firm's employee assistance program. Addicted employees are often experts at denial and deception, and they can fool even experienced counselors.

13 OBJECTIVE

Describe the impact of smoke-free workplaces.

Smoke-Free Workplaces

An important health issue facing employers today is environmental tobacco smoke. Although some smokers and advocates remain adamant that passive cigarette smoke is not harmful, the Surgeon General recently concluded that there is no safe level of secondhand smoke exposure.[99] The evidence that secondhand tobacco smoke causes serious harm becomes more concrete every day.[100] A research committee of the World Health Organization reported that secondhand smoke can increase the risk of cancer by as much as 20 to 30 percent. Passive smokers are breathing in the same carcinogens as active smokers and this affects their health. Exposure to secondhand smoke for individuals who have never smoked is responsible for about 3,000 lung cancer deaths and more than 35,000 coronary heart disease deaths in the United States annually.[101] A study released by the University of Minnesota Cancer Center revealed that nonsmoking employees had up to 25 times more nicotine in their bodies on days when they worked in restaurants and bars than on days they were not at work.[102] In a recent study of 115,000 restaurants goers, 89 percent of them believe smoking should be banned in restaurants.[103]

Numerous studies have concluded that workplace smoking is not only hazardous to employees' health, but is also detrimental to the firm's financial health. Smoking cessation programs are usually cost-effective and today 36 percent of employers offer them.[104] They achieve greater-than-average gains in health for each dollar invested; five hundred thousand dollars spent on smoking-cessation counseling is likely to save more years of life for many people than $500,000 spent on open-heart surgery. It is, therefore, more cost-effective on a per-dollar basis.[105]

To date, 14 states ban smoking in the workplace and others are sure to follow.[106] Nine states now are covered by smoke-free restaurant and bar laws, four states are covered by bans that include restaurants but exempt most bars, and several more states and major cities are in the process of negotiating their own solutions.[107] Anti-smoking ordinances also seem to improve heart health. Heart attack rates fell by 27 percent in the 18 months after a 2003 ban on smoking in all public spaces took effect in Pueblo, Colorado, a city of 104,000 people. Neighboring communities with no-smoking bans showed no change over the same period.[108]

Some business owners have taken a personal stand against smoking in general, not just smoking in the workplace. Four employees from Weyco, a firm that manages benefit plans for workers on behalf of other companies, were fired after refusing to take a nicotine test on whether they had smoked. President Howard Weyers said, "Some call this a violation of privacy, pointing to the principle that what you do in your own home is your own business. But they forget the part about so long as it doesn't harm anyone else."[109] In late 2006, employees at Scotts Miracle-Gro were subject to an aggressive smoke-free policy; employees who smoke, even when not at work, can lose their jobs.[110] Weyco Union Pacific Corporation and Alaska Airlines reject employment applications on the grounds that the would-be employee is a smoker. Union Pacific said that it wanted to save on employee health care insurance costs, which have jumped 10 percent annually over the past three years.[111] At Crown Laboratories smokers are given a deadline to stop smoking or they will have to pay their own health insurance premiums.[112] Companies with a policy of not hiring smokers see it as increasing productivity due to the extra time taken on smoke breaks, increased sick days, and increased health care costs.[113]

A Global Perspective

Global Safety Programs

Global companies continue to face global safety risks. That is one of the lessons learned after the 1984 disaster in Bhopal, India, affected Union Carbide's worldwide operations. The Bhopal Disaster of 1984 was the worst industrial disaster in the history of the world. It was caused by the accidental release of 40 metric tons of methyl isocyanate from a Union Carbide India, Limited (UCIL), pesticide plant located in the heart of the city of Bhopal, in the Indian state of Madhya Pradesh. UCIL was a joint venture between Union Carbide and a consortium of Indian investors. The accident in the early hours produced heavier-than-air toxic MIC gas, which rolled along the ground through the surrounding streets killing thousands outright and injuring anywhere from 150,000 to 600,000 others, at least 15,000 of whom died later from their injuries. Some sources give much higher fatality figures.[114]

Health and safety professionals with international experience say one of the most important trends sweeping through successful multinational companies is the shift to a single safety management system that applies to all their operations throughout the world. Although the example of Bhopal revealed the risks of safety failures, experts emphasize that taking a global approach to safety and health is not only about avoiding problems. It also opens up a wealth of opportunities to improve performance.[115] Seiji Machida, coordinator of the occupational safety cluster at the International Labor Organization in Geneva, Switzerland, said, "Multinationals should have a policy applicable to all operations, regardless of the site. Such global systems don't have to be detailed, but there should be a framework or a set of principles."[116]

Although events on the scale of Bhopal are rare, many companies have discovered that the way they treat their workers anywhere on the planet can pose a risk to their corporate reputation. "On an ethical basis, it doesn't make sense to do one thing in one country and something different elsewhere," says Zack Mansdorf, Ph.D., senior vice president for safety, health, and environment at L'Oréal North America and Worldwide, a cosmetics company with operations in more than 200 countries and headquartered in Paris. "We're going to do it because it's the right thing to do." Mansdorf also notes the financial savings and morale and productivity improvements that always result from safety improvements. "In addition, the business argument is that for some companies, brand is everything." This rationale is especially powerful for consumer companies such as L'Oréal. A global system also offers many operational efficiencies, according to James Forsman, vice president and general manager of DuPont Safety Resources, a safety consulting business unit of the global chemical company based in Wilmington, Delaware. "The advantages are profound: You have a single set of standards now, as opposed to multiple standards, say one for Brazil, one for China and one for the U.S."[117] The result is a far simpler management process.

Understanding the local culture and how it affects safety is critical for success, and not always easy. "Take Italy, where drivers are known for driving too fast," says Mansdorf. "When they get in your factory and drive a forklift, you expect them to behave in a different fashion." It can be hard to find the right people in the right places with the right skills and this sometimes requires difficult choices. Is it more important to know the local culture and language, or safety and health expertise? It is easier to teach someone the company global standards than the local mores.[118]

Summary

1. Describe the nature and role of safety and health.

Safety involves protecting employees from injuries due to work-related accidents. Health refers to the employees' freedom from physical or emotional illness.

2. Explain the role of the Occupational Safety and Health Administration.

The role of the administration is to assure a safe and healthful workplace for every American worker.

3. Describe the economic impact of safety and explain the focus of safety programs in business operations.

Job-related deaths and injuries of all types extract a high toll not only in terms of human misery, but also in economic loss. The significant financial costs are often passed along to the consumer in the form of higher prices. Thus, job-related deaths and injuries affect everyone, directly or indirectly. Safety risks can be significant for employers. In addition to workers' compensation costs, OSHA can levy major fines.

Safety programs may be designed to accomplish their purposes in two primary ways. The first approach is to create a psychological environment and attitudes that promote safety. The second approach to safety program design is to develop and maintain a safe physical working environment.

4. Describe the consequences of repetitive stress injuries.

The U.S. Bureau of Labor Statistics reports that repetitive stress injuries account for 25 percent of cases involving days away from work and that disorders associated with repetitive stress account for nearly 60 percent of all work-related illness.

5. Explain the purpose of ergonomics.

Ergonomics is the study of human interaction with tasks, equipment, tools, and the physical environment. Through ergonomics, the goal is to fit the machine and work environment to the person, rather than require the person to make the adjustment.

6. Explain the effect of workplace and domestic violence on businesses.

The fastest-growing form of homicide is murder in the workplace. Homicide is the leading cause of on-the-job death for women and the number-two cause of death for men. Spillover from domestic violence is an unexpected threat to both women and their companies.

7. Describe the nature of stress and means of managing stress.

Stress is the body's nonspecific reaction to any demand made on it. Three general areas from which stress may emanate include the organization (including the firm's culture), the jobs people perform, and working conditions. Personal factors focus on the family and financial problems. Finally, the general environment also contains elements that may produce stress.

Stress may be coped with through numerous means including exercise, following good diet habits, knowing when to pull back, putting the stressful situation into perspective, finding someone who will listen, establishing some structure to your life, recognizing your own limitations, being tolerant, pursuing outside diversions, and avoiding artificial control.

8. Explain burnout.

Burnout, although rarely fatal, is an incapacitating condition where individuals lose a sense of the basic purpose and fulfillment of their work.

9. Describe the purposes of wellness programs.

The traditional view is changing. No longer is health considered to be dependent on medical care and the absence of disease. Today, the prevailing opinion is that optimal health can generally be achieved through environmental safety, organizational changes, and changed lifestyles.

10. Describe the importance of physical fitness programs.

Many U.S. business firms have exercise programs designed to help keep their workers physically fit. These programs often reduce absenteeism, accidents, and sick pay.

11. Explain substance abuse and describe substance-abuse-free workplaces.

Substance abuse involves the use of illegal substances or the misuse of controlled substances such as alcohol and drugs. The Drug-Free Workplace Act of 1988 requires some federal contractors and all federal grantees to agree that they will provide drug-free workplaces as a condition of receiving a contract or grant from a federal agency.

12. Describe employee assistance programs.

An employee assistance program is a comprehensive approach that many organizations develop to deal with marital or family problems; job performance problems; stress, emotional, or mental health issues; financial troubles; alcohol and drug abuse; and grief.

13. Describe the impact of smoke-free workplaces.

Workplace smoking is not only hazardous to employees' health, but is also detrimental to the firm's financial health.

Key Terms

- Safety, 352
- Health, 352
- Job hazard analysis (JHA), 356
- Repetitive stress injuries, 359
- Carpal tunnel syndrome (CTS), 359

- Ergonomics, 360
- Workplace violence, 361
- Negligent retention, 362
- Stress, 364
- Burnout, 368

- Substance abuse, 372
- Alcoholism, 372
- Employee assistance program (EAP), 375

Questions for Review

1. Define safety and health.
2. What is the purpose of the Occupational Safety and Health Act?
3. What is the current thrust of OSHA?
4. What are the primary ways in which safety programs are designed? Discuss.
5. What is the purpose of job hazard analysis?
6. What is the purpose of the Superfund Amendments Reauthorization Act, Title III (SARA)?
7. Why are companies concerned with repetitive stress injuries? What is carpal tunnel syndrome?
8. Define ergonomics. What is the purpose of ergonomics?
9. What effect does workplace and domestic violence have on an organization?
10. Why should a firm attempt to identify stressful jobs?
11. Why should a firm be concerned with employee burnout?
12. What are the major sources of stress?
13. What are the purposes of wellness programs?
14. Why might physical fitness programs be established in organizations?
15. What is the purpose of substance-abuse-free workplaces in organizations?
16. What are the steps for establishing a substance-abuse-free workplace?
17. What is an employee assistance program?
18. What concerns should a manager have regarding smoking in the workplace?

HRM Incident 1

What a Change!

"Just leave me alone and let me do my job," said Manuel Gomez. Dumbfounded, Bill Brown, Manuel's supervisor, decided to count to 10 and did not respond to Manuel's comment. As he walked back to his office, Bill thought about how Manuel had changed over the past few months. He had been a hard worker and extremely cooperative when he started working for Bill two years earlier. The company had sent Manuel to two training schools and had received glowing reports about his performance in each of them.

Until about a year ago, Manuel had a perfect attendance record and was an ideal employee. At about that time, however, he began to have personal problems, which resulted in a divorce six months later. Manuel had requested a day off several times to take care of personal business. Bill attempted to help in every way he could without getting directly involved in Manuel's personal affairs. But, Bill was aware of the strain Manuel must have experienced as his marriage broke up, and he and his wife engaged in the inevitable disputes over child custody, alimony payments, and property.

During the same time period, top management initiated a push for improving productivity. Bill found it necessary to put additional pressure on all his workers, including Manuel. He tried to be considerate, but he had to become much more performance oriented, insisting on increased output from every worker. As time went on, Manuel began to show up late for work, and actually missed two days without calling Bill in advance. Bill attributed Manuel's behavior to extreme stress. Because Manuel had been such a good worker for so long, Bill excused the tardiness and absences, only gently suggesting that Manuel should try to do better.

Sitting at his desk, Bill thought about what might have caused Manuel's outburst a few minutes earlier. Bill had suggested to Manuel that he shut down the machine he was operating and clean up the surrounding area. This was a normal part of Manuel's job and something he had been careful to do in the past. Bill felt the disorder around Manuel's machine might account for the increasing number of defects in the parts he was making. "This is a tough one. I think I'll talk to the boss about it," thought Bill.

Questions

1. What do you think is likely to be Manuel's problem? Discuss.

2. How might use of an employee assistance program help in this situation?

HRM Incident 2

A Commitment to Safety?

Wanda Zackery was extremely excited a year ago when she joined Landon Electronics as its first safety engineer. She had graduated from Florida State University with a degree in electrical engineering and had a strong desire to enter business. Wanda had selected her job at Landon Electronics over several other offers. She believed that it would provide her with a broad range of experiences that she could not receive in a strictly engineering job. Also, when the company president, Martha Lincoln, interviewed her, she promised her that the firm's resources would be at her disposal to correct any safety-related problems.

Her first few months at Landon were hectic but exciting. She immediately identified numerous safety problems. One of the most dangerous involved a failure to install safety guards on all exposed equipment. Wanda carefully prepared her proposal, including expected costs, to make needed minimum changes. She estimated that it would take approximately $50,000 to complete the necessary conversions. Wanda then presented the entire package to Ms. Lincoln. She explained the need for the changes to her, and Ms. Lincoln cordially received her presentation. She said that she would like to think it over and get back to her.

But that was six months ago! Every time Wanda attempted to get some action on her proposal, Ms. Lincoln was friendly but still wanted some more time to consider it. In the meantime, Wanda had become increasingly anxious. Recently, a worker had barely avoided a serious injury. Some workers had also become concerned. She heard through the grapevine that someone had telephoned the regional office of OSHA.

Her suspicions were confirmed the very next week when an OSHA inspector appeared at the plant. No previous visits had ever been made to the company. Although Ms. Lincoln was not overjoyed, she permitted the inspector access to the company. Later she might have wished that she had not been so cooperative. Before the inspector left, he wrote violations for each piece of equipment that did not have the necessary safety guards. The fines could total $70,000 if the problems were not corrected right away. The inspector cautioned that repeat violations could cost $700,000 and possible imprisonment.

As the inspector was leaving, Wanda received a phone call. "Wanda, this is Ms. Lincoln. Get up to my office right now. We need to get your project under way."

Questions

1. Discuss Ms. Lincoln's level of commitment to occupational safety.

2. Is there a necessary trade-off between Landon's need for low expenses and the workers' need for safe working conditions? Explain.

Notes

1. Agency Group 09, "USAA Educational Foundation Offers Identity-Protection Tips," *FDCH Regulatory Intelligence Database* (May 25, 2006).

2. T. McCollum, "Flaws Found in Identity Protection," *Internal Auditor* 62 (August 2005): 20–21.

3. Susan J. Wells, "Stolen Identity," *HR Magazine* 47 (December 2002): 31.

4. Anne Fisher, "Job Offer or Identity-Theft Scam?" *Fortune* 152 (September 2005): 162.

5. Carol A. Mangis, "Caveats for Job Seekers," *PC Magazine* 24 (November 8, 2005): 25.

6. Paul McNamara, "Have Identity Thieves Stolen My Judgment?" *Network World* 23 (June 5, 2006): 54.

7. Kathy Gurchiek, "ID Theft Services Emerge as New Employee Benefit," *HR Magazine* 50 (October 2005): 29–32.

8. Erika Rosenfeld, "The Growing Crisis of Identity Theft," *Insurance Advocate* 116 (August 15, 2005): 17–20.

9. http://www.osha.gov/as/opa/oshafacts.html, June 30, 2006.

10. http://www.osha.gov/StratPlanPublic/strategicmanagementplan-final.html, June 30 2006.

11. http://www.osha.gov/StratPlanPublic/index.html, June 30, 2006.

12. http://www.osha.gov/StratPlanPublic/wheredowegofromhere.html, June 30, 2006.

13. Ibid.

14. http://www.osha.gov/StratPlanPublic/index.html, May 3, 2006.

15. James L. Nash, "Criminal Enforcement: Agency Looks Beyond OSH Act," *Occupational Hazards* 67 (June 2005): 8–13.

16. "Customers Give OSHA High Marks," *Job Safety and Health Quarterly* 13 (Winter 2002): 16.

17. Mark A. Hofmann, "OSHA Launches 5-Year Plan," *Business Insurance* 37 (May 19, 2003): 3.

18. "Serious Workplace Injuries Decrease, but Financial Impact Remains High," *Industrial Safety & Hygiene News* 39 (November 2005): 10.

19. "Steep Price Tag for Workplace Injuries," *Occupational Hazards* 67 (December 2005): 12.

20. Ibid.

21. "Workplace Fatality Rates Up Slightly," *Pit & Quarry* 98 (October 2005): 36.

22. http://www.nsc.org/aboutus.htm, June 30, 2006.

23. http://www.osha.gov/pls/oshaweb/owadisp.show_document?p_table=PREAMBLES&p_id=1085, June 30, 2006.

24. www.osha.gov/recordkeeping/new-osha300form, June 30, 2006.

25. Dan Petersen, "Setting Goals Measuring Performance," *Professional Safety* 50 (December 2005): 43–48.

26. "Ergo Claims & Costs Keep Climbing," *Industrial Safety & Hygiene News* 39 (March 2005): 12.

27. "Research Shows Computer Use Does Not Increase CTS Risk, Harvard Report Says," *Professional Safety* 51 (June 2006): 6.

28. "Carpal Tunnel Syndrome: Common Ailment, Many Treatments," *Safety Compliance Letter* (February 1, 2006): 12–13.

29. "Lost-Worktime Injuries and Illnesses: Characteristics and Resulting Time Away from Work," *Medical Benefits* 21 (April 30, 2004): 4.

30. Milford Prewitt, "Workers' Comp for RSI-related Injuries More Costly Overall," *Nation's Restaurant News* 39 (June 13, 2005): 1.

31. William H. Kincaid, "Realistic, Cost-Effective Ergonomics for Real People," *Occupational Hazards* 67 (August 2005): 44–46.

32. John G. Falcioni, "Finding the Right Fit," *Mechanical Engineering* 125 (April 2003): 4.

33. "Ergonomics Yield Benefits for Schneider," *Traffic World* 270 (April 10, 2006): 27.

34. Kathy Gurchiek, "Workplace Violence on the Upswing," *HR Magazine* 50 (July 2005): 27–28.

35. "Workplace Violence Has Increased," *Security Director's Report* 5 (October 2005): 9.

36. Gurchiek, "Workplace Violence on the Upswing."

37. Anne Fisher, "How to Prevent Violence at Work," *Fortune* 151 (February 21, 2005): 42.

38. "Study Quantifies Cost of Workplace Violence," *Safety Compliance Letter* (January 1, 2006): 12–13.

39. Mariene Piturro, "Workplace Violence," *Strategic Finance Magazine* 82 (May 2001): 35.

40. "Employees Concerned About Workplace Violence," *Occupational Hazards* 63 (September 2001): 27.

41. James E. Crockett, "Minimizing the Risk of Workplace Violence," *Business Insurance* 33 (July 1999): 35.

42. Kevin Dobbs, "The Lucrative Menace of Workplace Violence," *Training* 37 (March 2000): 54–62.

43. Linda Wasmer Andrews, "When It's Time for Anger Management," *HR Magazine* 50 (June 2005): 31–36.

44. Paul Viollis and Doug Kane, "Bark or Bite?" *Security: For Buyers of Products, Systems & Services* 43 (March 2006): 68.

45. Todd Henneman, "Ignoring Signs of Violence Can Be a Fatal, Costly Mistake," *Workforce Management* 85 (February 27, 2006): 10–11.

46. "How to Predict and Prevent Workplace Violence," *HR Focus* 82 (April 2005): 10–11.

47. "Employers Need Clear Policy as First Step in Workplace Violence Program," *HR Focus* 83 (May 2006): 8–9.

48. William Atkinson, "Keeping Violent Employees out of the Workplace," *Risk Management* 47 (February 2000): 12.

49. Kathy Gurchiek, "Domestic Abuse: Serious Hidden Workplace Problem," *HR Magazine* 51 (March 2006): 38.

50. "How Domestic Violence Affects Workplaces—and What to Do," *HR Focus* 82 (January 2005): 9.

51. Lydell C. Bridgford, "Piercing the Veil of Silence: Domestic Violence and the Workplace," *Employee Benefit News* 20 (August 2006): 21.

52. Anthony Urbaniak, "Managing Stress," *Supervision* 67 (August 2006): 7–9.

53. Meg Fletcher, "Addressing Stress Key to Reducing Absence," *Business Insurance* 39 (October 10, 2005): 32.

54. Dale Collie, "Pressure Points," *Business West* 21 (February 2005): 66–73.

55. Lynn Gresham, "When Employees Give Too Much," *Employee Benefit News* 18 (July 2004): 9.

56. Cora Daniels, "The Last Taboo," *Fortune* 146 (October 28, 2002): 138.

57. "Is Your Employee Benefits Program Adequately Addressing Stress? *Managing Benefits Plans* 6 (March 2006): 10.

58. Ibid.

59. "Why You Should Consider Elder-Care Benefits as a Retention Tool," *HR Focus* 83 (May 2006): 5–6.

60. Shane R. Premeaux, R. Wayne Mondy, and Arthur Sharplin, "Stress and the First-Line Supervisor," *Supervisory Management* 30 (July 1985): 36–40.

61. "Many Workers Are Burning Out, and Here's Why," *HR Focus* 83 (July 2006): 9.

62. Scott Westcott, "Beat Back Burnout," *Black Enterprise* 37 (August 2006): 116.

63. "Virtual Work: It's Not Just for Members of the Jedi Council," *T+D* 59 (August 2005): 12–13.

64. Katherine Spencer Lee, "Battling Back from Burnout," *Certification Magazine* 7 (November 2005): 13.

65. Michael Malone, "No Sick Pay," *Restaurant Business* 104 (January 15, 2005): 29–32.

66. Ibid.

67. Ibid.

68. Ibid.

69. "Wellness Programs on the Rise in the Workplace," *HR Focus* 83 (March 2006): 12.

70. Lori Chordas, "Here's to Your Health," *Best's Review* 106 (April 2006): 52–56.

71. Miles White, "The Cost-Benefit of Well Employees," *Harvard Business Review* 83 (December 2005): 22.

72. Joanne Wojcik, "Employers Trying Prevention as Cure to Health Care Costs," *Business Insurance* 40 (March 27, 2006): 14.

73. Josh Cable, "From Warm Fuzzies to Fitness Culture," *Occupational Hazards* 68 (April 2006): 35–37.

74. Jessica Marquez, "Programs Offer Cash Incentives to Encourage Employee Wellness," *Business Insurance* 39 (September 1, 2005): 36–37.

75. Leah Carlson Shepherd, "Mandatory Health Screenings Heap Huge Rewards," *Employee Benefit News* 20 (April 2006): 32.

76. Marquez, "Programs Offer Cash Incentives to Encourage Employee Wellness."

77. Stephenie Overman, "Lincoln Plating Benefits from Strategic Wellness Program," *Employee Benefit News* 19 (October 1, 2005): 67–68.

78. http://www.wbgh.org/about/index.cfm, June 30, 2006.

79. Molly Bernhart, "Wellness Winners Share Their Success Strategies," *Employee Benefit News* 20 (September 2006): 54–55.

80. http://www.wbgh.org/about/index.cfm, June 30, 2006.

81. Anne Fisher, "Helping Employees Stay Healthy," *Fortune* 152 (August 8, 2005): 114.

82. "Executives Give Weight to Fitness," *HR Magazine* 51 (January 2006): 16.

83. "Most Popular Wellness Plans Involve Exercise," *HR Focus* 82 (February 2005): 12.

84. Michael Barrier, "How Exercise Can Pay Off," *Nation's Business* 85 (February 1997): 41.

85. Lynn Gresham, "Benefits That Keep Mature Workers and Their Companies Going Strong," *Employee Benefit News* 19 (October 1, 2005): 9.

86. Jodi Schneider, "More Fit in Less Time," *U.S. News & World Report* 132 (May 13, 2002): 50–51.

87. Diane Cadrain, "Helping Workers Fool Drug Tests Is a Big Business," *HR Magazine* 50 (August 2005): 29–32.

88. Ibid.

89. Eric Newhouse, "Alcoholism: Its Origins, Consequences and Costs," *Nieman Reports* 57 (Spring 2003): 28.

90. Todd Nighswonger, "Just Say Yes to Preventing Substance Abuse," *Occupational Hazards* 62 (April 2000): 39.

91. "Workplace Drug Use Declined in 2005, Index Shows," *Occupational Hazards* 68 (July 2006): 14.

92. http://www.dol.gov/elaws/asp/drugfree/drugs/screen1.asp, July 1, 2006.

93. http://www.dol.gov/elaws/asp/drugfree/drugs/supervisor/screen45.asp, June 30, 2006.

94. http://www.dol.gov/elaws/asp/drugfree/drugs/employee/screen72.asp, July 1, 2006.

95. http://www.dol.gov/elaws/asp/drugfree/drugs/screen15.asp?selection_list=, December 29, 2006.

96. "Employee Assistance Programs Fill Many Needs," *Employee Benefit News* 19 (December 2005): 19.

97. Kelley M. Butler, "Mending Mind and Body," *Employee Benefit News* 20 (September 2006): 26–29.

98. Steve Davolt, "Comcast Employees Tune into Employee Assistance Program," *Employee Benefit News* 20 (April 2006): 57.

99. "Expect More Workplace Smoking Bans After Surgeon General's Report," *HR Focus* 83 (September 2006): 9.

100. Paul McIntyre, "A Smoking Ban Isn't About Your Bottom Line, It's About Protecting Your Workers' Health," *Nation's Restaurant News* 39 (December 5, 2005): 24–34.

101. Kathy Gurchiek, "Study: Smoking Ban Improved Air," *HR Magazine* 50 (January 2005): 34.

102. McIntyre, "A Smoking Ban Isn't About Your Bottom Line, It's About Protecting Your Workers' Health."

103. Tim Zagat, "Happier, Healthier Employees and Guests Prove Smoke Bans Are Better for Business," *Nation's Restaurant News* 40 (August 7, 2006): 24.

104. Leah Carlson Shepherd, "States, Businesses Snuff Out Smoking," *Employee Benefit News* 20 (August 2006): 1/38.

105. Bill Gillette, "Promoting Wellness Programs Results in a Healthier Bottom Line," *Managed Healthcare Executive* (February 11, 2001): 45–46.

106. "Workplace Smoking Ban Passed in 14th State," *HR Focus* 83 (July 2006): 2.

107. McIntyre, "A Smoking Ban Isn't About Your Bottom Line, It's About Protecting Your Workers' Health."

108. Catherine Arnst, "Of Smoking Bans and Nicotine Fits," *Business Week* (November 28, 2005): 85.

109. Monica Dobie, "Quit Smoking or Lose Your Job," *World Tobacco* (May 2005): 20–21.

110. A. E. Smith, "Stubbing Out Smoke Breaks," *Incentive* 180 (June 2006): 10.

111. Ibid.

112. Dee Gill, "Get Healthy . . . or Else," *Inc.* 28 (April 2006): 35–37.

113. Gurchiek, "Study: Smoking Ban Improved Air."

114. http://en.wikipedia.org/wiki/Bhopal_disaster, November 29, 2005.

115. James L. Nash, "Managing Global Safety: The Power of One," *Occupational Hazards* 67 (September 2005): 28–32.

116. Ibid.

117. Ibid.

118. Ibid.

PART SEVEN

Labor Unions and Collective Bargaining

CHAPTER OBJECTIVES

After completing this chapter, students should be able to:

1 Discuss the Change to Win Coalition.

2 Describe the broad objectives that characterize the labor movement as a whole and describe organized labor's strategies for a stronger movement.

3 Explain the reasons why employees join unions and describe the basic structure of the union.

4 Define collective bargaining and identify the steps involved in establishing the collective bargaining relationship.

5 Describe the collective bargaining process and explain the psychological aspects of collective bargaining.

6 Describe the factors involved in preparing for negotiations.

7 Explain typical bargaining issues and describe the process of negotiating the agreement.

8 Identify ways to overcome breakdowns in negotiations.

9 Describe what is involved in ratifying and administering the agreement.

10 Describe collective bargaining in the public sector.

11 Explain union decertification.

12 Describe the state of unions today.

Labor Unions and Collective Bargaining

HRM IN *Action:*

Change to Win Coalition

1 **OBJECTIVE**

Discuss the Change to Win Coalition.

Change to Win Coalition:
New union federation consisting of seven unions that broke from the AFL-CIO and formally launched a rival labor federation representing about 6 million workers in 2005.

The **Change to Win Coalition** is a new union federation consisting of seven unions that broke from the AFL-CIO and formally launched a rival labor federation representing about 6 million workers in 2005.

The Coalition, led by the Service Employees International Union (SEIU), intends to focus its energies on new membership growth and not as much on lobbying.[1] Also included in the new coalition are the Teamsters, the United Food and Commercial Workers, Unite Here (the labor union representing textile and apparel workers), Carpenters' Union, Laborers' International Union of North America, and the United Farm Workers.[2] The Change to Win Coalition broke with the AFL-CIO because of frustration with the leadership of AFL-CIO President John J. Sweeney, who had been unable to stop the decline of union membership during his 10-year term.[3] The coalition wants to be a labor movement that recruits more members and negotiates better wages and benefits. If this goal is achieved, the coalition should significantly impact industries with heavily unionized workforces and employers with low-wage workers.[4] As stated on the coalition's homepage, "Change to Win unions are building a movement of working people with the power to provide workers: a paycheck that supports a family, affordable health care, a secure retirement, and dignity on the job. By marshalling the collective strength of our unions, we will develop and implement strategies to organize tens of millions of workers. Only when millions more American workers belong to unions will a pro-worker political consensus to support our goals emerge."[5]

The central objective of the Change to Win Strategic Organizing Center is to unite the more than 50 million American workers who work in industries that cannot be outsourced or shipped overseas into strong unions that can win them a place in the American middle class—where their jobs provide good wages, good health care, good pensions, and a voice on the job.[6] Terence M. O'Sullivan,

Web Wisdom

Change to Win Coalition

**http://www.changetowin
.org/**

Topics related to "What they say they stand for, Campaigns, Strategic Organizing, Key Facts, and Who We Are" are included on the Website.

president of the Laborers' International Union of North America, said, "persistent and lengthy attempts to reform the AFL-CIO Building and Construction Trades Department were not successful. Needed reforms included changing the department's governance structure and changing jurisdictional rules that dictate which union members can do what type of work. Those rules no longer reflect the construction industry and hurt union contractors."[7]

This chapter begins by discussing the Change to Win Coalition; then union objectives are discussed and organized labor's strategies for a stronger movement are described. The reasons why employees join unions are explained, the basic structure of the union is described, and collective bargaining is defined. This is followed by a discussion of the steps involved in establishing the collective bargaining relationship. Then topics related to the psychological aspects of collective bargaining, preparing for negotiations, and bargaining issues are discussed. Next, topics related to negotiating the agreement, breakdowns in negotiations, and ratifying the agreement are presented; and sections on administration of the agreement, collective bargaining in the public sector, and union decertification are provided. There is a section called "Unions Today," and the chapter concludes with a Global Perspective entitled "The ICFTU Says Union Organizing Can Be Dangerous."

2 OBJECTIVE

Describe the broad objectives that characterize the labor movement as a whole and describe organized labor's strategies for a stronger movement.

Union Objectives

The labor movement has a long history in the United States. Although each union is a unique organization seeking its own objectives, several broad objectives characterize the labor movement as a whole:

1. To secure and, if possible, improve the living standards and economic status of its members.

2. To enhance and, if possible, guarantee individual security against threats and contingencies that might result from market fluctuations, technological change, or management decisions.

3. To influence power relations in the social system in ways that favor and do not threaten union gains and goals.

4. To advance the welfare of all who work for a living, whether union members or not.

5. To create mechanisms to guard against the use of arbitrary and capricious policies and practices in the workplace.[8]

The underlying philosophy of the labor movement is that of organizational democracy and an atmosphere of social dignity for working men and women. There are numerous strategies that unions use to accomplish their objectives.

Organized Labor's Strategies for a Stronger Movement

Even though the labor movement has suffered setbacks over the last few decades, with private-sector membership dropping below 8 percent, it is likely that the percentage would have been even lower if the following strategies had not been used.

Strategically Located Union Members

The importance of the jobs held by union members significantly affects union power. For instance, an entire plant may have to be shut down if unionized machinists performing critical jobs decide to strike. Thus, a few strategically located union members may exert a disproportionate amount of power. The type of firm that is unionized can also determine a union's power. Unionization of truckers or dock workers can affect the entire country and, subsequently, enhance the union's power base. This is precisely what the longshoremen did in the West Coast strike of 2002, which affected commerce from San Francisco to Maine. Through control of key industries, a union's power may extend to firms that are not unionized.

Organizing Several Big Companies at Once

The Service Employees International Union (SEIU) in Houston organized janitors at several big companies at the same time. Rather than having a campaign for each workplace, it negotiated a big, industry-wide contract. This eliminated each company's fear of being undercut by competitors if it allowed higher wages. Essentially, the companies stayed neutral. The strategy bypassed the National Labor Relations Board, which usually oversees the unionization of workers.[9]

Pulling the Union Through

One union tactic that has worked effectively is to put pressure on the end user of a company's product in order to have a successful organizing attempt. UAW President Ronald A. Gettelfinger authorized a strike against four Johnson Controls Inc. (JCI) factories that make interior parts for some of the country's best-selling vehicles. The quick two-day strike cost workers little lost income, but it hurt General Motors Corporation and DaimlerChrysler Group by shutting down production of their popular Chevy Trail Blazer and Jeep Liberty sport-utility vehicles. Worried about lost sales in a profitable segment and desiring to preserve good relations with the UAW, GM and DaimlerChrysler played an active behind-the-scenes role by pressuring JCI to settle the dispute. The result was a major UAW victory. Not only did raises increase up to $6 an hour, but the strikers won a promise from Johnson Control not to interfere with UAW efforts to organize some 8,000 workers at the 26 other JCI factories that supply the Big Three.[10]

Political Involvement

The political arm of the AFL-CIO is the Committee on Political Education (COPE). Founded in 1955, its purpose is to support politicians who are friendly to the cause of organized labor. The union recommends and assists candidates who will best serve its interests. Union members also encourage their friends to support those candidates. The union's political influence increases as the size of the voting membership grows. With *friends* in government, the union is in a stronger position to maneuver against management. Political involvement now means more than endorsing candidates at all levels of politics, and then attempting to deliver the union membership's vote. Unions are giving money to candidates who pledge to help pass pro-labor legislation. Remember from the Change to Win Coalition discussion that they broke away from the AFL-CIO to focus less on lobbying and more on new membership growth.

Union Salting

Union salting:
Process of training union organizers to apply for jobs at a company and, once hired, working to unionize employees.

Union salting is the process of training union organizers to apply for jobs at a company and, once hired, working to unionize employees.[11] Although traditionally used by blue-collar labor unions within the construction and building industries, it is a strategy labor unions are also using in other sectors, such as the hotel and restaurant industries. The U.S. Supreme Court has ruled that employers cannot discriminate against *union salts* (*NLRB v Town & Electric Inc.*). Therefore, a company cannot terminate these employees solely because they also work for a union.[12]

Flooding the Community

Flooding the community:
Process of the union inundating communities with organizers to target a particular business.

Flooding the community is the process of the union inundating communities with organizers to target a particular business. With their flooding campaigns, unions typically choose companies in which nonunionized employees have asked for help in organizing. Generally, organizers have been recruited and trained by the national union. They are typically young, ambitious, college-educated people with a passion for the American labor movement. Organizers meet with employees in small groups and even visit them at home. They know every nuance of a company's operations and target weak managers' departments as a way to appeal to dissatisfied employees who may be willing to organize.

Public Awareness Campaigns

Public awareness campaigns:
Labor maneuvers that do not coincide with a strike or organizing campaign to pressure an employer for better wages, benefits, and the like.

Public awareness campaigns involve labor maneuvers that do not coincide with a strike or an organizing campaign to pressure an employer for better wages, benefits, and the like. Increasingly, these campaigns are used as an alternative to strikes because more employers are willing to replace their striking employees. Employers have less recourse against labor campaigns that involve joining political and community groups that support union goals or picketing homes of a company's board of directors. They are also defenseless in dealing with the union's initiating proxy challenges to actions negative to labor, writing letters to the editors of the local newspapers, and filing charges with administrative agencies such as OSHA,[13] the Department of Labor, and the NLRB. These types of public awareness campaigns, which are not tied directly to labor gains, are often effective methods of developing union leverage. Also, fighting such campaigns is time consuming and costly for companies.

In 2006, the janitors in the Service Employees International Union engaged in a public awareness campaign called "Make Work Pay!" The campaign was intended to show the need for Americans to be paid enough to sustain a middle-class lifestyle. It comes as a national debate that involves a major gap between the pay of top executives and typical workers.[14]

Building Organizing Funds

To encourage workers to come together, the AFL-CIO often asks its affiliates to increase organizing funds. The federation may also increase funding to its Organizing Institute, which trains organizers, and even launched an advertising campaign to create wider public support for unions.[15] National unions are also creating organizing funds.

An interesting development is the use of a *market recovery fund*, a tool used by U.S. construction unions in their battle with nonunion contractors. The funds use members' dues to subsidize a unionized contractor bidding for work against nonunion competitors, who typically offer lower wage rates. Union contractors hire union plumbers, union electricians, and union artisans from many other crafts. The funds make up the difference in labor costs between a union and nonunion contractor. For instance, if a union shop paid a $1 more an hour, the market recovery fund would make up the $1 difference. Union workers would get paid the same, and the contractor would be on an even footing with his or her nonunion competition. Nonunion firms are eligible for market recovery money only if they sign collective bargaining agreements.[16]

Befriending Laid-Off Workers

The AFL-CIO hopes the castoffs from Enron, WorldCom, and others will become advocates for organizing. John Challenger, head of the national recruiting firm Challenger, Gray & Christmas, said telecom workers who manage to keep their jobs may be more receptive to unions in the future. "When you have an environment like you do in this industry, the fear and stress breaks down relationships between management and workers," Challenger said. "It's an environment ripe for conflict."[17]

Organizing through the Card Check

Card check:

Organizing approach by labor where employees sign a card of support if they want unionization, and if 50 percent of the work force plus one worker sign a card, the union considers it a victory.

The **card check** is an organizing approach by labor where employees sign a card of support if they want unionization, and if 50 percent of the workforce plus one worker sign a card, the union considers it a victory.[18] Card checks are an expedited way of polling workers on union representation but no secret-ballot election takes place.[19] As might be expected, unions strongly support the card check because no secret ballot is used.[20] It remains to be seen what will become of the card check in the future.

Ethical Dilemma

A Strategic Move

You are the plant manager for a medium-sized manufacturing company that has been experiencing growing employee tensions and there has been a lot of talk among workers about forming a union. You have even seen what appear to be authorization cards being passed out around the plant. Sandy Marshall, one of the workers in your plant, has been seen talking to many of the workers, obviously about forming a union. Sandy is very influential with the workers throughout the plant and appears to be a natural leader. You believe that if Sandy continues to promote the union, she will have a major impact among the workers in organizing the union. You have a supervisory position that has just come open. It pays a lot more than Sandy makes. You think, "If I make her a supervisor, she won't be able to use her influence to help get the union started." However, there is another worker in your department who is more qualified and has been with the firm several years longer than Sandy, although he is less influential with other workers throughout the plant.

What would you do?

3 **OBJECTIVE**

Explain the reasons why
employees join unions and
describe the basic structure of
the union.

Why Employees Join Unions

Individuals join unions for many different reasons, which tend to change over time, and may involve job, personal, social, or political considerations. It would be impossible to discuss them all, but the following are some of the major reasons.

Dissatisfaction with Management

Every job holds the potential for real dissatisfaction. Each individual has a boiling point that can cause him or her to consider a union as a solution to real or perceived problems. Unions look for arbitrary or unfair management decisions and then emphasize the advantages of union membership as a means of solving these problems. "Ninety percent of it is not a money issue," said Ron Hreha, president of Local 339 in Port Huron, Michigan. "Issues like seniority, favoritism, grievance procedures, and other quality of work life issues often loom as more important than wages."[21] Some of the other common reasons for employee dissatisfaction are described below.

Compensation. Employees want their compensation to be fair and equitable.[22] Wages are important because they provide both the necessities and pleasures of life. If employees are dissatisfied with their wages, they may look to a union for assistance in improving their standard of living. An important psychological aspect of compensation involves the amount of pay an individual receives in relation to that of other workers performing similar work. If an employee perceives that management has shown favoritism by paying someone else more to perform the same or a lower-level job, the employee will likely become dissatisfied. Union members know precisely the basis of their pay and how it compares with others'. In the past, union members have accepted pay inequities if seniority was the criterion used.

Job Security. Historically, young employees have been less concerned with job security than older workers. The young employee seemed to think, "If I lose this job, I can always get another." But if young employees witness management consistently terminating older workers to make room for younger, more aggressive employees, they may begin to think differently about job security. If the firm does not provide its employees with a sense of job security, workers may turn to a union. Remember also from Chapter 3 that age discrimination is illegal for individuals aged 40 and older.

Attitude of Management. People like to feel that they are important. They do not like to be considered a commodity that can be bought and sold. Thus, employees do not like to be subjected to arbitrary and capricious actions by management. In some firms, management is insensitive to the needs of its employees. In such situations, employees may perceive that they have little or no influence in job-related matters. Workers who feel that they are not really part of the organization are prime targets for unionization.[23]

Management's attitude may be reflected in even small actions. Employees may begin to feel they are being treated more as machines than people. Supervisors may fail to give reasons for unusual assignments and may expect employees to dedicate their lives to the firm without providing adequate rewards. The prevailing philosophy may be: "If you don't like it here, leave." A management philosophy that does not consider the needs of employees as individuals makes the firm ripe for unionization. Management must keep in mind that unions would never have gained a foothold if management had not abused its power. Companies that are pro-employees are not likely to be unionized.[24]

Social Outlet

By nature, many people have strong social needs. They generally enjoy being around others who have similar interests and desires. Some employees join a union for no other reason than to take advantage of union-sponsored recreational and social activities that members and their families find fulfilling. Some unions now offer day-care centers and other services that appeal to working men and women and increase their sense of solidarity with other union members. People who develop close personal relationships, whether in a unionized or union-free organization, will likely stand together in difficult times.

Opportunity for Leadership

Some individuals aspire to leadership roles, but it is not always easy for an operative employee to progress into management. However, employees with leadership aspirations can often satisfy those aspirations through union membership. As with the firm, the union also has a hierarchy of leadership that begins with the union steward, and individual members have the opportunity to work their way up through its various levels.

Forced Unionization

Right-to-work laws:

Laws that prohibit management and unions from entering into agreements requiring union membership as a condition of employment.

In the 28 states without right-to-work laws, it is legal for an employer to agree with the union that a new employee must join the union after a certain period of time (generally 30 days) or be terminated. This is referred to as a *union shop agreement*. **Right-to-work laws** prohibit management and unions from entering into agreements requiring union membership as a condition of employment. These laws are state statutes or constitutional provisions that ban the practice of requiring union membership or financial support as a condition of employment. They establish the legal right of employees to decide for themselves whether or not to join or financially support a union.[25] Twenty-two states, located primarily in the South and West, have adopted such laws, which are a continuing source of irritation between labor and management.[26] Oklahoma became the most recent right-to-work state.[27] The National Right to Work Committee, based in Springfield, Virginia, provides much of the impetus behind the right-to-work movement.

Peer Pressure

Some individuals will join a union because they are urged to do so by other members of the workgroup. Friends and associates may constantly remind an employee that he or she is not a member of the union. In extreme cases, union members have threatened nonmembers with physical violence and sometimes have carried out these threats.

Union Structure

The labor movement has developed a multilevel organizational structure. This complex of organizations ranges from local unions to the two principal federations, the AFL-CIO and the Change to Win Coalition. Each level has its own officers and ways of managing its affairs. Many national unions have intermediate levels between the national and the local levels. However, in this section we describe only the three primary elements of union organization: the local union; the national union; and the federation, or AFL-CIO. As was discussed in the opening HRM in Action, another federation, the Change to Win Coalition, consisting of national unions that bolted from the AFL-CIO, was created.

Local Union

Local union:
Basic element in the structure of the U.S. labor movement.

The basic element in the structure of the American labor movement is the **local union** (or, the *local*). To the individual union member, it is the most important level in the structure of organized labor. Through the local, the individual deals with the employer on a day-to-day basis. A local union may fill a social role in the lives of its members, sponsoring dances, festivals, and other functions. It may be the focal point of the political organization and activity of its members.

Craft union:
Bargaining unit, such as the Carpenters and Joiners union, which is typically composed of members of a particular trade or skill in a specific locality.

There are two basic kinds of local unions: craft and industrial. A **craft union**, such as the Carpenters and Joiners union, is typically composed of members of a particular trade or skill in a specific locality. Members usually acquire their job skills through an apprenticeship-training program. An **industrial union** generally consists of all the workers in a particular plant or group of plants. The type of work they do and the level of skill they possess are not a condition for membership in the union. An example of an industrial union is the United Auto Workers.

Industrial union:
Bargaining unit that generally consists of all the workers in a particular plant or group of plants.

The local union's functions are many and varied. Administering the collective bargaining agreement and representing workers in handling grievances are two very important activities. Other functions include keeping the membership informed about labor issues, promoting increased membership, maintaining effective contact with the national union, and, when appropriate, negotiating with management at the local level.

National Union

National union:
Organization composed of local unions, which it charters.

The most powerful level in the union structure is the national union. As stated previously, most locals are affiliated with national unions. A **national union** is composed of local unions, which it charters. As such, it is the parent organization to local unions. The local union, not the individual worker, holds membership in the national union. Each local union provides financial support to the national union based on its membership size. The Service Employees International Union is the largest and fastest-growing national union in North America, with 1.8 million members; it focuses on uniting workers in the key service sectors.[28] The International Brotherhood of Teamsters has about 1.4 million members and represents trade groups, including truckers, UPS workers, warehouse employees, cab drivers, airline workers, construction crews, and other workers. There are nearly 1,900 Teamster affiliates throughout the United States, Canada, and Puerto Rico.[29]

The national union is governed by a national constitution and a national convention of local unions, which usually meets every two to five years. Elected officers, aided by an administrative staff, conduct the day-to-day operations of the national union. The national union is active in organizing workers within its jurisdiction, engaging in collective bargaining at the national level, and assisting its locals in their negotiations. In addition, the national union may provide numerous educational and research services for its locals, dispense strike funds, publish the union newspaper, provide legal counsel, and actively lobby at national and state levels.

American Federation of Labor and Congress of Industrial Organizations (AFL-CIO)

American Federation of Labor and Congress of Industrial Organizations (AFL-CIO):
Central trade union federation in the United States.

The **AFL-CIO** is the central trade union federation in the United States. Until 2005, the AFL-CIO had membership of approximately 13.5 million workers and 57 national and international labor unions.[30] Then, the Change to Win Coalition broke away from the AFL-CIO, taking with it approximately 40 percent of the AFL-CIO membership. The AFL-CIO represents the interests of labor and its member national unions at the highest level. The federation does not engage in collective bargaining; however, it provides the means by which member unions can cooperate to pursue common objectives and attempt to resolve internal problems faced by organized labor. The federation is financed by its member national unions and is governed by a national convention, which meets every two years.

As shown in Figure 12-1, the structure of the AFL-CIO is complex. National unions can affiliate with one or more of the trade and industrial departments. These departments seek to promote the interests of specific groups of workers who are in different unions but have common interests. The federation's major activities include the following:

1. Improving the image of organized labor.

2. Extensive lobbying on behalf of labor interests.

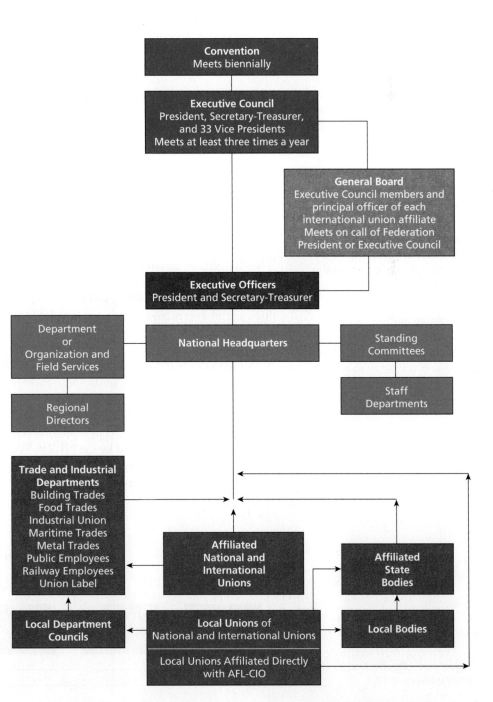

Figure 12-1 Structure of the AFL-CIO

Source: Bureau of Labor Statistics, *Directory of National Unions and Employee Associations.*

3. Politically educating constituencies and others through COPE.
4. Resolving disputes between national unions.
5. Policing internal affairs of member unions.

The AFL-CIO is a loosely knit organization of national unions that has little formal power or control. The member national unions remain completely autonomous and decide their own policies and programs.

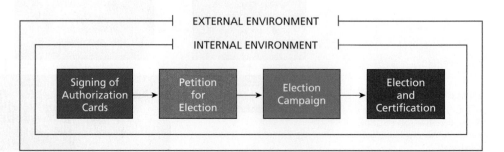

4 OBJECTIVE

Define collective bargaining and identify the steps involved in establishing the collective bargaining relationship.

Collective bargaining:
Performance of the mutual obligation of the employer and the representative of the employees to meet at reasonable times and confer in good faith with respect to wages, hours, and other terms and conditions of employment, or the negotiation of an agreement, or any question arising there under, and the execution of a written contract incorporating any agreement reached if requested by either party; such obligation does not compel either party to agree to a proposal or require the making of a concession.

Bargaining unit:
Group of employees, not necessarily union members, recognized by an employer or certified by an administrative agency as appropriate for representation by a labor organization for purposes of collective bargaining.

Establishing the Collective Bargaining Relationship

Before a union can negotiate a contract, it must first be certified. The primary law governing the relationship of companies and unions is the National Labor Relations Act, as amended. Collective bargaining is one of the key parts of the Act. Section 8(d) of the act defines **collective bargaining** as:

> *The performance of the mutual obligation of the employer and the representative of the employees to meet at reasonable times and confer in good faith with respect to wages, hours, and other terms and conditions of employment, or the negotiation of an agreement, or any question arising there under, and the execution of a written contract incorporating any agreement reached if requested by either party, but such obligation does not compel either party to agree to a proposal or require the making of a concession.*

The Act further provides that the designated representative of the employees shall be the exclusive representative for all the employees in the unit for purposes of collective bargaining. A **bargaining unit** consists of a group of employees, not necessarily union members, recognized by an employer or certified by an administrative agency as appropriate for representation by a labor organization for purposes of collective bargaining.

A unit may cover the employees in one plant of an employer, or it may cover employees in two or more plants of the same employer. Although the act requires the representative to be selected by the employees, it does not require any particular procedure to be used so long as the choice clearly reflects the desire of the majority of the employees in the bargaining unit. The employee representative is normally chosen in a secret-ballot election conducted by the NLRB. When workers desire to become the bargaining representative for a group of employees, several steps leading to certification have to be taken (see Figure 12-2).

Figure 12-2 Steps That Lead to Forming a Bargaining Unit

Signing of Authorization Cards

Authorization card:
Document indicating that an employee wants to be represented by a labor organization in collective bargaining.

A prerequisite to forming a recognized bargaining unit is to determine whether there is sufficient interest on the part of employees to justify the unit. Evidence of this interest is expressed when at least 30 percent of the employees in a workgroup sign an authorization card. The **authorization card** is a document indicating that an employee wants to be represented by a labor organization in collective bargaining. Most union organizers will not proceed unless at least 50 percent of the workers in the group sign cards. An authorization card used by the International Association of Machinists is shown in Figure 12-3.

Petition for Election

After the authorization cards have been signed, a petition for an election may be made to the appropriate regional office of the NLRB. When the petition is filed, the NLRB will conduct an investigation. The purpose of the investigation is to determine, among other things, the following:

1. Whether the Board has jurisdiction to conduct an election.
2. Whether there is a sufficient showing of employee interest to justify an election.
3. Whether a question of representation exists (for example, the employee representative has demanded recognition, which has been denied by the employer).
4. Whether the election will include appropriate employees in the bargaining unit (for instance, the Board is prohibited from including plant guards in the same unit with the other employees).
5. Whether the representative named in the petition is qualified (for example, a supervisor or any other management representative may not be an employee representative).
6. Whether there are any barriers to an election in the form of existing contracts or prior elections held within the past 12 months.[31]

YES, I WANT THE IAM

I, the undersigned, an employee of

(Company) _____,
hereby authorize the International Association of Machinists and Aerospace Workers (IAM) to act as my collective bargaining agent with the company for wages, hours, and working conditions.

NAME (print) _____ DATE _____
ADDRESS (print) _____
CITY _____ STATE _____ ZIP _____
DEPT. _____ SHIFT _____ PHONE _____
Classification _____
SIGN HERE ✗ _____

NOTE: THIS AUTHORIZATION IS TO BE SIGNED AND DATED IN EMPLOYEE'S OWN HANDWRITING. YOUR RIGHT TO SIGN THIS CARD IS PROTECTED BY FEDERAL LAW.

Figure 12-3 An Authorization Card
Source: The International Association of Machinists and Aerospace Workers.

National Labor Relations Board

http://www.nlrb.gov/

The NLRB is a federal agency that administers the National Labor Relations Act.

If these conditions have been met, the NLRB will ordinarily direct that an election be held within 30 days. Election details are left largely to the agency's regional director.

Election Campaign

When an election has been ordered, both union and management usually promote their causes actively. Unions will continue to encourage workers to join the union, and management may begin a campaign to tell workers the benefits of remaining union-free. The supervisor's role during the campaign is crucial. Supervisors need to conduct themselves in a manner that avoids violating the law and committing unfair labor practices. Specifically, they should be aware of what can and cannot be done in the pre-election campaign period. In many cases, it is not so much *what* the supervisor says as *how* it is said.[32] Throughout the campaign, supervisors should keep upper management informed about employee attitudes.

Theoretically, both union and management are permitted to tell their stories without interference from the other side. At times, the campaign becomes quite intense. Election results will be declared invalid if the campaign was marked by conduct that the NLRB considers to have interfered with the employees' freedom of choice. Examples of such conduct include the following:

- An employer or a union threatens loss of jobs or benefits to influence employees' votes or union activities.
- An employer or a union misstates important facts in the election campaign when the other party does not have a chance to reply.
- Either an employer or a union incites racial or religious prejudice by inflammatory campaign appeals.
- An employer fires employees to discourage or encourage their union activities or a union causes an employer to take such an action.
- An employer or a union makes campaign speeches to assembled groups of employees on company time within 24 hours of an election.

Election and Certification

The NLRB monitors the secret-ballot election on the date set. Its representatives are responsible for making sure that only eligible employees vote, and for counting the votes. Following a valid election, the board will issue a certification of the results to the participants. If a union has been chosen by a majority of the employees voting in the bargaining unit, it will receive a certificate showing that it is now the official bargaining representative of the employees in the unit. Remember in our earlier discussion, that the card check was being used as a means of eliminating the use of a secret election by the NLRB. However, the right to represent employees does not mean the right to dictate terms to management that would adversely affect the organization. The bargaining process does not require either party to make concessions; it only compels them to bargain in good faith in collective bargaining. Recently, the number of representation elections held was 2,117 and the union won 61.5 percent of them.[33]

Collective Bargaining

Once the NLRB certifies the union, efforts can begin to negotiate a contract. The collective bargaining process is fundamental to union and management relations in the United States. Most union/management agreements in the United States are for a three-year period. Thus, on average, one-third of collective bargaining agreements occur each year. The bargaining structure can affect the conduct of collective bargaining. The four major structures are one company dealing with a single union, several companies dealing with a single union, several unions dealing with a single company, and several companies dealing with several unions. Most contract bargaining is carried out under the first type of structure. The process can become quite complicated when several companies and unions are involved in the same negotiations. However, even when there is only one industry involved and one group of workers with similar skills, collective bargaining can be very difficult.

5 OBJECTIVE

Describe the collective bargaining process and explain the psychological aspects of collective bargaining.

Collective Bargaining Process

Regardless of the current state of labor management relations, the general aspects of the collective bargaining process are the same and are illustrated in Figure 12-4. Depending on the type of relationship encountered, the collective bargaining process may be relatively simple, or it may be a long, tense struggle for both parties. Regardless of the complexity of the bargaining issues, the ability to reach agreement is the key to any successful negotiation.

As you can see, both external and internal environmental factors can influence the process. The first step in the collective bargaining process is preparing for

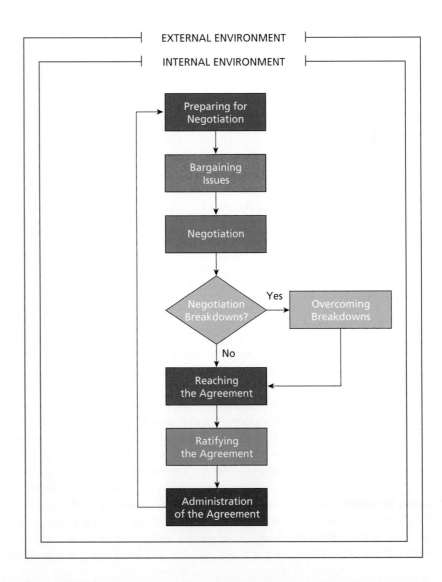

Figure 12-4 Collective Bargaining Process

negotiations. This step is often extensive and ongoing for both union and management. After the issues to be negotiated have been determined, the two sides confer to reach a mutually acceptable contract. Although breakdowns in negotiations can occur, both labor and management have at their disposal tools and arguments that can be used to convince the other side to accept their views. Eventually, however, management and the union usually reach an agreement that defines the rules for the duration of the contract. The next step is for the union membership to ratify the agreement. Note the feedback loop from "Administration of the Agreement" to "Preparing for Negotiation" in Figure 12-4. Collective bargaining is a continuous and dynamic process, and preparing for the next round of negotiations often begins the moment a contract is ratified.

Psychological Aspects of Collective Bargaining

Prior to collective bargaining, both management and union teams have to prepare positions and accomplish certain tasks. Vitally important for those involved are the psychological aspects of collective bargaining. Psychologically, the collective bargaining process is often difficult because it is an adversarial situation and must be approached as such. It is a situation that is fundamental to law, politics, business, and government, because out of the clash of ideas, points of view, and interests come agreement, consensus, and justice.

In effect, those involved in the collective bargaining process will be matching wits with the competition, will experience victory as well as defeat, and will still usually resolve problems, resulting in a contract. The role of those who meet at the bargaining table essentially involves the management of aggression in a manner that allows them to hammer out a collective bargaining agreement. The personalities of those involved have a major impact on the negotiation process. The attitudes of those who will be negotiating have a direct effect on what can be accomplished and how quickly a mutually agreed-on contract can be finalized. Finally, the longer, more involved, and intense the bargaining sessions are, the greater the psychological strain on all concerned. As psychological pressures intensify, the gap between labor and management can easily widen, further compounding the problem of achieving mutual accommodation.

Scare tactics intensify the psychological pressures of collective bargaining. Labor may threaten to strike; management may threaten a lockout. Most likely, neither side wants either a strike or a lockout, but it is hoped that the psychological impact of the threat will bring the other side back to the bargaining table.

6 OBJECTIVE
Describe the factors involved in preparing for negotiations.

Preparing for Negotiations

Because of the complex issues facing labor and management today, the negotiating teams must carefully prepare for the bargaining sessions. Prior to meeting at the bargaining table, the negotiators should thoroughly know the culture, climate, history, present economic state, and wage and benefits structure of both the organization and similar organizations. Because the length of a typical labor agreement is three years, negotiators should develop a contract that is successful both now and in the future. This consideration should prevail for both management and labor, although it rarely does. During the term of an agreement, the two sides usually discover contract provisions that need to be added, deleted, or modified. These items become proposals to be addressed in the next round of negotiations.

Bargaining issues can be divided into three categories: mandatory, permissive, and prohibited. **Mandatory bargaining issues** fall within the definition of wages, hours, and other terms and conditions of employment (see Table 12-1). These issues generally have an immediate and direct effect on workers' jobs. A refusal to bargain in these areas is grounds for an unfair labor practice charge. In many industries, collective

Mandatory bargaining issues: Bargaining issues that fall within the definition of wages, hours, and other terms and conditions of employment.

Table 12-1 Mandatory Bargaining Issues

Wages	Plant closedown and relocation
Hours	Change in operations resulting in
Discharge	reclassifying workers from incentive to
Arbitration	straight time, or a cut in the workforce,
Paid holidays	or installations of cost-saving machinery
Paid vacations	Price of meals provided by company
Duration of agreement	Group insurance—health, accident, life
Grievance procedure	Promotions
Layoff plan	Seniority
Reinstatement of economic strikers	Layoffs
Change of payment from hourly base to	Transfers
salary base	Work assignment and transfers
Union security and checkoff of dues	No-strike clause
Work rules	Piece rates
Merit wage increase	Stock purchase plan
Work schedule	Workloads
Lunch periods	Change of employee status to
Rest periods	independent contractors
Pension plan	Motor carrier-union agreement
Retirement age	providing that carriers use own
Bonus payments	equipment before leasing outside
Cancellation of seniority upon relocation of	equipment
plant	Overtime pay
Discounts on company products	Agency shop
Shift differentials	Sick leave
Contract clause providing for supervisors	Employer's insistence on clause giving an
keeping seniority in unit	arbitrator the right to enforce an award
Procedures for income tar withholding	Management rights clause
Severance pay	Plant closing
Nondiscriminatory hiring hall	Job posting procedures
Plant rules	Plant reopening
Safety	Employee physical examination
Prohibition against supervisor doing unit	Arrangement for negotiation
work	Change in insurance carrier and benefits
Superseniority for union stewards	Profit-sharing plan
Partial plant closing	Company houses
Hunting on employer's forest reserve where	Subcontracting
previously granted	Union production imposed ceiling

Source: Read Richardson, "Positive Collective Bargaining," Chapter 7.5 of ASPA *Handbook of Personnel and Industrial Relations,* 7–121. Copyright 1979 by The Bureau of National Affairs, Inc., Washington, DC. Reprinted by permission.

bargaining toward new wage, rules, and benefits agreements typically drags on for a long time. One of the biggest issues today is the rising health costs and who will to pay for them. **Permissive bargaining issues** may be raised, but neither side may insist that they be bargained over. For example, the management may want to bargain over health benefits for retired workers, but the union may choose not to bargain over the issue. Another permissive bargaining issue might be the union wanting child-care arrangements.

Prohibited bargaining issues, such as the issue of the closed shop, an arrangement whereby union membership is a prerequisite, are statutorily outlawed.

The Taft-Hartley Act made the closed shop illegal. However, the Act was modified 12 years later by the Landrum-Griffin Act to permit a closed shop in the construction industry. This is the only exception allowed.

The union must continuously gather information regarding membership needs to isolate areas of dissatisfaction. The union steward is normally in the best position to collect such data. Because they are usually elected by their peers, stewards should be well informed regarding union members' attitudes. The union steward constantly funnels information up through the union's chain of command, where the data are compiled and analyzed. Union leadership attempts to uncover any areas of

Permissive bargaining issues: Issues may be raised, but neither side may insist that they be bargained over.

Prohibited bargaining issues: Issues that are statutorily outlawed from collective bargaining.

dissatisfaction because the general union membership must approve any agreement before it becomes final. Because they are elected, union leaders will lose their positions if the demands they make of management do not represent the desires of the general membership.

Management also spends long hours preparing for negotiations. The many interrelated tasks that management must accomplish are presented in Figure 12-5. In this example, the firm allows approximately six months to prepare for negotiations. All aspects of the current contracts are considered, including flaws that should be corrected. When preparing for negotiations, management should listen carefully to first-line managers. These individuals administer the labor agreement on a day-to-day basis and must live with errors made in negotiating the contract. An alert line manager is also able to inform upper management of the demands unions may plan to make during negotiations.

Management also attempts periodically to obtain information regarding employee attitudes. Surveys are often administered to workers to determine their feelings toward their jobs and job environment. Union and management representatives like to know as much as possible about employee attitudes when they sit down at the bargaining table.

Another part of preparation for negotiations involves identifying various positions that both union and management will take as the negotiations progress. Each usually takes an initially extreme position, representing the conditions union or management would prefer. The two sides will likely determine absolute limits to their offers or demands before a breakdown in negotiations occurs. They also usually prepare fallback positions based on combinations of issues. Preparations should be detailed, because clear minds often do not prevail during the heat of negotiations.

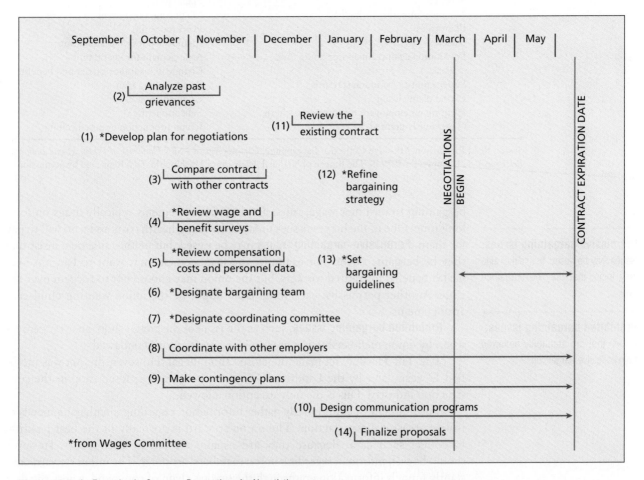

Figure 12-5 An Example of a Company Preparations for Negotiations
Source: Adapted from Ronald L. Miller. "Preparations for Negotiations," *Personnel Journal* 57: 38. Copyright January 1978. Reprinted with Permission.

A major consideration in preparing for negotiations is the selection of the bargaining teams. The makeup of the management team usually depends on the type of organization and its size. Normally, labor relations specialists, with the advice and assistance of operating managers, conduct bargaining. Sometimes, top executives are directly involved, particularly in smaller firms. Larger companies utilize staff specialists (a human resource manager or industrial relations executive), managers of principal operating divisions, and, in some cases, an outside consultant, such as a labor attorney.

The responsibility for conducting negotiations for the union is usually entrusted to union officers. At the local level, rank-and-file members who are elected specifically for this purpose will normally supplement the bargaining committee. In addition, the national union will often send a representative to act in an advisory capacity or even to participate directly in the bargaining sessions. The real task of the union negotiating team is to develop and obtain solutions to the problems raised by the union's membership.

Finally, it is imperative that both groups appreciate the environment in which companies in the industry must operate. Although there are environmental differences between industries, some basic similarities do exist. There have been rapid technological changes and ever-increasing competitive global pressures. Union membership has fallen and management does not hesitate to transfer jobs overseas. More and more, the jobs remaining in the United States require specific skills, adaptability, and flexibility. Also, worker involvement is a reality and not an option for many corporations.

 OBJECTIVE

Explain typical bargaining issues and describe the process of negotiating the agreement.

Bargaining Issues

The document that emerges from the collective bargaining process is known as a *labor agreement* or *contract*. It regulates the relationship between employer and employees for a specified period of time. It is still an essential but difficult task because each agreement is unique, and there is no standard or universal model. Despite much dissimilarity, certain topics are included in virtually all labor agreements.

Recognition

This section usually appears at the beginning of the labor agreement. Its purpose is to identify the union that is recognized as the bargaining representative and to describe the bargaining unit, that is, the employees for whom the union speaks. A typical recognition section might read as follows:

> *The XYZ Company recognizes the ABC Union as the sole and exclusive representative of the bargaining unit employees for the purpose of collective bargaining with regard to wages, hours, and other conditions of employment.*

Management Rights

A section that is often but not always written into the labor agreement spells out the rights of management. If no such section is included, management may reason that it retains control of all topics not described as bargainable in the contract. The precise content of the management rights section will vary by industry, company, and union. When included, management rights generally involve three areas:

1. Freedom to select the business objectives of the company.
2. Freedom to determine the uses to which the material assets of the enterprise will be devoted.
3. Power to take disciplinary action for cause.

In a brochure the company publishes for all its first-line managers, AT&T describes management's rights when dealing with the union, including the following:

You should remember that management has all such rights except those restricted by law or by contract with the union. You either make these decisions or carry them out through contact with your people. Some examples of these decisions and actions are:

- *To determine what work is to be done and where, when, and how it is to be done.*
- *To determine the number of employees who will do the work.*
- *To supervise and instruct employees in doing the work.*
- *To correct employees whose work performance or personal conduct fails to meet reasonable standards. This includes administering disciplinary action.*
- *To recommend hiring, dismissing, upgrading, or downgrading of employees.*
- *To recommend employees for promotion to management.[34]*

Union Security

Union security is typically one of the first items negotiated in a collective bargaining agreement. The objective of union security provisions is to ensure that the union continues to exist and perform its functions. A strong union security provision makes it easier for the union to enroll and retain members. Some basic forms of union security clauses are next described.

Closed shop:
Arrangement making union membership a prerequisite for employment.

Closed Shop. A **closed shop** is an arrangement whereby union membership is a prerequisite for employment.

Union shop:
Requirement that all employees become members of the union after a specified period of employment (the legal minimum is 30 days) or after a union shop provision has been negotiated.

Union Shop. A **union shop** arrangement requires that all employees become members of the union after a specified period of employment (the legal minimum is 30 days) or after a union shop provision has been negotiated. Employees must remain members of the union as a condition of employment. The union shop is generally legal in the United States, except in states that have right-to-work laws.

Maintenance of Membership. Employees who are members of the union at the time the labor agreement is signed or who later voluntarily join must continue their memberships until the termination of the agreement, as a condition of employment. This form of recognition is also prohibited in most states that have right-to-work laws.

Agency shop:
Labor agreement provision requiring, as a condition of employment, that each nonunion member of a bargaining unit pay the union the equivalent of membership dues as a service charge in return for the union acting as the bargaining agent.

Agency Shop. An **agency shop**, provision does not require employees to join the union; however, the labor agreement requires that, as a condition of employment, each nonunion member of the bargaining unit pay the union the equivalent of membership dues as a kind of tax, or service charge, in return for the union acting as the bargaining agent. The National Labor Relations Act requires the union to bargain for all members of the bargaining unit, including nonunion employees. The agency shop is outlawed in most states that have right-to-work laws.

Open shop:
Employment on equal terms to union members and nonmembers alike.

Open Shop. An open shop describes the absence of union security, rather than its presence. The **open shop**, strictly defined, is employment on equal terms to union members and nonmembers alike. Under this arrangement, no employee is required to join or contribute to the union financially.

Dues Checkoff. Another type of security that unions attempt to achieve is the check-off of dues. A checkoff agreement may be used in addition to any of the previously mentioned shop agreements. Under the **checkoff of dues** provision, the company agrees to withhold union dues from members' paychecks and to forward the money directly to the union. Because of provisions in the Taft-Hartley Act, each union member must voluntarily sign a statement authorizing this deduction. Dues checkoff is important to the union because it eliminates much of the expense, time, and hassle of collecting dues from each member every pay period or once a month.

> **Checkoff of dues:**
> Agreement by which a company agrees to withhold union dues from members' paychecks and to forward the money directly to the union.

Compensation

This section typically constitutes a large portion of most labor agreements. Virtually any item that can affect compensation may be included in labor agreements. Some of the items frequently covered include the following:

Wage Rate Schedule. The base rates to be paid each year of the contract for each job are included in this section. At times, unions are able to obtain a cost-of-living allowance (COLA), or escalator clause, in the contract in order to protect the purchasing power of employees' earnings (discussed in Chapter 9).

Overtime and Premium Pay. Another section of the agreement may cover hours of work, overtime pay, hazard pay, and premium pay, such as shift differentials (discussed previously in Chapter 10).

Jury Pay. For some firms, jury pay amounts to the employee's entire salary when he or she is serving jury duty. Others pay the difference between the amount employees receive from the court and the compensation that would have been earned. The procedure covering jury pay is typically stated in the contract.

Layoff or Severance Pay. The amount that employees in various jobs and/or seniority levels will be paid if they are laid off or terminated is a frequently included item.

Holidays. The holidays recognized and the amount of pay that a worker will receive if he or she has to work on a holiday are specified. In addition, the pay procedure for times when a holiday falls on a worker's normal day off is provided.

Vacation. This section spells out the amount of vacation that a person may take, based on seniority. Any restrictions as to when the vacation may be taken are also stated.

Family Care. This is a benefit that has been included in recent collective bargaining agreements, with child care expected to continue to be a hot bargaining issue.

Grievance Procedure

A portion of most labor agreements is devoted to a grievance procedure. It contains the means whereby employees can voice dissatisfaction with and appeal specific management actions.[35] Also included in this section are procedures for disciplinary action by management and the termination procedure that must be followed.

Employee Security

This section of the labor agreement establishes the procedures that cover job security for individual employees. Seniority is a key topic related to employee security. *Seniority* is the length of time an employee has been associated with the company, division, department, or job. Seniority may be determined company-wide, by division, by department, or by job. Agreement on seniority is important because the person with the most seniority, as defined in the labor agreement, is typically the last to be laid off and the first to be recalled. The seniority system also provides a basis for promotion decisions. When qualifications are met, employees with the greatest seniority will likely be considered first for promotion to higher-level jobs.

Job-Related Factors

Many of the rules governing employee actions on the job are also included. Some of the more important factors are company work rules, work standards, and rules related to safety. This section varies, depending on the nature of the industry and the product manufactured. Work rules are vitally important to both employers and employees, with companies tending to favor less restrictive work rules.

Negotiating the Agreement

There is no way to ensure speedy and mutually acceptable results from negotiations. At best, the parties can attempt to create an atmosphere that will lend itself to steady progress and productive results. For example, the two negotiating teams usually meet at an agreed-on neutral site, such as a hotel. When a favorable relationship can be established early, eleventh-hour (or last-minute) bargaining can often be avoided. It is equally important for union and management negotiators to strive to develop and maintain clear and open lines of communication. Collective bargaining is a problem-solving activity; consequently, good communication is essential to its success. Negotiations should be conducted in the privacy of the conference room, not in the news media. Often in the media, the unions belittle management and naturally management strikes back. The media love it because it sells. The results are harmful, often to both sides.[36] If the negotiators feel that publicity is necessary, joint releases to the media may avoid unnecessary conflict.

The negotiating phase of collective bargaining begins with each side presenting its initial demands. Because a collective bargaining settlement can be expensive for a firm, the cost of various proposals should be estimated as accurately as possible. Some changes can be quite expensive, and others cost little or nothing, but the cost of the various proposals being considered must always be carefully deliberated. The term *negotiating* suggests a certain amount of give-and-take, the purpose of which is to lower the other side's expectations. For example, the union might bargain to upgrade its members' economic and working conditions and the company might negotiate to maintain or enhance profitability.

One of the most costly components of any collective bargaining agreement is a wage increase provision. An example of the negotiation of a wage increase is shown in Figure 12-6. In this example, labor initially demands a 40-cent-per-hour increase. Management counters with an offer of only 10 cents per hour. Both labor and management, as expected, reject each other's demand. Plan B calls for labor to lower its demand to a 30-cents-per-hour increase. Management counters with an offer of 20 cents. The positions in plan B are feasible to both sides, as both groups are in the bargaining zone. Wages within the bargaining zone are those that management and labor can both accept, in this case, an increase of between 20 cents and 30 cents per hour. The exact amount will be determined by the power of the bargaining unit and the skills of the negotiators.

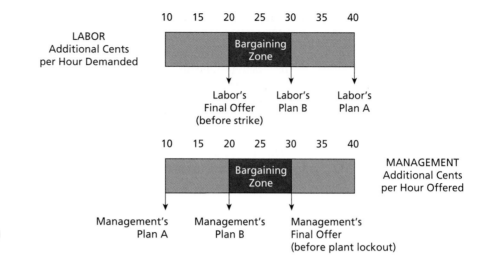

Figure 12-6 Example of Negotiating a Wage Increase

The realities of negotiations are not for the weak of heart and at times are similar to a high-stakes poker game. A certain amount of bluffing and raising the ante takes place in many negotiations. The ultimate bluff for the union is when a negotiator says, "If our demands are not met, we are prepared to strike." Management's version of this bluff would be to threaten a lockout. Each of these tactics will be discussed later as a means of overcoming breakdowns in negotiations. The party with the greater leverage can expect to extract the most concessions.

Even though one party in the negotiating process may appear to possess the greater power, negotiators often take care to keep the other side from losing face. They recognize that the balance of power may switch rapidly. By the time the next round of negotiations occurs, the pendulum may be swinging back in favor of the other side. Even when management appears to have the upper hand, it may make minor concessions that will allow the labor leader to claim gains for the union. Management may demand that workers pay for grease rags that are lost (assuming that the loss of these rags has become excessive). In order to obtain labor's agreement to this demand, management may agree to provide new uniforms for the workers if the cost of these uniforms would be less than the cost of lost rags. Thus, labor leaders, although forced to concede to management's demand, could show the workers that they have obtained a concession from management. Each side usually does not expect to obtain all the demands presented in its first proposal. Labor can lose a demand and continue to bring it up in the future. Demands for benefits that the union does not expect to receive when they are first made are known as **beachhead demands**.

Beachhead demands:
Demands that the union does not expect management to meet when they are first made.

 OBJECTIVE

Identify ways to overcome breakdowns in negotiations.

Breakdowns in Negotiations

At times negotiations break down, even though both labor and management may sincerely want to arrive at an equitable contract settlement. Several means of removing roadblocks may be used in order to get negotiations moving again.

Third-Party Intervention

Often an outside person can intervene to provide assistance when an agreement cannot be reached and the two sides reach an impasse. The reasons behind each party's position may be quite rational, or the breakdown may be related to emotional disputes that tend to become distorted during the heat of negotiations. Regardless of the cause, something must be done to continue the negotiations. The two basic types of third-party intervention are mediation and arbitration.

Mediation:
Neutral third party enters the negotiations and attempts to facilitate a resolution to a labor dispute when a bargaining impasse has occurred.

Mediation. In **mediation**, a neutral third party enters the negotiations and attempts to facilitate a resolution to a labor dispute when a bargaining impasse has occurred.[37] A mediator basically acts like a facilitator. The objective of mediation is to persuade the parties to resume negotiations and reach a settlement. A mediator has no power to force a settlement but can help in the search for solutions, make recommendations, and work to open blocked channels of communication. Successful mediation depends to a substantial degree on the tact, diplomacy, patience, and perseverance of the mediator.[38] The mediator's fresh insights are used to get discussions going again. Mediation is voluntary at every step of the process. The mediator serves as an informal coach, helping to ensure that the discussions are fair and effective.

The principal organization involved in mediation efforts, other than some state and local agencies, is the Federal Mediation and Conciliation Service (FMCS). In 1947, the Taft-Hartley Act established the FMCS as an independent agency. Either one or both parties involved in negotiations can seek the assistance of the FMCS, or the agency can offer its help if it feels that the situation warrants it. Federal law requires that the party wishing to change a contract must give notice of this intention to the other party 60 days prior to the expiration of a contract. If no agreement has been reached 30 days prior to the expiration date, the FMCS must be notified.

Arbitration:
Process in which a dispute is submitted to an impartial third party for a binding decision; an arbitrator basically acts as a judge and jury.

Arbitration. In **arbitration**, a dispute is submitted to an impartial third party for a binding decision; an arbitrator basically acts as a judge and jury. There are two principal types of union management disputes: rights disputes and interest disputes. Disputes over the interpretation and application of the various provisions of an existing contract are submitted to **rights arbitration**. This type of arbitration is used in settling grievances. Grievance arbitration is common in the United States. The other type of arbitration, **interest arbitration**, involves disputes over the terms of proposed collective bargaining agreements.

Rights arbitration:
Arbitration involving disputes over the interpretation and application of the various provisions of an existing contract.

In the private sector, the use of interest arbitration as an alternative procedure for impasse resolution is not a common practice. Unions and employers rarely agree to submit the basic terms of a contract (such as wages, hours, and working conditions) to a neutral party for disposition. They prefer to rely on collective bargaining and the threat of economic pressure (such as strikes and lockouts), to decide these issues.

Interest arbitration:
Arbitration that involves disputes over the terms of proposed collective bargaining agreements.

In the public sector, most governmental jurisdictions prohibit their employees from striking. As a result, interest arbitration is used to a greater extent than in the private sector, although there is no uniform application of this method. A procedure used in the public sector is *final-offer arbitration*, which has two basic forms: package selection and issue-by-issue selection. In package selection, the arbitrator must select one party's entire offer on all issues in dispute. In issue-by-issue selection, the arbitrator examines each issue separately and chooses the final offer of one side or the other on each issue. Final-offer arbitration is often used to determine the salary of a professional baseball player. Both players and management present a dollar figure to an arbitrator. The arbitrator chooses one figure or the other.

In arbitration, the disputants are free to select any person as their arbitrator, so long as they agree on the selection. Most commonly, however, the two sides make a request for an arbitrator to either the American Arbitration Association (AAA) or the FMCS. The AAA is a nonprofit organization with offices in many cities. Both the AAA and the FMCS maintain lists of arbitrators. Only arbitrators who can show, through references, experience in labor management relations and acceptance by both labor and management as neutral parties, are selected for inclusion on these lists.

Human Resource Links

http://www.lir.msu.edu/
hotlinks/

The homepage sites for numerous human resource links are identified.

Union Strategies for Overcoming Negotiation Breakdowns

There are times when a union believes that it must exert extreme pressure to get management to agree to its bargaining demands. Strikes, boycotts, and activism are the primary means that the union may use to overcome breakdowns in negotiations.

Strike:

Action by union members who refuse to work in order to exert pressure on management in negotiations.

Strikes. When union members refuse to work in order to exert pressure on management in negotiations, their action is referred to as a **strike**. A strike halts production, resulting in lost customers and revenue, which the union hopes will force management to submit to its terms. In reality, the United States has always had the lowest percentage of days lost due to strikes of all industrialized nations. There are fewer strikes today than at any time since such statistics were gathered. The number of strikes involving 1,000 or more workers in 2004 was 17 compared to over 200 each year in the 1970s.[39]

The timing of a strike is important in determining its effectiveness. An excellent time is when business is thriving and the demand for the firm's goods or services is expanding. However, the union might be hard-pressed to obtain major concessions from a strike if the firm's sales are down and it has built up a large inventory. In this instance, the company would not be severely damaged.

Contrary to many opinions, unions prefer to use the strike only as a last resort. During a strike, workers have little income. The strike fund may only pay for items such as food, utilities, and motor fuel.[40] In recent years, many union members have been even more reluctant to strike because of the fear of being replaced. When a union goes on an economic strike and the company hires replacements, the company does not have to lay off these individuals at the end of the strike. For example, Edw. C. Levy Co., headquartered in Detroit, Michigan, hired permanent replacements for the 130 members of the International Union of Operating Engineers Local 150 striking the contractor's operations at Mittal Steel Co.'s Burns Harbor plant.[41]

A union's treasury is often depleted by payment of strike benefits to its members. In addition, members suffer because they are not receiving their normal pay. Striking workers during one General Motors strike got paid about $150 a week strike pay instead of the roughly $1,000 a week that they might be taking home with all of their overtime. Although strike pay helps, union members certainly cannot maintain a normal standard of living from these minimal amounts. Sometimes during negotiations (especially at the beginning), the union may want to strengthen its negotiating position by taking a strike vote. Members often give overwhelming approval to a strike. This vote does not necessarily mean that there will be a strike, only that the union leaders now have the authority to call one if negotiations reach an impasse. This was the case at Dominick Stores, a grocery store chain in Chicago, when union officials rejected an offer and a strike vote was approved by 80 percent of the union workers.[42] A strike vote with Delta Airline pilots was approved by 94 percent of the union membership in 2006. A favorable strike vote can add a sense of urgency to efforts to reach an agreement.

Successful passage of a strike vote has additional implications for union members. Virtually every national union's constitution contains a clause requiring the members to support and participate in a strike if one is called. If a union member fails to comply with this requirement, he or she can be fined. Therefore, union members place themselves in jeopardy if they cross a picket line without the consent of the union. Fines may be as high as 100 percent of wages for as long as union pickets remain outside the company. However, the Supreme Court has ruled that an employee on economic strike may resign from the union during a strike and avoid being punished by the union. In today's economy, union members are using more subtle measures, such as sick outs and work slowdowns, to successfully avoid the impact of a strike while still bringing pressure on the company to meet union demands.

Members of the Association of Flight Attendants were threatening intermittent, random strikes, called CHAOS strikes, for Creating Havoc Around Our System. Those actions are designed to strangle the airline's global service network by creating bottlenecks at key airports. The plan calls for attendants at certain airports to walk off their jobs for only an hour or two before returning to work. That is long enough to throw off the carrier's schedule, but not long enough for the airline to replace them.[43]

Trends & Innovations

Virtual Strikes

It is well known that when labor calls a strike, more than labor and management are hurt. Suppliers, customers, stockholders, and possibly others are also affected. *Virtual strikes* have been proposed as a means to avoid hurting others. In a virtual strike only labor and management suffer. Here, worker wages, management *salaries*, and company profits go into a separate account from which neither side gets anything back unless they settle within a certain period of time. Production continues as usual, so the suffering hits only those directly involved.[44]

Virtual strikes, also known as nonstoppage strikes, have been around for a while. The U.S. Navy put an end to a strike at a valve plant in Bridgeport, Connecticut, during World War II. The Navy ordered the company to turn its receipts over to the Navy along with the wages it would otherwise have paid to its workers. This essentially turned a traditional strike into a virtual one.[45] Italy used the virtual strike in 1999 when Italian pilots and flight attendants staged a virtual strike against Meridiana Airlines. Workers wore white bows on their sleeves to signal their participation and told passengers that the action would not interrupt service. The airline, meanwhile, donated its revenues to charity, including the wages it would have paid to the cabin crews. In 2000, the Italian transport union scored a public relations coup when it donated 100 million lire forfeited in a virtual strike by 300 pilots to a children's hospital to buy medical equipment.[46]

The virtual strike has not been embraced in the United States, although every time labor strife occurs, the topic is brought up. Both labor and management must agree in advance to the limitations of a virtual strike. Individual managers who do not lose income during traditional strikes usually resist the idea. When the virtual strike has been tried in the United States, it has not been very successful. In 1960, after a three-day walkout by bus drivers in Miami, both sides agreed to turn the dispute into a virtual strike. The drivers went back to work for no pay, and riders got free service. After another four days, however, the bus company found that riders were giving drivers tips, and it ordered the buses off the streets. The strike lasted another 33 days.[47]

Boycott:
Agreement by union members to refuse to use or buy the firm's products.

Boycotts. The boycott is another of labor's weapons to get management to agree to its demands. A **boycott** involves an agreement by union members to refuse to use or buy the firm's products.

A boycott exerts economic pressure on management, and the effect often lasts much longer than that of a strike. Once shoppers change buying habits, their behavior will likely continue long after the boycott has ended. At times, significant pressures can be exerted on a business when union members, their families, and their friends refuse to purchase the firm's products. This approach is especially effective when the products are sold at retail outlets and are easily identifiable by brand name. For instance, the boycott against Adolph Coors Company was effective because the name of the product, Coors beer, was directly associated with the company. Ultimately, the AFL-CIO signed an agreement with Coors that ended a labor boycott of the company.[48]

Taco Bell was another easily identifiable brand name that succumbed to the pressure of a boycott. In 2005, the Coalition of Immokalee Workers (CIW) in Immokalee, Florida, won a significant victory to increase the wages of migrant tomato pickers. In a precedent-setting move, fast-food giant Yum! Brands Inc., the world's largest restaurant corporation, agreed to all the farm workers' demands if the CIW would end the four-year-old boycott of its subsidiary Taco Bell, the largest fast-food chain serving Mexican-style food in the United States. CIW targeted the company because it is a major tomato purchaser. In 2004, the company bought approximately 10 million pounds of Florida tomatoes. Churches joined the boycott against Taco Bell; among those were: the United Church of Christ, the United Methodist Church, the Christian Church (Disciples of Christ), the Presbyterian Church (U.S.A.), and the National Council of Churches.[49] Taco Bell ultimately agreed to a penny-per-pound increase in wages.[50]

The practice of a union attempting to encourage third parties (such as suppliers and customers) to stop doing business with the company is known as a **secondary boycott**. The Taft-Hartley Act declared this type of boycott to be illegal.

Other Tactics. Press editorial employees have used a byline strike to show their anger over the lack of progress in talks with the Newspaper Guild.[51] A **byline strike** is where newspaper writers withhold their names from stories. Writers at the *Washington Post* staged a byline strike in 2002.[52] **Informational picketing** is the use of union members to display placards and hand out leaflets, usually outside their place of business, depicting information the union wants the general public to see.

The flight attendants at United Airlines launched a global informational picketing campaign. Members of the Association of Flight Attendants-CWA were protesting United's unilateral termination of their pension plan.[53] In 2006, Delta pilots were using informational picketing over Delta's efforts to achieve concessions from pilots. Informational picketing is not the same as when workers are on strike.

Management Strategy for Overcoming Negotiation Breakdowns

There are times when management believes that it must exert extreme pressure to get the union to back away from a demand. The lockout and operating the firm by placing management and nonunion workers in the striking workers' jobs are the primary means that management may use to overcome breakdowns in negotiations.

Lockout. Management may use the lockout to encourage unions to come back to the bargaining table. In a **lockout**, management keeps employees out of the workplace and runs the operation with management personnel and/or replacements. Unable to work, the employees do not get paid and the fear of a lockout may bring labor back to the bargaining table. A lockout is particularly effective when management is dealing with a weak union, when the union treasury is depleted, or when the business has excessive inventories. The lockout is also used to inform the union that management is serious regarding certain bargaining issues. In March 2006, AK Steel Holding Corporation of Middletown, Ohio, locked out nearly 2,700 union employees and replaced them with salaried and replacement workers. Negotiations had come to a standstill over pension plans, health care costs, and a streamlining of job classifications so that workers can handle more duties.[54] After six weeks of picketing a Mallinckrodt Inc., plant in St. Louis, members of United Auto Workers Local 1887 resumed their jobs. During the lockout, hundreds of nonunion managers and supervisors filled 12-hour shifts to keep the plant running and filling orders. The union had ratified a four-year contract that includes a 3 percent annual wage increase plus improved pension benefits.[55]

Continue Operations without the Striking Workers. Another course of action that a company can take if the union goes on strike is to operate the firm by placing management and nonunion workers in the striking workers' jobs. When the Aircraft Mechanics Fraternal Association struck Northwest Airlines in 2005, the company hired replacements for the union's 4,300 mechanics.[56] The union leadership had

---

Secondary boycott:

Union attempt to encourage third parties (such as suppliers and customers) to stop doing business with a firm; declared illegal by the Taft-Hartley Act.

Byline strike:

Newspaper writers withhold their names from stories.

Informational picketing:

Use of union members to display placards and hand out leaflets usually outside their place of business depicting information the union wants the general public to see.

Lockout:

Management decision to keep union workers out of the workplace and runs the operation with management personnel and/or replacement workers to encourage the union to return to the bargaining table.

ordered the strike over the airline's demand that the union accept $176 million in wage concessions, including 2,000 job cuts.[57] Management prepared for a potential strike, setting up agreements with third-party maintenance contractors and hiring substitute workers from a private company.[58] Hiring replacements on either a temporary or a permanent basis is legal when the employees are engaged in an economic strike, that is, one that is part of a collective bargaining dispute. However, a company that takes this course of action risks inviting violence and creating bitterness among its employees, which may adversely affect the firm's performance long after the strike ends.

The type of industry involved has considerable effect on the impact of this maneuver. If the firm is not labor intensive and if maintenance demands are not high, such as at a petroleum refinery or a chemical plant, this practice may be quite effective. When appropriate, management may attempt to show how using nonunion employees can actually increase production. At times, management personnel will actually live in the plant and have food and other necessities delivered to them. This was the situation that occurred when the 900 members of local 470 of the International Association of Machinists struck the PPG Plant in Lake Charles, Louisiana, on May 26, 2006. Management continued to run the plant with management and contract labor personnel. They struck because of an increase in insurance payments and a new hiring-in rate for entry-level workers. Prior to the strike, the local had taken a strike vote and an overwhelming number of workers had voted in favor of the strike. On August 9, 2006, the union permitted the workers to vote on whether to accept or reject management's proposal. It was turned down by a majority of the workers. Then management sent registered letters to all union members suggesting that they were not willing to maintain the current work situation and the company was considering hiring replacement workers. Another vote was taken and the contract was accepted. Prior to the final vote, approximately 100 workers had resigned from the union and crossed the picked line.

9 **OBJECTIVE**

Describe what is involved in ratifying and administering the agreement.

Ratifying the Agreement

Most collective bargaining leads to an agreement without a breakdown in negotiations or disruptive actions. Typically, agreement is reached before the current contract expires. After the negotiators have reached a tentative agreement on all contract terms, they prepare a written agreement covering those terms, complete with the effective and termination dates. The approval process for management is often easier than for labor. The president or CEO has usually been briefed regularly on the progress of negotiations. Any difficulty that might have stood in the way of obtaining approval has probably already been resolved with top management by the negotiators.

However, the approval process is more complex for the union. Until a majority of members voting in a ratification election approve it, the proposed agreement is not final. At times, union members reject the proposal and a new round of negotiations must begin. Many of these rejections might not occur if union negotiators are better informed of the desires of the membership.

Administration of the Agreement

Negotiating, as it relates to the total collective bargaining process, may be likened to the tip of an iceberg. It is the visible phase, the part that makes the news. The larger and perhaps more important part of collective bargaining is administration of the agreement, which the public seldom sees. The agreement establishes the union–management relationship for the duration of the contract. Usually, neither party can change the contract's language until the expiration date, except by mutual consent. However, the main problem encountered in contract administration is uniform interpretation and application of the contract's terms. Administering the contract is a day-to-day activity. Ideally, the aim of both management and the union is to make the agreement work to the benefit of all concerned. Often, this is not an easy task.

Management is primarily responsible for explaining and implementing the agreement. This process should begin with meetings or training sessions not only to point out significant features but also to provide a clause-by-clause analysis of the contract. First-line supervisors, in particular, need to know their responsibilities and what to do when disagreements arise. Additionally, supervisors and middle managers should be encouraged to notify top management of any contract modifications or new provisions required for the next round of negotiations.

The human resource manager or industrial relations manager plays a key role in the day-to-day administration of the contract. He or she gives advice on matters of discipline, works to resolve grievances, and helps first-line supervisors establish good working relationships within the terms of the agreement. When a firm becomes unionized, the human resource manager's function tends to change rather significantly, and may even be divided into separate human resource and industrial relations departments. In such situations, the vice president of human resources may perform all human resource management tasks with the exception of industrial relations. The vice president of industrial relations would likely deal with all union-related matters.

OBJECTIVE

Describe collective bargaining in the public sector.

Collective Bargaining in the Public Sector

Executive Order 10988 established the basic framework for collective bargaining in federal government agencies. Title VII of the Civil Service Reform Act of 1978 regulates most of the labor management relations in the federal service. It establishes the Federal Labor Relations Authority (FLRA), which is modeled after the National Labor Relations Board. The intent of the FLRA is to bring the public-sector model in line with that of the private sector. Requirements and mechanisms for recognition and elections, dealing with impasses, and handling grievances are covered in the Act. Collective bargaining for federal unions has traditionally been quite different from private-sector bargaining because wages were off the table. Title V of the U.S. Code, the law that dictates rules for federal employees, did not allow bargaining over wage issues, except for the U.S. Postal Service.

There is no uniform pattern to state and local bargaining rights. Forty-one states and the District of Columbia have collective bargaining statutes covering all or some categories of public employees. Also, 38 states have some form of legislation that obligates state agencies and local governments to permit their public employees to join unions and to recognize bona fide labor organizations. However, the diversity of state labor laws makes it difficult to generalize about the legal aspects of collective bargaining at the state and local levels.

OBJECTIVE

Explain union decertification.

Decertification:
Reverse of the process that employees must follow to be recognized as an official bargaining unit.

Union Decertification

Until 1947, once a union was certified, it was certified forever. However, the Taft-Hartley Act made it possible for employees to decertify a union. **Decertification** is the reverse of the process that employees must follow to be recognized as an official bargaining unit. It results in a union losing its right to act as the exclusive bargaining representative of a group of employees. As union membership has declined, the need for decertification elections has also diminished.

Decertification Procedure

The rules established by the NLRB spell out the conditions for filing a decertification petition and it is essentially the reverse of obtaining union recognition. At least 30 percent of the bargaining unit members must petition for an election. As might be expected, this task by itself may be difficult because union supporters are likely to strongly oppose the move. Few employees know about decertification and fewer still know how to start the process. Also, although the petitioners' names are supposed to remain confidential, many union members are fearful that their signatures on the petition will be discovered. Timing of the NLRB's receipt of the decertification petition is also critical. The petition must be submitted between 60 and 90 days prior to the expiration of the current contract. When all these conditions have been met, the NLRB regional director will schedule a decertification election by secret ballot.

The NLRB carefully monitors the events leading up to the election. Current employees must initiate the request for the election. If the NLRB determines that management initiated the action, it will not certify the election. After a petition has been accepted, however, management can support the decertification election attempt. If a majority of the votes cast is against the union, the employees will be free from the union. Strong union supporters are all likely to vote. Thus, if a substantial numbers of employees are indifferent to the union and choose not to vote, decertification may not occur.

Management and Decertification

When management senses employee discontent with the union, it often does not know how to react. Many times, management decides to do nothing, reasoning that it is best not to get involved or that doing so may even be illegal. But if it does want to get involved, management can use a variety of legal tactics. If management really wants the union decertified, it must learn how to be active rather than passive. However, care must be taken to ensure that management's actions do not prompt an unfair labor practice complaint.[59]

Meetings with union members to discuss the benefits of becoming union-free have proven beneficial. In fact, such discussions are often cited as being the most effective campaign tactic. These meetings may be with individual employees, small groups, or even entire units. Management explains the benefits and answers employees' questions.

Management may also provide workers with legal assistance in preparing for decertification. Because the workers probably have never been through a decertification election, this type of assistance may prove invaluable. For example, the NLRB may not permit an election if the paperwork has not been properly completed. Management must always remember that it cannot initiate the decertification action; that is the workers' responsibility.

The most effective means of accomplishing decertification is to improve the corporate culture so workers no longer feel the need to have a union. This cannot be done overnight, as mutual trust and confidence must be developed between workers and the employer. If decertification is to succeed, management must eliminate the problems that initially led to unionization. Although many executives believe that pay and benefits are the primary reasons for union membership, other factors are probably more important. For example, failure to treat employees as individuals is often the

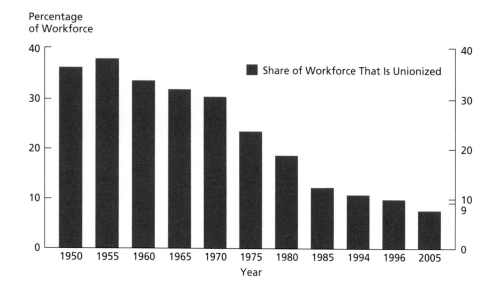

Percentage
of Workforce

Figure 12-7 Percentage of the Private Workforce That Is Unionized
Source: U.S. Department of Labor.

primary reason for unionization. The real problems often stem from practices such as failing to listen to employees' opinions, dealing with workers unfairly and dishonestly, and treating employees as numbers and not as people. Employers who desire to remain or become union-free can employ certain strategies and tactics that benefit both employers and employees.

12 OBJECTIVE

Describe the state of unions today.

Unions Today

Overall, the fall of *Big Labor* has been dramatic.[60] As shown in Figure 12-7, private-sector union membership has fallen from 39 percent of all workers in 1958 to about 7.8 percent in 2005,[61] the lowest percentage since 1901. Recent statistics show that 36.5 percent of all public employees are union members.[62] The United Steelworkers of America's membership was a major loser as dozens of steelmakers filed for Chapter 11 bankruptcy protection. Likewise, organized labor in the capital-goods sector saw membership fall, as businesses cut capital-investment spending, prompting manufacturers to make layoffs.[63] In 2006 both General Motors and Ford Motor Company made major cuts in their labor force.[64] In the United States, where all workers are facing cuts in health care and pension benefits, labor leaders have not had much success in winning public or political backing. Also, any growth that unions experience will not likely be in manufacturing but in the service sector where wages and benefits are typically lower.[65] For example, at the end of 2005, 5,000 janitors (cleaners and caretakers) in Houston joined the Service Employees International Union (SEIU).[66]

There are numerous examples where unions have experienced difficulties. The aircraft machinists' union that seems unwilling to bend any more is facing extinction, along with several thousand of its members who could lose their jobs.[67] Unionized workers in the airline passenger industry have been particularly hard hit. Northwest and Delta Airlines have reorganized under Chapter 11 bankruptcy protection, and United exited bankruptcy in February 2006. All have negotiated lower wages and stricter work rules with unions. Pilots at Northwest ratified a contract that cuts wages 24 percent. Flight attendants at United took two rounds of wage cuts at about 9 percent each. Pilots at Delta took a 32.5 percent pay cut in 2004 and are considering additional concessions. Once, the battles were just among the Big Three automakers. Today, cars and trucks built by nonunion workers account for almost half the volume of vehicles. UAW membership has dwindled by hundreds of thousands among the Big Three, and the companies are struggling for market share.[68] Ever since President Reagan's dismissal of the striking air traffic controllers, labor clout has seriously diminished. Reasons vary, but today, people's preference to bargain for themselves and ignore the interests of the collective members of the workforce is becoming more common. Some workers do not like paying union dues and some believe that unionized firms might be less competitive and could go out of business (not a problem for public-sector workers).

The ICFTU Says Union Organizing Can Be Dangerous

According to the International Confederation of Free Trade Unions, thousands of trade unionists were arrested, jailed, tortured, fired, or intimidated, and 223 were murdered or disappeared, across the world. The ICFTU survey, which draws on data from 132 countries, concluded that over 4,000 trade unionists were arrested, 1,000 injured, and 10,000 fired. Violations were particularly severe in many export-processing zones. Guy Ryder, secretary general of the ICFTU, said, "In places like Belarus, Zimbabwe and China, we find that undemocratic governments target trade unions first when their legitimacy is challenged."[69] The Belgium-based ICFTU represents 145 million workers in 234 affiliated organizations, including the AFL-CIO, in 154 countries and territories.[70]

The report documents a long list of abuses, including many in textile and apparel plants in Asia, Africa, Latin America, and also in developed nations like the United States. Juan Somavia, director general of the International Labor Organization, said the report showed that while labor advocates have worked for decades to improve the treatment of workers, "the situation in many countries today shows that the struggle continues." The study alleged that management of JAR Kenya, a clothing maker in Nairobi, embarked on "a hostile attack on the Tailors and Textile Workers Union." It said active union members were "constantly harassed and intimidated. Some were locked up in the factory cell and handed over to the police on fabricated charges." The report added that some were fired solely for joining the union. The survey pointed out that trade union rights are severely violated in many Far Eastern countries. It said police have attacked workers protesting in state-owned textile plants in China. "Any attempt to form a free trade union can be rewarded with huge prison sentences and even life imprisonment," it reported. The ICFTU survey also documented harsh anti-union policies by management of garment and footwear factories in Indonesia and Pakistan, and fierce anti-union tactics in export-promotion zones in the Philippines, Sri Lanka, and other countries.[71] According to ICFTU, in Bangladesh, some of the mostly female employees at International Knitwear and Apparel who took part in actions for better working conditions lost their jobs, were threatened with death if they joined a union, and were beaten up by hired thugs.[72]

With regard to the Americas, the report shows that hostility toward trade unions is a recurrent problem in many Central and South American countries. In Guatemala, it said, freedom of association "is virtually nonexistent" and added that employers in textile factories or the big multinationals refuse to recognize trade unions. No Guatemalan textile or apparel plants are currently unionized. In the case of the United States, the report estimated that "80 percent of employers engage consultants to assist in anti-union campaigning." ICFTU analysts alleged in the report that "some of the most extreme exploitation" takes place in territories controlled by the United States, such as the Northern Mariana Islands. The report argued the conditions there amount to a system of servitude: "Local authorities permit foreign-owned companies to recruit thousands of foreign workers, mainly young women from Thailand, China, the Philippines and Bangladesh." The report contended workers in that region are forced to sign contracts that stipulate they must refrain from asking for wage increases, from seeking other work, or from joining a union. If they violate the contract, they face deportation, the report added.[73]

Summary

1. Discuss the Change to Win Coalition.

The Coalition, led by the Service Employees International Union (SEIU), intends to focus its energies on new membership growth and not as much on lobbying. Included in the new coalition are the Teamsters, the United Food and Commercial Workers, Unite Here (the labor union representing textile and apparel workers), Carpenters' Union, Laborers' International Union of North America, and the United Farm Workers.

2. Describe the broad objectives that characterize the labor movement as a whole and describe organized labor's strategies for a stronger movement.

The underlying philosophy of the labor movement is that of organizational democracy and an atmosphere of social dignity for working men and women.

Organized labor's new strategies for a stronger movement include pulling the union through, political involvement, union salting, flooding the community with organizers, political awareness campaigns, building organizing funds, befriending laid-off workers, and organizing through the card check.

3. Explain the reasons why employees join unions and describe the basic structure of the union.

Employees join unions due to dissatisfaction with management, need for a social outlet, need for avenues of leadership, forced unionization, and social pressure from peers.

The basic element in the structure of the American labor movement is the local union. The national union is the most powerful level, and the American Federation of Labor and Congress of Industrial Organizations (AFL-CIO) is the central trade union federation in the United States.

4. Define collective bargaining and identify the steps involved in establishing the collective bargaining relationship.

The primary law governing the relationship of companies and unions is the National Labor Relations Act, as amended. Collective bargaining is one of the key parts of the Act. Section 8(d) of the act defines collective bargaining as: The performance of the mutual obligation of the employer and the representative of the employees to meet at reasonable times and confer in good faith with respect to wages, hours, and other terms and conditions of employment, or the negotiation of an agreement, or any question arising there under, and the execution of a written contract incorporating any agreement reached if requested by either party, but such obligation does not compel either party to agree to a proposal or require the making of a concession.

The steps involved include signing authorization cards, petitioning for election, campaigning, winning the election, and being certified.

5. Describe the collective bargaining process and explain the psychological aspects of collective bargaining.

Both external and internal environmental factors can influence the process. The first step in the collective bargaining process is preparing for negotiations. After the issues to be negotiated have been determined, the two sides confer to reach a mutually acceptable contract. Although breakdowns in negotiations can occur, both labor and management have at their disposal tools and arguments that can be used to convince the other side to accept their views. Eventually, however, management and the union usually reach an agreement that defines the rules for the duration of the contract. The next step is for the union membership to ratify the agreement.

Psychologically, the collective bargaining process is often difficult for both labor and management because an adversarial situation may exist.

6. Describe the factors involved in preparing for negotiations.

Because of the complex issues facing labor and management today, the negotiating teams must carefully prepare for the bargaining sessions. Prior to meeting at the bargaining table, the negotiators should thoroughly know the culture, climate, history, present economic state, and wage and benefits structure of both the organization and similar organizations.

7. Explain typical bargaining issues and describe the process of negotiating the agreement.

Mandatory bargaining issues are those issues that fall within the definition of wages, hours, and other terms and conditions of employment. Permissive bargaining issues are those issues that may be raised, but neither side may insist that they be bargained over.

The negotiating phase of collective bargaining begins with each side presenting its initial demands. Because a collective bargaining settlement can be expensive for a firm, the cost of various proposals should be estimated as accurately as possible. The term *negotiating* suggests a certain amount of give-and-take, the purpose of which is to lower the other side's expectations.

8. Identify ways to overcome breakdowns in negotiations.

Breakdowns in negotiations can be overcome through third-party intervention (mediation and arbitration), union tactics (strikes and boycotts), and management recourse (lockouts and continued operation without striking workers).

9. Describe what is involved in ratifying and administering the agreement.

The president of the organization can make the decision for the firm. However, until a majority of union members voting in a ratification election approve it, the proposed agreement is not final. Ideally, the aim of both management and the union is to make the agreement work to the mutual benefit of all concerned. Management is primarily responsible for explaining and implementing the agreement. The human resource manager or industrial relations manager plays a key role in the day-to-day administration of the contract.

10. Describe collective bargaining in the public sector.

Collective bargaining for workers in the public sector has traditionally been quite different from private-sector bargaining because wages have been off the table.

11. Explain union decertification.

Decertification is essentially the reverse of the process that employees must follow to be recognized as an official bargaining unit.

12. Describe the state of unions today.

Overall, the fall of *Big Labor* has been dramatic.

Key Terms

- Change to Win Coalition, 385
- Union salting, 388
- Flooding the community, 388
- Public awareness campaigns, 388
- Card check, 389
- Right-to-work laws, 391
- Local union, 392
- Craft union, 392
- Industrial union, 392
- National union, 392
- American Federation of Labor and Congress of Industrial Organizations (AFL-CIO), 392

- Collective bargaining, 394
- Bargaining unit, 394
- Authorization card, 395
- Mandatory bargaining issues, 398
- Permissive bargaining issues, 399
- Prohibited bargaining issues, 399
- Closed shop, 402
- Union shop, 402
- Agency shop, 402
- Open shop, 402
- Checkoff of dues, 403
- Beachhead demands, 405

- Mediation, 406
- Arbitration, 406
- Rights arbitration, 406
- Interest arbitration, 406
- Strike, 407
- Boycott, 408
- Secondary boycott, 409
- Byline strike, 409
- Informational picketing, 409
- Lockout, 409
- Decertification, 411

Questions for Review

1. What is the Change to Win Coalition?
2. What are the broad objectives that characterize the labor movement as a whole?
3. What are organized labor's strategies for a stronger movement?

4. What are the primary reasons for employees joining labor unions?

5. Define the following terms:
   a. Local union
   b. Craft union
   c. Industrial union
   d. National union

6. What steps must a union take in attempting to form a bargaining unit? Briefly describe each step.

7. What are the basic steps involved in the collective bargaining process?

8. With regard to collective bargaining, interpret the statement, "The realities of negotiations are not for the weak of heart and at times are similar to a high-stakes poker game."

9. Distinguish among mandatory, permissive, and prohibited bargaining issues.

10. What are the topics included in virtually all labor agreements?

11. Define each of the following:
    a. Closed shop
    b. Union shop
    c. Agency shop
    d. Maintenance of membership
    e. Checkoff of dues

12. What are the primary means by which breakdowns in negotiations may be overcome? Briefly describe each.

13. What is involved for both management and labor in ratifying the agreement?

14. What is involved in the administration of a labor agreement?

15. How is the collective bargaining process different in the public sector?

16. Define decertification. What are the steps in decertification?

17. What is the status of unions today?

HRM Incident 1

Break Down the Barrier

Yesterday, Angelica Angulo was offered a job as a waitress with GEM Hotel Corporation, located in Las Vegas, Nevada. She had recently graduated from high school in Milford, a small town in New Mexico. Since Angelica had no college aspirations upon graduation, she had moved to Las Vegas to look for a job.

Angelica's immediate supervisor spent only a short time with her before turning her over to Laurie Rader, an experienced waitress, for training. After they had talked for a short time, Laurie asked, "Have you given any thought to joining our union? You'll like all of our members."

Angelica had not considered this. Moreover, she had never associated with union members and her parents had never been members either. At Milford High, her teachers had never really talked about unions. The fact that this union operated as an open shop meant nothing to her. Angelica replied, "I don't know. Maybe. Maybe not."

The day progressed much the same way, with several people asking Angelica the same question. They were all friendly, but there seemed to be a barrier that separated Angelica from the other workers. One worker looked Angelica right in the eyes and said, "You're going to join, aren't you?" Angelica still did not know, but she was beginning to lean in that direction.

After the end of her shift, Angelica went to the washroom. Just as she entered, Stephanie Clements, the union steward, also walked in. After they exchanged greetings, Stephanie said, "I hear that you're not sure about joining our union. You, and everyone else, reap the benefits of the work we've done in the past. It doesn't seem fair for you to be rewarded for what others have done. Tell you what, why don't you join us down at the union hall tonight? We'll discuss it more then."

Angelica nodded yes and finished cleaning up. "That might be fun," she thought.

Questions

1. Why does Angelica have the option of joining or not joining the union?

2. How are the other workers likely to react toward Angelica if she chooses not to join? Discuss.

| HRM Incident 2 | **You Are Out of What?**

Marcus Ned eagerly drove his new company pickup onto the construction site. His employer, Kelso Construction Company, had just assigned him to supervise a crew of 16 equipment operators, oilers, and mechanics. This was the first unionized crew Marcus had supervised, and he was unaware of the labor agreement in effect that carefully defined and limited the role of supervisors. As he approached his work area, he noticed one of the cherry pickers (a type of mobile crane with an extendable boom) standing idle with the operator beside it. Marcus pulled up beside the operator and asked, "What's going on here?"

"Out of gas," the operator said.

"Well, go and get some," Marcus said.

The operator reached to get his thermos jug out of the toolbox on the side of the crane and said, "The oiler's on break right now. He'll be back in a few minutes."

Marcus remembered that he had a five-gallon can of gasoline in the back of his pickup. So he quickly got the gasoline, climbed on the cherry picker, and started to pour it into the gas tank. As he did so, he heard the other machines shutting down in unison. He looked around and saw all the other operators climbing down from their equipment and standing to watch him pour the gasoline. A moment later, he saw the union steward approaching.

Questions

1. Why did all the operators shut down their machines?
2. If you were Marcus, what would you do now?

Notes

1. Aaron Bernstein, "Labor's New Face, New Tactics," *Business Week Online* (September 28, 2005).
2. Matt Miller, "Blowing Up the Union to Save the Union," *Fortune* 152 (August 22, 2005): 36.
3. "Disorganized Labor," *Global Agenda* (September 10, 2005).
4. Tom Anderson, "Splitting Headache," *Employee Benefit News* 19 (October 1, 2005): 50–52.
5. http://www.changetowin.org/what.html, May 14, 2006.
6. http://www.changetowin.org/organizing.html, May 14, 2006.
7. http://www.liuna.org/,News Release, "Labors' Union, Operating Engineers to Disaffiliate from AFL-CIO's Building and Construction Trade," February 14, 2006.
8. Edwin F. Beal and James P. Begin, *The Practice of Collective Bargaining*, 5th ed. (Homewood, IL: Richard D. Irwin, 1982): 91.
9. "There's Money in Mopping," *Economist* 377 (December 10, 2005): 32–36.
10. Joann Muller, "Has the UAW Found a Better Road?" *Business Week* 3791 (July 15, 2002): 108.
11. Jeffrey A. Mello, "Salts, Lies and Videotape: Union Organizing Efforts and Management's Response," *Labor Law Journal* 55 (Spring 2004): 42–52.
12. "Salt's Right to Lie Is Protected," *Management Report for Nonunion Organizations (Wiley)* 28 (November 2005): 4–5.
13. Bill Schmitt, "Union Safety Initiative Survives a Big Test," *Chemical Week* 164 (July 3–July 10, 2002): 59.
14. Jane M. Von Bergen, "Labor Coalition Kicks Off Public-awareness Campaign on Wages," *Philadelphia Inquirer* (April 25, 2006).
15. Sharon Leonard, "Unions Could Be Staging a Comeback," *HR Magazine* 44 (December 1999): 207.
16. Mike Hughlett, "Unions Use Fund in Bidding Battle Against Non-Union Contractors," *Saint Paul Pioneer Press* (April 7, 2002): 1.
17. Kathy Brister, "AFL-CIO Befriends WorldCom Jobless Labor Federation: Has Eye on Future," *Atlanta Journal and Constitution* (November 13, 2002): D1.
18. Lindsey Chappell, "Group Thwarts Steel Union," *Automotive News* 79 (January 17, 2005): 32.
19. Mark Schoeff Jr., "NLRB'S Kirsanow Vows to Address Cases Objectively," *Workforce Management* 85 (February 13, 2006): 14.
20. "The Democrats and Big Labor," *Washington Times* (December 21, 2006).
21. John Gallagher, "Workers Consider Much More Than Wages When Deciding to Join Union," *Detroit Free Press* (December 27, 2002): 1.
22. Dina Berta, "Winkler: Recent Union Developments Can't Be Ignored," *Nation's Restaurant News* 39 (September 19, 2005): 32.
23. Jim Johnson, "Two Waste Execs Explain How to Beat Labor Pains," *Waste News* 11 (May 9, 2005): 4.
24. Keith Ecker, "State of the Union," *Corporate Legal Times* 15 (September 2005): 10.
25. Robert P. Hunter, "Executive Summary of the Effect of Right-to-Work Laws on Economic Development," *Government Union Review and Public Policy Digest* 20 (2002): 27–30.
26. Ibid.
27. Charles W. Baird, "Unions on the Run," *Government Union Review and Public Policy Digest* 20 (2002): 21–24.
28. http://www.seiu.org/faqs/faq_whatisseiu.cfm, August 10, 2006.
29. http://org.teamster.org/whoare.htm, August 10, 2006.
30. Kim Clark, "Disorganized Labor," *U.S. News & World Report* 138 (June 27, 2005): 38.

31. *A Guide to Basic Law and Procedures Under the National Labor Relations Act* (Washington, D.C: U.S. Government Printing Office, October 1978): 11–13.

32. Art Bethke, R. Wayne Mondy, and Shane R. Premeaux, "Decertification: The Role of the First-Line Supervisor," *Supervisory Management* 31 (February 1986): 21–23.

33. "Fewer NLRB Elections, but More Union Wins in 2005," *HR Focus* 83 (August 2006): 9.

34. *Management/Employee/Union Relations* (Dallas, Texas: Southwestern Bell Telephone Company): 3.

35. T. L. Stanley, "Running at Peak Performance," *Supervision* 66 (March 2005): 10–13.

36. Stephen J. Cabot, "United We Stand," *Executive Excellence* 18 (October 2001): 9.

37. Philip Zimmerman, "A Practical Guide to Mediation," *The CPA Journal* 73 (January 2003): 66.

38. Llona Geiger, "The Value of Professional Mediation," *Association Management* 54 (November 2002): 87.

39. http://www.bls.gov/news.release/wkstp.t01.htm, July 1, 2006.

40. Repps Hudson, "Spectrulite Steelworkers Rally over Wage Cuts, Health Benefits," *St. Louis Post-Dispatch* (January 18, 2003): 4.

41. Andrea Holecek, "Levy Co. Replaces Striking Steel Workers, Fires Others," *The Times* (March 29, 2006).

42. Patrick Waldron, "Union OKs Strike on Dominick's Store: No New Offer Will Be Made," *Chicago Daily Herald* (November 11, 2002): 1.

43. Dan Reed, "United Racks up $1.4B Loss," *USA Today* (July 29, 2005): Money, b.

44. Roberta Burnette, "Walking Out on Wages," *Workforce Management* 84 (August 2005): 12–13.

45. Ibid.

46. Ibid.

47. Ibid.

48. Heather Draper, "Coors Facing New Boycott: Workers at Brewer's Supplier Locked Out After Pact Expired," *Rocky Mountain News* (September 24, 2002): 6B.

49. "Labor Agreement Ends Boycott of Taco Bell," *Christian Century* 122 (April 5, 2005): 17.

50. "Taco Bell Cracks," *Multinational Monitor* 26 (March/April 2005): 4.

51. Joe Strupp, "AP, Guild Have Contract Issues," *Editor & Publisher* 136 (January 20, 2003): 4.

52. Todd Shields, "Bye-Bye, Bylines," *Editor & Publisher* 135 (October 7, 2002): 5.

53. Reed, "United Racks up $1.4B Loss."

54. Thomas Gnau, "AK: Production Will Go On and Improve," *Middletown Journal (OH)* April 26, 2006).

55. Rachel Melcer, "Mallinckrodt Workers Set to Return," *St. Louis Post-Dispatch* (April 21, 2006).

56. Anne Newman and Robert Berner, "Mechanical Failure," *Business Week* (September 9, 2005): 52.

57. Robert Berner, "This Hardball Union Is Striking Out," *Business Week Online* (September 1, 2005).

58. James Ott, "Clash of Wills," *Aviation Week & Space Technology* 163 (September 9, 2005): 39–40.

59. Satish P. Deshpande and Jacob Joseph, "Decertification Elections in Health Care: Some Recent Evidence," *The Health Care Manager* 22 (April-June 2003): 108–112.

60. Robert J. Flanagan, "Has Management Strangled U.S. Unions?" *Journal of Labor Research* (Winter 2005): 33–63.

61. "Union Members in 2005," U.S Department of Labor, Bureau of Labor Statistics, January 20, 2006.

62. Ibid.

63. Carlos Tejada, "Decline in Union Membership in 2002 Was Biggest Since 1995," *Wall Street Journal* (February 26, 2003): A10.

64. Scott Miller, "Unions: Are They Losing Their Clout?" *The Pantagraph,* (April 16, 2006).

65. Tami J. Friedman, "The Workers Aren't Nontraditional—But the Strategy Should Be," *Dollars & Sense* (September 1, 2002): 8.

66. "There's Money in Mopping," *Economist* 377 (December 10, 2005): 32–36.

67. Dan Reed, "Northwest Seeks Court OK to Reject Contracts," *USA Today* (October 13, 2005): Money, 5b.

68. Keith Crain, "It's Time for the UAW to Change," *Automotive News* 80 (September 2005): 12.

69. John Zarocostas, "Organizing in the Third World a Dangerous Job, Study Finds," *International Confederation of Free Trade Unions Reports* (June 25, 2002): 8.

70. Ibid.

71. Ibid.

72. Ibid.

73. Ibid.

Appendix
CHAPTER 12

History of Unions in the United States

Labor Movement before 1930

Unions are not a recent development in American history. The earliest unions originated toward the end of the eighteenth century, about the time of the American Revolution. Although these early associations had few of the characteristics of present-day labor unions, they did bring workers in craft or guild-related occupations together to consider problems of mutual concern. These early unions were local in nature and usually existed for only a short time.[1]

Development of the labor movement has been neither simple nor straightforward; unionism has experienced as much failure as success. Employer opposition, the impact of the business cycle, the growth of American industry, court rulings, and legislation have exerted their influence in varying degrees at different times. As a result, the history of the labor movement has somewhat resembled the swinging of a pendulum. At times, the pendulum has moved in favor of labor and, at other times, it has swung toward the advantage of management.

Prior to the 1930s, the trend definitely favored management. The courts strongly supported employers in their attempts to thwart the organized labor movement. This was first evidenced by the use of criminal and civil conspiracy doctrines derived from English common law. A **conspiracy** is two or more persons who band together to prejudice the rights of others or of society (such as by refusing to work or demanding higher wages).

An important feature of the conspiracy doctrine is that an action by one person, though legal, may become illegal when carried out by a group. In 1806, the year in which the conspiracy doctrine was first applied to labor unions, the courts began to influence the field of labor relations.[2] From 1806 to 1842, 17 cases charging labor unions with conspiracies went to trial. These cases resulted in the demise of several unions and certainly discouraged other union activities. The conspiracy doctrine was softened considerably by the decision in the landmark case *Commonwealth v Hunt* in 1842. In that case, Chief Justice Shaw of the Supreme Judicial Court of Massachusetts contended that labor organizations were legal. Thus, in order for a union to be convicted under the conspiracy doctrine, it had to be shown that the union's objectives were unlawful or the means employed to gain a legal end were unlawful. To this day, the courts continue to exert a profound influence on both the direction and character of labor relations.

Other tactics used by employers to stifle union growth were injunctions and yellow-dog contracts. An **injunction** is a prohibited legal procedure used by employers to prevent certain union activities, such as strikes and unionization attempts. A **yellow-dog contract** was a written agreement between the employee and the company, made at the time of employment, that prohibits a worker from joining a union or engaging in union activities. Each of these defensive tactics, used by management and supported by the courts, severely limited union growth.

In the latter half of the nineteenth century, the American industrial system started to grow and prosper. Factory production began to displace handicraft forms of manufacturing. The Civil War gave the factory system a great boost. Goods were demanded in quantities that only mass production methods could supply. The railroads developed new networks of routes spanning the continent and knitting the country into an economic whole. Employment was high, and unions sought to organize workers in both new and expanding enterprises. Most unions during this time were small and rather weak, and many did not survive the economic recession of the 1870s. Union membership rose to 300,000 by 1872 and then dropped to 50,000 by 1878.[3] This period also marked the rise of radical labor activity and increased industrial strife as unions struggled for recognition and survival.[4]

Out of the turbulence of the 1870s emerged the most substantial labor organization that had yet appeared in the United States. The Noble Order of the Knights of Labor was founded in 1869 as a secret society of the Philadelphia garment workers. After its secrecy was abandoned and workers in other areas were invited to join, it grew rapidly, reaching a membership of more than 700,000 by the mid-1880s. Internal conflict among the Knights' leadership in 1881 gave rise to the nucleus of a new organization that would soon replace it on the labor scene.[5] That organization was the American Federation of Labor (AFL).

Devoted to what is referred to as either *pure and simple unionism* or *business unionism*, Samuel Gompers of the Cigarmakers Union led some 25 labor groups representing skilled trades to found the AFL in 1886.[6] Gompers was elected the first president of the AFL, a position he held until his death in 1924 (except for one year, 1894–1895, when he adamantly opposed tangible support for the Pullman group strikers). He is probably the single most

---

Conspiracy:
Two or more persons who band together to prejudice the rights of others or of society (such as by refusing to work or demanding higher wages).

Injunction:
Prohibited legal procedure used by employers to prevent certain union activities, such as strikes and unionization attempts.

Yellow-dog contract:
Written agreement between an employee and a company made at the time of employment, that prohibits a worker from joining a union or engaging in union activities.

important individual in American trade union history. The AFL began with a membership of some 138,000 and doubled that number during the next 12 years.

In 1890, Congress passed the Sherman Anti-Trust Act, which marked the entrance of the federal government into the statutory regulation of labor organizations. Although the primary stimulus for this Act came from public concern over the monopoly power of business, court interpretations soon applied its provisions to organized labor. Later, in 1914, Congress passed the Clayton Act (an amendment to the Sherman Act), which, according to Samuel Gompers, was the Magna Carta of labor. The intent of this Act was to remove labor from the purview of the Sherman Act. Again, judicial interpretation nullified that intent and left labor even more exposed to lawsuits.[7] Nonetheless, as a result of industrial activity related to World War I, the AFL grew to almost 5 million members by 1920.[8]

During the 1920s, labor faced legal restrictions on union activity and unfavorable court decisions. The one exception to such repressive policies was the passage and approval of the Railway Labor Act of 1926. Passage of this legislation marked the first time that the government declared without qualification the right of private employees to join unions and bargain collectively through representatives of their own choosing, without interference from their employers. It also set up special machinery for the settlement of labor disputes. Although the Act covered only employees in the railroad industry (a later amendment extended coverage to the airline industry), it foreshadowed the extension of similar rights to other classes of employees in the 1930s.

Labor Movement after 1930

The 1930s found the United States in the midst of the worst depression in its history. The unemployment rate rose as high as 25 percent.[9] The sentiment of the country began to favor organized labor, as many people blamed business for the agony that accompanied the Great Depression. The pendulum began to swing away from management and toward labor. This swing was assisted by several acts and actions that supported the cause of unionism.

Anti-Injunction Act (Norris-LaGuardia Act), 1932

The Great Depression caused a substantial change in the public's thinking about the role of unions in society. Congress reflected this thinking in 1932 with the passage of the Norris-LaGuardia Act. It affirms that U.S. public policy sanctions collective bargaining and approves the formation and effective operation of labor unions. While this Act did not outlaw the use of injunctions, it severely restricted the federal courts' authority to issue them in labor disputes. It also made yellow-dog contracts unenforceable in the federal courts.[10]

National Labor Relations Act (Wagner Act), 1935

In 1933, Congress made an abortive attempt to stimulate economic recovery by passing the National Industry Recovery Act (NIRA). Declared unconstitutional by the U.S. Supreme Court in 1935, the NIRA did provide the nucleus for legislation that followed it. Section 7a of the NIRA proclaimed the right of workers to organize and bargain collectively. Congress did not, however, provide procedures to enforce these rights.

Undeterred by the Supreme Court decision and strongly supported by organized labor, Congress speedily enacted a comprehensive labor law, the National Labor Relations Act (Wagner Act). This Act, approved by President Roosevelt on July 5, 1935, is one of the most significant labor management relations statutes ever enacted. Drawing heavily on the experience of the Railway Labor Act of 1926 and Section 7a of the NIRA, the Act declared legislative support, on a broad scale, for the right of employees to organize and engage in collective bargaining. The spirit of the Wagner Act is stated in Section 7, which defines the substantive rights of employees:

> *Employees shall have the right to self-organization, to form, join, or assist labor organizations, to bargain collectively through representatives of their own choosing, and to engage in other concerted activities, for the purpose of collective bargaining or other mutual aid or protection.*

The rights defined in Section 7 were protected against employer interference by Section 8, which detailed and prohibited five management practices deemed to be unfair to labor:

1. Interfering with or restraining or coercing employees in the exercise of their right to self-organization.

2. Dominating or interfering in the affairs of a union.

3. Discriminating in regard to hire or tenure or any condition of employment for the purpose of encouraging or discouraging union membership.

4. Discriminating against or discharging an employee who has filed charges or given testimony under the Act.

5. Refusing to bargain with chosen representatives of employees.

The National Labor Relations Act created the National Labor Relations Board (NLRB) to administer and enforce the provisions of the Act. The NLRB was given two principal functions: (1) to establish procedures for holding bargaining-unit elections and to monitor the election procedures, and (2) to investigate complaints and prevent unlawful acts involving unfair labor practices. Much of the NLRB's work is delegated to 33 regional offices throughout the country.

Following passage of the Wagner Act, union membership increased from approximately 3 million to 15 million between 1935 and 1947.[11] The increase was most conspicuous in industries utilizing mass-production methods. New unions in these industries were organized on an industrial basis rather than a craft basis, and members were primarily unskilled or semiskilled workers. An internal struggle developed within the AFL over the question of whether unions should be organized to include all workers in an industry or strictly on a craft or occupational basis. In 1935, 10 AFL-affiliated unions and the officers of two other AFL unions formed a new group. Called the Committee for Industrial Organization, its purpose was to promote the organization of workers in mass-production and unorganized industries. The controversy grew to the point that in 1938 the AFL expelled all but one of the Committee for Industrial Organization unions. In November 1938, the expelled unions held their first convention in Pittsburgh, and reorganized as a federation of unions under the name of Congress of Industrial Organizations (CIO). The new federation included the nine unions expelled from the AFL and 32 other groups established to recruit workers in various industries. John L. Lewis, president of the United Mine Workers, was elected the first president of the CIO.

The rivalry generated by the two large federations stimulated union-organizing efforts in both groups. With the ensuing growth, the labor movement gained considerable influence in the United States. However, many individuals and groups began to feel that the Wagner Act favored labor too much. This shift in public sentiment was in part related to a rash of costly strikes following World War II. Whether justified or not, much of the blame for these disruptions fell on the unions.

Labor Management Relations Act (Taft-Hartley Act), 1947

In 1947, with public pressure mounting, Congress overrode President Truman's veto and passed the Labor Management Relations Act (Taft-Hartley Act). The Taft-Hartley Act extensively revised the National Labor Relations Act and became Title I of that law. A new period began in the evolution of public policy regarding labor. The pendulum had begun to swing toward a more balanced position between labor and management.

Some of the important changes introduced by the Taft-Hartley Act included the following:

1. Modifying Section 7 to include the right of employees to refrain from union activity as well as engage in it.

2. Prohibiting the closed shop (the arrangement requiring that all workers be union members at the time they are hired) and narrowing the freedom of the parties to authorize the union shop (the situation in which the employer may hire anyone he or she chooses, but all new workers must join the union after a stipulated period of time).

3. Broadening the employer's right of free speech.

4. Providing that employers need not recognize or bargain with unions formed by supervisors.

5. Giving employees the right to initiate decertification petitions.

6. Providing for government intervention in *national emergency strikes*.

Another significant change extended the concept of unfair labor practices to unions. Labor organizations were to refrain from the following:

1. Restraining or coercing employees in the exercise of their guaranteed collective bargaining rights.

2. Causing an employer to discriminate in any way against an employee in order to encourage or discourage union membership.

3. Refusing to bargain in good faith with an employer regarding wages, hours, and other terms and conditions of employment.

4. Engaging in certain types of strikes and boycotts.

5. Requiring employees covered by union-shop contracts to pay initiation fees or dues in an amount which the Board finds excessive or discriminatory under all circumstances.

6. *Featherbedding*, or requiring that an employer pay for services not performed.

One of the most controversial elements of the Taft-Hartley Act is its Section 14b, which permits states to enact right-to-work legislation. *Right-to-work laws* are laws that prohibit management and unions from entering into agreements requiring union membership as a condition of employment. These laws are state statutes or constitutional provisions that ban the practice of requiring union membership or financial support as a condition of employment. They establish the legal right of employees to decide for themselves whether or not to join or financially support a union. Twenty-two states, located primarily in the South and West, have adopted such laws, which are a continuing source of irritation between labor and management. Oklahoma became the most recent right-to-work state. The National Right to Work Committee, based in Springfield, Virginia, provides much of the impetus behind the right-to-work movement.

For about 10 years after the passage of the Taft-Hartley Act, union membership expanded at about the same rate as nonagricultural employment. But all was not well within the organized labor movement. Since the creation of the CIO, the two federations had engaged in a bitter and costly rivalry. Both the CIO and the AFL recognized the increasing need for cooperation and reunification. In 1955, following two years of intensive negotiations between the two organizations, a merger agreement was ratified, the AFL-CIO became a reality, and George Meany was elected president. In the years following the merger, the labor movement faced some of its greatest challenges.

Labor-Management Reporting and Disclosure Act (Landrum-Griffin Act), 1959

Corruption had plagued organized labor since the early 1900s. Periodic revelations of graft, violence, extortion, racketeering, and other improper activities aroused public indignation and invited governmental investigation. Even though the number of unions involved was small, every disclosure undermined the public image of organized labor as a whole.[12] Corruption had been noted in the construction trades, and in Laborers', Hotel and Restaurant workers', Carpenters', Painters', East Coast Longshoremen's, and Boilermakers' unions.

Scrutiny of union activities is a focal point in today's labor environment, but it began to intensify immediately after World War II. Ultimately, inappropriate union activities led to the creation in 1957 of the Senate Select Committee on Improper Activities in the Labor or Management Field, headed by Senator McClellan of Arkansas. Between 1957 and 1959, the McClellan Committee held a series of nationally televised public hearings that shocked and alarmed the entire country. As evidence of improper activities mounted, primarily against the Teamsters and Longshoremen/Maritime unions, the AFL-CIO took action. In 1957, the AFL-CIO expelled three unions (representing approximately 1.6 million members) for their practices. One of them, the Teamsters, was the largest union in the country.

In 1959, largely as a result of the recommendations of the McClellan Committee, Congress enacted the Labor-Management Reporting and Disclosure Act (Landrum-Griffin Act). This Act marked a significant turning point in the involvement of the federal government in internal union affairs. The Landrum-Griffin Act spelled out a *Bill of Rights for Members of Labor Organizations* designed to protect certain rights of individuals in their relationships with unions. The Act requires extensive reporting on numerous internal union activities and contains severe penalties for violations. Employers are also required to file reports when they engage in activities or make expenditures that might undermine the collective bargaining process or interfere with protected employee rights. In additionn, the Act amended the Taft-Hartley Act by adding additional restrictions on picketing and secondary boycotts.[13]

In 1974, Congress extended coverage of the Taft-Hartley Act to private, not-for-profit hospitals. This amendment brought within the jurisdiction of the National Labor Relations Board some 2 million employees. Proprietary (profit-making) health care organizations were already under NLRB jurisdiction. The amendment does not cover government-operated hospitals; it applies only to the private sector.

Key Terms

- Conspiracy, 421
- Injunction, 421
- Yellow-dog contract, 421

Notes

1. *Brief History of the American Labor Movement*, Bulletin 1000 (Washington, DC: U.S. Department of Labor Statistics, 1970): 1.
2. Benjamin J. Taylor and Fred Witney, *Labor Relations Law*, 5th ed. (Englewood Cliffs, NJ: Prentice Hall, 1987): 12–13.
3. *Brief History of the American Labor Movement*, 9.
4. Foster Rhea Dulles, *Labor in America*, 3rd ed. (New York: Crowell, 1966): 114–125.
5. Ibid., 126–149.
6. James Ryan, "The Merger of the AFL & the CIO," *Merger of the AFL & the CIO* (2005): 1–2.
7. E. Edward Herman, Alfred Kuhn, and Ronald L. Seeber, *Collective Bargaining and Labor Relations* (Englewood Cliffs, NJ: Prentice Hall, 1987): 32–34.
8. *Brief History of the American Labor Movement*, 27.
9. *Historical Statistics of the United States, Colonial Times to 1970*, bicentennial ed. Part I (Washington, DC: U.S. Bureau of the Census, 1975): 126.
10. Taylor and Witney, *Labor Relations Law*, 78–81.
11. *Brief History of the American Labor Movement*, 65.
12. Dulles, *Labor in America*, 382–383.
13. *Brief History of the American Labor Movement*, 58–61.

CHAPTER OBJECTIVES

After completing this chapter, students should be able to:

1 Define internal employee relations.

2 Explain the concept of employment at will.

3 Explain discipline and disciplinary action.

4 Describe the disciplinary action process, discuss the various approaches to disciplinary action, and describe the problems in the administration of disciplinary action.

5 Explain how grievance handling is typically conducted under a collective bargaining agreement and how grievance handling is typically conducted in union-free firms.

6 Explain the use of ombudspersons.

7 Describe termination and describe how termination conditions may differ with regard to nonmanagerial/ nonprofessional employees, executives, and middle and lower-level managers and professionals.

8 Describe demotion as an alternative to termination.

9 Describe transfers, promotions, resignations, and retirements as factors involved in internal employee relations.

Internal Employee Relations

Employee background checks are not just for pre-employment any more. The techniques and attitudes companies employ to maintain a law-abiding workforce is being upgraded to meet real-world requirements. In certain industries such as banking and health care, employers are required by regulation to routinely research the criminal records of employees.[1] However, few employers are screening their employees on an ongoing basis.[2] Perhaps they assume that if an employee did not engage in criminal activity before hiring, it will not happen in the future. But, people and events are ever-changing. For example, financial devastation, marital collapse, or a medical crisis can send a person with the cleanest record over the edge.[3]

It has been estimated that every year one to two out of every 1,000 existing employees acquire a new criminal record. In certain industries such as transportation, health care, and financial services, keeping a convicted worker can be disastrous. Since only 5 percent of convictions lead to jail time, the employer may never know of a conviction unless there is an ongoing background check.[4] At one U.S. hospital system, the backgrounds of 12,000 employees were rechecked and 74 criminal infractions were discovered that had occurred after those employees were hired. Some of the convictions included aggravated assault/battery, rape, grand theft, forgery, drug distribution, driving under the influence, prostitution, and fraud.[5] At a finance company where employees had access to sensitive customer information, 160 after-hire convictions were discovered.[6]

Online grocery company Fresh Direct, which delivers provisions to apartment-dwelling New Yorkers, suffered a financial blow when one of its drivers was charged with, and later pled guilty to, stalking and harassing female customers. Jim Moore, Fresh Direct's senior vice president for human resources, hired Verified Person, which now sends automated biweekly updates to Moore that alert him to any new misdemeanor or felony convictions of the company's employees. Anyone, from the CEO to the company's drivers and food packagers, is subject to the search. "We want to be seen as being ultra-vigilant," says Moore.[7] Verified Person charges $1 to $2 per month per employee screened.[8]

Even CEOs of major corporations have been shown to have false credentials. James Minder, chairman of the board of the parent company of Smith & Wesson, the second-biggest handgun maker in the United States, resigned under pressure after it was discovered that he had spent 15 years in Michigan prisons for a string of armed robberies and an attempted prison break.[9] RadioShack CEO David Edmondson stepped down after it was shown that he inflated his educational credentials. RadioShack had conducted a background check on Edmondson when he was hired as a vice president but did not check his education. Joseph McCool, senior contributing editor at ExecuNet, an online resource for recruiters, said, "The real mistake that RadioShack made was failing to do another background check on Edmondson before it promoted him to CEO. Like many employers, RadioShack only incorporated the background check into its recruiting, but not its talent management process." Now, all top-level Radio Shack managers are required to verify their educational experience.[10]

"Many employers are hesitant to screen current employees for fear of finding something wrong," says Garry Mathiason, an employment law attorney and the chair of the compliance and litigation group at Littler Mendelson in San Francisco. "If you have an employee who has been doing a great job for the last 10 years and then you find they fibbed on their résumé, you have a dilemma," he says. "On one hand the company may have a policy to terminate employees who lie on their résumés, but then again, you don't want to lose 50 percent of your top performers."[11]

In this chapter, continuous background checking is first discussed and internal employee relations and employment at will are presented. Discipline and disciplinary action are then described, followed by a discussion of the disciplinary action process. Next, approaches to disciplinary action are discussed, and grievance handling under a collective bargaining agreement and union-free organizations are presented. This is followed by a discussion of alternative dispute resolution, ombudspersons, and how termination differs for various groups of workers. We then examine demotion as an alternative to termination, and the topics of transfers, promotion, resignation, and retirement are discussed. This chapter concludes with a Global Perspective entitled "Getting Information to Support Disciplinary Action."

1 OBJECTIVE

Define internal employee relations.

Internal employee relations:
Those human resource management activities associated with the movement of employees within the organization.

Internal Employee Relations Defined

The status of most workers is not permanently fixed in an organization. Employees constantly move upward, laterally, downward, and out of the organization. To ensure that workers with the proper skills and experience are available at all levels, constant and concerted efforts are required to maintain good internal employee relations. **Internal employee relations** comprise the human resource management activities associated with the movement of employees within the organization. These activities include promotion, transfer, demotion, resignation, discharge, layoff, and retirement. Discipline and disciplinary action are also crucial aspects of internal employee relations.

OBJECTIVE

Explain the concept of employment at will.

Employment at will:

Unwritten contract created when an employee agrees to work for an employer but no agreement exists as to how long the parties expect the employment to last.

Employment at Will

In Chapter 3 we discussed the numerous hiring standards to avoid. You learned that factors such as race, religion, sex, national origin, age, and disabilities should not be considered as a hiring standard unless the factor was a BFOQ. The same rationale should be used as a means for terminating employees. For instance, the fact that a person is a certain age should not be used as a rationale for termination. Not withstanding various employment standards to avoid that are based on laws, court decisions, and executive orders, approximately two of every three U.S. workers depend almost entirely on the continued goodwill of their employer.[12] Individuals falling into this category are known as *at-will employees*. Not included are individuals with a contract for a specified period of time such as with collective bargaining agreements between labor and management. Teachers usually have an annual contract and are not at-will employees. Also, employees who report an illegal act, like whistleblowers, are not subject to employment at will.[13] Remember from Chapter 2, the Sarbanes-Oxley Act contained broad employee whistleblower protections. **Employment at will** is an unwritten contract created when an employee agrees to work for an employer but no agreement exists as to how long the parties expect the employment to last. Generally, much of the U.S. legal system presumes that the jobs of such employees may be terminated at the will of the employer and that these employees have a similar right to leave their jobs at any time.[14] Historically, because of a century-old common-law precedent in the United States, employment of indefinite duration could, in general, be terminated at the whim of either party.[15]

Although the concept of employment at will has eroded somewhat in the past few years, a recent California Supreme Court decision may have reversed the trend. Previously, in the landmark 1988 ruling in *Foley v Interactive Data Corporation*, employees who met certain criteria, including longevity, promotions, raises, and favorable reviews, could show an *implied-in-fact* contract and could be dismissed only for good cause.[16] Later, in the case of *Guz v Bechtel National, Inc.*, the *Foley* criteria established years earlier did not, in and of themselves, "constitute a contractual guarantee of future employment security," the justices said. Since Bechtel's own written personnel documents "imposed no restrictions upon the company's prerogatives to eliminate jobs or work units, for any or no reason," Guz had no implied-contract case to take to a jury.[17]

Time will tell regarding the employment-at-will concept. In 1987, Montana effectively ended employment at will with its Wrongful Discharge from Employment Act (WDEA). Following a probationary period (six months if not otherwise specified), a Montana employee may not be terminated except for *good cause*.[18] Although the WDEA effectively ended employment at will, it also effectively eliminated huge damages awards. General compensatory, emotional distress, and pain and suffering damages are gone. With only an extremely limited exception, it also prohibits punitive damages. Lost wages and benefits are capped at four years—minus what the employee could have earned with reasonable diligence.[19]

The courts have made certain exceptions to the employment-at-will doctrine. Some of these include prohibiting terminations in violation of public policy, permitting employees to bring claims based on representations made in employment handbooks, and permitting claims based on the common-law doctrine of good faith and fair dealing.[20] Employers can do certain things to help protect them against litigation for wrongful discharge based on a breach of implied employment contract.[21] Statements in documents such as employment applications[22] and policy manuals that suggest job security or permanent employment should be avoided if employers want to minimize charges of wrongful discharge.[23] Telling a person during a job interview that he or she can expect to hold the job as long as they want could be considered a contractual agreement and grounds for a lawsuit.[24] A person should not be employed without a signed acknowledgment of the at-will disclaimer (recall the Conoco Inc., application shown in Chapter 6).[25] In addition, the policy manual should have it clearly stated in bold, larger-than-normal print, so it is very clear to the employee that this is an at-will relationship. Other guidelines that may assist organizations in avoiding wrongful termination suits include clearly defining the worker's duties, providing good feedback on a regular basis, and conducting realistic performance appraisals on a regular basis.

Ethics was discussed in Chapter 2 and there are those who contend that even though an employer has a legal right to terminate an employee at will, there are ethical boundaries to be considered. Some of these include: terminate only as a last resort, after all other options have been exhausted; give as much notice as possible; provide as much severance pay and other help as one can; never terminate an employee for anything other than a legitimate business reason (not for personal reasons, such as replacing him with the owner's children or in-laws); never lie to an employee about the reason for his termination; always tell the truth. Treat the employee with as much dignity and respect as possible.[26] However, there is no law that says these ethical considerations have to be followed.

OBJECTIVE

Explain discipline and disciplinary action.

Discipline:
State of employee self-control and orderly conduct that indicates the extent of genuine teamwork within an organization.

Disciplinary action:
Invoking a penalty against an employee who fails to meet established standards.

Discipline and Disciplinary Action

Discipline is the state of employee self-control and orderly conduct that indicates the extent of genuine teamwork within an organization.[27] A necessary but often trying aspect of internal employee relations is the application of disciplinary action. **Disciplinary action** invokes a penalty against an employee who fails to meet established standards. Keith Ayers, president of Integro Leadership Institute, a consultancy in West Chester, Pennsylvania, says his studies indicate that poor performers make up between 11 and 16 percent of workers.[28] Poor performers are like a cancer that spreads throughout the entire workplace. "Actively disengaged workers tend to spread discontent. The impact on profitability can be enormous," says Robert Moore, CEO of the Effectiveness Connection, a consulting firm in Tampa, Florida. It is toward these workers that disciplinary action is primarily directed.[29]

Effective disciplinary action addresses the employee's wrongful behavior, not the employee as a person. Incorrectly administered disciplinary action is destructive to both the employee and the organization. Thus, disciplinary action should not be applied haphazardly. Disciplinary action is not usually management's initial response to a problem. Normally, there are more positive ways of convincing employees to adhere to company policies that are necessary to accomplish organizational goals.[30] However, managers at times must administer disciplinary action when company rules are violated.[31] Disciplinary action policies afford the organization the greatest opportunity to accomplish organizational goals, thereby benefiting both employees and the corporation. Written policies should be available regarding disciplinary action so that everyone knows the company philosophy regarding it.

OBJECTIVE

Describe the disciplinary action process, discuss the various approaches to disciplinary action, and describe the problems in the administration of disciplinary action.

Disciplinary Action Process

The disciplinary action process is dynamic and ongoing. Because one person's actions can affect others in a workgroup, the proper application of disciplinary action fosters acceptable behavior by other group members. Conversely, unjustified or improperly administered disciplinary action can have a detrimental effect on other group members.

The disciplinary action process is shown in Figure 13–1. The external environment affects every area of human resource management, including disciplinary policies and actions. Changes in the external environment, such as technological innovations, may render a rule inappropriate and may necessitate new rules. Laws and government regulations that affect company policies and rules are also constantly changing. For instance, the Occupational Safety and Health Act caused many firms to establish safety rules.

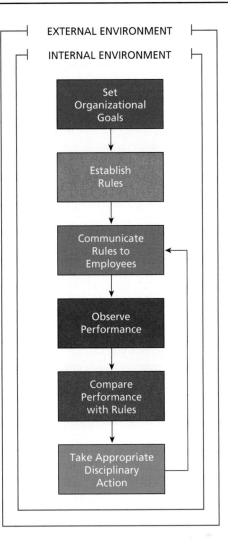

Figure 13-1 Disciplinary Action Process

Changes in the internal environment of the firm can also alter the disciplinary action process. Through organizational development, the firm may change its brand or culture. As a result of this shift, first-line supervisors may handle disciplinary action more positively. Organization policies can also have an impact on the disciplinary action process.

The disciplinary action process deals largely with infractions of rules. Notice in Figure 13-1 that rules are established to better facilitate the accomplishment of organizational goals. Rules are specific guides to behavior on the job. The *do's* and *don'ts* associated with accomplishing tasks may be highly inflexible. For example, a company rule may forbid employees to use the Internet for personal use at work.

After management has established rules, it must communicate these rules to employees. All employees must know the standards in order to be disciplined persons. Individuals cannot obey a rule if they do not know it exists. The manager then observes the performance of workers and compares performance with rules. As long as employee behavior does not vary from acceptable practices, there is no need for disciplinary action, but when an employee's behavior violates a rule, corrective action may be necessary. Taking disciplinary action against someone often creates an uncomfortable psychological climate. However, managers can still sleep well the night after taking disciplinary action if the rules have been clearly articulated to everyone. The purpose of disciplinary action is to alter behavior that can have a negative impact on achievement of organizational objectives, not to chastise the violator. The word *discipline* comes from the word *disciple*, and when translated from Latin, it means, *to teach*. Thus, the intent of disciplinary action should be to ensure that the recipient sees disciplinary action as a learning process rather than as something that merely inflicts pain.

Note that the process shown in Figure 13-1 includes feedback from the point of taking appropriate disciplinary action to communicating rules to employees. When appropriate disciplinary action is taken, all employees should realize that certain behaviors are unacceptable and should not be repeated. However, if appropriate disciplinary action is not taken, employees may view the behavior as acceptable and repeat it.

Approaches to Disciplinary Action

Several concepts regarding the administration of disciplinary action have been developed. Three of the most important concepts are the hot stove rule, progressive disciplinary action, and disciplinary action without punishment.

Hot Stove Rule

One approach to administering disciplinary action is referred to as the *hot stove rule*. According to this approach, disciplinary action should have the following consequences, which are analogous to touching a hot stove:

1. *Burns immediately.* If disciplinary action is to be taken, it must occur immediately so that the individual will understand the reason for it.

2. *Provides warning.* It is also extremely important to provide advance warning that punishment will follow unacceptable behavior. As individuals move closer to a hot stove, its heat warns them that they will be burned if they touch it; therefore, they have the opportunity to avoid the burn if they so choose.

3. *Gives consistent punishment.* Disciplinary action should also be consistent in that everyone who performs the same act will be punished accordingly. As with a hot stove, each person who touches it with the same degree of pressure and for the same period of time is burned to the same extent.

4. *Burns impersonally.* Disciplinary action should be impersonal. The hot stove burns anyone who touches it, without favoritism.[32]

If the circumstances surrounding all disciplinary action situations were the same, there would be no problem with this approach. However, situations are often quite different, and many variables may be present in each individual disciplinary action case. For instance, does the organization penalize a loyal 20-year employee the same way as an individual who has been with the firm less than six weeks? A supervisor often finds that he or she cannot be completely consistent and impersonal in taking disciplinary action. Because situations do vary, progressive disciplinary action may be more realistic and more beneficial to both the employee and the organization.

Progressive Disciplinary Action

Progressive disciplinary action:
Approach to disciplinary action designed to ensure that the minimum penalty appropriate to the offense is imposed.

Progressive disciplinary action is intended to ensure that the minimum penalty appropriate to the offense is imposed. The progressive disciplinary model was developed in response to the National Labor Relations Act (NLRA) of 1935. The goal of progressive disciplinary action is to formally communicate problem issues to employees in a

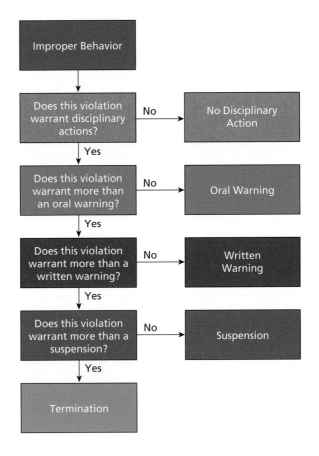

Figure 13-2 Progressive Disciplinary Action Approach

direct and timely manner so that they can improve their performance. Its use involves answering a series of questions about the severity of the offense. The manager must ask these questions, in sequence, to determine the proper disciplinary action, as illustrated in Figure 13-2. After the manager has determined that disciplinary action is appropriate, the proper question is, "Does this violation warrant more than an oral warning?" If the improper behavior is minor and has not previously occurred, perhaps only an oral warning will be sufficient. Also, an individual may receive several oral warnings before a *yes* answer applies. The manager follows the same procedure for each level of offense in the progressive disciplinary process. The manager does not consider termination until each lower-level question is answered *yes*. However, major violations, such as assaulting a supervisor or another worker, may justify immediate termination of the employee.

To assist managers in recognizing the proper level of disciplinary action, some firms have formalized the procedure. One approach is to establish progressive disciplinary action guidelines, as shown in Table 13-1. In this example, a worker who is absent without authorization will receive an oral warning the first time it happens and a written warning the second time; the third time, the employee will be terminated. Fighting on the job is an offense that normally results in immediate termination. However, specific guidelines for various offenses should be developed to meet the needs of the organization. For example, the wearing of rings or jewelry for aircraft mechanics is strictly prohibited. There would likely be no such rule in an office environment. Basically, the rule should fit the need of the situation.

Disciplinary Action without Punishment

The process of giving a worker time off with pay to think about whether he or she wants to follow the rules and continue working for the company is called **disciplinary action without punishment**. The approach is to throw out formal punitive

Web Wisdom

PROGRESSIVE DISCIPLINARY ACTION

http://humanresources. about.com/od/discipline/

Numerous articles related to disciplinary action and progressive disciplinary action.

Disciplinary action without punishment:

Process in which a worker is given time off with pay to think about whether he or she wants to follow the rules and continue working for the company.

Table 13-1 Suggested Guidelines for Disciplinary Action

Offenses Requiring First, an Oral Warning;
Second, a Written Warning; and Third, Termination

Negligence in the performance of duties
Unauthorized absence from job
Inefficiency in the performance of job

Offenses Requiring a Written Warning and Then Termination

Sleeping on the job
Failure to report to work one or two days in a row without notification
Negligent use of property

Offenses Requiring Immediate Discharge

Theft
Fighting on the job
Falsifying time cards
Failure to report to work three days in a row without notification

disciplinary policies for dilemmas such as chronic tardiness or a bad attitude in favor of affirming procedures that make employees want to take personal responsibility for their actions and be models for the corporate mission and vision. When an employee violates a rule, the manager issues an oral reminder. Repetition brings a written reminder, and the third violation results in the worker having to take one, two, or three days off (with pay) to think about the situation. During the first two steps, the manager tries to encourage the employee to solve the problem. If the third step is taken, upon the worker's return, the worker and the supervisor meet to agree that the employee will not violate a rule again or the employee will leave the firm. When disciplinary action without punishment is used, it is especially important that all rules be explicitly stated in writing. At the time of orientation, new workers should be told that repeated violations of different rules will be viewed in the same way as several violations of the same rule. This approach keeps workers from taking undue advantage of the process.

Today, numerous organizations have abandoned warnings, reprimands, probations, demotions, unpaid disciplinary suspensions, and all other punitive responses to discipline problems in favor of disciplinary action without punishment. Consider the following examples:

- The Texas Department of Mental Health saw turnover drop from 48.5 to 31.3 to 18.5 percent in the two years following implementation. The system has now been in place for over two decades. In this time, employee turnover has consistently remained at a manageable 20 percent or less per year.

- A Vermont General Electric plant, one of many GE facilities that have adopted discipline without punishment, reported written warnings/reminders dropping from 39 to 23 to 12 in a two-year period.

- GTE's Telephone Operations reduced all grievances by 63 percent and disciplinary grievances by 86 percent in the year after management installed the approach.

- Tampa Electric Co., reduced sick-leave hours per employee from 66.7 in the year before implementation to 31.2 eight years later.[33]

Problems in the Administration of Disciplinary Action

As might be expected, administering disciplinary action is not a pleasant task, but it is a job that managers sometimes have to do. Although the manager is in the best position to take disciplinary action, many would rather avoid it.[34] The reasons managers want to avoid disciplinary action include the following issues.

1. *Lack of training.* The manager may not have the knowledge and skill necessary to handle disciplinary problems.

2. *Fear.* The manager may be concerned that top management will not support a disciplinary action.

3. *Being the only one.* The manager may think, "No one else is disciplining employees, so why should I?"

4. *Guilt.* The manager may think, "How can I discipline someone if I've done the same thing?"

5. *Loss of friendship.* The manager may believe that disciplinary action will damage a friendship with an employee or the employee's associates.

6. *Time loss.* The manager may begrudge the valuable time that is required to administer and explain disciplinary action.

7. *Loss of temper.* The manager may be afraid of losing his or her temper when talking to an employee about a rule violation.

8. *Rationalization.* The manager may think, "The employee knows it was the wrong thing to do, so why do we need to talk about it?"[35]

These reasons apply to all forms of disciplinary action, from an oral warning to termination. Managers often avoid disciplinary action, even when it is in the company's best interest. Such reluctance often stems from breakdowns in other areas of the human resource management function. For instance, if a manager has consistently rated an employee high on annual performance appraisals, the supervisor's rationale for terminating a worker for poor performance would be weak. It is embarrassing to decide to fire a worker and then be asked why you rated this individual so high on the previous evaluation.[36] It could be that the employee's productivity has actually dropped substantially. It could also be that the employee's productivity has always been low, yet the supervisor may have trouble justifying to upper-level management that the person should be terminated. Rather than run the risk of a decision being overturned, the supervisor retains the ineffective worker.

Finally, some managers believe that even attempting to terminate women and minorities is useless. However, the statutes and subsequent court decisions were not intended to protect unproductive workers. Anyone whose performance is below standard can, and should, be terminated after the supervisor has made reasonable attempts to salvage the employee. Occasionally, there will be suits involving members of protected groups. One of the best ways for a company to protect itself against suits claiming discrimination or harassment is to ensure that it has proper, written policies barring unfair treatment of its staff, and a system for ensuring that the policies are followed.[37] Disciplinary actions should be fully documented, and managers should be trained in how to avoid bias claims.[38]

A supervisor may be perfectly justified in administering disciplinary action, but there is usually a proper time and place for doing so. For example, taking disciplinary action against a worker in the presence of others may embarrass the individual and actually defeat the purpose of the action. Even when they are wrong, employees resent

Ethical Dilemma

To Fire or Not to Fire

You are a first-line supervisor for Kwik Corporation, a medium-sized manufacturer of automotive parts. Workers in your company and also your department are quite close and you view them as family. The work in your department can be quite dangerous. It is especially important that all workers wear their safety glasses, because in the past there have been some serious injuries. The company has a rule that states that any employee who does not follow the stated policy will receive a written reprimand on the first offense, and will be terminated on the second violation. You have had to terminate several workers in the past because of similar violations. The other day, Allen Smith, one of your best and most influential employees, violated the safety glasses rule and you gave him a reprimand. You hated to do that because he is by far your best worker and he often helps you if you have a problem with the other workers. He has also been with the company for a long time. You would really be lost without him. You walk up to Allen's workstation and observe him not wearing his safety glasses again. He knows that he has been caught and quickly puts his glasses on and says in a pleading voice, "Please don't fire me. I promise it will never happen again. I have just had a lot on my mind lately."

What would you do?

---

disciplinary action administered in public. By disciplining employees in private, supervisors prevent them from losing face with their peers.

In addition, many supervisors may be too lenient early in the disciplinary action process and too strict later. This lack of consistency does not give the worker a clear understanding of the penalty associated with the inappropriate action. A supervisor will often endure an unacceptable situation for an extended period of time. Then, when the supervisor finally does take action, he or she is apt to overreact and come down excessively hard. However, consistency does not necessarily mean that the same penalty must be applied to two different workers for the same offense. For instance, employers would be consistent if they always considered the worker's past record and length of service. For a serious violation, a long-term employee might receive only a suspension, whereas a worker with only a few months' service might be terminated for the same act. This type of action could reasonably be viewed as being consistent.

5 OBJECTIVE

Explain how grievance handling is typically conducted under a collective bargaining agreement and how grievance handling is typically conducted in union-free firms.

Grievance Handling Under a Collective Bargaining Agreement

If a union represents employees in an organization, workers who believe that they have been disciplined or dealt with unjustly can appeal through the grievance and arbitration procedures of the collective bargaining agreement. The grievance system encourages and facilitates the settlement of disputes between labor and management.

Grievance:

Employee's dissatisfaction or feeling of personal injustice relating to his or her employment.

Grievance Procedure

A **grievance** can be broadly defined as an employee's dissatisfaction or feeling of personal injustice relating to his or her employment. A **grievance procedure** is a formal, systematic process that permits employees to express complaints without jeopardizing their jobs. It also assists management in seeking out the underlying causes of and solutions to grievances. Virtually all labor agreements include some form of grievance procedure. A grievance procedure under a collective bargaining agreement is normally well

Grievance procedure:

Formal, systematic process that permits employees to express complaints without jeopardizing their jobs.

defined. It is usually restricted to violations of the terms and conditions of the agreement. There are other conditions that may give rise to a grievance, including the following:

- A violation of law.
- A violation of the intent of the parties as stipulated during contract negotiations.
- A violation of company rules.
- A change in working conditions or past company practices.
- A violation of health and/or safety standards.

Grievance procedures have many common features. However, variations may reflect differences in organizational or decision-making structures or the size of a plant or company. Some general principles based on widespread practice can serve as useful guidelines for effective grievance administration:

- Grievances should be adjusted promptly.
- Procedures and forms used for airing grievances must be easy to utilize and well understood by employees and their supervisors.
- Direct and timely avenues of appeal from rulings of line supervision must exist.

The multistep grievance procedure shown in Figure 13-3 is the most common type. In the first step, the employee usually presents the grievance orally and

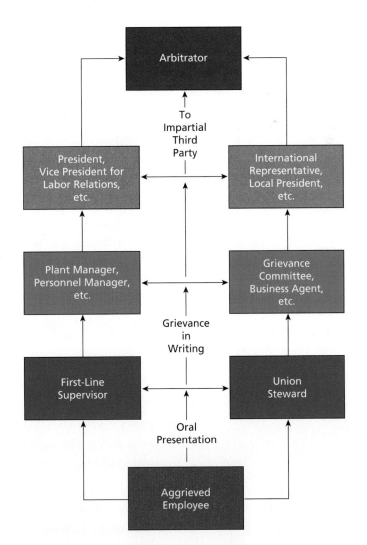

Figure 13-3 A Multistep Grievance Procedure
Source: Robert W. Eckles et al., *Essentials of Management for First-Line Supervision* (New York: John Wiley & Sons, 1974), p. 529. Reprinted by permission of John Wiley & Sons, Inc.

informally to the immediate supervisor in the presence of the union steward. This step offers the greatest potential for improved labor relations, and a large majority of grievances are settled here. The procedure ends if the grievance can be resolved at this initial step. If the grievance remains unresolved, the next step involves a meeting between the plant manager or human resource manager and higher union officials, such as the grievance committee or the business agent or manager. Prior to this meeting, the grievance is written out, dated, and signed by the employee and the union steward. The written grievance states the events, as the employee perceives them, cites the contract provision that allegedly has been violated, and indicates the settlement desired. If the grievance is not settled at this meeting, it is appealed to the third step, which typically involves the firm's top labor representative (such as the vice president of industrial relations) and high-level union officials. At times, depending on the severity of the grievance, the president may represent the firm. A grievance that remains unresolved at the conclusion of the third step may go to arbitration, if provided for in the agreement and the union decides to persevere.

Labor relations problems can escalate when a supervisor is not equipped to handle grievances at the first step. Since the union steward, the aggrieved party, and the supervisor usually handle the first step informally, the supervisor must be fully prepared. The supervisor should obtain as many facts as possible before the meeting, because the union steward is likely to have done his or her homework.

The supervisor needs to recognize that the grievance may not reflect the real problem. For instance, the employee might be angry with the company for modifying its pay policies, even though the union agreed to the change. In order to voice discontent, the worker might file a grievance for an unrelated minor violation of the contract.

AMERICAN ARBITRATION ASSOCIATION

http://www.adr.org

Vast source of information concerning arbitration rules and procedures, including international arbitration rules as well as individual state statutes, is provided.

Arbitration

Arbitration is a grievance procedure that has successfully and peacefully resolved many labor management problems. Arbitration is the final step in most grievance procedures. In arbitration, the parties submit their dispute to an impartial third party for binding resolution. Most agreements restrict the arbitrator's decision to application and interpretation of the agreement and make the decision final and binding on the parties. If the union decides in favor of arbitration, it notifies management. At this point, the union and the company select an arbitrator.[39]

Most agreements specify the selection method, although the choice is usually made from a list supplied by the Federal Mediation and Conciliation Service (FMCS) or the American Arbitration Association (AAA), both of which were discussed in Chapter 12. When considering potential arbitrators, both management and labor will study the candidates' previous decisions in an attempt to detect any biases. Obviously, neither party wants to select an arbitrator who might tend to favor the other's position.

When arbitration is used to settle a grievance, a variety of factors may be considered to evaluate the fairness of the management actions that caused the grievance. These factors include the following:

- Nature of the offense.
- Due process and procedural correctness.
- Double jeopardy.
- Past record of grievant.
- Length of service with the company.
- Knowledge of rules.
- Warnings.
- Lax enforcement of rules.
- Discriminatory treatment.

The large number of interacting variables in each case makes the arbitration process difficult. The arbitrator must possess exceptional patience and judgment in rendering a fair and impartial decision.

After the arbitrator has been selected and has agreed to serve, a time and place for a hearing will be determined. The issue to be resolved will be presented to the arbitrator in a document that summarizes the question(s) to be decided. It will also point out any contract restrictions that prohibit the arbitrator from making an award that would change the terms of the contract.

At the hearing, each side presents its case. Arbitration is an adversarial proceeding, so a case may be lost because of poor preparation and presentation. The arbitrator may conduct the hearing much like a courtroom proceeding. Witnesses, cross-examination, transcripts, and legal counsel may all be used. The parties may also submit or be asked by the arbitrator to submit formal written statements. After the hearing, the arbitrator studies the material submitted and testimony given and is expected to reach a decision within 30 to 60 days. The decision is usually accompanied by a written opinion giving reasons for the decision.

The courts will generally enforce an arbitrator's decision unless (1) the arbitrator's decision is shown to be unreasonable or capricious in that it did not address the issues; (2) the arbitrator exceeded his or her authority; or (3) the award or decision violated a federal or state law. In one arbitration case that ultimately went to the Supreme Court, the arbitrator's decision appeared to run counter to public policy, prohibiting workers who had tested positive for drugs from operating heavy machinery or being permitted to return to work. However, the Supreme Court wrote, "We recognize that reasonable people can differ as to whether reinstatement or discharge is the more appropriate remedy here. But both employer and union have agreed to entrust this remedial decision to an arbitrator."[40]

Proof That Disciplinary Action Was Needed

Any disciplinary action administered may ultimately be taken to arbitration, when such a remedy is specified in the labor agreement. Employers have learned that they must prepare records that will constitute proof of disciplinary action and the reasons for it. Although the formats of written warnings may vary, all should include the following information:

1. Statement of facts concerning the offense.
2. Identification of the rule that was violated.
3. Statement of what resulted or could have resulted because of the violation.
4. Identification of any previous similar violations by the same individual.
5. Statement of possible future consequences should the violation occur again.
6. Signature and date.

An example of a written warning is shown in Figure 13-4. In this instance, the worker has already received an oral reprimand. The individual is also warned that continued tardiness could lead to termination. It is important to document oral reprimands because they may be the first step in disciplinary action leading ultimately to arbitration.

Grievance Handling in Union-Free Organizations

In the past, few union-free firms had formalized grievance procedures. Today, this is not the case as most large and medium-sized nonunion firms have established formal grievance procedures and encouraged their use. Although the step-by-step procedure

Date: August 1, 2007

To: Wayne Sanders

From: Judy Bandy

Subject: Written Warning

We are quite concerned because today you were thirty minutes late to work and offered no justification for this. According to our records, a similar offense occurred on July 25, 2007. At that time, you were informed that failure to report to work on time is unacceptable. I am, therefore, notifying you in writing that you must report to work on time. It will be necessary to terminate your employment if this happens again.

 Please sign this form to indicate that you have read and understand this warning. Signing is not an indication of agreement.

_____
Name

_____
Date

Figure 13-4 An Example of a Written Warning

ALTERNATIVE DISPUTE RESOLUTION

http://www.opm.gov/er/ adrguide/toc.asp

Office of Personnel Management, Alternative Dispute Resolution: A Resource Guide.

OBJECTIVE

Explain the use of ombudspersons.

Ombudsperson:

Complaint officer who has access to top management and who hears employee complaints, investigates, and recommends appropriate action.

for handling union grievances is a common practice, the means of resolving complaints in nonunion firms vary. Generally, a well-designed grievance procedure ensures that the worker has ample opportunity to make complaints without fear of reprisal.[41] If the system is to work, employees must be well informed about the program and convinced that management wants them to use it. Some employees are hesitant to formalize their complaints and must be constantly urged to avail themselves of the process. The fact that a manager says, "Our workers must be happy because I have received no complaints," does not necessarily mean that employees have no grievances. In a closed, threatening corporate culture, workers may be reluctant to voice their dissatisfaction to management.

 Typically, an employee initiates a complaint with his or her immediate supervisor. However, if the complaint involves the supervisor, the individual is permitted to bypass the immediate supervisor and proceed to the employee-relations specialist or the manager at the next higher level. The grievance ultimately may be taken to the organization's top executive for a final decision.

Ombudspersons

An **ombudsperson** is a complaint officer who has access to top management and who hears employee complaints, investigates, and recommends appropriate action. More employers are using ombuds in their organizations to help defuse problems before they become lawsuits or scandals.[42] "The more internal mechanisms a corporation has to deal with internal problems, the less likely these problems are to wind up in court," said Allan Weitzman, a partner with law firm of Proskauer Rose LLP. Ombuds are impartial, neutral counselors who can give employees confidential advice about problems ranging from abusive managers to allegations of illegal corporate activity.[43]

Trends & Innovations

Alternative Dispute Resolution

As the number of employment-related lawsuits increases, companies have looked for ways to protect themselves against the costs and uncertainties of the judicial system. **Alternative dispute resolution (ADR)** is a procedure whereby the employee and the company agree ahead of time that any problems will be addressed by an agreed-upon means. Some of these include arbitration, mediation, mini-trials, and ombudspersons.[44] Whenever workers at Brown & Root, a Houston-based engineering, construction, and maintenance company, feel they need to resolve a dispute, the program allows them to choose one or all four options including an open-door policy, a conference, mediation, or arbitration. The idea behind ADR is to resolve conflicts between employer and employee through means less costly and contentious than litigation.[45] A successful program can save a company thousands of dollars in legal costs and hundreds of hours in managers' time. It has been estimated to cost an average of $100,000 to defend a case in court.[46] Just as important, perhaps, it can protect a company from the demoralizing tension and bitterness that employee grievances can spread through a workforce. Compared to litigation, ADR processes are less adversarial, faster and more efficient, relatively lower in cost, and private.[47]

Cases run the gamut from racial, gender, and age discrimination to unfair firings. Although ADR programs vary from employer to employer, many include informal methods that encourage workers to discuss their problem with their supervisor, a department head, or a panel of peers. The two best-known ADR methods are mediation and arbitration. Mediation is the preferred method for most people.[48] When parties agree to mediate, they are able to reach a settlement in 96 percent of the cases.[49] A Presidential Executive Order requires federal agencies to (1) promote greater use of mediation, arbitration, early neutral evaluation, agency ombudspersons, and other alternative dispute resolution techniques; and (2) promote greater use of negotiated rulemaking. Mediation in alternative dispute resolution cases has been credited with reducing the EEOC backlog of cases by 50 percent.[50]

The Supreme Court rendered an opinion in *Circuit City v Adams* that greatly enhanced an employer's ability to enforce compulsory alternative dispute resolution agreements. The Court held that the ADR was valid and enforceable and made clear that ADR applied to the vast majority of employees and was available to employers seeking to enforce compulsory arbitration agreements.

Alternative dispute resolution (ADR): Procedure whereby the employee and the company agree ahead of time that any problems will be addressed by an agreed-upon means.

Organizational ombuds are designated by employers so that all workers may seek informal, confidential assistance to work through problems without losing control over how their concerns will be addressed. The ombud is typically independent of line management and reports near or at the top of the organization.[51]

 OBJECTIVE

Describe termination and describe how termination conditions may differ with regard to nonmanagerial/nonprofessional employees, executives, and middle and lower-level managers and professionals.

Termination

Termination is the most severe penalty that an organization can impose on an employee; therefore, it should be the most carefully considered form of disciplinary action. The experience of being terminated is traumatic for employees regardless of their position in the organization. They can experience feelings of failure, fear, disappointment, and anger.[52] It is also a difficult time for the person making the termination decision. Knowing that termination may affect not only the employee but an entire family increases the trauma. Not knowing how the terminated employee will react also may create considerable anxiety for the manager who must do the firing. Recall from Chapter 11 that an individual who is terminated may respond with violence in the workplace.

When the decision is made to fire a worker, the individual should not really be surprised at the decision since he or she should have been given explicit warnings and counseling prior to being fired. The worker should have been advised of specific steps he or she needed to take to keep the job. Support should have been provided to show him or her what needed to be done to keep the job. The worker also should have been given a reasonable period of time to comply with the supervisor's expectations.[53]

Research has suggested that Friday afternoon is probably the best time to fire an employee, because it gives the employee the weekend to cool off. The final paycheck should be available at the time of firing. Further, firing a worker at the end of the day leaves little chance for discussion among the remaining staff that may interrupt the workplace. Managers should try to plan the termination and not make it based on emotions.[54] Certain steps should be followed in the termination process. In the first place, the manager of the worker should do the firing and do it in person. Second, the firing process should be kept short and done so in nonaccusatory language. Third, the manager should not go into the reason for the dismissal and should not answer any questions regarding the decision. Finally, another person should handle the mechanics of the exit such as the last paycheck and insurance.[55]

Regardless of the similarities in the termination of employees at various levels, distinct differences exist with regard to nonmanagerial/nonprofessional employees, executives, and middle and lower-level managers and professionals.

Termination of Nonmanagerial/Nonprofessional Employees

Individuals in this category are neither managers nor professionally trained individuals, such as engineers or accountants. They generally include such employees as steelworkers, truck drivers, salesclerks, and waiters. If the firm is unionized, the termination procedure is typically well defined in the labor management agreement. For example, drinking on the job might be identified as a reason for immediate termination. Absences, on the other hand, may require three written warnings by the supervisor before termination action can be taken.

When the firm is union-free, these workers can generally be terminated more easily since the worker is most likely an at-will employee. In most union-free organizations, violations justifying termination are included in the firm's employee handbook. At times, especially in smaller organizations, the termination process is informal, with the first-line supervisor telling workers what actions warrant termination. Regardless of the size of the organization, management should inform employees of the actions that warrant termination.

Termination of Executives

Unlike individuals in most organization positions, CEOs do not have to worry about their positions being eliminated. Their main concern is pleasing the board of directors because hiring and firing the CEO is a board's main responsibility.[56] In a study conducted to discover the reasons why organizations ousted their CEOs, it was found that the boards of directors lost confidence in them.[57] Tenure has become increasingly shaky for new CEOs, as the turnover in the *Fortune* 1000 companies is at a five-year high. In 1999 the number of chief executives who left their organizations was 42, but it has recently increased to 97.[58] Leslie Gaines-Ross, chief knowledge officer at the public relations firm of Burson-Marsteller, says the large number of firings of CEOs shows that it is the end of the *rubber-stamp* boards, as previously discussed in Chapter 2. Now, directors "don't want to be caught red-faced."[59]

Executives usually have no formal appeal procedure. The reasons for termination may not be as clear as those for lower-level employees. Some of the reasons include the following issues.

1. *Economic downturns.* At times, business conditions may force a reduction in the number of executives.

2. *Reorganization/downsizing.* In order to improve efficiency or as a result of merging with another company, a firm may reorganize or downsize, resulting in the elimination of some executive positions.

3. *Philosophical differences.* A difference in philosophy of conducting business may develop between an executive and other key company officials. In order to maintain consistency in management philosophy, the executive may be replaced.

4. *Decline in productivity.* The executive may have been capable of performing satisfactorily in the past but, for various reasons, can no longer perform the job as required.

This list does not include factors related to illegal activities such as sexual harassment or insider trading.[60] Under those circumstances, the firm has no moral obligation to the terminated executive. Consider such criminal actions as those of executives at Enron, WorldCom, Arthur Andersen, Global Crossing, Adelphia Communications, and Tyco International. Executives must now face a hostile board of directors that once was solidly in their corner. "Lousy performance won't be tolerated," says Barbara Franklin, who sits on five corporate boards. "Now we're trying to get ahead of the curve and make changes before you have an absolute crisis."[61]

An organization may derive positive benefits from terminating executives, but such actions also present a potentially hazardous situation for the company. Terminating a senior executive is an expensive proposition, often in ways more costly than just the separation package (discussed in Chapter 9). The impact on the organization should be measured in relationships, productivity, strategic integrity, and investor confidence, as well as dollars. Many corporations are concerned about developing a negative public image that reflects insensitivity to the needs of their employees. They fear that such a reputation would impede their efforts to recruit high-quality managers. Also, terminated executives have, at times, made public statements detrimental to the reputation of their former employers.

Termination of Middle and Lower-Level Managers and Professionals

Typically, the most vulnerable and perhaps the most neglected groups of employees with regard to termination have been middle and lower-level managers and professionals. Employees in these jobs may lack the political clout that a terminated executive has. Although certainly not recommended, termination may have been based on something as simple as the attitude or feelings of an immediate superior on a given day.

 **OBJECTIVE**

Describe demotion as an alternative to termination.

Demotion as an Alternative to Termination

Demotion is the process of moving a worker to a lower level of duties and responsibilities, which typically involves a reduction in pay. Termination may be the solution when a person is not able to perform his or her job satisfactorily. At times, however, demotions are used as an alternative to discharge, especially when a long-term employee is involved. The worker may have performed satisfactorily for many years,

Demotion:

Process of moving a worker to a lower level of duties and responsibilities and typically involves a reduction in pay.

but his or her productivity may then begin to decline for a variety of reasons. Perhaps the worker is just not physically capable of performing the job any longer or no longer willing to work the long hours that the job requires.

Emotions may run high when an individual is demoted. The demoted person may suffer loss of respect from peers and feel betrayed, embarrassed, angry, and disappointed. The employee's productivity may also decrease further. For these reasons, demotion should be used very cautiously. If demotion is chosen over termination, efforts must be made to preserve the self-esteem of the individual. The person may be asked how he or she would like to handle the demotion announcement. A positive image of the worker's value to the company should be projected.

The handling of demotions in a unionized organization is usually spelled out clearly in the labor–management agreement. Should a decision be made to demote a worker for unsatisfactory performance, the union should be notified of this intent and given the specific reasons for the demotion. Often the demotion will be challenged and carried through the formal grievance procedure. Documentation is necessary for the demotion to be upheld. Even with the problems associated with demotion for cause, it is often easier to demote than to terminate an employee. In addition, demotion is often less devastating to the employee. For the organization, however, the opposite may be true if the demotion creates lingering ill will and an embittered employee.

There is another reason for a demotion. As firms downsize and reduce the number of layers in the organizational structure, positions that may have been held by highly qualified employees may be eliminated. Rather than lose a valued employee, firms will, at times, offer this employee a lower-level position, often at the same salary.

9 **OBJECTIVE**

Describe transfers, promotions, resignations, and retirements as factors involved in internal employee relations.

Transfer:

Lateral movement of a worker within an organization.

Transfers

The lateral movement of a worker within an organization is called a **transfer**. A transfer may be initiated by the firm or by an employee. The process does not and should not imply that a person is being either promoted or demoted. Transfers serve several purposes. First, firms often find it necessary to reorganize. Offices and departments are created and abolished in response to the company's needs. In filling positions created by reorganization, the company may have to move employees without promoting them. Relocations for transfers are much more common than for promotions. A similar situation may exist when an office or department is closed. Rather than terminate valued employees, management may transfer them to other areas within the organization. These transfers may entail moving an employee to another desk in the same office or to a location halfway around the world.

A second reason for transfers is to make positions available in the primary promotion channels. Firms are typically organized into a hierarchical structure resembling a pyramid. Each succeeding promotion is more difficult to obtain because fewer positions exist. At times, very productive but unpromotable workers may clog promotion channels. Other qualified workers in the organization may find their opportunities for promotion blocked. When this happens, a firm's most capable future managers may seek employment elsewhere. To keep promotion channels open, the firm may decide to transfer employees who are unpromotable but productive at their organizational level.

Another reason for transfers is to satisfy employees' personal desires. The reasons for wanting a transfer are numerous. An individual may need to accompany a transferred spouse to a new location or work closer to home to care for aging parents, or the worker may dislike the long commute to and from work. Factors such as these may be of sufficient importance that employees may resign if a requested transfer is not approved. Rather than risk losing a valued employee, the firm may agree to the transfer.

Transfers may also be an effective means of dealing with personality clashes. Some people just cannot get along with one another. Because each of the individuals may be a valued employee, transfer may be an appropriate solution to the problem. But managers must be cautious regarding the *grass is always greener on the other side of the fence* syndrome. When some workers encounter a temporary setback, they immediately ask for a transfer before they even attempt to work through the problem.

Finally, because of a limited number of management levels, it is becoming necessary for managers to have a wide variety of experiences before achieving a promotion. Individuals who desire upward mobility often explore possible lateral moves so that they can learn new skills.

If the worker initiates the transfer request, it should be analyzed in terms of the best interests of both the firm and the individual. Disruptions may occur when the worker is transferred. For example, a qualified worker might not be available to step into the position being vacated. Management should establish clear policies regarding transfers. Such policies let workers know in advance when a transfer request is likely to be approved and what its ramifications will be. For instance, if the transfer is for personal reasons, some firms do not pay moving costs. Whether the organization will or will not pay these expenses should be clearly spelled out.

Promotions

Promotion:
Movement of a person to a higher-level position in an organization.

A **promotion** is the movement of a person to a higher-level position in the organization. The term *promotion* is one of the most emotionally charged words in the field of human resource management. An individual who receives a promotion normally receives additional financial rewards and the ego boost associated with achievement and accomplishment. Most employees feel good about being promoted. But for every individual who gains a promotion, there are probably others who were not selected. If these individuals wanted the promotion badly enough or their favorite candidate was overlooked, they may slack off or even resign. If the consensus of employees directly involved is that the wrong person was promoted, considerable resentment may result.

Resignations

Even when an organization is totally committed to making its environment a good place to work, workers will still resign. Some employees cannot see promotional opportunities, or at least not enough, and will therefore move on. A certain amount of turnover is healthy for an organization and is often necessary to afford employees the opportunity to fulfill career objectives. When turnover becomes excessive, however, the firm must do something to slow it. The most qualified employees are often the ones who resign because they are more mobile. On the other hand, marginally qualified workers never seem to leave. If excessive numbers of a firm's highly qualified and competent workers are leaving, a way must be found to reverse the trend.

Analyzing Voluntary Resignations

Exit interview:
Means of revealing the real reasons employees leave their jobs; it is conducted before an employee departs the company and provides information on how to correct the causes of discontent and reduce turnover.

Even during times of economic slowdown, unwanted employee turnover occurs. It is one of the biggest and most costly business problems companies face, and they are constantly striving to determine why outstanding producers quit to take another job elsewhere.[62] When a firm wants to determine the real reasons individuals decide to leave, it can use the exit interview and/or the postexit questionnaire. An **exit interview** is a means of revealing the real reasons employees leave their jobs; it is conducted before an employee departs the company, it provides information on how to correct the causes of discontent, and it reduces turnover.[63] The most common reason individuals give for taking a job with another company is more money or a better opportunity.[64] This explanation, however, may not reveal other weaknesses in the organization. For instance, in one study 57 percent of workers who were considering changing their jobs thought that they were underpaid; in reality, only 19 percent actually were underpaid.[65] Only after determining the *real* reason for leaving can a firm develop a strategy to overcome the problem. Employee departures from an organization are most likely explained by problems with their immediate supervisors, according to an ongoing Gallup survey of more than 1 million employees.[66]

Often a third party, such as a person in the HR department or an outsource party, will conduct the exit interview. A third party may be used because employees may not be willing to air their problems with their former bosses. Outsourcing the exit interviews may be beneficial because employers believe that the person who is leaving will be more honest when he or she is not speaking to a company employee.[67] The typical exit interview follows the following format:

- Establishing rapport.
- Stating the purpose of the interview.
- Exploring the employee's attitudes regarding the job.
- Exploring the employee's reasons for leaving.
- Comparing old and new jobs.
- Recording the changes recommended by the employee.
- Concluding the interview.[68]

Over a period of time, properly conducted exit interviews can provide considerable insight into why employees leave. Patterns are often identified that uncover weaknesses in the firm's management system. Knowledge of the problem permits corrective action to be taken. Also, the exit interview helps to identify training and development needs, to create strategic planning objectives, and to identify those areas in which changes need to be made.[69]

Postexit questionnaire:
Questionnaire sent to former employees several weeks after they leave the organization to determine the real reason they left.

A **postexit questionnaire** is sent to former employees several weeks after they leave the organization to determine the real reason they left. Usually, they have already started work at their new companies. Ample blank space is provided so that a former employee can express his or her feelings about and perceptions of the job and the organization. Since the individual is no longer with the firm he or she may respond more freely to the questions. A weakness is that the interviewer is not present to interpret and probe for more information.

Attitude Surveys: A Means of Retaining Quality Employees

Exit and postexit interviews can provide valuable information for improving human resource management practices. The problem, however, is that these approaches are reactions to events that were detrimental to the organization. The very people you want to save may be the ones being interviewed or completing questionnaires.

Attitude survey:
Survey that seeks input from employees to determine their feelings about topics such as the work they perform, their supervisor, their work environment, flexibility in the workplace, opportunities for advancement, training and development opportunities, and the firm's compensation system.

An alternative, proactive approach is administering attitude surveys (survey feedback was described in Chapter 7). **Attitude surveys** seek input from employees to determine their feelings about topics such as the work they perform, their supervisor, their work environment, flexibility in the workplace, opportunities for advancement, training and development opportunities, and the firm's compensation system. Since some employees will want their responses to be confidential, every effort should be made to guarantee their anonymity. To achieve this, it may be necessary to have the survey administered by a third party. Regardless of how the process is handled, it is clear that attitude surveys have the potential to improve management practices. For this reason, they are widely used throughout industry today.

Employees should be advised of the purpose of the survey. The mere act of giving a survey communicates to employees that management is concerned about their problems, wants to know what they are, and wants to solve them, if possible. Analyzing survey results of various subgroups and comparing them with the firm's total population may indicate areas that should be investigated and problems that need to be solved. For instance, the survey results of the production night shift might be compared to the production day shift. Should problems show up, management must be willing to make needed changes. It should be noted that if the survey does not result in some improvements, the process may be a real turn-off for employees and future surveys may not yield helpful data.[70]

Advance Notice of Resignation

Most firms would like to have at least a two-week notice of resignation from departing workers. However, a month's notice may be desired from professional and managerial employees who are leaving. When the firm desires notice, the policy should be clearly communicated to all employees. If they want departing employees to give advance notice, companies have certain obligations. For instance, suppose that a worker who gives notice is terminated immediately. Word of this action will spread rapidly to other employees. Later, should they decide to resign, they will likely not give any advance notice.

Recall from Chapter 5, on recruitment, that firms are now actively recruiting former employees. If the firm views a departing worker as eligible to return in the future, it should avoid treating that person like a second-class citizen. In some cases permitting a worker to remain on the job once a resignation has been submitted may create some problems. If bad feelings exist between the employee and the supervisor or the company, the departing worker may be a disruptive force. On a selective basis, the firm may wish to pay some employees for the notice time and ask them to leave immediately.

Retirements

Many long-term employees leave an organization by retiring. In a recent study, 55 percent of executives polled said their companies are concerned about losing key staff to retirement in the next 5 to 10 years.[71] Retirement plans may be based on the employee reaching a certain age, working a certain number of years with the firm, or both. The majority of today's employees are not planning for a traditional retirement, where they have an immediate and abrupt end to their working career at a specific age, such as 62. Most individuals expect to work in some capacity after retirement, or plan to take a more gradual approach to transition into retirement, such as in a bridge job.[72] Many want to *phase-in* retirement by working fewer hours as they near 65, or after.[73] Upon retirement, former employees usually receive compensation either from a defined benefits plan or a defined contributions plan, both of which were discussed in Chapter 10.

Sometimes employees will be offered early retirement before reaching the organization's normal length-of-service requirement. Historically, early retirement has been viewed as an attractive solution when workforce reductions had to be made. Early retirement plans, which gained popularity in the 1980s, appealed to older workers facing layoffs. They also gave companies an alternative to the negative press involving layoffs. Companies such as Procter & Gamble Co., Tribune Co., and Lucent Technologies Inc., offered early retirement to thousands of workers.[74] When the U.S. Agriculture Department reduced its workforce in 2005, buyout or early-out offers were provided. An incentive payment of up to $25,000 was provided in return for employees' resignation or retirement from the agency.[75]

From an organization's viewpoint, early employee retirement also has a negative side and companies are becoming reluctant to use them. "I'm seeing fewer early retirement windows," says Bernadette Kenny, of the outplacement firm Lee Hecht

Harrison. From a practical standpoint, with poor economic conditions, many companies cannot afford early retirement packages.[76] Another reason for the decline is that today's workers are more likely to have defined contribution plans, such as 401(k)s. Some workers are too young to use the account and others are afraid to use it because the amount may be too small as they approach older age. One of the major reasons for companies to accept layoffs as opposed to retirement packages is that layoffs are cheaper and they do not draw the publicity they did in the past. Further, often the best employees leave when early retirements are provided.[77]

A Global Perspective

Getting Information to Support Disciplinary Action

Multinational companies face significant challenges when they try to encourage whistle-blowing across a wide variety of cultures. There are a number of cultural factors that discourage international employees from reporting misconduct. In parts of East Asia, members of the corporation are a family; if you view them as family members, it is wrong to report them. In Japan, lifetime employment and a strict seniority system can discourage workers from questioning management decisions, dictating, instead, that employees show unbounded loyalty to their co-workers. In Korea, a subordinate's loyalty to a superior is even greater than his or her loyalty to the company. In China, attempts to introduce corporate hotlines can remind employees of the horrors of the Cultural Revolution when citizens were encouraged to report *illegal activities* to authorities, which included children reporting against parents, students against teachers, and neighbors against neighbors. In Germany, encouraging anonymous or confidential reporting can bring to mind Gestapo tactics from World War II. The aversion to whistle-blowing has been heightened by recent revelations of the far-reaching informant networks of the Stasi in former East Germany.[78]

Numerous time zones and languages also prevent international employees from using corporate whistle-blowing resources. International 800 numbers and international collect calls either do not work or are unknown in many countries. In some locations, even gaining access to a telephone can be difficult. Guy Dehn, Director of the U.K.-based Public Concern at Work, confirmed in a recent interview, "If you're in a village in Northern Indonesia, where are you going to get the telephone to call the Alert Line? At a public telephone with others listening?"[79]

Information tends to leak out though an informal network in Hong Kong, Taiwan, and China, and the whistle-blower's future becomes difficult. In addition to the real threat of losing a job, whistle-blowers can also be subject to legal sanctions and loss of personal reputation. Whistle-blowers in Russia subject themselves to possible persecution (legal or criminal) from company managers or owners. Finally, in certain parts of the world, there have been reports that employees have been murdered in countries from Russia to Guatemala for exposing corruption.[80]

Summary

1. Define internal employee relations.

Internal employee relations consist of the human resource management activities associated with the movement of employees within the firm after they have become organizational members. It includes the actions of promotion, transfer, demotion, resignation, discharge, layoff, and retirement. Discipline and disciplinary action are also included.

2. Explain the concept of employment at will.

Employment at will is an unwritten contract created when an employee agrees to work for an employer but no agreement exists as to how long the parties expect the employment to last.

3. Explain discipline and disciplinary action.

Discipline is the state of employee self-control and orderly conduct present within an organization. It indicates the extent of genuine teamwork that exists. Disciplinary action occurs when a penalty is invoked against an employee who fails to meet established standards.

4. Describe the disciplinary action process, discuss the various approaches to disciplinary action, and describe the problems in the administration of disciplinary action.

The external environment affects every area of human resource management, including disciplinary policies and actions. After management has established rules, it must communicate these rules to employees. The manager then observes the performance of workers and compares performance with rules. As long as employee behavior does not vary from acceptable practices, there is no need for disciplinary action, but when an employee's behavior violates a rule, corrective action may be necessary.

Three of the most important concepts are the hot stove rule, progressive disciplinary action, and disciplinary action without punishment.

Problems associated with the administration of disciplinary action include: lack of training, fear, being the only one, guilt, loss of friendship, time lost, loss of temper, and rationalization.

5. Explain how grievance handling is typically conducted under a collective bargaining agreement and how grievance handling is typically conducted in union-free firms.

The multistep grievance procedure is the most common type. In the first step, the employee usually presents the grievance orally and informally to the immediate supervisor in the presence of the union steward. If the grievance remains unresolved, the next step involves a meeting between the plant manager or human resource manager and higher union officials, such as the grievance committee or the business agent or manager. If the grievance is not settled at this meeting, it is appealed to the third step, which typically involves the firm's top labor representative (such as the vice president of industrial relations) and high-level union officials. A grievance that remains unresolved at the conclusion of the third step may go to arbitration, if provided for in the agreement and the union decides to persevere.

The means of resolving complaints in union-free firms vary. A well-designed union-free grievance procedure ensures that the worker has ample opportunity to make complaints without fear of reprisal.

6. Explain the use of ombudspersons.

An ombudsperson is a complaint officer with access to top management who hears employee complaints, investigates, and recommends appropriate action.

7. Describe termination and describe how termination conditions may differ with regard to nonmanagerial/nonprofessional employees, executives, and middle and lower-level managers and professionals.

The conditions for termination differ considerably with regard to nonmanagerial/nonprofessional employees, executives, and middle and lower-level managers and professionals.

8. Describe demotion as an alternative to termination.

At times demotions are used as an alternative to discharge, especially when a long-term employee is involved. Demotion is the process of moving a worker to a lower level of duties and responsibilities, which typically involves a reduction in pay. If demotion is chosen over termination, efforts must be made to preserve the self-esteem of the individual.

9. Describe transfers, promotions, resignations, and retirements as factors involved in internal employee relations.

The lateral movement of a worker within an organization is called a transfer. A promotion is the movement of a person to a higher-level position in the organization. Even when an organization is totally committed to making its environment a good place to work, workers will still resign. One of the last phases of internal employee relations is retirement.

Key Terms

- Internal employee relations, 428
- Employment at will, 429
- Discipline, 430
- Disciplinary action, 430
- Progressive disciplinary action, 432
- Disciplinary action without punishment, 433

- Grievance, 436
- Grievance procedure, 436
- Ombudsperson, 440
- Alternative dispute resolution (ADR), 441
- Demotion, 444
- Transfer, 444

- Promotion, 445
- Exit interview, 445
- Postexit questionnaire, 446
- Attitude survey, 446

Questions for Review

1. Define internal employee relations.
2. What is meant by the term employment at will?
3. What is the difference between discipline and disciplinary action?
4. What are the steps to follow in the disciplinary action process?
5. Describe the following approaches to disciplinary action:
   a. hot stove rule
   b. progressive disciplinary action
   c. disciplinary action without punishment
6. What are the problems associated with the administration of disciplinary action?
7. What is a grievance procedure? How are grievances handled under a collective bargaining agreement?
8. When arbitration is used to settle a grievance, what factors may be used to evaluate the fairness of management's actions that caused the grievance?
9. How would grievances typically be handled in a union-free firm? Describe briefly.
10. Define alternative dispute resolution (ADR). Describe briefly.
11. Define ombudsperson. Why might a firm want to use an ombudsperson?
12. How does termination often differ with regard to nonmanagerial/nonprofessional employees, executives, and middle and lower-level managers and professionals?
13. Briefly describe the techniques available to determine the real reasons that an individual decides to leave the organization.
14. Distinguish between demotions, transfers, and promotions.

HRM Incident 1

Should He Be Fired?

Toni Berdit is the Washington, D.C., area supervisor for Quik-Stop, a chain of convenience stores. She has full responsibility for managing the seven Quik-Stop stores in Washington. Each store operates with only one person on duty at a time. Although several of the stores stay open all night, every night, the Center Street store is open all night Monday through Thursday but only from 6:00 a.m. to 10:00 p.m., Friday through Sunday. Because the store is open fewer hours during the weekend, money from sales is kept in the store safe until Monday. Therefore, the time it takes to complete a money count on Monday is greater than normal. The company has a policy that when the safe is being emptied, the manager has to be with the employee on duty, and the employee has to place each $1,000 in a brown bag, mark the bag, and leave the bag on the floor next to the safe until the manager verifies the amount in each bag.

Bill Catron worked the Sunday night shift at the Center Street store and was trying to save his manager time by counting the money prior to his arrival. The store got very busy, and, while bagging a customer's groceries, Bill mistook one of the moneybags for a bag containing three sandwiches and put the moneybag in with the groceries. Twenty minutes later, Toni arrived, and both began to search for the money. While they were searching, a customer came back with the bag of money. Quik-Stop has a general policy that anyone violating the money-counting procedure could be fired immediately. However, the ultimate decision was left up to the supervisor and his or her immediate boss.

Bill was very upset. "I really need this job," Bill exclaimed. "With the new baby and all the medical expenses we've had, I sure can't stand to be out of a job."

"You knew about the policy, Bill," said Toni.

"Yes, I did, Toni," said Bill, "and I really don't have any excuse. If you don't fire me, though, I promise you that I'll be the best store manager you've got."

While Bill waited on a customer, Toni called his boss at the home office. With the boss's approval, Toni decided not to fire Bill.

Question

1. Do you agree with Toni's decision? Discuss.

HRM Incident 2

To Heck with Them!

Isabelle Anderson is the North Carolina plant manager for Hall Manufacturing Company, a company that produces a line of relatively inexpensive painted wood furniture. Six months ago Isabelle became concerned about the turnover rate among workers in the painting department. Manufacturing plant turnover rates in that part of the South generally averaged about 30 percent, which was the case at Hall. The painting department, however, had experienced a turnover of nearly 200 percent in each of the last two years. Because of the limited number of skilled workers in the area, Hall had introduced an extensive training program for new painters, and Isabelle knew that the high turnover rate was very costly.

Isabelle conducted exit interviews with many of the departing painters. Many of them said that they were leaving for more money, others mentioned better benefits, and some cited some kind of personal reasons for quitting. But, there was nothing to help Isabelle pinpoint the problem. Isabelle had checked and found that Hall's wages and benefits were competitive with, if not better than, those of other manufacturers in the area. She then called in Nelson Able, the painting supervisor, to discuss the problem. Nelson's response was, "To heck with them! They will do it my way or they can hit the road. You know how this younger generation is. They work to get enough money to live on for a few weeks and then quit. I don't worry about it. Our old-timers can take up the slack." After listening to Nelson for a moment, Isabelle thought that she might know what caused the turnover problem.

Questions

1. Do you believe that the exit surveys were accurate? Explain your answer.
2. What do you believe was the cause of the turnover problem?

Notes

1. Tal Moise, "Updated Background Checks Needed," *Business Insurance* 40 (February 13, 2006): 10.
2. Jessica Marquez, "RadioShack Gaffe Shows Need to Screen Current Employees," *Workforce Management* 85 (March 13, 2006): 3–4.
3. Moise, "Updated Background Checks Needed."
4. Ibid.
5. Ibid.
6. Ibid.
7. Jena McGregor, "Background Checks That Never Quit," *Business Week* (March 20, 2006): 40.
8. Ibid.
9. Julie Rawe, "It's 2004. Do You Know Who Your Chairman Is?" *Time Canada* 163 (March 8, 2004): 10.
10. Marquez, "RadioShack Gaffe Shows Need to Screen Current Employees."
11. McGregor, "Background Checks That Never Quit."
12. Jathan Janove, "Keep 'Em At Will, Treat 'Em for Cause," *HR Magazine* 50 (May 2005): 111–117.
13. Dan Van Bogaert and Arthur Gross-Schaefer, "Terminating the Employee-Employer Relationship: Ethical and Legal Challenges," *Employee Relations Law Journal (Aspen)* 31 (Summer 2005): 49–66.
14. Mary-Kathryn Zachary, "Labor Law for Supervisors," *Supervision* 66 (May 2005): 23–25.
15. "Tortious Breach of Contract," *Business Torts Reporter* 17 (September 2005): 348–349.
16. Matthew Heller, "A Return to At-Will Employment," *Workforce* 80 (May 2001): 42–46.
17. Ibid.
18. Janove, "Keep 'Em At Will, Treat 'Em for Cause."
19. Ibid.
20. Paul Salvatore, Daniel Halem, Allan Weitzman, Gershom Smith, and Lan Schaefer, "How the Law Changed HR," *HR Magazine* 50 (2005 Anniversary): 47–56.
21. "Employee Handbooks: Have You Updated Yours Lately?" *HR Focus* 83 (July 2006): 5–6.
22. "Engineer Was Hired and Fired 'At Will'," *ENR* 248 (April 22, 2002): 22.
23. Jane Easter Bahls, "Fire Power," *Entrepreneur* 34 (May 2006): 92.
24. Kent R. Davies, "Defensive Firing," *Dealernews* 41 (October 2005): 30–32.
25. Michele Begley, "Avoiding Employee Litigation," *Business West* 21 (March 21 2005): 44–52.
26. "Termination Procedures: Ethical Considerations," *Fair Employment Practices Guidelines* (July 1, 2005): 4–5.
27. Shane R. Premeaux, R. Wayne Mondy, and Lonnie D. Phelps, "The Need for Discipline," *Supervisory Management* 84 (March 1989): 39–41.
28. Kathryn Tyler, "One Bad Apple," *HR Magazine* 49 (December 2004): 77–86.
29. Ibid.
30. Jane F. Miller, "Motivating People," *Executive Excellence* 19 (December 2002): 15.
31. Fiona W. Ong, "Firing Union Supporter for Careless Work Not Unlawful," *HR Magazine* 50 (September 2005): 143–144.
32. Herff L. Moore and Helen L. Moore, "Discipline + Help = Motivation," *Credit Union Management* 21 (August 1998): 33.
33. Dick Grote, "Discipline Without Punishment," *Across the Board* 38 (September/October 2001): 52–57.
34. Aimee L. Franklin and Javier F. Pagan, "Organization Culture as an Explanation for Employee Discipline Practices," *Review of Public Personnel Administration* 26 (March 2006): 52–73.
35. Wallace Wohlking, "Effective Discipline in Employee Relations," *Personnel Journal* 54 (September 1975): 489.
36. Hugh A. McCabe, "The Art of Employee Discipline," *San Diego Business Journal* 25 (December 20, 2004): 5.
37. Robert Ankeny, "A Question of Fairness," *Crain's Detroit Business* 21 (August 8, 2005): 11–12.
38. Michael Nowicki and Jim Summers, "Poor Management Can Look Like Discrimination," *Healthcare Financial Management* 60 (April 2006): 118–119.
39. Charles A. Borell, "How Unions Can Improve Their Success Rate in Labor Arbitration," *Dispute Resolution Journal* 61 (February 2006): 28–38.
40. "Arbitrator's Decision Upheld," *Business Insurance* 34 (December 4, 2000): 2.
41. Mable H. Smith, "Grievance Procedures Resolve Conflict," *Nursing Management* 33 (April 2002): 13.
42. "Ombuds Can Help Address Conflicts, Potential Lawsuits," *HR Focus* 82 (October 2005): 8.
43. Ibid.
44. "Ombuds Can Help Address Conflicts, Potential Lawsuits," *HR Focus* 82 (October 2005): 8.
45. Wayne Hougland, "Keep Employment Disputes Out of Court," *Business Insurance* 39 (August 29, 2005): 9.
46. Dimitra Kessenides, "Can't We All Get Along?" *Inc.* 27 (June 2005): 34–36.
47. Claude Solnik, "*Mediation* Comes of Age . . . Will It Keep More Cases Out of Court?" *Long Island Business News* 52 (May 20, 2005): 3B–6B.
48. Amanda Bronstad, "Big-Ticket Cases Are Getting Low-Cost Solutions," *San Diego Business Journal* 26 (July 7, 2005): 24.
49. Michael Barrier, "The Mediation Disconnect," *HR Magazine* 48 (May 2003): 54–58.
50. Mark J. Keppler, "The EEOC's Alternative Dispute Resolution Program: A More Civil Approach to Civil Rights Disputes," *Review of Business* (Winter 2003): 38–42.
51. Kevin Jessar, "The Ombud's Perspective: A Critical Analysis of the ABA 2004 Ombuds Standards," *Dispute Resolution Journal* 60 (August–October 2005): 56–61.
52. "Firing: Letting People Go with Dignity Is Good for Business," *HR Focus* 77 (January 2000): 10.
53. Paul Glen, "You're Fired," *Computerworld* 39 (November 7, 2005): 48.
54. Chuck Jones, "When Is the Best Time to Fire an Employee?" *Advisor Today* 97 (December 2002): 78.
55. Paul Glen, "You're Fired," *Computerworld* 39 (November 7, 2005): 48.
56. Bill Roberts, "Shown the Door," *Electronic Business* 29 (January 2003): 44–48.
57. Mark Murphy, "Why CEOs Get Fired," *Leadership Excellence* 22 (September 2005): 14.
58. Kate Bonamici, "By the Numbers," *Fortune (Europe)* 151 (February 21, 2005): 15.
59. Del Jones, "More CEOs Jump Ship—or Walk the Plank," *USA Today* (June 13, 2005): Money, 1b.

60. Robert J. Grossman, "Executive Discipline," *HR Magazine* 50 (August 2005): 46–51.

61. Keith Naughton, "The CEO Party Is Over," *Newsweek* 141 (December 30, 2002/January 6, 2003): 55.

62. Craig R. Taylor, "Focus on Talent," *T + D* 56 (December 2002): 26–31.

63. Scott Westcott, "Goodbye and Good Luck," *Inc.* 28 (April 2006): 40–42.

64. Judith A. Ross, "Dealing with the Real Reasons People Leave," *Harvard Management Update* 10 (August 2005): 3–5.

65. "No Respect?" *Money* 35 (May 2006): 22.

66. "Poor Managers Hurt Productivity, Morale, and Worker Engagement," *HR Focus* 82 (May 2005): 8.

67. Martha Frase-Blunt, "Making Exit Interviews Work," *HR Magazine* 49 (August 2004): 109–113.

68. Wanda R. Embrey, R. Wayne Mondy, and Robert M. Noe, "Exit Interview: A Tool for Personnel Development," *Personnel Administrator* 24 (May 1979): 46.

69. Chris Penttila, "Exit Ramp," *Entrepreneur* 33 (December 2005): 112.

70. Joanne Earl, Melissa Dunn Lampe, and Andrew Buksin, "What to Do with Employee Survey Results," *Gallup Management Journal Online* (August 10, 2006): 1–6.

71. "How Will Retiring Employees Affect Your Organization's Workforce?" *HR Focus* 82 (July 2005): 8.

72. Mary Willett, "Early Retirement and Phased Retirement Programs for the Public Sector," *Benefits & Compensation Digest* 42 (April 2005): 31–35.

73. Mindy Fetterman, "Retirees Back at Work, with Flexibility," *USA Today* (June 9, 2005): Money, 5b.

74. Carlos Tejada, "A Special News Report About Life on the Job—and Trends Taking Shape There," *Wall Street Journal* (July 31, 2002): B9.

75. Forest Laws, "USDA Looks at Reducing FSA County Staffs," *Western Farm Press* 27 (October 1, 2005): 1–13.

76. Tejada, "A Special News Report About Life on the Job."

77. Ibid.

78. Lori Tansey Martin and Amber Crowell, "Whistleblowing: A Global Perspective (Part I)," *Ethikos* 15 (May 1, 2002): 6.

79. Ibid.

80. Ibid.

PART EIGHT

Operating in a Global Environment

CHAPTER OBJECTIVES

After completing this chapter, students should be able to:

1 Describe the evolution of global business and global human resource management.

2 Explain global staffing.

3 Describe global human resource development.

4 Explain global compensation.

5 Describe global safety and health.

6 Explain global employee and labor relations.

7 Describe political and legal factors affecting global human resource management.

8 Explain bribery, equal employment opportunity, and virtual teams in a global environment.

Global Human Resource Management

Throughout this chapter, cultural differences between countries will be identified as a major factor influencing global business. Culture is highlighted because in a recent survey, cultural differences were found to be the biggest barrier to doing business in the world market.[1] A **country's culture** is the set of values, symbols, beliefs, languages, and norms that guide human behavior within the country. It is a learned behavior that develops as individuals grow from childhood to adulthood.[2] The cultural norms of Asia promote loyalty and teamwork. In Japan, most managers tend to remain with the same company for life. In the United States, senior executives often change companies, but there are few second chances in Japan. The Japanese believe strongly that leaving a job is to be avoided out of respect for the business team.[3] Recognizing the cultural differences present in a workplace can help managers achieve maximum effectiveness.[4]

Country's culture:
Set of values, symbols, beliefs, languages, and norms that guide human behavior within the country.

In Chapter 8, the concept of the 360-degree feedback evaluation was addressed. Here, people all around the rated employee provide ratings, including senior managers, the employee himself or herself, supervisors, subordinates, peers, team members, and internal or external customers. But, in some countries the 360-degree approach would be difficult to implement. For example, in a Thai corporation, the 360-degree feedback process might be difficult to implement because subordinates would be uncomfortable. Thai workers do not see it as their business to evaluate their bosses, and the bosses would be insulted because Thai managers do not think subordinates are in any way qualified to assess them.[5]

Companies are recognizing that they need to understand the culture of host countries in which they do business. As a step in becoming a major global supplier, Hyundai Mobis, headquartered in Seoul, Korea, is attempting to foster a global culture among its employees. In countries where they may be doing business, teams of three employees design their own trip to study the country's culture, and they write a proposal explaining what they can learn. Then they compete for company sponsorship of a 15-day expedition. To date, 47 teams have visited about 70 countries. Itineraries have ranged from going to Peru to visiting cultural sites in Egypt, Turkey, and Greece. In the United States one team studied the culture of Alabama, where Hyundai Mobis was building a plant.[6]

Americans who will be doing business overseas need to understand that other cultures view us differently. Philip R. Harris and Robert T. Moran, in their book, *Managing Cultural Differences*, summarize feedback from Arab businesspeople regarding how they perceive many Westerners. To them, Westerners act superior, as if they know the answer to everything and are not willing to share credit for joint efforts; they are unable or unwilling to respect and adjust to local customs and culture, and prefer solutions based on their home cultures rather than meeting local needs; they resist working through local administrative and legal channels and procedures and they manage in an autocratic and intimidating way. Westerners are also thought of as too imposing and pushy.[7] At times, there can be tension between the organization's culture and the culture of the host country.[8] Successful international workers are able to find a balance between maintaining their own cultural values and accepting those of the host country. They essentially create a *third culture* style of doing business. In this third culture, expatriates do not have to abandon their own values or totally adopt the host country's value system.[9]

Web Wisdom
Cross-Cultural Training
http://www.
interchangeinstitute.org/
html/cross_cultural.htm#top

The Cross-Cultural Institute assists individuals and families in managing the transition to a new culture.

The importance of understanding the culture of a host country is discussed first, and the evolution of global business and global human resource management is described. Then, global staffing and global human resource development are explained, after which e-learning and virtual teams are presented. Global compensation and global safety and health are then examined, followed by a discussion of global employee and labor relations. This chapter concludes with a look at political and legal factors, global bribery, and equal employment opportunity in the global environment.

 OBJECTIVE

Describe the evolution of global business and global human resource management.

Evolution of Global Business

"Organizations must either globalize or they will die" is an apt description of the twenty-first-century economy. Much of the U.S. economy is based on exports and imports. Not long ago, Mercedes-Benz was still a *German* company, General Electric was *American*, and Sony was *Japanese*, but today these companies are truly global.[10] Years ago, a lot of U.S. multinational corporations had operations in Canada or perhaps Mexico, but not in many other countries. Now, U.S. firms such as Coca-Cola, Procter & Gamble, and Texas Instruments do most of their business and employ most of their workers outside the United States. Countless products of U.S. companies are made outside the country. Maytag refrigerators are no longer made in Galesburg, Illinois. Many non-U.S. companies make products here, such as Toyota American, which manufactures cars in Kentucky.[11] Companies still regularly do business in Canada and Mexico, but many now have operations in Hong Kong, Singapore, Japan, the United Kingdom, France, Germany, and Southeast Asia, to name a few. More and more U.S. global corporations are doing business in former Eastern Bloc countries. Vietnam, a country with which the United States was once at war, is now viewed as a potential marketplace. The globalization of the marketplace has created special human resource challenges that will endure well into this century. Today, globalization is not limited to only large organizations. It is now the main focus for both large and small firms.[12]

Normally, companies evolve to the point of being truly global over an extended period. Most companies initially become global without making substantial investments in foreign countries, by exporting, licensing, or franchising. **Exporting** entails selling abroad, either directly or indirectly, by retaining foreign agents and distributors. It is a way that many small businesses enter the global market.[13] **Licensing** is an arrangement whereby an organization grants a foreign firm the right to use intellectual properties such as patents, copyrights, manufacturing processes, or trade names for a specific period of time. **Franchising** is an option where the parent company grants another firm the right to do business in a prescribed manner. Franchisees must follow stricter operational guidelines than do licensees.[14] Licensing is usually limited to manufacturers, whereas franchising is popular with service firms, such as restaurants and hotels. Tricon Restaurants International reports a record-breaking 1,041 new international restaurant openings for its KFC, Pizza Hut, and Taco Bell brands.[15] Franchising possibilities are even available in China, where the rapid emergence of a middle class, led by a growing population of educated professionals, is paving the way for franchise development.[16]

Although exporting, licensing, and franchising are good initial entry options, in order to take full advantage of global opportunities, companies must make a substantial investment in another country. Companies can vary greatly in their degree of global involvement. A **multinational corporation (MNC)** is a firm that is based in one country (the parent or home country) and produces goods or provides services in one or more foreign countries (host countries). A multinational corporation directs manufacturing and marketing operations in several countries; these operations are coordinated by a parent company, usually based in the firm's home country.

A growing number of firms have evolved beyond being multinational to becoming a **global corporation (GC)**, an organization that has corporate units in a number of countries that are integrated to operate as one organization worldwide. The global corporation operates as if the entire world were one entity. Global corporations sell essentially the same products in the same manner throughout the world with components that may be made and/or designed in different countries. Expectations are that as the world becomes more globally open, the globalization of corporations will become much more commonplace. Not many years ago Procter & Gamble was still primarily a U.S. business investing heavily in food brands. Now it is a truly global corporation with operations in 140 countries and a tremendous variety of product categories. Its 30 corporate leaders are an extremely diverse group, representing many cultures and backgrounds.[17]

The importance of human resource management in the global environment is illustrated by the fact that the Human Resource Certification Institute now has an international component. The Global Professional in Human Resources certification focuses on six areas of international human resource management. These are: strategic international HR management, organizational effectiveness and employee development, global staffing, international assignment management, global compensation, and international employee relations and regulations.[18]

Global Human Resource Management

The world is experiencing an increasing global workforce.[19] Global human resource problems and opportunities are enormous and are expanding. **Global human resource management (GHRM)** is the utilization of global human resources to achieve organizational objectives without regard to geographic boundaries. Individuals dealing with

---

Exporting:
Selling abroad, either directly or indirectly, by retaining foreign agents and distributors.

Licensing:
Arrangement whereby an organization grants a foreign firm the right to use intellectual properties such as patents, copyrights, manufacturing processes, or trade names for a specific period of time.

Franchising:
Option whereby the parent company grants another firm the right to do business in a prescribed manner.

Multinational corporation (MNC):
Firm that is based in one country (the parent or home country) and produces goods or provides services in one or more foreign countries (host countries).

Global corporation (GC):
Organization that has corporate units in a number of countries that are integrated to operate as one organization worldwide.

Global human resource management (GHRM):
Utilization of global human resources to achieve organizational objectives without regard to geographic boundaries.

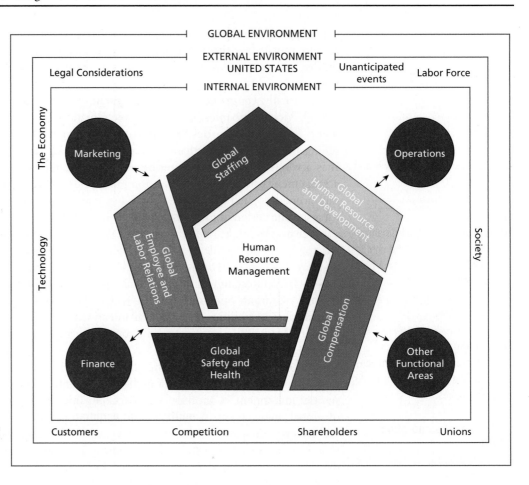

Figure 14-1 Environment of Global Human Resource Management

global human resource matters face a multitude of challenges beyond that of their domestic counterparts. These considerations range from cultural barriers to political barriers to international aspects such as compensation. Before upper management decides on a global move, it is vitally important that the critical nature of human resource issues be considered.

Companies that engage in the global economy place even greater emphasis on strategic HR. Those engaged in the management of global human resources develop and work through an integrated global human resource management system, and the functional areas associated with effective global human resource management are similar to the ones they experience domestically, as shown in Figure 14-1. Although the five areas are the same, the manner in which they are implemented may differ. Sound global human resource management practices are required for successful performance in each area. As with domestic human resources, the functional areas are not separate and distinct, but are highly interrelated.

Global Staffing

The recruitment, retention, and utilization of global talent are essential elements of modern-day corporate success.[20] Although expatriate failure or underperformance costs are difficult to quantify, most executives agree losses are substantial, affecting up to 40 percent of all expatriate assignments.[21] Before the staffing process for an international assignment begins, a thorough understanding of what is involved in the job should be developed (job analysis). A global organization must systematically match the internal and external supply of people with job openings anticipated in the

OBJECTIVE

Explain global staffing.

organization over a specified period of time (human resource planning). Individuals should be recruited and selected based upon the specific qualifications identified. Without proper identification of the qualities needed for an overseas assignment, an outstanding worker in the United States may fail on a global assignment.

Types of Global Staff Members

Companies must choose from various types of global staff members and may employ specific approaches to global staffing. Global staff members may be selected from among three different types: expatriates, host-country nationals, and third-country nationals. An **expatriate** is an employee who is not a citizen of the country in which the firm operations are located, but is a citizen of the country in which the organization is headquartered. A **host-country national (HCN)** is an employee who is a citizen of the country where the subsidiary is located. An example would be a U.S. citizen working for a Japanese company in the United States. Normally, the bulk of employees in international offices will be host-country nationals. Not only are companies staffed by locals less expensive, they also offer advantages from a cultural and business standpoint. In most industries, host-country nationals comprise more than 98 percent of the workforce in the foreign operations of North American and Western European multinational companies.[22] Hiring local people and operating the company like local companies whenever possible is good business. The ultimate goal of most foreign operations is to turn over control to local management. However, relying totally on local employees may, at times, pose problems. Chinese officials often think a foreign company (particularly a large multinational) is not taking them seriously if a local represents them with no links to the decision makers in the home country.[23] A **third-country national (TCN)** is a citizen of one country, working in a second country, and employed by an organization headquartered in a third country. An example would be an Italian citizen working for a French company in Germany.

Expatriate:
Employee who is not a citizen of the country in which the firm operations are located, but is a citizen of the country in which the organization is headquartered.

Host-country national (HCN):
Employee who is a citizen of the country where the subsidiary is located.

Third-country national (TCN):
Citizen of one country, working in a second country, and employed by an organization headquartered in a third country.

Approaches to Global Staffing

Using the three basic types of global staff, there are four major approaches to global staffing: ethnocentric, polycentric, regiocentric, and geocentric staffing.[24] These reflect how the organization develops its human resource policies and the preferred types of employees for different positions.

Ethnocentric staffing:
Staffing approach in which companies primarily hire expatriates to staff higher-level foreign positions.

Ethnocentric Staffing. With **ethnocentric staffing**, companies primarily hire expatriates to staff higher-level foreign positions. This strategy assumes that home-office perspectives and issues should take precedence over local perspectives and issues and that expatriates will be more effective in representing the views of the home office. Corporate human resources is primarily concerned with selecting and training managers for foreign assignments, developing appropriate compensation packages, and handling adjustment issues when managers return home. Generally, expatriates are used to ensure that foreign operations are linked effectively with parent corporations. However, the use of expatriate employees must be carefully considered since the cost of an international assignment may be high both in terms of financial compensation and resentment on the part of the host-country employees.

Expatriates are often selected from those already within the organization and the process involves four distinct stages: self-selection, creating a candidate pool, technical skills assessment, and making a mutual decision. In the self-selection stage, employees determine if they are right for a global assignment, if their spouses and children are interested in relocating internationally, and if this is the best time for a move. In a recent survey, family concerns were the major reason (47 percent) for refusal of a global assignment.[25] In the case of self-selection, the candidates assess themselves on all of the relevant dimensions for a job and then decide whether to pursue a global assignment. The self-assessment extends to the entire family. Basically, candidates must decide whether to go to the next step in the selection process. "Self-nomination is helpful. Someone who is interested in a country and a culture has a better chance to succeed. They're appreciative of being sent and aren't looking for other kinds of perks to make it worthwhile to go," says Melanie Young, director of global talent management at NCR.[26]

Stage two involves creating a candidate database organized according to the firm's staffing needs. Included in the database is information such as the year the employee is available to go overseas, the languages the employee speaks, the countries the employee prefers, and the jobs for which the employee is qualified. During stage three, the database is scanned for all possible candidates for a given global assignment; then the list is forwarded to the assigning department. There, each candidate is assessed on technical and managerial readiness relative to the needs of the assignment. In the final stage, one person is identified as an acceptable candidate based on his or her technical or managerial readiness and is tentatively selected.

If the decision is made to employ expatriates, certain selection criteria should be carefully considered in stages two and three. Expatriate selection criteria should include cultural adaptability, strong communication skills, technical competence, professional or operational expertise, global experience, country-specific experience, interpersonal skills, language skills, family flexibility, and country- or region-specific considerations.

Polycentric staffing:
Staffing approach where host-country nationals are used throughout the organization, from top to bottom.

Polycentric Staffing. When host-country nationals are used throughout the organization, from top to bottom, it is referred to as **polycentric staffing**. In developed countries such as Japan, Canada, and the United Kingdom, there has been more reliance on local executives, and less on traditional expatriate management.[27] The ultimate goal of most foreign operations is to turn over control to local management. Not only are locally run businesses less expensive, they also offer advantages from a cultural and business standpoint. The use of the polycentric staffing model is based on the assumption that host-country nationals are better equipped to deal with local market conditions. Organizations that use this approach will usually have a fully functioning human resource department in each foreign subsidiary responsible for managing all local human resource issues. Corporate human resource managers focus primarily on coordinating relevant activities with their counterparts in each foreign operation. Most global employees are usually host-country nationals because this helps to clearly establish that the company is making a commitment to the host country and not just setting up a foreign operation. Host-country nationals often have much more thorough knowledge of the culture, the politics, and the laws of the locale, as well as how business is done. There is no standard format in the selection of host-country nationals.

Regiocentric staffing:
Staffing approach that is similar to the polycentric staffing approach, but regional groups of subsidiaries reflecting the organization's strategy and structure work as a unit.

Regiocentric Staffing. **Regiocentric staffing** is similar to the polycentric approach, but regional groups of subsidiaries reflecting the organization's strategy and structure work as a unit. There is some degree of autonomy in regional decision making, and promotions are possible within the region but rare from the region to headquarters. Each region develops a common set of employment practices.

Geocentric staffing:
Staffing approach that uses a worldwide integrated business strategy.

Geocentric Staffing. **Geocentric staffing** is a staffing approach that uses a worldwide integrated business strategy. The firm attempts to always hire the best person available for a position, regardless of where that individual comes from. The geocentric staffing model is most likely to be adopted and used by truly global firms. Usually, the corporate human resource function in geocentric companies is the most complicated, since every aspect of HR must be dealt with in the global environment.

Background Investigation

We discussed in Chapter 6 the importance of conducting a background investigation on potential employees. Conducting background investigations when working in the global environment is equally, or even more, important but differences across cultures and countries often put up barriers to overcome. Each country has its own laws, customs, and procedures for background screenings.[28] For instance, Japanese law covers a person working at the Tokyo office of a U.S.-based company and includes privacy statutes that prohibit criminal checks on Japanese citizens. The United Kingdom does not allow third parties such as background-checking firms to have direct access to criminal records held by local police. Instead, the job applicant and the recruiting organization must sign and submit a formal request to a specific agency responsible for handling criminal records. It can take up to 40 business days to get information back.[29] Traci Canning, director of international operations for HireRight, a pre-employment screening company in Irvine, California, says, "It's important to understand the local context. In general, that means understanding how HR operations, law enforcement agencies, schools/universities and businesses operate outside the United States."[30] HireRight tells the story of a person who had been in the United States for two years and had applied for a job with a multinational firm. There were no gaps in the individual's employment history that would suggest he had ever been in jail. However, further check revealed that he had been convicted of murder in his home country and in accord with a practice that was legal at the time, had paid a proxy to serve his prison term while he remained free and in the workforce.[31]

3 OBJECTIVE

Describe global human resource development.

Global Human Resource Development

Many U.S. businesses operate under the assumption that American ways and business practices are standard across the globe. Similarly, some T&D professionals believe that training and consulting principles and strategies that work for a U.S. audience can be equally effective abroad. Unfortunately, nothing could be further from the truth. Global training and development is needed because people, jobs, and organizations are often quite different. Next, various aspects of global HRD will be discussed.

Expatriate Training and Development

The training of employees going on a global assignment has often been bleak, but appears to be improving. For instance, the proportion of companies offering language training to assignees and their spouses increased from 34 percent in 1999 to 42 percent in 2005. Also, about 48 percent of companies offered cross-cultural training to assignees, their spouses, and their children in 2005, compared to 33 percent in 1999.[32] The development process should start as soon as workers are selected; definitely before they begin the global assignment.

Global expansion into China has been particularly difficult for some companies such as McDonald's because the Cultural Revolution of the 1960s and 1970s closed most schools in China. As a result, an entire generation did not receive much education. McDonald's has had to personally develop its workforce. Bob Wilner, McDonald's director of international HR, says that McDonald's tries to develop local people in Asia, finding them more effective than expatriates because they better understand the Asian marketplace and customers.[33] David Hoff of Anheuser-Busch in Asia hires host-country nationals, develops their talents in the United States, and reassigns them abroad as local managers.[34]

Organizations are recognizing that expatriate employees and their families face special situations and pressure that training and development activities must prepare them to deal with. Employees and their families must have an effective orientation program and a readjustment-training program. In addition, the employee must have a program of continual development. Figure 14-2 illustrates the ideal expatriate preparation and development program, which includes pre-move orientation and training, continual development, and repatriation orientation and training.

Pre-move Orientation and Training

Pre-move orientation and training of expatriate employees and their families are essential before the global assignment begins. The pre-move orientation involves training and familiarization in language, culture, history, living conditions, and local customs and peculiarities. Continuing employee development, in which the employee's global skills are fitted into career planning and corporate development programs, makes the eventual transition to the host home country less disruptive.

Many organizations have established a formal *buddy system* to alleviate the stress new expatriates and their families normally endure, to reduce the time it takes for expatriates to operate at peak productivity. Buddies often inform expatriates of host-office norms and politics, invite them into their homes, introduce them to friends and networks, and help bolster their credibility in the office.[35]

Continual Development: Online Assistance and Training

Companies are now offering online assistance and training in such areas as career services, cross-cultural training, and employee assistance programs (EAP). The Internet offers troubled global employees assistance 24 hours a day, seven days a week. Technology is a time-saving and cost-effective solution for the stress experienced by employees who are on assignment or doing business travel. Even if the assignment is a short-term business trip, technology can be used to provide ongoing contact and support. For example, online career services can give expatriates and their spouses the opportunity to upgrade skills while on assignment.

Repatriation Orientation and Training

Repatriation:
Process of bringing expatriates home.

Orientation and training are also necessary prior to **repatriation**, which is the process of bringing expatriates home. According to a survey of leading *Fortune* 1000 companies, while nearly half of respondents stated that they selected their best employees for international assignments, only 35 percent stated that their respective companies managed the repatriation process successfully.[36] In fact, many expatriates were not even guaranteed a job upon their return.[37] Approximately one-third of repatriates leave their companies within two years of repatriation because their companies do a poor job of repatriating them. Reasons given for leaving include they were not being properly prepared to return to their work and not being able to utilize skills that were learned abroad.[38]

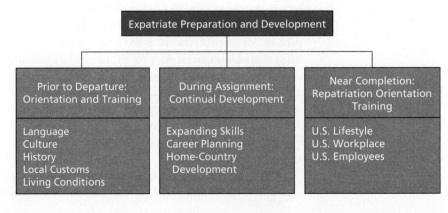

Figure 14-2 The Expatriate Preparation and Development Program

To counter the challenges of repatriation, firms need to have a formal in-house repatriation program in place. A dialogue regarding expectations and career planning upon return will help to manage expectations. Also, the exchange should continue after the employee has returned home. In addition, acknowledgment and recognition of the significant overseas contribution is a courtesy that the returning employee has earned and richly deserves. Ideally, there should be a clear career path or position identified for the expatriate employee upon his or her return.[39]

Global Compensation

4 OBJECTIVE

Explain global compensation.

Companies that are successful in the global environment align their human resources programs in support of their strategic business plans.[40] A major component is the manner in which the human resources total compensation program supports the way the business is structured, organized, and operated both globally and regionally.[41]

Trends & Innovations

Global E-learning

Globalization has created a special need for e-learning. By 2008, the e-learning market should more than double, rising to $21 billion globally, according to International Data Corporation.[42] In the past, a program for a *Fortune* 200 company in the Far East would likely cost between $250,000 and $500,000 for travel and related expenses. Many believe that live, instructor-led training is still more effective, but the question that must be asked is, "how much more effective?" The costs of a training program include the instructor's salary, materials costs, travel costs, meeting room expenses, and the salaries and benefits of the people attending the program, in addition to the costs of the program. E-learning allows companies to keep the money and still receive a good training product. At marketing communications firm Fleishman-Hillard, the company's 2,000 employees are spread across 80 locations in 22 countries, so Web-based technology is used to make information sharing and education more accessible and interactive.[43]

The most obvious challenges for any global e-learning implementation are language and localization issues. Many companies offer courses only in English or in English and one other language, usually Spanish. An English-only focus works for firms that routinely conduct their business all over the world in English. But others need courses in more than one language. Companies that want to offer courses in several languages usually turn to translators. Financial services provider GE Capital relies on translation companies to offer Web-based courses in English, French, German, and Japanese.[44]

Hilton's team members are scattered the world over. In a sector that sees high turnover rates, it is also hard to imagine that a classroom trainer could keep up with the demands of hundreds of new workers requiring training. Hilton, along with many multinational companies, realized that it could save money through online courses. Hilton first introduced e-learning in 2002 when the company launched its Hilton University with 60 generic business skills programs and 21 finance programs. Over the following year, Hilton put in place an additional 40 business skills courses and significantly increased the number of generic online courses offered. Hilton came a long way in a short period of time, from 5,000 course completions after the first year to over 40,000 completions in the third year, 2004. Andrea Kluit, director of international learning and development at Hilton International, points out another huge plus of e-learning by saying, "Where a classroom course cannot be re-visited after its completion, an e-learning course can be used as a reference tool, returned to when team members feel the need to refresh their memories. We have found that in the case of systems training especially, this tool is invaluable in offering learners a re-usable resource and so is hugely popular."[45]

Compensation for Host-Country Nationals

Certainly, in compensation-related matters, organizations should think globally but act locally. One reason that organizations relocate to other areas of the world is probably the high-wage pressures that threaten their ability to compete on a global basis.[46] Globally, the question of what constitutes a fair day's pay is not as complicated as it is in the United States; normally, it is slightly above the prevailing wage rates in the area. The same is often true of benefits and nonfinancial rewards. Variations in laws, living costs, tax policies, and other factors all must be considered when a company is establishing global compensation packages. For example, Puerto Rico has laws requiring the paying of severance pay and Christmas bonus.[47] Employers in Nigeria are required to provide a life insurance policy for employees at a rate of three times their salary. In Italy, a mandatory benefit is paid when an employee leaves an organization, regardless of whether this is due to resignation, termination, or retirement. In Belgium, employers offering a defined contribution pension scheme must provide a guaranteed investment return of 3.25 percent.[48]

The company will want to create a precise picture of employment and working conditions in order to establish appropriate practices in each country. Some of the factors that should be considered include: minimum wage requirements, which often differ from country to country and even from city to city within a country; working time information such as annual holidays, vacation time and pay, paid personal days, standard weekly working hours, probation periods, and overtime restrictions and payments; and hiring and termination rules and regulations covering severance practices.

Culture often plays a part in determining compensation. North American compensation practices encourage individualism and high performance; continental European programs typically emphasize social responsibility; the traditional Japanese approach considers age and company service as primary determinants of compensation. There is no guarantee that additional compensation will ensure additional output. It has been found that, in some countries, additional pay has resulted in employees' working less. As soon as employees have earned enough to satisfy their needs, time spent with family or on other noncompany activities is perceived as more valuable than additional cash. In former communist countries, people were used to a system where pay and performance were not related. Under the old system, good employees were paid the same as poor performers. With the collapse of the Iron Curtain, the idea that pay and performance should be related is now making its way into people's minds. In mainland China, workers who are paid by the hour often do not work hard. Under the communist system, working harder than anyone else did not result in additional pay. Therefore, there was no reason to do it.[49]

In countries where people value a steady income over the possibility of making a high income if their productivity is outstanding, a pay-for-performance scheme that includes a high variable fraction is often considered threatening. In countries like France and Greece, where the best graduates often choose government positions with secure paychecks for life, it is quite difficult to attract good employees with pay schemes that include high bonuses for achieving specific objectives. In places like Hong Kong, where people value risk and are motivated by personal financial gains, employees who have achieved a significant professional result expect a financial form of recognition (raise, bonus, or commission) within a matter of weeks. They are likely to look for another employer if they have to wait until their next annual performance review.

Because of these and other cultural differences, it is difficult to design a global, *one-size-fits-all* pay scheme that attracts the best talent in all countries. In particular, pay-for-performance schemes often need to be adapted to local preferences depending on whether income security or higher risks and returns are preferred.[50]

Expatriate Compensation

International assignments for expatriates cost three to five times an assignee's host-country salary per year and more if currency exchange rates become unfavorable.[51] In a recent survey, as an enticement, 44 percent of companies offered assignees a percentage of their base salary as a foreign-service bonus, while 19 percent gave assignees a lump sum at the beginning or end of the assignment and 34 percent did not provide a bonus.[52] For expatriate managers and professionals, the situation is more complex than simply paying at or slightly above local host-country compensation rates. Even minor changes in the value of the U.S. dollar may result in compensation adjustments for expatriates. The largest expatriate costs include overall remuneration, housing, cost-of-living allowances, and physical relocation.[53] Regarding tax equalization payments, U.S. citizens living overseas can exclude up to $80,000 of gross income earned abroad. Also, credits against U.S. income taxes are given for a portion of the foreign income taxes paid by U.S. expatriates beyond the $80,000 level. All these factors make global compensation extremely complex.

A country's culture can also impose significant constraints on the globalization of pay. Remember from Chapter 9 that the ratio of chief executives' compensation to the pay of the average production worker was 431 to one.[54] In Sweden, the spread is likely to be closer to eight to one. Whereas people in the United States derive great status from high pay, nations in large parts of Europe and Asia shun conspicuous wealth. In Italy, where teamwork is more valued than individual initiative, sales incentives for top sales professionals working in small teams can be demotivational. The recipient of a large award may feel awkward when receiving larger than a *fair share* of the reward pie.

American concepts such as employee stock ownership and linking executive compensation to corporate performance through equity and equity-based compensation techniques have caught on in an increasingly globalized marketplace. Successful companies around the world realize the importance of using long-term incentives and are making stock options a central feature of their remuneration programs. Several Japanese companies, including Sony, are now using compensation practices such as employee stock options for their employees in Japan. In a like manner, many U.S.-based companies have adopted equally radical foreign approaches such as profit sharing and team-based and skill-based pay. No one country has a monopoly on the best practices.

Global Safety and Health

5 OBJECTIVE

Describe global safety and health.

Safety and health aspects of the job are important because employees who work in a safe environment and enjoy good health are more likely to be productive and yield long-term benefits to the organization than those in less desirable circumstances. U.S.-based global operations are often safer and healthier than host-country operations, but frequently not as safe as similar operations in the United States. Safety and health laws and regulations often vary greatly from country to country. Such laws can range from virtually nonexistent to more stringent than those in the United States. Also, health care facilities across the globe vary greatly in their state of modernization. Companies are attempting to overcome this problem. For example, global health care provider CIGNA International has teamed up with CIGNA Behavioral Health to offer an employee assistance program for expatriate employees of multinational firms. The EAP program allows CIGNA International participants to access a multilingual support and counseling network. Employees and their dependents can receive assistance through telephone or personal visits for a wide range of behavioral health and work-life concerns. The program is designed to help employees better manage stress and anxiety, depression and substance abuse, as well as to help them lead healthy lifestyles.[55]

Additional considerations specific to global assignments are emergency evacuation services and global security protection. An international firm was preparing to evacuate 15 expatriate employees and dependents from a country that had suffered an earthquake. When it came time to meet at the departure point, 25 people showed up. Those arranging for the evacuation had not known that two technical teams were in the country supporting clients at the time.[56]

Often, evacuation and care of injured employees is done through private companies. Medical emergencies are frightening under any circumstances, but when an employee becomes sick or injured abroad, it can be a traumatic experience. If the travelers are assigned to more remote or less developed areas, companies should be aware that in many medical facilities needles are often reused, equipment is not properly used, and there is a lack of basic medical supplies.[57] Also, employees and their families living abroad must constantly be aware of security issues. Many firms provide bodyguards who escort executives everywhere. Some firms even have disaster plans to deal with evacuating expatriates if natural disasters, civil conflicts, or wars occur.

6 OBJECTIVE

Explain global employee and labor relations.

Global Employee and Labor Relations

Although unionism has waned in the United States, it has maintained much of its strength abroad. In Sweden, 96 percent of its employees are union members; it is 50 percent in the United Kingdom, 43 percent in Germany, 33.3 percent in Canada,[58] and 28 percent in Japan and France.[59] Although foreign unions are generally less adversarial with management and less focused on wage gains, they are still quite influential around the globe. For this reason, HR policies and practices must be geared toward dealing with the global differences in collective bargaining.

Obviously, the strength and nature of unions differ from country to country, with unions ranging from nonexistent to relatively strong. Codetermination, which requires firms to have union or worker representatives on their boards of directors, is very common in European countries. Even though they face global competition, unions in several European countries have resisted changing their laws and removing government protections. Laws make it hard to fire workers, so companies are reluctant to hire.[60] Generous and lengthy unemployment benefits discourage the jobless from seeking new work. Wage bargaining remains centralized and companies have little flexibility to fashion contracts that fit their needs. High payroll taxes raise labor costs and their laws mandating cumbersome layoff procedures increase the cost of the product.[61]

On the other hand, in some South American countries such as Chile, collective bargaining for textile workers, miners, and carpenters is prohibited. And unions are generally allowed only in companies of 25 workers or more. This practice has encouraged businesses to split into small companies to avoid collective bargaining, leaving workers on their own.

The North American Free Trade Agreement (NAFTA) between Canada, Mexico, and the United States facilitated the movement of goods across boundaries within North America. It forms a free-trade zone of over 400 million people with a combined gross domestic profit of about $12 trillion dollars.[62] Labor relations took a major step forward, with a *side agreement* on labor designed to protect workers in all three countries from the effects of competitive economic pressures. NAFTA established a Commission for Labor Cooperation with offices in each country, which is governed by a council made up of labor ministers of Canada, Mexico, and the United States. Each country is accountable for complying with its *own* labor laws when dealing with occupational safety and health; child labor; migrant workers; human resource development; labor statistics; work benefits; social programs for workers; productivity improvements; labor management relations; employment standards; the equality of men and women in the workplace; and forms of cooperation among workers, management, and government. A country that consistently fails to enforce its own labor laws could be fined up to $20 million per violation. There are also a number of principles identifying broad areas of common agreement to protect the rights and interests of each workforce. Since NAFTA was implemented, trade between the United States, Canada, and Mexico has grown dramatically as all three countries have seen increased volumes of trade.[63]

CAFTA, the Central American Free Trade Agreement, was finally ratified by America's Congress after a long political battle, and signed into law in 2005. If increases like those that occurred in Mexico in the wake of the North American Free Trade Agreement (NAFTA) do take place, it would provide a huge economic boost for a region whose infrastructure remains startlingly basic.[64]

7 OBJECTIVE

Describe political and legal factors affecting global human resource management.

Global Political and Legal Factors

A recent survey identified the growing complexity of legal compliance in the global environment as the most important trend affecting global business. Mangers working for global businesses have to contend with a growing tide of employment legislation that cuts across national boundaries.[65] Legal and political forces are unique to each country,[66] and sometimes, the laws of one contradict those of another. For instance, the French authorities acknowledge that their data protection laws are in direct conflict with the U.S. Sarbanes-Oxley Act, but they insist that multinationals comply with French law.[67] Further, the nature and stability of political and legal systems vary throughout the globe. U.S. firms enjoy relatively stable political and legal systems, and the same is true in many of the developed countries. In other nations, however, the political and legal systems are much less stable. Some governments are subject to coups, dictatorial rule, and corruption, which can substantially alter both the business and the legal environments. Legal systems can also become unstable, with contracts suddenly becoming unenforceable because of internal politics.

HR regulations and laws vary greatly among countries. As previously mentioned, merely conducting a background check is different from one country to another. In many Western European countries, laws on labor unions and employment make it difficult to lay off employees. Because of political and legal differences, it is essential that a comprehensive review of the political and legal environment of the host country is conducted before beginning global operations.

Some have asked the question, "Does operating under local laws and customs free a company of all ethical considerations?" Yahoo! said it was obeying Chinese law when it turned an e-mail from a private Yahoo! e-mail account over to the Chinese government. The e-mail revealed the identity of Shi Tao, an editorial department head at *Contemporary Business News* in China's Hunan province, leading to his conviction and 10-year sentence. Shi's crime was sending an e-mail to a New York–based Website regarding the Chinese government's warning to its representatives to watch for

Ethical Dilemma

Mordita

Your company, a distributor of heavy mining equipment, wants to trade in the Mexican market where cash under the table, *mordita* (a little bit), is part of doing business. This payoff practice is so ingrained in the Mexican culture that a business virtually cannot open a Mexican operation without going along. You have observed many companies that did not pay and they failed to enter the Mexican market, as well as those that paid and entered the market, and overall, did fairly well. You can continue to raise your stature with mining companies, farmers, and contractors, and encourage them to lobby the government to freely open the market, or you can pay the bribe.

What would you do?

dissident activity during the 15th anniversary of the Tiananmen Square massacre. Yahoo!, in a statement read by spokeswoman Mary Osako, gave the following reasoning: "Just like any other global company Yahoo must ensure that its local country sites must operate within the laws, regulations, and customs of the country in which they are based."[68] Each company will have to evaluate what it would do in instances such as Yahoo! encountered.

Americans may encounter laws that are routinely ignored by host countries, creating somewhat of a dilemma. For example, the laws in some countries that require a minimum age for factory workers are often not enforced. The U.S. Department of Labor report revealed continued child labor abuses in the apparel and textile industries. The report identified several countries such as Pakistan, the Philippines, Brazil, Bangladesh, Egypt, Cambodia, India, Indonesia, and Lesotho as the greatest abusers.[69] In addition, a form of indentured servitude exists for many foreign workers in Asian factories. Here, foreign workers are grossly overcharged by labor brokers just for the privilege of working.[70]

Also affecting the environment in which global companies operate are certain tariffs and quotas that can greatly impact business profitability. **Tariffs** are taxes collected on goods that are shipped across national boundaries. For example, in 2005, Mexico imposed a tariff on U.S. exports because Congress had not repealed the Byrd amendment, formally known as the Continued Dumping and Subsidy Offset Act of 2000. Mexico imposed tariffs of $20.9 million in three product categories including a 30 percent duty on dairy products, including baby formula; a 20 percent duty on wine; and a 9 percent duty on candy and chewing gum.[71] According to the 49-member World Trade Organization, the U.S. average tariffs for industrial goods was 4 percent, but for textiles and apparel the average was 9 percent and up to 37.7 percent for some products.[72] There is much talk about eliminating tariffs around the world but actions directed at eliminating them have been limited.[73] **Quotas** are policies that limit the number or value of goods that can be imported across national boundaries. In 2005, the United States imposed quotas on 46 percent of all textile imports from China, ranging from trousers to towels.[74] The agreement allows for shipments to gradually increase before expiring at the end of 2008.[75]

Global Bribery

Conducting business globally exposes U.S. companies to an environment that permits bribery, which is against the law in the United States. Since 1977, U.S. firms have been prohibited from bribing foreign officials under the Foreign Corrupt Practices Act.[76] Although unacceptable to most American multinational firms, paying bribes to foreign public officials is a generally accepted marketing ploy on the part of the traditional competitors of U.S. companies, multinational firms from other developed nations.[77] The law has teeth because Lockheed Corporation paid approximately $25 million for violating the Act after an executive was found to have bribed an Egyptian government official to win a contract for cargo jets.[78] Titan Corporation agreed in 2005 to pay $28.5 million in fines for lack of supervision and control of its 120 agents working in 60 countries. Douglas A. Murphy, president of American Rice Inc., was sentenced to 63 months in prison while David O. Kay, the company's vice president, was sentenced to 37 months.[79] When Lucent Technologies found that managers in its Chinese operations bribed government officials in order to do business there, the company fired its entire Chinese senior management team. Although this way of doing business may be very common in China, it is illegal in the United States.[80]

Berlin-based Transparency International, a nongovernmental organization dedicated to fighting bribery, finds signs of *rampant corruption* in no fewer than 60 countries. Bangladesh and Haiti are the worst of that group, and Russia and several other former Soviet republics are also included.[81] Companies other than the United States

Tariffs:
Taxes collected on goods that are shipped across national boundaries.

Quotas:
Policies that limit the number or value of goods that can be imported across national boundaries.

Web Wisdom

International Law Affecting HR

http://www.lir.msu.edu/hotlinks/IGO.php

Site hot-linked to numerous international law sites.

 OBJECTIVE

Explain bribery, equal employment opportunity, and virtual teams in a global environment.

face far fewer constraints when dealing with bribery. Although the 35 signatories of the Organization of Economic Cooperation and Development's 1997 convention made it a crime to bribe foreign officials, there has been little enforcement of new laws by national governments, other than by the United States. China, a country that is rapidly moving into free enterprise has yet to sign the OECD and it is said that the country's tough antibribery laws are underenforced.[82] Fritz Heimann, chairman of the U.S. branch of Transparency International, writes on its Website, "There is insufficient awareness in the business community that foreign bribery has become a crime, and relatively few non-U.S. companies have adopted antibribery compliance programs."[83]

Not having the ability to use bribery as a tool of doing business has been costly for American companies. According to a U.S. Commerce Department report, competition for 47 contracts worth $18 billion may have been affected by bribes that foreign firms paid to foreign officials. Because U.S. companies would not participate, the department estimates, at least eight of those contracts, worth $3 billion, were lost to them.[84]

A growing number of international organizations have developed guidelines to help curb future corruption. Several multinationals, including Switzerland's Ciba-Geigy, have encouraged other multinationals to band together and adopt policies on corrupt practices that will resemble those in U.S. law. Perhaps such voluntary codes will be effective in upgrading the standards of ethics practiced in international business.

Global Equal Employment Opportunity

The global assignment of women and members of racial/ethnic minorities can involve legal issues, as these individuals may be protected by EEO regulations. American workers employed by American-controlled businesses operating overseas are still protected under the American employment laws.[85] Presently, women constitute more than 20 percent of the total U.S. expatriate managerial workforce.[86] Unfortunately, these gains in female expatriate participation rates have not been equally distributed worldwide. There are some countries in which the sexist culture is so ingrained that women would have extreme difficulty participating on equal footing with the majority population in the workforce. In fact, there are some cultures today that will not accept a woman as a boss.[87]

Sexual harassment is also a global problem. A disproportionate number of cross-cultural sexual harassment complaints involve perpetrators and victims from different ethnic, racial, or national origin groups. When individuals from two different cultures interact, there is a potential for sexual harassment problems. Some behaviors that violate U.S. cultural norms may not be perceived as a problem in another culture. In many Mediterranean and Latin countries, physical contact and sensuality are a common part of socializing. The famous Cirque du Soleil, headquartered in Montreal, Canada, has had to adapt to the U.S. definition of sexual harassment when performing in the United States. While kissing good friends and co-workers on both cheeks is common in Montreal, such behavior could be considered a form of sexual harassment in the United States. Also, there are the semi-nude photos of Cirque performers hanging on the walls of the company's Montreal headquarters. Suzanne Gagnon, vice president of human resources, said, because of "America's stringent laws on pornography, sexual harassment and obscenity, those photos would never see the light of day in Las Vegas."[88]

Australia, Canada, the Netherlands, Sweden, and the United Kingdom are among jurisdictions that have laws specifying prohibited conduct and allowing employees to seek individual remedies. Italy, the Philippines, Taiwan, and Venezuela define sexual harassment as a criminal offense, and penalties and remedies are provided in special statutory penal codes. In Germany, Spain, and Thailand, sexual discrimination law is based on the concept of termination indemnity that allows employees to terminate their employment relationships due to discrimination or harassment. In turn, termination indemnity laws require employers to pay employees substantial severance pay if the cause of their termination is due to discrimination or harassment. In Japan, legislative initiatives are bolstered by U.S.-style regulations prohibiting sexual harassment.[89]

Virtual Teams in a Global Environment

The events of 9/11 accelerated the use of virtual teams. These teams operate across boundaries of time and geography and have become a necessity of everyday working life. Virtual global teams' members located in several countries regularly work together effectively in the absence of face-to-face interactions. The advantage of virtual teams is that membership is not restricted to a specific location.[90] In all other ways, virtual teams emulate traditional teams. Virtual teams have been defined in many ways, with the virtual component ranging from occasional to total reliance on technology as the medium for interaction.

Virtual teams enable companies to accomplish things more quickly and efficiently. The times when virtual team members are in one place are few, especially when members are located across the globe. This often makes global teams more difficult to manage effectively. Communication is the key to keeping teams working effectively together. Some of the difficulties that virtual teams confront with regard to communication are discussed next. First, dispersed team members often do not feel as connected or committed to the team. "Out of sight, out of mind" may apply. Virtual team members need to get together from time to time.[91] Second, communication problems between team members appear to be directly proportional to the number of time zones that separate them. If it is only a couple of zones, teammates will be in their offices earlier or later than one another, but their workdays still overlap enough to allow phone calls. If the distance stretches from 9 to 12 time zones, workdays do not overlap at all, and e-mail and voice mail must be used. Third, there is the language problem. Since English is becoming the world language, those for whom English is a second language may be placed at a disadvantage. Many Asians are concerned with saving face if they do not understand something. They may be hesitant to ask questions that would reveal their ignorance, thus widening the communication gap. Leading global virtual teams is certainly challenging.

Countless tools are available these days to help dispersed teams stay in close communication. They include e-mail, voice mail, video- and teleconferencing, groupware, and various aids to communication and decision making. In one survey, videoconferencing was viewed as one of the richest communication media, second only to face-to-face communication.[92] Global organizations can also use Instant Messaging (IM) when they need a fast and secure way to communicate with their counterparts around the world.[93] No single tool is best for all situations. Some tools, such as phone calls or face-to-face meetings, provide real-time communication. Others, such as e-mail or voice mail, have a brief delay.

Summary

1. Describe the evolution of global business and global human resource management.

Most companies initially become global without making substantial investments in foreign countries by exporting, licensing, or franchising. A multinational corporation is a firm that is based in one country (the parent or home country) and produces goods or provides services in one or more foreign countries (host countries). A global corporation has corporate units in a number of countries that are integrated to operate as one organization worldwide. The functions are global human resource planning, recruitment, and selection; global human resource development; global compensation; global safety and health; and global employee and labor relations.

2. Describe global staffing.

Companies must choose from various types of global staff members and may employ specific approaches to global staffing. Global staff members may be selected from among three different types: expatriates, host-country nationals, and third-country nationals. There are four major approaches to global staffing: ethnocentric, polycentric, regiocentric, and geocentric staffing.

3. Describe global human resource development.

Many T&D professionals believe that training and consulting principles and strategies that work for a U.S. audience can be equally effective abroad. Nothing could be further from the truth. Global training and development is needed because people, jobs, and organizations are often quite different. The ideal expatriate preparation and development program includes pre-move orientation and training, continual development, and repatriation orientation and training.

4. Explain global compensation.

Companies that are successful in the global environment align their human resources programs in support of their strategic business plans. A major component is the manner in which the human resources total compensation program supports the way the business is structured, organized, and operated both globally and regionally. Certainly, in compensation-related matters, organizations should think globally but act locally. One reason that organizations relocate to other areas of the world is probably the high-wage pressures that threaten their ability to compete on a global basis. International assignments for expatriates cost three to five times an assignee's host-country salary per year and more if currency exchange rates become unfavorable.

5. Describe global safety and health.

U.S.-based global operations are often safer and healthier than host-country operations, but frequently not as safe as similar operations in the United States. Safety and health laws and regulations often vary greatly from country to country. Such laws can range from virtually nonexistent to more stringent than those in the United States.

6. Explain global employee and labor relations.

Although unionism has waned in the United States, it has maintained much of its strength abroad.

7. Describe political and legal factors affecting global human resource management.

Legal and political forces are unique for each country.

8. Explain bribery, equal employment opportunity, and virtual teams in a global environment.

Conducting business globally exposes U.S. companies to an environment permitting bribery, which is illegal in the United States. Since 1977, U.S. firms have been prohibited from bribing foreign officials under the Foreign Corrupt Practices Act.

The global assignment of women and members of racial/ethnic minorities can involve legal issues. Sexual harassment is also a global problem.

The events of 9/11 accelerated the use of virtual teams. These teams operate across boundaries of time and geography and have become a necessity of everyday working life. Virtual global teams' members located in several countries regularly work together effectively in the absence of face-to-face interactions.

Key Terms

- Country's culture, 455
- Exporting, 457
- Licensing, 457
- Franchising, 457
- Multinational corporation (MNC), 457
- Global corporation (GC), 457

- Global human resource management (GHRM), 457
- Expatriate, 459
- Host-country national (HCN), 459
- Third-country national (TCN), 459
- Ethnocentric staffing, 459

- Polycentric staffing, 460
- Regiocentric staffing, 460
- Geocentric staffing, 460
- Repatriation, 462
- Tariffs, 468
- Quotas, 468

Questions for Review

1. How do cultural differences affect global human resource management?
2. How has global business evolved?
3. Define the following terms:
   a. exporting
   b. licensing
   c. franchising
4. What are the various types of global staff members?
5. What are the approaches to global staffing?
6. Why is repatriation orientation and training needed?
7. What is meant by the statement, "Organizations should think globally but act locally"?
8. What is the state of affairs for international unions?
9. What are some political and legal factors affecting global human resource management?
10. What is meant by the statement, "Conducting business globally exposes U.S. companies to an environment involving bribery that they are not exposed to in the United States"?
11. Globally, what is the state of equal employment opportunity?

HRM Incident 1

The Overseas Transfer

In college, Pat Marek majored in industrial management and was considered by his teachers and peers to be a good all-around student. Pat not only took the required courses in business, but he also learned French. After graduation, Pat took an entry-level management training position with Tuborg International, a multinational corporation with offices and factories in numerous countries, including the United States. His first assignment was in a plant in Chicago. His supervisors quickly identified Pat for his ability to get the job done and still maintain good rapport with subordinates, peers, and superiors. In only three years, Pat had advanced from a manager trainee to the position of assistant plant superintendent.

After two years in this position, he was called into the plant manager's office one day and told that he had been identified as ready for a foreign assignment. The move would mean a promotion. The assignment was for a plant in Haiti, a predominantly French-speaking country; but Pat wasn't worried about living and working there. He was excited and wasted no time in making the necessary preparations for the new assignment.

Prior to arriving at the plant in Haiti, Pat took considerable time to review his French textbook exercises. He was surprised at how quickly the language came back to him. He thought that there wouldn't be any major difficulties in making the transition from Chicago to Haiti. However, Pat found, on arrival, that the community where the plant was located did not speak the pure French that he had learned. There were many expressions that meant one thing to Pat but had an entirely different meaning to the employees of the plant.

When meeting with several of the employees a week after arriving, one of the workers said something to him that Pat interpreted as uncomplimentary. Actually, the employee had greeted him with a rather risqué expression but in a different tone than Pat had heard before. All of the other employees interpreted the expression to be merely a friendly greeting. Pat's disgust registered in his face.

As the days went by, this type of misunderstanding occurred a few more times, until the employees began to limit their conversation with him. In only one month, Pat managed virtually to isolate himself from the workers within the plant. He became disillusioned and thought about asking to be relieved from the assignment.

Questions

1. What problems had Pat not anticipated when he took the assignment?

2. How could the company have assisted Pat to reduce the difficulties that he confronted?

3. Do you believe the situation that Pat confronted is typical of an American going to a foreign assignment? Discuss.

HRM Incident 2

Was There Enough Preparation?

"Hi, Sam. How are the preparations going for your assignment in Japan?"

"Well, Elvis, I really feel prepared for the assignment, and the high level of apprehension I first experienced is gone."

"What exactly did the preparation program involve, Sam?"

"The experience was really exhaustive. First, I spent a good deal of time in a comprehensive orientation and training program. The program covered training and familiarization in the language, culture, history, living conditions, and local customs of Japan. Then, to make the transition back to home easier and better for my career, I have developed a plan with my boss that includes several trips back here to remain a key part of this operation. Also, my career development training will include the same training as the other managers in the home office. Finally, I was completely briefed on repatriation orientation and training that I would experience when I returned. Also, I was fully briefed on the compensation package, which appears to be fairly generous."

"That is great, Sam. Have you found a place to live yet?"

"Not yet, Elvis, but my wife and children are leaving in three days to meet with the company's relocation person to consider the various possibilities."

"How did the family like the orientation training, Sam?"

"Well, my wife ordered some Japanese language tapes, and I think she read all of the information that was covered in the class. She and the children will be fine because they have time to adapt; they don't have to hit the ground running like I do."

Questions

1. Do you believe that Sam's family is adequately prepared for the move to Japan? Why or why not?

2. Should the company's orientation program have included training for Sam's family?

3. Is repatriation orientation and training necessary for Sam's family on their return to the United States?

Notes

1. K. Pan Fan and K. Zhang Zigang, "Cross-Cultural Challenges When Doing Business in China," *Singapore Management Review* 26 (2004): 81–90.

2. Zoe Fielding, "Culture Shock: Confusion Sours Export Deals," *Manufacturers' Monthly* (June 2005): 52–53.

3. Mark Wolfendale, "Doing Business in the Asia Pacific," *Strategic Finance* 84 (December 2002): 26–30.

4. Rich Thomaselli, "Learning Culture May Help Seal Business Deal," *Hudson Valley Business Journal* 16 (September 5, 2005): 3.

5. David A. Light, "Cross-Cultural Lessons in Leadership," *MIT Sloan Management Review* 45 (Fall 2003): 5–6.

6. Norman Thorpe, "Employees Take Trips to Understand Other Cultures," *Automotive News* (July 1, 2005): 24I.

7. Gary Wederspahn, "Expatriate Training: Don't Leave Home Without It," *T&D* 56 (February 2002): 67.

8. Diane Nilsen, Brenda Kowske, and Kshanika Anthony, "Managing Globally," *HR Magazine* 50 (August 2005): 111–115.

9. Dana Breitenstein, "Helping New Assignees Swim When They're Thrown in the Cultural Deep End," *T&D* 8 (September 2002): 9.

10. Zachary Karabell, "Wake Up and Smell the Performance Gap," *Harvard Business Review* 84 (February 2006): 59–60.

11. Geoffrey Colvin, "America Isn't Ready," *Fortune (Europe)* 152 (August 8, 2005): 22–31.

12. Michael Brennan and Paul Braswell, "Developing and Leading Effective Global Teams," *Chief Learning Officer* 4 (March 2005): 44–48.

13. John D. Mittelstaedt, George N. Harben, and William A. Ward, "How Small Is Too Small? Firm Size as a Barrier to Exporting from the United States?" *Journal of Small Business Management* 41 (January 2003):

14. Carl E. Zwisler, "Finding the Right International Master Franchise Partner," *Franchising World* 37 (April 2005): 43–48.

15. Polly Larson, "International Growth Patterns Remain Strong," *Franchising World* 34 (April 2002): 6–8.

16. Stacey Mieyal Higgins, "Brands Focus on Worldwide Growth," *Hotel & Motel Management* 221 (March 6, 2006): 30–32.

17. Kevin T. Higgins, "P&G Reinvents Itself," *Marketing Management* 11 (November/December 2002): 12–15.

18. Beth McConnell, "HRCI to Offer Global HR Certification in 2004," *HR Magazine* 48 (March 2003): 115, 117.

19. Elissa Tucker, Tina Kao, and Nihdi Verma, "Next-Generation Talent Management: Insights on How Workforce Trends Are Changing the Face of Talent Management," *Business Credit* 106 (July 2005): 20–27.

20. Jeffrey Pfeffer, "Recruiting for the Global Talent War," *Business 2.0* 6 (August 2005): 56–56.

21. "Success Strategies for Expats," *T+D* 59 (September 2005): 48–51.

22. Calvin Reynolds, "Global Compensation and Benefits in Transition," *Compensation and Benefits Review* 32 (January/February 2000): 28.

23. Pauline Loong, "The Search for New Rainmakers," *Asiamoney* 13 (October 2002): 38–41.

24. This section was developed based on Anne Marie Francesco and Barry Allen Gold, *International Organizational Behavior* (Upper Saddle River, NJ: Prentice Hall, 1998): 165.

25. Leah Carlson, "Complications Abound in Managing Expatriate Benefits," *Employee Benefit News* 19 (June 15, 2005): 28–39.

26. Andrea C. Poe, "Selection Savvy," *HR Magazine* 47 (April 2002): 77–83.

27. Dianne S. Jacobini, "Expatriate Administration: New Realities and HR Challenges," *Employee Benefit News* 19 (March 1, 2005): 11.

28. Russell Flannery, "Get Me Personnel!" *Forbes* 177 (April 17, 2006): 50.

29. Pamela Babcock, "Foreign Assignments," *HR Magazine* 50 (October 2005): 91–98.

30. Ibid.

31. Ibid.

32. Carlson, "Complications Abound in Managing Expatriate Benefits."

33. Clifford C. Hebard, "Managing Effectively in Asia," *Training & Development* 50 (April 1996): 34.

34. Ibid.

35. Eric Krell, "Budding Relationships," *HR Magazine* 50 (June 2005): 114–118.

36. "Top Employees Get Overseas Jobs," *Westchester County Business Journal* 41 (August 26, 2002): 15.

37. Kathryn Tyler, "Retaining Repatriates," *HR Magazine* 51 (March 2006): 97–102.

38. Jan Nelson, "The Benefits of a Formal Repatriation Program for the Organization and the Expatriate," *Employee Benefit News* 19 (November 1, 2005): 20.

39. Shirley Puccino, "The Right Mix of Expatriate Employee Compensation Components," *Benefits & Compensation Digest* 42 (September 2005): 30–33.

40. Ann Pomeroy, "Global Compensation Strategies and HR," *HR Magazine* 50 (May 2005): 14–18.

41. Jessica Marquez, "McDonald's Rewards Program Leaves Room for Some Local Flavor," *Workforce Management* 85 (April 10, 2006): 26.

42. Michael A. Tucker, "E-Learning Evolves," *HR Magazine* 50 (October 2005): 74–78.

43. Ibid.

44. Ibid.

45. Hanif Sazen, "Keeping It Fresh," *e.learning age* (June 2005): 28–29.

46. Gina Ruiz, "Kimberly-Clark: Developing Talent in Developing World Markets," *Workforce Management* 85 (April 10, 2006): 34.

47. Lawson D. Thurston, "Severance Payment and Christmas Bonus Changes Increase Cost of Doing Business," *Caribbean Business* 34 (May 11, 2006): 58.

48. Vicki Taylor, "Benefits Around the World," *Employee Benefits* (February 2006): Special Section, 8–9.

49. Tim Richardson, "Entertaining the Culture," *Cabinet Maker* (August 12, 2005): 22–23.

50. Lionel Laroche, "Hiring Abroad," *CMA Management* 76 (March 2002): 57–58.

51. Eric Krell, "Evaluating Returns on Expatriates," *HR Magazine* 50 (March 2005): 60–65.

52. Carlson, "Complications Abound in Managing Expatriate Benefits."

53. Virginia A. Hulme, "Short Staffed," *China Business Review* 33 (March/April 2006): 18–56.

54. "Too Many Turkeys," *Economist* 337 (November 26, 2005): 75–76.

55. "CIGNA Launches EAP for Expatriates," *Business Insurance* 38 (June 14, 2004): 37.

56. Moray J. Taylor-Smith, "Do You Know Where Your Employees Are?" *Security Management* 46 (July 2002): 74–80.

57. "Global Protection," *Occupational Health & Safety* 67 (October 1998): 182.

58. "Unions Show Slight Growth in 2002," *Canadian HR Reporter* 15 (September 23, 2002): 2.

59. M.E. Sharpe, "Labor's Future," *Challenge* 39 (March 1996): 65.

60. Thomas Sowell, "Job Security Laws Do Nothing but Redistribute Insecurity," *Enterprise/Salt Lake City* 34 (February 21, 2005): 18.

61. Carol Matlack, Michael Arndt, and Adrienne Carter, "Time to Cut Their Losses," *Business Week* (May 5, 2005): 56–56.

62. "Regional Overview: Membership of Organizations," *Country Profile, United States* (December 2005): 60.

63. Roger Morton, "NAFTA: Twelve Years After," *Logistics Today* 47 (February 2006): 10.

64. "Nothing's Free in This World," *Economist* 376 (August 6, 2005): 30.

65. "HR's Response to the Top 10 Workplace Trends," *Strategic HR Review* 3 (September/October 2004): 14–15.

66. "Global Benefits Laws You Need to Know," *HR Focus* 82 (February 2005): 7–11.

67. Bill Goodwin, "Lawyers Little Help in International Minefield," *Computer Weekly* (May 5, 2005): 10.

68. Ephraim Schwartz, "On Business and Ethics," *InfoWorld* 27 (October 10, 2005): 12.

69. Kristi Ellis, "Child Labor Report the Good and Bad," *Fairchild Publications, Inc.* (August 2, 2002): 14.

70. Nicholas Stein, "No Way Out," *Fortune* 147 (January 20, 2003): 102–108.

71. "Mexico Hits U.S. Exports with Tariffs in Retaliation for Byrd Amendment," *Metal Center News* 45 (September 2005): 71.

72. John Zarocostas, "U.S. Tariffs Cited in WTO Trade Review," *WWD: Women's Wear Daily* 191 (March 27, 2006): 15.

73. Ernesto Zedillo, "A Trade Fiction," *Forbes* 176 (September 19, 2005): 41.

74. "Stuck with the Second Best," *Economist* 377 (November 12, 2005): 78.

75. Evan Clark, "China Restrained but Undaunted," *Women's Wear Daily* 191 (February 14, 2006): 12–14.

76. Laetitia Tjoa, Jianyu Ouyang, and Like Pykstra, "Complying with PRC Antibribery Laws," *China Business Review* 32 (March/April 2005): 34–37.

77. Roger Chen and Chia-Pei Chen, "Chinese Professional Managers and the Issue of Ethical Behaviour," *Ivey Business Journal* 69 (May/June 2005): 1–5.

78. Mike Koehler, "Does Your Target Have Clean Hands Overseas?" *Mergers & Acquisitions: The Dealermaker's Journal* 40 (April 2005): 53–56.

79. Benjamin Norris, "Don't Ignore the FCPA," *Journal of Commerce* 27 (February 27, 2006): 42.

80. David M. Katz, "The Bribery Gap," *CFO* 21 (January 2005): 59–61.

81. Ibid.

82. Tom Leander, "Dungeons and the Dragon," *CFO* 22 (April 2006): 46–48.

83. Katz, "The Bribery Gap."

84. Ibid.

85. David Drickhamer, "Employment Laws Apply Abroad: Americans Overseas Have Same Rights as U.S. Counterparts," *Industry Week* 251 (May 2002): 12.

86. "Expatriate Workforce Demographics," *HR Magazine* 51 (May 2006): 16.

87. Barry R. Weissman, "English Only Training," *Industrial Safety & Hygiene News* 39 (October 2005): 37.

88. Cindy Waxer, "Life's a Balancing Act for Cirque du Soleil's Human Resources Troupe," *Workforce Management* 84 (January 2005): 52–53.

89. Gerald L. Maatmann Jr., "Harassment, Discrimination Laws Go Global," *National Underwriter* 104 (September 11, 2000): 34–35.

90. Jenny Goodbody, "Critical Success Factors for Global Virtual Teams," *Strategic Communication Management* 9 (February/March 2005): 18–21.

91. "Virtual Work: It's Not Just for Members of the Jedi Council," *T+D* 59 (August 2005): 12–13.

92. Vicki R. McKinney and Mary M. Whiteside, "Maintaining Distributed Relationships," *Communications of the ACM* 49 (March 2006): 82–86.

93. Dan Caterinicchia, "IM in the Business World," *HR Magazine* 50 (September 2005): 131–135.

Glossary

Adverse impact: Concept established by the Uniform Guidelines it occurs if women and minorities are not hired at the rate of at least 80 percent of the best-achieving group.

Affirmative action: Stipulated by Executive Order 11246, it requires employers to take positive steps to ensure employment of applicants and treatment of employees during employment without regard to race, creed, color, or national origin.

Affirmative action program (AAP): Approach developed by organizations with government contracts to demonstrate that workers are employed in proportion to their representation in the firm's relevant labor market.

Agency shop: Labor agreement provision requiring, as a condition of employment, that each nonunion member of a bargaining unit pay the union the equivalent of membership dues as a service charge in return for the union acting as the bargaining agent.

Alcoholism: Medical disease characterized by uncontrolled and compulsive drinking that interferes with normal living patterns.

Alternative dispute resolution (ADR): Procedure whereby the employee and the company agree ahead of time that any problems will be addressed by an agreed-upon means.

American Federation of Labor and Congress of Industrial Organizations (AFL-CIO): Central trade union federation in the United States.

Applicant pool: Number of qualified applicants recruited for a particular job.

Applicant tracking system (ATS): Software application designed to help an enterprise recruit employees more efficiently.

Apprenticeship training: Training method which combines classroom instruction with on-the-job training.

Arbitration: Process in which a dispute is submitted to an impartial third party for a binding decision; an arbitrator basically acts as a judge and jury.

Assessment center: Selection technique that requires individuals to perform activities similar to those they might encounter in an actual job.

Attitude survey: Survey that seeks input from employees to determine their feelings about topics such as the work they perform, their supervisor, their work environment, flexibility in the workplace, opportunities for advancement, training and development opportunities, and the firm's compensation system.

Authorization card: Document indicating that an employee wants to be represented by a labor organization in collective bargaining.

Autonomy: Extent of individual freedom and discretion employees have in performing their jobs.

Availability forecast: Determination of whether the firm will be able to secure employees with the necessary skills, and from what sources.

Baby boomers: People born between just after World War II through the mid-1960s.

Bargaining unit: Group of employees, not necessarily union members, recognized by an employer or certified by an administrative agency as appropriate for representation by a labor organization for purposes of collective bargaining.

Beachhead demands: Demands that the union does not expect management to meet when they are first made.

Behavior modeling: T&D method that permits a person to learn by copying or replicating behaviors of others to show managers how to handle various situations.

Behavioral interview: Structured interview where applicants are asked to relate actual incidents from their past relevant to the target job.

Behaviorally anchored rating scale (BARS) method: Performance appraisal method that combines elements of the traditional rating scale and critical incident methods; various performance levels are shown along a scale with each described in terms of an employee's specific job behavior.

Benchmark job: Well-known job in the company and industry and one performed by a large number of employees.

Benchmarking: Process of monitoring and measuring a firm's internal processes, such as operations, and then comparing the data with information from companies that excel in those areas.

Benefits: All financial rewards that are not included in direct financial compensation (indirect financial compensation).

Board interview: An interview approach in which several of the firm's representatives interview a candidate at the same time.

Bonus: One-time annual financial award based on productivity that is not added to base pay.

Bottom-up approach: Forecasting method in which each successive level in the organization, starting with the lowest, forecasts its requirements, ultimately providing an aggregate forecast of employees needed.

Boycott: Agreement by union members to refuse to use or buy the firm's products.

Branding: Firm's corporate image or culture.

Broadbanding: Compensation technique that collapses many pay grades (salary grades) into a few wide bands in order to improve organizational effectiveness.

Burnout: Incapacitating condition in which individuals lose a sense of the basic purpose and fulfillment of their work.

Business games: T&D method that permits participants to assume roles such as president, controller, or marketing vice president of two or more similar hypothetical organizations and compete against each other by manipulating selected factors in a particular business situation.

Byline strike: Newspaper writers withhold their names from stories.

Card check: Organizing approach by labor where employees sign a card of support if they want unionization, and if 50 percent of the workforce plus one worker sign a card, the union considers it a victory.

Career: General course that a person chooses to pursue throughout his or her working life.

Career development: Formal approach used by the organization to ensure that people with the proper qualifications and experiences are available when needed.

Career path: Flexible line of progression through which an employee may move during his or her employment with a company.

Career planning: Ongoing process whereby an individual sets career goals and identifies the means to achieve them.

Career security: Requires developing marketable skills and expertise that help ensure employment within a range of careers.

Carpal tunnel syndrome: Common repetitive stress injury, resulting from pressure on the median nerve in the wrist due to repetitive flexing and extending the wrist.

Case study: T&D method in which trainees are expected to study the information provided in the case and make decisions based on it.

Cash balance plan: Retirement plan with elements of both defined benefit and defined contribution plans.

Central tendency error: Evaluation appraisal error that occurs when employees are incorrectly rated near the average or middle of a scale.

Change to Win Coalition: New union federation consisting of seven unions that broke from the AFL-CIO and formally launched a rival labor federation representing about 6 million workers in 2005.

Checkoff of dues: Agreement by which a company agrees to withhold union dues from members' paychecks and to forward the money directly to the union.

Classification method: Job evaluation method in which classes or grades are defined to describe a group of jobs.

Closed shop: Arrangement making union membership a prerequisite for employment.

Coaching: Often considered a responsibility of the immediate boss who provides assistance much as a mentor.

Cognitive aptitude tests: Tests that determine general reasoning ability, memory, vocabulary, verbal fluency, and numerical ability.

Collective bargaining: Performance of the mutual obligation of the employer and the representative of the employees to meet at reasonable times and confer in good faith with respect to wages, hours, and other terms and conditions of employment, or the negotiation of an agreement, or any question arising there under, and the execution of a written contract incorporating any agreement reached if requested by either party; such obligation does not compel either party to agree to a proposal or require the making of a concession.

Comparable worth: Determination of the values of dissimilar jobs (such as company nurse and welder) by comparing them under some form of job evaluation, and the assignment of pay rates according to their evaluated worth.

Compensation: Total of all rewards provided employees in return for their services.

Compensation policy: Policies that provide general guidelines for making compensation decisions.

Compensation survey: A means of obtaining data regarding what other firms are paying for specific jobs or job classes within a given labor market.

Competencies: Broad range of knowledge, skills, traits, and behaviors that may be technical in nature, relate to interpersonal skills, or be business oriented.

Competency-based pay: Compensation plan that rewards employees for the capabilities they attain.

Compressed work week: Any arrangement of work hours that permits employees to fulfill their work obligation in fewer days than the typical five-day work week.

Conspiracy: Two or more persons who band together to prejudice the rights of others or of society (such as by refusing to work or demanding higher wages).

Construct validity: Test validation method that determines whether a test measures certain constructs, or traits, that job analysis finds to be important in performing a job.

Content validity: Test validation method whereby a person performs certain tasks that are actually required by the job or completes a paper-and-pencil test that measures relevant job knowledge.

Contingency search firms: Executive search firm that receives fees only upon successful placement of a candidate in a job opening.

Contingent workers: Described as the "disposable American workforce" by a former secretary of labor, work as part-timers, temporaries, or independent contractors.

Corporate career Websites: Job sites accessible from a company homepage that list available company positions and provide a way for applicants to apply for specific jobs.

Corporate social responsibility (CSR): Implied, enforced, or felt obligation of managers, acting in their official capacity, to serve or protect the interests of groups other than themselves.

Corporate university: T&D delivery system provided under the umbrella of the organization.

Cost-of-living allowance (COLA): Escalator clause in a labor agreement that automatically increases wages as the U.S. Bureau of Labor Statistics cost-of-living index rises.

Country's culture: Set of values, symbols, beliefs, languages, and norms that guide human behavior within the country.

Craft union: Bargaining unit, such as the Carpenters and Joiners union, which is typically composed of members of a particular trade or skill in a specific locality.

Criterion-related validity: Test validation method that compares the scores on selection tests to some aspect of job performance determined, for example, by performance appraisal.

Critical incident method: Performance appraisal method that requires keeping written records of highly favorable and unfavorable employee work actions.

Customized benefit plan: Benefit plan that permits employees to make yearly elections to largely determine their benefit package by choosing between taxable cash and numerous benefits.

Cyberwork: Possibility of a never-ending workday.

Decertification: Reverse of the process that employees must follow to be recognized as an official bargaining unit.

Defined benefit plan: Retirement plan that provides the participant with a fixed benefit upon retirement.

Defined contribution health care plan: System where companies give each employee a set amount of money annually with which to purchase health care coverage.

Defined contribution plan: Retirement plan that requires specific contributions by an employer to a retirement or savings fund established for the employee.

Demotion: Process of moving a worker to a lower level of duties and responsibilities and typically involves a reduction in pay.

Development: Learning that goes beyond today's job and has a more long-term focus.

Direct financial compensation: Pay that a person receives in the form of wages, salary, commissions, and bonuses.

Disciplinary action: Invoking a penalty against an employee who fails to meet established standards.

Disciplinary action without punishment: Process in which a worker is given time off with pay to think about whether he or she wants to follow the rules and continue working for the company.

Discipline: State of employee self-control and orderly conduct that indicates the extent of genuine teamwork within an organization.

Disparate treatment: Employer treats some people less favorably than others because of race, religion, sex, national origin, or age.

Diversity: Any perceived difference among people: age, race, religion, functional specialty, profession, sexual orientation, geographic origin, lifestyle, tenure with the organization or position, and any other perceived difference.

Diversity management: Ensuring that factors are in place to provide for and encourage the continued development of a diverse workforce by melding these actual and perceived differences among workers to achieve maximum productivity.

Downsizing: Reverse of a company growing and suggests a one-time change in the organization and the number of people employed (also known as restructuring, and rightsizing).

Dual-career family: A situation in which both husband and wife have jobs and family responsibilities.

Dual-career path: Career path that recognizes that technical specialists can and should be allowed to contribute their expertise to a company without having to become managers.

E-learning: T&D delivery system for online instruction.

Employability doctrine: Employees owe the company their commitment while employed and the company owes its workers the opportunity to learn new skills, but that is as far as the commitment goes.

Employee assistance program (EAP): Comprehensive approach that many organizations have taken to deal with burnout, alcohol and drug abuse, and other emotional disturbances.

Employee equity: Equity that exists when individuals performing similar jobs for the same firm receive pay according to factors unique to the employee, such as performance level or seniority.

Employee requisition: Document that specifies job title, department, the date the employee is needed for work, and other details.

Employee self-service (ESS): Processes that automate transactions that previously were labor-intensive for both employees and HR professionals.

Employee stock option plan (ESOP): Defined contribution plan in which a firm contributes stock shares to a trust.

Employment agency: Organization that helps firms recruit employees and at the same time aids individuals in their attempt to locate jobs.

Employment at will: Unwritten contract created when an employee agrees to work for an employer but no agreement exists as to how long the parties expect the employment to last.

Employment interview: Goal-oriented conversation in which an interviewer and an applicant exchange information.

Equity theory: Motivation theory that people assess their performance and attitudes by comparing both their contribution to work and the benefits they derive from it to the contributions and benefits of comparison others whom they select—and who in reality may or may not be like them.

Ergonomics: Study of human interaction with tasks, equipment, tools, and the physical environment.

Essay method: Performance appraisal method in which the rater writes a brief narrative describing the employee's performance.

Ethics: Discipline dealing with what is good and bad, or right and wrong, or with moral duty and obligation.

Ethnocentric staffing: Staffing approach in which companies primarily hire expatriates to staff higher-level foreign positions.

Event recruiting: Recruiters going to events that individuals the company is seeking attend.

Exclusive provider organization (EPO): Managed-care health organization that offers a smaller preferred provider network and usually provides few, if any, benefits when an out-of-network provider is used.

Executive: A top-level manager who reports directly to a corporation's chief executive officer or to the head of a major division.

Executive order (EO): Directive issued by the president that has the force and effect of law enacted by Congress as it applies to federal agencies and federal contractors.

Exempt employees: Employees categorized as executive, administrative, professional, or outside salespersons.

Exit interview: Means of revealing the real reasons employees leave their jobs; it is conducted before an employee departs the company and provides information on how to correct the causes of discontent and reduce turnover.

Expatriate: Employee who is not a citizen of the country in which the firm operations are located, but is a citizen of the country in which the organization is headquartered.

Exporting: Selling abroad, either directly or indirectly, by retaining foreign agents and distributors.

External environment: Factors outside an organization's boundaries that affect a firm's human resources.

External equity: Equity that exists when a firm's employees receive pay comparable to workers who perform similar jobs in other firms.

Factor comparison method: Job evaluation method that assumes there are five universal factors consisting of mental requirements, skills, physical requirements, responsibilities, and working conditions; and the evaluator makes decisions on these factors independently.

Feedback: Information employees receive about how well they have performed the job.

Financial equity: Perception of fair pay treatment for employees.

Flexible spending account: Benefit plan established by employers that allows employees to deposit a certain portion of their salary into an account (before paying income taxes) to be used for eligible expenses.

Flextime: Practice of permitting employees to choose their own working hours, within certain limitations.

Flooding the community: Process of the union inundating communities with organizers to target a particular business.

Forced distribution method: Performance appraisal method in which the rater is required to assign individuals in a workgroup to a limited number of categories similar to a normal frequency distribution.

401(k) plan: Defined contribution plan in which employees may defer income up to a maximum amount allowed.

Franchising: Option whereby the parent company grants another firm the right to do business in a prescribed manner.

Free agents: People who take charge of all or part of their careers, by being their own bosses or by working for others in ways that fit their particular needs or wants.

Gainsharing: Plans designed to bind employees to the firm's productivity and provide an incentive payment based on improved company performance.

Generalist: A person who may be an executive and performs tasks in a variety of HR-related areas.

Generation I: Internet-assimilated children born after the mid-1990s.

Generation X: Label affixed to the 40 million American workers born between the mid-1960s and late 1970s.

Generation Y: Comprises people born between the late 1970s and early 1990s.

Genetic testing: Tests given to identify predisposition to inherited diseases, including cancer, heart disease, neurological disorders, and congenital diseases.

Geocentric staffing: Staffing approach that uses a worldwide integrated business strategy.

Glass ceiling: Invisible barrier in organizations that impedes women and minorities from career advancement.

Global corporation (GC): Organization that has corporate units in a number of countries that are integrated to operate as one organization worldwide.

Global human resource management (GHRM): Utilization of global human resources to achieve organizational objectives without regard to geographic boundaries.

Golden parachute contract: Perquisite that protects executives in the event that another company acquires their firm or the executive is forced to leave the firm for other reasons.

Graphoanalysis: Use of handwriting analysis as a selection factor.

Grievance: Employee's dissatisfaction or feeling of personal injustice relating to his or her employment.

Grievance procedure: Formal, systematic process that permits employees to express complaints without jeopardizing their jobs.

Group interview: Meeting in which several job applicants interact in the presence of one or more company representatives.

Halo error: Evaluation error that occurs when a manager generalizes one positive performance feature or incident to all aspects of employee performance, resulting in a higher rating.

Hay guide chart-profile method (Hay Plan): Refined version of the point method used by approximately 8,000 public and private-sector organizations worldwide to evaluate clerical, trade, technical, professional, managerial and/or executive level jobs.

Hazard pay: Additional pay provided to employees who work under extremely dangerous conditions.

Health: Employees' freedom from physical or emotional illness.

Health maintenance organization (HMO): Managed-care health organization that covers all services for a fixed fee but control is exercised over which doctors and health facilities a member may use.

Health savings account: A tax-sheltered savings account similar to the IRA, but earmarked for medical expenses with high-deductible health plans that have annual deductibles of at least $1,050 for individuals and $2,100 for families.

Horn error: Evaluation error that occurs when a manager generalizes one negative performance feature or incident to all aspects of employee performance, resulting in a lower rating.

Host-country national (HCN): Employee who is a citizen of the country where the subsidiary is located.

Human capital metrics: Measures of HR performance.

Human resource development: Major HRM function consisting not only of training and development but also of individual career planning and development activities, organization development, and performance management and appraisal.

Human resource ethics: Application of ethical principles to human resource relationships and activities.

Human resource information system (HRIS): Any organized approach for obtaining relevant and timely information on which to base human resource decisions.

Human resource management (HRM): Utilization of individuals to achieve organizational objectives.

Human resource manager: Individual who normally acts in an advisory or staff capacity, working with other managers to help them deal with human resource matters.

Human resource planning (HRP): Systematic process of matching the internal and external supply of people with job openings anticipated in the organization over a specified period of time.

In-basket training: T&D method in which the participant is asked to establish priorities for and then handle a number of business papers, e-mail messages, memoranda, reports, and telephone messages that would typically cross a manager's desk.

Indirect financial compensation (benefits): All financial rewards that are not included in direct financial compensation.

Industrial union: Bargaining unit that generally consists of all the workers in a particular plant or group of plants.

Informational picketing: Use of union members to display placards and hand out leaflets, usually outside their place of business depicting information the union wants the general public to see.

Injunction: Prohibited legal procedure used by employers to prevent certain union activities, such as strikes and unionization attempts.

Interest arbitration: Arbitration that involves disputes over the terms of proposed collective bargaining agreements.

Internal employee relations: Those human resource management activities associated with the movement of employees within the organization.

Internal equity: Exists when employees receive pay according to the relative value of their jobs within the same organization.

Internet recruiter: Person whose primary responsibility is to use the Internet in the recruitment process (also called cyber recruiter).

Internship: Special form of recruitment that involves placing a student in a temporary job with no obligation either by the company to hire the student permanently or by the student to accept a permanent position with the firm following graduation.

Job: Group of tasks that must be performed for an organization to achieve its goals.

Job analysis: Systematic process of determining the skills, duties, and knowledge required for performing jobs in an organization.

Job bidding: Procedure that permits employees who believe that they possess the required qualifications to apply for a posted position.

Job characteristics theory: Employees experience intrinsic compensation when their jobs rate high on five core job dimensions: skill variety, task identity, task significance, autonomy, and feedback.

Job description: Document that provides information regarding the essential tasks, duties, and responsibilities of a job.

Job design: Process of determining the specific tasks to be performed, the methods used in performing these tasks, and how the job relates to other work in an organization.

Job enlargement: Increasing the number of tasks a worker performs, with all of the tasks at the same level of responsibility.

Job enrichment: Changes in the content and level of responsibility of a job so as to provide greater challenge to the worker.

Job evaluation: Process that determines the relative value of one job in relation to another.

Job evaluation ranking method: Job evaluation method in which the raters examine the description of each job being evaluated and arrange the jobs in order according to their value to the company.

Job fair: Recruiting method engaged in by a single employer or group of employers to attract a large number of applicants to one location for interviews.

Job hazard analysis (JHA): Multistep process designed to study and analyze a task or job and then break down that task into steps that provide a means of eliminating associated hazards.

Job-knowledge tests: Tests designed to measure a candidate's knowledge of the duties of the job for which he or she is applying.

Job posting: Procedure for informing employees that job openings exist.

Job pricing: Placing a dollar value on the job's worth.

Job rotation: T&D method where employees move from one job to another to broaden their experience.

Job security: Implies security in one job, often with one company.

Job sharing: Two part-time people split the duties of one job in some agreed-on manner and are paid according to their contributions.

Job specification: A document that outlines the minimum acceptable qualifications a person should possess to perform a particular job.

Just-in-time training: Training provided anytime, anywhere in the world when it is needed.

Keyword résumé: Résumé that contains an adequate description of the job seeker's characteristics and industry-specific experience presented in keyword terms in order to accommodate the computer search process.

Keywords: Words or phrases that are used to search databases for résumés that match.

Labor market: Potential employees located within the geographic area from which employees are recruited.

Lateral skill path: Career path that allows for lateral moves within the firm; taken to permit an employee to become revitalized and find new challenges.

Learning organization: Firm that recognizes the critical importance of continuous performance-related T&D and takes appropriate action.

Leniency: Giving an undeserved high performance appraisal rating to an employee.

Licensing: Arrangement whereby an organization grants a foreign firm the right to use intellectual properties such as patents, copyrights, manufacturing processes, or trade names for a specific period of time.

Likes and dislikes survey: Procedure that helps individuals recognize restrictions they place on themselves.

Line managers: Individuals directly involved in accomplishing the primary purpose of the organization.

Local union: Basic element in the structure of the U.S. labor movement.

Lockout: Management decision to keep union workers out of the workplace and runs the operation with management personnel and/or replacement workers to encourage the union to return to the bargaining table.

Management development: Consists of all learning experiences provided by an organization, resulting in upgrading skills and knowledge required in current and future managerial positions.

Manager self-service: The use of software and the corporate network to automate paper-based human resource processes that require a manager's approval, record-keeping or input, and processes that support the manager's job.

Mandatory bargaining issues: Bargaining issues that fall within the definition of wages, hours, and other terms and conditions of employment.

Market (going) rate: Average pay that most employers provide for a similar job in a particular area or industry.

Mediation: Neutral third party enters the negotiations and attempts to facilitate a resolution to a labor dispute when a bargaining impasse has occurred.

Mentoring: Approach to advising, coaching, and nurturing, for creating a practical relationship to enhance individual career, personal, and professional growth and development.

Merit pay: Pay increase added to employees' base pay based on their level of performance.

Mission: Unit's continuing purpose, or reason for being.

Multinational corporation (MNC): Firm that is based in one country (the parent or home country) and produces goods or provides services in one or more foreign countries (host countries).

NACElink: National, Web-based system for recruiting college students for all types of employment such as full-time, part-time, internship, co-op, work-study, and alumni.

National union: Organization composed of local unions, which it charters.

Negligent hiring: Liability a company incurs when it fails to conduct a reasonable investigation of an applicant's background, and then assigns a potentially dangerous person to a position where he or she can inflict harm.

Negligent referral: Liability former employers may incur when they fail to offer a warning about a particularly severe problem with a past employee.

Negligent retention: Liability an employer may incur when a company keeps persons on the payroll whose records indicate strong potential for wrongdoing and fails to take steps to defuse a possible violent situation.

Network career path: Method of career progression that contains both a vertical sequence of jobs and a series of horizontal opportunities.

Niche sites: Websites that cater to a specific profession.

Nonfinancial compensation: Satisfaction that a person receives from the job itself or from the psychological and/or physical environment in which the person works.

Norm: Frame of reference for comparing an applicant's performance with that of others.

Objectivity: Condition that is achieved when everyone scoring a given test obtains the same results.

Ombudsperson: Complaint officer with access to top management who hears employee complaints, investigates, and recommends appropriate action.

Onboarding: Process companies use to help new executives quickly learn an organization's structure, culture, and politics so that they can start making contributions to the organization as soon as possible.

Online higher education: Educational opportunities including degree and training programs that are delivered, either entirely or partially, via the Internet.

On-the-job training (OJT): An informal T&D method that permits an employee to learn job tasks by actually performing them.

Open shop: Employment on equal terms to union members and nonmembers alike.

Organization development (OD): Planned process of improving an organization by developing its structures, systems, and processes to enhance effectiveness and achieve desired goals.

Organizational career planning: Planned succession of jobs worked out by a firm to develop its employees.

Organizational fit: Management's perception of the degree to which the prospective employee will fit in with the firm's culture or value system.

Organizational stakeholder: Individual or group whose interests are affected by organizational activities.

Orientation: Initial T&D effort for new employees that inform them about the company, the job, and the workgroup.

Outplacement: A procedure whereby laid-off employees are given assistance in finding employment elsewhere.

Outsourcing: Process of hiring an external provider to do the work that was previously done internally.

Paid time off (PTO): Means of dealing with the problem of unscheduled absences by providing a certain number of days each year that employees can use for any purpose.

Paired comparison: Variation of the ranking method in which the performance of each employee is compared with that of every other employee in the group.

Pay compression: Situation that occurs when less experienced employees are paid as much as or more than employees who have been with the organization a long time due to a gradual increase in starting salaries and limited salary adjustment for long-term employees.

Pay followers: Companies that choose to pay below the going rate because of a poor financial condition or a belief that they do not require highly capable employees.

Pay grade: Grouping of similar jobs to simplify pricing jobs.

Pay leaders: Organizations that pay higher wages and salaries than competing firms.

Pay range: Minimum and maximum pay rate with enough variance between the two to allow for a significant pay difference.

Performance appraisal (PA): Formal system of review and evaluation of individual or team task performance.

Performance management: Goal-oriented process directed toward ensuring that organizational processes are in place to maximize productivity of employees, teams, and ultimately, the organization.

Permissive bargaining issues: Issues may be raised, but neither side may insist that they be bargained over.

Perquisites (perks): Special benefits provided by a firm to a small group of key executives and designed to give the executives something extra.

Personality tests: Self-reported measures of traits, temperaments, or dispositions.

Piecework: Incentive pay plan in which employees are paid for each unit they produce.

Point method: Job evaluation method where the raters assign numerical values to specific job factors, such as knowledge required, and the sum of these values provides a quantitative assessment of a job's relative worth.

Point-of-service (POS): Managed-care health organization that requires a primary care physician and referrals to see specialists, as with HMOs, but permits out-of-network health care access.

Polycentric staffing: Staffing approach where host-country nationals are used throughout the organization, from top to bottom.

Position: Collection of tasks and responsibilities performed by one person.

Postexit questionnaire: Questionnaire sent to former employees several weeks after they leave the organization to determine the real reason they left.

Preferred provider organization (PPO): Managed-care health organization in which incentives are provided to members to use services within the system; out-of-network providers may be utilized at greater cost.

Premium pay: Compensation paid to employees for working long periods of time or working under dangerous or undesirable conditions.

Profession: Vocation characterized by the existence of a common body of knowledge and a procedure for certifying members.

Professional employer organization (PEO): A company that leases employees to other businesses.

Profit sharing: Compensation plans that result in the distribution of a predetermined percentage of the firm's profits to employees.

Progressive disciplinary action: Approach to disciplinary action designed to ensure that the minimum penalty appropriate to the offense is imposed.

Prohibited bargaining issues: Issues that are statutorily outlawed from collective bargaining.

Promotion: Movement of a person to a higher-level position in an organization.

Promotion from within (PFW): Policy of filling vacancies above entry-level positions with current employees.

Psychomotor abilities tests: Tests that measure strength, coordination, and dexterity.

Public awareness campaigns: Labor maneuvers that do not coincide with a strike or organizing campaign to pressure an employer for better wages, benefits, and the like.

Quality circles: Groups of employees who voluntarily meet regularly with their supervisors to discuss problems, investigate causes, recommend solutions, and take corrective action when authorized to do so.

Quotas: Policies that limit the number or value of goods that can be imported across national boundaries.

Ranking method: Performance appraisal method in which the rater places all employees from a group in order of overall performance.

Rating scales method: Performance appraisal method that rates employees according to defined factors.

Realistic job preview (RJP): Method of conveying both positive and negative job information to an applicant in an unbiased manner.

Recruitment: Process of attracting individuals on a timely basis, in sufficient numbers, and with appropriate qualifications, to apply for jobs with an organization.

Recruitment methods: Specific means used to attract potential employees to the firm.

Recruitment sources: Where qualified candidates are located.

Reengineering: Fundamental rethinking and radical redesign of business processes to achieve dramatic improvements in critical, contemporary measures of performance such as cost, quality, service, and speed.

Reference checks: Information from individuals who know the applicant and who provide additional insight into the information furnished by the applicant, as well as verification of its accuracy.

Regiocentric staffing: Staffing approach that is similar to the polycentric staffing approach, but regional groups of subsidiaries reflecting the organization's strategy and structure work as a unit.

Reliability: Extent to which a selection test provides consistent results.

Relocation benefits: Company-paid shipment of household goods and temporary living expenses, covering all or a portion of the real estate costs associated with buying a new home and selling the previously occupied home.

Repatriation: Process of bringing expatriates home.

Repetitive stress injuries: Group of conditions caused by placing too much stress on a joint when the same action is performed repeatedly.

Requirements forecast: Determining the number, skill, and location of employees the organization will need at future dates in order to meet its goals.

Results-based system: Performance appraisal method in which the manager and subordinate jointly agree on objectives for the next appraisal period; in the past a form of management by objectives.

Résumé: Goal-directed summary of a person's experience, education, and training developed for use in the selection process.

Retained search firms: Executive search firm considered as consultants to their client organizations, serving on an exclusive contractual basis; typically recruit top business executives.

Reverse mentoring: A process where older employees learn from younger ones.

Right-to-work laws: Laws that prohibit management and unions from entering into agreements requiring union membership as a condition of employment.

Rights arbitration: Arbitration involving disputes over the interpretation and application of the various provisions of an existing contract.

Role-playing: T&D method where participants are required to respond to specific problems they may encounter in their jobs by acting out real-world situations.

Sabbaticals: Temporary leaves of absence from an organization, usually at reduced pay.

Safety: Protection of employees from injuries caused by work-related accidents.

Scanlon plan: Gainsharing plan that provides a financial reward to employees for savings in labor costs resulting from their suggestions.

Secondary boycott: Union attempt to encourage third parties (such as suppliers and customers) to stop doing business with a firm; declared illegal by the Taft-Hartley Act.

Selection: Process of choosing from a group of applicants the individual best suited for a particular position and the organization.

Selection ratio: Number of people hired for a particular job compared to the number of individuals in the applicant pool.

Self-assessment: Process of learning about oneself.

Seniority: Length of time an employee has been associated with the company, division, department, or job.

Sensitivity training: Organization development technique that is designed to help individuals learn how others perceive their behavior (also know as T-group training).

Sequencing moms: New mothers who leave the labor force only to return later.

Severance pay: Compensation designed to assist laid-off employees as they search for new employment.

Shared service centers (SSCs): Centers that take routine, transaction-based activities dispersed throughout the organization and consolidate them in one place.

Shareholders: Owners of a corporation.

Shift differential: Additional money paid to employees for the inconvenience of working undesirable hours.

Simulation: Forecasting technique for experimenting with a real-world situation through a mathematical model.

Simulators: T&D delivery system comprised of devices or programs that replicate actual job demands.

Skill variety: Extent to which work requires a number of different activities for successful completion.

Skill-based pay: System that compensates employees for their job-related skills and knowledge, not for their job titles.

Social audit: Systematic assessment of a company's activities in terms of its social impact.

Social contract: Set of written and unwritten rules and assumptions about acceptable interrelationships among the various elements of society.

Social responsibility: Implied, enforced, or felt obligation of managers, acting in their official capacity, to serve or protect the interests of groups other than themselves.

Specialist: Individual who may be an HR executive, a human resource manager, or a nonmanager, and who is typically concerned with only one of the five functional areas of human resource management.

Spot bonus: Relatively small monetary gift provided employees for outstanding work or effort during a reasonably short period of time.

Staffing: Process through which an organization ensures that it always has the proper number of employees with the appropriate skills in the right jobs, at the right time, to achieve organizational objectives.

Standardization: Uniformity of the procedures and conditions related to administering tests.

Stock option plan: Incentive plan in which executives can buy a specified amount of stock in their company in the future at or below the current market price.

Strategic planning: Process by which top management determines overall organizational purposes and objectives and how they are achieved.

Strength/weakness balance sheet: Self-evaluation procedure, developed originally by Benjamin Franklin, that assists people in becoming aware of their strengths and weaknesses.

Stress: Body's nonspecific reaction to any demand made on it.

Stress interview: Form of interview in which the interviewer intentionally creates anxiety.

Strictness: Being unduly critical of an employee's work performance.

Strike: Action by union members who refuse to work in order to exert pressure on management in negotiations.

Structured interview: Interviewer asks each applicant for a particular job the same series of job-related questions.

Substance abuse: Use of illegal substances or the misuse of controlled substances such as alcohol and drugs.

Succession planning: Process of ensuring that qualified persons are available to assume key managerial positions once the positions are vacant.

Supplemental unemployment benefits: Provide additional income for employees receiving unemployment insurance benefits.

Survey feedback: Process of collecting data from an organizational unit through the use of questionnaires, interviews, and objective data from other sources such as records of productivity, turnover, and absenteeism.

Tariffs: Taxes collected on goods that are shipped across national boundaries.

Task identity: Extent to which the job includes an identifiable unit of work performed from start to finish.

Task significance: Impact that the job has on other people.

Team building: Conscious effort to develop effective work-groups and cooperative skills throughout the organization.

Team equity: Equity that is achieved when teams are rewarded based on their group's productivity.

Telecommuting: Work arrangement whereby employees, called teleworkers or telecommuters, are able to remain at home (or otherwise away from the office) and perform their work using computers and other electronic devices that connect them with their offices.

Third-country national (TCN): Citizen of one country, working in a second country, and employed by an organization headquartered in a third country.

360-degree feedback evaluation method: Popular performance appraisal method that involves evaluation input from multiple levels within the firm as well as external sources.

Traditional career path: Employee progresses vertically upward in the organization from one specific job to the next.

Training: Activities designed to provide learners with the knowledge and skills needed for their present jobs.

Training and development: Heart of a continuous effort designed to improve employee competency and organizational performance.

Transfer: Lateral movement of a worker within an organization.

Type I ethics: Strength of the relationship between what an individual or an organization believes to be moral and correct and what available sources of guidance suggest is morally correct.

Type II ethics: Strength of the relationship between what one believes and how one behaves.

Union: Employees who have joined together for the purpose of dealing with their employer.

Union salting: Process of training union organizers to apply for jobs at a company and, once hired, working to unionize employees.

Union shop: Requirement that all employees become members of the union after a specified period of employment (the legal minimum is 30 days) or after a union shop provision has been negotiated.

Unstructured interview: Interview in which the job applicant is asked probing, open-ended questions.

Validity: Extent to which a test measures what it claims to measure.

Vestibule system: T&D delivery system that takes place away from the production area on equipment that closely resembles equipment actually used on the job.

Virtual job fair: Online recruiting method engaged in by a single employer or group of employers to attract a large number of applicants.

Virtual reality: Unique extension of e-learning that permits trainees to view objects from a perspective otherwise impractical or impossible.

Vocational interest tests: Tests that indicate the occupation a person is most interested in and the one likely to provide satisfaction.

Wage curve: Fitting of plotted points to create a smooth progression between pay grades (also known as the pay curve).

Work standards method: Performance appraisal method which compares each employee's performance to a predetermined standard or expected level of output.

Workplace violence: Violent acts, including physical assaults and threats of assault, directed toward employees at work or on duty.

Work-sample tests: Tests that require an applicant to perform a task or set of tasks representative of the job.

Yellow-dog contract: Written agreement between an employee and a company made at the time of employment that prohibits a worker from joining a union or engaging in union activities.

Zero-base forecasting: Forecasting method which uses the organization's current level of employment as the starting point for determining future staffing needs.

Name Index

Company Index

Subject Index